Principles of Macroeconomics
Version 4.0

Libby Rittenberg, Alan Grant, and Timothy Tregarthen

978-1-4533-3902-2

Principles of Macroeconomics
Version 4.0

Libby Rittenberg, Alan Grant, and Timothy Tregarthen

Published by:

FlatWorld
292 Newbury Street
Suite #282
Boston, MA 02115-2832

Gen: 202109091656

Brief Contents

Contents

About the Authors

Tim and I are so pleased to introduce our new co-author, Alan Grant. With both of us now retired, we were eager to bring in a new voice to carry the text into the third decade of the 21st century. As you will see, this new edition is not only thoroughly updated and includes some new topics but also has some added features that we are confident will enrich the student learning experience. We are grateful to Alan for all of these enhancements. About halfway through the revision, Alan even admitted that he was having a good time working on the book! We look forward to an extended collaboration with him.

Libby Rittenberg

Libby Rittenberg began teaching economics at Colorado College in Colorado Springs in 1989. She taught principles of economics (always her favorite course to teach), intermediate macroeconomic theory, comparative economic systems, and international political economy. She received her BA in economics-mathematics and Spanish from Simmons College and her PhD in economics from Rutgers University.

Tim Tregarthen and Libby Rittenberg

Prior to joining the faculty at Colorado College, she taught at Lafayette College and at the Rutgers University Graduate School of Management. She served as a Fulbright Scholar in Istanbul, Turkey, and as a research economist at Mathematica, Inc., in Princeton, New Jersey.

Dr. Rittenberg specializes in the internationally oriented areas of economics, with numerous articles in journals and books on comparative and development economics. Much of her work focuses on development and transition, and on the Turkish economy.

Throughout her career, she was very involved in study abroad education and directed programs in central Europe and Turkey.

She recently became professor emerita.

Alan Grant

Alan Grant (PhD, Kansas State University) is the Barbara and Charles A. Duboc University Professor at Baker University. In addition to the principles courses, he teaches general education courses in economic issues and in game theory. His research has been published in many professional journals, including *Public Finance Review*, *National Tax Journal*, *Economics Letters*, and the *Journal of Economic Education*, and has been highlighted in *The Wall Street Journal*, *Businessweek*, *The Economist*, and *The New York Times*. Alan is also the author of *Economic Analysis of Social Issues*, and is co-author of *Seinfeld and Economics: Lessons on Everything from the Show about Nothing*. He is currently writing a second mass-market economics book, *Game Theory of Thrones*.

Tim Tregarthen

There is one word that captures the essence of Dr. Timothy Tregarthen—inspiring. Tim was first diagnosed with multiple sclerosis (MS) in 1975. Yet, he continued a remarkable academic career of teaching and research. In 1996, he published the first edition of his principles of economics textbook to great acclaim, and it became widely used in colleges around the country. That same year, MS made him wheelchair-bound. The disease forced his retirement from teaching at the University of Colorado at Colorado Springs in 1998. He lost the use of his arms in 2001 and has been quadriplegic ever since. In 2002, Tim's doctor expected him to die.

He was placed in the Pikes Peak Hospice program and was twice given his last rites by his priest. Former UCCS Chancellor Shockley-Zalabak says, "I really thought that Tim would die in hospice. That's what the doctors told me, and I really believed that. I remember one day they called me and told me to try to come see him. They didn't expect him to live through the night."

Not only did he live through the night, but he eventually recovered to the point that he moved from hospice to a long-term care facility. There, he never let his disease get him down. In fact, he turned back to his love of writing and teaching for inspiration. He obtained a voice-activated computer, recruited a co-author, Libby Rittenberg of Colorado College, and turned his attention to revising his principles of economics book. FlatWorld was honored to publish a new, first-edition relaunch of this wonderful book, which has remained a most important part of its textbook offerings since its founding.

Tim has also written an autobiography about the 32 years he has had MS, titled *Suffering, Faith, and Wildflowers*. Remarkably, in 2007, he was able to return for a semester to the classroom at UCCS, where he had taught economics for 27 years. In 2009, Tim returned to California to be closer to his supportive extended family. He now lives in Pasadena.

Perhaps Tim's approach to life is best summed up by an observation by UCCS English Professor Thomas Naperierkowski: "One of the remarkable things is, heck, I can wake up with a headache and be a pretty grouchy character, but given his physical trials, which he faces every minute of his life these days, I've never seen him grouchy, I've never seen him cranky." Carry on, Tim.

Acknowledgments

Writing a book is never a solo effort. Without a team of wonderful people to shepherd the development of the book and bring it to market, this book would never have seen the light of day. We are lucky to have such a talented, cheerful, patient, and responsive group of FlatWorld people to work with, including the Digital Project Manager for this title, Lindsey Kaetzel, and Vice President of Product and Editorial, Sean Wakely. In addition, we would like to thank Ann West for her copyediting expertise, Stephanie Campbell for checking the accuracy of the text, Dana Weightman for helping us to square away permissions, and the team at Circle Graphics, Inc., Reisterstown, MD, for their efforts in proofreading the text and designing our new art program for this version.

Finally, we would like to thank the following individuals who reviewed this and previous editions of the text and whose contributions were invaluable in shaping the final product:

Robb Freeman	Eastern Maine Community College
Gary L. Stone	Winthrop University
Kyle Hoy	Shepherd University
Lauren Imperiale	Marist College
Christopher Boucher	University of New England
Colleen Callahan	American University
Christina Edmundson	North Idaho College
Paul Hettler	California University of Pennsylvania
Sean Malloy	Stuart Country Day School
Christopher Stiffler	University of Denver
Carlos Aguilar	El Paso Community College
Jeff Ankrom	Wittenberg University
Lee Ash	Skagit Valley Community College
Randall Bennett	Gonzaga University
Joseph Calhoun	Florida State University
Richard Cantrell	Western Kentucky University
Gregg Davis	Flathead Valley Community College
Kevin Dunagan	Oakton Community College
Mona El Shazly	Columbia College
Jose Esteban	Palomar College
Maurita Fawls	Portland Community College
Fred Foldvary	Santa Clara University
Richard Fowles	University of Utah
Doris Geide-Stevenson	Weber State University
Sarmila Ghosh	University of Scranton, Kania School of Management
David Gordon	Illinois Valley Community College
Clinton Greene	University of Missouri-St. Louis
James Holcomb	University of Texas at El Paso

Phil Holleran	Mitchell Community College
Yu Hsing	Southeastern Louisiana University
Thomas Hyclak	Lehigh University
Bruce Johnson	Centre College
James Kahiga	Georgia Perimeter College
Andrew Kohen	James Madison University
Kristen Monaco	California State University–Long Beach
Mark Maier	Glendale Community College
David McClough	Bowling Green State University
Ann McPherren	Huntington University
John Min	Northern Virginia Community College
Shahriar Mostashari	Campbell University, Lundy-Fetterman School of Business
Francis Mummery	Fullerton College
Robert Murphy	Boston College
Kathryn Nantz	Fairfield University
Paul Okello	Tarrant County College-South Campus
Nicholas Peppes	St. Louis Community College
Ramoo Ratha	Diablo Valley College
Teresa Riley	Youngstown State University
Michael Robinson	Mount Holyoke College
Anirban Sengupta	Texas A&M University
John Solow	The University of Iowa
John Somers	Portland Community College
Charles Staelin	Smith College
Richard Stratton	The University of Akron
Kay E. Strong	Bowling Green State University–Firelands
Della Sue	Marist College
John Vahaly	University of Louisville
Robert Whaples	Wake Forest University
Mark Wheeler	Western Michigan University
Leslie Wolfson	The Pingry School
Sourushe Zandvakili	University of Cincinnati

Dedication

Tim and Libby would like to thank their families for their support over the decades that this book has been part of their lives.

As the newest author of this book, I'd also like to thank my father, an engineer and author who was a constant source of support and encouragement to me as a writer. Whatever I've contributed to this already fine text can be traced back, in one way or another, to a lifetime of talking about books with him. Thanks, Chief!

—Alan Grant

Preface

Greek philosopher Heraclitis said more than 2,500 years ago that "Nothing endures but change." Forecasting is a tricky business, but this sentiment strikes us as being as safe a bet as one can make. Change—rapid change—underlies all our lives. As this revision was getting underway, both economic and political uncertainty had taken center stage. A once-in-a-century pandemic had swept the globe, an event that is likely (we hope!) to be the most extraordinary economic event of your lives. The recent COVID-19 pandemic intensified an existing political divide that culminated in a contested presidential election and the subsequent storming of the Capitol in the days before President Joe Biden's inauguration. None of these events were widely predicted, and their long-run impact on the global economy is still uncertain. And yet, those events give us the opportunity to share economics principles and the economic way of thinking in a way that emphasizes their relevance to today's world.

Economics is about people making decisions as they go about the ordinary business of life. To that end, we use applications from sports, politics, campus life, current events, and other familiar settings to illustrate the links between whiteboard theory and common experience. We've explored the sometimes odd, sometimes predictable behavior of macro variables throughout the COVID-19 recession, the perverse effects of means-testing public assistance, the wild and painful impacts of Venezuelan hyperinflation, and the "money-ness" of Bitcoin. As in previous editions, we have provided a balance between current issues and historical context in an attempt to provide a sense of the intellectual excitement of the field and an appreciation for the gains it has made (as well as an awareness of the challenges that lie ahead). Because of the increasingly global nature of economic activity, we've maintained a clear and consistent international focus.

In this new edition, we have stayed true to what we believe are the elements that make this text effective. To ensure students realize that economics is a unified discipline and not a bewildering array of seemingly unrelated topics, we develop the presentation of macroeconomics around integrating themes.

The integrating theme for macroeconomics is the model of aggregate demand and aggregate supply. Following its presentation in an early chapter, this model allows us to look at both short-run and long-run concepts and to address a variety of policy issues and debates.

Recognizing that a course in economics may seem daunting to some students, we have tried to make the writing clear and engaging. Clarity comes in part from the intuitive presentation style, but each chapter contains pedagogical features that make learning economic concepts and principles easier and more fun:

- *Start Up*—Each chapter begins with a real-world example that motivates readers to study the material that follows. These essays, on topics such as the value of a college degree in the labor market or how policymakers reacted to a particular economic recession, lend themselves to the type of analysis explained in the chapter. We often refer to these examples later in the text to demonstrate the link between theory and reality.

- *Learning Objectives*—These succinct statements serve as guides to the content of each section. Instructors can use them as a snapshot of the important points of the section. After completing the section, students can return to the learning objectives to see if they have mastered the material.

- *Heads Up!*—Notes to warn of common errors and explain how to avoid making them are included throughout the text. This feature provides additional clarification and shows students how to navigate potentially treacherous waters.

- *Key Takeaways*—These statements review the main points covered in each content section.

- *Key Terms*—Defined within the text, students can review these terms in context.

- *Pop! Goes the Econ* features—These features include links to contemporary and engaging examples that instantly connect with students from movies such as *Forrest Gump* or television shows such as *The Simpsons*.

- *Try It!* questions—At the end of every content section is a *Try It!* question. These problems are answered completely in the text and give students the opportunity to be active learners. They are designed to give students a clear signal as to whether they understand the material before they go on to the next topic. Each *Try It!* question is linked to a similar end-of-chapter problem.

- *Cases in Point*—These essays, included at the end of each content section, illustrate the influence of economic forces on real issues and real people. Unlike other texts that use boxed features to present interesting new material or newspaper articles, we have written each case ourselves to integrate them more clearly with the rest of the text.

- *Summary*—The information presented in the chapter is pulled together in a way that allows for a quick review of the material in just a few paragraphs.

- *End-of-chapter Concept Problems* and *Numerical Problems*—These are bountiful and are intended to check understanding, to promote discussion of the issues raised in the chapter, and to engage students in critical thinking about the material. Included are not only general review questions to test basic understanding but also examples drawn from the news and from results of economics research. Some have students working with real-world data.

- *Chapter quizzes*—Each chapter of the online version of the text includes embedded multiple choice questions that provide students with feedback on both correct and incorrect responses. The quizzes provide yet another way for students to test themselves on the material at the most teachable moments.

We hope that users will find this text an engaging and enjoyable way of becoming acquainted with economics principles and that mastery of the material will lead to looking at the world in a deeper and more meaningful way. We welcome all feedback.

—Libby Rittenberg, Alan Grant, and Timothy Tregarthen

What's New in Version 4.0

This new edition builds on the solid foundation and structure of the previous versions, but brings fresh new content.

- The book content has been significantly reorganized and streamlined, including the addition of several new macroeconomics chapters on output, inflation, and unemployment.

- New *Pop! Goes the Econ* video links let students see economics in their daily lives by connecting theory with movies, television, music, and the news.

- Over twenty new *Case in Point* boxes highlight news items, academic research, and economic curiosities that help students connect theory with the real world.

- For instructors who emphasize long-run economic growth, a new appendix develops a simple version of the Solow growth model.

- New sections devoted to taxes and the functions of financial instruments have been included.

- Links to supporting video from Khan Academy have been added at point-of-use throughout the text.

- Several new *Start Up* features have been added to this version.

Supplements

Principles of Macroeconomics v4.0 is accompanied by a robust supplements program that augments and enriches both the teaching and student learning experiences. The authors personally prepared all of the supplements to ensure accuracy and full alignment with the book's narrative. Faculty should contact their FlatWorld sales representative or FlatWorld support at support@flatworld.com for more information or to obtain access to the supplements upon adoption.

Sample Syllabi

Sample syllabi based on either 16-week or 10-week terms provide useful templates that help new adopters transition from their current course textbook to *Principles of Macroeconomics* v4.0. Faculty can download the syllabi from the FlatWorld website or they can be obtained by contacting your local FlatWorld representative or FlatWorld support (support@flatworld.com).

Instructor's Manual

The instructor's manual (IM) includes the following for each chapter: Overview and Outline, Learning Objectives, Common Student Difficulties, Suggestions for Active Learning, Lecture Supplements, and Lecture Extensions, along with Additional Materials when applicable.

PowerPoint Slides

PowerPoint Slides organized by chapter include a concise and thorough outline, a list of Learning Objectives, and figures and tables contained in the text. These slides work well for both face-to-face and online learning environments, enliven lectures, and stimulate class discussions. Adopters can use the slides as composed to support lectures or customize and build upon them to suit their particular teaching goals.

Test Item File

The author-written Test Item File (TIF) includes more than 200 questions per chapter in multiple-choice, true/false, and short answer formats. All answers are provided, including possible responses to the short answer questions. The items have been written specifically to reinforce the major topics covered in each chapter and to align with FlatWorld Homework and in-text quiz items. The Test Item File questions are also available in pre-formatted form for easy export into popular learning management systems such as Canvas or Blackboard.

Test Generator—Powered by Cognero

FlatWorld is pleased to provide a computer-generated test program powered by the leading assessment provider Cognero to assist instructors with selecting, randomizing, formatting, loading online, or printing exams. Please contact your local FlatWorld representative or FlatWorld support (support@flatworld.com) for more information or to request the program.

FlatWorld Homework

Accompanying author-reviewed FlatWorld Homework for this text is provided in an easy-to-use interface. Multiple choice, fill-in-the-blank, matching, graphing, and other question types are available for use and are all auto-gradable. Students who utilize the homework questions should see their performance improve on examinations that are given using the Test Item File questions that accompany this book.

Solutions Manual

The Solutions Manual contains answers for all Concept Problems and Numerical Problems found at the end of each text chapter.

Online Quizzes and Flashcards

Author-created Quiz questions and Flashcards for student self-evaluation are organized by chapter and section and embedded in the online version of the book. Students can use the Quizzes and Flashcards to test themselves on their comprehension by section as they read and learn, once they have completed a chapter, or for test review.

CHAPTER 1
Economics: The Study of Choice

1.1 Start Up: Economics in the News

In the best of times and in the worst of times, economic issues dominate the news. What's happening in the job market, how fast the economy is growing, the prices and availability of the products we want, the level of the national debt—these are just a few examples of economic topics you're likely to find discussed on your favorite news site's homepage. These issues not only affect us as individuals, but also affect the overall well-being of society.

If you're interested in learning more about these topics, this book covers them extensively. But economics is a field that encompasses so much more! As scientists who study how people make choices, economists investigate the nature of family life, obesity, education, discrimination, and even crime. There are weather economists, traffic economists, sports economists—there's even an Association of Wine Economists! The list of things economists study is practically limitless, because so much of our lives involves making choices.

Consider some of the choices you face. Would you like better grades? More time to binge-watch Netflix? There's a choice: Getting better grades probably requires more time studying, time you could have spent binge-watching *Game of Thrones*. We face these kinds of choices as individuals, but we also must make choices as a society. Do we want a cleaner environment? Faster economic growth? Both are desirable, but efforts to ratchet up economic growth may take a toll on the natural world we enjoy. Society, like you, must make choices.

Economics is defined less by the subjects economists investigate than by *how* economists investigate them. Economists look differently at the world than ordinary people, or even scholars in other disciplines, do. This special perspective—the *economic way of thinking*—is the subject of this chapter.

Winter is coming: Are you willing to sacrifice the strategy, intrigue, and double dealing of the Seven Kingdoms to get a better econ grade?

Source: tomertu/Shutterstock.com

1.2 Defining Economics

Learning Objectives

1. Define economics.
2. Define the concepts of scarcity and opportunity cost and explain how they relate to the definition of economics.
3. Explore the three fundamental economic questions: What should be produced? How should goods and services be produced? For whom should goods and services be produced?

Not all economists spend their days fearlessly braving the markets on Wall Street.

Source: quietbits/Shutterstock.com

economics

A social science that examines how people choose among the alternatives available to them.

Is this your first course in economics? If so, you may be wondering exactly what economics *is*. Once your friends and acquaintances have discovered you are studying economics, many will ask you what the stock market is going to do. Your parents may expect you to show up for Thanksgiving dinner in a grey flannel business suit; students majoring in education or English literature may speculate admiringly about your post-graduation earning potential.

But despite the preconception that economists generally end up on Wall Street (and some, of course, actually do), most economists consider their field to be less a sub-field of business administration and more a study of human behavior—a social science rather than a professional discipline.

Economics is a social science that examines how people choose among the alternatives available to them. It is *social* because it involves people and their behavior. It is a *science* because it uses, as much as possible, a scientific approach in its investigation of choices.

Scarcity and Opportunity Cost

All choices mean that someone must pick one alternative over another. Selecting among competing alternatives involves two ideas central to economics: scarcity and opportunity cost.

Scarcity

The people we share our lives with are all different—different shapes, different colors, different goals, different dreams. Despite those differences, we all share two important things. First among them is that we all desire things we don't currently have. Sometimes those things are material: reliable transportation, nicer clothes, sufficient food. Sometimes those things are intangible: a loving relationship, more charisma, the athletic ability of Lebron James, a summer internship. Whether we like it or not, this fundamental desire for more is part of the human condition, present from the minute we're born—"It was warm and safe *in there*; it's cold and scary *out here*! Put me back!" Nobody—not you, not me, not even billionaires like Jeff Bezos and Warren Buffet—has everything they want.

Pop! Goes the Econ: Kramer and the Human Condition

In this episode of *Seinfeld*, friends Kramer and George discuss the fundamental human condition of filling unlimited wants with scarce resources. How do Kramer and George describe it?

And why not? Because the things we want don't materialize out of thin air! It takes what economists call *resources* to produce them: raw materials, land, workers, machinery, and energy are just a few examples. If our resources were unlimited, we could say "Yes!" to each of our wants—and there would be no reason to study economics. The problem, of course, is that at any given time, there is only so much land, so many tractors, so many workers. That's the second thing that everybody, rich and poor alike, shares: We all have limited resources—even the mega-rich, who get exactly the same 24 hours to binge-watch *Tiger King* and work on their jump shots as the rest of us. And because of those limitations, saying yes to one thing generally means that we have to say no to another. Whether we like it or not, we must make choices.

scarcity

A condition in which people attempt to meet unlimited wants with limited resources.

Our unlimited wants are continually colliding with the limits of our resources. That intersection—trying to meet unlimited wants with limited resources—reflects what economists call **scarcity**. It's scarcity that forces us to pick some activities and to reject others.

A resource is a **scarce good** if using the resource for one purpose means we can't use it for something else. Consider, for example, a small parcel of land. That land has several alternative uses: We could build a house on it; we could put a gas station on it; we could create a small park on it. We could even leave the land undeveloped in order to keep our future options open. Choosing one use for the land (building a house, for example) means giving up the chance to use that land for any of its alternatives. Land is a scarce good, and when a good is scarce, you're forced to choose.

But the choices scarcity forces upon us don't end there. Suppose we have decided the land should be used for housing. Should we build a large and expensive house, or should we build several modest ones? If we build a large and expensive house, we have to choose who should live in the house: If the Lees live in it, the Nguyens cannot. There are alternative uses of the land both in terms of what we use it for and in terms of who gets to enjoy it. If there were no scarcity, we wouldn't have to make such tough decisions.

Even the air we breathe is a scarce good—despite the fact that it comes to us at no charge! The true test of whether a good is scarce is whether it has alternative uses. Is this true for air? Clearly, people need to breathe it. But we also pollute it when we drive our cars, heat our houses, and operate our factories. In other words, we use it as a garbage dump! Those two uses are competing alternatives: The more pollution we dump in the air, the less desirable—and healthy—it is to breathe. If we decide we want to breathe cleaner air, we must limit the (also) desirable activities that generate pollution. Air, even at zero charge, is a scarce good because it has alternative uses.

Almost everything is scarce. The extent of a good's scarcity depends on how available that good is and how badly that good is desired. The scarcest goods are both rare and highly desired. Not all goods, however, confront us with such choices. A good is a **free good** if the decision to use that good for one purpose does not require that we give up another.[1] One example of such a good is gravity. The fact that gravity is holding you to the earth does not mean that your neighbor is forced to drift up into space! One person's use of gravity isn't an alternative to another person's use.

There aren't many free goods. Outer space, for example, may have been a free good when the only use we made of it was to gaze at it. But now, our use of space has reached the point where one use is an alternative to another. There are conflicts, for example, over who gets orbital slots for communications satellites. And, like our airspace, now outer space is becoming a dumping ground for space junk, a hazard to passing satellites and spacecraft. So parts of outer space are already scarce, and will surely become more so as as we find new ways to use it. The (ironic) lesson in all this? *Scarcity is everywhere.* That makes the scope of economics wide, indeed!

> **scarce good**
>
> A good for which the choice of one alternative requires that another be given up.

In Jiujiang, China, clean air is *most definitely* a scarce good!

Source: humphery/Shutterstock.com

> **free good**
>
> A good for which the choice of one use does not require that another be given up.

The Economy, Scarcity, and Three Fundamental Economic Questions

If you listen to a lot of newscasts, you've probably heard lots of experts—both actual and self-proclaimed—discussing the state of the economy. But despite the fact that everyone seems to be an expert on "the economy," nobody ever really defines what the economy *is*. Listen to enough newscasts and you may have some notion that the economy is some vague entity whose performance is measured by the health of the stock market and the unemployment rate.

But the economy is much more than that—it encompasses, in one way or another, almost all human activity. At its most basic, an **economy** is any organization that produces goods and services and then allocates them to people for use. Economies can be as small as households: *"I made this pot of chili; you take a small bowl and leave the big bowl for your sister."* In fact, the word "economy" comes from the Greek *oikonomia*, which roughly translates to "household management." So, economies can be small organizations like households, but they can be big organizations, too—like

> **economy**
>
> Any organization that produces goods and services and then allocates them to people for use.

the United States, Central America, or the European Union, each of which produces hundreds of thousands of different products and then distributes them in some fashion for people to use.

Because of scarcity, every economy must make choices about what should be produced, how it should be produced, and for whom it should be produced. We will return to these questions again and again throughout this book.

Big or small, every economy must deal with scarcity. That means that every economy has to answer these fundamental questions:

Pop! Goes the Econ:
Allocation and *The Hunger Games*
In Panem, an oppressive government selects 24 children each year to participate in a battle to the death called the Hunger Games. The sole survivor is celebrated nationwide, and is given preferential housing and food. In this clip from the movie, Katniss and Peeta are chosen to represent Panem's District 12. What allocation mechanism(s) is Panem using to distribute housing and food? (If you're familiar with the story, how are non-participants allocated food and housing?)

View in the online reader

1. ***What* should be produced?** Using the economy's scarce resources to produce one thing generally requires giving up another. That's true in the household economy: "*I only have four cups of flour—I can bake you a warm, crusty sourdough loaf, or I can make chocolate chip cookies.*" It's true at the national level, too, where producing better schools may require cutting back on other services, such as health care. Every economy must decide what it will produce with its scarce resources.

2. ***How* should goods and services be produced?** Once an economy has decided what to produce, it must then decide how production will be arranged. For example, at the household level, "You wash and I'll dry" is a common arrangement—but not the only possible arrangement—that partners use to produce clean, dry dishes. Business firms such as automakers have to decide whether it's better to have a lot of workers assembling automobiles, or whether to replace some of those workers with robots. Governments make the same decisions. Today's military, for example, produces national defense using much less human power and much more high-tech weaponry than it used to.

3. ***For whom* should goods and services be produced?** Once production is complete, we have to decide how to divide up, or *allocate,* the pile of goodies that we've made. A decision to have one person or group receive a good or service usually means it will not be available to someone else. In the United States, we generally leave those decisions to the *market system,* where individual buyers and sellers determine who will receive the goods and services we've produced based on who is willing and able to pay for them. That's one possible answer to the allocation question, but it's not the only possible answer. For example, we could allocate goods on a first-come, first-served basis, or we could allocate goods by lottery, or perhaps by tournament. Another possible solution to the allocation question is to divide the goods we've produced equally: That's the system many countries have chosen to allocate health care services, which ensures that everybody, rich and poor alike, has access to some basic care. In contrast, in the United States, a good chunk of our health care services are allocated by the market system—meaning those services are more available to the rich than to the poor. Critics of that system often argue that health care should be more evenly allocated. Should it? That is a "for whom" question.

Opportunity Cost

opportunity cost

The value of the best alternative forgone in making any choice.

Scarcity forces us to make choices. That implies that we face trade-offs: More of one thing necessarily means less of another. Economists have a special name for these trade-offs: opportunity cost. When you choose one activity over another, the value of the option you sacrificed is the opportunity cost. Specifically, **opportunity cost** is the value of the *best* alternative forgone in making any choice.

Suppose, for example, you're down to your last $20, and you decide to spend it on a meal for you and your BFF at Chipotle. That $20 could have bought you a movie ticket (and popcorn!); it could have bought you morning coffee for a week; it could even have bought you tickets to see Cardi B perform at a local bar. But because you decided to use it at Chipotle, you lost the chance to do those other things.

But $20 won't buy you movie tickets *and* coffee *and* Cardi B; it will only buy you *one* of those things! So to determine the true opportunity cost of Chipotle, ask yourself this hypothetical question: If you'd gone to Chipotle, and found it closed, what would you have done with your $20? If you don't like movies and don't care for coffee, the real opportunity cost of going to Chipotle is losing your next-best alternative—an evening with Cardi B.

Sometimes it's easy to confuse opportunity cost with money, or to attempt to measure opportunity cost in dollars (or euros, or pesos). Resist that temptation when you can! One reason to resist is because money itself does not make us particularly happy. When you accidentally turn a hundred-dollar bill into lint by running it through the laundry, you're probably not sad about losing the bill—after all, the bill's just a colorful piece of paper. You're more likely disappointed because you were planning to *use* that bill to go out with your friends, or to buy your Calc II textbook, or to put gas in your Corolla. It's the loss of those *opportunities* that is important to you.

More important, thinking of opportunity cost only in terms of money may lead you to confuse the cost of an item with that item's purchase price. "*What?*" you may be saying. "*I thought cost and price were the same thing!*" And while even economists sometimes use these terms interchangeably in their daily lives, they're really two distinct notions.[2] Consider, for example, the cost of your college education. That cost includes the money (let's say, $100,000) you'll spend for four years' worth of tuition, fees, and books—money you could have spent on other things. But perhaps the biggest cost of a college education is the *time* you sacrifice—time that could be spent developing your social media empire, training for an Ironman, or even just working. Suppose, for example, that you'd never gone to college and instead went straight to work. At a modest $15 per hour wage, you could have made $120,000 during the time you spent sleeping in your applied numerology class. That brings the total cost of college up substantially—from the $100,000 sticker *price* to the $220,000 total *cost*.

That kind of thinking helps us solve an important question: Why are so many NBA superstars college dropouts? The less-than-obvious answer is that college is much more expensive for basketball hotshots than it is for the rest of us. That's not because they pay more to attend college (in fact, many college standouts receive excellent scholarships), but because every year spent in college means forgoing an opportunity—an NBA salary—that's *way* more lucrative than the opportunities you and I likely have.

There is one final reason to resist the temptation to express all costs in terms of money: Not all costs are easily measured in dollars. That's true when your roommate talks you into his 21st birthday party at the expense of studying for your particle physics final. It's equally true when you and your significant other decide to become exclusive: You lose the chance to date anyone else who may catch your eye. Those opportunities—study time, other romantic partners—are genuine costs, but costs that are hard to assign a dollar value to.

Let's link the pieces: Scarcity exists because our desires are unlimited but our resources aren't. That scarcity forces us to make choices, and all of those choices involve opportunity cost. These concepts—scarcity, choice, and opportunity cost—are at the heart of economics. We'll revisit them often throughout this book.

Poor Offset—he could have had Chipotle!

Source: Featureflash Photo Agency/Shutterstock.com

Pop! Goes the Econ: Sheldon Cooper Discovers Opportunity Cost

In this clip from *The Big Bang Theory*, Sheldon can't decide which gaming system to buy. What resources are scarce in this scene? What is the opportunity cost of buying the PS4?

View in the online reader

Opportunity cost, man—don't forget the opportunity cost!

Source: Antonio Guillem/ Shutterstock.com

Key Takeaways

- Economics is a social science that examines how people choose among the alternatives available to them.

- Scarcity implies that we must give up one alternative in selecting another. A good that is not scarce is a free good.
- The three fundamental economic questions are: What should be produced? How should goods and services be produced? For whom should goods and services be produced?
- Every choice has an opportunity cost, and opportunity costs affect the choices people make. The opportunity cost of any choice is the value of the best alternative that had to be forgone in making that choice.

Try It!

Identify the elements of scarcity, choice, and opportunity cost in each of the following:

1. The Environmental Protection Agency is considering an order to preserve a 500-acre area on the outskirts of a large city in its natural state, because the area is home to an endangered rodent. Developers had planned to build tract housing on the land.
2. The manager of an automobile assembly plant is considering whether to produce cars or sport utility vehicles (SUVs) next month. Assume that the quantities of labor and other materials required would be the same for either type of production.
3. A young man who went to work as a nurse's aide after graduating from high school leaves his job to go to college. There, he will obtain training as a registered nurse.

See related Concept Problem 5 at the end of this chapter.

Case in Point: The Opportunity Cost of COVID-19

2020 Vision: Nobody saw the coronavirus coming.

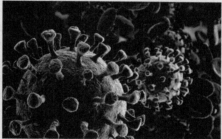

Source: creativeneko/Shutterstock.com

Everything was going just fine . . . until a single microscopic organism brought the world to its knees.

In early 2020, the U.S. economy was vibrant—unemployment was at a historical low; the stock market had just hit record highs. But a new bug was on the loose—a new virus that nobody in the world had ever seen before. The coronavirus, a deadly, easily transmissible virus, slowly but surely began spreading to the rest of the globe from its epicenter in Wuhan, China.

As March 2020 unfolded, it became apparent that the virus was both real and deadly. COVID-19 (the official name for the illness) cases mounted; the death toll climbed as the numbers of afflicted overwhelmed hospitals throughout Italy and Spain. How, policymakers wondered, could such a virus be beaten? And at what cost?

In the United States, the federal government followed the lead most European nations had taken: It closed borders to outsiders and then empowered state governments to shutter all but essential businesses. Schools closed; residents were ordered home to keep the virus from spreading. That choice undoubtedly saved lives, but it came at a great cost: Millions lost their jobs, and wealth evaporated as the stock market lost one-third of its value.

That cost was too high for many American policymakers to bear. By the beginning of May, state governments began re-opening businesses and people began resuming their pre-corona routines. As the economy recovered through May and June, cases mounted. By early July, many states began hitting record daily highs for new cases; the states that had re-opened the earliest were the hardest hit. The silver lining on this dark viral cloud was that while cases mounted, death rates stabilized.

Countries that endured stricter lockdowns and widespread containment measures saw dramatic reductions in coronavirus transmission. The state/local patchwork of lockdown measures in the United States likely contributed to a longer surge in the spring and summer of 2020.

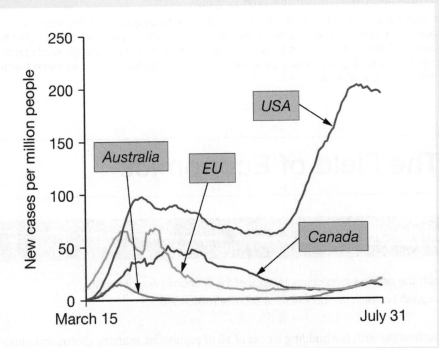

Source: Adapted from Our World in Data, "Coronavirus (COVID-19) Cases." COVID-19 Data Explorer. Retrieved from: https://ourworldindata.org/covid-cases. Reproduced via Creative Commons Attribution 4.0 International (CC BY 4.0) license: https://creativecommons.org/licenses/by/4.0/.

False Advertising: Any economist worth her egg salad sandwich can tell you there are no free lunches!

Source: lukeruk/Shutterstock.com

All choices are made at a cost—there is no proverbial "free lunch." Countries that endured stricter lockdowns saw dramatic declines in infection rates. Countries that relaxed restrictions early, like the United States (and the United States was not alone—Sweden and Brazil, for example, imposed relatively few restrictions), paid a different price—a price measured in hospital visits and lost lives.

See related Concept Problems 15 and 16 at the end of this chapter.

Answers to Try It! Problems

1. The 500-acre area is scarce because it has alternative uses: preservation in its natural state or a site for homes. A choice must be made between these uses. The opportunity cost of preserving the land in its natural state is the forgone value of the land as a housing development. The opportunity cost of using the land as a housing development is the forgone value of preserving the land.

2. The scarce resources are the plant and the labor at the plant. The manager must choose between producing cars and producing SUVs. The opportunity cost of producing cars is the profit that could be earned from producing SUVs; the opportunity cost of producing SUVs is the profit that could be earned from producing cars.

3. The man can devote his time to his current career or to an education; his time is a scarce resource. He must choose between these alternatives. The opportunity cost of continuing as a nurses' aide is the forgone benefit he expects from training as a registered nurse; the opportunity cost of going to college is the forgone income he could have earned working full-time as a nurses' aide.

1.3 The Field of Economics

Learning Objectives

1. Identify the distinguishing characteristics of the economic way of thinking.
2. Distinguish between microeconomics and macroeconomics.

You are now familiar with the building blocks of all of economics: scarcity, choice, and opportunity cost. In this section, we'll look at economics as a field of study. We begin with the characteristics that distinguish economics from other social sciences.

The Economic Way of Thinking

Economists study choices that scarcity requires us to make. But *all* social scientists are interested in choices. An anthropologist might study the choices of ancient peoples: *Will we be nomadic hunter-gatherers, or will we raise crops and live in permanent settlements?* Likewise, a political scientist might study the choices of legislatures; a psychologist might study how people choose a mate; a sociologist might study the factors that have led to an increase in single-parent households. So, if everybody studies choices, what is it that separates economics from these other social sciences?

Three features distinguish the economic approach to choice from the approaches taken in other social sciences:

1. Economists give special emphasis to the role of opportunity costs in their analysis of choices.

2. Economists assume that individuals make self-interested choices in order to attain some clearly defined objective—a process called *optimization*. Optimization can be interpreted as maximizing (making as large as possible) the value of desirable things or minimizing (making as small as possible) the value of undesirable things.

3. Economists argue that individuals pay attention to the consequences of small changes in the levels of the activities they pursue; that individuals achieve their objectives through incremental decisions about pursuing a bit more or a bit less of their activities.

The emphasis economists place on opportunity cost, the idea that people make choices in order to achieve the ideal level of a clear objective, and a focus on the effects of small changes are ideas of great power. They constitute the core of economic thinking. The next three sections examine these ideas in greater detail.

Opportunity Costs Are Important

If doing one thing requires giving up another, then the value of the alternatives we face can affect our choices. Economists argue that an understanding of opportunity cost is crucial to understanding the choices people make.

As the value or number of available alternatives changes, economists expect to see individual choices change—and change in predictable ways! The surprise announcement that Disney+ would air the original Broadway recording of *Hamilton* over the 2020 July 4th weekend changed, for millions, the opportunity cost of spending that weekend at the lake. An unexpectedly warm winter day might change your opportunity cost of going to class; your econ professor likely expects lower attendance when the weather is particularly delightful. In the same vein, a high income makes it more costly to take a day off; economists expect highly paid individuals to work more hours than those who are not paid so well. In each of these examples, and in millions more each day, the emphasis economists place on opportunity cost helps us better understand peoples' choices by pushing us to think about the relative values of the alternatives they face.

Fireworks, schmireworks. Come spend your Independence Day with me, your obedient servant, A. Ham.

Source: SeaRick1/Shutterstock. com

Self-Interested Individuals Optimize

What motivates people as they make choices? Perhaps more than anything else, it is the economist's answer to this question that distinguishes economics from other fields.

Economists assume that individuals, first and foremost, pursue their own self-interest—doing things that make them, as individuals, better off; avoiding things that make them worse off. Economists assume that in chasing those rainbows, people make choices that will ultimately bring them the greatest possible benefits, given the constraints they face.

Economists assume, for example, that the owners of business firms try to maximize their profits. That assumption gives economists power to predict how firms in an industry will respond to changes in the markets where they operate. For example, as new U.S. tariffs (a fancy word for taxes) on imported steel and aluminum drove up prices for those metals in early 2018, economists were not surprised to see heavy users of those metals, such as Harley-Davidson Motor Company, shuttering U.S. plants and shifting production to countries where tariff rates were lower and steel cheaper.

Pop! Goes the Econ: Ferris Bueller Optimizes
Ferris Bueller desperately needs a day off! Locate and explain the illustrations of opportunity cost and optimization in this clip. Bonus points if you can read ahead and pick out the marginal analysis!

View in the online reader

A solid understanding of economics can help you explain this man's portion sizes!

Source: Poznyakov/Shutterstock. com

Assumptions about the profit-maximizing behavior of business firms give economists great power to explain how firms behave in the real world. Likewise, assumptions about the goals of people who *buy* products (often referred to as *consumers*) shed similar light on those peoples' behavior. Of course, consumers don't maximize profits. Instead, economists assume that individual consumers make choices in order to maximize their satisfaction, or *utility*. That utility-maximization assumption, again, gives economists great power to explain all kinds of interesting consumer behavior—like why birthday celebrants often prefer cash to gifts, and why we tend to overeat when the restaurant we choose happens to offer a buffet.

A cautionary note: Study economics long enough, and sooner or later you'll be accused of endorsing greed. But good economists know that there's a difference between self-interest and self-ishness. People clearly gain satisfaction by helping others—just ask any parent, or anyone who has ever volunteered their time or donated to a charity. So, when economists make the assumption that consumers maximize their satisfaction, they include such seemingly altruistic activities among the choices consumers face.

People Make Choices at the Margin

margin

The current level of an activity.

choice at the margin

A decision to do a little more or a little less of something.

The third thing that sets economics apart from other disciplines is that in economics, we argue that most choices are made "at the margin." The **margin** is the current level of an activity. Think of it as the "edge" from which a choice is to be made. A **choice at the margin** is a decision to do a little more or a little less of something.

Here's an example of a choice made at the margin: Imagine you pull into the drive-thru at your favorite fast-food joint. You scan the menu and see the following:

MENU

Burger	$5
Drink	$2
Fries	$2

Based on those prices, the cash in your wallet, and your particular preferences, you decide to get a burger and a drink; the fries just aren't worth the $2. And then, the clown's mouth asks you an all-important question, a question you've probably often been asked: "*Would you like burger/fry/drink combo meal for $8?*"

"Would you like fries with that?" is a question no longer reserved just for fast-food workers!

Source: Sorbis/Shutterstock.com

This is an interesting question—you've now got a new option to evaluate, one that wasn't even on the menu! And notice that you don't really have to think about whether the combo meal is worth the $8, because you've already committed to a $7 purchase of a burger and drink either way. Instead, all you have to determine is whether the extra food (fries) is worth the extra money (now $1 rather than $2!). The idea of only evaluating *extra or additional* costs and benefits in decision-making is the essence of marginal thinking, and the good news is that such marginal thinking will automatically guide you to the best choice between just the burger and drink or the combo meal.[3]

Evaluating choices at the margin can lead to extremely useful insights. Consider, for example, the problem of curtailing water consumption when, say, a drought makes water increasingly scarce. Economists argue that one way to induce people to conserve water is to raise its price. But non-economists often disagree with this assessment, claiming that prices won't affect water consumption because water is a necessity.

But choices in water consumption, like virtually all choices, are made at the margin. Individuals don't make all-or-nothing decisions about whether they should or should not consume water. Instead, they decide whether to consume a little *more* or a little *less* water. For example, the typical person in the United States uses about 100 gallons of water each day. If the price of water doubled, could some of those people cut consumption to, say, 95 gallons per day by taking slightly shorter showers, or maybe flushing less often? High prices might also make people evaluate choices about what they use their water *for*: Few of us would eliminate toothbrushing at any price (we hope?), but many of us might stop washing our cars and watering our lawns with precious liquid gold. When we examine the choice to consume water at the margin, the notion that a higher price would reduce consumption seems much more plausible. Prices affect our consumption of water because choices in water consumption, like other choices, are made at the margin.

You're now acquainted with the three key elements of the economic way of thinking—opportunity cost, optimization, and decision-making at the margin. We'll revisit and expand on these concepts repeatedly as we analyze the inner workings of the market system and the economy as a whole.

Pop! Goes the Econ: Are *Super Troopers* Marginal Thinkers?

Find the marginal thinking (both costs and benefits) in this clip from the movie *Super Troopers*.

Microeconomics and Macroeconomics

When you enrolled in your econ course, you probably signed up for either a "macro" or a "micro" course. If you're uncertain what you've gotten yourself into (and don't worry—most econ newbies are), you might find it helpful to know that economics is typically divided into two broad categories: microeconomics and macroeconomics.

Microeconomics is the branch of economics that focuses on the choices made by individual decision-making units in the economy—typically consumers and firms—and the impacts those choices have on individual markets, like the market for cheese and the market for recorded music. In your micro course, you might dig into questions such as why tickets to the musical *Hamilton* cost so much, how global warming is affecting real estate prices, why women end up doing a disproportionate share of the housework, and why popcorn costs so much at the movies.

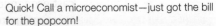
Quick! Call a microeconomist—just got the bill for the popcorn!

Source: BlueSkyImage/Shutterstock.com

Macroeconomics is the branch of economics that focuses on the impact of choices on the total, or *aggregate*, level of economic activity. Rather than looking at what's happening in just the cheese market or just the market for bottled water, macroeconomists look at the big picture and attempt to measure and evaluate the performance of *all* markets—the cheese market, the bottled water market, the markets for sports merchandise and gasoline and hundreds of thousands of other goods and services—all at the same time. Is overall production in the United States rising or falling? What's happening to the cost of living—and why? How will the unemployment rate change this month? These are the questions that macroeconomists attempt to answer. And those answers are important: Policymakers rely on macroeconomists to help them in their attempts to steer the broad economy toward desirable goals such as economic growth and the full employment of workers.

microeconomics

The branch of economics that focuses on the choices made by consumers and firms and the impacts those choices have on individual markets.

macroeconomics

The branch of economics that focuses on the impact of choices on the total, or aggregate, level of economic activity.

Putting Economics to Work

You now have a passing acquaintance with the types of issues economists address, and the types of questions economists are interested in answering. You're also acquainted with some of the building blocks of economics: scarcity, opportunity cost, and marginal analysis. But you may still be curious about what it is that economists actually *do*. Is economics something a person can actually make a living doing?

Yes! Because the economic way of thinking has proven to be both insightful and useful, training in economics can be put to work in a wide range of fields. Of course, people with training in econ can become economists (we'll talk briefly about what that entails in a second), but even if you don't want to become an economist, you'll find the economic training extremely useful both in other careers and in your personal life.

Careers in Economics

Suppose you decide to become an economist. Where can you find a job? Economists work in all kinds of places, but most of those places can be generally categorized in one of three ways: government agencies, business firms, and colleges and universities.

One dollar out of every five that gets spent in the economy is spent by some unit of government—either federal, state, or local. For all the highbrow talk about the dignity of public service, most government work reduces to making decisions about how to bring in tax money and then how to send it out again. In other words, your legislators, your governors, your president are all making the same kinds of choices you make about your own income and expenditures, but on a much larger scale.[4] Governments employ economists to help them make decisions about how to spend this money: *"Will we get the biggest bang for our buck building a border wall, or should we spend that money on an aircraft carrier?"* Governments also employ economists to help them forecast economic activity, to measure the cost of living and other important variables, and to advise them on matters of policy: *"If we give each taxpayer a $1,200 tax rebate, how many retail jobs will be saved?"* or *"Will more support for Head Start pre-K programs increase future SAT scores?"*

Economists work for businesses, too, and businesses beyond the stereotypical Wall Street firms like Goldman Sachs and Deutschebank. Hallmark employs economists to forecast sales of greeting cards. World Series champions employ economists to help them strategically price their tickets. BMW employs economists to help develop more efficient production processes (remember the choice of human power vs. robot power we talked about earlier? That's just one piece of building the greatest number of cars out of the fewest resources). And economists' training makes them particularly well suited for the rapidly growing field of data analytics, where the exploding world of internet data is used to determine the best location for a new Walgreens, Netflix's best recommendations for those who loved *The Good Place*, and the best products for Amazon to discount on Cyber Monday.

But we're getting ahead of ourselves. After all, you're young, and you probably haven't met many industry or government economists yet. The economists *you* know probably work at your college or university. And yes, colleges and universities employ thousands and thousands of economists. In addition to teaching you about economic theory, those economists help guide your senior theses; they help faculty members in other disciplines crunch numbers for research projects; they conduct research projects of their own.[5] In fact, the most brilliant economists in the world aren't found on Wall Street or at the Federal Reserve; you'll find most of our Nobel laureates in economics in university classrooms, teaching students by day and cultivating brilliance by night.

Pop! Goes the Econ: The Relentless Pursuit of Greater Efficiency
That state of the art Xbox Kinect you loved so much? Economists were using that same technology a hundred years ago to improve efficiency in manufacturing!

View in the online reader

Applying Economics to Other Fields

"Okay, but I don't really want to become an economist. I'm just taking this course because it's required for my Social Influencing minor. Will training in econ still be useful?"

While we're sorry you're not really interested in becoming a working economist, the good news is that your time in the econ classroom isn't likely to be wasted. The economic way of thinking is both insightful and incisive; it helps people in all kinds of professions to make better decisions.

Suppose, for example, that you are considering law school. The study of law requires keen analytical skills; studying economics sharpens such skills. Not only do students with training in economics tend to do better in law school than students who lack such training, but students with econ training tend to have an easier time getting *into* law school in the first place!

One of the big litmus tests aspiring law students must pass is getting a good score on the Law School Admission Test (LSAT). Because econ students are taught to think carefully and logically through somewhat messy problems, year after year, students with economics training excel on this exam. That excellence is summarized in Table 1.1, which shows scores by major for entering law school students.

TABLE 1.1 LSAT Scores for Students Taking the Exam in 2017–2018
Here are the average LSAT scores and rankings for the thirteen undergraduate majors with more than 1,000 students taking the test to enter law school in the 2017–2018 academic year.

Rank	Major	Average LSAT Score	Number of Students
1	Economics	158.9	2,757
2	Philosophy	157.2	2,238
3	International Relations	156.7	1,104
4	History	156.3	3,138
5	Finance	155.0	1,471
6	English	154.8	3,151
7	Political Science	153.6	11,947
8	Psychology	152.5	3,736
9	Business Marketing	151.3	1,002
10	Communications	150.8	1,838
11	Sociology	150.6	1,870
12	Business Administration	149.3	1,489
13	Criminal Justice	145.9	3,629

Source: Based on University of Manitoba, "Average LSAT Scores by Major in 2018," with data from the Law School Admissions Council. Retrieved from: https://umanitoba.ca/faculties/arts/departments/philosophy/media/Average_LSAT_Scores_by_Major.pdf.

Of course, you may not be interested in going to law school. But people with training in economics have lots of other great options and tend to do very well in terms of their lifetime earnings. The Georgetown Center on Education and the Workforce surveyed a large group of college graduates at various stages in their careers regarding both their earnings and their undergraduate major. Their study found that people with degrees in economics (but who weren't necessarily working as economists) earned much more than people with degrees in the other social sciences. They also found economics to be the only non-STEM discipline among the top twenty-five highest-paid majors (that list is dominated by engineering and computer sciences).[6] So whether you decide to become a production manager, an aircraft refurbisher, a personal financial planner, a baseball analyst, or a wedding planner, the skills you learn in the economics classroom will be both useful in advancing your career and financially rewarding.

Of course, your choice of a major isn't likely to be based solely on considerations of potential earnings or the prospect of landing a spot in law school. You are surely also considering your interests and abilities, and hopefully you're also considering the benefits (both monetary and non-monetary) of other possible degree paths. What is *your* opportunity cost of pursuing a degree in economics? Does studying more economics serve your interests? Will doing so maximize your utility, now and over your lifetime? These considerations may be on your mind as you begin to study economics at the college level. But, should you decide to pursue further study in economics, you can rest assured that a background in this field is likely to serve you well.

Key Takeaways

- Economists focus on the opportunity costs of choices; they assume that individuals pursue their own self-interest and attempt to optimize their choices; and they assume that individuals make those choices at the margin.
- Economics is divided into two broad areas: microeconomics and macroeconomics.
- A wide range of career opportunities is open to economics majors. Empirical evidence suggests that students with a degree in economics tend to have an edge in getting into graduate programs and tend to have relatively high lifetime earnings.

Try It!

The Department of Agriculture estimated that the expenditures a middle-income, husband–wife family of three would incur to raise one additional child from birth in 2015 to age 17 would be $284,570. In what way does this estimate illustrate the economic way of thinking? Would the Department's estimate be an example of microeconomic or of macroeconomic analysis? Why?

See related Concept Problem 10 at the end of this chapter.

Case in Point: Opportunity Cost with *The Simpsons*

Source: Victoria 1/Shutterstock.com

In the animated television comedy *The Simpsons*, Homer's father, Grampa Simpson, faced a classic problem in the allocation of a scarce resource—his time. He wanted to spend the day with his girlfriend, Bea—it was, after all, her birthday. His alternative was to spend the day with Homer and the family, which he did not really want to do, partly because they never visited him anyway.

Homer and his family prevailed, however, and insisted on taking Grampa to "Discount Lion Safari," a local amusement park. The cost of Grampa's day with his family is the enjoyment he anticipated from spending time with Bea. It all ends up badly for Grampa—Homer's car breaks down on the way to the park. As for the forgone alternative, Bea dies that day, possibly because of a broken heart from not being able to spend the day with Grampa.

See related Concept Problem 8 at the end of this chapter.

Sources: Based on R. Andrew Luccasen and M. Kathleen Thomas, "Simpsonomics: Teaching Economics Using Episodes of The Simpsons," The Journal of Economic Education, 41(2), Spring

2010, 136–149. The Simpsons, Episode no. 30, first broadcast 28 March 1991 by Fox, directed by David Silverman and written by Jay Kogen and Wallace Wolodarsky.

Answer to Try It! Problem

The information given suggests one element of the economic way of thinking: assessing choices at the margin. The estimate reflects the cost of one *additional* child for a family that already has one. (Economists often use the words "extra" or "additional" as synonyms for the word "marginal.")

It is not clear from the information given how close the estimate of cost comes to the economic concept of opportunity cost. The Department of Agriculture's estimate included such costs as housing, food, transportation, clothing, health care, child care, and education. An economist would add the value of the best alternative use of the additional time that will be required to raise the child. If the couple is looking far ahead, it may want to consider the opportunity cost of sending that marginal child to college. And, if it is looking *very* far ahead, it may want to consider the fact that nearly half of all parents over the age of 50 support at least one child over the age of 21. This is a problem in microeconomic analysis, because it focuses on the choices of individual households.

1.4 The Economist's Tool Kit

Learning Objectives

1. Explain how economists test hypotheses, develop economic theories, and use models in their analyses.
2. Explain how the all-other-things unchanged (*ceteris paribus*) problem and the fallacy of false cause affect the testing of economic hypotheses, and how economists try to overcome these problems.
3. Distinguish between normative and positive statements.

Thank the plague! Pulled home from college in Cambridge to shelter in place as the bubonic plague ravaged England, Isaac Newton made fundamental discoveries in physics, astronomy, and calculus. But nobody can resist the world of economics: Newton finished his career at the royal treasury; his life's biggest challenge was tracking down a serial counterfeiter! Here, this little guy sits under the very apple tree that inspired Newton's theory of gravitational attraction.

Source: Photo courtesy of Alan Grant

variable

Something whose value can change.

constant

Something whose value does not change.

scientific method

A systematic set of procedures through which knowledge is created.

hypothesis

An assertion of a relationship between two or more variables that could be proven to be false.

Oops . . . too much sunlight. Theory = falsified!

Source: Lolostock/Shutterstock. com

Now that we have a sense of *what* economists do, let's talk about *how* they do it. Economists are in the business of creating theories about how the world works, and then testing those theories to see if they do a good job of describing what we actually see. We already know that economics differs from other social sciences because of its emphasis on opportunity cost, the assumption of maximization in terms of one's own self-interest, and the analysis of choices at the margin in explaining decisions. But despite those differences, much of the basic methodology of economics—theorizing and then testing—is common to every science. This section explores how economists test and refine their knowledge of the choices people make.

Researchers in the sciences are often interested in the relationships between variables. A **variable** is something whose value can change. So, for example, a nutritionist might be interested in the relationship between zinc intake (one variable) and the length of the common cold (a second variable). By contrast, a **constant** is something whose value does not change, such as the number of minutes in an hour. While that makes constants sound less important in science, nothing could be further from the truth—just ask Isaac Newton, whose constant of gravitational attraction appears in hundreds of thousands of research articles in physics and engineering.

Scientific research is generally conducted within a framework called the **scientific method**, a systematic set of procedures that we use to advance our knowledge of the world. In the scientific method, hypotheses about how the world works are suggested and then tested. A **hypothesis** is a claim about the relationship between two or more variables that could potentially be proven false. *A statement is not a hypothesis if no conceivable test could show it to be false.* For example, the statement "Plants like sunshine" is not a hypothesis; there is no way to test whether plants like sunshine or not, so it's impossible to prove the statement false. The statement "Increasing exposure to sunlight causes plants to grow more quickly" *is* a hypothesis because it's possible to test the relationship between sunlight and plant growth with some kind of experiment, and it's possible the results of your experiment might show your claim to . be false.

"So, I've developed my theory and conducted a test, and darned if the test didn't prove my theory wrong! What now?!" Well, there's good news and bad news. Here's the bad: If a test reveals that your hypothesis is false, then your theory is either flat-out wrong or needs work. Here's the good: You now have new knowledge—data—that you can use to help improve your theory. For example, let's suppose you wanted to test the hypothesis about sunlight and plant growth. You might carefully pot some plants and expose each plant to different amounts of sunlight. If you found that your theory was true over some range, but that too much sunlight eventually caused your plants to wither, that information could be used to create a different (and possibly more nuanced) hypothesis about the relationship between those two variables.

If the tests of a hypothesis yield results consistent with it, then further tests are conducted. A hypothesis that has not been rejected after widespread testing and that wins general acceptance is commonly called a **theory**, like the big bang theory. A theory that has been subjected to even more testing and that has won virtually universal acceptance becomes a **law**, like Newton's laws of motion . . . or the economists' law of demand, which you'll explore in Chapter 3.

No matter how strong a theory or a law might appear, there is *always* a possibility that someone, someday, might find a case that invalidates the hypothesis.[7] That possibility means that nothing in economics, or in any other social science, or in any science at all, can ever be *proven* true. We can have great confidence in a particular proposition, but it is always a mistake to say that it's been "proven."

> **theory**
>
> A hypothesis that has not been rejected after widespread testing and that wins general acceptance.

> **law**
>
> A theory that has been subjected to even more testing and that has won virtually universal acceptance.

Models in Economics

The real world is a messy place, with lots of things all happening at once. In fact it's far too complex for the human mind—or the most powerful computer—to account for all of the possibilities, contingencies, combinations, and permutations that might affect our understanding of the relationships between variables. So, to simplify the world to a manageable scale, scientists use models. A **model** is a set of simplifying assumptions about some aspect of the real world.

> **model**
>
> A set of simplifying assumptions about some aspect of the real world.

Have you ever used a road map (or the Maps app on your phone)? That map is a model—it doesn't show every house, every stream, every fire hydrant, every driveway, even though knowing where those things are might help you navigate from A to B. Instead, it filters those things out, simplifies the world, and only shows the big picture—roads, rivers, major landmarks. That keeps the size of the map manageable, and makes it more useful to people trying to navigate to a destination. Like the map, the economic models we'll use are always simplifications of the real world. But in generalizing about the world, we gain the power to explain how the world generally works, without having to account for every possible contingency.

Which *looks* more like a real airplane? Which *flies* more like a real airplane? Sometimes our models don't have to perfectly mimic the real world to be useful in explaining complex ideas!

Sources: conrado/Shutterstock.com; Vasilyev Alexandr/ Shutterstock.com

You will encounter your first economic model in Chapter 2. That model assumes, for example, that an economy can produce only two goods. (Economists often use graphs to represent economic models, and the model in Chapter 2 is no exception. The appendix to this chapter provides a quick refresher course on graphs if you need one.) What we've discovered is that even though we know that even the simplest real-world economies can produce hundreds or thousands of goods, trying to incorporate those extra products into our model makes the mathematics really hard, but doesn't shed any additional insight into the choices people make. And remember that understanding peoples' choices is what economic science is all about!

Testing Hypotheses in Economics

Models in economics help us generate hypotheses about the real world. In this section, we will examine some of the problems we encounter in testing those hypotheses.

Here is a hypothesis suggested by the model of demand and supply, which you'll see in Chapter 3: A decrease in the price of gasoline will lead consumers to buy more gasoline. How could we test this hypothesis? One way would be to go out into the real world and gather data about peoples' actual behavior.

Let's look for some convenient data: a time when the price of gasoline was dropping sharply. For example, between May 2014 and January 2015, the average retail price of gasoline in the United

States plummeted from $3.68 per gallon to $2.06. Over that same few months, the number of gallons of gasoline consumed by U.S. motorists rose 16.7 percent. So, real-world data from that time period seems to be consistent with our theory.[8]

Just for fun, let's gather some more data from a more recent time period and see if the theory still holds. Between February and April 2020, the retail price of gasoline fell from $2.45 per gallon to $1.77. Over the same time period, gasoline consumption *fell* by 52%! Can you say, "*Oops!*" This data is inconsistent with our hypothesis that lower gas prices lead to increased gas consumption.

Does that mean that we should dismiss our original hypothesis? Not so fast! There are lots of pitfalls in interpreting any set of economic data. One potential problem is that at any time, several things other than just gas prices may be changing—and some of those other things might be affecting consumers' choices about how much gas to buy. Pitfalls like these can sometimes make economic analysis difficult, but being able to recognize such pitfalls and explain the real-world data is what makes economics so useful. The next two sections examine these potential pitfalls in detail.

The All-Other-Things-Unchanged Problem

ceteris paribus

A Latin phrase that means, "all other things unchanged."

The hypothesis that a decrease in the price of gasoline produces an increase in the quantity of gas desired by consumers carries with it the assumption that there are no other changes that might also affect consumers' desire for gasoline. A better statement of the hypothesis might be: "*A decrease in the price of gasoline will increase the quantity consumers want to buy, ceteris paribus.*" **Ceteris paribus** is a Latin phrase that means "all other things unchanged, or held constant."

L.A. traffic is notoriously bumper-to-bumper . . . but during the coronavirus lockdown even cheap gas couldn't get drivers back on the road.

Source: Hyperlapse Media/Shutterstock.com

While our data from early 2020 seems to invalidate our theory, it's worth noting that we didn't test our theory while holding all other things constant. In fact, lots of very important things changed between February and April 2020. During that time, you may recall, businesses were being shuttered and people ordered to stay home to prevent the spread of the coronavirus. So, even if rapidly decreasing gasoline prices made consumers *want* to drive more, the order to shelter in place *forced* them to drive less! The *ceteris paribus* assumption we made when formulating our hypothesis wasn't cooperating in the real world.

In laboratory sciences such as chemistry and biology, it is relatively easy to conduct experiments in which only selected things change and all other factors are held constant. But the economists' laboratory is the real world, and as we mentioned before, it's a messy place. It's hard to test theories in such an environment—after all, we can't ask the world to stand still while we collect our data.[9] So most of the time, economists end up testing their theories with messy real-world data, and then use special statistical methods to help them isolate the impact of a change in one variable (like the price of gasoline) on another (like gas consumption), even while other factors are waving their hands in the background.

The Fallacy of False Cause

Here's another pitfall economists often encounter when testing theory with real-world data: *Just because two things happen at the same time doesn't mean that one causes the other.*

Here's an example: Do you remember the discussion in Section 3 about how well economics majors did on the Law School Admission Test (LSAT)? Does the strong performance by economics majors mean that training in economics sharpens analytical skills, enabling ordinary students to become LSAT superperformers? Or, might it be possible that the type of person who is predisposed to do well on the LSAT possesses the keen analytical skills that draw her to study, and enable her to succeed in, economics? Truthfully, both are probably at work: Economics tends to attract students with good analytical skills—and studying economics helps to develop those skills.

Here's why this situation poses such a problem for economic science: Hypotheses in economics typically specify a relationship in which a change in one variable causes another to change. We call the variable that causes (or *induces*) the change the **independent variable**, and the variable that responds to the change the **dependent variable**.

Sometimes, though, when two variables (like major and LSAT score) display some relationship (or, are *correlated*), the fact that the two variables move together might falsely suggest that one of the variables *causes* changes in the other variable. Consider the following (ridiculous!) hypothesis: *People wearing shorts cause warm weather.* Even though we know our apparel choices can't possibly influence Mother Nature, the data we see in the real world certainly seems to support our hypothesis. This is a case where our (misguided) theory probably gets it backward: Rather than shorts causing warm weather, warm weather likely causes shorts.

False Cause: Has there ever been a Nicolas Cage film that *didn't* cause despair? The correlation presented here, from Tyler Vigen's magnificent Spurious Correlations website, is simply a coincidence—an artifact of the time period Vigen chose. Adding earlier or later data would have destroyed the (coincidental) pattern!

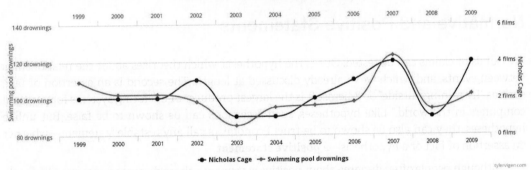

Number of people who drowned by falling into a pool
correlates with
Films Nicolas Cage appeared in

Source: Tyler Vigen. "Number of people who drowned by falling into a pool correlates with Films Nicolas Cage appeared in (1999-2009)." Spurious Creations.com. Retrieved from: https://tylervigen.com/spurious-correlations. Reproduced via Creative Commons Attribution 4.0 International (CC BY 4.0): https://creativecommons.org/licenses/by/4.0/.

Reaching the incorrect conclusion that one event causes another because the two events tend to occur together is called the **fallacy of false cause**. You may have heard the fallacy of false cause expressed in a different way: *Correlation doesn't imply causation.* Because of the danger of the fallacy of false cause, economists test their theories using special statistical techniques that are designed to determine whether changes in one thing actually *do* cause changes observed in another. Those tests, however, are not perfect, and don't always offer convincing evidence that one thing does, in fact, cause changes in another.

independent variable

A variable that causes or induces a change in another variable.

dependent variable

A variable that responds to change.

fallacy of false cause

The incorrect assumption that one event causes another because the two events tend to occur together.

Pop! Goes the Econ: Fallacy of False Cause Discovered in *The West Wing*

In this clip from *The West Wing*, President Jed Bartlett discusses the post-hoc fallacy. Explain how the post-hoc fallacy is a special case of the fallacy of false cause.

View in the online reader

Normative and Positive Statements

positive statement

A statement of fact or a hypothesis.

normative statement

A statement that makes a value judgment.

Two kinds of claims can be tested. One is the hypothesis, which theorizes about the relationships between events, and which we've already discussed at length. The second is an assertion of fact, such as "It's raining outside" or "Microsoft is the largest producer of operating systems for personal computers in the world." Like hypotheses, such assertions can be shown to be false. But unlike hypotheses, they can also be shown to be true! Economists call any testable statement—whether an assertion of fact or a hypothesis—a **positive statement**.

Although people often disagree about positive statements, those disagreements can ultimately be resolved by testing. There is another category of assertions, however, where testing is useless in resolving differences. A **normative statement** is one that makes some kind of value judgment. Here are some examples of normative statements:

- *There is too much income inequality.*
- *People should save more for their retirement.*
- Tiger King *is the greatest TV series of all time.*

These statements aren't testable; they can't be proven right or wrong. They're judgments, or opinions, that depend on the values of the person who asserts them.

Because people have different values, normative statements often provoke disagreement. An economist whose values lead him or her to conclude that we should provide more help for the poor will disagree with one whose values lead to a conclusion that we should not. Because no test exists for these values, these two economists will continue to disagree, unless one persuades the other to change values.

The good news for you, as a student of economics, is that your values are your own, and we're not going to try to change them: This book focuses on positive, rather than normative, economics. We won't indoctrinate you, but we will help inform you. And as you gain a more sophisticated understanding of how the world works and become acquainted with what real-world data shows to be true, you may see your values changing, or becoming more nuanced. By the end of the term, you may well feel differently about policies like the minimum wage, universal basic income, or taxes on imported goods.

Key Takeaways

- Economists try to employ the scientific method in their research.
- Scientists cannot prove a hypothesis to be true; they can only fail to prove it false.
- Economists, like other social scientists and scientists, use models to assist them in their analyses.
- Two problems inherent in tests of hypotheses in economics are the all-other-things-unchanged (ceteris paribus) problem and the fallacy of false cause.
- Positive statements are factual and can be tested. Normative statements are value judgments that cannot be tested. Many of the disagreements among economists stem from differences in values.

Try It!

Look again at the data in Table 1.1. Now consider the hypothesis: "Majoring in economics will result in a higher LSAT score." Are the data given consistent with this hypothesis? Do the data prove that this hypothesis is correct? What fallacy might be involved in accepting the hypothesis?

See related Concept Problem 17 at the end of this chapter.

Case in Point: Does Baldness Cause Heart Disease?

A patient walks into his doctor's office and asks the following: "I seem to be going bald. I've read that this means I'm more likely to have a heart attack. If I take a drug to prevent hair loss, will it reduce that risk?"

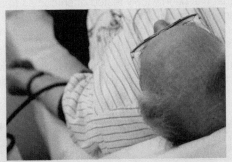

Source: Zsolt Biczo/Shutterstock.com

How might the doctor reply? Do you suppose the correlation between baldness and heart disease indicates that a lack of hair causes your heart to fail (those winters can be *cold!*)? Or is it more likely that both baldness and heart disease are affected by underlying factors, such as hypertension, high cholesterol, and smoking?

Science seems to point to the second explanation as the most likely. The good news for balding men (particularly for those whose baldness begins at the top of their head) is that their baldness serves as an early-warning system that might alert them to cardiovascular problems down the road.

See related Concept Problem 14 at the end of this chapter.

Source: Based on Nicholas Bakalar, "Risks: Male Baldness and Heart Disease," The New York Times, April 9, 2013, p. D4.

Answer to Try It! Problem

The data are consistent with the hypothesis, but it is never possible to prove that a hypothesis is correct. Accepting the hypothesis could involve the fallacy of false cause; students who major in economics may already have the analytical skills needed to do well on the exam.

1.5 Review and Practice

Summary

Economists study the choices that people make—choices that are forced on us by scarcity. Scarce goods are those for which the choice of one alternative requires giving up another. The opportunity cost of any choice is the value of the best alternative forgone in making that choice.

Some key choices assessed by economists include what to produce, how to produce it, and for whom it should be produced. Economics is distinguished from other academic disciplines that also study choices by its emphasis on the central importance of opportunity costs in evaluating choices, the assumption of optimizing behavior that serves the interests of individual decision makers, and its focus on evaluating choices at the margin.

Economic analyses may be aimed at explaining individual choice or choices in an individual market; such investigations are largely the focus of microeconomics. The analysis of the impact of those individual choices on such aggregates as total output, the level of employment, and the price level is the concern of macroeconomics.

Working within the framework of the scientific method, economists formulate hypotheses and then test them. These tests can only refute a hypothesis; hypotheses in science cannot be proved. A hypothesis that has been widely tested often comes to be regarded as a theory; one that has won virtually universal acceptance is a law. Because of the complexity of the real world, economists rely on models that rest on a series of simplifying assumptions. The models are used to generate hypotheses about the economy that can be tested using real-world data.

Statements of fact and hypotheses are positive statements. Normative statements, unlike positive statements, cannot be tested, and they provide a source for potential disagreement.

Concept Problems

1. Why does the fact that something is scarce require that we make choices?
2. Does the fact that something is abundant mean it is not scarce in the economic sense? Why or why not?
3. In some countries, such as Cuba and North Korea, the government makes most of the decisions about what will be produced, how it will be produced, and for whom. Does the fact that these choices are made by the government eliminate scarcity in these countries? Why or why not?
4. Explain what is meant by the opportunity cost of a choice.
5. (Related to "Try It!" in Section 1.2.) What is the approximate dollar cost of the tuition and other fees associated with the economics course you are taking? Does this dollar cost fully reflect the opportunity cost to you of taking the course?
6. Indicate whether each of the following is a topic of microeconomics or macroeconomics:

   a. The impact of higher oil prices on the production of steel

b. The increased demand in the last 15 years for exotic dietary supplements

c. The surge in aggregate economic activity that hit much of Asia late in the early 2000s

d. The sharp increases in U.S. employment and total output that occurred between 2003 and 2007

e. The impact of preservation of wilderness areas on the logging industry and on the price of lumber

7. Determine whether each of the following raises a "what," "how," or "for whom" issue. Are the statements normative or positive?

   a. A requirement that aluminum used in cars be made from recycled materials will raise the price of automobiles.

   b. The federal government does not spend enough for children.

   c. An increase in police resources provided to the inner city will lower the crime rate.

   d. Automation destroys jobs.

   e. Efforts to improve the environment tend to reduce production and employment.

   f. Japanese firms should be more willing to hire additional workers when production rises and to lay off workers when production falls.

   g. Access to health care should not be limited by income.

8. (Related to "Case in Point: Opportunity Cost with The Simpsons " in Section 1.3.) Your time is a scarce resource. What if the quantity of time were increased, say to 48 hours per day, and everyone still lived as many days as before? Would time still be scarce?

9. Most college students are under age 25. Give two explanations for this—one based on the benefits people of different ages are likely to receive from higher education and one based on the opportunity costs of a college education to students of different ages.

10. (Related to "Try It!" in Section 1.3.) Some municipal water companies charge customers a flat fee each month, regardless of the amount of water they consume. Others meter water use and charge according to the quantity of water customers use. Compare the way the two systems affect the cost of water use at the margin.

11. How might you test each of the following hypotheses? Suggest some problems that might arise in each test due to the ceteris paribus (all-other-things-unchanged) problem and the fallacy of false cause.

    a. Reducing the quantity of heroin available will increase total spending on heroin and increase the crime rate.

    b. Higher incomes make people happier.

    c. Higher incomes make people live longer.

12. Many models in physics and in chemistry assume the existence of a perfect vacuum (that is, a space entirely empty of matter). Yet we know that a perfect vacuum cannot exist. Are such models valid? Why are models based on assumptions that are essentially incorrect?

13. Suppose you were asked to test the proposition that publishing students' teacher evaluations causes grade inflation. What evidence might you want to consider? How would the inability to carry out controlled experiments make your analysis more difficult?

14. (Related to "Case in Point: Does Baldness Cause Heart Disease?" in Section 1.4.) Explain the possible fallacy of false cause in concluding that baldness makes a person more likely to have heart disease.

15. (Related to "Case in Point: The Opportunity Cost of COVID-19" in Section 1.2.) In early 2021, several European countries removed access to the Oxford-Astra Zeneca COVID-19 vaccine because of worries that it might be linked to an increased risk of blood clots. Explain the tradeoff regulators faced.

16. (Related to "Case in Point: The Opportunity Cost of COVID-19" in Section 1.2.) In late 2020, the U.S. began its long COVID-19 vaccine rollout. Each state developed its own plan, and had to prioritize access to the scarce vaccine. Discuss the tradeoffs, costs, and benefits inherent in these two options:

a. Begin the vaccination program by providing vaccine to the elderly, who are most vulnerable.

b. Begin the vaccination program by providing vaccine to the young, who are the most likely to spread the disease to others.

17. (Related to "Try It!" in Section 1.4.) Doctors have noticed that in any month, sales of ice cream are positively related to the number of drownings. *"Didn't your mother tell you to wait 30 minutes after eating before you jump in the pool?"* Explain the nature of causation in this observation.

Endnotes

1. A reasonable test of whether a good is a free good is to ask whether there would be any left if the good were given away.

2. Get ready for it—you'll spend way more time than you want to discussing the distinctions between price and cost beginning in just a few chapters!

3. If you're math-phobic but understand how the burger/drink/combo analysis leads you to your best outcome, pat yourself on the back—you've just demonstrated mastery of something that would ordinarily take a course in calculus to understand!

4. The scale is huge: The federal government is set to spend well over $4 trillion this year. If you counted two hundred-dollar bills each second (one in each hand), 24/7/365, it would take you well over 600 years to count the money your federal government spends in one.

5. Some of them even write textbooks!

6. See the full report at https://1gyhoq479ufd3yna29x7ubjn-wpengine.netdna-ssl.com/wp-content/uploads/The-Economic-Value-of-College-Majors-Full-Report-web-FINAL.pdf

7. Even Newton's law of gravitational attraction has been proven invalid in special circumstances (though it's still quite useful in everyday application). If Isaac Newton—astronomer, physicist, inventor of calculus—couldn't come up with a universal law, what hope is there for the rest of us?!

8. Data is from the U.S. Energy Information Administration.

9. That's not entirely true—a group of *experimental economists* regularly tests basic theory by conducting controlled experiments (usually with undergraduate econ students as test subjects) in a laboratory. That kind of testing, however, is the exception rather than the rule.

CHAPTER 2

Confronting Scarcity: Choices in Production

2.1 Start Up: An Attempt to Produce Safer Air Travel

Two decades after the terrorist attacks of September 11, 2001, American taxpayers continue to give up a great deal of money, and airline passengers continue to give up a great deal of time—and a great deal of privacy—to ensure that other terrorists will not turn their travel into tragedy.

The U.S. effort is run by the Transportation Security Administration (TSA), a federal agency created in response to the 2001 attacks. TSA requirements became a bit more onerous after Richard Reid, an Englishman and member of al-Qaeda, tried in December of that same year to blow up an American Airlines flight with a bomb he had concealed in his shoe. Reid was unsuccessful, but his legacy remains: Even today, passengers must remove their shoes so TSA agents can check them for bombs.

TSA restrictions became dramatically more stringent after Umar Farouk Abdulmutallab, a jihadist from Nigeria, tried—again without success—to blow up a plane flying from Amsterdam to Detroit on Christmas Day, 2009, using a bomb concealed in his underwear. The subsequent tightening of TSA regulations, and the introduction of body-scan machines and "patdown inspections," were quick to follow. Each new procedure required additional money and time, and each new procedure further reduced passenger privacy. Those choices have frustrated many passengers, but they have also been successful, to date, in preventing subsequent terrorist attacks.

Because really, who *doesn't* love standing in line at airport security?

Source: Jim Lambert/Shutterstock.com

While the TSA procedures represent an unusual production choice, it is still a production choice—one that is being made all over the world as countries grapple with the danger of terrorist attacks. In this chapter we introduce our first model, the **production possibilities model**, to examine the nature of choices to produce more of some goods and less of others. As its name suggests, the production possibilities model shows the goods and services that an economy is capable of producing—its possibilities—with the factors of production and the technology it has available. Our production possibilities model specifies what it means to use resources fully and efficiently, and it suggests some important implications for international trade. We'll also use the model to discuss what's necessary for economic growth—an increase in the overall productive capacity of an economy.

The production possibilities model illustrates the choices available to an economy. To see how decisions regarding those choices are made, we'll take a peek at various economic systems. An **economic system** is the set of rules that define how an economy's resources are to be owned and how decisions about their use are to be made. Economic systems differ in terms of how they answer the fundamental economic questions; those differences often stem from differing degrees of government involvement in planning, production, and distribution. In many countries, individuals

production possibilities model

A model that shows the goods and services that an economy is capable of producing—its opportunities—given the factors of production and the technology it has available.

economic system

The set of rules that define how an economy's resources are to be owned and how decisions about their use are to be made.

operating in a market economy decide what gets produced, and how. In other places, government makes those choices. Different economic systems result in different choices and different outcomes; that market economies generally outperform the others when it comes to providing more of the things that people want helps to explain the dramatic shift from government-dominated toward market-dominated economic systems that occurred throughout the world in the last half-century.

2.2 Factors of Production

Learning Objectives

1. Define the three factors of production—labor, capital, and natural resources.
2. Explain the role of technology and entrepreneurs in how the economy's factors of production are ultimately utilized.

factors of production

The resources available to the economy for the production of goods and services.

utility

The value, or satisfaction, that people derive from the goods and services they consume and the activities they pursue.

labor

The human effort that can be applied to the production of goods and services.

capital

A factor of production that has been produced for use in the production of other goods and services.

natural resources

The resources of nature that can be used for the production of goods and services.

An economy is an organization devoted to producing goods and services and then distributing what has been produced. But Albert Einstein proved that you can't make matter out of nothing—so if an economy is going to produce things, it's going to need some "ingredients." Those ingredients, the resources available for the production of goods and services, are often referred to as the economy's **factors of production**.

Why does an economy produce things? Because people get value from the goods and services they consume and the activities they pursue. Economists often refer to that value as **utility**. Ultimately, then, an economy's factors of production create utility; they serve the interests of actual people.

Even the simplest of products—like a bagel—has lots of "ingredients." Beyond the flour, yeast, water, and salt, it takes time and effort to mix and shape a bagel; it takes a stove to boil the bagel and an oven to bake it. Rather than trying to account for all of these bits and pieces individually, economists often lump the factors of production into broader categories. **Labor** represents the human effort necessary to produce a good or service—like mixing and shaping our bagels. People who are employed—or are available to be—are considered part of the labor available to the economy. **Capital** encompasses products like ovens and stoves that are then used to produce other goods and services. The collection of buildings, machines, and other productive goods and services constitute an economy's *capital stock*. Finally, **natural resources** are the items found in nature that can be used for the production of goods and services. Natural resources might include the water, yeast, and salt that ended up in our bagels; they also might include the land needed to grow the wheat and the energy needed to fire the ovens.

The three basic building blocks of labor, capital, and natural resources may be combined in different ways to produce different goods and services. Figuring out the best way to use an economy's factors of production isn't a new problem: Two hundred fifty years ago, early economists grappling with the problems of scarcity, choice, and opportunity cost paid special attention to the factors of production. We still do today. And because the factors of production are themselves scarce, we're likely to *still* be focused on their best uses hundreds of years in the future. In the next three sections, we will take a closer look at these factors of production. We will then look at the roles played by technology and entrepreneurs in putting these factors of production to work.

Labor

Labor is the human effort that can be applied to production. People who work to repair tires, pilot airplanes, teach children, and enforce laws are all part of the economy's labor. People who would like to work but have not found employment—who are unemployed—are also considered part of the *labor force*, which measures the human power available to the economy.

You've probably already noticed how economists tend to assume away complications in order to make generalizations. Here's one big complication that you've probably already noticed in your own life: Not everybody has the same skills, talents, or productive abilities. Some can knit, some can dunk a basketball, and others seem to struggle with even the simplest tasks. Trying to account for those differences in economic models is extremely difficult, so economists often lump labor together into two broad types. The first type is the human equivalent of a natural resource. It consists of the natural ability an untrained, uneducated person brings to a particular production process. But most workers do eventually acquire some education, training, or experience that can be used in production. Those productivity-enhancing measures are called **human capital**. Believe it or not, you're acquiring some human capital at this very moment!

The amount of labor power available to an economy, then, depends on two things: How many workers are there? And how much human capital do those workers possess?[1] An economy that wants to increase its available labor power, then, can go about it in two ways: It can increase the number of people available to work (by, perhaps, allowing more immigration, increasing the retirement age, rolling back child labor laws, or ratcheting up the typical number of hours worked each week). Or, the economy can increase its labor power by increasing the amount of human capital those workers possess (perhaps by expanding federal student loan programs).

Even Einstein's can't make bagels out of nothing—it took labor, capital, and natural resources to create these delicious treats.

Source: Brent Hofacker/Shutterstock.com

human capital

The knowledge and skills people accumulate through experience, education, and training.

Pop! Goes the Econ: Mike Rowe on Human Capital

Human capital makes you more productive . . . and that will show up in your paycheck. But there's more than one way to obtain it!

View in the online reader

Capital

"Stone tools? A capital idea! Once this dagger is finished, I'll use it to prepare my mammoth carpaccio!"

Source: Gorodenkoff/Shutterstock.com

Yes, you can fold a dollar bill into an awesome jet fighter. No, that doesn't make that dollar capital!

Source: shutter2photos/Shutterstock.com

financial capital

Forms of funding including money and other "paper" assets (such as stocks and bonds) that represent claims on future payments.

Long ago, when the first human beings walked the earth, they produced food by picking leaves or fruit off of plants or by catching animals. But very early on, humans began shaping stones into tools for use in hunting and butchering animals. Those stone tools were the first capital—goods made for use in producing other goods, such as food and clothing.

And those stone tools stood the test of time! Stone knives, axes, hooks, and shovels still exist today, but they have been updated with modern materials. We've added new tools, too, like hammers, screwdrivers, and wrenches. But there's no need to limit our definition of capital to hand tools: Chainsaws are capital, semi-trucks are capital, workplace computers are considered capital, and so are the buildings they're used in. Even roads, bridges, ports, and airports are included in our capital stock.

And capital doesn't consist solely of physical objects, either! The score for Ariana Grande's new song is capital—it will be used to produce both concerts and downloads. The software that controls robotic welders at BMW's factory in Spartanburg, South Carolina, is capital. Even the proprietary research and development that takes place within pharmaceutical firms is considered capital. In short, any resource is considered capital if it satisfies two criteria:

- The resource must have been produced.
- The resource can be used to produce other goods and services.

Economists are careful to distinguish between the kind of capital we've just been discussing and financial capital. **Financial capital** includes money and other "paper" assets (such as stocks and bonds) that represent claims on future payments. They are not, in the economist's sense, capital, because they are not directly used to produce other goods and services—in other words, they don't satisfy the second criterion listed above. That doesn't mean that financial capital is unimportant: Firms often use financial capital to raise the funds they need to *acquire* economic capital.

Natural Resources

You don't have to turn this giant redwood into a thousand backyard decks for it to be considered a natural resource!

Source: Sam Spicer/Shutterstock.com

So our economy has machinery (capital) and people to turn the machines on (labor). But that labor and capital needs something to transform into a finished product. Economists categorize the collection of raw materials we might use to create other products as natural resources. Technically, natural resources have two essential characteristics: First, they are originally found in nature. Second, they can be used for the production of goods and services. That requires knowledge; we must know how to use the things we find in nature before they truly can be considered resources.

Consider oil. Oil in the ground is a natural resource because it is found (not manufactured) and can be used to produce goods and services like the gasoline that powers your car, the plastic your AirPods are made from, and the propane you'll use to fire up your grill on Independence Day.

Two hundred fifty years ago, Pennsylvania farmers who found oil oozing up through their soil were dismayed, not delighted. No one knew what could be done with the oil—it was a problem, not an opportunity. It wasn't until the mid-nineteenth century that a method was found for refining oil into kerosene, which in turn could be used to light homes and generate electricity. Oil *became* a natural resource because people discovered and implemented a way to use it.

Defining something as a natural resource only if it can be used to produce goods and services does not mean that a tree has value only for its wood or that a mountain has value only for its minerals. If people gain utility from the existence of a beautiful wilderness area, then that wilderness provides a service. It's a natural resource!

The natural resources available to us can be expanded in three ways. One is the discovery of new natural resources, like the Gold Rush of '49, or the discovery of a deposit of uranium. The second is the discovery of new *uses* for resources, as in the case of oil discussed above. The third is the discovery of new ways to *extract* natural resources in order to use them. Horizontal boring and hydraulic fracturing (fracking), for example, have opened up new reserves of oil and natural gas across the Midwest, and they have made the United States a global energy superpower in the process.

Wind: Once a nuisance; now a resource.

Source: majeczka/Shutterstock.com

Technology and the Entrepreneur

Goods and services are produced using the factors of production available to the economy. Two things play a crucial role in putting these factors of production to work. The first is technology. It's tempting to think of technology as things involving microchips and circuitry, but in economics, we speak more broadly about production technology, which is our ability to transform *inputs* like labor, capital, and natural resources into *outputs* like goods and services. At any given time, our stock of **technology** is limited by our knowledge of how best to go about this.

The second key ingredient in putting the factors of production to work is an individual in the market economy called an entrepreneur. An **entrepreneur** is a person who, operating within the context of a market economy, seeks to earn profits by finding new ways to organize or combine the factors of production. An entrepreneur might find a better, less costly, or more efficient way to produce an item society already enjoys (have you ever heard the phrase, "Build a better mousetrap and the world will beat a path to your door?"). But entrepreneurs also play a critical role in shepherding new products and services to the marketplace—life-improving things like smartphones, hip hop music, hoverboards, and cronuts. Entrepreneurs risk their savings and their reputations in hopes of earning high profits from the goods and services they bring to the marketplace.

Of course, not all economies are market based. In non-market economies, the role of the entrepreneur is played by bureaucrats and other decision makers who respond to incentives other than profit to guide their choices about resource allocation. We'll spend considerable time talking about how well those bureaucrats perform later in this book.

technology

Knowledge that can be applied to the production of goods and services.

entrepreneur

A person who, operating within the context of a market economy, seeks to earn profits by finding new ways to organize the factors of production.

Pop! Goes the Econ: *Young Sheldon* and the Candy Entrepreneur

Entrepreneurs bear risks in pursuit of outsized rewards. In this clip from *Young Sheldon*, Georgie takes a big risk . . . and the potential rewards are better than he'd ever imagined. Discuss how this clip illustrates the role of the entrepreneur in finding better and more efficient ways to do things, and in introducing life-improving products to the market.

The interplay of entrepreneurs and technology affects us all. Entrepreneurs put new technologies to work every day, changing the way factors of production are used to produce the goods and services we enjoy. Farmers and factory workers, engineers and electricians, technicians and teachers all work differently than they did just a few years ago, using new technologies introduced by entrepreneurs. The music you enjoy, the food you eat, the clothes you wear, the social media you scan; they're all produced differently than they were just five short years ago. Even the book you are reading was written using technologies that didn't exist a decade ago! You may wonder whether all of these changes have made our lives better (*except the book . . . right?*). What we *cannot* dispute is that they have made our lives different, and it's entrepreneurs who get the credit (or who bear the blame).

Key Takeaways

- Factors of production are the resources the economy has available to produce goods and services.
- Labor is the human effort that can be applied to the production of goods and services. Labor's contribution to an economy's output of goods and services can be increased either by increasing the quantity of labor or by increasing human capital.
- Capital is a factor of production that has been produced for use in the production of other goods and services.
- Natural resources are those things found in nature that can be used for the production of goods and services.
- Two keys to the utilization of an economy's factors of production are technology and, in the case of a market economic system, the efforts of entrepreneurs.

Try It!

Explain whether each of the following is labor, capital, or a natural resource.

1. An unemployed factory worker
2. A college professor
3. The library building on your campus
4. Yellowstone National Park
5. An untapped deposit of natural gas
6. The White House
7. The local power plant

See related Concept Problem 1 at the end of this chapter.

Case in Point: Technology and Economic Progress

Quick . . . how much better off are you today than someone a century ago? Twice as well off? Five times?

That kind of improvement in well-being can be hard even for economists to measure. Oh, sure, we can compare today's income to incomes from a century ago. But even that's not a perfect metric, because today's income can buy so many more things, and so many better things, than were available in the past. How much would Cornelius Vanderbilt have loved to travel by air? How much would John D. Rockefeller have loved access to even the simplest of modern medicines? And the smartphone?! It may not be exaggerating to say that the richest man a hundred years ago would gladly trade his life for an average lifestyle today.

The Egg: One constant in a changing universe.

Source: rangizzz/Shutterstock.com

The new and better goods we enjoy today make us much better off than a simple income comparison can show. But just for the sake of argument, let's ignore new goods, and ignore the fact that the goods we enjoy today are generally better than those of a century ago. Instead, let's focus on a good that's produced exactly the same today as it was then, a good that is essentially unchanged in terms of its quality: the egg.

One good measure of how much better off we are is to measure how long we have to work to afford the things we want. One hundred years ago, a typical schoolteacher had to work for an hour to earn enough money to buy a dozen eggs. But over time, that has changed, and it's changed because of technology.

Long ago, farmers let their chickens run free and then sent their kids out to find the eggs. But then some enterprising farmer discovered that if he kept his hens fenced in, the eggs were easier to find, and fewer got lost. Believe it or not, that's a new technology!

Before long, chickens moved indoors out of the weather, and egg production increased even more. Soon, farmers were partially burying their henhouses for climate control—cool in the summer; warm in the winter. And egg production increased again: A happy hen is a productive hen! Farmers began experimenting with better foods and better medicines. Some even fitted their hens with red contact lenses, which calmed chickens and increased egg production even further. The chicken that laid your morning omelet may well have been viewing the world through rose-colored glasses!

Imitation is the sincerest form of flattery: Producers, watching their competitors prosper with these new technologies, adopted them for themselves. And those technologies made chickens more productive: The typical free-range chicken of a century ago produced just 50 eggs per year; today's modern chicken produces 300 in the same year, a six-fold improvement!

And so, Americans today find themselves awash in a sea of cheap eggs, as ever-increasing production drives prices downward. Ironically, innovations that were motivated by profits ended up producing gains not for competing producers—those profits dwindled as competition increased and prices fell—but for consumers. If our schoolteacher of a century ago were alive today, she'd have found that it takes not an hour of work to buy a dozen eggs, but less than three minutes—a twenty-fold improvement in her standard of living, even holding quality constant!

To an economist, technology is just the way we transform inputs into outputs—like chickens into eggs. And improvements in technology—even in places as pedestrian as the henhouse—are in one way or another responsible for the lion's share of comfort and quality of our daily lives.

See related Concept Problem 14 at the end of this chapter.

Sources: Based on Roberts, Russell. The Price of Everything: A Parable of Possibility and Prosperity. Princeton: Princeton University Press, 2008.

Answers to Try It! Problems

1. An unemployed factory worker could be put to work; he or she counts as labor.

2. A college professor is labor.

3. The library building on your campus is part of capital.

4. Yellowstone National Park. Those areas of the park left in their natural state are a natural resource. Facilities such as visitors' centers, roads, and campgrounds are capital.

5. An untapped deposit of natural gas is a natural resource. Once extracted and put in a storage tank, natural gas is capital.

6. The White House is capital.

7. The local power plant is capital.

2.3 The Production Possibilities Curve

Learning Objectives

1. Explain the concept of the production possibilities curve and discuss the implications of its downward slope and bowed-out shape.

2. Use the production possibilities model to distinguish between full employment and situations of idle factors of production and between efficient and inefficient production.

3. Define specialization and describe its relationship to the production possibilities model and comparative advantage.

Let's briefly recap where we've been: In Chapter 1, we learned that everyone faces scarcity, and because of scarcity we are forced to accept trade-offs. In the first few sections of this chapter, we learned how the factors of production are combined to produce goods and services.

Now, let's mash those ideas together: Almost everything is scarce, and that scarcity begins with our economy's *factors of production*. And because the factors of production are scarce, they can't be used to produce an unlimited quantity of goods and services. That forces us to make choices about how they are used. Before we make those choices, it would be nice if we could look at a "menu" to see what kinds of goods and services our economy *could* produce if it wanted to. Lucky for us, we've got just such a menu. A **production possibilities curve** (or PPC) is a graph that shows different combinations of goods and services that an economy can produce. The PPC also shows us the trade-offs available to us, the "*more of this means less of that*" that exists because of scarcity.

The production possibilities curve is a very basic economic model, and like all models it is built on simplifying assumptions. In particular, when we create an economy's PPC, we'll assume the following:

- There are only two goods or services produced in the economy.

- The quantities of labor, capital, and natural resources are "fixed"; there is only so much of each available.

- Today's production technology is fixed.

production possibilities curve

A graphical representation of the alternative combinations of goods and services an economy can produce.

Our production possibilities are limited by the amount of labor, capital, and natural resources available to us. Which of these factors of production is limiting the amount of candy we can enjoy?

View in the online reader

Building the Model: Constructing a Production Possibilities Curve

To construct a production possibilities curve, we'll begin with the case of a hypothetical firm, Alpine Sports, Inc., a specialized sports equipment manufacturer. Christie Ryder began the business twenty years ago with a single ski production facility near Killington Ski Resort in central Vermont. Ski sales grew, and she also saw demand for snowboards rising—particularly after snowboard competition events were included in the 2002 Winter Olympics in Salt Lake City. She added a second plant in a nearby town. The second plant, while smaller than the first, was designed to produce snowboards as well as skis. She also modified the first plant so that it could produce both snowboards and skis. Two years later she added a third plant in another town. While even smaller than the second plant, the third was primarily designed for snowboard production, but could also produce skis.

We can think of Alpine Sports' three plants as three miniature economies, and we can analyze each mini-economy using the production possibilities model. We'll assume here, as indicated in the bullet points above, that the factors of production and the technology available to each of the plants operated by Alpine Sports are fixed. That doesn't mean they're identical across plants, however—each plant has a different number of workers and machines, and each plant has different production technology.

Suppose the first plant, Plant 1, can produce 200 pairs of skis per month when it produces only skis. When devoted solely to snowboards, it produces 100 snowboards per month. It can produce both goods simultaneously—a blend of skis and snowboards—as well.

The table in Figure 2.1 gives three combinations of skis and snowboards that Plant 1 can produce each month. Combination A involves devoting the plant entirely to ski production; combination C means shifting all of the plant's resources to snowboard production; combination B involves devoting equal time (and resources) to the production of skis and the production of snowboards. These values are then plotted in a production possibilities curve for Plant 1. The curve is a downward-sloping straight line, which reflects an implicit assumption that there is a linear, negative relationship between the production of the two goods.[2]

FIGURE 2.1 A Production Possibilities Curve

The table shows the combinations of Pairs of skis and Snowboards that Plant 1 is capable of producing each month. These combinations are then shown graphically as a production possibilities curve. Notice that this curve is a straight line.

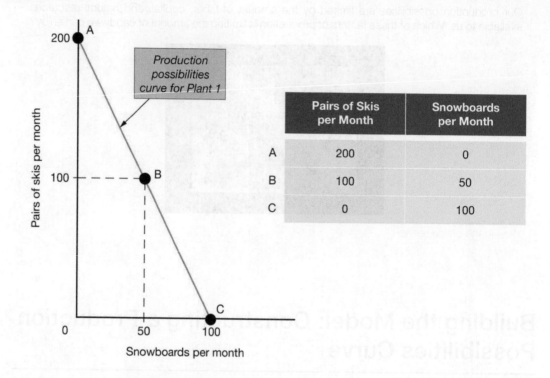

	Pairs of Skis per Month	Snowboards per Month
A	200	0
B	100	50
C	0	100

The negative slope of the production possibilities curve reflects the trade-offs Alpine Sports faces because of scarce capital and labor. Producing more snowboards requires shifting those resources out of ski production and into snowboard production. Likewise, producing more skis requires shifting resources out of snowboard production and into ski production. Alpine Sports can't have it all!

Americans learned that you can't have it all during the coronavirus crisis of early 2020. An uncertainty-driven panic of expectations (see Chapter 3) emptied store shelves of toilet paper. The empty shelves lasted for weeks, as anxious, locked-down consumers wondered, "Why aren't they making more?"

Wiped Clean: Shoppers in Australia looking for TP during the coronavirus crisis of 2020 found only empty shelves.

Source: Zorro Stock Images/Shutterstock.com

The answer, of course, is that they couldn't. Toilet paper producers faced short-term constraints on resources that hindered production. Toilet paper is made primarily from eucalyptus trees grown in South America; it's hard to get those trees (or their pulp) here in the space of a few short weeks. And toilet paper use is generally predictable, which has led manufacturers to adopt just-in-time production techniques that keep their machinery running at over 90% capacity in normal times: They simply don't have extra pulp, nor extra machines, sitting around.[3]

But generally predictable doesn't mean predictable in a lockdown: In addition to panic demand, millions of consumers found that they were . . . using the facilities . . . at home rather than at work. And, if you haven't noticed at your own college, institutional TP is generally skimpy 1-ply; we want beefier, cushier 2-ply at home. So, Americans wanted more paper, and they wanted better paper; more than TP manufacturers could supply. Simply put, the desire for TP lay well beyond the limitations of producers' capital, labor, and natural resources; consumers were panicked to find that no matter how badly they wanted their TP, the economy couldn't escape its PPC.

The *slope* of Plant 1's production possibilities curve measures the trade-off between ski production and snowboard production. Because the production possibilities curve for Plant 1 is a straight line, we can compute the slope between any two points on the curve and get the same answer. So, let's make our work easy: Suppose Alpine Sports is producing at point A (all skis) and decides to shift production to point C (all snowboards). In the move from A to C, ski production falls by 200, and snowboard production increases by 100. So, the slope of the PPC between points A and C is (-200)/(+100), or -2. If we had used points A and B, or points B and C, we would have gotten the same -2 result. (If you need a brief refresher on slope, see Appendix A Section 1).

That -2 that we got for the slope of the PPC is important, not because we're interested in making you jump through a bunch of algebraic hoops, but because it has an economic interpretation: The slope of the PPC measures the opportunity cost of producing another snowboard!

To see why that's the case, examine Figure 2.2. Suppose Plant 1 is producing 100 pairs of skis and 50 snowboards per month at point B. Now consider what would happen if Alpine Sports decided to produce 1 more snowboard per month. The segment of the PPC around point B is magnified in Figure 2.2. The slope between points B and B′ is -2 pairs of skis/snowboard. Producing one additional snowboard at point B′ requires giving up two pairs of skis. So, two pairs of skis is the opportunity cost of producing an additional snowboard at Plant 1.

On the PPC or on the mountain—there's always an opportunity cost when you're talking slopes.

Source: sirtravelalot/Shutterstock.com

FIGURE 2.2 The Slope of a Production Possibilities Curve

The slope of the linear production possibilities curve in Figure 2.1 is constant; it is –2 pairs of skis/snowboard. In the section of the curve shown here, the slope can be calculated between points B and B′. Expanding snowboard production to 51 snowboards per month from 50 snowboards per month (an increase of one) requires a reduction in ski production from 100 pairs of skis to 98 (a decrease of 2). To shift from B′ to B″, Alpine Sports must give up two more pairs of skis per snowboard. The absolute value of the slope of a production possibilities curve measures the opportunity cost of an additional unit of the good on the horizontal axis measured in terms of the quantity of the good on the vertical axis.

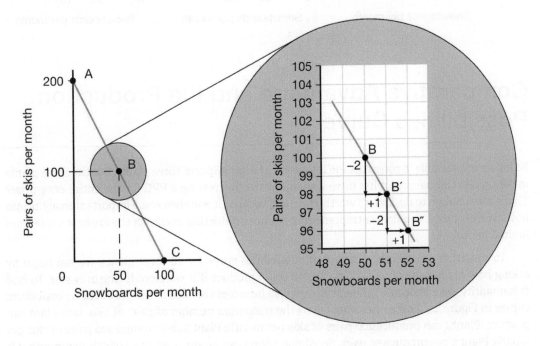

Generally speaking, the absolute value of the slope of a PPC measures the amount of the good on the vertical axis that must be given up in order to free up the resources needed to produce one more unit of the good on the horizontal axis. In other words, the slope of the PPC equals the opportunity cost of an additional unit of the good on the horizontal axis. We will make use of this important fact as we continue exploring the nature of the PPC.

Figure 2.3 shows production possibilities curves for each of the firm's three plants. Remember that each of these plants has a different size; each has a different set of production equipment that is perhaps better suited to one product than the other. For simplicity, we're assuming that each of the plants, if devoted entirely to snowboards, could produce 100 snowboards. Plants 2 and 3, if devoted exclusively to ski production, could produce 100 and 50 pairs of skis per month, respectively.

At each plant, the (absolute value of the) slope of each production possibilities curve measures the opportunity cost of an additional snowboard (that is, the number of pairs of skis that must be given up to make one more snowboard) at that plant. So, the opportunity cost of an additional snowboard at Plant 1 is 2 sets of skis; the opportunity cost of an additional snowboard at Plant 2 is 1 pair of skis; and at Plant 3, the opportunity cost of an additional snowboard is 1/2 of a pair of skis.

FIGURE 2.3 Production Possibilities at Three Plants
The slopes of the production possibilities curves for each plant differ. The steeper the curve, the greater the opportunity cost of an additional snowboard. Here, the opportunity cost is lowest at Plant 3 and greatest at Plant 1.

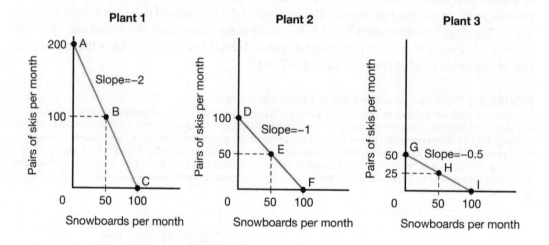

Comparative Advantage and the Production Possibilities Curve

So far we've been able to construct PPCs for each of Alpine Sports' three plants. But the three plants make up one company; so what if we were interested in creating a PPC for the entire enterprise? That's easy enough to do, and it's worthwhile, too, because it will shed some important insights into how careful choices can help entrepreneurs organize production to extract the greatest value from limited resources.

To construct a combined production possibilities curve for all three plants, we can begin by asking how many pairs of skis Alpine Sports could produce if it were producing only skis. To find this quantity, we add up the values at the vertical intercepts of each of the production possibilities curves in Figure 2.3. These intercepts tell us the maximum number of pairs of skis each plant can produce. Plant 1 can produce 200 pairs of skis per month; Plant 2 can produce 100 pairs of skis per month; Plant 3 can produce 50 pairs. So, Alpine Sports can produce 350 pairs of skis per month if it devotes its all of its resources to ski production and produces no snowboards.

Now suppose the firm decides to produce 100 snowboards. That will require shifting one of its plants out of ski production. Which one will it choose to shift? The sensible thing for it to do is to choose the plant in which snowboards have the lowest opportunity cost: Plant 3. After all, why give up 2 pairs of skis to make a snowboard (by switching over Plant 1), or 1 pair of skis to make a snowboard (by switching over Plant 2), when you can get the same snowboard and only sacrifice half a pair of skis by switching Plant 3?!

Economists say that Plant 3 has a *comparative advantage* in producing snowboards because it is the plant for which the opportunity cost of producing snowboards is lowest (you'll notice that Plant 3's PPC, correspondingly, is the flattest, too). More generally, and sticking with our earlier notion of viewing each plant as its own little mini-economy, economists say that an economy has a **comparative advantage** in producing a good or service if the opportunity cost of producing that good or service is lower for that economy than for any other.

Plant 3's comparative advantage in snowboard production makes a crucial point about the nature of comparative advantage in general: Comparative advantage need not imply that a particular plant is especially good at an activity! In fact, all three of Alpine Sports' plants are equally good at snowboard production. Plant 3, though, is the *least* efficient of the three in ski production. Ironically, that relative inefficiency is the *source* of its comparative advantage in snowboards!

> **comparative advantage**
>
> In producing a good or service, the situation that occurs if the opportunity cost of producing that good or service is lower for that economy than for any other.

FIGURE 2.4 The Combined Production Possibilities Curve for Alpine Sports
The curve shown combines the production possibilities curves for each plant. At point A, Alpine Sports produces 350 pairs of skis per month and no snowboards. If the firm wishes to increase snowboard production, it will first use Plant 3, which has a comparative advantage in snowboards. See text for details.

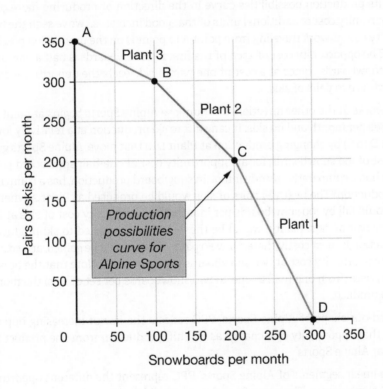

Let's use the notion of comparative advantage to create the PPC for the combined enterprise, Alpine Sports. That production possibilities curve is shown in Figure 2.4. It reflects not only the labor and capital available to Alpine Sports, but also wise decision-making on the part of its owner:

- We begin at point A, with all three plants producing only skis. Production totals 350 pairs of skis per month and zero snowboards.

- Now, ratchet up production of snowboards by 100 units. What's the best way to do that? We've already determined that those 100 snowboards will come at the lowest (opportunity) cost if we build them at Plant 3. If the firm were to produce 100 snowboards at Plant 3, ski production would fall by 50 pairs per month to 300 pairs, at point B.

- Let's keep going: We've now got Plants 1 & 2 making skis, and Plant 3 making snowboards. To increase snowboard production by another hundred units, we'll need to switch production at either Plant 1 or Plant 2. Because the opportunity cost of a snowboard is lower at Plant 2, let's use it to make another 100 snowboards, at a cost of 100 pairs of skis. That brings us to 200 snowboards and 200 skis, at point C.

- Finally, we complete the PPC at point D, where even the least-efficient plant (Plant 1, with an opportunity cost of 2 pairs of skis per snowboard) is building snowboards. There, Alpine Sports produces 300 snowboards, and no skis.

Notice that this production possibilities curve, which is made up of linear segments representing each assembly plant, ends up with a bowed-out shape: Its slope gets steeper and steeper as Alpine Sports produces more and more snowboards. We'll examine the significance of that bowed-out shape in the next section.

The Law of Increasing Opportunity Cost

law of increasing opportunity cost

As an economy moves along its production possibilities curve in the direction of producing more of a particular good, the opportunity cost of additional units of that good will increase.

We see in Figure 2.4 that, beginning at point A, the more snowboards Alpine Sports makes, the higher the opportunity cost of producing them. This reflects an important economic law, the law of increasing opportunity cost. The **law of increasing opportunity cost** says that as an economy moves along its production possibilities curve in the direction of producing more of a particular good, the opportunity cost of additional units of that good increases. We've seen the law of increasing opportunity cost at work traveling from point A to point D on the production possibilities curve in Figure 2.4: The opportunity cost of each of the first 100 snowboards is half a pair of skis; each of the next 100 snowboards comes at a cost of one pair of skis each; the opportunity cost of the last 100 snowboards is two pairs of skis.

The law works in the other direction, too. Suppose Alpine Sports begins at point D, producing 300 snowboards per month and no skis. It can shift to ski production at a relatively low cost at first (moving from D to C) by changing production at Plant 1. In that move, Alpine Sports gains 200 pairs of skis at a cost of 100 snowboards, for an opportunity cost of one-half snowboard per pair of skis. Plant 1, which had a comparative *disadvantage* in snowboard production, has a comparative *advantage* in ski production! The next 100 pairs of skis would be produced at Plant 2, where snowboard production would fall by 100 snowboards per month; the opportunity cost of skis at Plant 2 is one snowboard per pair of skis. Plant 3 would be the last plant converted to ski production, because altering production is most costly there: Only 50 pairs of skis would be gained, at a cost of 100 snowboards, for an opportunity cost of two snowboards per pair of skis. Note that the opportunity cost of making skis rises (from one-half, to one, to two snowboards per set of skis) the more skis Alpine Sports tries to produce.

The bowed-out shape of Alpine Sports' PPC reflects the law of increasing opportunity cost. But why does that opportunity cost change as we shift production from one product to the other? Remember that Alpine Sports'

The three linear segments of Alpine Sports' PPC represent the different opportunity costs at Alpine Sports' three plants. The more factories we consider, the more linear segments we'll get . . . and the smoother the PPC will appear. Panel (a) in Figure 2.5 illustrates a much smoother production possibilities curve, for example, with ten linear segments. In an actual economy, with a tremendous number of firms and workers, the PPC is even smoother, like the one in Panel (b). This production possibilities curve represents an entire economy that produces only skis and snowboards. (For those of you who are wondering what the snow bunnies in this economy *eat*, remember that it is a just a model. You could just as easily call one product "food" and the other "clothing." Now, pass the mustard; my snowboard sandwich is almost ready.) Notice these key features of the economy-wide PPC:

- The economy-wide PPC still has a bowed-out shape (reflecting the law of increasing opportunity cost).

- The economy-wide PPC still has a negative slope (reflecting scarcity and trade-offs).
- This particular economy-wide PPC has no numbers. Economists often care more about capturing the essence of the economy (like the downward slope and concave shape mentioned above) than they do about using specific numbers.

FIGURE 2.5 Production Possibilities for the Economy
As we combine the production possibilities curves for more and more units being produced at more and more factories, the curve becomes smoother. It retains its negative slope and bowed-out shape. Panel (a) shows a PPC for a company with ten plants producing skis and snowboards. Even though each plant is represented with a linear segment, the PPC appears almost as a smooth curve. In drawing production possibilities curves for the entire economy, we will generally assume they are smooth and "bowed out," as in Panel (b). This curve depicts an entire economy that produces only skis and snowboards.

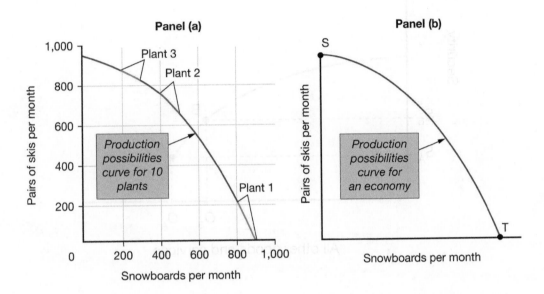

Movements Along the Production Possibilities Curve

We can use the production possibilities model to examine choices in the production of goods and services. Let's revisit our chapter opener by considering two goods and services: national security and a category we'll call "all other goods and services." That second category includes all of the various goods and services the economy is capable of producing other than national security.

In the wake of the 9/11 attacks in 2001, nations across the globe increased their spending for national security: At the national level, countries increased their defense spending and devoted additional resources to border security and immigration. State and local governments also increased spending in an effort to prevent terrorist attacks. And airports around the world installed new screening equipment and hired additional agents to inspect luggage and passengers.

Devoting more resources to security meant using fewer resources to produce other goods and services. This is depicted in Figure 2.6 as a movement from A to B.

FIGURE 2.6 Spending More for Security

Here, an economy that can produce two categories of goods, "security" and "all other goods and services," begins at point A on its production possibilities curve. The economy produces S_A units of security and O_A units of all other goods and services per period. Increasing security from S_A to S_B requires shifting resources out of the production of all other goods and services and into spending on security. Production of all other goods and services falls from O_A to O_B, and the economy moves from point A to point B.

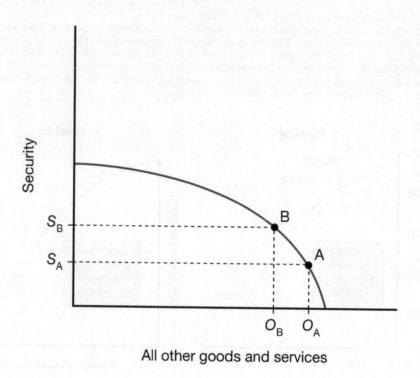

All other goods and services

At point A, which you might view as the pre-9/11 allocation of resources, the economy was producing S_A units of security (measured on the vertical axis) and O_A units of other goods and services (measured on the horizontal axis). The decision to devote more resources to security and fewer to other goods and services represents the choice discussed in the chapter opener. With a fixed quantity of resources available, ramping up security to level S_B meant reducing the production of other goods and services to O_B. The economy moves along its PPC from point A to point B.

The law of increasing opportunity cost tells us that as the economy shifts production toward greater security, the opportunity cost of security will increase. The first security improvements are cheap, because some security measures are relatively effective and easy to implement (think: a few extra scanning machines at a few hundred airports). But the cost increases as we exhaust the "low-hanging fruit" and begin to implement measures that are both less effective and more difficult, like developing sophisticated internet technologies to detect and deter potential terrorist activity.

The production possibilities model tells us about the trade-offs an economy faces. It doesn't, however, tell us where on the curve a particular economy will operate—it simply presents the possibilities. Many countries—the United States and Israel, for example—choose a point high on their respective PPCs where each produces a relatively large amount of national security. Other countries, for various reasons, choose to devote relatively fewer resources to security and relatively more to other goods and services, and end up at points farther to the right on their PPCs.

Producing On Versus Producing Inside the Production Possibilities Curve

An economy's PPC shows what is *possible* for the economy to produce. Whether the economy lives up to its potential or not is another question. If the economy doesn't use all of its resources to the best of their capacity, the economy will not end up on its PPC. Instead, it will produce less than it is capable of, and end up at a point inside its production possibilities curve. As a result, some material well-being for its people will be sacrificed—an opportunity loss.

Two things could leave an economy operating at a point inside its production possibilities curve. First, the economy might fail to use all of the resources available to it. Second, the economy might not allocate the resources it has to their best use. In either case, production within the production possibilities curve implies that the economy could improve its performance.

Idle Factors of Production

Suppose an economy fails to put all its factors of production to work—maybe there are workers without jobs, or machinery sitting idle. Because an economy's production possibilities curve assumes the full use of the factors of production available to it, the failure to use some productive resources results in the economy operating inside the production possibilities curve.

If all the factors of production that are available for use under current market conditions are being utilized, the economy has achieved the **full employment** of its resources. (Note that "full employment" applies to *all* productive resources, and not just labor.) An economy cannot operate on its production possibilities curve unless it has full employment.

Figure 2.7 illustrates the effect of underemployed resources in an economy that can produce food and clothing. If it chooses to produce at point A, for example, it can produce F_A units of food and C_A units of clothing. Now, suppose that a large fraction of the economy's workers lose their jobs, so the economy no longer makes full use of its labor. Because workers are sitting at home filling out job apps instead of making T-shirts and chalupas, the economy produces less food (F_B) and less clothing (C_B), and moves to point B. Unemployment is hard on the laid-off workers, but it also has a second hidden cost: a loss of material well-being for the rest of society.

full employment

Situation in which all the factors of production that are available for use under current market conditions are being utilized.

FIGURE 2.7 Idle Factors and Production

This production possibilities curve shows an economy that can produce two goods, food and clothing. It's possible for this economy to produce at point A, with C_A units of clothing and F_A units of food. But because of unemployment, the economy operates *inside* its PPC at B, producing C_B units of clothing and F_B units of food. If this economy could put its idled labor to work, it would be possible to increase the production of both food *and* clothing.

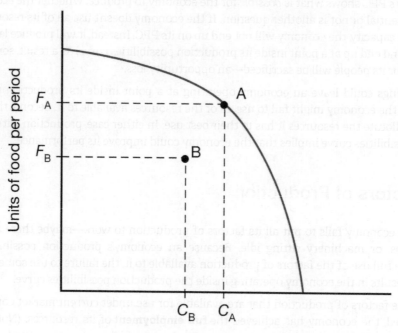

Inefficient Production

Don't screw up: Use the wrong tool for the job and you'll ruin your productivity!

Source: maxuser/Shutterstock. com

There's another way an economy might end up inside its PPC, even if all of its resources are fully employed: It might *misallocate* those resources, the economy-wide equivalent of driving nails with a saw while cutting lumber with a hammer. In other words, the *choices* we make not only affect where *on* the PPC we might operate, but also affect whether we'll get to the PPC at all.

To show how that might happen, let's return to Alpine Sports and show that even if it fully employs its factors of production, the choice of *how* to employ those factors can drive production inside the PPC. The key to this puzzle lies in the nature of comparative advantage: An economy achieves a point on its production possibilities curve *only if* it allocates its factors of production on the basis of comparative advantage. If it fails to do that, it will operate inside the curve.

Suppose that, as before, Alpine Sports is only producing skis. With all three of its plants churning out skis, Alpine Sports will make 350 pairs of skis per month and no snowboards.

Now, as before, let's let Alpine Sports begin producing snowboards. But instead of using Plant 3 to produce them (you'll recall that Plant 3 has a comparative advantage in making snowboards), Alpine Sports decides to make its snowboards in Plant 1, and then shift production at Plant 2, before it ever makes a single snowboard in Plant 3.

Figure 2.8 illustrates the result. Instead of the bowed-out production possibilities curve ABCD that we replicate here from Figure 2.4, Alpine sports makes choices that result in a curve that bows *inward*, AB'C'D. This happens because when Alpine Sports decides to make that first 100 snowboards, it uses resources from Plant 1, where the opportunity cost of each snowboard is two pairs of skis. The 100 snowboards cost Alpine Sports 200 pairs of skis (point B'). Alpine Sports *could* have shifted resources from Plant 3, where the opportunity cost of snowboards is lower (1/2 pair of skis per snowboard) and gotten the same 100 snowboards at a sacrifice of only 50 pairs of skis . . . but it didn't! Alpine Sports sent production to a plant with a comparative *disadvantage*. As a result, Alpine Sports ended up at B′ when it could have, with better decision-making, reached point B: Same snowboards; more skis.

When an economy is operating on its production possibilities curve, we say that it is engaging in **efficient production**. If it uses the same quantities of factors of production but operates *inside* its production possibilities curve, it is engaging in **inefficient production**. Simply put, inefficient production means wasted resources; the economy could produce more goods and services without using any additional labor, capital, or natural resources.

efficient production

When an economy is operating on its production possibilities curve.

inefficient production

Situation in which the economy is using the same quantities of factors of production but is operating inside its production possibilities curve.

FIGURE 2.8 Efficient Versus Inefficient Production

When factors of production are allocated contrary to their comparative advantage, the result is inefficient production. Suppose Alpine Sports operates the three plants illustrated in Figure 2.3, and that all three plants are devoted exclusively to ski production with the firm operating at A. If Alpine Sports wants to increase snowboard production and begins switching production at Plant 1 first, then Plant 2, and finally Plant 3, the result is the bowed-in curve AB′C′D, which lies below the production possibilities curve ABCD. Alpine Sports could get the same snowboards and *more* skis if it began producing snowboards at Plant 3 first.

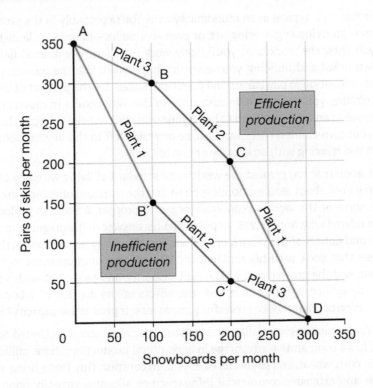

Points on the production possibilities curve thus satisfy two conditions: the economy is using all of its factors of production, and it is using them in the most efficient way possible. So, the production possibilities curve not only shows what can be produced; it provides insight into how goods and services *should* be produced. It suggests that to avoid wasting resources, factors of production should be allocated on the basis of comparative advantage.

Specialization

specialization

Situation in which an economy is producing the goods and services in which it has a comparative advantage.

The production possibilities model suggests natural forces will eventually move an economy toward the specialized use of its resources. **Specialization** implies that an economy is devoting all of its resources to producing the goods and services in which it has a comparative advantage.

To see why specialization is an outcome that an economy will naturally gravitate toward, let's revisit the three mini-economies (Plant 1, Plant 2, and Plant 3) of Alpine Sports. If Alpine Sports wants to produce 100 snowboards this year, it will do so by switching production from skis to snowboards at Plant 3 (because Plant 3 has a comparative advantage in making snowboards). Any other allocation of resources (say, switching production at Plant 1 or Plant 2) will result in the same 100 snowboards, but fewer skis. That's an outcome that costs Alpine Sports lost profit, and one that likely gets middle management fired!

Alpine Sports, driven by profits, ends up *creating* specialization: Rather than having some ski production and some snowboard production at each plant, we see Plants 1 and 2 solely devoted to ski production, and Plant 3 solely devoted to snowboard production. That's specialization.

Such specialization is typical in an economic system. You're probably in the process of specialization right now—studying engineering, art, or even economics—in order to launch a specialized career. When you enter the workforce, you'll likely work in a narrowly defined field; rather than baking your own bread and building your own furniture, you'll use the income you earn from your specialized occupation to pay bakers and furniture makers for the product of their specialized occupation. Exploiting your comparative advantage in this way results in much greater material wealth for everyone to enjoy—if you had to build your own shelter, bake your own bread, milk your own cow, sew your own clothes, there wouldn't be any time left in the day for doing what you're best at . . . much less relaxing with an episode or two of *Ozark*.

Not many economists have statues erected in their honor . . . but Adam Smith was no ordinary economist!

Source: Travel Telly/Shutterstock.com

It's specialization that has created the wealth and standard of living we enjoy today. From the beginning of time until about 1600, economic growth and the standard of living were stagnant. But then, suddenly, some of the world's economies began to prosper. A Scottish philosopher named Adam Smith wondered why, and in 1776, he published his answer in his magnum opus, *An Inquiry into the Nature and Causes of the Wealth of Nations*. Smith, widely proclaimed as the world's first economist, opens that book with his explanation: "The greatest improvement in the productive powers of labour, and the greater part of the skill, dexterity, and judgment with which it is anywhere directed, or applied, seem to have been the effects of the division of labour."[4] And what, exactly, *is* the division of labor that so powerfully improves our productive capacity? Specialization!

You specialize, businesses specialize, and nations specialize, too: The United States, with its abundant land, has a comparative advantage in agricultural production; there, millions of acres of land are sown in corn, wheat, and soybeans each year. In contrast, tiny Hong Kong, with its highly educated people and extensive commercial infrastructure, allocates virtually none of its land to agricultural use; that option would be too costly. Instead, it exploits its comparative advantage in commerce and uses its limited land for office buildings.

Key Takeaways

- A production possibilities curve shows different combinations of two goods that an economy is capable of producing.
- The downward slope of the production possibilities curve reflects scarcity.
- The bowed-out shape of the production possibilities curve reflects the law of increasing opportunity cost, and results from allocating resources based on comparative advantage.

- An economy that fails to make full and efficient use of its factors of production will operate inside its production possibilities curve.
- Specialization means that an economy is producing the goods and services in which it has a comparative advantage.

Try It!

Suppose a manufacturing firm is equipped to produce radios or calculators. It has two plants, Plant R and Plant S, at which it can produce these goods. Given the labor and the capital available at both plants, it can produce the combinations of the two goods at the two plants shown.

Output per Day, Plant R		
Combination	Calculators	Radios
A	100	0
B	50	25
C	0	50

Output per Day, Plant S		
Combination	Calculators	Radios
D	50	0
E	25	50
F	0	100

Put calculators on the vertical axis and radios on the horizontal axis. Draw the production possibilities curve for Plant R. On a separate graph, draw the production possibilities curve for Plant S. Which plant has a comparative advantage in calculators? In radios? Now draw the combined curves for the two plants. Suppose the firm decides to produce 100 radios. Where will it produce them? How many calculators will it be able to produce? Where will it produce the calculators?

See related Numerical Problem 5 at the end of this chapter.

Case in Point: Your Econ Grade and the Law of Increasing Opportunity Costs

By now, you're hip-deep in your economics course—we hope you're enjoying the subject (and, of course, we hope you're reading your book!). But if you're like many of our students, the big questions on your mind are "Is this going to be on the test?" and "How hard will I have to study to get an A?"

We can't answer the first question for you—after all, we don't write your exams. But we can offer some insights about studying, guided by our own experiences as students and by years of watching people just like you preparing for exams of their own.

Our biggest insight is that no matter what your grade target happens to be, your efforts will likely reflect the nature of increasing opportunity cost. If your target grade is a C, for example, you might achieve that through diligent class attendance coupled with a couple of hours spent reviewing notes, working some basic problems, and reviewing key terms.

But taking your grade to the next level (remember marginal thinking?) is likely to be much more costly. "B" thinking requires a more refined understanding of the nuances of economics; those fine points are much harder to pin down than "C" basics. So, raising your grade to a B might require another four hours of study, on top of the two you already invested in getting your "C."

Intellectual power means putting in the hours—those grades won't get themselves!

Source: Stock-Asso/Shutterstock.com

And the "A?" The "A" requires not just understanding, but mastery—the same kind of mastery it takes to perfect a jump shot or become a concert violinist. While some of us might be able to squeak into "A" range with a couple of hard days of study, your author's experience in his own General Psych course lays bare the possibility that some of us might simply bump into the limits of our "grade production possibilities" curve before we ever get to the 4.0.

So if you're determined to walk away from college *summa cum laude*, the law of increasing opportunity costs advises you to prepare to devote ever-increasing amounts of time for ever-smaller improvements in your grade. After all, there's a reason that the academic high-fliers are often the same people you see hunched over their books in the library late at night . . . while the rest of us mere mortals are catching up on the lost episodes of *Jane the Virgin*.

See related Concept Problem 3 at the end of this chapter.

Answer to Try It! Problem

The production possibilities curves for the two plants are shown, along with the combined curve for both plants. Plant R has a comparative advantage in producing calculators. Plant S has a comparative advantage in producing radios, so, if the firm goes from producing 150 calculators and no radios to producing 100 radios, it will produce them at Plant S. In the production possibilities curve for both plants, the firm would be at M, producing 100 calculators at Plant R.

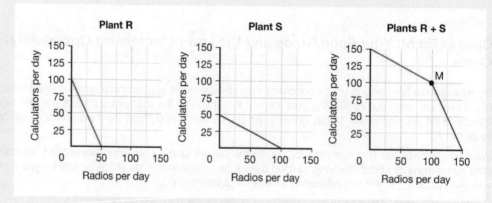

2.4 Applications of the Production Possibilities Model

Learning Objectives

1. Describe the argument for unrestricted international trade in terms of economic specialization and comparative advantage.
2. Define economic growth in terms of the production possibilities model and discuss factors that make such growth possible.
3. Explain the classification of economic systems, the role of government in different economic systems, and the strengths and weaknesses of different systems.

The production possibilities curve is a model of an economy. It's a simple model, but it can provide powerful insights about the real world, insights that help us to answer some important questions: Why does trade between individuals and countries occur, and who wins from trade? What can account for the world's ever-increasing standard of living? And what is the value of economic freedom? In this section, we'll explore applications of the production possibilities model to international trade, economic growth, and economic systems.

Comparative Advantage and International Trade

The market system that forms the basis of most modern economies is based on exchange. Why have most countries gravitated toward exchange economies? And what lies behind the increasing volume of global trade between countries? These are questions we can answer with our new-found understanding of production possibilities and comparative advantage.

At first glance, the gains from exchange, especially exchange between nations, seem obvious. It makes perfect sense, for example, for the United States to send airplanes to Guatemala and accept Guatemala's bananas in return: The United States has a lot of skilled labor that is well suited to making 747s; Guatemala has a climate that's much more suitable for growing bananas. Exchange between the United States and Guatemala, in this case, can be driven by the fact that each country is simply better at producing a particular product—an edge that Adam Smith called "absolute advantage." Each country specializing in making the product they've got an absolute advantage in and then trading for the other one makes a lot more sense than each country trying to do a bit of everything: Bananas just don't grow that well in Minnesota greenhouses.

But what happens to the obvious benefits from exchange when one country is better at producing *everything*—in the case of our model, not better at producing one good, but at producing *both* goods? Does trade make sense? Let's use our model of production possibilities to explore this question. Let's keep things simple by talking about two individuals, Andre and Cheryl, who are both capable of making both pizza and beer, and who both desire to live self-sufficiently. In the space of a week:

- Andre can make 5 pizzas and brew no beer; he can brew five beers if he makes no pizza. He usually divides his time so that he can enjoy 3 pizzas and 2 beers each week.

- Cheryl can make 6 pizzas if she brews no beer; she can brew 12 beers if she makes no pizza. Cheryl usually divides her time so that she can enjoy 2 pizzas and 8 beers each week.

Earlier in this chapter, we learned that the reason we produce things is so that we can later enjoy them—and, generally speaking, the more the better! In this world of self-sufficiency and isolation, both Andre and Cheryl have consumption possibilities that are identical to their production possibilities: They can only eat and drink the food they, themselves, produce. Those production and consumption possibilities are illustrated in Figure 2.9.

FIGURE 2.9 Production and Consumption Possibilities
Andre and Cheryl can produce both pizza and beer. The production possibilities curves for each indicate that Cheryl is better at producing both pizza and beer. Without trade, Andre and Cheryl are limited to consuming what they produce for themselves: Andre produces and consumes 2 beers and 3 pizzas; Cheryl produces and consumes 8 beers and 2 pizzas.

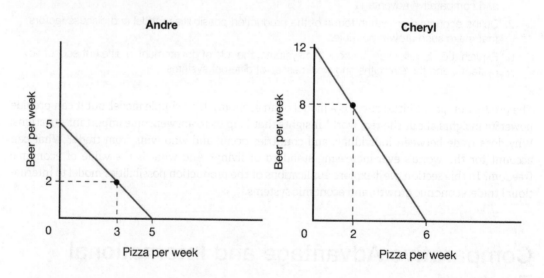

Now, we've got some important observations to make and some important questions to ask! It's clear that Cheryl is better at making pizza than Andre (she can produce more in a week's time). It's also clear that she's better at brewing beer, for the same reason. That's the absolute advantage Adam Smith talked about! But Cheryl's clear superiority leaves us with a few questions:

1. Does Cheryl's absolute advantage in producing both beer and pizza mean that there's nothing for her to gain by trading with Andre?

2. If Cheryl *can* gain by trading with Andre, do her gains come at Andre's expense? Or if Andre gains, are those gains at Cheryl's expense?

Let's explore these questions with a hypothetical trade, one that Andre and Cheryl might reach on their own were they given the freedom to negotiate: Andre agrees to specialize in making pizza, and at the end of the week he'll trade two pizzas to Cheryl (who has specialized in beer production) for 3 of her beers.

What does this leave Cheryl with at the end of the week? Because Cheryl has specialized in beer production, at the end of the workweek she has a 12-pack of beer sitting on her dining room table. She gives away three of those beers (leaving her with nine beers) in exchange for two of Andre's pizzas. That leaves her with two pizzas and nine beers to consume. But remember that when Cheryl produced only for herself, she could only enjoy two pizzas and *eight* beers; trade with Andre has made Cheryl one beer richer!

Is Cheryl's gain Andre's loss? Let's find out. Andre, you'll remember, specializes in pizza production. At the end of the week, he's got a stack of five pizzas ready for eating. He trades two of them away to Cheryl, leaving him with three for himself. Cheryl, in turn, sends him three beers. That leaves Andre to enjoy three pizzas and three beers. But remember that when Andre produced only for himself, he could only enjoy three pizzas and *two* beers! So, trade between Andre and Cheryl makes Cheryl one beer richer, but it makes Andre one beer richer, too. Somehow, Andre and Cheryl have managed to produce two more beers out of thin air! And that enables Andre and Cheryl to consume at a point outside their PPC—they consume quantities that are unavailable to them in isolation, as shown in Figure 2.10.

FIGURE 2.10 The Gains from Exchange
When Andre and Cheryl specialize in pizza and beer, respectively, each can escape their production possibilities and consume more than they ever could when self-sufficient.

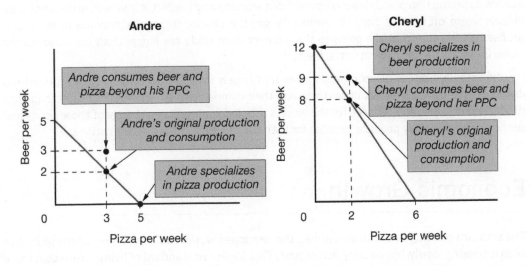

This is an interesting result—and an outcome that isn't obvious to the casual observer: Even when one party is better than the other at producing everything, *both* stand to gain from specialization and exchange! Why does that happen?

If you know the answer, you're one step ahead of Adam Smith, who measured the "best" producer of a good by who could produce the most. But Section 3 taught us the importance of comparative advantage, and it's comparative advantage that's at work in the case of Andre and Cheryl. Who is "best" at producing a product isn't measured by who is fastest; *it's measured by who gives up the least to produce it*—that's comparative advantage!

Let's see if that holds true in this case. Remember that the slope of the PPC measures the opportunity cost of whatever's on the horizontal axis. Andre's opportunity cost of producing pizza is one beer per pizza; Cheryl's is two beers per pizza. So, Andre has a comparative advantage in making pizzas. Now let's turn that upside down to see who has the comparative advantage in brewing beer. Andre gives up one pizza for every beer he produces; Cheryl only gives up half a pizza, so Cheryl has a comparative advantage in beer brewing. That's not a coincidence: If Andre has a comparative advantage in pizza, Cheryl *must* have a comparative advantage in beer.[5] In other words, everybody has a comparative advantage in something!

And that leads us to one of economics' greatest (and least obvious) theories, attributed to David Ricardo, an English economist from the early 1800s: Each person should specialize in the good

"D'oh! I could have had more beer if I'd spent more time making pizza!"

Source: UKRAINE/Shutterstock. com

in which he has a comparative advantage, and trade for the other good. Exploiting comparative advantage, as we saw in the case of Alpine Sports, allows an economy to maximize its production; the process of exchange distributes that extra production among the people who live in that economy.

Ricardo's insight is true for individuals like Andre and Cheryl, but it's also true at the national level, too—say, for the Republic of Andre and the Commonwealth of Cheryl. Nations stand to gain through specialization and exchange—what is commonly referred to as *international trade*. Restrictions on trade, then, foreclose the opportunity to specialize in what a country is good at and gain from the process of exchange—they prevent people from using their comparative advantage. We'll discuss such restrictions further in Chapter 5.

The theory of trade and comparative advantage isn't necessarily obvious. Here's a second non-obvious lesson: A nation's trade policy has nothing to do with how fully it utilizes its factors of production. Before trade, Andre and Cheryl were working full time. When they began to specialize and trade, they still worked full time—they just worked more efficiently by exploiting their comparative advantage! That's true if we extend our analysis to countries—trade doesn't necessarily create or destroy jobs, but it does cause jobs to move between the pizza industry and the beer industry. And to be honest, that transition can be painful: Expert pizza chefs may not have any particular talent for brewing beer; your local brewmeister may not know the first thing about making tasty crust. While we know trade makes the country as a whole better off (because it gets to consume outside its production possibilities curve without working any harder), it may well make some individuals worse off, even if they do eventually get the chance to acquire training in their new profession. Knowing that the gains to the winners from trade are bigger than the losses to the losers is likely little consolation to the losers.[6]

Nevertheless, nearly all economists agree that largely unrestricted trade between countries is desirable. Free trade allows countries to exploit their comparative advantage and results in greater production of goods and services for the world's people to enjoy. The exchange of those goods and services can potentially produce benefits for both the richest and the poorest nations.

Pop! Goes the Econ: Milton Friedman on Restricting Trade

Nobel Prize winner and champion of free markets Milton Friedman talks about the hidden costs of restricting trade in steel. Why do you suppose so many non-economists resist moving toward freer trade? Identify the movement along the PPC discussed in this classic bit of economics!

View in the online reader

Economic Growth

economic growth

An increase in the productive ability of an economy, represented by outward shift in an economy's production possibilities curve.

The standard of living in the United States, the developed world, and across most of the globe has been increasing slowly, but steadily, across time. That improved standard of living means that there are more goods and services to enjoy, even on a per capita basis. We can represent that increase in production as an outward shift in the production possibilities curve, a shift economists call **economic growth**. Just such a shift is represented in Figure 2.11.

In Panel (a), a point such as N is unattainable; it lies outside the production possibilities curve. Growth shifts the curve outward, as in Panel (b), making previously unattainable levels of production possible.

FIGURE 2.11 Economic Growth and the Production Possibilities Curve

An economy capable of producing two goods, A and B, is initially operating at point M on production possibilities curve QMR in Panel (a). Given this production possibilities curve, the economy could not produce a combination like the one represented by point N, which lies outside the curve. An increase in the factors of production available to the economy, or an improvement in technology, would shift the curve outward to SNT, allowing the choice of a point such as N. That extra production is economic growth.

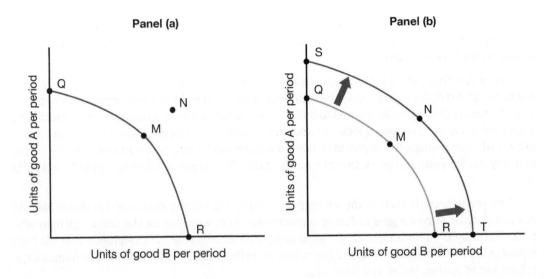

The Sources of Economic Growth

Economic growth implies an outward shift in an economy's production possibilities curve. But *how* does such an outward shift occur? Remember that when we draw a PPC, we are drawing it at a point in time. At that time, the economy only has so many workers, so much capital, and some existing level of technology. But as time passes, those things change: Factories may invest in new capital, the population may grow, and the relentless pursuit of profits by entrepreneurs may result in improvements in production technology. Anything that increases the quantity or quality of the factors of production available to the economy, or that improves the technology available to the economy, contributes to economic growth and shifts the PPC outward.

Consider, for example, worker quality. We've seen dramatic gains in human capital over the last century. For example, in 1900, about 3.5% of U.S. workers had completed a high school education. Today, over 90% have their diploma. In 1900, fewer than 1% of the workers had graduated from college; today, over 30% have. Today's workers are better educated and receive more and better training on the job than workers of even a few decades ago. They bring far more economically useful knowledge and skills to their work than did workers a century ago, and their productivity reflects it.

Moreover, the technological changes that have occurred within the past 100 years have greatly reduced the time and effort required to produce most goods and services. The assembly lines of the early 1900s (themselves a major innovation) have given way to today's automated production. Innovations in transportation (automobiles, trucks, airplanes, and intermodal rail transportation) have made moving goods and people cheaper and faster. A dizzying array of new materials is available for manufacturing. And as anyone who completed their schooling by Zoom during the coronavirus crisis of 2020 can attest, the exploding development of modern information technology is transforming both the way we live and the way we work.

Look at the big technological changes described in the "Case in Point: Is Economic Growth Over?" at the end of this section. Technology has historically played a large role in the United States' increasing prosperity, and today's advances in computer and information technology—from new

Go on, I dare you: Find a human being in this car factory!

Source: Jenson/Shutterstock.com

ways of mapping oil deposits to new methods of milking cows—are only just beginning to show their true value in increasing economic growth.

Waiting for Growth

One big way for an economy to increase productivity and spur growth is to make sure that its workers have plenty of tools to work with. In other words, an economy that builds its capital stock is an economy that is likely to grow.

Remember that capital goods are goods that are used not for personal pleasure or enjoyment, but to produce still *more* products in the future. Creating capital goods, then, comes at an opportunity cost today: The resources we used to build a new robotic welder or to expand a port could have been used to create consumer goods like Roomba vacuums and ribeye steaks. But the payoff to a juicy steak is immediate; the payoff to building a robotic welder or a new port comes in the future and may last for years and years. In other words, steaks don't promote economic growth, and ports do.

One key to growth, then, is the willingness to postpone current consumption (Roombas and ribeyes) in order to create greater future consumption. That was true for the Stone Age man who took time away from hunting to chip a stone dagger; it's equally true for an eighteen-year-old high school graduate who decides to spend her money on college tuition (an investment in human capital) instead of clothes, booze, and fireworks.

Figure 2.12 illustrates this notion using the production possibilities curves. Let's compare two countries with identical production possibilities (labeled PPC$_{NOW}$), each of which can produce both consumer goods (Roombas and ribeyes) and capital goods (robots and ports). In Yololia, people live as if there's no tomorrow, and heavily emphasize the production of utility-generating consumer goods, as shown by point A on PPC$_{NOW}$ in Panel (a). In contrast, the residents of Investia heavily emphasize the production of capital goods; their production point is shown as point B on PPC$_{NOW}$ in Panel (b).

FIGURE 2.12 Capital and Economic Growth
The choices an economy makes today can affect that economy's well-being in the future. Yololia empasizes production of consumption goods today (Panel (a), point A on PPC$_{NOW}$), and experiences small economic growth. Investia produces more capital goods (Panel (b), point B on PPC$_{NOW}$), and as a result, experiences a large outward shift of its PPC over time. The choices an economy makes today can affect that economy's well-being in the future. Yololia emphasizes production of consumption goods today (Panel (a), point A on PPC$_{NOW}$), and experiences small economic growth. Investia produces more capital goods (Panel (b), point B on PPC$_{NOW}$), and as a result experiences a large outward shift of its PPC over time.

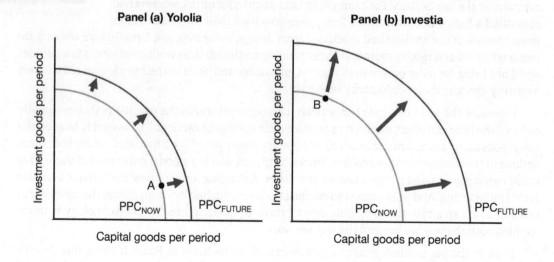

Panel (a) Yololia   **Panel (b) Investia**

Investment goods per period   Investment goods per period

Capital goods per period   Capital goods per period

The choice of where to operate on your PPC has implications for your happiness today, but it also has implications for your happiness tomorrow. Because residents in Yololia don't produce many capital goods, they're limited in what they can produce tomorrow: Their economic growth (indicated by the shift from PPC$_{NOW}$ to PPC$_{FUTURE}$) is small. In Investia, the emphasis on producing capital goods today pays big dividends tomorrow: Their PPC shifts outward dramatically, enabling residents to enjoy a bit less consumption today but a lot more in the future.

Pop! Goes the Econ: Economic Growth in *Castaway*

In this clip from the movie *Castaway*, Tom Hanks struggles to eke out an existence. Pinpoint the choice between current and future consumption Hanks makes, then explain how human capital and improvements in production technology help Hanks survive.

How important is the accumulation of capital in the real world? Table 2.1 summarizes the factors that have contributed to post-WWII U.S. economic growth. On average, the economy's ability to produce goods and services grew by about 3% per year. This table shows the contribution toward that growth of increases in the *quantity* of labor and capital, increases in the *quality* of labor and capital, and changes in technology. The story those numbers tell is fascinating—for all of the increases in technology the last seventy years have brought, for all of the improvements in educational attainment, it is simple additions to capital that are responsible for most of the economic growth we've enjoyed. Over 1.2% per year (twice the impact of any other contributing factor) was gained simply by giving workers more tools and equipment!

TABLE 2.1 Sources of U.S. Economic Growth, 1947–2012

Sources of Growth	% Contribution of Growth of Factor to Overall Growth Rate of 3.05%
Increase in quantity of labor	0.58
Increase in quantity of capital	1.24
Increase in quality of labor	0.24
Increase in quality of capital	0.38
Improved technology	0.61

Source: Based on Dale W. Jorgenson, Mun Ho, and Jon Samuels, "U.S. Economic Growth Retrospect and Prospect: Lessons from a Prototype Industry-Level Production Account from the United States, 1947–2012," in Dale W. Jorgenson, Kyoji Fukao, and Marcel P. Timmer, *The World Economy: Growth or Stagnation?* (Cambridge: Cambridge University Press:2017). Table based on Fig. 2.17, p. 58, underlying detail supplied by authors.

Arenas for Choice: A Comparison of Economic Systems

We learned in Section 3 that in order to operate on its PPC, an economy must fully employ its resources, and it must employ them in the most efficient way. That involves someone, somewhere, making a choice of how best to use the factors of production. But is it realistic to assume the person or people making that choice can or will make the perfect decisions necessary to produce on the PPC?

Under what circumstances will a nation achieve efficiency in the use of its factors of production? Alpine Sports had an incentive to allocate its plants efficiently because in her quest to maximize profit, company owner Christie Ryder had an incentive to produce the greatest output of skis and snowboards at the lowest possible cost. But, in the real world, the decisions firms face are not always so clear-cut. The motivations decision-makers face may vary depending on the nature of the economic system in which they operate.

Classifying Economic Systems

market capitalist economy

Economy in which resources are generally owned by private individuals who have the power to make decisions about their use.

command socialist economy

Economy in which government is the primary owner of capital and natural resources and has broad power to allocate the use of factors of production.

mixed economy

Economy that combines elements of market capitalist and command socialist economic systems.

Each of the world's economies can be viewed as operating somewhere on a spectrum between market capitalism and command socialism. In a **market capitalist economy**, resources are generally owned by private individuals who have the power to make decisions about their use. A market capitalist system is often referred to as a free enterprise economic system. In a **command socialist economy**, the government is the primary owner of capital and natural resources and has broad power to allocate the use of factors of production. Between these two categories lie **mixed economies** that combine elements of market capitalist and of command socialist systems.

Figure 2.13 illustrates this spectrum of economic systems. Market capitalist economies lie toward the right end of this spectrum; command socialist economies appear toward the left. Mixed economies lie in between. The market capitalist end of the spectrum includes countries such as the United States, the United Kingdom, New Zealand, and Singapore. Countries at the command socialist end of the spectrum include Cuba, Venezuela, and North Korea.

FIGURE 2.13 Economic Systems
The world's economies range from highly capitalist economies to heavily socialist economies. There are no purely capitalist economies; nor are there any purely socialist economies.

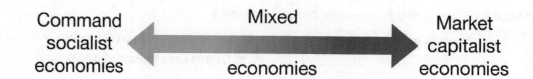

Many economies operate somewhere in the middle of this spectrum, with some resources controlled by individuals and others controlled by government. The tightly regulated economies of France, Germany, and Sweden, for example, probably lie in the center of this spectrum. Russia and China, which long operated at the command socialist end of the spectrum, have moved toward the center over the past few decades. Most economies in Latin America also once operated toward the left end of the spectrum, not because their governments exercised the extensive ownership of capital and natural resources once found in Russia and China, but because of extensive regulations. Many of these nations are in the process of carrying out economic reforms that will move them further in the direction of market capitalism.

The global shift toward market capitalist economic systems that occurred in the 1980s and 1990s was driven by three factors. First, the kind of desire for personal freedom that brought down the iconic Berlin Wall sparked a global movement for individual liberty, a liberty largely unavailable in command socialist and heavily regulated mixed economies. People seeking political, religious, and economic freedom have gravitated toward market capitalism. Second, market economies are more likely than other systems to allocate resources on the basis of comparative advantage. That efficiency results in higher levels of production and material well-being than is generally found in economies where decision-making is more centralized and bureaucratic. Finally, market capitalist–type systems appear to be the most conducive to entrepreneurial activity.

Suppose that Alpine Sports' owner, Christie Ryder, had the same three plants we considered earlier in this chapter, but was operating in a mixed economic system with extensive government regulation. In such a system, she might be prohibited from transferring resources from one use (skis) to another (snowboards) to achieve the gains possible from comparative advantage. If she were operating under a command socialist system, she wouldn't be allowed to own the plants at all—instead, she would manage the plants as a bureaucrat with any profits going to the state. Without any personal "skin in the game," Christie Ryder would have little incentive to ensure the efficient use of the three plants.

Market capitalist economies rely on economic freedom—the freedom to own private property and pursue personal gain, and the freedom to control productive resources. One good way to assess whether an economy falls more toward the capitalist or socialist end of the spectrum is to examine the degree of economic freedom it permits. One of the most extensive comparisons of global freedom is an annual effort by the Heritage Foundation that assigns each country's economy an overall economic freedom score based on such things as the degree of regulation of firms, tax levels, and restrictions on international trade. In the 2020 rankings, Singapore ranked as the freest economy in the world; North Korea received the dubious honor of being named the least free, while the United States ranked seventeenth.

Pop! Goes the Econ: Command Socialist Fashion Show
This Cold War commercial spoofs command socialism. Why do you suppose market capitalism appears to be more responsive to the desires of consumers than command socialism? How does that responsiveness manifest itself?

View in the online reader

FIGURE 2.14 Economic Freedom and Income
The graph shows the relationship between economic freedom and per capita income. The bars show the average per capita income for five equally sized groups, ranked in order from least free to most free. Countries with higher degrees of economic freedom tend to have higher per capita incomes. Income ranges from 0 to $60,000 on the vertical axis. The horizontal axis shows least free to most free.

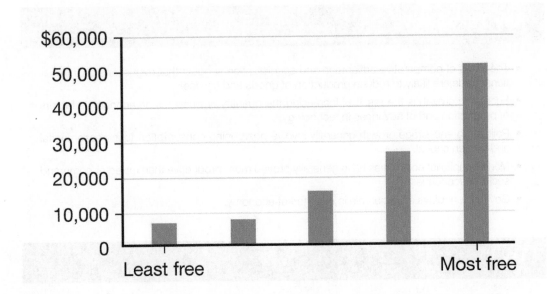

Source: Data from the Heritage Foundation's *2020 Index of Economic Freedom* at www.heritage.org/index.

Figure 2.14 illustrates the direct relationship between economic freedom and per capita income (a solid measure of an economy's overall level of production) based on the Heritage Foundation's index of economic freedom. Simply put, the richest places on the planet are also the freest places on the planet. The Heritage data also shows a direct association between the degree of economic freedom and economic growth and an inverse association between the degree of economic freedom and poverty and food insecurity. Of course, correlation doesn't equal causation—after all, it could be that higher incomes lead nations to opt for greater economic freedom. But in this case, it seems reasonable to conclude that, in general, economic freedom does lead to greater production and higher incomes.

Government in a Market Economy

The production possibilities model provides a menu of choices among alternative combinations of goods and services. Given those choices, which combinations will be produced?

In a market economy, this question is answered through the decentralized interactions of thousands, or even millions, of individual buyers and sellers. But even in a market economy, government plays a role: It encourages greater consumption of some goods (say, solar panels) by subsidizing their purchase; it discourages consumption of other goods (cigarettes, gasoline, and entertainment at "gentlemen's clubs") by levying taxes that drive up their price. Government may also try to stop the production and consumption of some goods—like heroin and cocaine—altogether. And government may supplement the private production of some goods: You may have swum in a public pool, learned in a public school, or golfed on a public course. And in some cases, there may be no private market for a good or service at all: Government agencies are virtually the sole providers of security and national defense.

Even the most capitalistic economies rely on government for at least a few key things—defense, law enforcement, education, environmental protection, and infrastructure. And even the strictest command socialist economies rely on private production and markets to provide key goods, such as food. Most economies operate with a blend of private and government production, so while government's role may be somewhat limited in a market economy, it is still fundamentally important.

Key Takeaways

- The ideas of comparative advantage and specialization suggest that restrictions on international trade are likely to reduce production of goods and services.
- Economic growth is the result of increasing the quantity or quality of an economy's factors of production and of advances in technology.
- Policies to encourage growth generally involve postponing consumption to increase capital and human capital.
- Market capitalist economies have generally proved more productive than mixed or command socialist economies.
- Government plays a crucial role in any market economy.

Try It!

Draw a production possibilities curve for an economy that can produce two goods, smartphones and jackets. You do not have numbers for this one—just draw a curve with the usual bowed-out shape. Put the quantity of smartphones per period on the vertical axis and the quantity of jackets per period on the horizontal axis. Now mark a point A on the curve you have drawn; extend dotted lines from this point to the horizontal and vertical axes. Mark the initial quantities of the two goods as CD_A and J_A, respectively. Explain why, in the absence of economic growth, an increase in jacket production requires a reduction in the production of smartphones. Now show how economic growth could lead to an increase in the production of both goods.

See related Concept Problem 5 at the end of this chapter.

Case in Point: Is Economic Growth Over?

Source: ESB Professional/Shutterstock.com

The message Robert Gordon delivered in his recent book, *The Rise and Fall of American Growth*, is not one that many Americans want to hear. The Northwestern University professor uses the term "secular stagnation" to describe the future of economic growth, which he predicts will be sluggish compared to what it was in the not-so-distant past. Gordon doesn't see a world without technological innovation, but believes that the innovations of today just won't have the same punch that ones from the past did: "Some inventions are more important than others—and the most important ones happened decades ago."[7]

This echoes the sentiments of George Mason University economist Tyler Cowen, whose 2011 book *The Great Stagnation* argues that for centuries, the United States benefited from free land, lots of immigration, and remarkable technological progress. Cowen calls these fortuitous gifts "low-hanging fruit" that America was in the right place, at the right time, to pluck.

Gordon and Cowen both point to innovations that were more "powerful" than the innovations of today: steam power, railroads and cars to move goods and people, airplanes, electricity, modern sanitation and medical care. Those innovations had deep, far-reaching impacts that made them not just useful, but transformative: They gave private citizens the elements of a modern, industrious life.

But during the last half-century, Cowen argues, the low-hanging fruit got plucked. New innovations just aren't as life-changing. Gordon points out that a car produced today is not much different than a car produced forty years ago; that our cellphones (as much as we enjoy them) don't have nearly the impact that the original telephone did.

Not all economists agree. Erik Brynjolfsson, an economist at Massachusetts Institute of Technology, thinks that it takes time for some of the current innovations, such as those related to artificial intelligence, to show their impact on the economy, but that they will eventually. Others have argued that growth isn't impossible, but it may take more spending on research and innovation today to maintain it (remember the law of increasing opportunity costs?).

Gordon remains skeptical, and cautions equal skepticism in evaluating the promises of government: "Growth has been our American mantra, but it might just prove to be an elusive slogan. So beware politicians bearing promises of a return to a vanished past."

See related Concept Problem 13 at the end of this chapter.

Sources: Based on Robert Gordon, "American Growth Has Slowed Down. Get Used to it," Politico Magazine, September/October 2016, p. 78–80; Greg Ip, "Are We Out of Big Ideas?" The Wall Street Journal, December 7, 2016, pp. A1 and A12; and Tyler Cowen's The Great Stagnation: How America Ate All the Low-hanging Fruit of Modern History, Got Sick, and Will (Eventually) Feel Better (New York: Dutton, 2011).

Your first production possibilities curve should resemble the one in Panel (a). Starting at point A, an increase in jacket production requires a move down and to the right along the curve, as shown by the arrow, and thus a reduction in the production of smart phones. Alternatively, if there is economic growth, it shifts the production possibilities curve outward, as in Panel (b). This shift allows an increase in production of both goods, as suggested by the arrow.

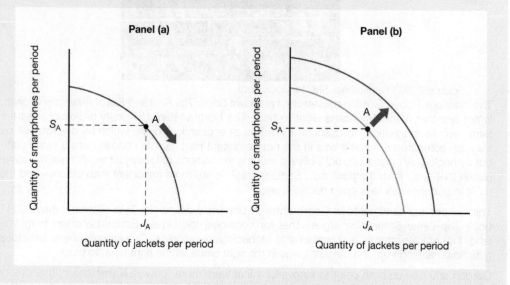

2.5 Review and Practice

Summary

Economics deals with choices. In this chapter, we examined the range of choices in production that must be made in any economy. In particular, we looked at choices involving the allocation of an economy's factors of production: labor, capital, and natural resources. In any economy, the level of technology plays a key role in determining how productive those factors of production will be. In a market economy, entrepreneurs organize factors of production and introduce technological change.

The production possibilities model assists us in thinking about the choices of resource allocation in an economy. Given the economy's factors of production and technology, the economy can produce various combinations of two goods. If the economy uses its factors of production efficiently and has full employment, it will operate on the production possibilities curve.

The production possibilities curve is downward sloping. This reflects the scarcity of the factors of production; producing more of one good requires producing less of the other. The slope of the PPC reflects the opportunity cost of the good on the horizontal axis. Because the production possibilities curve gets steeper as we move from left to right, each additional unit we produce of the good on the horizontal axis requires a greater sacrifice of the good on the vertical axis. This is the law of increasing opportunity cost, and is the inevitable result of choices in production based on comparative advantage.

The production possibilities model has important implications for international trade. It suggests that free trade will allow countries to specialize in the production of goods and services in which they have a comparative advantage. This specialization increases the production of all goods and services, and creates gains for both parties to trade.

Increasing the quantity or quality of factors of production and/or improving technology will cause economic growth, an outward shift of the production possibilities curve. In the last half century, economic growth in the United States has resulted chiefly from increases in capital.

Choices concerning the use of scarce resources take place within the context of a set of institutional arrangements that define an economic system. In a market capitalist system, resources are owned and controlled by private individuals. In a command socialist system, resources are owned and controlled by the government. Most economies are a blend of market capitalism and command socialism. An increasing body of evidence suggests that market capitalist economies tend to be most productive; many command socialist and mixed economies are moving in the direction of market capitalist systems. Even in such systems, government provides the system of laws on which market systems are founded, and may also provide certain goods and services and regulate the actions of individuals and firms.

Concept Problems

1. (Related to "Try It!" in Section 2.2.) Are the skills you develop during your college education more accurately described as labor or capital? If possible, argue both sides.

2. Why does the downward-sloping production possibilities curve imply that factors of production are scarce?

3. (Related to "Case in Point: Your Econ Grade and the Law of Increasing Opportunity Costs" in Section 2.3.) Draw a hypothetical production possibilities curve for grades, assuming that each hour you spend studying costs you the chance to watch one episode of *Jane the Virgin*. Is your production possibilities curve bowed out? In general, how does the shape of a bowed-out production possibilities curve reflect the law of increasing opportunity cost?

4. What is the relationship between the concept of comparative advantage and the law of increasing opportunity cost?

5. (Related to "Try It!" in Section 2.5.) Suppose an economy can produce two goods, A and B. It is now operating at point E on production possibilities curve RT. An improvement in the technology available to produce good A shifts the curve to ST, and the economy selects point E'. How does this change affect the opportunity cost of producing an additional unit of good B? Can you add a new point to curve ST that reflects increased consumption of both good A and good B?

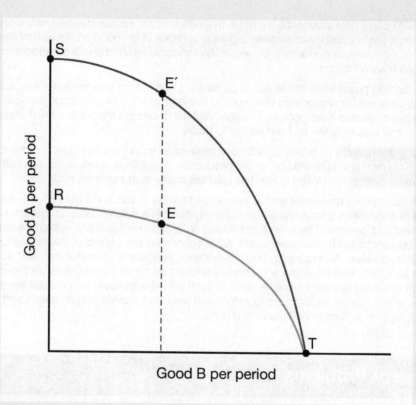

6. Could a nation's production possibilities curve ever shift inward? Explain what such a shift would mean, and discuss events that might cause such a shift to occur.

7. Suppose blue-eyed people were banned from working. How would this affect a nation's production possibilities curve?

8. Evaluate this statement: "The U.S. economy could achieve greater growth by devoting fewer resources to consumption and more to investment; it follows that such a shift would be desirable."

9. Two countries, Sportsland and Foodland, have similar total quantities of labor, capital, and natural resources. Both can produce two goods, figs and footballs. Sportsland's resources are particularly well suited to the production of footballs but are not very productive in producing figs. Foodland's resources are very productive when used for figs but are not capable of producing many footballs. In which country is the cost of additional footballs generally greater? Explain.

10. Suppose a country is committed to using its resources based on the reverse of comparative advantage doctrine: It first transfers those resources for which the cost is greatest, not lowest. Describe this country's production possibilities curve.

11. The U.S. Constitution bans states from restricting imports of goods and services from other states. Suppose this restriction did not exist and that states were allowed to limit imports of goods and services produced in other states. How do you think this would affect U.S. output? Explain.

12. By 1993, nations in the European Union (EU) had eliminated all barriers to the flow of goods, services, labor, and capital across their borders. Even such things as consumer protection laws and the types of plugs required to plug in appliances have been standardized to ensure that there will be no barriers to trade. How do you think this elimination of trade barriers affected EU output?

13. (Related to "Case in Point: Is Economic Growth Over?" in Section 2.4.) How did the technological changes described in this Case in Point affect the production possibilities curve for the United States? According to Gordon and Cowen, what is happening to the size of those changes as time passes?

14. (Related to "Case in Point: Technology and Economic Progress" in Section 2.2.) Using the egg as a metaphor, explain the role of both capital and entrepreneurship in creating a better standard of living.

Numerical Problems

1. Nathan can mow four lawns in a day or plant 20 trees in a day.

   a. Draw Nathan's production possibilities curve for mowing lawns and planting trees. Assume the production possibilities curve is linear and put the quantity of lawns mowed per day on the horizontal axis and the quantity of trees planted per day on the vertical axis.

   b. What is Nathan's opportunity cost of planting trees?

   c. What is Nathan's opportunity cost of mowing lawns?

2. David can mow four lawns in a day or plant four trees in a day.

   a. Draw David's production possibilities curve for mowing lawns and planting trees. Again, assume a linear production possibilities curve and put the quantity of lawns mowed per day on the horizontal axis.

   b. What is David's opportunity cost of planting trees?

   c. What is David's opportunity cost of mowing lawns?

3. Given the production information in problems 1 and 2 above, who has the comparative advantage in planting trees? Mowing lawns?

4. The exhibits below describe the production possibilities for Germany and Turkey.

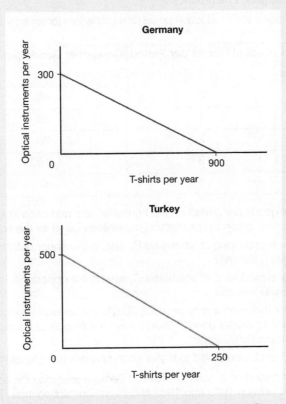

a. What is the slope of Germany's production possibilities curve?

b. What is the slope of Turkey's production possibilities curve?

c. What is the opportunity cost of producing T-shirts in Germany?

d. What is the opportunity cost of producing T-shirts in Turkey?

e. What is the opportunity cost of producing optical instruments in Germany?

f. What is the opportunity cost of producing optical instruments in Turkey?

g. In which good does Germany have a comparative advantage?

h. In which good does Turkey have a comparative advantage?

5. (Related to "Try It!" in Section 2.3.) The nation of Leisureland can produce two goods, bicycles and bowling balls. The western region of Leisureland can, if it devotes all its resources to bicycle production, produce 100 bicycles per month. Alternatively, it could devote all its resources to bowling balls and produce 400 per month—or it could produce any combination of bicycles and bowling balls lying on a straight line between these two extremes.

a. Draw a production possibilities curve for western Leisureland (with bicycles on the vertical axis).

b. What is the opportunity cost of producing an additional bowling ball measured in terms of forgone bicycles in western Leisureland?

c. Suppose that eastern Leisureland can, if it devotes all its resources to the production of bicycles, produce 400. If it devotes all its resources to bowling ball production, though, it can produce only 100. Draw the production possibilities curve for eastern Leisureland (again, assume it is linear and put bicycles on the vertical axis).

d. What is the opportunity cost of producing an additional bowling ball measured in terms of forgone bicycles in eastern Leisureland?

e. Explain the difference in opportunity cost between western and eastern Leisureland. Which region has a comparative advantage in producing bowling balls? Bicycles?

f. Draw the production possibilities curve for Leisureland, one that combines the curves for western and eastern Leisureland.

g. Suppose it is determined that 400 bicycles must be produced in the nation of Leisureland. How many bowling balls can be produced?

h. Where will these goods be produced?

6. The table below shows the production possibilities schedule for an economy.

Production Alternatives	Capital Goods per Period	Consumer Goods per Period
A	0	40
B	1	36
C	2	28
D	3	16
E	4	0

a. Putting capital goods per period on the horizontal axis and consumer goods per period on the vertical axis, graph the production possibilities curve for the economy.

b. If the economy is producing at alternative B, what is the opportunity cost to it of producing at alternative C instead?

c. If the economy is producing at alternative C, what is the opportunity cost to it of producing at alternative D instead?

d. Is it possible for this economy to produce 30 units of consumer goods per period while producing 1 unit of capital goods? Would this combination of goods represent efficient or inefficient production? Explain.

e. Which point, B or C, would lead to higher economic growth? Explain your answer.

7. The table below is based on a study by Edward Denison analyzing the sources of growth in the United States between 1929 and 1982 and for various subperiods. The numbers in the first row show the average annual rate of growth for the period and subperiods and those

in the subsequent rows show the contribution of each factor to the overall rate of growth. Note that the numbers are percentage points and do not add up to the average annual rate of growth due to a variety of other factors not shown.[8]

	1929–1982	1929–1948	1948–1973	1973–1982
Growth rate for the period	2.92	2.54	3.70	1.55
Increase in quantity of labor	0.94	1.04	1.00	0.66
Increase in quantity of capital	0.56	0.11	0.77	0.69
Increase in human capital	0.40	0.38	0.40	0.47
Technological improvement	0.66	0.50	1.09	-0.05

a. Approximately what percentage of U.S. growth between 1929 and 1982 was due to increases in the quantities of factors of production?

b. Approximately what percentage of U.S. growth between 1929 and 1982 was due to increases in quality of labor and technological improvement?

c. In which of the subperiods shown did the increase in the quantity of labor make the largest percentage contribution to the overall average annual growth rate?

d. In which of the subperiods shown did technological change make the largest contributor to the overall average annual growth rate?

Endnotes

1. If you're inclined to think mathematically, you might view the total labor power available, L, to be the product of the number of workers, W, multiplied by some number that reflects those workers' average human capital, H. So, L = W * H.

2. Neither skis nor snowboards is an independent or a dependent variable in the production possibilities model; we can assign either one to the vertical or to the horizontal axis. Here, we have placed the number of pairs of skis produced per month on the vertical axis and the number of snowboards produced per month on the horizontal axis.

3. For more on this, see "The Case of the Missing Toilet Paper: How the Coronavirus Exposed U.S. Supply Chain Flaws," in *Fortune* magazine, May 18, 2020.

4. Smith, Adam. (1827). *An Inquiry into the Nature and Causes of the Wealth of Nations*. Edinburgh: Printed at the University Press for T. Nelson and P. Brown, p2.

5. This is true because opportunity costs for two goods are reciprocals of one another. Suppose Drew and Maya produce cheese and board games. If Drew gives up 3 cheeses per board game, then he must give up 1/3 board game per cheese. Similarly, if Maya gives up 2 cheeses per board game, then she must give up 1/2 board game per cheese. So, because 2 < 3, Maya has a comparative advantage in cheese; because 1/3 < 1/2, Drew has a comparative advantage in board games. The nature of reciprocals guarantee that if opportunity costs differ; each party has a comparative advantage in something.

6. In the real world, production possibilities curves are concave, and the real-location of resources required by trade will not be nearly as dramatic. Still, moving toward free trade does result in some resources being shifted from one activity to another.

7. Robert Gordon. "American Growth Has Slowed Down. Get Used to it," *Politico Magazine*, September/October 2016. Retrieved from: https://www.politico.com/magazine/story/2016/09/economic-growth-jobs-recession-slowed-technology-214220/.

8. Edward Denison, *Trends in American Growth*, 1929–1982 (Washington, D.C.: Brookings Institution, 1985). Data from Table 8.1 Sources of Growth of Total Actual National Income, Selected periods, 1929–1982, p. 111.

CHAPTER 3
Demand and Supply

3.1 Start Up: Crazy for Coffee

Starbucks Coffee Company has revolutionized the coffee-drinking habits of people all over the world. Starbucks, whose green-and-white logo is almost as familiar as the golden arches of McDonald's, began in Seattle in 1971. Fifteen years later, it had grown into a small chain of four stores in the Seattle area. In 1987, Howard Schultz, a former Starbucks manager who had become intrigued by the culture of Italian coffee bars, bought the company from its founders for $3.8 million. Schultz launched an aggressive expansion campaign and took the company public. By 2019, Starbucks had become an international chain with over 30,000 stores in seventy-eight countries. The company had grown from its humble roots into a Fortune 500 company with over $22 billion in annual sales revenue.

Coffee Shops: More than one on every corner.

Source: rblfmr/Shutterstock.com

The change in American consumers' taste for gourmet coffee and Starbucks' outsized profits lured other companies to get into the game. Retailers such as Seattle's Best Coffee and Gloria Jean's Coffees entered the market, and today there are coffee bars, coffee carts, drive-throughs, and coffee kiosks in downtowns, malls, and airports all around the country. Even McDonald's sells specialty coffee drinks in its McCafes.

Starbucks' empire is built on a foundation of coffee beans. The price of those coffee beans can be quite volatile: Over the last decade, the price of fresh coffee beans has been as low as $1.22 per pound and as high as $3.02. Starbucks then roasts those beans and distributes them through grocery stores and through its huge network of cafes, where Americans may pay $5 or more for a cappuccino or a latte. What determines the price of raw coffee beans? How is the price of a cappuccino set? And how do producers of coffee beans decide how much to produce? What happens if growers don't produce enough, or if they harvest too much?

We'll learn the answers to those questions by studying the inner workings of markets. **Markets** are the institutions that bring together buyers and sellers, the places where those people meet. Markets can be physical spaces—you may buy your morning latte from a kiosk in your student union. Markets can also be virtual spaces: Someone interested in buying Indonesian civet coffee may have a hard time finding it in her local supermarket, but can easily find a seller on the internet. Some markets are centralized—someone who wants to buy shares of stock in Starbucks will ultimately see their purchase routed through the NASDAQ stock exchange. Other markets are decentralized: Muffin lovers, for example, get their morning fix at groceries, bakeries, cafes, and convenience stores all across the country. This chapter explains how buyers and sellers in markets, no matter what form those markets take, interact to determine not only the prices of the things we buy, but also how much of those things society will produce and consume. Even more important, this chapter gives you the tool you need to understand how those prices and quantities are likely to change in response to events elsewhere in the economy.

> **markets**
>
> The institutions that bring together buyers and sellers.

The tool we'll use to understand those things is a model of markets called the demand and supply model. The demand and supply model is a powerful workhorse that is used by Nobel Prize winners and first-semester college students alike. This chapter develops that model. We begin by looking at the buyers' side, or *demand* side, of the market. There, we discuss the factors that influence buyers' decisions about what to buy and how much. Then we examine the sellers' side, or *supply* side, of the market, where we look at the factors that determine what sellers want to produce and how much they want to offer for sale. Finally, we put demand and supply together to see how markets determine the prices of the products and services bought and sold in the economy—whatever those products and services may be. We'll find the demand and supply model so versatile that we can apply it in situation after situation, whether we're talking about brides-to-be looking for wedding venues, craft brewers sourcing a supply of hops, or even college students buying coffee to help them stay awake while they study for final exams.

3.2 Demand

Learning Objectives

1. Define the quantity demanded of a good or service and illustrate it using a demand schedule and a demand curve.
2. Distinguish between the following pairs of concepts: demand and quantity demanded; demand schedule and demand curve; movement along and shift of a demand curve.
3. Identify demand shifters and determine whether a change in a demand shifter causes the demand curve to shift to the right or to the left.

The demand and supply model is an extremely useful tool economists can use to explain what they see happening in the world around them. You may have heard something like this: "Avocado prices soared as unexpected hailstorms ravaged growers in the San Diego area." The demand and supply model can also be used to make predictions: "Peanut butter producers are ramping up production in anticipation of a coming recession."

Models are useful simplifications of reality, and the demand and supply model is no exception. The broad applicability of the demand and supply model for explanation and prediction relies on a few simplifying assumptions. In the demand and supply model, we assume the following:

Does it make that bell any less annoying to know that your customers' demands for coffee stem from a natural desire for more?

Source: beeboys/Shutterstock. com

- There are many sellers in competition with one another. That gives buyers choice over whom to complete transactions with, or the freedom to seek the best deal. No single seller can dictate the price.
- There are lots of potential buyers competing with one another. This ensures that sellers don't feel pressure to accept lowball offers simply because there's no other buyer available. No single buyer can dictate the price.
- Prices are free to move up and down in response to events in the market; there are no laws, regulations, or social norms that fix prices at some level.
- All sellers are selling an identical product. This ensures that sellers compete by offering consumers the best price, rather than adding features that make their product different than every other seller's products.

We begin our dive into the demand and supply model by looking at the buyers' side of the market for a particular good or service. How many pizzas will people eat this year? How many doctor visits will people make? How many houses will people buy? Consumers' desire and willingness to purchase a product is referred to as their *demand* for that product.

Each good or service has its own special characteristics that together determine consumers' demand for that product. One is the price of the good or service itself. Other factors that influence consumers' demand for a product include:

- buyers' preferences and available information about the product;

- the prices of related products or services;
- buyers' income;
- demographic factors such as the number of potential buyers; and
- buyers' expectations about the future.

The number of pizzas people will purchase, for example, depends very much on how much they like pizza. It also depends on the prices for alternatives such as hamburgers or spaghetti. The number of doctor visits is likely to vary with income—people with higher incomes are likely to see a doctor more often than people with lower incomes. The demands for pizza, for doctor visits, and for housing are certainly affected by the age distribution of the population and its size.

While many factors play a role in determining buyers' demands for a product or service, economists pay special attention to one: the price of the good or service. Given the values of all the other variables that affect demand, a higher price tends to reduce the quantity people demand, and a lower price tends to increase it. A medium pizza typically sells for about $10. But suppose the price were $30. Chances are, you would buy fewer pizzas at that price than you do now. And what if pizzas sold for $3? At that price, you would be likely to buy more pizzas than you do now.

Because price plays such a big role in determining how much of a product people will buy, we will discuss first how price affects the quantity demanded of a good or service. Then, we'll talk about each of the other variables listed above and see how changes in those variables affect consumers' demand for a product.

Reliably Related: Even in Brazil, Black Friday price cuts lead frenzied shoppers to buy more TVs.

Source: Nelson Antoine/Shutterstock.com

Price and the Demand Curve

Because people will purchase different quantities of a good or service at different prices, economists must be careful when speaking of the "demand" for something. They have therefore developed some specific terms for expressing the general concept of demand.

The **quantity demanded** of a good or service is the quantity buyers are willing and able to buy at various prices during a particular time period, *all other things unchanged*. (As we learned in Chapter 1, we can substitute the Latin phrase *ceteris paribus* for "all other things unchanged.") Suppose, for example, that 100,000 movie tickets are sold each month in a particular town at a price of $8 per ticket. That quantity—100,000—is the quantity of movie admissions demanded per month at a price of $8. If the price were $12, we would expect the quantity demanded to be less than 100,000. If the price were $4, we would expect the quantity demanded to be greater than 100,000. (The quantity demanded at each price would be different if *other* things that might affect it, such as the population of the town, were to change. That is why we added the qualifier that other things have not changed to the definition of quantity demanded.)

A **demand schedule** is a table that shows the quantities of a good or service demanded at different prices during a particular time period, all other things unchanged. To introduce the concept of a demand schedule, let's consider the demand for coffee in the United States. We will ignore differences among types of coffee beans and roasts, and speak simply of coffee. The table in Figure 3.1 shows quantities of coffee that will be demanded each month at prices ranging from $9 to $4 per pound; the table is a demand schedule. Note that the higher the price, the lower the quantity demanded.

quantity demanded

The quantity buyers are willing and able to buy of a good or service at a particular price during a particular period, all other things unchanged.

demand schedule

A table that shows the quantities of a good or service demanded at different prices during a particular period, all other things unchanged.

FIGURE 3.1 A Demand Schedule and a Demand Curve

The table is a demand schedule; it shows quantities of coffee demanded per month in the United States at particular prices, all other things unchanged. These data are then plotted on the demand curve. At point A on the curve, 25 million pounds of coffee per month are demanded at a price of $6 per pound. At point B, 30 million pounds of coffee per month are demanded at a price of $5 per pound.

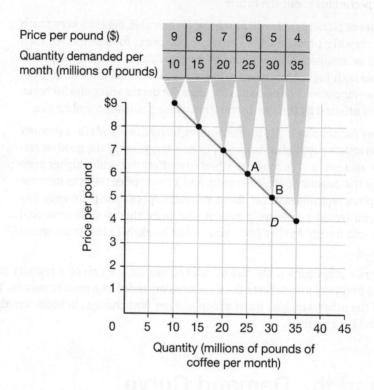

Price per pound ($)	9	8	7	6	5	4
Quantity demanded per month (millions of pounds)	10	15	20	25	30	35

demand curve

A graphical representation of a demand schedule.

The information given in a demand schedule can be presented with a **demand curve**, which is a graphical representation of a demand schedule. A demand curve thus shows the relationship between the price and quantity demanded of a good or service during a particular period, all other things unchanged. The demand curve in Figure 3.1 shows the prices and quantities of coffee demanded that are given in the demand schedule. At point A, for example, we see that 25 million pounds of coffee per month are demanded at a price of $6 per pound. By convention, economists graph price on the vertical axis and quantity on the horizontal axis.

Price alone does not determine the quantity of coffee or any other good that people buy. To isolate the effect of changes in price on the quantity of a good or service demanded, however, we show the quantity demanded at each price, assuming that those other variables remain unchanged. We do the same thing in drawing the demand curve: We assume that the other factors that may affect consumers' demand for a product (such as income or population) remain unchanged for the period under consideration.

change in quantity demanded

A movement along a demand curve that results from a change in price.

A change in price, with no change in any of the other variables that affect demand, results in a movement *along* the demand curve. For example, if the price of coffee falls from $6 to $5 per pound, consumption rises from 25 million pounds to 30 million pounds per month. That is a movement from point A to point B along the demand curve in Figure 3.1. A movement along a demand curve that results from a change in price is called a **change in quantity demanded**. Note that a change in quantity demanded is not a change or shift in the *position* of the demand curve; it is a movement *along* the demand curve.

The negative slope of the demand curve in Figure 3.1 suggests a key behavioral relationship in economics. All other things unchanged, the **law of demand** says that, for virtually all goods and services, a higher price leads to a decrease in quantity demanded, and a lower price leads to an increase in quantity demanded.

The law of demand is called a law because it's been confirmed by the results of countless studies. Undoubtedly, you have seen the law of demand in action. Suppose a clothing store finds itself with an overstock of ugly Christmas sweaters at the end of the holiday season, and needs to make room on its shelves for summer swimwear. How does it get rid of the ugly sweaters? It slashes prices and puts the sweaters on sale, secure in the knowledge that lower prices lead to increases in quantity demanded. What's true for clothing stores holds more generally: Given the values of other variables that influence demand, a higher price reduces quantity demanded. A lower price increases quantity demanded. Demand curves, in short, slope downward.

law of demand

For virtually all goods and services, a higher price leads to a reduction in quantity demanded, and a lower price leads to an increase in quantity demanded.

Changes in Demand

Of course, price alone does not determine the quantity of a good or service that people consume. Coffee consumption, for example, will certainly be affected by income: The richer you are, the more affordable $5 Starbucks lattes will be. Preferences also play a role. Starbucks' phenomenal expansion was successful in large part because coffee drinkers began developing an appreciation for gourmet coffee during the 1990s. Coffee consumption is also affected by the prices or availability of other products. For example, people often eat doughnuts with their coffee, so a decrease in the price of doughnuts might well encourage people to eat more doughnuts . . . and also buy more coffee to dunk them in! On the other hand, an alternative to coffee is tea, so a decrease in the price of tea might cause some coffee drinkers to cut back their coffee consumption and switch to Earl Grey instead. So, a change in any one of the variables that we held constant when we constructed the demand schedule for coffee will change the quantity of coffee demanded, even if the price doesn't change. In other words, the entire demand curve will *shift*. A shift in a demand curve is called the **change in demand**.

change in demand

The shift in a demand curve.

Suppose, for example, that something happens to increase the quantity of coffee demanded at each price. Several events could produce such a change: an increase in incomes, an increase in population, or publication of a study that shows coffee prevents male-pattern baldness. Each of these events would be likely to increase the quantity of coffee demanded at any given price. Such a change produces a new demand schedule, as shown in Figure 3.2. Notice that the quantity of coffee demanded is greater at each price than before; such a change is called an *increase in demand*. We can illustrate this increase in demand on our graph: The original curve, labeled D_1, shifts to the right, to D_2. At a price of $6 per pound, for example, the quantity demanded rises from 25 million pounds per month (point A) to 35 million pounds per month (point A′). So, an increase in demand shifts the demand curve to the right.

"Want. More. Coffee."

Source: Ranta Images/ Shutterstock.com

FIGURE 3.2 An Increase in Demand

An increase in the quantity of a good or service demanded at each price is shown as an increase in demand. Here, the original demand curve D_1 shifts to D_2. Point A on D_1 corresponds to a price of $6 per pound and a quantity demanded of 25 million pounds of coffee per month. On the new demand curve D_2, the quantity demanded at this price rises to 35 million pounds of coffee per month (point A').

Price ($)	Old Quantity Demanded	New Quantity Demanded
9	10	20
8	15	25
7	20	30
6	25	35
5	30	40
4	35	45

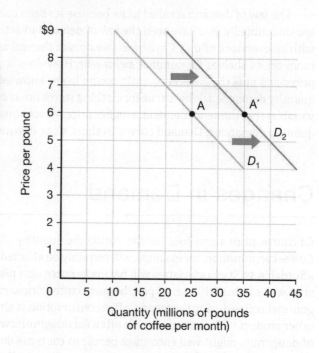

Just as demand can increase, it can decrease. We say there is a *decrease in demand* when buyers want less of a product at any given price. In the case of coffee, demand might decrease as a result of events such as an economic recession that reduces consumers' incomes, an increase in the price of doughnuts, or a decrease in the price of tea.

A decrease in the demand for coffee is illustrated in Figure 3.3. The demand schedule shows that less coffee is demanded at each price than in Figure 3.1. The result is a shift in demand from the original curve D_1 to D_3. For example, the quantity of coffee demanded at a price of $6 per pound falls from 25 million pounds per month (point A) to 15 million pounds per month (point A''). Note, again, the distinction between a decrease in quantity demanded and a decrease in demand: A *decrease in the quantity demanded* of coffee (discussed earlier) is an upward *movement* along the existing demand curve, and is caused by an increase in the price of coffee. In contrast, a *decrease in demand* (as shown here) is a leftward *shift* of the entire demand curve, and is caused by a change in some factor other than the price of coffee.

FIGURE 3.3 A Decrease in Demand

A decrease in demand occurs when the quantities of a good or service demanded fall at each price. Here, the demand schedule shows a lower quantity of coffee demanded at each price than we had in Figure 3.1. The reduction shifts the demand curve for coffee to D_3 from D_1. The quantity demanded at a price of $6 per pound, for example, falls from 25 million pounds per month (point A) to 15 million pounds of coffee per month (point A").

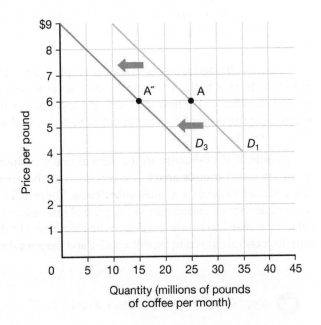

Price ($)	Old Quantity Demanded	New Quantity Demanded
9	10	0
8	15	5
7	20	10
6	25	15
5	30	20
4	35	25

What Factors Cause Demand to Shift?

A factor or variable that can change the quantity of a good or service demanded at each price is called a **demand shifter**. When these other variables change, the all-other-things-unchanged condition behind the original demand curve no longer holds. Although different goods and services will have different demand shifters, the following demand shifters generally apply to most of the goods and services people buy. They include (1) consumer preferences and available information, (2) the prices of related goods and services, (3) income, (4) demographic characteristics, and (5) buyer expectations. Let's take a look at each of these.

demand shifter

A variable that can change the quantity of a good or service demanded at each price.

Preferences and Information

Changes in the preferences of buyers can have important consequences for demand. We have already seen how growth in the retail coffee market was fueled by a growing taste for gourmet coffee (or a growing distaste for gas station brew . . .). While tastes often change slowly and gradually, the *information* available to consumers often changes rapidly. Changes in information about the quality or attributes of a product can cause dramatic changes in demand for that product, even over short time horizons. Consider, for example, the vape scare of 2019 in which, for reasons still unknown, nine e-cigarette users died suddenly and over 500 were sickened. As news of these casualties spread, the demand for vaping oils containing the psychoactive compound THC (which had been linked to the illnesses) decreased dramatically; retail sales plummeted by up to 60% in some states.

Prices of Related Goods and Services

Consider the market for peanut butter. Lots of people love peanut butter and jelly sandwiches. Suppose the price of jelly were to decrease. The law of demand tells us that PB&J lovers would buy more jelly . . . and then want more peanut butter to go with it. So, a decrease in the price of jelly will cause the demand for peanut butter to increase. The peanut butter demand curve would shift to the right.

Here's an alternative scenario: Lots of people like to slather pancakes with either peanut butter or Nutella (but not both). A decrease in the price of Nutella would likely convince some peanut butter users to switch to the now-more-affordable Nutella instead. So, a decrease in the price of Nutella might cause the demand for peanut butter to decrease; the demand curve for peanut butter would shift to the left.

complements

Two goods for which an increase in price of one reduces the demand for the other.

substitutes

Two goods for which an increase in price of one increases the demand for the other.

In general, if a reduction in the price of one good increases the demand for another, the two goods are called **complements**. If a reduction in the price of one good reduces the demand for another, the two goods are called **substitutes**. These definitions hold in reverse as well: two goods are complements if an increase in the price of one reduces the demand for the other, and they are substitutes if an increase in the price of one increases the demand for the other. Coffee and doughnuts, for example, are complements; coffee and tea are substitutes.

 Pop! Goes the Econ: Perfect Substitutes?

The Paperless Society: Your tablet is a pretty good substitute for some things . . . and not so much for others! Does the couple in this ad agree on the degree of substitutability?

View in the online reader

Complementary goods are goods that are best used in conjunction with one another. Tennis rackets and tennis balls, eggs and bacon, and iPhones and AirPods are complementary goods. Substitute goods are goods used *instead* of one another. Netflix, for example, is a substitute for television broadcasts; breakfast cereal is a substitute for eggs; text messages are a substitute for both email and phone calls.

FIGURE 3.4 Complements, Substitutes, and Demand
Coffee and doughnuts are often purchased together while tea can be substituted for coffee.

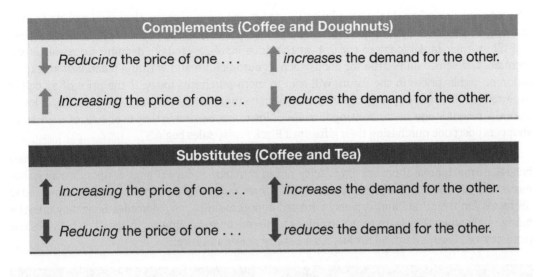

Income

As incomes rise, people increase their consumption of many goods and services (and as incomes fall, so does people's consumption of those goods and services). For example, an increase in income is likely to increase the demand for AirPods, ski trips, movie tickets, and jewelry. A good for which demand increases when income increases is called a **normal good**.

There are, however, goods and services for which consumption *falls* as income rises (and rises as income falls). As incomes rise, for example, people tend to consume less macaroni and cheese. A good for which demand decreases when income increases is called an **inferior good**. An increase in income shifts the demand curve for macaroni and cheese (an inferior good) to the left. But if someone's income decreases—perhaps because they took a pay cut or quit their job—it might cause their demand for macaroni and cheese to increase; the demand curve would shift to the right.

> **normal good**
>
> A good for which demand increases when income increases.

> **inferior good**
>
> A good for which demand decreases when income increases.

> ### Pop! Goes the Econ: Normal and Inferior Goods in *South Park*
>
> *South Park* is in a recession, and Randy suggests some ways to cope. Watch this clip and then indicate whether cable TV is a normal or inferior good. How about margaritas?

Demographic Characteristics

The number of buyers in a market affects the total quantity of a good or service that will be bought; in general, the greater the population, the greater the demand. Other demographic characteristics can affect demand as well. As the share of the population over age 65 increases, the demand for medical services, ocean cruises, and motor homes increases. On the other hand, the birth rate in the United States began falling sharply in 2007; university administrators are already planning for a 15% decrease in college enrollments beginning in 2025. Demand can thus shift as a result of changes in both the number of buyers and the characteristics of buyers.

Buyer Expectations

The consumption of goods that can be easily stored, or whose consumption can be postponed, is strongly affected by a buyer's expectations. If people expect gasoline prices to rise tomorrow, they will fill up their tanks today to try to beat the price increase—today's demand for gasoline will increase. The same will be true for goods such as automobiles and washing machines: an expectation of higher prices in the future will lead to more purchases today. If the price of a good is expected to fall, however, people are likely to postpone their purchases and await tomorrow's lower prices. A recent study by accounting firm PwC, for example, shows that over half of Christmas shoppers postpone purchasing their gifts until Black Friday sales begin.

It's not only expectations about future prices that may cause consumers to change their behavior. Smartphone shoppers may decide not to purchase today's iPhone 11 upon learning that next year's iPhone 12 will have much faster 5G connectivity. The demand for smartphones today decreases. On the other hand, drivers interested in purchasing a new Mercedes-Benz may take the plunge early when they learn that Benz plans to discontinue gasoline engines and go fully electric from now on. Today's demand for Mercedes cars increases as a result.

Heads Up!

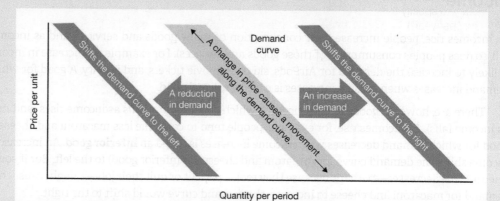

It is crucial to distinguish between a change in quantity demanded, which is a movement along the demand curve caused by a change in price, and a change in demand, which implies a shift of the demand curve itself. A change in demand is caused by a change in a demand shifter. An increase in demand is a shift of the demand curve to the right. A decrease in demand is a shift in the demand curve to the left. This drawing of a demand curve highlights the difference.

Key Takeaways

- The quantity demanded of a good or service is the quantity buyers are willing and able to buy at a particular price during a particular period, all other things unchanged.
- A demand schedule is a table that shows the quantities of a good or service demanded at different prices during a particular period, all other things unchanged.
- A demand curve shows graphically the quantities of a good or service demanded at different prices during a particular period, all other things unchanged.
- All other things unchanged, the law of demand holds that, for virtually all goods and services, a higher price induces a reduction in quantity demanded, and a lower price induces an increase in quantity demanded.
- A change in the price of a good or service causes a change in the quantity demanded—a movement *along* the demand curve.

- A change in a demand shifter causes a change in demand, which is shown as a *shift* of the demand curve. An increase in demand shifts the demand curve to the right. A decrease in demand shifts the demand curve to the left.

- Demand shifters include preferences and information, the prices of related goods and services, income, demographic characteristics, and buyer expectations.

- Two goods are substitutes if an increase in the price of one causes an increase in the demand for the other. Two goods are complements if an increase in the price of one causes a decrease in the demand for the other.

- A good is a normal good if an increase in income causes an increase in demand. A good is an inferior good if an increase in income causes a decrease in demand.

Try It!

All other things unchanged, what happens to the demand curve for streaming video rentals if there is (a) an increase in the price of movie theater tickets, (b) a decrease in family income, or (c) an increase in the price of streaming video rentals?

For each event described above, draw a graph of the demand for streaming video rentals, and then show how the graph changes as a result of the event described.

- On the horizontal axis of your graph, show the quantity of streaming video rentals. It is necessary to specify the time period to which your quantity pertains (e.g., "per period," "per week," or "per year").

- On the vertical axis, show the price per streaming video rental.

- Make a freehand drawing of the demand for streaming video rentals. Because you do not have specific data on prices and quantities demanded, focus on the general shape and position of the demand curve.

- For each event described above, draw a new curve, if necessary, to show how the event changes the demand for streaming video rentals. In each case, the demand curve for streaming video rentals could shift to the left, to the right, or remain where it is.

- Briefly explain your reasoning in each case.

See related Concept Problem 7 at the end of this chapter.

Case in Point: Is Beer a Normal Good?

In the late 1990s, a craft beer revolution began to transform the brewing industry. Adventurous palates abandoned Budweiser and began drinking crisp Belgian blondes, bitter India Pale Ales, and creamy oatmeal stouts instead.

Just as the craft beer explosion was reviving Americans' interest in beer, the Great Recession of 2007 hit. It was a doozy: Millions of people lost their jobs; others had their hours cut or their salaries slashed. As incomes fell, consumers cut back on travel, postponed buying automobiles, and stopped dining out.

How do changes in income—like the Great Recession and the long recovery that followed—affect the demand for beer? When we analyze demand shifters, sometimes theory is a clear guide to how the demand curve shifts. For example, we can use reason to figure out how an increase in the price of one good will affect the demand for a complementary good.

But theory doesn't help us determine whether a good is normal or inferior. One reason is because, at different stages of your life, you may regard the same product differently. For example, hungry college students may view hamburger as a normal good. But after they're out of college and earning good money, those same students (with fatter wallets) may buy less hamburger and more steak. Without theory to help us, we have to rely on data to figure out whether a good is normal or inferior.

Whoever placed this order was either really, really rich . . . or really, really poor.

Source: WildThingShoot/Shutterstock.com

Economists Daniel Toro-González, Jill McCluskey, and Ron Mittelhammer set out to do just that for beer. They analyzed seven years of sales data for 340 beer products at sixty different stores. Those stores were located in neighborhoods with different incomes, which allowed Toro-González, McCluskey, and Mittelhammer to see how consumption of beer varied with income.

Did lower incomes lead beer drinkers to economize on beer consumption? Or did beer drinkers drown their sorrows in *more* beer as their income fell? Toro-González, McCluskey, and Mittelhammer found that, on the whole, beer is a normal good: A 10% increase in income leads to about a 6% increase in beer consumption.

That means that during the Great Recession, brewers suffered as their sales dried up. But it's important to note that not all beers are created equal: While beer sales declined *overall* during the Great Recession, a few brands did remarkably well. Sales of sub-premium brands like Keystone, Natural Lite, and Busch grew as budget-conscious beer drinkers cut back their consumption of snooty craft beers and substituted toward lower-quality, mass-produced, but inexpensive beer instead. The big winner? Pabst Blue Ribbon, long a cellar-dweller in the American beer industry, saw sales grow by over 25%.

See related Concept Problem 6 at the end of this chapter.

Sources: Based on Daniel Toro-González, Jill McCluskey, and Ron Mittelhammer "Beer Snobs Do Exist: Estimation of Beer Demand by Type," Journal of Agricultural and Resource Economics, Vol. 39, no. 2, 2014, pp. 174–187; Johan Swinnen's The Economics of Beer (Oxford University Press, 2011), and "When is Beer an Inferior Good?" The Economist, July 27, 2009.

Answer to Try It! Problem

Since going to the movies is a substitute for watching a streaming video at home, an increase in the price of going to the movies should cause more people to switch from going to the movies to staying at home and renting streaming videos. Thus, the demand curve for streaming video rentals will shift to the right when the price of movie theater tickets increases [Panel (a)].

A decrease in family income will cause the demand curve to shift to the left if streaming video rentals are a normal good but to the right if streaming video rentals are an inferior good. The latter may be the case for some families, since staying at home and watching streaming videos is a cheaper form of entertainment than taking the family to the movies. For most others, however, streaming video rentals are probably a normal good [Panel (b)].

An increase in the price of streaming video rentals does not shift the demand curve for streaming video rentals at all; rather, an increase in price, say from P_1 to P_2, is a movement upward to the left along the demand curve. At a higher price, people will rent fewer streaming videos, say Q_2 instead of Q_1, *ceteris paribus* [Panel (c)].

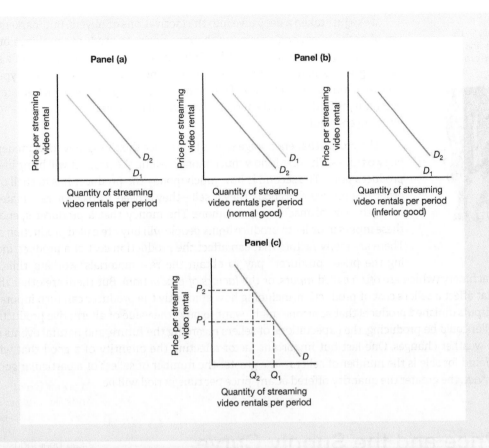

Panel (a)

Price per streaming video rental

D_2
D_1

Quantity of streaming video rentals per period

Panel (b)

Price per streaming video rental

D_1
D_2

Quantity of streaming video rentals per period (normal good)

Panel (c)

Price per streaming video rental

P_2
P_1

D_2
D_1

Quantity of streaming video rentals per period (inferior good)

D

Q_2 Q_1

Quantity of streaming video rentals per period

Khan Academy Links

The law of demand

Prices of related goods and shifts in demand

Normal and inferior goods

Expected future prices

3.3 Supply

Learning Objectives

1. Define the quantity supplied of a good or service and illustrate it using a supply schedule and a supply curve.

2. Distinguish between the following pairs of concepts: supply and quantity supplied; supply schedule and supply curve; movement along and shift in a supply curve.

3. Identify supply shifters and determine whether a change in a supply shifter causes the supply curve to shift to the right or to the left.

Producers can smell a potential profit like a drug dog sniffing out pot. The higher the price, the higher the profit—and the harder producers will work!

Source: New Africa/Shutterstock.com

We've just taken a deep dive into the motivations of buyers. But markets consist of both buyers *and* sellers—without someone to produce the things buyers want, they'll go home empty-handed. What determines the willingness of a seller to bring goods and services to the market and offer them for sale? Typically, they're driven by self-interest: They want to earn a profit! And the greater the potential profit they see, the more willing they'll be to produce the goods and services buyers want.

The profits that encourage sellers to produce the things buyers want depend on two things. The first is how much money selling the product will bring in—the product's price. The second is how much money the producer has to shell out in order to produce the goods they'll sell—they'll need to pay for raw materials, labor, the use of machinery, and more. The money that a producer spends on these inputs in order to produce items people will buy are called *production costs*. There are many factors that can affect the production cost of a product, including the prices producers pay to obtain the raw materials, workers' time, and machinery (which are often called *inputs*, or the *factors of production*). But there are other things that affect a seller's cost of production, including how efficiently the producer can turn inputs into *outputs* (finished products that someone might want to buy), the value of alternative products the seller could be producing, the expectations of sellers regarding the future, and natural events such as weather changes. One last but important factor affecting the quantity of a good that will be offered for sale is the number of sellers—the greater the number of sellers of a particular good or service, the greater the quantity offered at any price per time period will be.

Price and the Supply Curve

The **quantity supplied** of a good or service is the quantity producers are willing to sell at a particular price during a particular time period, all other things unchanged. *Ceteris paribus*, a higher price implies greater potential profits; the lure of those higher profits encourages sellers to increase the quantity they produce and offer for sale, which is referred to generally as *supply*.

Usually, as long as there are many sellers of a good, an increase in the price of a good or a service results in an increase in the quantity supplied of that good or service. This relationship is often referred to as the **law of supply**. There are a few cases, however, in which a higher price will not induce an increase in quantity supplied. For example, goods that cannot be produced, such as additional land on the corner of Park Avenue and 56th Street in Manhattan, are fixed in supply—a higher price cannot induce an increase in the quantity supplied. There are also a few uncommon cases in which a higher price might actually cause a decrease in the quantity supplied.

Those rare exceptions aside, an increase in price generally results in a greater quantity supplied. The relationship between price and quantity supplied can be represented in a **supply schedule**, a table that shows quantities supplied at different prices during a particular time period, all other things unchanged. Figure 3.5 shows a supply schedule for the quantities of coffee that will be supplied per month at various prices, *ceteris paribus*. At a price of $4 per pound, for example, producers are willing to supply 15 million pounds of coffee per month. A higher price, say $6 per pound, induces sellers to supply a greater quantity—25 million pounds of coffee per month.

FIGURE 3.5 A Supply Schedule and a Supply Curve
The supply schedule shows the quantity of coffee that will be supplied in the United States each month at particular prices, all other things unchanged. The same information is given graphically in the supply curve. The values given here suggest a positive relationship between price and quantity supplied.

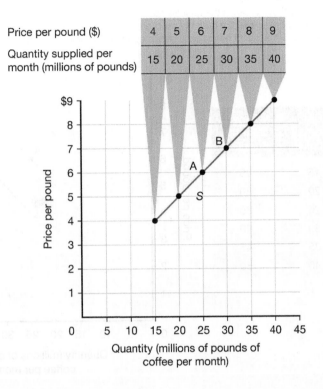

A **supply curve** is a graphical representation of a supply schedule. It shows the relationship between price and quantity supplied during a particular period, all other things unchanged. Because the relationship between price and quantity supplied is generally positive, supply curves are generally upward sloping. The supply curve for coffee in Figure 3.5 shows graphically the values given in the supply schedule.

A change in price causes a movement *along* the supply curve; such a movement is called a **change in quantity supplied**. For example, if the price rises from $6 per pound to $7 per pound, the quantity supplied rises from 25 million pounds per month to 30 million pounds per month. That's a movement from point A to point B along the supply curve in Figure 3.5. As was the case with a change in quantity demanded, a change in quantity supplied does *not* shift the supply curve.

supply curve

A graphical representation of a supply schedule.

change in quantity supplied

Movement along the supply curve caused by a change in price.

Changes in Supply

When we draw a supply curve, we assume that other variables that affect the willingness of sellers to supply a good or service are unchanged. But when one of those other variables *does* change, it causes a shift in the position of the entire supply curve. We call such a shift a **change in supply**. A change that increases the quantity of a good or service supplied at each price shifts the supply curve to the right. We call that rightward shift of the supply curve an *increase in supply*. Suppose, for example, that the price of fertilizer falls. That will reduce the cost of producing coffee (and make growing coffee more profitable); coffee growers will respond by offering more coffee for sale at each price. The supply schedule in Figure 3.6 shows such an increase: The quantity supplied at each price increases by 10 million pounds of coffee per month.

The increase in supply can be shown graphically as a rightward shift in the supply curve from S_1 to S_2. At point A on the original supply curve S_1, for example, 25 million pounds of coffee per

change in supply

A shift in the supply curve.

month were supplied at a price of $6 per pound. After the increase in supply, 35 million pounds per month are supplied at the same price (point A' on curve S_2).

FIGURE 3.6 An Increase in Supply

If there is a change in supply that increases the quantity supplied at each price, the supply curve shifts to the right. At a price of $6 per pound, for example, the quantity supplied rises from the previous level of 25 million pounds per month on supply curve S_1 (point A) to 35 million pounds per month on supply curve S_2 (point A').

Price ($)	Old Quantity Supplied	New Quantity Supplied
4	15	25
5	20	30
6	25	35
7	30	40
8	35	45
9	40	50

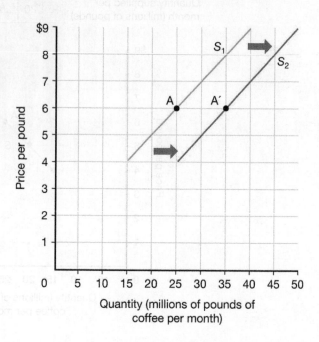

FIGURE 3.7 A Decrease in Supply

A change in supply that reduces the quantity supplied at each price shifts the supply curve to the left. At a price of $6 per pound, for example, the original quantity supplied was 25 million pounds of coffee per month (point A). With a new supply curve S_3, the quantity supplied at that price falls to 15 million pounds of coffee per month (point A").

Price ($)	Old Quantity Supplied	New Quantity Supplied
4	15	5
5	20	10
6	25	15
7	30	20
8	35	25
9	40	30

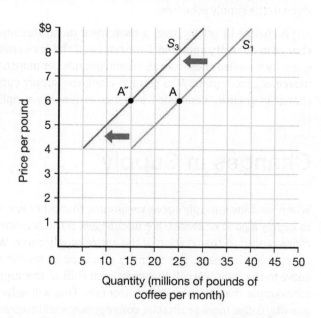

An event that reduces the quantity supplied at each price shifts the supply curve to the left. We call this a *decrease in supply*. Figure 3.7 shows a decrease in the supply of coffee. An increase in production costs or a drought that reduces the yields from coffee plants are examples of events that might cause such a decrease in supply. We see in the supply schedule that the quantity of coffee supplied falls by 10 million pounds of coffee per month at each price; the supply curve shifts leftward from S_1 to S_3.

A variable that can change the quantity of a good or service supplied at each price is called a **supply shifter**. Supply shifters include (1) the cost of inputs, (2) improvements in technology, (3) returns from alternative activities, (4) sellers' expectations, (5) natural events, and (6) the number of sellers. When these factors change, the all-other-things-unchanged condition behind the original supply curve no longer holds, and the supply curve will shift. Let's take a look at each of these supply shifters in turn.

The Cost of Inputs

Inputs are the resources producers use to make goods and services. Inputs include what economists refer to as the *factors of production*: human power, or *labor*; tools and equipment, called *capital* or *physical capital*; and land. Inputs also include the other resources necessary to make a product, such as raw materials, energy, packaging, and transportation.

Even the simplest products can require lots of inputs. Your morning coffee, for example, required land to grow the coffee trees, labor to harvest the ripe beans, and capital and energy to shell and roast the beans. Then, the beans were packaged and shipped from distant lands to your local Starbucks, where still more machinery was used to grind the beans, and yet more energy and human power turned it into your cup of Pike's Place Roast.

When inputs get more expensive, producers have to spend more to make their product. As a result, their profits shrink. They typically respond by producing less and offering a smaller quantity for sale. Supply decreases, and the supply curve shifts to the left. But when the price of inputs *decreases*, producers' potential profits increase. They respond by offering more for sale at any price, and the supply curve shifts to the right.

Suppose coffee growers must pay a higher wage to the workers they hire to harvest coffee, or must pay more for fertilizer. Those increases in production cost will cause growers to produce a smaller quantity at each price, shifting the supply curve for coffee to the left. On the other hand, a decrease in any of these costs will increase the supply of coffee and shift the supply curve to the right.

Technology

When most people hear the word "technology," they think of things like smartphones, AirPods, and video cameras—things that have have circuitry and microchips. But to an economist, technology means something very different. **Technology** is the process that turns inputs into *outputs*—the goods and services that are ultimately sold to buyers in the market. An improvement in technology generally means that you can produce the same quantity of outputs using fewer inputs, or that you can get more output from the same number of inputs. In other words, an improvement in technology should reduce the cost of producing a good or service, raising profits and causing producers to supply a greater quantity at any given price. Supply increases, and the supply curve will shift to the right.

supply shifter
A variable that can change the quantity of a good or service supplied at each price.

inputs
The resources producers use to make goods and services.

You can't make an omelet without breaking a few eggs . . . but the more expensive the eggs, the fewer omelets you'll make!

Source: Mike_shots/Shutterstock.com

technology
Knowledge that can be applied to the production of goods and services.

Even producers of simple products like coffee can benefit from improvements in technology. Development of drought-resistant varieties of coffee plants, for example, can increase yields when the weather is uncooperative. New machinery can reduce the need to hand-pick coffee beans. Improvements in packaging can reduce spoilage. Each of these events represents an improvement in production technology. Each makes it possible to grow more coffee more efficiently, getting more coffee beans to market using fewer inputs. That improves coffee growers' profitability, and encourages them to bring more beans to market at any price.

We usually think of changes in technology as improvements—after all, if a new production process made a good *more* expensive to produce, producers would simply refuse to adopt it and stick with whatever method they are using before. But there's one case where producers may choose to adopt an inferior production process—when a rule or regulation forces them too. Government, for example, may prohibit certain production processes because of safety or environmental concerns, leaving producers little choice but to use more costly methods. For example, several European countries have prohibited farmers from planting highly productive genetically modified corn. That regulation reduces yields and makes farming less profitable; the supply of corn decreases and the supply curve shifts to the left.

Returns from Alternative Activities

In Chapter 1, we learned there is no free lunch: Every choice involves an opportunity cost. That principle applies to everyone, including producers. Making one good or service means giving up the chance to produce another: A farmer who plants wheat gives up the opportunity to use that land for growing corn. The money he could have earned growing corn, then, is the opportunity cost of growing wheat.

But what happens when that opportunity cost changes? What if the market value of corn suddenly skyrockets? That change increases the (opportunity) cost of growing wheat. Some farmers will likely plow under their wheat crop and replant that land in corn. So, an increase in the price of corn may cause the supply of wheat to decrease. On the other hand, a decrease in the price of corn may tempt some corn farmers to plant wheat, instead; in that case, the supply of wheat would increase.

Seller Expectations

All supply curves are based in part on sellers' expectations about future market conditions. Many decisions about production and selling are typically made long before a product is ready for sale. Think, for example, about a distiller making fine whisky. That distiller must decide today which products to make, how much equipment to install, and what inputs to buy. He distills whisky and stores it in barrels to mellow and age; that whisky may not be ready to sell for another eighteen years! Decisions like how much whisky to produce *necessarily* depend on expectations about the future value of a bottle of good bourbon.

Changes in expectations about the future can have important effects on supply today, even for products that *don't* need to be stored for decades before sale. Consider the owners of oil deposits. Oil pumped out of the ground and used today will be unavailable in the future. If a change in the international political climate leads many owners to expect higher oil prices in the future, they may decide to leave their oil in the ground today and plan to offer it for sale later when prices are higher. In other words, speculation about higher future oil prices can cause today's oil supply to decrease.

Natural Events

Storms, insect infestations, and drought affect agricultural production and thus the supply of agricultural goods. If something destroys a substantial part of an agricultural crop, the supply curve will shift to the left. A terrible cyclone that killed more than 50,000 people in Myanmar in 2008 also destroyed some of the country's prime rice-growing land. That shifted the supply curve for rice to the left. On the other hand, if great weather brings an unusually good harvest, the supply curve for rice will shift to the right.

The Number of Sellers

The supply curve for a product, such as coffee, includes all the sellers in the market. A change in the number of sellers in the market will change the quantity available at each price, and therefore will change supply. An increase in the number of sellers supplying a good or service will shift the supply curve to the right; a decrease in the number of sellers will shift the supply curve to the left.

We often see sellers entering some markets and leaving others. Today, for example, we're seeing increasing entry (and more competition!) in the market for video streaming. The elder statesman, Netflix, has had to make room for Hulu, HBO Now, Amazon Prime, Sling TV, and, most recently, Disney+, which signed up 10 million users on its very first day! At the same time, sellers are leaving other industries: There are 25% fewer movie theaters than there were twenty years ago, digital camera makers have abandoned the industry as smartphones become more capable, and newspapers are shuttering their offices on an almost daily basis. This cycle of entry and exit from various markets plays an important role in a dynamic economy.

Heads Up!

In this chapter, we've been very careful to describe increases in demand or supply as rightward shifts, and decreases in demand or supply as leftward shifts. Wouldn't it be easier just to say, "Supply goes up," when there's an increase in supply?

It might be easier, but it might also be wrong! To understand why we're so fussy about our "rights" and our "lefts," consider the following picture, which represents an increase in demand.

Notice that when demand increases (when more units of a product or service are desired by consumers), the demand curve shifts to the right, but that you could also view the shift in the demand curve as an *upward* shift. So far, so good: When demand goes up, the demand curve goes up.

When demand increases, the demand curve shifts rightward or upward.

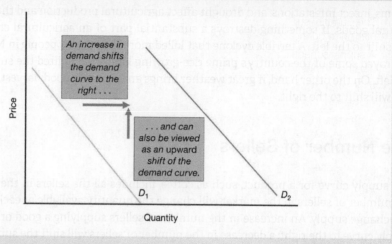

But now let's look at an increase in supply, where at each price, more units are offered for sale. This shifts the supply curve to the right, as shown next.

When supply increases, the supply curve shifts rightward or downward.

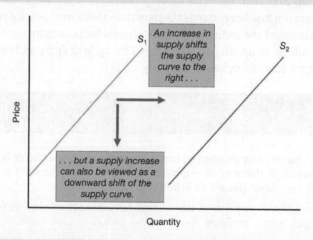

Here's the issue: Supply increased, and the supply curve shifted to the right. But you could also view the shift in the supply curve as a *downward* shift!

So let's recap: When demand increases, the demand curve shifts up, but when supply increases, the supply curve shifts down! That's accurate, but it's also confusing, and students often find it difficult to remember which curve moves in which direction.

Using "left" and "right" instead "up" and "down" eliminates that confusion:

- When demand increases, the demand curve shifts right; when supply increases, the supply curve shifts right.

- Similarly, when demand *decreases*, the demand curve shifts left; when supply decreases, the supply curve shifts left, too.

Everything consistent, everything moving the same direction, no mixed messages. So resist the temptation to use "up" and "down" when describing moves in demand and supply; your grade may depend on it!

Key Takeaways

- The quantity supplied of a good or service is the quantity sellers are willing to sell at a particular price during a particular period, all other things unchanged.
- A supply schedule shows the quantities supplied at different prices during a particular period, all other things unchanged. A supply curve shows this same information graphically.
- A change in the price of a good or service causes a change in the quantity supplied—a movement *along* the supply curve.
- A change in a supply shifter causes a change in supply, which is shown as a *shift* of the supply curve. Supply shifters include prices of factors of production, returns from alternative activities, technology, seller expectations, natural events, and the number of sellers.
- An increase in supply is shown as a shift to the right of a supply curve; a decrease in supply is shown as a shift to the left.

Try It!

If all other things are unchanged, what happens to the supply curve for haircuts if there is (a) an increase in wages paid to hairstylists, (b) an increase in the price of a haircut, or (c) an increase in the number of hair salons? Draw a graph that shows what happens to the supply curve in each circumstance. The supply curve can shift to the left or to the right, or stay where it is. Remember to label the axes and curves, and remember to specify the time period (e.g., "Haircuts per week").

See related Concept Problem 11 at the end of this chapter.

Case in Point: The Monks of St. Benedict's Get Out of the Egg Business

Even monks aren't immune to supply and demand.

Source: © 2010 Jupiterimages Corporation

It was cookies that lured the monks of St. Benedict's out of the egg business, and now private retreat sponsorship is luring them away from cookies.

St. Benedict's is a Benedictine monastery, nestled on a ranch high in the Colorado Rockies, about twenty miles down the road from Aspen. The monastery's twenty monks operate the ranch to support themselves and to provide help for poor people in the area. They lease out about 3,500 acres of their land to cattle and sheep grazers, produce cookies, and sponsor private retreats. They used to produce eggs.

Attracted by potential profits and the peaceful nature of the work, the monks went into the egg business in 1967. They had 10,000 chickens producing their Monastery Eggs brand. For a while, business was good. Very good. Then, in the late 1970s, the price of chicken feed started to rise rapidly.

"When we started in the business, we were paying $60 to $80 a ton for feed—delivered," recalls the monastery's abbot, Father Joseph Boyle. "By the late 1970s, our cost had more than doubled. We were paying $160 to $200 a ton. That really hurt, because feed represents a large part of the cost of producing eggs."

The monks adjusted to the blow. "When grain prices were lower, we'd pull a hen off for a few weeks to molt, then return her to laying. After grain prices went up, it was twelve months of laying and into the soup pot," Fr. Joseph says.

Grain prices continued to rise in the 1980s and increased the costs of production for all egg producers. It caused the supply of eggs to fall. Demand fell at the same time, as Americans worried about the cholesterol in eggs. Times got tougher in the egg business.

"We were still making money in the financial sense," Fr. Joseph says. "But we tried an experiment in 1985 producing cookies, and it was a success. We finally decided that devoting our time and energy to the cookies would pay off better than the egg business, so we quit the egg business in 1986."

The mail-order cookie business was good to the monks. They sold 200,000 ounces of Monastery Cookies in 1987.

By 1998, however, they had limited their production of cookies, selling only locally and to gift shops. Since 2000, they have switched to "providing private retreats for individuals and groups—about forty people per month," according to Fr. Micah Schonberger.

The monks' calculation of their opportunity costs revealed that they would earn a higher return through sponsorship of private retreats than in either cookies or eggs. This projection has proved correct.

And there is another advantage as well.

"The chickens didn't stop laying eggs on Sunday," Fr. Joseph chuckles. "When we shifted to cookies we could take Sundays off. We weren't hemmed in the way we were with the chickens." The move to providing retreats is even better in this regard. Since guests provide their own meals, most of the monastery's effort goes into planning and scheduling, which frees up even more of their time for other worldly as well as spiritual pursuits.

See related Concept Problem 10 at the end of this chapter.

Source: Based on personal interviews and the monastery's website at http://www.snowmass.org.

Answer to Try It! Problem

Hairstylists are a factor of production in the market for haircuts. An increase in their wages raises the cost of production, causing the supply curve for haircuts to shift to the left [Panel (a)]. (*Caution*: It is possible that you thought of the wage increase as an increase in income, a demand shifter, that would lead to an increase in demand, but this would be incorrect. The question refers only to wages of hairstylists. They may get their own hair cut, but their impact on total demand would be negligible. Besides, we have no information on what has happened overall to incomes of all of the other people who get their hair cut. We do know, however, that the cost of a factor of production, which is a supply shifter, increased.)

An increase in the price of haircuts doesn't shift the supply curve at all; rather, it corresponds to a movement upward to the right along the supply curve. At a higher price of P_2 instead of P_1, a greater quantity of haircuts, say Q_2 instead of Q_1, will be supplied [Panel (b)].

An increase in the number of hair salons offering haircuts will cause the supply curve to shift to the right [Panel (c)].

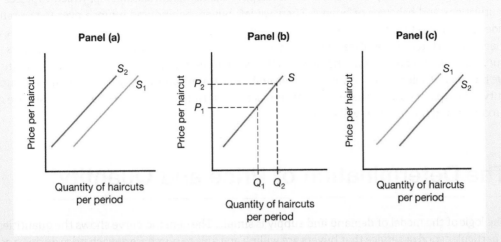

3.4 Demand, Supply, and Equilibrium

Learning Objectives

1. Use demand and supply to explain how equilibrium price and quantity are determined in a market.
2. Understand the concepts of surpluses and shortages and the pressures on price they generate.
3. Explain the impact of a change in demand or supply on equilibrium price and quantity.
4. Apply the four-step process to analyze the impact on equilibrium price and quantity of events related to a particular market.
5. Explain the impact on equilibrium price and quantity of simultaneous shifts in demand and supply.

On the Catwalk: These models *might* be able to tell you how the weather will affect the price of coffee, but none of them can outperform the model of demand and supply.

Source: Paolo Bona/Shutterstock. com

model of demand and supply

Model that uses demand and supply curves to explain the determination of price and quantity in a market.

We began our study of markets by developing the demand relationship, which captures the motivations and behavior of buyers. Then, we left buyers behind and jumped over to the sellers' side of the market to explore the supply relationship, which depicts the behavior of producers. But markets, you'll recall, are places where buyers and sellers *interact*. It's time to put our buyers and our sellers together to see what happens. In this section we combine the demand and supply curves we have just studied into a new model. The **model of demand and supply** uses demand and supply curves to explain how buyers and sellers interact to determine how much of a good or service gets produced, and how much it will sell for.

The Determination of Price and Quantity

The logic of the model of demand and supply is simple. The demand curve shows the quantities of a particular good or service that buyers are willing and able to purchase at each price during a specified period. The supply curve shows the quantities that sellers will offer for sale at each price during that same period. By putting the two curves together, we should be able to find a price at which the quantity buyers are willing and able to purchase equals the quantity sellers will offer for sale.

Figure 3.8 combines the demand and supply data introduced in Figure 3.1 and Figure 3.5. Notice that the two curves intersect at a price of $6 per pound—at this price the quantities demanded and supplied are equal. Buyers want to purchase, and sellers are willing to offer for sale, exactly 25 million pounds of coffee per month.

FIGURE 3.8 The Equilibrium Price and Quantity
When we combine the demand and supply curves for a good in a single graph, the point at which they intersect identifies the equilibrium price and equilibrium quantity. Here, the equilibrium price is $6 per pound. Consumers demand, and suppliers supply, 25 million pounds of coffee per month at this price.

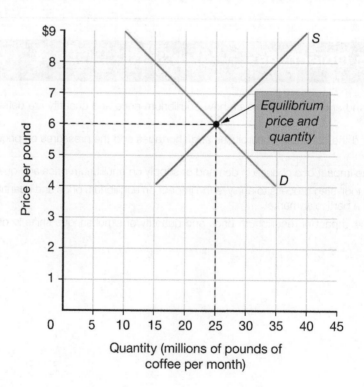

At a price of $6 and a quantity of 25 million pounds, the market for coffee is in *equilibrium*—a state of rest where neither price nor quantity has any tendency to change. In the demand and supply model of markets, the **equilibrium price** is the price at which quantity demanded equals quantity supplied. Here, the equilibrium price of coffee is $6 per pound. The **equilibrium quantity** is the quantity demanded and supplied at the equilibrium price. Here, that's 25 million pounds of coffee per month.

We've claimed that $6 is the equilibrium price. But to fully understand what that means, it's important to show (1) that the market tends to automatically gravitate to that equilibrium price, and (2) that once the equilibrium price is reached, it tends to stay there. To do that, let's see what happens at prices *other* than the equilibrium price.

> **equilibrium price**
>
> The price at which quantity demanded equals quantity supplied.
>
> **equilibrium quantity**
>
> The quantity demanded and supplied at the equilibrium price.

Surpluses

Figure 3.9 shows the same demand and supply curves we have just examined. To see how the market manages to work its way to equilibrium, let's pick a different price—say, $8 instead of $6—and see what happens.

First, let's see how buyers will respond to an $8 price. Here's how to do that: Work your way up the vertical axis until you find the price of $8. Then, read over horizontally to the demand curve, which indicates that consumers would be willing to buy exactly 15 million pounds of coffee per month at that price.

FIGURE 3.9 A Surplus in the Market for Coffee
At a price of $8, the quantity supplied is 35 million pounds of coffee per month and the quantity demanded is 15 million pounds per month; there is a surplus of 20 million pounds of coffee per month. Given a surplus, the price will fall quickly toward the equilibrium level of $6.

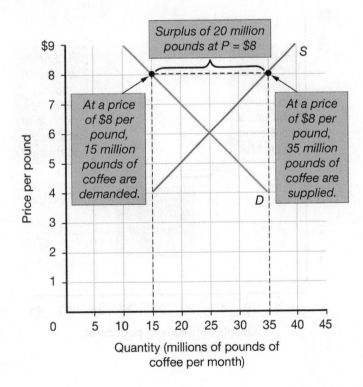

Now, let's see how sellers will respond to an $8 price. Again, read up the vertical axis until you hit an $8 price. Then, read over horizontally at that price until you hit the supply curve. At that point, you'll find that sellers would offer 35 million pounds of coffee for sale at a price of $8.

surplus

The amount by which the quantity supplied exceeds the quantity demanded at the current price.

Notice that at a price of $8, sellers are producing more than buyers want to buy! The difference, 20 million pounds of coffee per month, is called a surplus. More generally, a **surplus** is the amount by which the quantity supplied exceeds the quantity demanded at a particular price.

A surplus in the market for coffee is unlikely to last long. With too many sellers and not enough buyers, competing sellers will begin to reduce their prices in an attempt to undercut their rivals and get rid of their unsold coffee. In other words, a surplus tends to put downward pressure on prices. As the price of coffee begins to fall, the quantity of coffee supplied begins to decline and the quantity of coffee demanded begins to increase: The surplus shrinks. The price will continue to fall until it reaches its equilibrium level; there, quantity demanded equals quantity supplied; the surplus has disappeared entirely. At that point, there will be no tendency for price to fall further—sellers will be able to get rid of every unit they produce for $6, with no need to cut prices further.

Shortages

shortage

The amount by which the quantity demanded exceeds the quantity supplied at the current price.

While prices above the equilibrium price cause a surplus, prices below the equilibrium price will cause a shortage. A **shortage** is the amount by which the quantity demanded exceeds the quantity supplied at the current price.

Figure 3.10 shows a shortage in the market for coffee. Suppose the price is $4 per pound. At that price, 15 million pounds of coffee would be supplied per month, and 35 million pounds would be demanded per month. There are too many customers and not enough coffee to satisfy them all!

FIGURE 3.10 A Shortage in the Market for Coffee
At a price of $4 per pound, the quantity of coffee demanded is 35 million pounds per month and the quantity supplied is 15 million pounds per month. The result is a shortage of 20 million pounds of coffee per month.

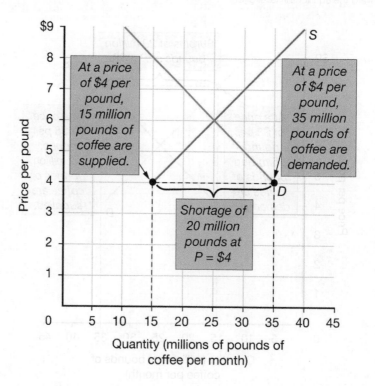

Let's think how this shortage might look in the real world. With too many customers and not enough coffee to go around, caffeine cravers will start lining up early to help ensure they get their cappuccinos. Those farther back in the line will start trying to outbid the early risers—competing for scarce coffee by offering a higher price. And sellers, seeing long lines of potential customers, will start to see dollar signs: They'll gladly increase their prices. So, the shortage tends to put upward pressure on prices.

As the price of coffee increases, two things begin to happen. First, some buyers cut back on their coffee consumption; they were only interested in coffee because it was so artificially cheap. So, quantity demanded falls as buyers work their way upward along the demand curve. Second, sellers respond to rising prices by producing more coffee. They increase the quantity of coffee supplied to the market and work their way upward along the supply curve. With buyers wanting less, and sellers offering more, the shortage begins to shrink. By the time the price hits the equilibrium price of $6, the shortage has disappeared entirely.

Equilibrium

Our look at the market equilibrium has shown us some pretty amazing things:

- When the price of a product is above the equilibrium price, surpluses result. Those surpluses tend to push prices downward, toward the equilibrium price.
- When the price of a product is below the equilibrium price, shortages result. Those shortages tend to push prices upward, toward the equilibrium price.
- When the price is at its equilibrium level, there are neither shortages nor surpluses. Because there are no shortages or surpluses, there is no pressure on prices to move up or down.

So, as long as there is competition in the market—lots of buyers competing with one another, and lots of sellers competing with one another—prices will adjust to get rid of shortages and surpluses. The market will gravitate to the only price where buyers' and sellers' interests are aligned: the equilibrium price. There, every buyer willing to pay the market price will find a seller willing to sell. Every seller willing to accept the market price will find a buyer for her product. And once the market has "found" the equilibrium price, it will tend to stay there as long as demand and supply remain unchanged.

Of course, demand and supply *can* change and *do* change in response to all kinds of events—changes in buyers' tastes or incomes, changes in the prices of related goods, changes in producers' costs of production. How will a change in the price of tea affect the price of coffee? How will an increase in consumers' incomes affect the quantity of bicycles sold? What will happen to the price of a hamburger if Congress increases the minimum wage? While the demand and supply model is useful in determining the equilibrium price and quantity in a market, its true power lies in showing how the markets for goods and services respond to events like these.

Equilibrium is a place of rest, where the forces of demand and supply are in balance. Markets, like these stones, tend to stay at their equilibrium until disturbed. Don't let your kid brother get too close!

Source: Aleksandr Simonov/
Shutterstock.com

Shifts in Demand and Supply

A change in one of the variables (shifters) held constant in any model of demand and supply will create a change in demand or supply. A shift in a demand or a supply curve changes the equilibrium price and equilibrium quantity for a good or service. Figure 3.11 illustrates the four possible cases: an increase in demand, a decrease in demand, an increase in supply, and a decrease in supply. We'll discuss each of these cases in turn, beginning at the initial equilibrium of 25 million pounds of coffee sold each month for a price of $6. After we've seen how a shift in one curve or the other affects the market, we'll extend our analysis to see what happens when *both* curves shift at the same time.

FIGURE 3.11 Changes in Demand and Supply
A change in demand or in supply changes the equilibrium solution in the model. Panels (a) and (b) show an increase and a decrease in demand, respectively; Panels (c) and (d) show an increase and a decrease in supply, respectively. Text provides further description.

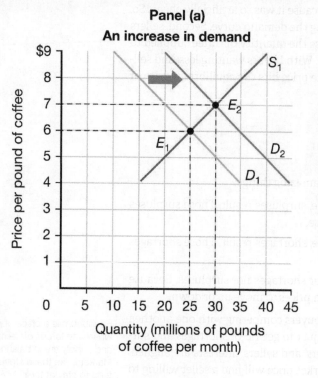

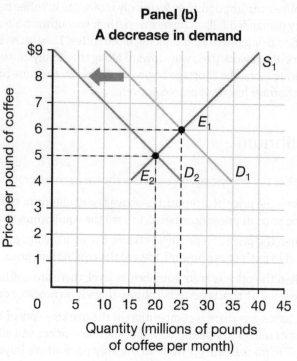

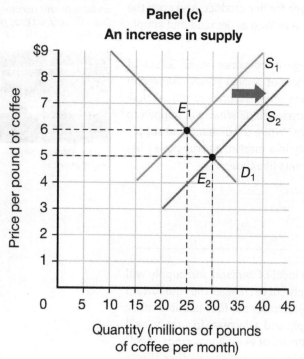

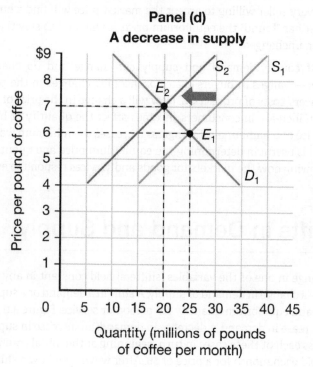

An Increase in Demand

Let's suppose that for some reason, coffee drinkers suddenly find coffee more desirable—the demand for coffee increases. This increase in demand for coffee shifts the demand curve to the right, as shown in Panel (a) of Figure 3.11. Our initial equilibrium ($6, 25 million pounds) was found at the intersection of D_1 and S_1. But the change in demand means that D_1 no longer really exists (although we leave it in the graph for comparison purposes). Instead, consumers' desires are now represented by the new demand curve, D_2. So, the new equilibrium can be found where D_2 and S_1 intersect: The equilibrium price is now $7 per pound, and the equilibrium quantity is 30 million pounds of coffee per month. The increase in demand causes the equilibrium price to increase (from $6 to $7); the equilibrium quantity increases as well (from 25 million pounds of coffee per month to 30 million pounds).

How and why do these price changes come about? How do we move from one equilibrium to another? Let's take a deeper look into how the market adjusts to an increase in demand. In Figure 3.12, we begin at our initial equilibrium E_1. But then consumers decide they want more coffee, and demand increases from D_1 to D_2.

Here's something interesting: Sellers are initially oblivious to the fact that buyers want more coffee. They continue to bring 25 million pounds of coffee to the market and offer it for sale at a price of $6. But at that price, buyers now want *more* than 25 million pounds; they want 35 million pounds. There is a shortage in the coffee market!

FIGURE 3.12 An Increase in Demand
An increase in demand creates a shortage that exerts upward pressure on prices. As prices increase, sellers increase the quantity supplied to the market.

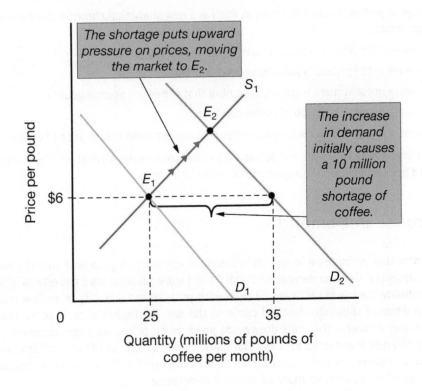

Consumer Sovereignty: "It's good to be the king—now, bring me more burgers!

Source: Sunshine Seeds/Shutterstock.com

consumer sovereignty

The principle that in a market system, the desires of consumers control the output of producers.

It's this sudden shortage that helps the coffee market move to its new equilibrium. Shortages, you may recall, put upward pressure on prices. As the price increases, suppliers begin offering more coffee for sale—there is an increase in quantity supplied. Notice that the supply curve does not shift; nothing has happened to change producers' costs. Rather, there is an upward movement *along* the supply curve, caused by the rising price of coffee. That upward movement stops when the shortage disappears; when quantity supplied equals quantity demanded at the new equilibrium point E_2.

This adjustment is part of the magic of the market! Consumers decided they wanted more coffee, but producers were oblivious to that desire. The shortage that resulted placed upward pressure on prices, and those rising prices communicated consumers' new desire for coffee to producers. Consumers wanted more coffee, and because of the workings of the market system, producers responded by bringing more coffee to the market! This principle, that in a market system the desires of consumers control the output of producers, is known as **consumer sovereignty**, which literally means that the "consumer is king."

We've been discussing the effects of a generic increase in demand: Whenever the demand for a good increases, it causes the equilibrium price of that good to increase and the equilibrium quantity of that good to increase. But demand doesn't shift for no reason; something causes demand to increase. Let's revisit our demand shifters to see what might have caused demand to increase:

- A change in preferences or information, such as a new study that shows coffee reduces the risk of heart attack
- A decrease in the price of a complementary good, like doughnuts
- An increase in the price of a substitute good, like tea
- An increase in consumers' incomes, assuming that coffee is a normal good
- An increase in the population of coffee drinkers
- A change in expectations, such as an increase in the expected future price of coffee

All of these events will cause the demand for coffee to increase. All of them, then, will cause the equilibrium price and equilibrium quantity of coffee to increase.

A Decrease in Demand

Now we know that an increase in demand causes the equilibrium price and quantity to increase. But what happens if demand decreases? Panel (b) of Figure 3.11 illustrates the effects of a demand decrease. Initially, the market is in equilibrium with price $6 and quantity 25 million pounds. The decrease in demand shifts the demand curve to the left. At the initial price of $6, the demand decrease creates a surplus that puts downward pressure on prices. As prices decrease, producers respond by offering fewer units for sale. The market moves from its initial equilibrium to a new equilibrium at a lower price and quantity ($5, 20 million pounds). The decrease in demand causes both the price of coffee and the quantity of coffee to decrease.

What could cause such a change? Demand shifters that could reduce the demand for coffee include the following:

- A change in preferences that makes people want to consume less coffee
- An increase in the price of a complementary good, such as doughnuts
- A decrease in the price of a substitute, like tea
- A decrease in income (assuming coffee is a normal good)
- A decrease in the coffee-drinking population
- A change in expectations that leads people to anticipate lower prices in the future

Any of the changes described above will cause the demand for coffee to decrease and will ultimately cause a decrease in the equilibrium price and quantity of coffee.

An Increase in Supply

We've seen how changes in demand affect the market. Now let's look at the impact of changes in *supply*. We'll start by looking at the effects of an increase in the supply of coffee, as shown in Panel (c) of Figure 3.11.

When the supply of coffee increases, the supply curve shifts to the right. At the initial price, there is now a surplus of coffee that puts downward pressure on prices. As the price falls to its new equilibrium level ($5, found where the demand and the new supply curve intersect), buyers respond by purchasing more coffee: the quantity of coffee demanded increases to 30 million pounds of coffee per month. (Notice that the demand curve does not shift; rather, there is movement along the demand curve.) Ultimately, the increase in supply causes the equilibrium price of coffee to decrease and the equilibrium quantity of coffee to increase.

What could cause supply to increase in such a way? Possible supply shifters that could increase supply include the following:

- A decrease in the price of an input, such as labor
- A decrease in the value of alternative products that coffee growers could produce using the same inputs
- An improvement in coffee production technology
- Good weather
- An increase in the number of coffee producers
- A change in expectations: Coffee producers believe coffee prices will be lower in the future than previously expected

Whatever the cause, the effect is the same: The increase in supply leads to more coffee sold at a lower price.

A Decrease in Supply

We've seen that an increase in supply causes the equilibrium price to decrease and the equilibrium quantity to increase. A decrease in supply has just the opposite effect: the equilibrium price increases and the equilibrium quantity decreases. This is shown in Panel (d) of Figure 3.11. Initially, the market is in equilibrium at the intersection of D_1 and S_1. The decrease in supply shifts the supply curve leftward to S_2. The new equilibrium, found at the intersection of D_1 and S_2, corresponds to a price of $7 per pound and 20 million pounds of coffee per month.

Anything that causes supply to decrease will cause an increase in the price and a decrease in the quantity. Possible supply shifters that could reduce supply include the following:

- An increase in the price of inputs used to produce coffee
- An increase in the value of alternative products that could be made using the same inputs
- An adverse technology shock such as a new restriction on pesticides used to protect coffee beans
- A decrease in the number of coffee growers
- A natural event that adversely impacts coffee production, such as a drought
- A change in expectations: Coffee producers believe coffee prices will be higher in the future than previously expected

All of the events listed above cause the supply of coffee to decrease; all of these events will lead to a higher equilibrium coffee price and a lower equilibrium quantity of coffee sold.

Pop! Goes the Econ: *Always Sunny* and the Price of Fish

In this clip from *It's Always Sunny in Philadelphia*, what is causing the price of snapper to rise—a change in demand or a change in supply? And in which direction?

Heads Up!

Many students struggle when using graphs to analyze the impact of changes in demand or supply on the equilibrium price and quantity of a good sold. When you're asked to do this, let your intuition and experience help you check your work. Here are a couple of common-sense notions you might find helpful:

- *The demand for a good reflects consumers' desire. All else equal, the more desirable a good is, the more buyers will be willing to pay and the higher the price it will fetch in the market.* This is why Rolex watches are so expensive and Timex watches so cheap.
- *The supply of a good reflects scarcity. All else equal, the more scarce a good is, the higher the price it will fetch in the market.* This is why diamonds (which are pure carbon) are so expensive and charcoal (also pure carbon) so cheap.

An increase in demand means that a good has become more desirable—like when a toy such as a hoverboard suddenly becomes *the* hot Christmas gift item. The more desirable a product is, the more buyers are willing to pay; they line up outside of Best Buy in hopes of obtaining a hoverboard to put under the tree. Best Buy, sensing profits waiting to be made, responds by placing orders for more hoverboards at the factory. So, when hoverboards become more desirable, the price and quantity increase.

Let's see what happens when the supply of a good decreases—like when a hailstorm ruins the Iowa corn crop. The supply decrease means that, all else equal, corn has become more scarce. Because scarce things are more valuable, the price of corn will increase. And because there's less corn (it has become more scarce), the equilibrium quantity of corn will decrease.

As a college student, it's likely that you have been participating in markets for years. You've probably seen products become hot Christmas gift items; you've also probably seen bad weather ruin crops. Remember those experiences and let them serve as a check on your graphing work. If you need to, don't think of the S and the D in your graph as reflecting "supply" and "demand." Instead, think of them as "scarcity" and "desire," and then let your intuition and experience with those notions be your guide.

Analyzing the Impact of Events on the Market

The real power of the demand and supply model of markets is its ability to show how various events will affect things we can see and measure: prices and quantities. You are likely to be asked to assess the impact of some event on the market for a good or service, a job many economics students find challenging. When you're faced with a problem like this, try applying the following four-step method:

1. Draw a demand and supply graph of the market you're interested in, and find the equilibrium price and quantity.
2. Determine *which* curve the event will affect—generally, it's either the supply curve *or* the demand curve, but not both. Referring to your lists of demand shifters and supply shifters will help you do this.

3. Determine the *direction* that the curve will shift.

4. Draw the new curve on your graph and find the new equilibrium. Compare to the initial equilibrium to see the effects of the event on price and quantity.

Let's apply this four-step algorithm to see how an increase in the price of jelly will affect the market for peanut butter. We start by drawing a graph of our market of interest, the peanut butter market, in equilibrium. We don't know the *actual* price and quantity of peanut butter, so let's just call them P_1 and Q_1, as in Figure 3.13.

FIGURE 3.13 The Peanut Butter Market in Equilibrium
The market for peanut butter is initially in equilibrium at price P_1 and quantity Q_1.

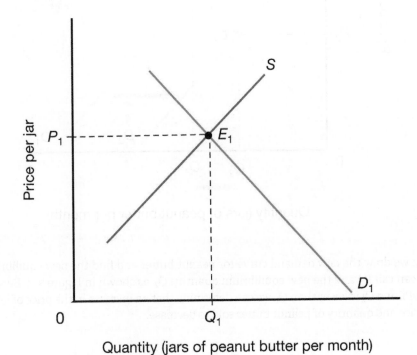

Now we have to determine whether the increase in the price of jelly will cause the demand for peanut butter to change, or the supply of peanut butter to change. Those two products are related on the buyers' side of the market: Many people like to consume peanut butter and jelly together. When we look at our lists of demand shifters and supply shifters, we find that a change in price of a complementary good is a demand shifter. So, the demand curve will move.

Third, we have to figure out in which direction the demand curve will shift. Because the price of jelly, a complementary good, increased, the demand for peanut butter will *decrease.* (Be sure to keep in mind that even though the price of *jelly* changed, it's the market for *peanut butter* that we're actually interested in!) So, the demand for peanut butter will shift to the left, as shown in Figure 3.14.

FIGURE 3.14 The Four-Step Process to Analyzing Events in the Demand and Supply Model
An increase in the price of jelly causes the demand for peanut butter to decrease. The price of peanut butter decreases from P_1 to P_2. The quantity of peanut butter sold decreases from Q_1 to Q_2.

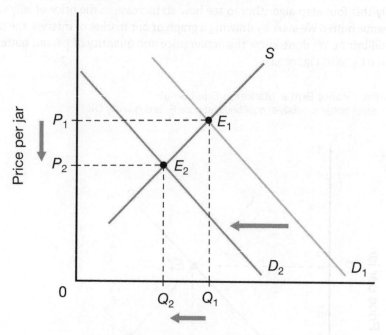

Quantity (jars of peanut butter per month)

Finally, we draw the new demand curve for peanut butter and find the new equilibrium price (which we can call P_2) and the new equilibrium quantity, Q_2, as shown in Figure 3.14. Because P_2 is lower than P_1, and Q_2 is lower than Q_1, we can determine that an increase in the price of jelly causes both the price and quantity of peanut butter sold to decrease.

Simultaneous Shifts

As we have seen, when *either* the demand or the supply curve shifts, the results are unambiguous; that is, we know what will happen to both equilibrium price and equilibrium quantity. However, in practice, several events may occur at around the same time that cause *both* the demand and supply curves to shift. To figure out what happens to equilibrium price and equilibrium quantity, we must know not only in which direction the demand and supply curves have shifted but also the relative amount by which each curve shifts.

For example, all three panels of Figure 3.15 show a decrease in demand for coffee (caused perhaps by a decrease in the price of a substitute good, such as tea) and a simultaneous decrease in the supply of coffee (caused perhaps by bad weather). Since reductions in demand and supply, considered separately, each cause the equilibrium quantity to fall, the impact of both curves, shifting simultaneously to the left means that the new equilibrium quantity of coffee will be lower than the original equilibrium quantity. The effect on the equilibrium price, though, is ambiguous: The decrease in demand tends to put downward pressure on the price, while the decrease in supply tends to force prices upward. Whether the equilibrium price ends up higher, lower, or unchanged depends on the extent to which each curve shifts.

FIGURE 3.15 Simultaneous Decreases in Demand and Supply
Both the demand and the supply of coffee decrease. Since decreases in demand and supply, considered separately, each cause equilibrium quantity to decrease, the new equilibrium quantity of coffee will be lower than the original equilibrium quantity. In Panel (a), the demand curve shifts farther to the left than does the supply curve, so equilibrium price falls. In Panel (b), the supply curve shifts farther to the left than does the demand curve, so the equilibrium price rises. In Panel (c), both curves shift to the left by the same amount, so equilibrium price stays the same.

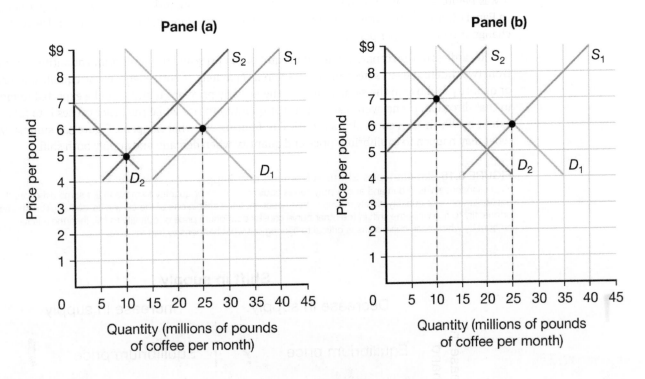

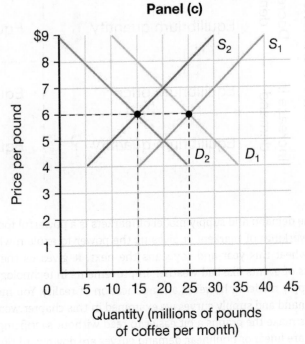

If the demand curve shifts farther to the left than does the supply curve, as shown in Panel (a) of Figure 3.15, then the equilibrium price will be lower than it was before the curves shifted. In this case the new equilibrium price falls from $6 per pound to $5 per pound. If the shift to the left of the supply curve is greater than that of the demand curve, the equilibrium price will be higher than it was before, as shown in Panel (b). In this case, the new equilibrium price rises to $7 per pound. In Panel (c), since both curves shift to the left by the same amount, the equilibrium price does not change; it remains $6 per pound.

Regardless of the scenario, changes in equilibrium price and the equilibrium quantity resulting from two different events need to be considered separately. If both events cause equilibrium price or quantity to move in the same direction, then clearly price or quantity can be expected to move in that direction. If one event causes price or quantity to rise while the other causes it to fall, the extent by which each curve shifts is critical to figuring out what happens. Figure 3.16 summarizes what may happen to equilibrium price and quantity when demand and supply both shift.

FIGURE 3.16 Simultaneous Shifts in Demand and Supply
If simultaneous shifts in demand and supply cause equilibrium price or quantity to move in the same direction, then equilibrium price or quantity clearly moves in that direction. If the shift in one of the curves causes equilibrium price or quantity to rise while the shift in the other curve causes equilibrium price or quantity to fall, then the relative amount by which each curve shifts is critical to figuring out what happens to that variable.

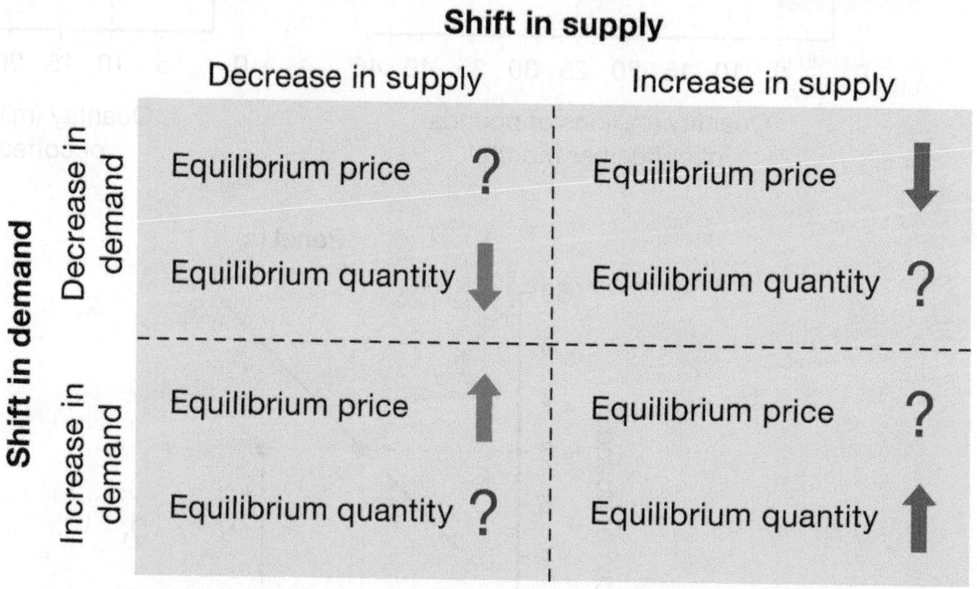

The demand and supply model of markets is a powerful tool that you can use to describe the inner workings of markets. It gives us the power to explain why prices rise or fall, why farmers plant wheat this year and soybeans the next. It gives us the power to predict the impact on markets of events like bad weather, improvements in technology, or falling incomes. The demand and supply model *is*, however, a simplification of reality. You may have noticed, for example, that the demand and supply curves we examined in this chapter were all straight lines. Simplifications like this make the graphs a bit easier to read without sacrificing the essential point: Whether the curves are linear or nonlinear, demand curves are downward sloping and supply curves are generally upward sloping. Such simplifications allow us to make broad predictions without the trouble of incorporating every nuance into our analysis. In other words, the simplifications make the model more versatile. And versatile it is: We'll apply the concepts of demand and supply over and over again throughout the rest of this book.

Key Takeaways

- The equilibrium price is the price at which the quantity demanded equals the quantity supplied. it is determined by the intersection of the demand and supply curves.
- A surplus exists if the quantity of a good or service supplied exceeds the quantity demanded at the current price. A surplus causes downward pressure on price. A shortage exists if the quantity of a good or service demanded exceeds the quantity supplied at the current price. A shortage causes upward pressure on price.
- An increase in demand, all other things unchanged, will cause the equilibrium price and quantity to increase. A decrease in demand will cause the equilibrium price and quantity to decrease.
- An increase in supply, all other things unchanged, will cause the equilibrium price to decrease and equilibrium quantity to increase. A decrease in supply will cause the equilibrium price to increase and equilibrium quantity to decrease.
- To analyze the impact of events on a market, figure out which curve shifts, which direction the curve shifts, and the impact of that shift.

Try It!

Suppose that an enterprising engineering student invents a peanut sheller that reduces wasted peanuts by half. Use the four-step method above to analyze the impact of this invention on the market for peanut butter.

See related Numerical Problem 19 at the end of this chapter.

Case in Point: Uber Finds the Market Equilibrium

If you live in a big city and don't own a car, getting from Point A to Point B can sometimes be problematic. That's especially true if neither of those points is located near a bus line or a subway. For decades, car-less city dwellers in those situations relied on taxis. But taxi service can be expensive, and because most big cities limit the number of taxi licenses, sometimes there just aren't enough taxis to go around: Too many commuters, not enough cabs.

> *Unplanned obsolescence: You can never find a taxi when you need one, but you can always summon an Uber...for the right price!*

Source: Jirapong Manustrong/Shutterstock.com

Enter Uber, the ride-sharing service made possible by the smartphone. Uber works by enabling ordinary people like you and me to drive other people around for money—anyone with a clean history, a decent car, and a smartphone can qualify. And drivers *need* a smartphone, because Uber uses a powerful app to match people who need to get places with nearby drivers looking to earn a buck. The app proposes a fixed price to both driver and rider; if they both agree, the deal is done.

Riders have found Uber to be much more convenient than taxi service. There's almost always an Uber within a few minutes' drive; you never have to remember the number of a taxi service; the cars are generally quite clean and comfortable; and an Uber ride often costs much less than the same ride in a taxi. At the same time, millions of people have found driving for Uber a great way to supplement the income from their day job, and many drive for Uber full-time.

But sometimes, on cold, rainy winter evenings, even Uber drivers don't want to brave the elements. With too many people in search of rides, and not enough cars to take them, there's a classic example of a shortage.

Our demand and supply model of markets tells us that shortages put upward pressure on prices. In ordinary markets—the market for oil, or gold, or wheat—the ordinary interactions of competition between buyers and sellers would drive up prices until the shortages disappeared.

But buyers and sellers in the "Point A to Point B" market don't have a great way to communicate with one another. After all, taxicabs and buses have regulated, fixed fares. And in the ride-sharing market that Uber created, riders and drivers don't communicate until a request is made, and neither buyer nor seller has any power to change the price that's offered—they only have the chance to accept a ride or decline.

But the economists at Uber (and it employs a ton of them!) understand demand and supply. Even though the market mechanism can't increase prices when there are too many riders and not enough drivers, the computers at Uber automatically start to ratchet up prices in response to shortages in a practice that Uber calls "surge pricing."

It should come as no surprise that riders hate surge pricing. A midnight ride from Times Square that costs $10 on December 30 might be $50 or $100 on New Year's Eve. Uber riders often feel that surge pricing takes advantage of them just when they need rides the most. But riders should really be thankful—without surge pricing, they might not get a ride home at all! When there are too many riders and not enough cars, Uber's surge pricing tempts drivers to leave their living rooms and start ferrying passengers. Economist Chris Nosko estimates that surge pricing can double the number of drivers on the streets at critical hours.

To consumers, surge pricing looks like exploitation. But it's really the linchpin that ensures everyone gets to where they want to be. In this way, Uber's pricing behavior mimics what would happen naturally in the more competitive markets for soybeans, metals, and oil. So the next time you hail an Uber and see that a six-block ride will cost you $50, don't be mad—be grateful for the surge pricing that insures you against a long, cold, wet walk home.

See related Concept Problem 12 at the end of this chapter.

Answer to Try It! Problem

1. Here is the peanut butter market in equilibrium, at price P_1 and quantity Q_1.

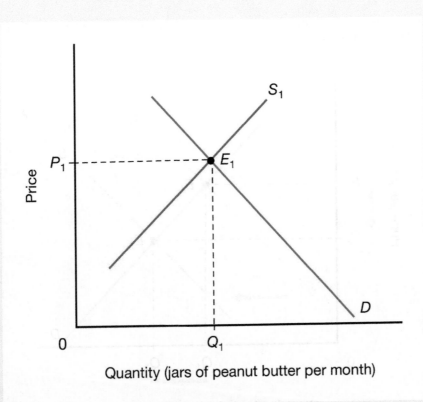

Quantity (jars of peanut butter per month)

2. The new peanut sheller makes it easier to produce peanut butter. Looking at our lists of demand and supply shifters, we can pinpoint the new peanut sheller as a change in technology, a supply shifter.

3. The new peanut sheller is an *improvement* in technology, so it will cause the supply of peanut butter to increase, or shift to the right.

4. The new supply curve is S_2. The new equilibrium price of peanut butter is P_2, and the new quantity of peanut butter is Q_2. The technology improvement causes the price of peanut butter to decrease and the quantity to increase.

A supply increase causes the equilibrium price to fall from P_1 to P_2, and the equilibrium quantity to increase from Q_1 to Q_2.

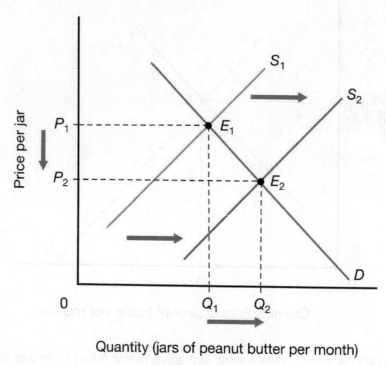

Quantity (jars of peanut butter per month)

See related Numerical Problem 19 at the end of this chapter.

Khan Academy Links

Market equilibrium

Changes in demand or supply

Changes in market equilibrium

3.5 Review and Practice

Summary

In this chapter we developed the demand and supply model of markets. A demand curve shows the quantity demanded at each price, all other things unchanged. The law of demand says that an increase in price reduces the quantity demanded, and a decrease in price increases the quantity demanded, all other things unchanged. The supply curve shows the quantity of a good or service that sellers will offer at various prices, all other things unchanged. Supply curves are generally upward sloping: an increase in price generally increases the quantity supplied, all other things unchanged.

The equilibrium price occurs where the demand and supply curves intersect. At this price, the quantity demanded equals the quantity supplied. A price higher than the equilibrium price increases the quantity supplied and reduces the quantity demanded, causing a surplus. A price lower than the equilibrium price increases the quantity demanded and reduces the quantity supplied, causing a shortage. Usually, market surpluses and shortages are short-lived. Changes in demand or supply, caused by changes in the determinants of demand and supply otherwise held constant, change the equilibrium price and output in the market.

Concept Problems

1. What do you think happens to the demand for pizzas during the Super Bowl? Why?

2. Which of the following goods are likely to be classified as normal goods or services? Inferior? Defend your answer.

   a. Beans

   b. Tuxedos

   c. Used cars

   d. Used clothing

   e. Computers

   f. Books reviewed in *The New York Times*

   g. Macaroni and cheese

   h. Calculators

   i. Cigarettes

   j. Caviar

   k. Legal services

3. Which of the following pairs of goods are likely to be classified as substitutes? Complements? Defend your answer.

   a. Peanut butter and jelly

   b. Eggs and ham

   c. Nike brand and Reebok brand sneakers

   d. IBM and Apple Macintosh brand computers

   e. Dress shirts and ties

   f. Airline tickets and hotels

   g. Gasoline and tires

   h. Beer and wine

   i. Faxes and first-class mail

   j. Cereal and milk

   k. Cereal and eggs

4. A study found that lower airfares led some people to substitute flying for driving to their vacation destinations. This reduced the demand for car travel and led to reduced traffic fatalities, since air travel is safer per passenger mile than car travel. Using the logic suggested by that study, suggest how each of the following events would affect the number of highway fatalities in any one year.

   a. An increase in the price of gasoline

   b. A large reduction in rental rates for passenger vans

   c. An increase in airfares

5. Children under age 2 are now allowed to fly free on U.S. airlines; they usually sit in their parents' laps. Some safety advocates have urged that they be required to be strapped in infant seats, which would mean their parents would have to purchase tickets for them. Some

economists have argued that such a measure would actually increase infant fatalities. Can you say why?

6. (Related to "Case in Point: Is Beer a Normal Good?" in Section 3.2.) The research summary in this case discusses how income changes affect a broad market category, beer. It also discusses how income changes affect specific beers. From the discussion, is Pabst Blue Ribbon beer normal or inferior? How about Dogfish Head Brewery's 90-Minute IPA, a craft beer? Show, using a diagram, how rising incomes would affect the demand for each of these beers.

7. (Related to "Try It!" in Section 3.2.) Consider the demand for Apple iPhones. Draw a graph to illustrate how the following events will affect the demand for iPhones.

   a. An increase in the price of cellular service

   b. A decrease in the price of Apple Music, a subscription service that gives iPhone users unlimited access to an extensive library of music

   c. A decrease in the price of Android-based phones from Samsung

   d. An increase in consumer incomes

   e. An increase in the price of AirPods, Apple's cordless earbuds

   f. An announcement that the next iPhone will have 5G connectivity and longer battery life, at a lower price than expected

8. Inner cities have a big traffic problem: Too many cars trying to drive on too few streets. Some cities, like Kansas City, are attempting to reduce congestion by adding mass transit services like light rail. Other cities, like London, Stockholm, and Singapore, have attempted to reduce congestion by charging tolls for access to the inner city. On a crowded day in London, for example, it can cost a driver over $25 to enter the central city. Do these congestion reduction schemes attempt to shift the demand curve for driving, or move along the existing demand curve for driving? Explain.

9. The graphs below show four possible shifts in demand or in supply that could occur in particular markets. Relate each of the events described below to one of them.

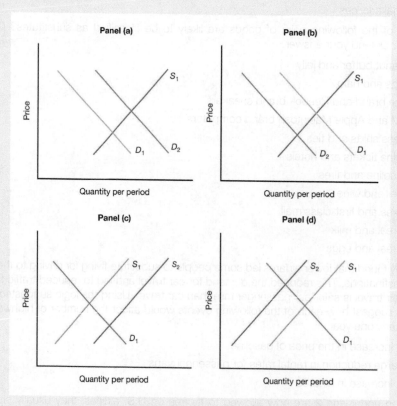

   a. How did heavy rains and flooding in South America in 1997 affect the market for coffee?

   b. The Surgeon General decides french fries are not bad for your health after all and issues a report endorsing their use. What happens to the market for french fries?

   c. How do you think rising incomes affect the market for ski vacations?

   d. A new technique is discovered for manufacturing computers that greatly lowers their production cost. What happens to the market for computers?

   e. How would a ban on smoking in public affect the market for cigarettes?

10. (Related to "Case in Point: The Monks of St. Benedict's Get Out of the Egg Business" in Section 3.3.)

   As low-carb diets increased in popularity, egg prices rose sharply. How might this affect the monks' supply of cookies or private retreats?

11. (Related to "Try It!" in Section 3.3.) Describe what would happen to the supply of chocolate in each of the following circumstances. Illustrate your answers with a graph.

   a. There is an increase in the price of chocolate.

   b. There is an increase in the price of cacao nibs, the primary ingredient in chocolate.

   c. New engineered fats make it cheaper to produce outstanding chocolate bars.

   d. A fungus decimates the cacao harvest; again, cacao is the primary ingredient in chocolate.

   e. There is a large increase in the price of coffee, which grows in the same places as cacao trees.

12. (Related to "Case in Point: Uber Finds the Market Equilibrium" in Section 3.4.) Gasoline prices typically rise during the summer, a time of heavy tourist traffic. A "street talk" feature on a radio station sought tourist reaction to higher gasoline prices. Here was one response: "I don't like 'em [the higher prices] much. I think the gas companies just use any excuse to jack up prices, and they're doing it again now." How does this tourist's perspective differ from that of economists who use the model of demand and supply?

13. While consumers' preferences for artisanal coffee were growing in the 1990s, excessive rains and flooding in South America were adversely affecting the coffee harvest. Show and explain the effects of these two events on the coffee market.

14. With preferences for coffee remaining strong in the early part of the century, Vietnam entered the market as a major exporter of coffee. Show and explain the effects of these two circumstances on the coffee market.

15. Economists who study obesity have noted that one factor behind rising obesity is the decline in cigarette smoking as the price of cigarettes has risen. Show and explain the effect of higher cigarette prices on the market for food. What does this finding imply about the relationship between cigarettes and food?

16. In 2004, *The New York Times* reported that India might be losing its outsourcing edge due to rising wages.[1] The reporter noted that a recent report "projected that if India continued to produce college graduates at the current rate, demand would exceed supply by 20% in the main outsourcing markets by 2008." Using the terminology you learned in this chapter, explain what he meant to say was happening in the market for Indian workers in outsourcing jobs. In particular, is demand for Indian workers increasing or decreasing? Is the supply of Indian workers increasing or decreasing? Which is shifting faster? How do you know?

17. For more than a century, milk producers have produced skim milk, which contains virtually no fat, along with regular milk, which contains 4% fat. But a century ago, skim milk accounted for only about 1% of total production, and much of it was fed to hogs. Today, skim and other reduced-fat milks make up the bulk of milk sales. What curve shifted, and what factor shifted it?

18. Consider the clip below, from the movie *Joe Dirt*. What principle is lead actor David Spade trying to clue Kicking Wing in on?

Pop! Goes the Econ: *Joe Dirt* and Fireworks

It's hard to make a living selling snakes and sparklers! What principle from this chapter can help Kicking Wing get to vet school?

View in the online reader

Numerical Problems

Problems 1–5 are based on the graph below.

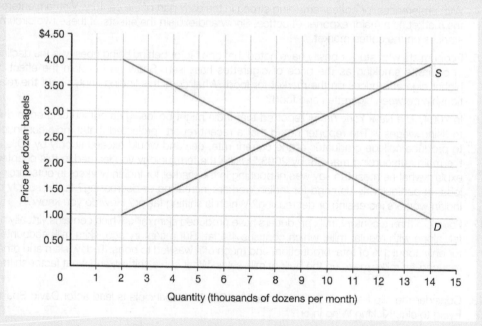

1. At a price of $1.50 per dozen, how many bagels are demanded per month?
2. At a price of $1.50 per dozen, how many bagels are supplied per month?
3. At a price of $1.50 per dozen, is there a surplus or a shortage of bagels? If so, how big is it?
4. At a price of $3.00 per dozen, how many bagels are demanded per month?
5. At a price of $3.00 per dozen, how many bagels are supplied per month?
6. At a price of $3.00 per dozen, is there a surplus or a shortage of bagels? If so, how big is it?

7. What is the equilibrium price of bagels? What is the equilibrium quantity per month?

8. At the equilibrium price, is there a surplus or a shortage of bagels? If so, how big is it?

Problems 9–12 are based on the model of demand and supply for coffee as shown in Figure 3.11. You can graph the initial demand and supply curves by using the following values, with all quantities in millions of pounds of coffee per month:

Price per Dozen ($)	Quantity Demanded	Quantity Supplied
3	40	10
4	35	15
5	30	20
6	25	25
7	20	30
8	15	35
9	10	40

9. Suppose the quantity demanded rises by 20 million pounds of coffee per month at each price. Draw the initial demand and supply curves based on the values given in the table above. Then draw the new demand curve given by this change, and show the new equilibrium price and quantity.

10. Suppose the quantity demanded falls, relative to the values given in the above table, by 20 million pounds per month at prices between $4 and $6 per pound; at prices between $7 and $9 per pound, the quantity demanded becomes zero. Draw the new demand curve and show the new equilibrium price and quantity.

11. Suppose the quantity supplied rises by 20 million pounds per month at each price, while the quantities demanded retain the values shown in the table above. Draw the new supply curve and show the new equilibrium price and quantity.

12. Suppose the quantity supplied falls, relative to the values given in the table above, by 20 million pounds per month at prices above $5; at a price of $5 or less per pound, the quantity supplied becomes zero. Draw the new supply curve and show the new equilibrium price and quantity.

Problems 13–18 are based on the demand and supply schedules for gasoline below (all quantities are in thousands of gallons per week):

Price per Gallon ($)	Quantity Demanded	Quantity Supplied
1	8	0
2	7	1
3	6	2
4	5	3
5	4	4
6	3	5
7	2	6
8	1	7

13. Graph the demand and supply curves and show the equilibrium price and quantity.

14. At a price of $3 per gallon, would there be a surplus or shortage of gasoline? How much would the surplus or shortage be? Indicate the surplus or shortage on the graph.

15. At a price of $6 per gallon, would there be a surplus or shortage of gasoline? How much would the surplus or shortage be? Show the surplus or shortage on the graph.

16. Suppose the quantity demanded increased by 2,000 gallons per month at each price. At a price of $3 per gallon, how much would the surplus or shortage be? Graph the demand and supply curves and show the surplus or shortage.

17. Suppose the quantity supplied decreased by 2,000 gallons per month at each price for prices between $4 and $8 per gallon. At prices less than $4 per gallon the quantity supplied becomes zero, while the quantities demanded retain the values shown in the table. At a price of $4 per gallon, how much would the surplus or shortage be? Graph the demand and supply curves and show the surplus or shortage.

18. If the demand curve shifts as in problem 16 and the supply curve shifts as in problem 17, without drawing a graph or consulting the data, can you predict whether equilibrium price increases or decreases? What about equilibrium quantity? Now draw a graph that shows what the new equilibrium price and quantity are.

19. (Related to "Try It!" in Section 3.4.) Consider the market for beer. Use the four-step method to show the impact of each of these events on the equilibrium price and quantity of beer.

   a. There is an increase in the price of barley, the primary ingredient in beer.

   b. There is a decrease in the price of wine, a substitute for beer.

   c. There is a decrease in the price of pizza, a complement to beer.

   d. Consumers' incomes increase.

   e. A new brewing process reduces the time needed to brew beer by 20%.

Endnotes

1. Noam Scheiber, "As a Center for Outsourcing, India Could Be Losing Its Edge," *New York Times*, May 9, 2004, p. BU3.

CHAPTER 4
Applications of Demand and Supply

4.1 Start Up: A Composer Logs On

"Since the age of seven, I knew that I would be a musician. And from age fourteen, I knew that I would be a composer," says Israeli-born Ofer Ben-Amots. What he did not know was that he would use computers to carry out his work. He is now a professor of music at Colorado College; his compositions and operas have been performed in the United States, Europe, and Japan.

For over thirty years, Dr. Ben-Amots has used musical composition software in creating his music. "The output is extremely elegant. Performers enjoy looking at such a clear and clean score. The creation of parts out of a full score is as easy as pressing the <ENTER> key on the keyboard." Changes can easily be inserted into the notation file, which eliminates the need for recopying. Dr. Ben-Amots also uses computers for playback. "I can listen to a relatively accurate 'digital performance' of the score at any given point, with any tempo or instrumentation I choose. The sound quality has improved so much that digital files sound almost identical to real performance."

Ben-Amots was an early adopter of computers, using them to produce his own CDs. Today, he mostly streams his music on online sites such as YouTube, SoundCloud, and Facebook, so that anyone in the world can hear his music. He self-publishes and self-markets his musical scores. "In my case, I get to keep the copyrights on all of my music. This would have been impossible ten to twelve years ago when composers transferred their rights to publishers. Home pages on the World Wide Web allow me to promote my own work." Professor Ben-Amots also harnessed ever-increasing computing power to change the way he teaches music composition. New software, such as GarageBand, has opened the way for anyone interested to try to compose music: Ben-Amots' music composition classes used to have music theory prerequisites, but today, his classes are open to all.

Dr. Ben-Amots began integrating tech into his musical career in 1989. His first computer, a Macintosh SE30 with 4 megabytes of random access memory (RAM) and an 80-megabyte hard drive, cost him $3,000. Today, he uses a $2,200 MacBook Pro with several gigabytes of RAM (a gigabyte is slightly more than 1,000 megabytes). His first computer had a cost per megabyte of RAM of about $750. Measured in the same way, his current machine cost less than a thousandth of that amount and is far more powerful besides: His first computer could execute 18 million instructions per second; his MacBook Pro can carry out 280 *billion*.

Computers are better, more portable, and faster than ever—even the tiny computer in your iPhone is over 100,000 times more powerful than the computer that landed man on the moon. And yet, despite those quality improvements, and despite the fact that the demand for computers is stronger than ever, computers' prices continue to fall.[1] That story is just one of the stories about markets we will tell in this chapter, which aims to help you apply the model of demand and supply to the real world.

Pop! Goes the Econ: Ofer Ben-Amots' Klezmer Concerto
The Chamber Orchestra of the Springs plays Ofer Ben-Amots' thrilling concerto featuring Kliment Krylovskiy on clarinet.

View in the online reader

The computer in this thing is a marvel—this single credit-card-sized device has replaced the camera, the calculator, the road atlas, the television, the stereo, the flashlight, and the notepad. Oh, and the phone—it's replaced the phone, too!

Source: Daniel M Ernst/ Shutterstock.com

We begin this chapter by looking at several markets you are likely to be familiar with—the market for personal computers, the markets for crude oil and for gasoline, and the stock market. After all, as a college student, you most likely own (or at least have access to) a computer—and in the wake of the coronavirus crisis, computing power has proven to be more important than ever. You've probably also been affected by sharp swings in the prices of oil and gasoline: Even if you don't drive, the price of fuel shows up in your heating bill and in the cost of transporting the goods you buy. And, while you may not *yet* have a stock portfolio, it's probably only a matter of time before you start building a retirement nest egg. A big part of that nest egg would likely consist of stock. (Besides, remember that the first thing many people ask when they learn you've studied econ is, "What's the stock market going to do?") Demand and supply are very useful in explaining the behavior of these markets; learning to apply them here is great practice for explaining the behavior of markets for other things you're interested in—music downloads, heirloom seeds, skin care products, and thousands of other goods and services you might care about.

Beginning in the third section of this chapter, we'll start looking at how various government policies affect the market. One set of government policies replaces the price-setting abilities of buyers and sellers with mandates that establish either minimum or maximum prices that sellers can charge. You may not be familiar with *those* kinds of policies, but odds are you've paid a tax a time or two: Just like minimum and maximum mandates, a tax affects both the quantity and price of a good traded in the market. We will look at the rationales for these policies and explore those policies' consequences. And, as you'll see, sometimes those consequences are both unintended and counterproductive!

4.2 Putting Demand and Supply to Work

Learning Objectives

1. Apply the model of demand and supply to the behavior of equilibrium prices and output in a variety of markets.
2. Identify and define the key terms related to the organization of firms and explain how the model of demand and supply can be used to understand prices of shares of stock.

Economic models are simplifications of reality that economists use for three main purposes: To *explain* what's going on around us; to *predict* how markets will react to events; and to *prescribe* solutions to what we perceive as economic problems.

In Chapter 3, you developed the model of demand and supply, and you learned that shifts in demand and supply lead to changes in equilibrium prices and equilibrium quantities. In this section, we'll use the demand and supply model to *explain* the behavior of prices and quantities in a few special markets—the market for computers, the market for oil and gasoline, and the stock market. The oil, gas, and stock markets are particularly interesting because prices in those markets are volatile—changes in prices can be both rapid and large. But before we get to those stories, let's unravel another interesting puzzle: the behavior of prices in personal computing.

The Personal Computer Market

In the 1960s, personal computers (not to mention laptops and smartphones) didn't exist. Computers were large mainframe computers—machines big enough to fill an entire room—and IBM was the undisputed king of mainframe computing.

This is the one that started the personal computing revolution, the Apple II.

Source: Anton_Ivanov/ Shutterstock.com

But in 1976, two upstart computer junkies working out of a garage did something revolutionary that transformed the entire industry. Those entrepreneurial techies—Steve Wozniak and Steven Jobs—created the Apple I, a desktop computer with a single motherboard that came pre-assembled. Novel, right? By the next year, they'd taken it to the next level: The Apple II was born, and the era of the personal computer began. Now, computing power was available to everyone, not just governments and big companies with deep pockets. Between 1976, when Apple Computer introduced its first desktop computer, and 1981, when IBM produced its first personal computers (PCs), computer usage expanded dramatically. Even though computers were quite expensive by today's standards (the Apple II sold for about $3,500 in today's dollars—today, you can get a decent used Camry for less!), by 1984, 8.2% of U.S. households owned a personal computer. Twenty-three years later, 92% of households had some type of computer, and access to the internet had grown to 84% from virtually zero at the World Wide Web's inception in 1989. Let's use the tools of demand and supply to tell the story of the personal computer that has become so familiar and affordable to most people in the United States.

Let's begin on the demand side of the market. In 1976, Apple brought personal computing to the masses. But what, those masses wondered, could these things actually *do*? Unless you could write your own programs (what you probably know today as apps), you had to spend a fair chunk of money to access a library of software small enough to list on a notepad. A few of those programs were extremely useful, though—including early spreadsheet, database, and word processing programs—and that spurred sales of *both* the software and the computers to run them on. (Remember complementary goods?) Computer makers and software producers found themselves in a virtuous spiral—more software meant more things to do with computers; more computers meant greater opportunities for software developers. Systems became more user-friendly as applications became increasingly graphically driven and mouse-controlled. By the 1990s, rising incomes and the exploding internet had sealed the deal: Demand was stronger than ever, and the computer was here to stay.

Pop! Goes the Econ: Steve Jobs on Apple's Early Success
Apple computers were just toys until software developers turned them into something useful. In this video, Steve Jobs credits the success of Apple's first personal computer to the spreadsheet. In econ-speak, how are spreadsheet software and computer hardware related?

View in the online reader

While the demand side of the computer market was exploding, big changes were also under way on the supply side, driven primarily by technological change. Chips, hard drives, and other components were becoming easier and easier to engineer and manufacture. At the same time, they were also getting better and better. Between 1993 and 1998—the golden age of personal computing—the Bureau of Labor Statistics estimates that central processing unit (CPU) speed rose 1,263%, system memory increased 1,500%, hard drive capacity soared by 3,700%, and monitor size went up 13%. The trajectory of those performance metrics continues to this day: Computers are faster, better, and yet smaller and easier to produce with each passing year.

You'd think those desirable attributes would make computers more valuable in the marketplace . . . but you'd be wrong! Computers are getting faster, better, and smaller, but they're also getting cheaper. Let's see how those prices have evolved . . . but let's compare apples to apples. Because a computer today is not the same good as a computer even five years ago, we'll look at the price of a computer holding its speed and capabilities constant—what we'll call a "quality-adjusted" computer, or generically, "computing power." Those prices have done nothing but decline: The price per unit of quality-adjusted desktop computers fell by about half every 50 months during the period 1976–1989; in the first half of the 1990s, those prices fell by half every 28 months; in the second half of the 1990s, the "halving time" fell to every 24 months. As a buyer of computers, that's money in your pocket: Figure 4.1 shows just how cheap computing power has become. While you may bemoan the cost of your college laptop, that laptop is incredibly capable: To have purchased the same amount of computing power in 1992, you'd have had to spend over 750 times as much. By that metric, computing power today is practically free!

FIGURE 4.1 Producer Price Index for Computing Power, 1992–2020

Craziness! Between 1992 and 2020, the price of computers fell dramatically. Computing power you'd have spent $11,751 on in 1992 could be bought in June of 2020 for an amazing $15.50.

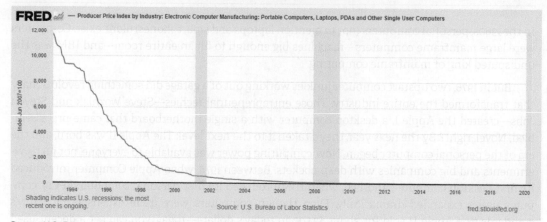

Source: U.S. Bureau of Labor Statistics, Producer Price Index by Industry: Electronic Computer Manufacturing: Portable Computers, Laptops, Tablets and Other Single User Computers [PCU33411133411172], retrieved from FRED, Federal Reserve Bank of St. Louis; https://fred.stlouisfed.org/series/PCU33411133411172

Back trouble? This 1950s IBM mainframe computer was far less capable than the cheapest laptop today . . . and really hard to fit in your book bag!

Source: Everett Collection/Shutterstock.com

So part of the story on the supply side has to do with improvements in production technology. The second part of the story is a tale of increased competition. Initially, most personal computers were manufactured by only two firms: Apple and Compaq. Those companies, with a lock on the personal computing market, were very profitable. But unlike large mainframe computers, personal computer clones turned out to be fairly easy to manufacture, which meant that almost anyone could build and sell machines. Starry-eyed entrepreneurs, agog at the profitability of Apple and Compaq, entered the industry. And the big dogs weren't about to leave those profits on the table, either—computing giant IBM rapidly started up a personal computing division to complement its mainframe business. As time passed and prices fell, many of the smaller players left the industry, but there is still cutthroat competition among the remaining firms. As shown in Table 4.1, the top two personal computer manufacturers, Lenovo (which bought out IBM's rights to make personal computers) and Hewlett-Packard (HP) each produced about a quarter of the personal computers sold in the world in the fourth quarter of 2019, with another 36% produced by the next four companies. This is a far cry from the more than 90% of the mainframe computer market that IBM once held. The market has become far more competitive.

TABLE 4.1 Personal Computer Shipments, Market Percentage Shares by Vendors, World and United States, 4th Quarter 2019

Company	Percentage of World Shipments	Company	Percentage of U.S. Shipments
Lenovo	24.8	HP	31.2
HP	22.8	Dell	26.8
Dell	17.2	Lenovo	14.9
Apple	7.5	Apple	13.6
Asus	5.8	Asus	4.6
Acer Group	5.7	Others	8.9
Others	16.7		

Source: Based on data from "Gartner Says Worldwide PC Shipments Grew 2.3% in 4q19 and 0.6% for the Year, at https://www.gartner.com/en/newsroom. Due to rounding, totals may not add to exactly 100.

Let's look at the impact of these important events on the personal computing market, using our demand and supply model of the market. Figure 4.2 applies that model to illustrate changes in the personal computer market. In the figure, the horizontal axis shows the quantity of quality-adjusted personal computers sold in a given year. The vertical axis shows the price per unit of computing power.

Our story began with increasing demand for computing power as incomes rose and new uses for computers were developed. Households discovered that computers were good for things like typing term papers, sending email, selling crafts on Etsy, and watching *The Good Place* on Netflix. Businesses found computers invaluable for things like managing inventory, predicting sales, and designing bridges. The increase in demand on the part of both consumers and businesses is shown in Figure 4.2 as a shift from D_1 to D_2, where D_1 represents the demand for computing power in 1976, and D_2 represents the demand for computing power in 2020.

On the supply side of the market, the rapid increase in the number of firms, together with dramatic technological improvements, led to an increase in the supply of personal computing power, shifting the supply curve in Figure 4.2 to the right from S_1 in 1976 to S_2 in 2020.

FIGURE 4.2 The Personal Computer Market
Both the demand for and the supply of quality-adjusted personal computers increased between 1976 and 2020. But the shift in supply was much larger, resulting in lower prices (from P_1 to P_2) and an increase in the equilibrium quantity (from Q_1 to Q_2).

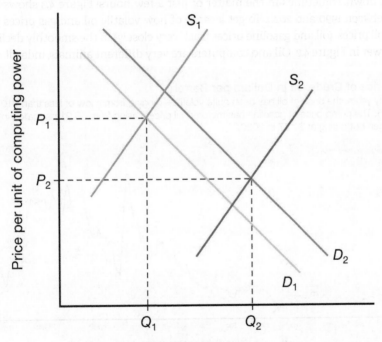

Familiar? Today's fast computers and great apps keep families together and students learning . . . even while the world falls apart around them!

Source: Cabeca de Marmore/Shutterstock.com

An increase in demand tends to cause prices to increase; an increase in supply tends to cause prices to *decrease*. (Both tend to cause the equilibrium quantity to increase.) Because the price of computers has been falling as the equilibrium quantity sold increases, the rightward shift in supply must have been much larger than the rightward shift in demand.

So who do you have to thank for the incredible computing power you (often) hold right in the palm of your hand? The demand and supply model tells us that the only way to explain ever-falling prices coupled with ever-increasing quantities is by looking to the supply side of the market. So . . . *thanks, Apple! Thanks Lenovo! The computing power you keep sending us at lower and lower prices makes us more productive, better informed, and maybe most important, it's kept us sane and connected in COVID-19 quarantine!*

The Markets for Crude Oil and Gasoline

If you own a car and regularly fill up with gas, you may find the experience frustrating: Some days, you'll pay $3.35 or $3.50 for each gallon; some days, you'll pay $2.60 or even less. The price of gasoline, like the price of the oil it is made from, is exceptionally volatile—it makes large and sudden moves up and down, sometimes in the matter of just a few hours! Figure 4.3 shows the behavior of oil prices between 1990 and 2020. To get a sense of how volatile oil and gas prices are, compare the nature of oil prices (oil and gasoline prices track very closely) to the smoothly declining price of computing power in Figure 4.2. Oil and computers are very different animals, indeed!

FIGURE 4.3 Price of Crude Oil in Dollars per Barrel
Over the last thirty years, the price of oil has been quite volatile—ranging from a low of less than $10 per barrel to a high of over $133. The pump price of gasoline has mirrored oil prices, rising from $0.91 per gallon in 1999 to over $4.10 in 2008, then bottoming at $1.77 in 2020.

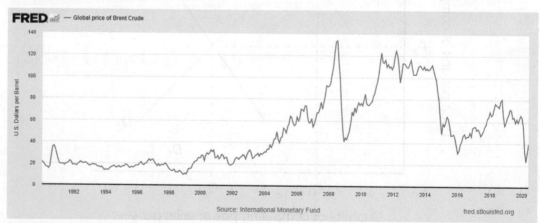

Source: International Monetary Fund, Global price of Brent Crude [POILBREUSDM], retrieved from FRED, Federal Reserve Bank of St. Louis; https://fred.stlouisfed.org/series/POILBREUSDM.

What's responsible for this price volatility? To answer that question, we'll draw once again on the model of demand and supply, where we'll find partial answers on both sides of the market.

Let's look at the demand side of the market first, where the biggest part of the story is an insatiable and growing thirst for gasoline. Part of that growing thirst is attributable to Americans' driving habits: They are driving more than ever before. And even though the fleet of American cars is becoming increasingly fuel-efficient, gasoline consumption continues to rise steadily: In 1980, American drivers logged about 1.5 trillion miles, consuming about 264 million gallons of gasoline each day in the process; by 2020, total miles driven had just about doubled to 3.2 trillion miles and gasoline consumption had increased to 390 million gallons per day. As big as those increases are, they're dwarfed by the growth in gasoline demand in other countries—especially in the developing world. The developing world's standard of living has risen sharply over the past forty years, and gasoline consumption has moved in lockstep with it. As a result, the U.S. share of global gas consumption has fallen from 45% to 38%.

The impact on oil prices of that steadily increasing global demand for gasoline (and the oil it's made from) is illustrated in Figure 4.4. Remember that an increase in demand causes both prices and quantities to increase: That's exactly what we've seen in the oil and gas markets. The growth in global demand over the last few decades is likely responsible for the long-run trend in oil prices: In the 1990s, oil averaged about $18 per barrel; over the last ten years it's averaged about $77.

Pop! Goes the Econ: Uncontrolled Intersection, Miraculous Coordination
Rising standards of living in developing countries have made driving a genuine possibility for billions. In busy Addis Ababa, Ethiopia, the demand for gasoline is outstripping the demand for stoplights.

View in the online reader

FIGURE 4.4 Increasing Demand for Crude Oil
The price of oil averaged $18 per barrel through the 1990s, as determined by the intersection of world demand, D_1, and world supply, S_1. Increasing world demand for oil and its primary product, gasoline, is illustrated by the rightward shift in demand to D_2. As a result, oil prices in the past ten years have increased to an average of $77 per barrel.

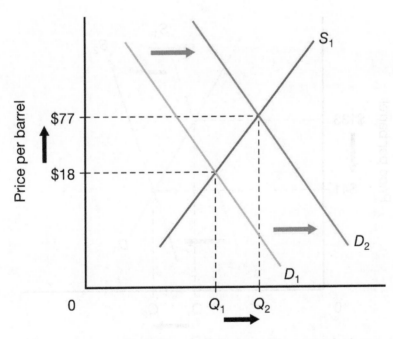

Quantity of oil (in barrels) per period

But if the steady growth in demand explains the upward trend in gas and oil prices, what explains the huge swings we sometimes see? To answer that question, we'll need to look to the supply side of the market, where world oil and gas production has historically been controlled by a small group of large producers. That group, the Organization of the Petroleum Exporting Countries (OPEC), works to keep oil prices high by restricting overall production across the globe. When they're successful, they're *very* successful; sharp restrictions in supply, for example, are responsible for the huge run-up in oil prices from $54 per barrel to $133 in 2007–2008.

OPEC sounds like it has a license to print money. But OPEC consists of various member nations, and those nations don't always get along with one another. Furthermore, there's some economic tension: Each member nation wants to sell more oil, but also wants the *other* nations to restrict *their* production to keep prices high. That's a recipe for disagreement! And when those disagreements occur and each country ramps up output, prices collapse—just like they did at the end of 2008, when oil collapsed from $133 per barrel to $41 over the span of a few weeks.

Pop! Goes the Econ: Dividing Territory in *Narcos*

The Netflix series *Narcos* documents Pablo Escobar's control of the Colombian drug trade. In this clip from the series, drug lords discuss how they've divided up territory to reduce competition. Draw parallels between their conversation and the behavior of OPEC. Pay special attention to the incentives to form such a cartel, and to break such agreements.

The impact of an OPEC collapse is shown in Figure 4.5. As countries expand production, the global supply of oil increases from S_1 to S_2. That causes the equilibrium quantity to increase and the equilibrium price to decrease (we'll explore how *much* the price decreases in the next chapter). Should OPEC get its collective act back together, supply will return to S_1 and prices will increase again.

FIGURE 4.5 The Collapse of an OPEC Agreement
As an OPEC agreement to restrict output collapsed in late 2007, OPEC member countries each tried to expand production. The supply of oil increased from S_1 to S_2, driving prices down from $133 per barrel to just $41.

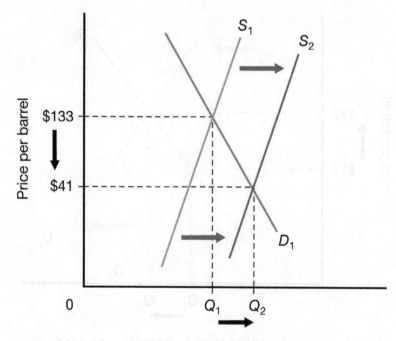

Interesting things are always happening on one side of the oil/gas market or the other. But what if interesting things are happening on *both* sides of the market at the same time? What if, for example, drivers suddenly stopped driving, while suppliers of oil and gas happened to be ramping up production? What? Drive less? That sounds...counter to our experience, but that's exactly what happened in April of 2020, when the coronavirus crisis hit. Freeways emptied as states went on lockdown; total miles driven fell dramatically both in the United States and worldwide. And at just that moment, two of the world's largest oil producers, Saudi Arabia and Russia, entered a spat over Russia's refusal to abide by an OPEC agreement to curtail oil production. As the Saudis ramped up production to punish the Russians, worldwide production increased.

All gassed up, no place to go: Global coronavirus lockdowns kept drivers off freeways and pushed gas prices downward.

Source: Kirill Neiezhmakov/Shutterstock.com

Figure 4.6 shows the impact of the simultaneous events. The decrease in the demand for oil and gas as drivers sheltered in place put downward pressure on oil prices. The increase in supply as Saudi Arabia and Russia duked it out over oil production put even further downward pressure on oil prices. Over the space of a few short weeks, oil prices fell by two-thirds, and the price of gas at the pump followed, dropping from $2.42 per gallon to just $1.77. Americans felt the irony: Gas was as cheap as it had been in years, but there was nowhere open to drive to!

FIGURE 4.6 Oil and Gas: Simultaneous Decrease in Demand & Increase in Supply

In early 2020, coronavirus lockdowns caused the demand for oil and gas to decrease (shown here as a decrease from D_1 to D_2). At the same time, feuding OPEC members Saudi Arabia and Russia were increasing oil production in a costly game of chicken (shown as an increase in supply from S_1 to S_2). The result was a double dose of downward pressure on prices, as oil fell from $66 per barrel to just $23.

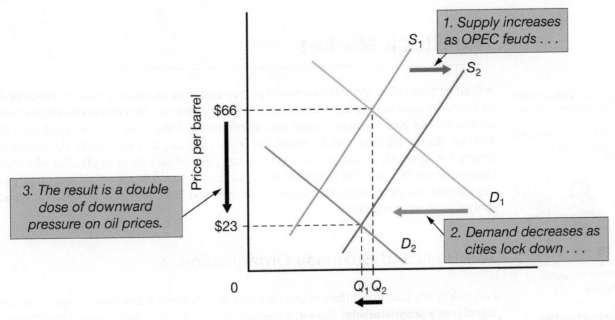

Accounting for simultaneous shifts on both sides of the market can be daunting. Don't be shy about breaking down your analysis into two pieces; you'll end up in the same place, eventually! But our look at the coronavirus episode was a useful one because the double pressure on prices we saw there gave us our first hint as to why oil and gas prices might be so volatile compared to many of the other things we buy. Oil and gas markets frequently get these double-shots of price pressure, and that's due to one important factor: expectations.

View in the online reader

If you return to Chapter 3 and look at the lists of demand shifters and supply shifters, you'll find one factor (and only one factor!) that is common to both: expectations. Let's suppose, for example, that some tidbit of news leads people in the oil market to believe the price of oil will fall by half tomorrow. That causes demand to decrease as buyers attempt to postpone their purchases; after all, why pay full price today when you can pay half tomorrow? But on the seller's side of the market, supply is increasing as producers attempt to sell their oil today before the price drops tomorrow. A small tidbit of news—perhaps news of increasing tensions within OPEC or new discoveries of oil under the Statue of Liberty—has caused the same double-dose of downward pressure that we illustrated in Figure 4.6. This is a fascinating result: Nothing has fundamentally changed—consumers' driving habits are the same; sellers' production capacity is unchanged. Instead, prices are being driven by a self-fulfilling prophecy: *A mere inkling that prices will fall tomorrow causes prices to fall today!*

And the process works in reverse too. If market participants suddenly come to believe that the price of oil will double tomorrow, buyers will rush to the proverbial oil store to stock up today. There, they'll likely be met with, "*No, we're all sold out; not even a single quart of Quaker State,*" as sellers hoard inventory today to sell for money tomorrow. Increased demand + decreased supply = higher prices now.

We opened this section with a question: Why are oil and gas prices more volatile than computer prices? And now we have at least a partial answer: For storable commodities that can be easily stockpiled until an opportune moment arises, or that can be bought now and resold later, price behavior is heavily driven, doubly driven, by changes in future expectations.

The Stock Market

Feel the power! With the click of a mouse, ordinary people like you and me can own shares of corporate titans like Google, Amazon, and Microsoft.

Source: WAYHOME studio/ Shutterstock.com

In Chapter 2, we talked about the factors of production: labor, capital, and natural resources. Chapter 2 also discussed market capitalism, an economic system in which individuals own the factors of production. But you may have a sense that there's no way individuals can own the factors of production—it's the big dogs, the Amazons, the Fords, the Googles, that control the capital in our society. And, generally speaking, that's true: Big companies own a lot of capital. But who owns the big companies? You might be surprised: Even giants like Microsoft are owned by ordinary people like you and me. So, through their ownership of business firms, households in market economies control the stock of capital.

The Basics of Business Organization

sole proprietorship

A firm owned by one individual.

partnership

A firm owned by several individuals.

corporation

A firm owned by shareholders who own stock in the firm.

Let's talk briefly about the different ways to organize a business. A firm may be owned by one individual (a **sole proprietorship**), like social media influencer James Charles, or your local flower shop. A firm may also be owned by several individuals (a **partnership**), like Ben and Jerry's once was and your economics textbook company still is. Doctors, accountants, and other professionals often create such partnerships to share overhead. Sole proprietorships and partnerships share two unique characteristics. First, the earnings of the business generally are treated as personal income to the owners. Second, if the business happens to fail, the business's creditors can come after the personal assets of the owners in payment.

There's a third type of business organization: A business firm can be owned by a larger number of individuals (potentially millions of different people!), each of whom owns a bigger or smaller share of the company. That kind of business is called a **corporation**, and each of the owners is called a shareholder or *stockholder*. Corporations have features very different from those of sole proprietorships and partnerships. First, the corporation is treated a lot like an individual for tax purposes—the income of the corporation is taxed by the government . . . and then if the corporation distributes any of its profits to its shareholders, those distributions are treated as income to the stockholder and get taxed again (in what is called *double taxation*) as personal income! That's certainly a disadvantage to the corporate form of ownership, but there are some benefits. One of the big benefits is that if the corporation goes under, the corporation's creditors cannot attempt to recoup their losses by coming after the personal assets of the shareholders (a feature known as *limited liability*). You're probably intimately familiar with corporations, because although most firms in the United States are sole proprietorships or partnerships, the bulk of the nation's total output (about 90%) is produced and sold by corporations, which makes it likely that most of the things you buy (Chipotle? Budweiser? Nike?) originated from within a corporation. Corporations also own most of the country's capital.

This section describes how the prices of shares of **corporate stock**, which represent ownership shares in a corporation, are determined by the interaction of demand and supply. Ultimately, the same forces that determine the value of a firm's stock determine the value of a sole proprietorship or partnership.

Suppose a corporation—say, the Boston Beer Company—needs funds to build a new facility to brew hard seltzer, and then to launch its hard seltzer with a huge media blitz. One way to raise those funds is to issue new stock in the Boston Beer Company. In other words, the firm can sell off new pieces of ownership in exchange for cold, hard cash![2] Once the new shares have been sold in what is called an *initial public offering* (IPO), the people who now own those shares are free to sell them to *other* people who'd like the chance to own part of the Boston Beer Company in what is called the *secondary market*. That's the market for stocks that have been issued in the past, and what you've probably heard generally referred to on the news and in your social media feed as "the stock market." Sales of "used" stock in the secondary market are like sales of used cars: When a schoolteacher from Moline buys a share of Boston Beer stock from a machinist in Minneapolis, the Boston Beer Company receives nothing, in the same way that Honda receives nothing when you sell your 25-year-old Civic hatchback to your next-door neighbor.

More precisely, the **stock market** is the set of institutions in which shares of stock are bought and sold. The New York Stock Exchange (NYSE) is one such institution. There are others all over the world, such as the DAX in Germany and the Bolsa in Mexico. The exchanges exist to match buyers of stock with sellers. To buy a share of stock in Yum! Brands, for example, you place an order with a broker, who in turn relays the order to a trader at the stock exchange. There, you'll be matched with a seller who is willing to accept your offer, and before you know it you'll be up to your eyeballs in double chalupa boxes, while the price of your transaction gets reported almost instantly throughout the world.

Demand and Supply in the Stock Market

Figure 4.7 applies the model of demand and supply to the secondary market in stocks. Suppose, for example, that some people are hoping to buy shares of ownership in chip maker Intel for their retirement portfolio. Those people are represented by the demand curve D_1. Others currently own Intel and have decided to get rid of it; those potential sellers are represented by the supply curve S_1.[3] The equilibrium price for shares of Intel is $60, and Q_1 shares change hands. If the price were higher, more shares would be offered for sale than would be demanded, and the price would quickly fall. If the price were lower, more shares would be demanded than would be supplied, and the price would quickly rise. In general, we expect the prices of shares of stock to move quickly to their equilibrium levels.

corporate stock

Shares in the ownership of a corporation.

Pop! Goes the Econ: Open Outcry Trading Pits in *Trading Places*
Out of chaos comes order! Until recently, both stocks and commodities were traded in pits like these, the orange juice pits from the movie *Trading Places*. Somehow, the traders understand and keep track of everything going on around them. Pay particular attention to the role that expectations play in determining the price of orange juice in this clip. How do we know the Duke brothers' firm is a partnership and not a corporation?

View in the online reader

stock market

The set of institutions in which shares of stock are bought and sold.

FIGURE 4.7 Demand and Supply in the Stock Market

The equilibrium price of stock shares in Intel Corporation is initially $60, found at the intersection of demand and supply curves D_1 and S_1. Q_1 million shares are traded each day.

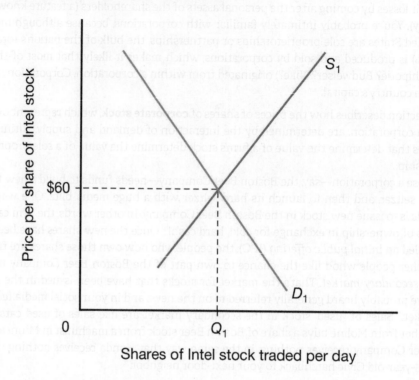

retained earnings

Profits kept by a company.

dividends

Profits distributed to shareholders.

All of this begs an important question: Why does someone want to buy stock in a corporation like Intel in the first place? (In other words, where do the demand and supply come from?) The short answer is this: If you own a share of the company, and the company earns a profit, then because you're an owner, you'll receive a share of the profits! Sometimes, a corporation will retain and reinvest some of its profits to increase its future profitability—that makes stock in Intel more valuable because whoever owns that stock will share in those future profits. Profits kept by a company in this manner are called **retained earnings**. On the other hand, sometimes a profitable corporation will turn right around and send a check to each of its shareholders. Profits distributed in this way are called **dividends**.

Whether the firm retains earnings or distributes dividends, because a share of stock gives its owner an immediate claim on the company's future earnings, the level of expected future earnings plays an important role in determining the value of its stock. Of course, those future profits cannot be known with certainty; investors can only predict what they might be based on information about future demand for the company's products, future costs of production, information about the soundness of a company's management, and so on. So, stock prices today reflect the market's guesses about what the company's profits will look like far into the future.

The downward slope of the demand curve suggests that at lower prices for the stock, more prospective buyers believe the firm's future earnings will justify the stock's purchase. The upward slope of the supply curve tells us that at higher stock prices, more current stockholders believe that the firm's future earnings don't justify holding the stock: Time to sell while the selling's good! And, of course, at the equilibrium price, the number of shares supplied by people who think holding the stock no longer makes sense just balances the number of shares demanded by people who think it does.

Pop! Goes the Econ: Expectations and the Demand for Stock in *Seinfeld*

In this clip from *Seinfeld's* "The Stock Tip," George has heard about a firm's pending merger and decides to invest in the company. How do expectations of future profits affect George's willingness to pay for a share of stock? How will George's actions influence stock prices today?

Digital Downloads

Seinfeld_The Stock Tip Transcript.docx
https://catalog.flatworldknowledge.com/a/35275/
Seinfeld_The_Stock_Tip_Transcript-2603.docx

What factors, then, cause the demand or supply curves for shares of stocks to shift? The most important factor is a change in the expectations of a company's future profits. Suppose Intel announces a fast new generation of computer chips that send signals by light impulses. Revolutionary! Prospective sellers (current owners) of Intel stock now think, *"Wow! These new chips are really gonna have Intel rolling in dough. I don't wanna miss out on my share of the profits."* The supply of stock available on the market decreases. At the same time, buyers are lining up around the block to purchase shares in innovative Intel's future profits: The demand for Intel stock increases.

Just as we saw in the oil market, a change in expectations has caused both the supply and the demand for stock to change, and to change in ways that place double pressure on prices, as shown in Figure 4.8. There, supply decreases from S_1 to S_2; demand increases from D_1 to D_2, and driven by expectations, the price skyrockets from $60 to $90 in a matter of minutes.

FIGURE 4.8 A Change in Expectations Affects the Price of Intel's Corporate Stock
Intel's new chip makes it likely to be more profitable in the future. The supply of Intel stock shifts to the left (in this case, from S_1 to S_2), and the demand for Intel stock increases from D_1 to D_2, resulting in an increase in price from $60 to $90.

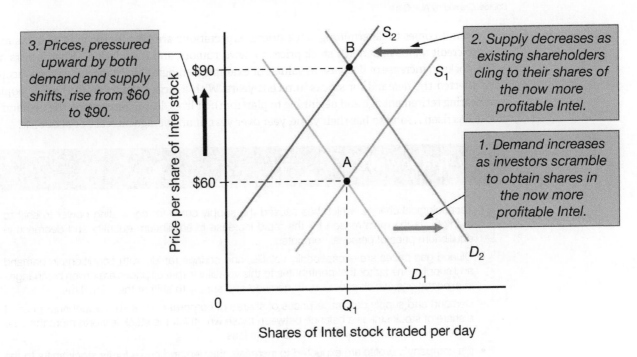

Being driven primarily by expectations, it should come as no surprise that stock prices are more volatile than the prices of ordinary goods and services like hardwood flooring and cat food.

The stock market is bombarded with new information every minute of every day, information that has implications for firms' future profitability. News of a land war in Asia? Stock prices immediately tank. Rumors that the Senate has proposed a corporate income tax cut for next year? Stock prices rebound. Jobs figures show a weakening economy? Stock prices plummet again, only to rebound on rumors of an OPEC feud brewing that might result in cheaper energy. In short, any information that may affect a company's profits next month, next year, or even in the next century causes a flurry of buying and selling that immediately incorporates that information into stock prices today!

A meal few will have the stomach for: With the double-price-pressure of expectations, this dish can make a dog's breakfast of your portfolio!

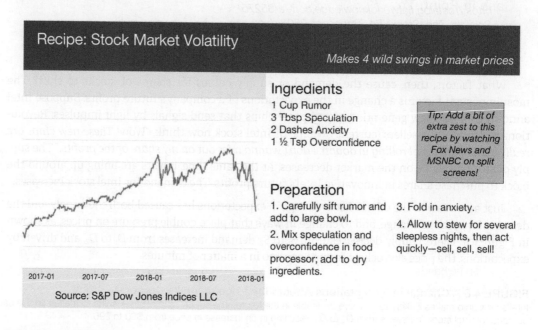

Recipe: Stock Market Volatility

Makes 4 wild swings in market prices

Ingredients
1 Cup Rumor
3 Tbsp Speculation
2 Dashes Anxiety
1 ½ Tsp Overconfidence

Tip: Add a bit of extra zest to this recipe by watching Fox News and MSNBC on split screens!

Preparation
1. Carefully sift rumor and add to large bowl.

2. Mix speculation and overconfidence in food processor; add to dry ingredients.

3. Fold in anxiety.

4. Allow to stew for several sleepless nights, then act quickly—sell, sell, sell!

2017-01   2017-07   2018-01   2018-07   2018-01

Source: S&P Dow Jones Indices LLC

Source: Created by Alan Grant

When it comes to determining stock prices, expectations are king. But it may be oversimplifying to credit *all* movements in stock prices to news, rumors, and speculation. Other factors may cause stocks to increase or decrease in value. For example, demographic change and rising incomes have affected the demand for stocks in recent years: With a large proportion of the U.S. population nearing retirement age and beginning to plan for their lives during retirement, the demand for stocks has risen ... and so has their value, year over year, at an average increase of about 9%.

Key Takeaways

- Technological change, which has caused the supply curve for computing power to shift to the right, is the main reason for the rapid increase in equilibrium quantity and decrease in equilibrium price of personal computers.

- Oil and gas prices are exceptionally volatile, and change rapidly with conditions in demand and supply. One factor that contributes to this volatility is that oil prices are driven by changes in expectations, which causes both demand and supply to shift at the same time.

- Demand and supply determine prices of shares of corporate stock. The equilibrium price of a share of stock strikes a balance between those who think the stock is worth more than the current price and those who think it is worth less.

- If a company's profits are expected to increase, the demand curve for its stock shifts to the right and the supply curve shifts to the left, causing the equilibrium price to rise. The opposite would occur if a company's profits were expected to decrease.

Try It!

Suppose an airline announces that its earnings this year are lower than expected due to reduced ticket sales. The airline spokesperson gives no information on how the company plans to turn things around. Use the model of demand and supply to show and explain what is likely to happen to the price of the airline's stock.

See related Concept Problem 2 at the end of this chapter.

Case in Point: The Topsy-Turvy World of 2020 Oil Prices

Everything I've learned about prices in this econ course just got turned a** over oilcan!

Source: Leila Ablyazova/Shutterstock.com

Imagine this: You're in the market for a pair of new shoes. You go to the Foot Locker and pick out an awesome pair of Chuck Taylors. At the register, the clerk tells you, "That comes to $65."

And then he hands you three twenties and a five!

Now just hold on a minute—that doesn't happen in the world *we* live in! Except, of course, when it does . . . in circumstances so unprecedented and unusual that prices actually go negative, *and sellers actually pay buyers to take product off their hands!*

It's just that kind of bizarre circumstance—the confluence of two extreme events, actually, that led to oil prices dropping below zero in the spring of 2020. The first event, of course, was the coronavirus crisis, as governors across the country called off school for students and shuttered all but essential businesses, while telling families to "shelter in place." In just days, the total miles U.S. drivers were racking up fell by 40%. And across the Pacific, China's 1.7 billion consumers were on heavy lockdown too, as were most people in the European Union. Global demand for gasoline plummeted . . . which in turn reduced the demand for the oil from which gasoline is refined.

The second event was a fairly regular, but particularly severe, dispute between members of the Organization of Petroleum Exporting Countries (OPEC), a cartel of major producers who generally try to restrict oil production to drive up prices. In early 2020, two major players within OPEC, Saudi Arabia and Russia, were playing a punishing game of chicken; each was expanding output in violation of previous agreements, while both watched prices plummet.

So, just as the demand for oil was declining, the supply was increasing. It only took one small institutional detail to set the stage for negative prices: Oil is generally bought and sold in what's called the *forward market*—buyers and sellers agree on prices today for oil that will be delivered in the future.

That's where the United States found itself in late April of 2020: Oil contracts were being bought and sold for May delivery . . . but *May was just around the corner, and nobody was driving!* Gasoline refiners had bought oil for May delivery anticipating that the oil they'd bought for delivery in March and April would have been turned into gasoline already. But it hadn't, and refiners were sitting on huge, unused inventories of oil. With no place to store any more, refiners frantically tried to offload their May contracts to someone else, anyone else, who had room for the oil that was scheduled to be delivered.

You'd think that with too much oil being produced, with nowhere to put it, producers would simply turn off the oil spigot until normalcy returned. But in the oilfields of Texas, Oklahoma, and Kansas, oil continued to flow: Shutting down an oil well is a costly operation; starting one back up is even more costly. Pumpers calculated that they'd lose less money by just flooding the market for a few weeks than they would if they tried to shut down the pumps and then turn them on again.

So that's where the market for West Texas Intermediate Crude (a particular grade of oil commonly pumped in the lower Midwest) found itself: No demand . . . in fact, negative demand . . . as refiners tried to offload their scheduled deliveries to someone else with the room to store it. High supply as producers refused to hit the "Off" button. The result? On April 20, 2020, the price of a 42-gallon barrel of West Texas Intermediate Crude oil went negative for the first time in history, hitting -$37 per barrel. Just like your imaginary Chuck Taylors, *producers and refiners were paying people to take product off their hands!*

If only we consumers could be so lucky all the time!

On April 20, 2020, the price of May crude oil temporarily plummeted into negative territory—an unprecedented event caused by the oddities of the oil market.

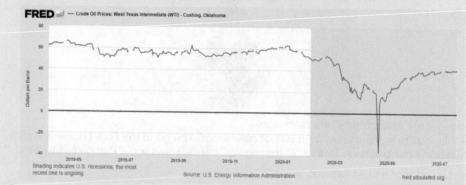

Source: U.S. Energy Information Administration, Crude Oil Prices: West Texas Intermediate (WTI) - Cushing, Oklahoma [DCOILWTICO], retrieved from FRED, Federal Reserve Bank of St. Louis; https://fred.stlouisfed.org/series/DCOILWTICO.

See related Concept Problem 4 at the end of this chapter.

Answer to Try It! Problem

The information given in the problem suggests that the airline's profits are likely to fall below expectations. Current owners of the airline's stock and potential buyers of the stock would adjust downward their estimates of what the value of the corporation's stock should be. As a result, the supply curve for the stock would increase, shifting it to the right, while the demand curve for the stock would decrease, shifting it to the left; the equilibrium price of the stock falls from P_1 to P_2. What happens to equilibrium quantity depends on the extent to which each curve shifts. In the diagram, equilibrium quantity is shown to decrease from Q_1 to Q_2.

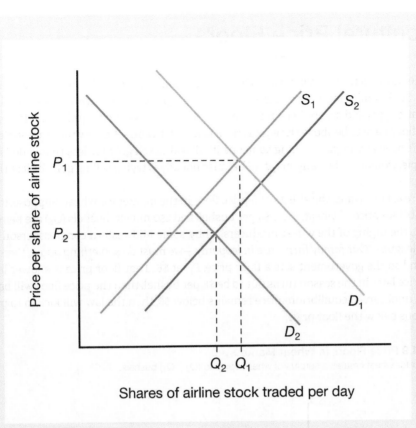

4.3 Government Intervention in Markets: Price Floors and Price Ceilings

Learning Objectives

1. Use the demand and supply model to explain what happens when the government imposes price floors or price ceilings.
2. Discuss the reasons why governments sometimes choose to control prices and the consequences of price-control policies.

So far, we've seen how the natural forces of demand and supply tend to push prices and quantities toward their equilibrium levels. In some markets, however, the government intervenes to keep prices higher than their equilibrium levels; in others, the government holds prices lower than they would naturally be. In this section, we'll see how government controls prices in these ways, and we'll examine two common examples of government intervention in markets: agricultural markets and apartment rental markets. In each case, we'll look at reasons why governments have chosen to control prices and the consequences of these policies.

Agricultural Price Floors

Governments often try to assist farmers by setting minimum allowable prices for agricultural commodities. Such a minimum allowable price is called a **price floor**. Price floors generally raise the prices that buyers and sellers "see" in the marketplace to above their equilibrium levels. Why does the price floor have to be above the equilibrium price? If it were set below the market-clearing price, it wouldn't have any impact: Telling someone it's illegal to sell gold for less than a dollar an ounce, for example, wouldn't affect anyone at all because nobody *is* trying selling gold for less than a dollar an ounce.

Figure 4.9 illustrates the effects of a price floor in the market for wheat. Suppose, initially, that the equilibrium price of wheat, P_E, is $4 per bushel, and 250 million bushels (Q_E) are being sold each month. At the urging of the wheat producers' lobby, some Midwestern congressperson announces to her colleagues, "*Our family farms are in jeopardy—we must do something about these low wheat prices!*" And so the government sets a floor price, P_F, at $6. That floor price is a lower limit—if the market price later in the season turns out to be $8 per bushel, then the price floor will be irrelevant. But if the unobserved equilibrium price remains below $6, then the law will kick in to prohibit any transactions below the floor price.

Pop! Goes the Econ: Chris Rock on Setting Price Floors

The minimum wage is a price floor in the labor market. Chris Rock nails the notion that price floors have to be above the free-market equilibrium to work!

View in the online reader

FIGURE 4.9 Price Floors in Wheat Markets
A price floor for wheat creates a surplus of wheat equal to ($Q_2 - Q_1$) bushels.

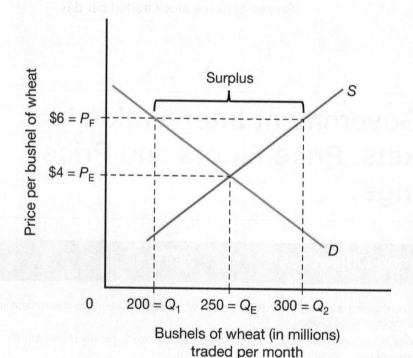

Figure 4.9 shows the impact of the $6 price floor on a market in which the price "wants to be" $4.

- At the floor price of $6, go straight over to the demand curve and then straight down to find that buyers will be willing to purchase 200 million bushels (Q_1).

- At the floor price, go straight over to the supply curve and then straight down to find that at $6, sellers will be willing to offer 300 million bushels for sale (Q_2).

- Because the quantity supplied (300 million bushels) is greater than the quantity demanded (200 million bushels), there is a surplus of 100 million (300 million minus 200 million, or $Q_2 - Q_1$) bushels of wheat.

In other words, one of the immediate side effects of a price floor is that the price floor creates surplus production. A **surplus** exists any time, at the going price, quantity supplied is greater than quantity demanded. With excess wheat on the market, there is market pressure on the price of wheat to fall … but selling wheat for below the floor price is against the law. So, to prevent farmers from turning into criminals by selling their extra wheat at below-floor prices in the black market (just imagine trench-coated farmers in dark alleys, accosting passersby with, "*Pssst! Hey, buddy … wanna buy some $4 wheat?*"), most governments that institute price floors end up promising to purchase any surplus production. In this case, the government buys the 100 million bushels of surplus production so that only 200 million bushels are actually available to private consumers for purchase. And what does the government do with the crops it buys? It can store the surpluses or find special uses for them. In the United States, surplus crop production has often been shipped to developing countries at discounted prices, or has been distributed to the federal school lunch programs. Governments often require farmers who participate in price-support programs to reduce the number of acres of ground they plant, in hopes of limiting the size of these surpluses.

Many governments around the world actively use price floors in agricultural markets. One important question is, "Why?" Part of the answer lies on the supply side of the market. Farming has changed dramatically over the past two centuries. Technological improvements in the form of new equipment, fertilizers, pesticides, and varieties of crops have led to dramatic increases in both overall production and in output per acre. Those supply increases have reduced the equilibrium price of food, and while such price reductions have been celebrated in computer markets, farmers have successfully lobbied for government programs aimed at keeping their prices from falling.

While the supply curve for agricultural goods has shifted to the right, rising population and rising income has caused the demand for agricultural goods to increase, too. But as incomes rise, people spend a smaller and smaller fraction of their incomes on food, so the increase in demand has not been nearly as great as the increase in supply. Figure 4.10 shows that the supply curve has shifted much farther to the right (from S_1 to S_2) than the demand curve has (D_1 to D_2). As a result, equilibrium quantity has risen dramatically (from Q_1 to Q_2), and equilibrium price has fallen from P_1 to P_2. This accords well with actual experience: In May 2020, farmers received less for a bushel of wheat than they did in February of 1974 … while the cost of everything farmers buy with their wheat dollars went up five-fold.[4] It's hard to make ends meet when everything you buy gets more expensive, while the goods you sell get cheaper!

Prunes, anyone? In the 1930s, surplus foods were offered for sale by the government; hungry shoppers could pay with cash or the newly created federal food stamps.

Source: National Archives. *Surplus Commodities*. National Archives Identifier: 195893. Franklin D. Roosevelt Library Public Domain Photographs, 1882 - 1962. Via Wikimedia: https://commons.wikimedia.org/wiki/File:Surplus_Commodities_-_NARA_-_195893.tif.

surplus

A situation where, at a given price, $Q_S > Q_D$.

Less work; more pay! Long before Google developed the self-driving car, farmers used GPS and self-driving tractors to maximize the ground planted and prevent wasteful overlapping rows. Autosteer cuts machine time by 5% and increases yields by 1%—a big win come harvest time!

Source: itn_akira/Shutterstock.com

FIGURE 4.10 Demand and Supply Shifts for Agricultural Products
A relatively large increase in the supply of agricultural products, accompanied by a relatively small increase in demand, has reduced the price received by farmers and increased the quantity of agricultural goods.

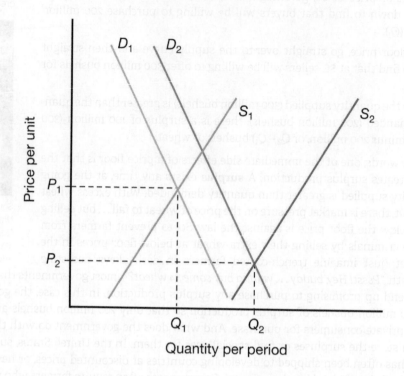

On top of this long-term historical trend in agriculture, agricultural prices are subject to wide swings over shorter periods. Droughts or freezes can sharply reduce supplies of particular crops, causing sudden increases in prices. Demand for agricultural goods of one country can suddenly dry up if the government of another country imposes trade restrictions against its products (as happened during a global trade war in 2018), and prices can fall. Such dramatic shifts in prices and quantities make incomes of farmers unstable.

American farmers fell victim to that kind of price instability during the Great Depression of the 1930s. Prices received by farmers plunged nearly two-thirds from 1930 to 1933. Many farmers had a tough time keeping up mortgage payments, and by 1932, more than half of all farm loans were in default. Concerns about food security and stability led to a variety of farm programs, including price supports, designed to stabilize farm production and income. These programs have been generally accompanied by government purchases of any crop surpluses, or by requirements to restrict acreage or production in order to limit those surpluses.

After 1973, the government stopped buying the surpluses (with some exceptions) and simply guaranteed farmers a "target price." If the average market price for a crop fell below the crop's target price, the government paid the difference. If, for example, the market price of wheat was $4 per bushel and the target price was $6, the government would pay farmers the $2 difference for each bushel sold. For farmers to receive these payments, they had to agree to remove acres from production and to comply with certain conservation provisions, both of which reduced the size of the surplus. In recent years, the government has replaced these programs with subsidized crop insurance programs that guarantee farmers a certain amount of revenue from each acre of crops; while the details differ slightly from the price floors discussed above, the impact to farmers is largely the same: The government guarantees farmers a price for crops sold in the marketplace that is often above the market equilibrium price.

Different programs do have a slightly different impact on consumers. With simple price floors, consumers pay more for food than they would otherwise, and governments spend heavily to finance the programs. But government spending doesn't materialize out of nowhere—those dollars come largely out of taxpayers' pockets, which means consumers take a double hit for price floors: once in the supermarket, the second on tax day, April 15. Replacing the price floor with a target or reference price changes this: Consumers see *lower* prices in supermarket aisles, but still take a hit when they pay their taxes.

Do these programs do their intended job? Well, yes, and no. Help to farmers has often been justified on the grounds that it boosts incomes of "small" farmers. However, because farm aid has generally been allotted on the basis of how much farms produce rather than on a per-farm basis, most federal farm support has gone to the largest farms. If the goal is to eliminate poverty among farmers, farm aid could be redesigned to supplement the incomes of small or poor farmers rather than to alter the functioning of agricultural markets. Using such an indirect means to solve a problem is called a *second-best solution*.

Rental Price Ceilings

Sometimes the government thinks something is selling too inexpensively, and the solution is to mandate a price that is more expensive. But sometimes the opposite happens: The government thinks something is too expensive, and so it mandates a price that is *below* the market price. That kind of policy, which establishes the maximum allowable price in the market, is called a **price ceiling**.

> **price ceiling**
>
> A government price control that specifies the maximum allowable price at which a good or service may sell.

Governments often impose price ceilings to keep necessities affordable. Governments around the world have imposed price ceilings in the markets for pharmaceuticals, bread, gasoline, and more. One such policy in the United States is *rent control*, a price ceiling designed to ensure a supply of affordable housing. Unlike agricultural price controls, rent control in the United States has been largely a local phenomenon. Currently, about 200 cities and counties have some type of rent control provisions, and about 10% of rental units in the United States are now subject to price controls. New York City's rent control program, which began in 1943, is among the oldest in the country. Many other cities in the United States adopted some form of rent control in the 1970s. Rent controls have been pervasive in Europe since World War I, and many large cities in poorer countries have also adopted rent controls.

Price ceilings and real ceilings: This man, like prices, is being held lower than he'd like by the ceiling. Price ceilings are below equilibrium!

Source: Viacheslav Nikolaenko/Shutterstock.com

The essence of rent control is that once you move into an apartment, the law limits your landlord's ability to raise your rent. As time passes, this often results in rents, being held well below market rates. Rent controls in different cities do differ in terms of their flexibility, however. Some cities allow rent increases for specified reasons, such as to make improvements in apartments or to allow rents to keep pace with price increases elsewhere in the economy. Often, rental housing constructed after the imposition of the rent control ordinances is exempted. For simplicity, the model presented here assumes that apartment rents are controlled at a price that does not change.

Figure 4.11 shows the market for rental apartments. The demand curve slopes downward: The lower the rent, the more people who will choose an apartment over home ownership; the more young people will choose to rent an apartment rather than live in their parents' basement; the more people will lease an apartment for themselves rather than trying to share an apartment with roommates.

FIGURE 4.11 Effect of a Price Ceiling on the Market for Apartments

A $550 price ceiling on apartment rents set below the $800 equilibrium rent creates a 1,000-unit shortage ($Q_2 - Q_1$) of apartments.

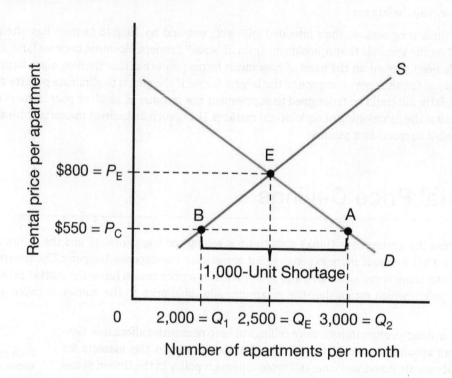

The supply curve in Figure 4.11 slopes upward: The higher the rents, the more apartment buildings will be built; the greater the number of warehouses converted into lofts; the greater the number of homeowners who will rent rooms, convert basement, attic, and garage space to apartments, and so on.

Suppose in Figure 4.11 that in the absence of any government intervention, the equilibrium price (P_E) of an apartment is $800, and 2,500 units are being occupied each month (point E). Decrying the lack of affordable housing, the mayor says, "*We must do something to help our lower-income residents—they're the backbone of our local economy!*" In response, the local government sets a ceiling price (P_C) for apartments at $550.[5] And what's the impact of this policy? As the ceiling forces down the rental rate from $800 to $550, more people start looking for apartments, and there's an increase in quantity demanded. We move downward along the demand curve from point E to point A, where 3,000 people (Q_1) are scouring Craigslist and Zillow looking for apartments.

On the supply side of the market, the price ceiling has the opposite effect. As the price falls, some apartments get taken off the market: Read over at the ceiling price of $550 to the supply curve and down; the quantity supplied (Q_2) shrinks from 2,500 at equilibrium to just 2,000 at the ceiling price. As a result of a policy designed to ensure affordable housing, there is less housing available! And what happened to that housing? Some may have been converted from rentals to condominiums. In other cases, some homeowners decided the low ceiling price wasn't worth the trouble of having a tenant living in their attic. Or, perhaps the rent control laws discouraged a developer from building a new complex.

shortage

A situation in which, at the prevailing price, quantity demanded is greater than quantity supplied.

A **shortage** exists any time quantity demanded is greater than quantity supplied. With 3,000 (Q_1) people looking for apartments and only 2,000 available (Q_2), there's a 1,000-unit shortage of apartments ($Q_1 - Q_2$). In markets experiencing shortages, we typically see lines form (though in today's world, we might instead see people frantically sending endless strings of text messages and emails rather than waiting in a physical line) in hopes that the goods won't run out before they've made it to the front.

That kind of first-come, first-served allocation mechanism is one way to ration the reduced quantity of apartments available. That wouldn't be necessary in the absence of the price control: There would be enough apartments to go around if apartment rents were at the $800 equilibrium. Of course, in a world with rent control, the first people in line for apartments are the people who are already living in them: Current occupants cling more tightly to their apartments, and move less often. And rent control prevents the most efficient allocation of apartments—the person who gets an available apartment isn't necessarily the person who gets the greatest value from having it.

"Pssst! Hey buddy—wanna rent an apartment?" Rent control laws may turn ordinary people into criminals—something that wouldn't happen in a world with freely floating prices that brought quantity demand, and quantity supplied into equilibrium. For example, sometimes the person who has leased a rent-controlled apartment subleases the apartment at illegally high rents. In Figure 4.12, rent control has reduced the number of apartments available from 2,500 to 2,000. It has created scarcity. And that scarcity drives up prices: In the figure, there are 2,000 people willing to pay $1,200 or more for an apartment (go up from 2,000 on the horizontal axis to the demand curve, point C, and then read over to the left). If all rent-controlled apartments were subleased in this way, the rent control law would actually drive rents *up* instead of down! Of course, not all apartments are likely to end up being subleased—some lucky leaseholders need a place to stay for themselves; others are inherently law-abiding. But there are other ways for apartment owners to extract cash from renters, including large security deposits, payments for things renters may not want (such as furniture), simple bribes, or so-called key payments (*"The monthly rent is $550, but I'll need to get a new key made for you. That costs $5,000."*). All of these are common practice in places with rent control.

Even dictators can't rewrite the laws of demand and supply: Venezuelan president Hugo Chavez won the popular vote by promising price ceilings for food, fuel, and toilet paper. Store shelves emptied as goods purchased cheap in Venezuela were smuggled into neighboring Colombia for resale at market rates. The irony? Even with price controls, because of price controls, Venezuelans who needed toilet paper had to pay the market price . . . *and had to travel to Colombia to find it!*

Source: sunsinger/Shutterstock.com

FIGURE 4.12 The Unintended Consequences of Rent Control
Controlling apartment rents at $550 (*P*c) creates scarcity, with only 2,000 apartments available. Scarcity drives up prices: There are 2,000 people willing to pay $1,200 (*P*illegal) or more for those apartments (point C). So apartments get subleased at illegally high prices on the black market, or landlords require illegal backdoor payments of renters.

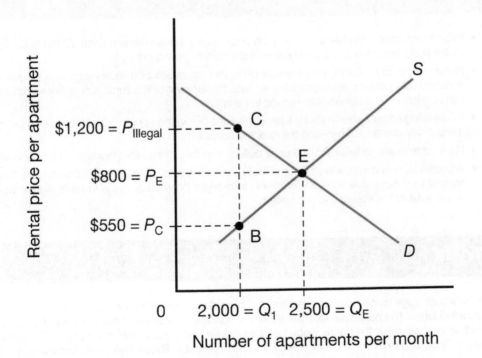

Pop! Goes the Econ: Rent Control in *Seinfeld*

Jerry's friend Elaine needs a new apartment, and lucky for everyone there's one open in Jerry's building. In this clip, what has to happen for Elaine to find this rent-controlled steal? Does rent control make it easy for low-income people to find affordable housing? Why or why not?

Digital Downloads

Seinfeld_The Apartment (Rent Control) Transcript.docx
https://catalog.flatworldknowledge.com/a/35275/
Seinfeld_The_Apartment_Rent_Control_Transcript-7c3a.docx

There are other side effects, too. Rent controls may make it more difficult for landlords to maintain their buildings (and in fact, landlords sometimes have an incentive *not* to maintain their rent-controlled apartments—if you can drive your current tenants out, you can raise the rent for the next ones. In one spectacular episode, a landlord desperate to remove a rent-controlled tenant hired hit men to kill the renter![6]). Rent controls may also discourage new construction in places where new construction will be subject to rent-control regulations. So, a policy designed to help lower-income people acquire affordable housing turns into a system (because of scarcity) that makes apartments harder to find and often more costly to get into. In the end, rent controls and other price ceilings often end up hurting some of the very people they are intended to help. And many of the people that rent control *does* help (primarily current occupants, regardless of their income, and those lucky enough to find apartments) are not necessarily those they are intended to help (the poor). Again, by taking an indirect route to making life more livable for the poor, government has chosen a second-best policy; a more direct means of helping poor tenants would be to simply subsidize their incomes, rather than attempting to micromanage the housing system.

Key Takeaways

- Price floors create surpluses by fixing the price above the equilibrium price. At the price set by the floor, the quantity supplied exceeds the quantity demanded.
- In agriculture, price floors have created persistent surpluses of a wide range of agricultural commodities. Governments typically purchase the amount of the surplus or impose production restrictions in an attempt to reduce the surplus.
- Price ceilings create shortages by setting the price below the equilibrium. At the ceiling price, the quantity demanded exceeds the quantity supplied.
- Rent controls are an example of a price ceiling, and they create shortages of rental housing.
- Sometimes, rent controls lead to "backdoor" arrangements, ranging from requirements that tenants rent items that they do not want, to outright bribes that result in rents higher than would exist in the absence of the ceiling.

Try It!

A minimum wage law is another example of a price floor. Draw demand and supply curves for unskilled labor. The horizontal axis will show the quantity of unskilled labor per period, and the vertical axis will show the hourly wage rate for unskilled workers, which is the price of unskilled labor. Show and explain the effect of a minimum wage that is above the equilibrium wage.

See related Numerical Problem 2 at the end of this chapter.

Case in Point: Thank Goodness for Gouging?

A bargain at twice the price! During the coronavirus crisis, shortages of toilet paper and hand sanitizer became acute. In your author's hometown, the only store that reliably had toilet paper for those in need was the one that charged $12 a roll!

Source: Jaimieandkyleshootstock/Shutterstock.com

It's a story you'll hear repeated often—any time there's some kind of natural disaster, in fact. It's a story of greed versus government, with government generally winning . . . and consumers often losing.

A hurricane destroys a gulf coast town. The power's out; the water treatment plant is inoperable. People have lost their homes, they've got no food, they've got no water.

But a man in Kentucky offers a solution: He fills the back of his pickup truck with water bottles and drives through the night to provide relief. Arriving just as the sun comes up, he pulls into a parking lot and starts selling his inventory. *"Get your bottled water here—five bucks a bottle!"* And the morning passes, and the man makes money, and then the local constabulary shows up, dumps his water out on the ground, and ushers our hero away to jail for violating the state's anti-gouging laws. Those laws prevent "profiteering" from a disaster—in other words, they prohibit sellers from increasing the prices of necessities in moments of crisis.

But while the states can keep *prices* from changing during crises like hurricanes, and tornadoes, and raging novel viruses, governments are powerless to stop the forces of demand and supply. During a disaster, supplies of necessities dry up while demand may be higher than ever. That combination would ordinarily cause prices to rise, but anti-gouging laws act as a price ceiling, taking a situation of acute scarcity and making it worse by creating shortages.

Sometimes, in a crisis, we tend to lose track of what's really important. It's probably not fair for sellers to take advantage of buyers by charging $5 a bottle for water, or $50 for a four-pack of toilet paper. But the real problem in a disaster isn't fairness, it's getting enough water, enough food, enough electricity, enough hand sanitizer to the places where they're needed most desperately. And so while it may not be *fair* for sellers to charge high prices, it may be exactly what is *needed*—to encourage people living in disaster areas to think carefully about what they need (instead of buying and hoarding everything they can get their hands on), and to encourage Kentuckians to drive more water to the gulf, more generators to tornado alley, and more hand sanitizer to New York hospitals.

And so our enterprising and admittedly self-interested Kentuckian performs a service that is desperately needed precisely *because* he can gouge. Without that opportunity, he'll be just as happy to watch the crisis unfold . . . fairly and equitably . . . on TV, from the comfort of his living room couch.

See related Concept Problem 11 at the end of this chapter.

Source: Based on Jack Nicas, "He Has 17,700 Bottles of Hand Sanitizer and Nowhere to Sell Them," The New York Times, March 14, 2020.

Answer to Try It! Problem

A minimum wage (W_{min}) that is set above the equilibrium wage would create a surplus of unskilled labor equal to ($L_2 - L_1$). That is, L_2 units of unskilled labor are offered at the minimum wage, but companies only want to use L_1 units at that wage.

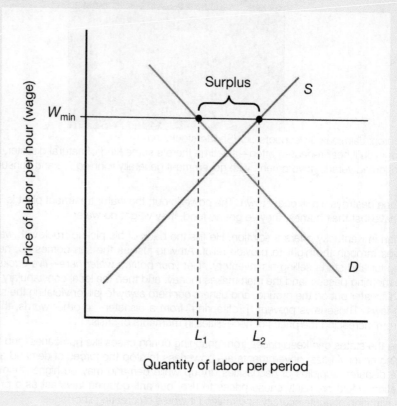

4.4 Government Intervention in Markets: Taxes

Learning Objectives

1. Use the demand and supply model to show the effects of a tax on equilibrium prices and quantity.
2. Discuss the reasons why governments impose taxes.

tax

A mandatory payment to the government that is generally coupled with some sort of economic activity.

Price ceilings and price floors are direct, forceful interventions by government into the marketplace. Because of their blunt nature, they're not used very often. But there's another government policy that is less direct, that creates less economic chaos, and that is so common it touches virtually every aspect of our lives. That policy is the **tax**, a mandatory payment to the government that is generally coupled with some sort of economic activity. Here are just a few places you might see taxes:

- Buy a Red Bull at the mini-mart? *Pay a sales tax.*
- Put a gallon of gas in your car? *Pay an excise tax.*
- Earn a buck? *Pay an income tax.*
- Buy a house? *Pay a property tax.*
- Drink French wine? *Pay an import tax.*
- Live? *Pay a head tax.*
- Die? *Pay an estate tax.*

Taxes are everywhere—even if, as a consumer, you don't really "see" them, as is the case with the gas tax, where the price you pay at the pump already has the amount of the tax built in. And taxes are important—they're the primary way governments raise the cash necessary to fund their operations. The roads you drive on, the schools you attend, the safety and security you enjoy—they're all paid for by taxes. For that reason, a basic understanding of the effects of a tax is useful knowledge.

Pop! Goes the Econ: Ron Swanson on Taxes
In this episode of *Parks and Rec*, cynical libertarian Ron Swanson teaches a young lady about the reach of government. Taxes are everywhere!

View in the online reader

A Tax on Sellers: The Supply Curve

Each of the types of taxes listed above works slightly differently, but in the end, the effects are largely the same. For that reason, we'll dig only into the simplest type of tax, in which the government collects a set amount of tax for each unit of a good or service sold. That tax is called an excise, or per-unit, tax, and it's generally collected from the seller of a good or service.

To understand how the excise tax works, we need to take a second look at the nature of the supply curve. Let's look at the supply of kombucha, which is brewed by five different mom-and-pop cafes in an isolated mountain town. Each of our five cafes can brew one (and only one) big crock of kombucha each day, But not all cafes are created equal: Each cafe brews that crock at a different cost, as summarized in Table 4.2.

TABLE 4.2 The Cost of Kombucha
Five cafes can each brew one crock of kombucha each day, but their costs differ. Arlo's cafe brews kombucha at the lowest cost; Echo is the high-cost brewer.

Proprietor	Cost ($)
Arlo	1
Birch	2
Clover	3
Dharma	4
Echo	5

Those costs include all of the resources needed to brew a crock of kombucha, including compensation for the owner's time. Now, let's think about what the supply curve for kombucha will look like:

- If kombucha sells for $1, only Arlo will be willing to make kombucha—she is the only cafe owner who can cover her costs (including compensation for the value of her time) at that price.
- If kombucha sells for $2, both Arlo and Birch can cover their costs; 2 units will be offered for sale.
- If kombucha sells for $3, Arlo, Birch, and Clover are all able to cover their costs; 3 units will be offered for sale.

- If kombucha sells for $4, Arlo, Birch, Clover, and Dharma will be able to cover their costs; 4 units will be offered for sale.

- If kombucha sells for $5, all five producers will be able to cover their costs; 5 units will be offered for sale.

The supply curve for kombucha, based on the bullets above, is shown in Figure 4.13.

FIGURE 4.13 The Supply Curve for Kombucha
The supply curve for kombucha shows the quantity that producers stand willing to bring to market at various prices.

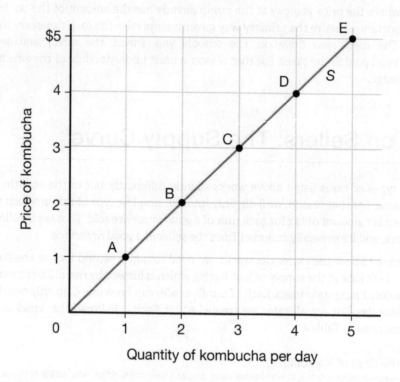

There's nothing particularly new in this—you've already worked extensively with supply curves in Chapter 3. Using the supply curve is simple: Go to a price you're interested in, travel over to the right until you hit the supply curve, and then go down to the horizontal axis to read how many units will be brought to market.

But in this chapter, we want to turn things upside down by looking at the supply curve in a slightly different way: Start instead on the horizontal (quantity) axis—looking first at a quantity of 1. Travel up until you hit the supply curve (at point A), and then over to the vertical axis, where you'll see $1. That very first unit of kombucha, you'll recall, is produced by the most efficient producer, Arlo, who could brew kombucha at a cost of $1—*exactly the number you read off the vertical axis!* The same is true for other quantities—the second unit is brought to market by Birch at a cost of $2 (point B), the third by Clover at $3 (point C), and so on. Notice that in this simplified case, each dot represents a different seller, arranged alphabetically.

Now we know something interesting about the supply curve: It shows the quantity brought to market at various prices, *but the supply curve also shows the cost of producing any particular unit of a good.* That interpretation is extremely useful, because when the government imposes a tax on kombucha, that's going to change producers' costs, and the supply curve will shift as a result.

Let's do that now! Government, sensing a gold mine of revenue in kombucha, decides to impose a $2 tax on each crock of kombucha. That increases each producer's cost by $2, as shown in Table 4.3.

TABLE 4.3 Taxes and Cost

When the government imposes a $2 tax on kombucha, the cost of each unit produced increases by the amount of the tax.

Producer	Cost ($)	New Cost with Tax ($)
Arlo	1	3
Birch	2	4
Clover	3	5
Dharma	4	6
Echo	5	7

Now, the market price is going to have to be $3 to convince even the lowest-cost producer to bring kombucha to market. Let's see how that alters the supply curve in Figure 4.14.

FIGURE 4.14 A Tax on Sellers Shifts the Supply Curve

A $2 tax on kombucha shifts the supply curve vertically by the amount of the tax at each quantity.

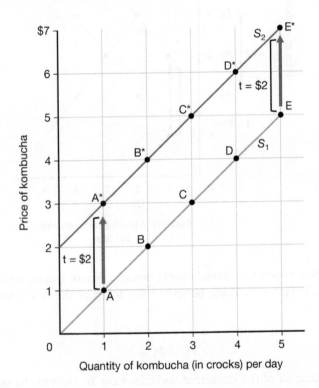

In the figure, each producer (Arlo, Birch, Clover, Dharma, Echo) sees their cost rise by the amount of the tax. (Point A moves to point A*, B to B*, and so on.) This shifts the supply curve upward (from S_1 to S_2) vertically, at each quantity, by exactly the amount of the tax.

So, the supply curve shifts upward, but don't let that confuse you: That upward shift is a *decrease* in supply! (That's because the supply curve can also be viewed as shifting to the left.) At each price, fewer producers are able to cost-effectively produce kombucha, thanks to the tax. Let your intuition be your guide: A tax *discourages* the activity being taxed!

So now we know that a tax on sellers causes supply to decrease. How will that tax impact the market for kombucha? Will sellers just build the tax into the price of their product and go on as before? Let's add a demand curve to our graph to see what happens.

In Figure 4.15, the free-market (no-tax) equilibrium is found at point C, with an equilibrium quantity of 3 and an equilibrium price of $3. And then, the government imposes its $2 tax, shifting S_1 to S_2. That supply shift brings us to a new equilibrium at B*, where two units are sold and the market price is $4. That price is the "price at the pump" that buyers end up paying. However, it's not the price sellers end up receiving! Sellers of kombucha arrive home in the evening to discover a bill from the government waiting in their mailbox: *"I want my two dollars!"* So sellers, who received $4 from their customers, walk away with only $2 after paying their $2 tax.

FIGURE 4.15 The Effects of the Tax

A $2 tax on kombucha causes the equilibrium quantity to decrease, and causes the price to rise by something less than the full amount of the tax. The tax drives a $2 wedge between the price buyers pay and the price sellers receive.

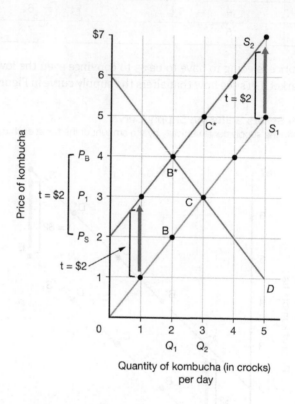

Let's call the $4 that buyers spend the buyer's price, and denote it as P_b. We'll call the $2 that the seller receives the seller's price, P_s. Those two prices are linked by the $2 amount of the tax, which we'll call t, in this way:

EQUATION 4.1

$$P_b = P_s + t$$

That makes finding all of the important variables easy. To analyze the tax, shift the supply curve upward by the amount of the tax. The new equilibrium is found where the new supply curve intersects the demand curve; that's point B* in Figure 4.15. From B*, look leftward to the vertical axis to find the $4 market (buyer's) price. Then, subtract the amount of the tax from the buyer's price to find the seller's price. This is easy, because we know the two supply curves in the graph are separated vertically by exactly the amount of the tax; simply travel from the new supply curve at B* vertically downward to point B on the original supply curve; looking leftward to the vertical axis shows the seller's price, $2.

"I thought I was making bank . . . until I got the bill for my kombucha tax."

Source: fizkes/Shutterstock.com

Let's make some key observations about the effects of the tax:

- The tax results in less kombucha being traded in the marketplace. Generally speaking, the tax discourages the activity being taxed.
- The tax drives a wedge between the price sellers receive and the price buyers pay—so there are now *two* prices in the market for kombucha—the buyer's price and the seller's price. Government captures the difference as tax revenue.
- The tax results in higher prices to buyers, who saw kombucha rise from $3 to $4. This happens because sellers try to pass some of the tax along to buyers.
- The market price doesn't rise by the full amount of the tax—buyers ended up paying $1 more when a $2 tax was imposed.
- Because sellers can't pass along the full amount of the tax to buyers, they end up receiving less for their product. In the example, the price sellers receive decreases from $3 to $2.

The tax wedge splits buyer's and seller's prices as neatly as this wedge splits firewood!

Source: Hans Christiansson/ Shutterstock.com

A Tax on Buyers: The Demand Curve

You're now acquainted with what happens when the government taxes the seller of an item. But what if the government collected the money from the buyer, instead? Would that turn our results inside-out?

To answer that, we'll need to take the same deep dive into the demand curve as we did the supply curve. So let's suppose we have five potential buyers of kombucha, each of whom has a different maximum amount they are willing to pay, as shown in Table 4.4. Buyer's willingness to pay reflects both their desire for the product and the size of their wallet—for our purposes, let's just assume these buyers are all very thirsty, but are limited by the money they've got available. Poor Jonah has only a dollar to spend!

TABLE 4.4 Willingness to Pay for Kombucha
Five buyers of kombucha have different willingnesses to pay. Flower values kombucha the most; Jonah values kombucha the least.

Buyer	Willing to Pay ($)
Flower	5
Graham	4
Henna	3
Indigo	2
Jonah	1

Just as we used producers' cost information to develop the supply curve, we can use buyers' willingness to pay to develop the demand curve. Note that at a price of $5, only Flower is willing to buy kombucha. At a price of $4, both Flower and Graham will buy kombucha and two units will be demanded; and so on until we find that at a price of $1, all five buyers would like to take some kombucha home. We can use this information to draw the demand for kombucha, as shown in Figure 4.16.

FIGURE 4.16 The Demand for Kombucha
The demand curve reflects the maximum willingness to pay for each unit of a good demanded.

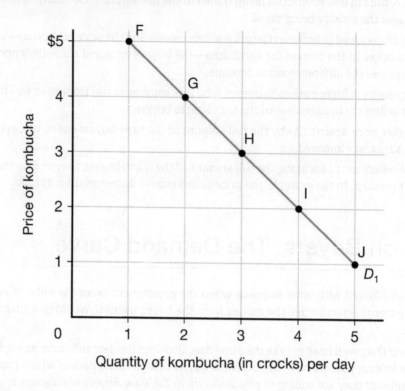

Of course, the demand curve tells us how many units will sell at various prices. But just as we did with supply, if we read the demand curve "backward," *it tells us how much each unit of kombucha is valued by consumers.* The first unit is the most valuable: If you go up from a quantity of 1 to the demand curve (at point F), and over to the vertical axis, you'll see it's valued at $5 (by Flower, which is why we've labeled this with an F). The second unit is not quite as highly valued; Graham (point G) is willing to pay $4 for it. Continuing in this way, we see that each consumer has his or her own "dot" on the demand curve (in alphabetic correspondence), reflecting how much he or she would be willing to pay for kombucha.

But what happens to those consumers' willingness to pay when government imposes a $2 tax on kombucha? Knowing that there will be a bill waiting on their doorstep when they get home—*I want my two dollars!*—consumers' willingness to pay at the store goes down by the amount of the tax, as shown in Table 4.5.

TABLE 4.5 The Effect of a Tax on Willingness to Pay
A $2 tax reduces buyers' willingness to pay by $2.

Buyer	Original Willingness to Pay ($)	Willing to Pay with $2 Tax ($)
Flower	5	3
Graham	4	2
Henna	3	1
Indigo	2	0

Each person's willingness to pay "at the pump" declines by the amount of the tax. Poor Indigo, with only $2 in her wallet, can now only buy kombucha if they're giving it away for free. And Jonah has been priced out of the market entirely—with only a dollar in his wallet to begin with, he can't even afford to pay the tax! And so, the new demand curve for kombucha with the tax incorporated is shown in Figure 4.17.

FIGURE 4.17 A Tax on Buyers of Kombucha Decreases Demand

Imposing a $2 tax on buyers of kombucha shifts the demand for kombucha vertically downward by the amount of the tax.

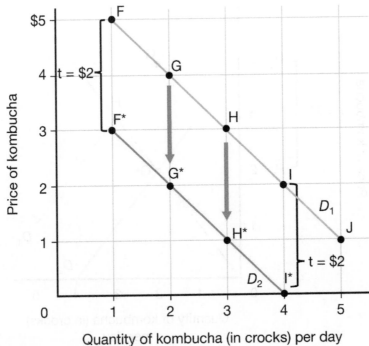

The $2 tax on kombucha reduces each buyer's willingness to pay (as shown by the change from F to F*; G to G*, and so on), and shifts the demand for kombucha vertically downward (from D_1 to D_2) by the amount of the tax. In other words, the tax discourages the activity being taxed; demand decreases. Surprise!

What will the impact of this tax be once we incorporate sellers into our analysis? Let's bring back our original supply curve and see what happens. The effect of the tax on the market is illustrated in Figure 4.18.

We initially start with no tax at point H, corresponding to an equilibrium quantity of 3 and an equilibrium price of $3. And then, government imposes the $2 tax on buyers. That causes demand to decrease to D_2, and takes us to a new equilibrium at point G*. The new market price is $2—the tax has caused the price to decrease (remember that when we taxed sellers, the market price *increased*)! But things are arranged a bit differently this time: Now, it's sellers who "see" the market price, because once customers hand over their cash, sellers are done. But the buyers aren't—they'll return home to find that the government wants an additional $2 from them. So, the buyer's price will be the $2 market price, plus another $2 tax, for a total of $4.

Drop the kombucha, Jonah—you've just been taxed out of the market!

FIGURE 4.18 A Tax on Buyers of Kombucha

A $2 tax on buyers of kombucha causes the market (seller's) price to fall from $3 to $2. The buyer's price rises from $3 to $4, while the equilibrium quantity falls from 3 to 2.

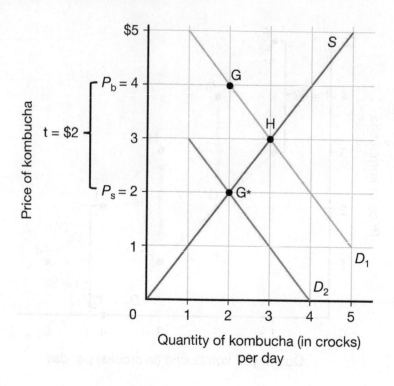

A Generic Tax: The Wedge Method

Let's review what we've learned from each of these examples:

1. When the government's $2 tax was collected from *sellers*, the buyer's price increased from $3 to $4, the seller's price decreased from $3 to $2, and the equilibrium quantity fell from 3 units to 2.

2. When the government's $2 tax was collected from *buyers*, the buyer's price increased from $3 to $4, the seller's price decreased from $3 to $2, and the equilibrium quantity fell from 3 units to 2.

The effects are the same no matter who you tax? Mind = Blown!

This is an interesting result! *It doesn't matter whether the government collects a tax from sellers or buyers, the outcome is the same.* That's not immediately intuitive, but you've proven it true here. And it begs some important questions, such as exactly why the government bothers to collect half of your Social Security taxes from you (the seller of labor services) and half from your employer (the buyer) when it could just collect from one or the other: We now know it doesn't make a hoot's bit of difference at all!

Knowing the outcome is the same also gives us the power to simplify the analysis. You might, in the heat of an exciting econ moment, find yourself having trouble remembering the mechanics of the process: "*When the government collects the tax from the seller, does the supply curve shift, or the demand curve? And, does it shift upward or downward? And is that an increase or a decrease? Oh, nuts!*"

That's a lot of stuff to keep straight! But knowing that the outcomes are identical is useful, because it eliminates the confusion associated with shifting curves. Instead, all you have to remember is that a tax drives a wedge between prices, and that the size of the wedge is the amount of the tax. Let's see what this means with a picture—a much simpler view of what we've already done.

FIGURE 4.19 The Wedge Method of Analyzing a Tax
A $2 tax discourages the activity being taxed, and drives a wedge between the buyer's and seller's prices equal to the $2 amount of the tax. There's only one quantity to the left of the free-market equilibrium where demand and supply are $2 apart. That's the new equilibrium quantity, and the buyer's and seller's prices can be read off the demand and supply curves at that quantity.

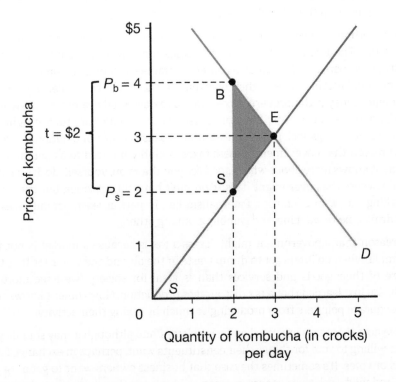

Figure 4.19 shows the simplified analysis of the tax. Here's how to use what we'll call the "wedge method" to figure out how the tax impacts the market.

1. Start at the free-market (no tax) equilibrium, shown as point E. Pinch your right index finger and thumb together and place them on point E, at a quantity of 3 and a price of $3.

2. The tax discourages the activity being taxed. So, begin to slide your fingers to the left (lower quantity). Let your index finger follow the demand curve and your thumb follow the supply curve. Be sure to keep your finger and thumb lined up on the same quantity!

3. The tax drives a $2 wedge between the buyer's price (on the demand curve) and the seller's price (on the supply curve). There's only one quantity to the left of point E where that's true. So keep sliding to the left until your finger and thumb are $2 apart and you'll have found it. You'll reach that point when your finger is on point B and your thumb is on point S.

4. Read off the equilibrium quantity from the horizontal axis. Here, that's 2 units. Then find the point (B) that's on the demand curve at that quantity (*Hint: Your finger is on it!*) and read over to the price axis; that's the buyer's price, $4. Finally, find the point (point S) that's on the supply curve at that quantity (*Hint: It's under your thumb!*); read over to the price axis to find the seller's price, $2.

You'll notice that the three important points in your graph—the initial equilibrium at E, the buyer's price at B, the seller's price S—all make a triangle (which is colored in blue here). That's the wedge! But just to be sure the wedge method works, go back to our earlier examples and make sure that the buyers always pay $4, the sellers always receive $2, and the equilibrium quantity always falls from 3 to 2. Once you've verified that for yourself, you can *always* use the wedge to do the analysis or to check your work.

Why Taxes?

So, governments impose taxes—lots of taxes—on lots of people. But why? There are a handful of reasons, and we'll mention them briefly here before discussing them more fully in later chapters.

First, the government needs money to operate, and one of the easiest methods to obtain money is to impose a tax. The U.S. federal government raises most of its money through the personal income tax (though there are thousands of other federal taxes, too). State and local governments often assess personal income taxes of their own, but on the whole, the biggest source of state and local government money is the property tax—that's a tax assessed against people who own property like land, houses, and cars. And then, of course, those revenues are turned right around and used to provide other things society deems essential—roads, schools, and national defense.

A second reason that governments assess taxes is kindly referred to as paternalism, the idea that government knows more about what's good for you than you, yourself, do. It's a parenting sort of relationship, where the government doesn't *prohibit* harmful activities, but tries to *discourage* you from making the "wrong" choices. Paternalism lies, in part at least, behind taxes on alcohol, tobacco, soft drinks, exotic dancing, and gambling, among others.

A third reason that a government might assess a tax is because a market is not functioning well. For example, when polluters get to dump waste in the air and the water for free, they tend to produce more of their goods and services than is ideal for society (we'll see more about this in Chapter 6). You just learned that a tax discourages production. Government knows this, too, and may try to discourage polluters from producing so much by taxing their activity.

Finally, we note that taxes are voted on by legislators, and although it may sound cynical, *some* legislators are willing to vote for things their constituents want, perhaps in exchange for campaign contributions or votes. It's sometimes the case that business owners want to get a leg up on their competition, and might ask their congressperson to pass a tax that helps them do that. For example, domestic manufacturers of dog collars might ask the government to tax foreign-sourced dog collars, in an attempt to reduce competition from abroad. This behavior—using the power of government to your own economic advantage—is called *rent seeking*, and it's our last motivation for a tax.

Pop! Goes the Econ: The Beatles and the "Taxman"

Here's the Beatles' commentary on the ubiquity of taxes in 1960s England, where the top marginal income tax rate was about 95%. Find a reference in the song to that 95% tax rate. Is it a surprise that the Beatles spent a fortune trying to avoid paying taxes?

View in the online reader

Key Takeaways

- A tax discourages the activity being taxed, resulting in a lower equilibrium quantity in the market.
- A tax drives a wedge between the price paid by buyers and the price received by sellers. The price paid by buyers generally increases; the price received by sellers generally decreases.
- The effects of a tax in a market are identical whether the tax is collected from buyers or from sellers.
- Governments use taxes to raise revenue, to discourage undesirable activity, to correct market failures, and as a tool of special interest politics.

Try It!

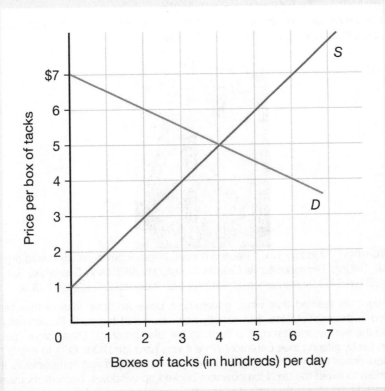

Consider the market for tacks shown above. Use the graph to answer the following:

a. What is the free-market equilibrium price and quantity of tacks?

b. If the government imposed a $3 tax on tacks, what would the equilibrium quantity be? (Hint: Use the wedge method!)

c. With a $3 tack tax, what is the buyer's price?

d. With a $3 tack tax, what is the seller's price?

See related Numerical Problems 10 and 11 at the end of this chapter.

Case in Point: A Look Through Britain's Window Tax

When a government depends on taxes to fund its operations, often the choice of the tax depends on the ease of assessment and collection. In today's developed, computerized world, it's relatively simple for governments to keep track of how much you work and how much you earn: The income tax is a straightforward way to collect government revenue. But keeping track of everybody's earnings wasn't so easy two hundred years ago—government needed an easier way to figure out how much money you had and how much you should owe. With the income tax impractical to implement, the British government decided on a fireplace tax: Richer people with bigger homes had more fireplaces; by assessing a tax per fireplace, the government could raise the revenue it needed.

Of course, counting how many fireplaces were in each residence in a block of row houses meant an intrusive visit inside each home. That was both politically unpopular and time consuming. But there was an easier way to figure out who had money and who didn't without a costly visit inside: Bigger residences had more windows. By replacing the fireplace tax with a tax on windows, which were easily counted from outside the home, the government could extract more money from the rich (who had bigger houses) than the poor. A homeowner paid no tax if the house had fewer than 10 windows; the homeowner paid 6 pence per window if the house had 10 to 14 windows; the tax increased to 9 pence per window if the house had 15 to 19 windows; it rose to 1 shilling per window if there were 20 or more windows.

Shedding light on bricked-up windows: The Southampton, England, landlord who bricked up these windows masterfully avoided the British window tax.

Source: Whilesteps. "Window Tax.." Retrieved from: https://commons.wikimedia.org/wiki/File:Window_Tax.jpg. Reproduced via Creative Commons Attribution-ShareAlike 3.0 Unported (CC BY-SA 3.0): Attribution-ShareAlike 3.0 Unported (CC BY-SA 3.0).

In this section, we learned that when government taxes an item, less of that item ends up being traded in the marketplace. But exactly how does that happen? Sometimes, people will try to *evade* the tax by purchasing the item on the black market. Other times, people will try to *avoid* the tax by altering their behavior. While it was hard for 1700s Brits to evade the window tax (a window doesn't do you much good unless you install it in a wall somewhere!), it was much easier for them to avoid the tax. Homeowners bricked up windows, because houses with more windows were taxed at a higher rate per window than houses with less. New homes were built with fewer windows; to maintain appearances, fake "windows" were often painted on the outside, with no (taxable) opening to the inside.

The tax avoidance becomes obvious when you look at a large number of homes and count the windows, as economists Wallace Oates and Robert Schwab did using historical tax data from hundreds of homes in Ludlow, England. Their findings show a disproportionate number of houses with 9 windows and 14 windows, rather than 10 or 15, when tax rates would jump considerably:

While the window tax benefited government, it made society as a whole poorer. The effects of the window tax were so devastating that Charles Dickens was compelled to comment on it: "*Neither air nor light have been free since the imposition of the window-tax. We are obliged to pay for what nature lavishly supplies to all . . . and the poor . . . are stinted in two of the most urgent necessities of life.*" And those necessities were important: Windows were important for light, but even more important for fresh air. Apartments with windows bricked shut turned out to be hotbeds of contagion. Dr. John Heysham commented on a particularly bad outbreak of typhus in an apartment house: "*In order to reduce the window tax, every window that even poverty could dispense with was built up, and all source of ventilation were thus removed. The smell . . . was overpowering. [The fever] was propagated from it to other parts of town, and 52 of the inhabitants were killed.*"

One would expect the number of windows in a home to be smoothly distributed . . . but one would be wrong, at least in 1760 England! Because window tax rates stairstepped upward when a home reached its tenth, fifteenth, and twentieth windows, records of this town's tax rolls show an unusually large number of houses with 9, 14, and 19 windows.

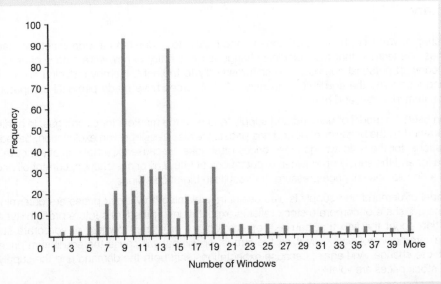

Source: Author-constructed histogram using historical data.

We'll revisit the window tax in our chapter devoted to international trade. In the meantime, let's recap the general lessons we can learn from the window tax: Government imposes taxes; people try to avoid taxes; society generally suffers as a result.

See related Concept Problem 14 at the end of this chapter.

Source: Based on Wallace Oates and Robert Schwab's "The Window Tax: A Case Study in Excess Burden," Journal of Economic Perspectives," 29, no. 1 (2015): 163–80.

Answers to Try It! Problems

a. Find the intersection of demand and supply to determine the equilibrium price ($5) and quantity (4).

b. Use the wedge method to find that demand and supply curves are exactly $3 apart when the quantity is 2.

c. At a quantity of 2, go up to the demand curve and read off the vertical axis: The buyer's price is $6.

d. At a quantity of 2, go up to the supply curve and read off the vertical axis: The seller's price is $3.

4.5 Review and Practice

Summary

In this chapter we used the tools of demand and supply to understand a wide variety of market outcomes. We learned that technological change and the entry of new sellers have caused the supply curve of personal computers to shift markedly to the right, thereby reducing equilibrium price and increasing the equilibrium quantity. Market forces have made personal computers a common item in offices and homes.

We then used the model of demand and supply to look at the markets for oil and gas. In addition to understanding the behavior of oil and gas prices, we also developed an explanation, based on expectations, for the wide swings those prices often take. Because expectations affect both the demand for and the supply of oil, when expectations of future oil prices change, current oil prices receive a double dose of price pressure that results in big price swings.

The model of demand and supply is also useful in explaining how stock prices are determined. The price per share of corporate stock reflects expectations of the firm's future profitability. Any information about the firm that causes potential buyers or current owners of corporate stock to reevaluate how profitable they think the firm is, or will be, will cause the equilibrium price of the stock to change. And again, because expectations shift both the demand and the supply of stocks, stock prices are volatile.

We then examined markets in which some form of government price control keeps the price permanently above or below equilibrium. A price floor leads to persistent surpluses because it is set above the equilibrium price, whereas a price ceiling, because it is set below the equilibrium price, leads to persistent shortages. Interfering with the market mechanism may solve one problem but often creates other problems. For example, agricultural price floors aimed at boosting farm income have also raised prices for consumers and cost taxpayers dearly, while the bulk of government payments have gone to large farms. Rent controls have lowered rents, but they have also reduced the quantity of rental housing supplied, created shortages, and sometimes led to various forms of "backdoor" payments that can make housing less affordable rather than more.

Finally, we looked at how a tax can affect the market for a good or service. Taxes drive a wedge between the price paid by buyers and the price received by sellers. When a new tax is imposed, the price faced by buyers generally increases, while the price received by sellers generally decreases. The tax also discourages the activity being taxed: The equilibrium quantity declines when a new tax is imposed. Finally, we discovered that it makes no difference whether a tax is collected from buyers or sellers; the impact is identical. That led us to a shortcut method for analyzing the impact of a tax, the wedge method.

Concept Problems

1. Like personal computers, smartphones have become a common household item. Smartphone prices have fallen steadily since they were first brought to the market. Use the model of demand and supply to explain the fall in price and increase in quantity.

2. (Related to "Try It!" in Section 4.2.) Enron Corp. was one of several corporations convicted of fraud in its accounting practices during the early part of this century. It had created dummy corporations to hide massive borrowing and to give it the appearance of extraordinary profitability. Use the model of demand and supply to explain the likely impact of such convictions on the stocks of other corporations.

3. During World War II there was a freeze on wages, and corporations found they could evade the freeze by providing other fringe benefits such as retirement funds and health insurance for their employees. The Office of Price Administration, which administered the wage freeze, ruled that the offer of retirement funds and health insurance was not a violation of the freeze. The Internal Revenue Service went along with this and ruled that employer-financed retire-

ment and health insurance plans were not taxable income. Was the wage freeze an example of a price floor or a price ceiling? Use the model of demand and supply to explain why employers began to offer such benefits to their employees.

4. (Related to "Case in Point: The Topsy-Turvy World of 2020 Oil Prices" in Section 4.2.) Outline briefly the reasons that oil prices dipped into negative territory in early 2020. Then, explain why it's unlikely that the price of tennis shoes will ever do the same.

5. Suppose that technological change affects the dairy industry in the same way it has affected the computer industry. However, suppose that dairy price supports remain in place. How would this affect government spending on the dairy program? Use the model of demand and supply to support your answer.

6. People often argue that there is a "shortage" of child care. Using the model of demand and supply, evaluate whether this argument is likely to be correct.

7. "During most of the past fifty years the United States has had a surplus of farmers, and this has been the root of the farm problem." Comment.

8. Suppose the Department of Agriculture ordered all farmers to reduce the acreage they plant by 10%. Would you expect a 10% reduction in food production? Why or why not?

9. Suppose that the United States and the European Union impose a price ceiling on crude oil of $25 per barrel. Explain, and illustrate graphically, how this would affect the markets for crude oil and for gasoline in the United States and in the European Union.

10. Given that rent controls can actually hurt low-income people, devise a housing strategy that would provide affordable housing for those whose incomes fall below the poverty line (in 2020, this was about $26,200 for a family of four).

11. (Related to "Case in Point: Thank Goodness for Gouging?" in Section 4.3.) Your university town believes that greedy landlords are making college students "house poor." The town council proposes capping apartment rents at $200 per month. As a college student, what are some pros of this proposal? What are some cons? Are there any likely consequences you would face as a result of this policy that are not captured by the model of demand and supply?

12. Suppose that the demand curve for water in your town is very steep, reflecting the fact that it's hard for consumers to cut back on their water use, but that the supply curve is very flat—producers can ramp up production fairly easily if prices increase. Who do you think would end up being hurt the most by a new $1 tax on water—buyers or sellers? (*Hint: Draw a graph, then use the wedge method to analyze the effects of the tax.*)

13. Social Security and Medicare taxes are split equally between an employee and an employer. You now know that it doesn't make any difference who a tax is collected from; the effects are the same. Why do you suppose the government decided to split these taxes in this way?

14. (Related to "Case in Point: A Look Through Britain's Window Tax" in Section 4.4.) Does the motivation for Britain's window tax shed any light on why many developing countries rely more heavily on import taxes (tariffs) for revenue than more common alternatives in the developed world, such as the income tax?

Numerical Problems

Problems 1–4 are based on the following demand and supply schedules for corn (all quantities are in millions of bushels per year).

Price per Bushel ($)	Quantity Demanded	Quantity Supplied
0	6	0
1	5	1
2	4	2
3	3	3
4	2	4

Price per Bushel ($)	Quantity Demanded	Quantity Supplied
5	1	5
6	0	6

1. Draw the demand and supply curves for corn. What is the equilibrium price? The equilibrium quantity?

2. (Related to "Try It!" in section 4.3.) Suppose the government now imposes a price floor at $4 per bushel. Show the effect of this program graphically. How large is the surplus of corn?

3. With the price floor, how much do farmers receive for their corn? How much would they have received if there were no price floor?

4. If the government buys all the surplus corn, how much will it spend?

Problems 5–9 are based on the following hypothetical demand and supply curves for apartments.

Rent/Month ($)	Number of Apts. Demanded/Month	Number of Apts. Supplied/Month
0	120,000	0
200	100,000	20,000
400	80,000	40,000
600	60,000	60,000
800	40,000	80,000
1,000	20,000	100,000
1,200	0	120,000

5. Draw the demand and supply curves for apartments.

6. What is the equilibrium rent per month? At this rent, what is the number of apartments demanded and supplied per month?

7. Suppose a ceiling on rents is set at $400 per month. Characterize the situation that results from this policy.

8. At the rent ceiling, how many apartments are demanded? How many are supplied?

9. How much are people willing to pay for the number of apartments supplied at the ceiling? Describe the arrangements to which this situation might lead.

Problems 10–12 are based on the following hypothetical demand and supply curves for coffee:

Price per Pound ($)	Quantity Demanded	Quantity Supplied
4.00	100	500
3.50	200	400
3.00	300	300
2.50	400	200
2.00	500	100
1.50	600	0
1.00	700	0
0.50	800	0

10. What is the equilibrium price and quantity of coffee?

11. (Related to "Try It!" in Section 4.4.) Suppose that the local government imposes a $1 tax. What will happen to the equilibrium quantity of coffee sold? (*Hint: When in doubt, draw a graph!*)

12. Related to "Try It!" in Section 4.4.) If the government imposes a $1 tax, how will the tax affect the price paid by buyers? The price received by sellers?

Endnotes

1. That price decline is even *more* notable if measured in terms of dollars per unit of processing speed or dollars per unit of memory.

2. There are, of course, other ways to raise money, including borrowing money or hanging onto recent earnings.

3. The market represents only active trading by buyers and sellers; that means that the supply curve shows only the shares that are potentially up for sale, and not the total number of shares in existence.

4. The dollar price of wheat declined just a few cents between 1974 and 2020, but because other products got more expensive, each bushel of wheat ended up being tradable for only 1/5 as many clothes, shoes, cars, and other things in 2020 as it was in 1974. Economists say that the *real* price of wheat (the price adjusted for the cost of other goods and services) fell by 80%.

5. Notice that in order to have any impact, the ceiling price must be below the equilibrium price. In a market where everyone's charging $800 for apartments, telling them, "You are forbidden to charge more than $2,000" is a waste of words: Nobody is *trying* to charge more than $2,000!

6. See "Queens Landlord Convicted in Plot to Kill Two Tenants," *New York Times*, December 8, 2004.

CHAPTER 5
Introduction to the Macroeconomy: Measuring the Economy's Output

5.1 Start Up: Your Uncertain Future

You've done all the right things. You've enrolled in college, you've chosen a degree path. You're taking a course in economics, and over the next few years you'll home in on a degree track—maybe in econ, maybe in business, or computer science, or literature. Just to give you perspective, you'll supplement those courses with work in philosophy and history and sociology, and when you emerge from college you'll be well on your way to being a critical thinker and a lifelong learner.

"Bring it on, world!"

Source: Greanlnw studio/Shutterstock.com

All of that learning, though, has come at a cost. You've invested money and time in making yourself more educated and more employable. Many of you have suffered through cafeteria food of questionable quality and roommates who never washed their stinky laundry. Now, having made all of these good but costly moves, you're about ready to graduate and start adulting, with all that it entails—a job, bills, a place to live, maybe a family to start. You're ready!

But is the world ready for *you*? Because despite all of the control you've exercised, despite the proactive way you took charge of your destiny, so much of your early adult life is going to be shaped by forces largely beyond your control. Not least among those forces is the state of the economy when you graduate. No matter how sharp you are, you'll be much better off graduating into an economy where employers are lined up looking for good workers than graduating into one where a long line of job-seekers competes for a few jobs. How eager employers are to hire new workers, in turn, depends on the overall health of the economy: If consumers are spending and business is booming, firms may be more willing to take a chance on more fresh college grads. A bleak outlook may prevent employers from hiring new workers, and may actually convince them to lay off some of their current workforce.

There are other variables in the overall economy that will impact your material future, too. High interest rates may make that new Jeep you've been wanting unaffordable, and steer you into a 20-year-old Camry instead. Rising prices may make the things you'd like to buy for your new apartment more expensive. And a falling dollar could price you out of your honeymoon in Greece... but there's nothing wrong with three romantic days in Toledo, right?

Output, employment, interest rates, the price level: These economic variables are fundamentally different than the ones we've looked at so far. In our micro-level study of the markets for a particular good, we were largely interested in the price of that product and the quantity of that product exchanged in the marketplace. As we move into our study of the macroeconomy, we're going to focus more on economic variables that summarize the performance of the economy as a whole. In other words, macroeconomists are going to try to assess the performance of the markets for bread, video streaming, hot-stone massages, and Tide pods all at the same time. We'll ask different questions than the ones we looked at in our earlier micro-level study of a single market—questions like why some economies are rich and others are poor, why your paycheck keeps getting bigger but seems to buy you less, and, yes, why looking for a good post-graduation job can be so frustrating.

As we write this in mid-2021, the United States and the rest of the world are coming to terms with a year-plus-long pandemic that significantly affected the world economy. Many of the economic variables that would have had you looking at your future through rose-colored glasses in early 2020 may look different today. Not least among those, the nation's (and the world's) total output of goods and services took a nosedive in 2020, with a subsequent recovery that was still incomplete by the time this book went to press.

"Remember when I said, 'Bring it on, world'? Well, thanks. Thanks a lot."

Source: Simone Hogan/ Shutterstock.com

5.2 Measuring Total Output: GDP and Its Components

Learning Objectives

1. Define gross domestic product and its four major spending components.
2. Distinguish between measuring GDP as the sum of the values of final goods and services and as the sum of values added at each stage of production.
3. Describe why the income approach to calculating GDP should result in the same figure as the expenditure approach.

The economy produces a *lot* of stuff, and it's the macroeconomist's job to add them all up. You're gonna need that coffee!

Source: Mangostar/Shutterstock. com

A developed economy produces a mind-boggling array of goods and services every year. Domino's Pizza produces hundreds of millions of pizzas; U.S. Steel makes tens of millions of tons of steel; AT&T transmits 3.2 trillion text messages; and across the United States, writers churn out over 300,000 new titles. A list of all the goods and services an economy produces in any year would be virtually endless. You think of it, someone's probably doing it!

You might remember that the fundamental economic problem any society faces is making the greatest amount of right stuff while using the smallest quantity of resources, and then handing all that stuff out to the right people so that it provides the greatest material happiness. So yes, the U.S. economy turns out lots of stuff. But it turns out that stuff by using lots of people, and the stuff it turns out provides those people their material happiness. So—are we producing what we're capable of? How good a job are we doing providing material comfort to the people in society? Those are the questions of the macroeconomist.

We'd like to answer those questions. But we'd also like to avoid having to enumerate the economy's entire output item by item: " . . . four calling birds, three French hens, two turtle doves . . ."[1] It would be helpful to have a single number that measures total output in the economy. Lucky for us, we've got it: That number is called *gross domestic product*, or GDP. GDP is often referred to as *nominal GDP*.

Gross Domestic Product: An Economy's Yardstick

In order to understand what gross domestic product tells us and what it doesn't, it's helpful to take a look at its technical definition. **Gross domestic product** (GDP) is *the market value of all final goods and services produced in an economy in a given year*. That sounds straightforward, but there are some hidden nuances. Let's break that definition down word by word and see what it tells us.

Market Value: Remember that GDP is supposed to measure total production in an economy. That sounds easy, except that adding up total production requires us, quite literally, to add apples and oranges, which math teachers have been warning us against for as long as we can remember. We simply can't add apples and oranges (much less rockets and pedicures) unless we can find some common unit to measure them in. That common unit turns out to be their market value, which is, of course, measured in dollars.

To measure the market value of an item like, say, pizza, simply multiply the quantity of pizzas (Q_{pizza}) sold times their price (P_{pizza}). In a simple economy that produces only beer and pizza, then, GDP is just the market value of all pizza sold in that year plus the market value of all beer sold in that year:

$$GDP_{2022} = (Q_{beer} \times P_{beer}) + (Q_{pizza} \times P_{pizza})$$

If, in 2022, 10 beers sold for $5 each, and 4 pizzas sold for $20 each, GDP for 2022 would be:

$$GDP_{2022} = (10 \times \$5) + (4 \times \$20) = \$130$$

Why is it that we bother to convert everything to market value? Because an economy that produces five $20 haircuts and one $50,000 Benz is very different from an economy that produces one $20 haircut and five $50,000 Benzes. Both economies produce 6 items, but the second economy is producing a lot more material value for its citizens, and measuring market value is a good way to capture that: The first economy has GDP of $50,100; the second's is almost five times higher at $250,020.[2]

Goods and Services: The definition of GDP includes both goods and services. That's because we get material comfort and satisfaction from both, and both are exchanged in the marketplace. When you buy a new bike to commute from home to school, GDP increases, but it also increases if you hire an Uber, instead. If your dorm floor is disgusting, you can buy a mop or you can hire someone to mop for you; GDP will increase in either case.

Final: GDP includes the market value of goods and services. But that doesn't mean *every* good or service traded in the economy is included in GDP. Instead, GDP only includes purchases made by the *final* consumers of a good or service.

Let's look at a brief example to see what that means. Suppose you *LOVE* the $3 cinnamon rolls from a local bakery, and every Monday morning (because, *Monday*) you treat yourself to one. If the purpose of GDP is to capture material comforts people enjoy, the $3 price of the cinnamon roll is a pretty good proxy for the value you place on your bit of Monday joy.

Suppose the baker used $0.50 of flour, $0.25 of butter, $0.25 of sugar, and $1 worth of snooty Ceylon cinnamon to make your cinnamon roll. Those ingredients are called *intermediate* goods, raw materials or components that will later be transformed into a final, finished product. Even though the baker bought them in the marketplace, their value isn't explicitly included in GDP. That's because their value is already built into the $3 price of the cinnamon roll they'll soon become. If we accidentally included them, we would end up counting them twice and overstating GDP. Remember that the purpose of GDP is to measure our material comfort; if we double-count these intermediate goods, GDP would rise by $5 every time you indulged your Monday sweet tooth, which is more than the $3 of actual value the cinnamon roll brings you.

gross domestic product

The market value of all final goods and services produced in an economy in a given year. Abbreviated GDP.

Cutting hair is honorable work . . . and lots of people need haircuts. Too bad a haircut doesn't have as much impact on GDP as a Benz.

Source: Olena Yakobchuk/
Shutterstock.com

Even Einstein's can't make bagels out of nothing—it takes flour, salt, yeast, and water. But the value of those intermediate goods won't be directly included in GDP.

Source: Ken Wolter/Shutterstock.com

Produced: GDP measures the market value of transactions taking place in the economy, but not the market value of *all* transactions. (In fact, you've already seen one example of a transaction that isn't included in GDP when we discussed intermediate goods.) The goal of GDP is to measure production, so when we compute GDP, we need to be sure we're only counting items at the time they're produced; we don't want to double-count them again, later. That means that when your neighbor buys a new Jeep, GDP increases, but when your 18-year-old sister buys a 1972 VW microbus to drive across-country during her so-called gap year, GDP doesn't change at all; the value of her "new" wheels was already included in the GDP for 1972. The same is true for things like used clothing and used housing (although the realtor that brings the buyer and seller of a pre-owned home together *has* performed a current service; his commission *will* be included in GDP).

In an Economy in a Given Year: GDP measures the output an economy, and generally, that means a particular country's economy.[3] The United States has its own GDP, as do Congo, Kuwait, and North Korea. Each country's GDP measures production that happens within its own borders, no matter who does the production. When German auto giant BMW builds a new 7-series at its Spartanburg, South Carolina, plant, U.S. GDP increases; Germany's does not. When a U.S. resident crosses the Canadian border to harvest timber, or when a prominent U.S. businessman produces neckties in a Bangladeshi factory, U.S. GDP does nothing, even though the proceeds end up in the pockets of a U.S. resident.[4]

 Pop! Goes the Econ: Ferris Bueller and the Ferrari

Ferris says, "It is so choice. If you have the means, I highly recommend picking one up." If you do, the salesperson's commission will appear in this year's GDP, but the value of the car won't—it was already included in 1961's . . . in Italy!

View in the online reader

GDP is also specific to a particular period of time—one year, to be exact. A variable like GDP that measures something over a time period is called a **flow variable**. The United States' $23 trillion GDP means that the United States produces $23 trillion worth of final goods and services *each year*. In practice, GDP is estimated four times each year, or *quarterly*, and then that quarterly figure is scaled by a factor of 4 to convert it to an annual estimate. (There are economic variables that, rather than measuring something over a period of time, are more like snapshots taken at a *point* in time. These variables, like your checking account balance or the price of gold, are called **stock variables**.)

flow variable

A variable that is measured over a specific period of time.

stock variables

Variables that measure something at a single point in time.

The Components of GDP and the Expenditures Approach

GDP is the market value of a country's production, and as such we can measure it by adding up the amount spent on the economy's goods and services by various buyers. Those buyers include households, which make personal consumption expenditures (C); businesses, which spend money on investment goods (I); government, which purchases all kinds of goods and services (G); and foreigners, who purchase U.S.-produced goods and services that we call *net exports* (X_n). GDP is the sum of the expenditures made by those four types of buyer:

$$GDP = \text{Consumption} + \text{Investment} + \text{Government Purchases} + \text{Net Exports}$$

EQUATION 5.1

$$GDP = C + I + G + X_n$$

Let's take a closer look at each of these components of GDP, see what their relative contribution to GDP is, and see how their behavior fits into the pattern of overall macroeconomic activity.

Personal Consumption

Personal consumption measures the value of goods and services purchased by households during a time period. Purchases by households include such things as:

- food and clothing, which are referred to as *consumer nondurables* because they don't last very long;
- televisions and motorcycles, which are called *consumer durables* because they generally last for several years; and
- tai chi lessons, which are a service.

In 2019, personal consumption expenditures amounted to about $14,544.6 billion, about 68% of the economy's $21.4 trillion GDP. That share of total expenditure has typically been quite stable over time, but because it accounts for such a big share of total spending, when it does increase or decrease sharply, it has a large impact on the economy.

> **personal consumption**
>
> A flow variable that measures the value of goods and services purchased by households during a time period.

Private Investment

Gross private domestic investment (often referred to as *private investment* or just *investment*) is the value of all goods produced during a period for use in the production of other goods and services. In other words, investment goods are stuff used to produce more stuff!

Investment goods are generally divided into four major categories. The first is *fixed investment*, which includes expenditures on production facilities (plants and factories) and the equipment (physical capital) that goes in them, like printing presses, conveyor belts, and sewing machines. Be sure to recognize the distinction between intermediate goods (which are goods that will eventually be transformed into final goods) and investment goods (which might be used to transform those intermediate goods into final goods).

> **gross private domestic investment**
>
> The value of all goods produced during a period for use in the production of other goods and services.

Heads Up!

The term *investment* can generate confusion. In everyday conversation, we use the term *investment* to refer to uses of money to earn income. We say we have invested in a stock or invested in a bond. Economists, however, restrict *investment* to activities that increase the economy's stock of capital. The purchase of a share of stock does not add to the capital stock; it is not investment in the economic meaning of the word. We refer to the exchange of financial assets, such as stocks or bonds, as financial investment to distinguish it from the creation of capital that occurs as the result of investment. Only when new capital is produced does investment occur.

The value of this new ship will be included in GDP's investment category. The steel it's made from is an intermediate good, and will not be directly included.

Source: Juozas Baltiejus/Shutterstock.com

The second category of investment is *inventory investment.* Suppose Levi Strauss produces 1 million pairs of jeans late in 2021 and distributes them to stores at the end of December. Those jeans will be added to stores' inventory, and will count as investment goods in 2021's GDP calculation. Now suppose those jeans are sold in January of 2022. Because we calculate GDP by adding up expenditures, they will then be counted as consumption expenditures in 2022's GDP. But now we've counted them twice—a big no-no that overstates actual production, and remember that we want to recognize production at the time it actually happens. So to offset that second entry into GDP, the Bureau of Economic Analysis (which is in charge of calculating GDP) will note that when those jeans sold, the existing inventory of jeans decreased. In other words, in 2022, consumption gets marked up, but is exactly offset by a decrease in inventory. The only time GDP actually rose and stayed that way was when the jeans were originally produced and added to inventory, in December of the year before.

Generally speaking, most investment spending is undertaken by businesses. But one big component of investment spending originates at the household level. That spending is called *residential fixed investment,* and it represents expenditures on new homes. This is categorized as investment spending rather than consumption because a new home is essentially a piece of equipment that will provide a stream of "housing services" far into the future. Residential fixed investment played a noteworthy role in the Great Recession of 2007–2009; we'll revisit that role later in this book.

Pop! Goes the Econ: Jerry Seinfeld on Intellectual Property

Fifteen years of R&D created intellectual property that will bring its creator profits for years to come. What category of GDP do those research expenditures belong to?

View in the online reader

Finally, the investment category of GDP includes spending on intellectual property—creations of the mind that can become someone's property through patents, trademarks, or copyrights. *Intellectual property investment* includes research and development expenditures by individuals and firms. It also includes expenditures devoted to creating or purchasing the rights to computer code, film, television, music, or other artistic or written works. Intellectual property investment was counted as an intermediate good until 2013, when it was reclassified as investment spending because, like factories and equipment, it can last a long time and produce a stream of profits for its owners.

In 2019, the $3,751.2 billion of investment spending accounted for about 17% of GDP. Despite its relatively small share of total economic activity, private investment plays a crucial role in the macroeconomy for two reasons:

1. Investment represents a choice to forgo current consumption in order to add to the economy's capital stock. Those additions to capital increase the economy's capacity to produce and shift its production possibilities curve outward. Investment, then, is a big contributor to economic growth, explored in another chapter.

2. Private investment is a relatively volatile component of GDP; it can change dramatically from one year to the next. Fluctuations in GDP are often driven by fluctuations in private investment. We'll examine the determinants of private investment in a later chapter.

Government Purchases

Government agencies at all levels purchase goods and services from firms. They purchase office equipment, vehicles, and buildings. They purchase labor services from astronauts, policemen, janitors, and legislators. Governments build roads and parks and bridges; they run clinics and staff schools.

Government purchases are the sum of purchases of goods and services from firms by government agencies plus the total value of output produced by government agencies themselves. Government purchases are not quite the same thing as *government spending*. That's because a lot of government spending takes the form of **transfer payments**, which are payments that do not require the recipient to produce a good or service in order to receive them. Transfer payments, which include Social Security and other types of assistance to retired people, welfare payments to poor people, and unemployment compensation to people who have lost their jobs, simply shift money from one person in the economy to another; when you pay your Social Security taxes, for example, those dollars are immediately turned around and sent to a retiree who likely produced absolutely nothing! Transfer payments, despite not being included in GDP, are significant—they account for roughly half of all federal government spending in the United States.

In 2019, government purchases totaled $3,747.9 billion, or about 17% of GDP. Economists pay particular attention to government purchases for a couple of big reasons. First, the government doesn't always have enough money to pay for the purchases it makes. When it doesn't, it generally borrows what it needs. This has happened frequently enough over the past half-century that there are some concerns about the repayment burden that growing government debt has created. Second, government expenditures are one of the tools that government uses to fight economic downturns. Both of those topics will be addressed later in the book. For now, it's sufficient to note that when a caterer puts together a fancy meal, it doesn't particularly matter whether the customer is a proud dad celebrating his daughter's college graduation (consumption spending), or the governor of a state hosting a formal meal for her cabinet (government spending). Either way, the spending will show up in GDP.

Net Exports

Sales of a country's goods and services to buyers in the rest of the world during a particular time period represent its **exports**. When a Japanese jogger buys a pair of New Balance shoes made in Maine, the value is included in U.S. exports. Exports also include such transactions as the purchase of accounting services from a New York firm by a shipping line based in Hong Kong, or the purchase of a ticket to Disney World by a tourist from Argentina.

Imports are purchases of foreign-produced goods and services by a country's residents. When a U.S. resident purchases a Chinese-made iPhone, the value is included in U.S. imports. So are purchases of Guatemalan bananas in your local grocery, and the value of the espresso an American might drink in a sidewalk cafe while visiting Paris.

Subtracting imports from exports yields **net exports**.

EQUATION 5.2

$$\text{Exports } (X) - \text{Imports } (M) = \text{Net Exports } (X_n)$$

It's easy to understand that when the United States exports a Caterpillar tractor to Brazil, exports, net exports, and GDP all increase. After all, the GDP represents production, and the Caterpillar tractor was produced in the United States. But in Equation 5.2, imports have a negative sign . . . does that mean that if we import a set of bagpipes from Scotland that GDP will go *down*?

government purchases

The sum of purchases of goods and services from firms by government agencies plus the total value of output produced by government agencies themselves during a time period.

transfer payments

Payments that do not require the recipient to produce a good or service in order to receive them.

Who doesn't love a good monument? The money spent on Dakar's African Renaissance monument was included in Senegal's GDP.

Source: Salvador Aznar/ Shutterstock.com

exports

Sales of a country's goods and services to buyers in the rest of the world during a particular time period.

imports

Purchases of foreign-produced goods and services by a country's residents during a period.

net exports

Exports minus imports.

"Like all bagpipe music, it was hard to tell if it was good music played horribly, or horrible music played well." One thing's certain, though: The pipes you imported from Scotland won't have any ultimate impact on U.S. GDP.

Sources: Photo from Zapp2Photo/Shutterstock.com; "The B-Team." *Arrested Development*. Imagine Television/20th Century Fox, 26 May 2013.

trade deficit

Negative net exports.

trade surplus

Positive net exports.

Nope, not at all. The negative treatment of imports in the calculation of net exports and GDP is an accounting device much like we saw with the treatment of inventories. Let's think about what happens when you buy a $200 set of bagpipes (besides your roommate locking you out for the forseeable future, that is). Because you are a consumer, and bagpipes are a consumption good, the Bureau of Economic Analysis (BEA) will mark up the consumption component of GDP by $200. If that were the end of it, GDP would rise by $200, suggesting that the United States had produced $200 more stuff. But, of course, it hasn't: The bagpipes were produced in Scotland. So, to prevent that from happening, the BEA makes a *second* entry: It marks up imports, which causes net exports to decrease. That decrease in net exports exactly offsets the increase in consumption, leaving overall GDP, appropriately, unchanged.

In 2019, foreign buyers purchased $2,514.7 billion worth of goods and services from the United States. In that same year, U.S. residents, firms, and government agencies purchased $3,125.2 billion worth of goods and services from foreign countries. The difference between these two figures, –$610.5 billion, represented the net exports of the U.S. economy. Net exports were negative because imports exceeded exports. Negative net exports constitute a **trade deficit**. The amount of the deficit is the amount by which imports exceed exports. When exports exceed imports there is a **trade surplus**. The magnitude of the surplus is the amount by which exports exceed imports.

The United States has recorded more deficits than surpluses since World War II, but the amounts have typically been relatively small, only a few billion dollars. The trade deficit began to soar, however, in the 1980s and again in the 2000s. We will examine the reasons for persistent trade deficits in another chapter. The rest of the world plays a key role in the domestic economy, and, as we will see later in the book, there is nothing particularly good or bad about trade surpluses or deficits. Goods and services produced for export represent roughly 13% of GDP, and the goods and services the United States imports add significantly to our standard of living.

Figure 5.1 shows the size of the components of GDP in 2019. We see that the production of goods and services for personal consumption accounted for nearly 70% of GDP. Imports exceeded exports, so net exports were negative.

FIGURE 5.1 Components of GDP, 2019, in Billions of Dollars
Consumption makes up the largest share of GDP. Net exports were negative in 2019. Total GDP—the sum of personal consumption, private investment, government purchases, and net exports—equaled $21,433.2 billion in 2019. See text for breakdown of numbers.

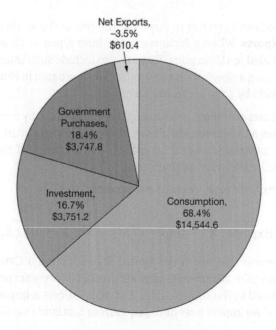

Source: Based on data from Bureau of Economic Analysis, from FRED Economic Data: https://fred.stlouisfed.org/series/PCE; https://fred.stlouisfed.org/series/GPDI; https://fred.stlouisfed.org/series/GCE; and https://fred.stlouisfed.org/series/NETEXP.

Final Goods and Value Added

GDP is the total value of all *final* goods and services produced during a particular period valued at prices in that period. That is not the same as the total value of *all* goods and services produced during that period. This distinction gives us another method of estimating GDP in terms of output.

Suppose, for example, that a logger cuts some trees and sells the logs to a sawmill. The mill makes lumber and sells it to a construction firm, which builds a house. The market price for the lumber includes the value of the logs; the price of the house includes the value of the lumber. As was true when we were discussing the intermediate goods that went into your cinnamon roll, if we try to estimate GDP by adding the value of the logs, the lumber, and the house, we would be counting the lumber twice and the logs three times. Oops!

This does, however, suggest another way to compute GDP. We can estimate, at each stage of production, the **value added**, which is the amount by which the value of a firm's output exceeds the value of the goods and services the firm purchases from other firms. Table 5.1 illustrates the use of value added in the production of a house.

> **value added**
>
> The amount by which the value of a firm's output exceeds the value of the goods and services the firm purchases from other firms.

TABLE 5.1 Final Value and Value Added

If we sum the value added at each stage of the production of a good or service, we get the final value of the item. The example shown here involves the construction of a house, which is produced from lumber that is, in turn, produced from logs.

Good	Produced By	Purchased By	Price ($)	Value Added ($)
Logs	Logger	Sawmill	12,000	12,000
Lumber	Sawmill	Construction firm	25,000	13,000
House	Construction firm	Household	125,000	100,000
		Final Value	**125,000**	
		Sum of Values Added		**125,000**

Suppose the logs produced by the logger are sold for $12,000 to a sawmill, and that the mill sells the lumber it produces from these logs for $25,000 to a construction firm. Then the logger created $12,000 of market value by cutting wild trees into logs, and the sawmill added another $13,000 ($25k – $12k) of value to those logs by transforming them into boards that a construction company values at $25,000. The construction firm, having paid $25,000 for boards, then transforms that lumber into a house worth $125,000 (for convenience, we'll ignore the other things that a house needs, like heat and a bathtub), adding $100,000 ($125k – $25k) of value along the way.

Notice that the sum of values added at each stage ($12,000 + $13,000 + $100,000) equals the final value of the house, $125,000. The value of an economy's output in any period can, therefore, be estimated in either of two ways: The values of final goods and services produced can be added directly, or the values added at each stage in the production process can be added. The Commerce Department uses both approaches in its estimate of the nation's GDP.

> The whole point of value added is that the whole is more than the sum of its parts. Paradoxically, the whole *IS* the sum of its value added!

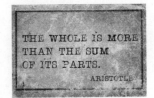

> THE WHOLE IS MORE THAN THE SUM OF ITS PARTS.
> ARISTOTLE

Source: Yury Zap/Shutterstock. com

The Income Approach

We've been measuring the value of a country's output by adding up buyers' expenditures. But every transaction has a buyer and a seller. If the purchase of a cinnamon roll represents $3 of expenditure to the buyer, it's just as accurate to say that it represents $3 of income to the seller. If you reframe every transaction that takes place in an economy in this way, you'll end up concluding that GDP not only represents the total expenditures in the economy; it also represents the economy's total income! In fact, adding up everyone's income is another way we can compute the economy's GDP, a method called the *income approach*.

Loving the Leftovers: "After we pay our baker and pay the rent, the rest is our profit to keep!"

Source: Rawpixel.com/Shutterstock.com

Earlier, we divided expenditure into categories like consumption, investment, and so on. We can do the same thing with income. Think about the $3 you spent on your cinnamon roll. Some of it will go to pay the worker who got up at 4 a.m. to bake the roll. That's called *wage* income. Some of it will be used to pay for the capital that helped make your roll, like the ovens and the storefront. Those payments to capital owners and landlords are called *rents*. And after everyone else has been paid, if there's any money left over, it will go straight into the bakery owner's pocket as *profit*. That's her reward for risking her savings opening up the business in the first place.

Of course, cinnamon rolls aren't made from nothing—there's $2 worth of flour, sugar, yeast, butter, and cinnamon in your cinnamon roll! Those ingredients (intermediate goods, right?) need to be paid for. What should we call *those* payments?

If the baker spends $2 on ingredients, then at the bakery, the remaining $1 will be divided up as wages, rents, and profit. But while the $2 purchase of ingredients represents an expenditure to the baker, it represents income to the flour mill, the spice merchant, and the sugar processor. Those sellers receive their money and divide it just like the baker did: Some goes to pay their workers (wages); some goes to pay for their buildings and equipment (rents) and anything left over becomes profit. Ultimately, the entire $3 purchase price of your cinnamon roll gets divvied up as income somewhere along the supply chain, which means GDP really does measure income, even though the recipients of that income may be scattered throughout the economy.

Key Takeaways

- GDP is the sum of final goods and services produced for consumption (*C*), investment (*I*), government purchases (*G*), and net exports (*X*ₙ). GDP = $C + I + G + X_n$
- Total output can be measured in two ways: as the sum of the values of final goods and services produced, and as the sum of the value added at each stage of production.
- GDP measures total production in an economy, but it also measures the total income received as a result of that production. That income can be broken down into wages, rents, and profits.

Try It!

Consider the following transactions from a small desert island:

- Households spend $100 on fish and coconuts
- Households hire maid services worth $20
- Three new huts are built, worth $70 each
- Two existing huts are sold for $50 each
- Four coconut stands are built for $30 each
- The government sends out Social Security payments totaling $150
- The government buys a $70 war canoe to defend its shores
- The government collects $30 in taxes
- $8 of fish is imported from a neighboring island
- Firms sell $12 of coconuts to a neighboring island

Calculate GDP, broken down by components.

See related Numerical Problem 7 at the end of this chapter.

Case in Point: Hidden Figures—GDP Surprises in the COVID-19 Recession

The COVID-19 recession of 2020 was unlike any other before. Almost literally overnight, output of goods and services plummeted. That decline was so steep that it dwarfed even the drop in output following the legendary Crash of 1929. While many of the features of the COVID-19 recession mimic those we've seen in recessions before, there *were* some hidden (and interesting!) surprises. Let's take a look at the behavior of real GDP and its components and see what tales they tell.

Source: Sam Wordley/Shutterstock.com

Consumption: Perhaps the most interesting story belongs to consumption spending, shown in the figure below. Between late February and April of 2020, consumption spending declined an astonishing 19%. That's not normal! Ordinarily, consumption spending is very stable, even in recessions. Consider, for example, the recession of 2007–2009, shown in the graph below. This was no mild recession—in fact, it's now referred to as the Great Recession. But even in a nasty recession like the Great Recession, consumption didn't start falling until a year after the recession began, and when it did start to decline, it fell gradually, and only by about 4%. What's responsible for the incredible decline in 2020? While uncertainty about the future did cause consumers to hold more tightly to their cash reserves, the lion's share of the decline can be attributed to lockdown measures designed to slow the spread of the coronavirus—there simply was no place to spend money! As quickly as lockdowns eased, spending resumed, returning to its pre-COVID-19 level by January of the next year.

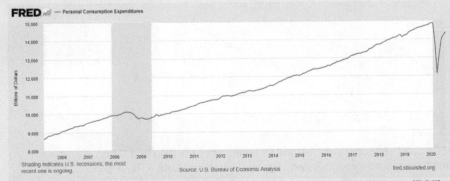

Source: U.S. Bureau of Economic Analysis, Personal Consumption Expenditures [PCE], retrieved from FRED, Federal Reserve Bank of St. Louis; https://fred.stlouisfed.org/series/PCE.

That's part of consumption's story, but not the entire story. One big surprise for market followers was the quick rebound in purchases of goods and services. Particularly telling was the behavior of consumer nondurables, which, after an initial decline, exploded to far beyond pre-pandemic levels. That explosion was driven primarily by tech goods (millions of people working from home need laptops, monitors, and cameras . . . and so did their children, who were suddenly thrust into distance learning whether they wanted to or not). Refrigerators and freezers also sold out rapidly as consumers sought storage for stockpiles of food. Sales of other home goods, including furniture (not normal!), increased rapidly as sheltered workers with little else to do undertook home renovations.

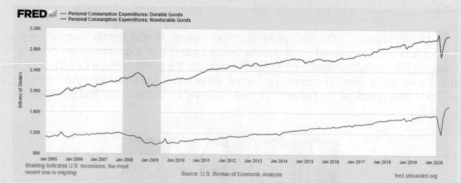

Source: Bureau of Economic Analysis, accessed through Federal Reserve Economic Data (FRED) at https://fred.stlouisfed.org/series/PCEDG and https://fred.stlouisfed.org/series/PCEND. FRED® Graphs ©Federal Reserve Bank of St. Louis. All rights reserved. All FRED® Graphs appear courtesy of Federal Reserve Bank of St. Louis. https://fred.stlouisfed.org/.

So if consumer nondurables quickly returned to their trend, and consumer durables skyrocketed above their trend, why did overall consumption fail to fully recover? The answer lies in the third type of consumption spending: services, which were slow to rebound due largely to social distancing guidelines in public spaces.

Investment: A recession is a lousy time to open or expand a business, and the COVID-19 recession was no exception. Investment has historically been the most volatile component of GDP, falling rapidly in downturns and rising quickly in expansions. As shown in the graph below, between February and April of 2020, overall investment spending declined by 15%. But again, the data contained surprises! For all the turmoil, the housing market remained strong. After a brief decline, existing home sales quickly returned to normal, and housing starts (which shows the number of new housing projects being initiated, shown by the green line below) quickly returned to their pre-pandemic path—an unusual development signaling great confidence in a quick recovery.

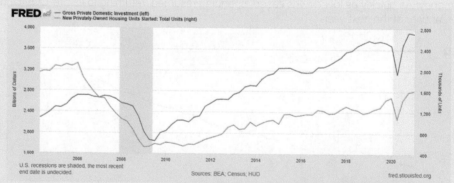

Source: Bureau of Economic Analysis and Department of Housing and Urban Development, accessed through Federal Reserve Economic Data (FRED) at https://fred.stlouisfed.org/series/GPDI and https://fred.stlouisfed.org/series/HOUST. FRED® Graphs ©Federal Reserve Bank of St. Louis. All rights reserved. All FRED® Graphs appear courtesy of Federal Reserve Bank of St. Louis. https://fred.stlouisfed.org/.

Government Purchases: Government purchases (shown in red in the following graph) remained stable during the COVID-19 recession, changing little between February and April. However, that doesn't mean the government was sitting idle hoping the recession would disappear! In fact, the government *was* spending money (as shown by the blue line); it was rapidly expanding transfer payments and other forms of assistance, which are included in government expenditures but not in government purchases or GDP. We'll detail more of the government's policy response in a later chapter.

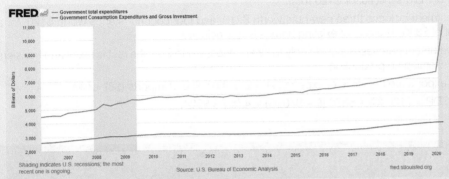

Source: Bureau of Economic Analysis, accessed through Federal Reserve Economic Data (FRED) at https://fred.stlouisfed.org/series/W068RCQ027SBEA and https://fred.stlouisfed. org/series/GCE. FRED® Graphs ©Federal Reserve Bank of St. Louis. All rights reserved. All FRED® Graphs appear courtesy of Federal Reserve Bank of St. Louis. https://fred. stlouisfed.org/.

Net Exports: The last component of GDP is net exports of goods and services. Often during recessions, imports dry up as spending slows, but exports remain on pace; that causes net exports to increase. In the COVID-19 recession, however, both imports *and* exports dried up as countries locked down borders to prevent the virus's spread. With both imports and exports plummeting in roughly equal proportions, net exports didn't change much at all, the only factor of GDP not to take even a temporary turn for the worse in the great coronavirus crisis of 2020.

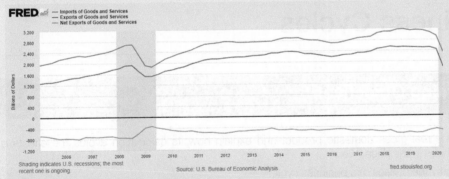

Source: Bureau of Economic Analysis, accessed through Federal Reserve Economic Data (FRED) at https://fred.stlouisfed.org/series/IMPGS; https://fred.stlouisfed.org/series/ EXPGS; and https://fred.stlouisfed.org/series/NETEXP. FRED® Graphs ©Federal Reserve Bank of St. Louis.All rights reserved. All FRED® Graphs appear courtesy of Federal Reserve Bank of St. Louis. https://fred.stlouisfed.org/.

In many ways, the COVID-19 recession ran true to form; almost every big-picture variable behaved like economists would expect: Consumption faltered, investment sagged, imports declined, government responded. In other ways, though, the COVID-19 recession was unprecedented; its speed and severity were unequaled, as was the speed of the rebound. (In ordinary recessions, it often takes about four years to return to trend—in the COVID-19 recession, the rebound in many spending categories was measured in months, not years.) Moreover, the policy response in the COVID-19 recession, as you'll see in later chapters, was orders of magnitude greater than in previous downturns. The atypical COVID-19 recession, then, gives us a new lens to think about the causes, consequences, and cures of recessions, lessons that economists will be learning from, no doubt, for years going forward.

See related Concept Problem 12 at the end of this chapter.

Answers to Try It! Problems

- Consumption spending includes the $100 households spent on fish and coconuts and the $20 of maid services, or $120 total.
- Investment includes three new huts worth $210, and four coconut stands worth $120, for a total of $330. The sale of existing homes is not included.
- Government purchases include only the war canoe, worth $70; the rest is taxes and transfers representing no production.
- Net exports are the value of exports ($12) less the value of imports ($8), or $4.
- So GDP = $120 (C) + $330 (I) + $70 (G) + 4 ($X_n$) = $524.

Khan Academy Links

Income and expenditure views of GDP

Value added view of GDP

Expenditure approach to GDP

Examples of expenditure approach to GDP

5.3 Real GDP, Economic Growth, and Business Cycles

Learning Objectives

1. Define real gross domestic product and explain how its calculation avoids the effects of changes in the price level.
2. Identify the phases of a business cycle.
3. Relate business cycles to the overall long-run trend in real GDP in the United States.

"Think how much hungrier I'd be if these $2 coconuts I've harvested only sold for a dollar."

Source: KOBE611/Shutterstock.com

The purpose of measuring GDP is to give us a sense of the material well-being of a nation's people. But nominal GDP doesn't always do a great job of that.[5] To illustrate, let's visit two Pacific islands, Fanna and Merir, where production is limited to just two goods, fish and coconuts. In 2022, residents of each island produced 100 fish and 100 coconuts, and both fish and coconuts sold for $1 each in the local market. So, in Fanna, GDP for 2022 was $200 (100 fish × $1 each + 100 coconuts × $1 each); in Merir, GDP was also $200.

Then, in 2023, something interesting happened:

- In Fanna, residents worked twice as hard and produced 200 coconuts and 200 fish, which both continued to fetch $1 each in the local market.
- In Merir, residents continued to produce 100 coconuts and 100 fish, but the price of both fish and coconuts doubled to $2 each.

When GDP was calculated, each island's GDP had doubled from $200 to $400. How much richer they'd all become!

Or had they? In Fanna, every resident had twice as many coconuts and fish to enjoy. They really were twice as well off, at least in terms of their material comfort. But what about Merir? It's true that everyone now made twice as much money, but when they took that money to market to buy fish and coconuts, they were dismayed to find that everything cost twice as much. People on Merir were no better off than before, because they had not increased their production of the things that create material happiness.

This raises a thorny problem: GDP is supposed to measure production, but when we see a country's GDP increasing, we can't tell whether it's rising because production is expanding or because prices are rising. To deal with that difficulty, we need to adjust GDP to filter out the effects of rising prices. The measure of output we get when we do this is called **real GDP**, short for real gross domestic product. Real GDP is the market value of all final goods and services produced during a particular year or period, adjusted to eliminate the effects of changes in prices.

To isolate the behavior of output only, we have to hold prices constant at some level. Generally, we pick one year and anchor the prices of goods and services in that year, which is called the *base year*. Real GDP, then, values each year's current output at base-year prices, or

$$\text{Real GDP in Current Period} = (Q_{coconuts_{current}} \times P_{coconuts_{base}} + (Q_{fish_{current}} \times P_{fish_{base}})$$

where a "current" subscript shows the current year's value of a quantity, and a "base" subscript indicates prices from the base-year. In Fanna, real GDP for 2022 would still be \$200,[6] and in 2023, real GDP would be:

$$\text{Fanna's Real GDP}_{2023} = (200 \times \$1) + (200 \times \$1) = \$400$$

Economists would say that Fanna's "real GDP in 2023 was \$400, measured in 2022 dollars." Fanna's output doubled between 2022 and 2023, and so did its real GDP. How about Merir, where current prices for fish and coconuts are \$2, but base year prices were \$1?

$$\text{Merir's Real GDP}_{2023} = (100 \times \$1) + (100 \times \$1) = \$200$$

Merir's residents produced no more fish or coconuts than they did in 2022; their real GDP, unchanged between 2022 and 2023, reflected that.

We want to determine whether the economy's output is growing or shrinking. If each final good or service produced, from hammers to haircuts, were valued at its current market price, and then we were to add the values of all such items produced, we would not know if the total had changed because output changed or because prices changed or both. The market value of all final goods and services produced can rise even if total output falls. To isolate the behavior of total output only, we must hold prices constant at some level. For example, if we measure the value of basketball output over time using a fixed price for valuing the basketballs, then only an increase in the number of basketballs produced could increase the value of the contribution made by basketballs to total output. By making such an adjustment for basketballs and all other goods and services, we obtain a value for real GDP. In contrast, **nominal GDP**, usually just referred to as gross domestic product (GDP), is the total value of final goods and services for a particular period valued in terms of prices for that period. For example, real GDP fell in the third quarter of 2008. But, because the **price level** in the United States was rising, nominal GDP rose 3.6%.

real GDP

The total value of all final goods and services produced during a particular year or period, adjusted to eliminate the effects of changes in prices.

nominal GDP

The total value of final goods and services for a particular period valued in terms of prices for that period.

price level

The average level of prices in an economy.

Business Cycles and the Growth of Real GDP in the United States

Now we know that real GDP tells us how much an economy produces each year. Let's see how real output in the United States has changed over time. Figure 5.2 shows movements in real GDP in the United States from 1960 to the first quarter of 2020. Measured in 2012 dollars, real GDP has increased over five-fold, from about $3,300 billion in 1960 to over $17,300 billion in early 2020. That growth, which has been reasonably steady, averages just under 3% per year.

But while that growth was reasonably steady, it wasn't *perfectly* steady. Over those years, the economy experienced nine economic slowdowns, called *recessions*, during which output generally fell. Those time periods are indicated as shaded areas in the chart, except for the COVID-19 recession of 2020, which began just at the end of the data series. Although periods of expansion have been more prolonged than periods of recession (58 months, on average, for expansions; 11 months, on average, for recessions), some of those recessions have been severe, including the Great Recession of 2007–2009, and the COVID-19 recession of 2020.

FIGURE 5.2 Expansions and Recessions, 1960–2020

The chart shows movements in real GDP since 1960. Recessions—periods of falling real GDP—are shown as shaded areas. On average, the annual rate of growth of real GDP between 1960 and 2020 was 2.8% per year.

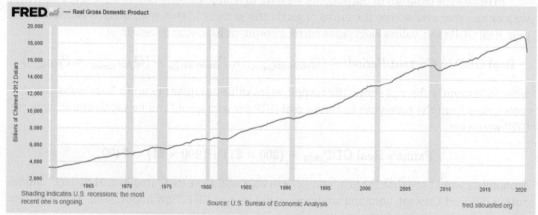

Source: U.S. Bureau of Economic Analysis, Real Gross Domestic Product [GDPC1], retrieved from FRED, Federal Reserve Bank of St. Louis; https://fred.stlouisfed.org/series/GDPC1.

Like San Francisco's famous Lombard Street, the economy gets you from A to B, but follows a winding path to do it.

Source: Maks Ershov/Shutterstock.com

expansion

A sustained period in which real GDP is rising.

recession

A sustained period in which real GDP is falling.

The fluctuations of real GDP around its long-term trend are referred to as the *business cycle*. That terminology, however, can be misleading, as the word "cycle" implies some degree of regularity and predictability, like the phases of the moon. Business cycles, in contrast, are anything but regular and predictable. Each recession, for example, varies in both length and severity. Each expansion does, too: Compare, for example, the long, sustained expansion between 2009 and 2020 to the short expansion that occurred between the "double-dip" recessions of the early 1980s.

Let's dig a bit deeper into the terminology and mechanics of the business cycle. Figure 5.3 shows a stylized picture of a typical business cycle. Like the real-world data shown in Figure 5.2, it shows an economy that goes through periods of increasing and decreasing real GDP, but one that, over time, shows an overall increase. It shows sustained periods in which real GDP is rising, called **expansions**; it also shows periods when real GDP is falling, called **recessions**. Typically, an economy is said to be in a recession when real GDP drops for two consecutive quarters, but in the United States, the responsibility of defining precisely when the economy is in recession is left to the Business Cycle Dating Committee of the National Bureau of Economic Research (NBER). The committee defines a recession as a "significant decline in economic activity spread across the economy, lasting more than a few months, normally visible in real GDP, real income, employment, industrial production, and wholesale-retail sales."[7]

At time t_1 in Figure 5.3, an expansion ends and real GDP turns downward. The point at which an expansion ends and a recession begins is called the **peak** of the business cycle. Real GDP then falls during a period of recession. Eventually, at time t_2, real GDP changes course and starts upward again. The point at which a recession ends and an expansion begins is called the **trough** of the business cycle. The expansion continues until another peak is reached at time t_3.[8] A complete business cycle is defined by the passage from one peak to the next.

FIGURE 5.3 Phases of the Business Cycle

The business cycle is a series of expansions and contractions in real GDP. The cycle begins at a peak and continues through a recession, a trough, and an expansion. A new cycle begins at the next peak. Here, the first peak occurs at time t_1, the trough at time t_2, and the next peak at time t_3. Notice that there is a tendency for real GDP to rise over time.

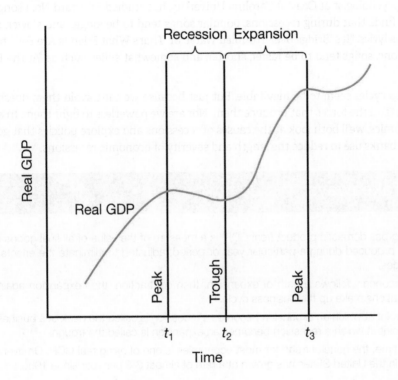

Because the Business Cycle Dating Committee dates peaks and troughs by specific months, and because real GDP is estimated only on a quarterly basis by the Bureau of Economic Analysis, the committee relies on a variety of other indicators that are published monthly, including real personal income, employment, industrial production, and real wholesale and retail sales. The committee typically determines that a recession has happened long after it has actually begun, and sometimes even after it has ended! In large part, that avoids problems when data released about the economy are revised, and the committee avoids having to reverse itself on its determination of when a recession begins or ends, something it has never done. For example, the recession that began in December 2007 wasn't announced until a full year later, in December 2008; in September 2010, the committee announced that this recession had ended over a year earlier, in June 2009. The NBER was much quicker to declare the COVID-19 recession of 2020: The collapse in economic activity that began in February was so large and so rapid that by early June the recession had been both declared and dated.

Economists have sought for centuries to explain the forces at work in a business cycle. Not only are the currents that move the economy up or down intellectually fascinating, but also an understanding of them is of tremendous practical importance. A business cycle is more than just a movement along a curve in a textbook. It is new jobs for people, or the loss of them. It is new income, or the loss of it. It is the funds to build new schools or to provide better health care—or the lack of funds to do all those things. The story of the business cycle is the story of progress and plenty, of failure and sacrifice.

The effects of recessions extend beyond the purely economic realm and influence the social fabric of society as well. Property crimes like burglary, larceny, and motor vehicle theft tend to rise during recessions. So-called deaths of despair, from suicide, alcoholism, and drug overdoses, are closely tied to economic conditions as well. Even popular music appears to be affected. Terry F. Pettijohn II, a psychologist at Coastal Carolina University, has studied Billboard No. 1 songs from 1955 to 2003. He finds that during recessions, popular songs tend to be longer and slower, and to have more serious lyrics. "It's 'Bridge over Troubled Water' or 'That's What Friends Are For'," he says. During expansions, songs tend to be faster, shorter, and somewhat sillier, such as "At the Hop" or "My Sharona."[9]

Business cycles seem to be inevitable. But just because we can't avoid them doesn't mean we can't understand the forces that produce them. Nor are we powerless to fight them. In our study of macroeconomics, we'll both look at the causes of recessions and explore policies that governments and central banks use to reduce the length and severity of economic recessions.

Key Takeaways

- Real gross domestic product (real GDP) is a measure of the value of all final goods and services produced during a particular year or period, adjusted to eliminate the effects of price changes.
- The economy follows a path of expansion, then contraction, then expansion again. These fluctuations make up the business cycle.
- The point at which an expansion becomes a recession is called the peak of a business cycle; the point at which a recession becomes an expansion is called the trough.
- Over time, the general trend for most economies is one of rising real GDP. On average, real GDP in the United States has grown at a rate of almost 3% per year since 1960.

Try It!

The data below show the behavior of real GDP in Iceland from 2005 through 2013. Use the data to plot real GDP in Iceland and indicate the phases of the business cycle.

Period	Real GDP (Billions of Icelandic Krona, 2010 Prices)
2005	397.43
2006	422.53
2007	458.26
2008	468.38
2009	432.49
2010	420.24
2011	427.99

Period	Real GDP (Billions of Icelandic Krona, 2010 Prices)
2012	432.55
2013	452.24

See related Numerical Problem 1 at the end of this chapter.

Case in Point: Predicting Recessions—Satisfaction (Not) Guaranteed

"An economist is an expert who will know tomorrow why the things he predicted yesterday didn't happen today." —Laurence Peter[10]

> *"C'mon, lady, tell me when the next recession will be: My career on Wall Street depends on it!"*

Source: Everett Collection/Shutterstock.com

It's good to be paid for being wrong, and for those who worry they don't have the stage presence to be a TV meteorologist, economics might be a good fallback. The truth is that economists make great money . . . and they do a lousy job of actually predicting what is going to happen in the economy! For example, in an impressive display of hindsight, the fifty-two economists that the *Wall Street Journal* polls each month *did* predict that the economy would slip into a recession in the third quarter of 2008. They made that prediction, however, in October—*after the third quarter had ended*!

Predicting business cycle turning points has always been a tricky business. Economists are so bad at it, in fact, the Nobel Prize winner Paul Samuelson once quipped they had "successfully predicted nine out of the last five recessions." But while Samuelson may sense that economists are too eager to predict a downturn, actual evidence suggests the opposite: Economists often fail to see them coming. In 2001, International Monetary Fund economist Prakash Loungani once said, "The record of failure to predict recessions is virtually unblemished."

More recently, Loungani put his money where his mouth is. Together with economists Zidong An and João Tovar Jalles, Loungani looked at a large number of GDP forecasts covering sixty-three countries for the twenty-two-year period between 1992 and 2014. During that time span, there were 153 recessionary years (where a recessionary year is a year of declining real GDP). At any given time, about 10% of the countries surveyed were experiencing one.

Surely, with 10% of countries in a recessionary year at any given moment, economists could forecast at least 10% of the recessions, right? Nope, not even close. According to Loungani, in April of the year before the recession, forecasters expected output to fall in only 5 of these 153 cases—a remarkable 3% success rate. So bad were professional forecasters at predicting recessions that in September 2008, when the Great Recession was well underway in the United States and had spread across the globe, the consensus was *still* that not a single economy would fall into recession by 2009. George Washington University economist Tara Sinclair says that's par for the course: "There's no economic data or research or analysis that suggests we can look 12 months into the future and predict recessions with any confidence."[11]

That doesn't mean that there aren't some economists who have made great calls. Case in point, Yale economist Robert Schiller, who forecast the 2000 stock market collapse and subsequent recession, as well as the looming housing market collapse that touched off the Great Recession of 2007–2009. But Schiller was a lone voice among many, and that's problematic, according to Loungani. He asserts that economists are often hesitant to risk their reputations by predicting a crisis that never materializes; far better to hedge your bets by publishing moderate forecasts more in agreement with your peers. In the words of economist Edgar Fiedler, "The herd instinct among forecasters makes sheep look like independent thinkers."

The truth is that the macroeconomy is an extremely complex web of interconnected markets, subject to meddling by policymakers, and largely driven by psychology and animal spirits. Forecasting where it will be a year in the future is incredibly difficult . . . especially now that we know how quickly the world can change. Events like raging new viruses can stymie even prominent experts like Schiller, who in September 2019 put the odds of a 2020 recession at less than half. So, for giving both amateur and professional prognosticators a better understanding of just how unpredictable recessions can be, "*Thanks, coronavirus?*"

See related Concept Problem 2 at the end of this chapter.

Sources: Based on Paul Davidson, "Robert Shiller, who predicted dot-com crash, sees less than 50% chance of recession in '20," USA Today, September 9, 2019; Ameila Thomson-DeVeaux, "Economists Are Bad at Predicting Recessions," Fivethirtyeight.com, August 21, 2019; and Prakash Loungani, Zidong An, and João Tovar Jalles, "How Well Do Economists Forecast Recessions," IMF Working Paper, March 5, 2018.

Answer to Try It! Problem

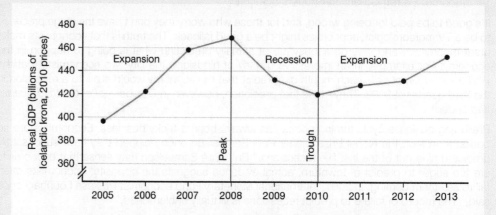

Khan Academy Links

Real and nominal GDP

Business cycles

5.4 GDP and Economic Well-Being

Learning Objectives

1. Discuss and give examples of measurement and conceptual problems in using real GDP as a measure of economic performance and of economic well-being.
2. Explain the use of per capita real GNP or GDP to compare economic performance across countries and discuss its limitations.

Let's recap what we've learned so far in this chapter:

- A country's material well-being depends on its output of goods and services.
- The measure most commonly used to capture the value of goods and services produced in an economy is (nominal) GDP.
- An even better measure of output, real GDP, filters out the influence of rising prices.

There's one more small wrinkle in the use of real GDP to capture a sense of how well people in a society live. Consider the economies, for example, of Brazil and the United Kingdom. Real GDP for 2020 in both these economies is about $3 trillion. Does that mean that the typical Brazilian has a standard of living (i.e., lives about as comfortably) roughly equivalent to the typical Brit?

Well, it would, if those economic pies were shared by the same numbers of people. But they're not! Brazil's real GDP has to be divided among 210 million people; Great Britain's is divided among only 67 million. That means that the typical Brazilian has a real income of about $14,000, while the typical Brit brings home about $45,000. We call this population-adjusted measure of output and income[12] *real GDP per capita*, and comparing these figures across nations (or even to your own real GDP per capita, which in the United States is about $63,000 per year) is a decent way to compare the standard of living people in different places enjoy.

$$\text{Real GDP Per Capita} = \frac{\text{Real GDP}}{\text{Population}}$$

Let's take a brief snapshot of real GDP and real GDP per capita across the globe. In 2020, the world's largest economy belonged to China, as shown in Panel (a) of Figure 5.4. Despite its tremendous aggregate performance, however, China still ranks as a middle-income country once adjusted for population, in Panel (b). China's real GDP per capita of $17,206 places it just behind Mexico's $18,804 and Argentina's $20,370. The United States is the world's second-largest economy overall, and ranks seventh overall in terms of GDP per capita, and the world's richest place in per capita terms is Luxembourg, with a per capita income over $112,000. The Democratic Republic of Congo, in contrast, is one of the world's poorer places with its per capita income of $4,233.

FIGURE 5.4 Real GDP and Real GDP Per Capita in Selected Countries, 2020

Panel (a) shows that the world's largest economy is China's, at over $24 trillion. Nevertheless, once adjusted for population, China is a fairly ordinary middle-income country, as shown in Panel (b). Luxembourg's small economy produces the highest standard of living on the planet, with per capita real GDP over $112,000.

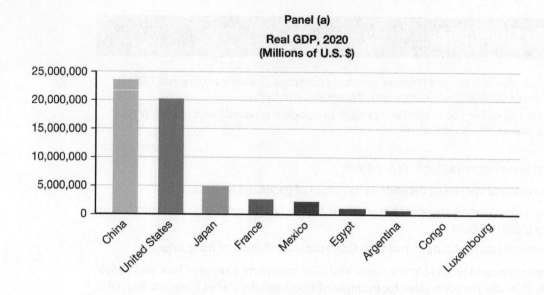

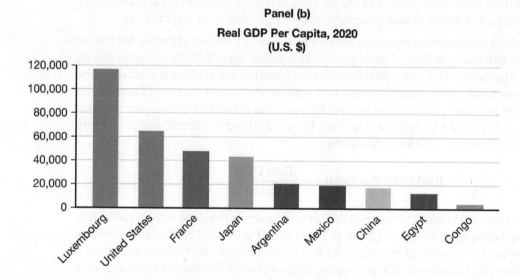

Source: Data from International Monetary Fund's International Financial Statistics database at data.imf.org.

That snapshot of real GDP per capita gives us a good idea of what it's like to live in various places around the world. But it's not a perfect idea, because as a measure of well-being, GDP has a few failings. The next sections explore those flaws in detail.

Pop! Goes the Econ: Life in Other Places

People in different countries live very different lives. Gapminder's Dollar Street website gives you a photo-based look at what other peoples' lives are like—from their wristwatches to their beds to their most cherished items. A visit to Dollar Street is a great way to spend a few hours!

Measurement Problems in Real GDP

GDP may provide a measure of a country's output, but it's not a perfect measure. That's because it would take too long to count up everything a country makes, so to save time and effort, the Bureau of Economic Analysis estimates GDP. That creates a couple of issues that may, at any given moment, paint a distorted picture of the economy's production.

Revisions

The first issue with using GDP as a guide to the true state of production deals with the quality of the data used in the BEA's estimate. Actually, the BEA estimates GDP for a particular time period not once, but *three* times.

The first estimate of real GDP for a calendar quarter is called the *advance estimate*. It is issued about a month after the quarter ends. To produce a measure so quickly, officials at the Department of Commerce must rely on information from relatively few firms and households. One month later, it issues a revised estimate drawn from more data points, and a month after that it issues its final estimate. Often, the advance estimate of GDP and the final estimate do not agree. Near the end of the Great Recession of 2007–2009, advance estimates of fourth-quarter 2008 GDP showed that the U.S. economy shrank by 3.8%. The first revision, however, showed a drop of 6.8%, and the second revision showed a drop of 8.9%—over twice the drop of the advance figures!

You'd think that two revisions would be plenty, but that's not good enough for the Department of Commerce, which oversees the BEA. Every summer, it goes back in time yet again and issues revised figures for the previous two or three years. And if that weren't enough, once every five years, the department conducts an extensive analysis that traces flows of inputs and outputs throughout the economy, and in the process of doing so, revises real GDP estimates for the previous five years once again! Sometimes those revisions can paint a picture of economic activity that is quite different from the one given even by the revised estimates of GDP. For example, revisions of the data for the 1990–1991 recession issued several years later showed that the recession had been much more serious than had previously been apparent, and the recovery more pronounced.

The Service Sector

Another problem lies in estimating production in the service sector. The output of goods in an economy is relatively easy to compute. There are so many bushels of corn, so many pounds of beef. But what is the output of a bank? Of a hospital? It's easy to record the dollar value of output to enter for nominal GDP, but estimating the quantity of output to use in real GDP is a different matter. In some cases, the Department of Commerce estimates service-sector output based on the quantity of labor used. For example, if this technique were used in the banking industry and banks used 10% more labor, the department would report that production rose by 10%. If the number of employees remained unchanged, reported output would remain unchanged. Unfortunately, this approach assumes that output per worker—productivity—in those sectors remains constant, yet studies have indicated that productivity has increased greatly in the service sector. Since 1990 extra effort has been devoted to measurement of services to allow for better estimation of productivity changes, but more remains to be done, and it's important to do so: Services make up a full 2/3 of all economic activity in the U.S. economy, so measuring them as accurately as possible is quite important.[13]

What a relief to dine out again! The COVID-19 crisis gave us a new understanding of how large a role services play in our lives, and how much happiness a vibrant service sector creates for us.

Source: Drazen Zigic/Shutterstock.com

Conceptual Problems with Real GDP

A second set of limitations of real GDP stems from problems inherent in the indicator itself. Real GDP measures market activity. Goods and services that are produced and exchanged in a market are counted; goods and services that are produced but that are not exchanged in markets are not.[14]

Household Production

You're hungry . . . and you need to take care of it fast! You're not a bad cook; with the food you've got in your cabinets and an hour of your time, you could whip up a pretty nice meal. But maybe you don't want to wait for an hour—maybe you'd rather just pick up some takeout from the local ramen shop. Hmmmm . . . the possibilities!

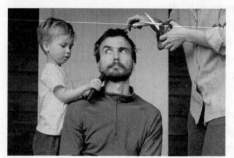

That quarantine haircut isn't doing much for GDP . . . or your hair.

Source: Gargonia/Shutterstock.com

Believe it or not, those possibilities have some pretty big implications for GDP. When you order takeout, GDP increases. But because no market transaction occurs when you cook for yourself, there's no impact on GDP. Either way, of course, work takes place—either you cook or someone else does, but only in the carryout case does GDP rise to reflect that work. In the same way, GDP does not count the value of your efforts to wash your own car, grow your own vegetables, or homeschool your children. As economist Greg Mankiw wryly notes, if you decide to marry your housekeeper, that may cause GDP to fall!

There's reason to believe this omission is serious. Economists J. Steven Landefeld and Stephanie H. McCulla once estimated that household production accounted for a full third of the nation's production at the end of World War II! That number has fallen over time, especially because more women entered the workforce and substituted market production for household production. But as recently as 2017, the BEA estimated that household production accounted for 1/5 of the country's total production.[15]

Household production generally makes up a much greater share of total production in developing economies, which makes international comparisons difficult. In Congo, for example, per capita GDP is only about $400 per month. But many Congolese grow their own food, raise and educate their own children, wash their own clothes, and cook their own meals, which means that they enjoy a higher material standard of living than their low (market-based) per capita GDP estimates may indicate.

The Underground Economy

Now we know that GDP understates true economic well-being because household production isn't based on market transactions. But sometimes, even transactions that take place in the market aren't included in GDP. Sometimes that happens because production goes unreported in order to evade taxes or the law. For example, a carpenter might build a small addition to a dentist's house in exchange for orthodontic work for the carpenter's children. Although income has been earned and output generated, this exchange won't appear in GDP.

There are other transactions that won't appear in GDP either, mainly because reporting them could earn buyer or seller an all-expenses-paid vacation to the local penitentiary. Consider, for example, a glaucoma sufferer in Coolidge, Kansas, who purchases a marijuana brownie from a trusted friend. That transaction won't be reported in GDP. Oddly, if she'd purchased the brownie at a legal dispensary in seven-miles-distant Holly, Colorado, GDP would have risen by the value of her treat!

Economic activity left unreported to avoid taxes or jail time generally takes place in what is referred to as the "underground economy." That activity isn't inconsequential: It is estimated that the underground economy in the United States might amount to as much as $2 trillion each year. But not all people who fail to report their transactions are trying to escape government scrutiny. In many countries, commerce isn't as organized and computerized as it is in the United States. In developing countries, a great deal of business is often conducted out of homes, carts, or on blankets spread out on the sidewalk. Governments often lack the means to track and record the transactions that take place in this "informal economy." Those transactions, like the underground transactions in the United States, are significant: In Zimbabwe and Bolivia, the informal economy is estimated to be almost 2/3 the size of the official economy.

So although GDP might measure a great deal of the economy's production, it likely doesn't measure it all. That can make international comparisons difficult. For example, if GDP per capita in the United States is $50,000, but there is no underground or informal activity, while GDP per capita in Uruguay is $30,000 but each person generates $20,000 of informal activity, too, then the United States and Uruguay will have identical standards of living, but Uruguayans will look much poorer than Americans on paper.

"How many times I gotta tell you: Never leave a paper trail!" Talk-show host Jerry Springer's political career was derailed in 1974 when police raiding a brothel found a bad check he'd written pinned to the wall. That's one transaction he doesn't want included in GDP . . . or in a campaign ad!

Source: s_bukley/Shutterstock.com

Leisure

Consider this paradox: Zoe enjoys a nice beer, and when she orders one at her favorite taproom, GDP rises by $5. Zoe also enjoys a good nap, and when she takes one, GDP doesn't rise at all. In fact, if she calls in sick to work for a "me day," GDP might actually fall!

In other words, GDP accounts for the fact that our well-being depends on our consumption of *things*, but it fails to account for the fact that well-being also depends on our consumption of *leisure*. Consider the problem that creates when making international comparisons: In the United States, the typical employed person works 35 hours each week, but in Germany, the typical worker only works 26. The problem is bigger than that, though, because some adults choose to consume only leisure and produce nothing. A couple might decide that a second earner's income isn't worth the trouble; a professor might retire early to enjoy some time in the woodshop. Once we include the leisure these people enjoy, the typical American adult puts in 25 hours; the typical Italian only 16. So Americans will have high reported incomes, but no time to enjoy them, Italians will look poor (and therefore unhappy?) on paper, but will enjoy lots of fulfilling idle time that is not reflected in GDP.

Better Than a Pedicure: This young lady is clearly enjoying her downtime, but its value won't be counted in GDP.

Source: 9nong/Shutterstock.com

GDP Ignores "Bads"

Suppose a wave of burglaries were to break out across the United States. One would expect people to respond by buying more and louder burglar alarms, better locks, fiercer German shepherds, and more guard services than they had before. Those transactions would cause GDP to increase. An epidemic might have much the same effect by driving up health-care spending. But that doesn't mean that crime and disease are good things; it means only that crime and disease may force an increase in the production of goods and services counted in the GDP.

Mixed Message: "No time to fix that catalytic converter—gotta get to work and make some GDP."

Similarly, the GDP accounts ignore the impact of pollution on the environment. We might produce an additional $200 billion in goods and services but create pollution that makes us feel worse off by, say, $300 billion. The GDP accounts simply report the $200 billion in increased production and neglect the environmental degradation. By failing to account for economic bads, GDP tends to overstate a country's true standard of living.

Source: LanaElcova/Shutterstock.com

GDP Says Nothing About the Income Distribution

Gross domestic product is a total, arrived at by adding up the value of all production. GDP per capita is an average, arrived at by dividing the total by the population. GDP per capita is supposed to tell us something about how the typical person lives. Unfortunately, the averaging process can distort the picture of what the average Josephine's life is actually like.

Consider two neighboring islands, each with five residents. On one island, each resident earns $200,000. Total GDP is $1 million, and GDP per capita is $200,000. Here, GDP does a great job of describing the life of the typical resident! But on the neighboring island, four people earn $20,000 each, while the fifth brings home $920,000. On this island, GDP is also $1 million and per capita GDP is also $200,000, but you'd be hard pressed to say that per capita GDP describes the life of the typical resident very well.

Ultimately, measures of GDP are expressed as a single number. A single number, even an average, may do a poor job of describing the life of the average person, and a simple average like GDP per capita has zero ability to describe the variation or distribution in the standard of living across individuals. We'll need another set of tools to do that; we develop those tools in our chapter on income inequality.

GDP, Redeemed

We now know that GDP has its flaws, and probably does only a fair job of measuring the material well-being of a nation's people. And yet, GDP and its variants are almost always our go-to statistics when we need to assess or compare standards of living. Why is it that we rely on such a flawed measure?

For one thing, flawed as it is, we haven't been able to come up with a measure that's *less* flawed. The second reason is more compelling: GDP may not capture *everything* we care about, but it is so strongly correlated with things we *do* care about that it provides a decent guide to how an economy is doing. For all its faults, GDP *does* measure the production of most goods and services. Those goods and services get produced, for the most part, because we want and enjoy them. It means more jobs and more income, and most people seem to place a high value on these things.

But it's not just jobs and material goods that GDP brings with it. Consider, for example, something that almost everyone cares about: children. Someday, you're likely to have one (or more) of your own. Wouldn't it be nice to know that your child is going to live a long life, and maybe even have children of her own someday? Of course! Yet, we know there are no guarantees—some children don't even make it to their first day of kindergarten.

Unfortunately, your child's chance of making it to kindergarten depends critically on where he or she happened to be born. Let's take a look at a hundred-odd countries' child mortality numbers, and see if we can pinpoint anything that might affect your own child's chances. That's done in Figure 5.5, where each dot represents a different country, arranged left to right in order of increasing real GDP per capita.

In Figure 5.5, the height of each dot measures the number of children out of every thousand born who fill fail to live until their fifth birthday. The unluckiest place to be born on earth is Chad, where 123 out of every thousand born will die before turning five. Compare that to Finland, with the lowest child mortality rate of less than two per 1,000 born.

FIGURE 5.5 Real GDP and Child Mortality, 2018
Real GDP per capita is highly correlated with meaningful life outcomes like child mortality. The higher a country's real GDP per capita, the lower the odds of a child's passing away before their fifth birthday.

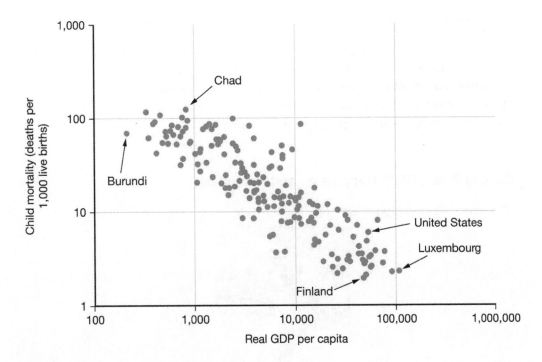

Source: Based on data from Gapminder.org via https://bit.ly/3uMxzb4.

Is it coincidence that Finland is relatively rich and Chad relatively poor? Not so much. The pattern in the graph shows clearly the general pattern of increased income reducing child mortality. Part of that is causal: Earning more money allows you to afford better food, clean water, and better health care. Part is less direct: Political strife and civil war tend to happen more often in lower-income countries, disrupting markets and increasing mortality. Nevertheless, GDP turns out to be so strongly correlated with so many indicators of well-being that, despite its flaws, it remains our go-to in assessing the quality of life across the globe.[16]

Pop! Goes the Econ: 200 Countries, 200 Years, and 4 Minutes of Wealth and Health
Late global health expert Hans Rosling demonstrates the importance of income in producing well-being. What measure of well-being does he use? And how does it change over time?

View in the online reader

Key Takeaways

- Real GDP (or real GDP per capita) is often used as an indicator of the economic well-being of a country.
- Problems in the measurement of real GDP, in addition to problems encountered in converting from nominal to real GDP, stem from revisions in the data and the difficulty of measuring output in some sectors, particularly the service sector.
- Conceptual problems in the use of real GDP as a measure of economic well-being include the facts that it does not include nonmarket production, doesn't include the underground and informal economies, fails to capture the income distribution, and does not properly adjust for "bads" produced in the economy.
- Per capita real GDP remains highly correlated with many desirable life outcomes, and it can be used to compare economic performance in different countries.

Try It!

What impact would each of the following have on real GDP? Would economic well-being increase or decrease as a result?

1. Locked down due to a pandemic, and with more time on their hands, people in a country decide to bake more bread at home and buy less from the store.
2. Spending on homeland security increases in response to a terrorist attack.
3. The price level and nominal GDP increase by 10%.

See related Concept Problem 9 at the end of this chapter.

Case in Point: GDP, Happiness, and Hemlines

"The economy's looking good, Bob. Real good."

Source: Julia Strekoza/Shutterstock.com

In 1926, economist George Taylor made an unusual observation: The length of a woman's skirt correlated well with the success or failure of the stock market. Stock prices rising? Hemlines up! Market plummeting? Hems at the floor! Taylor's observation soon became a theory both widely studied and widely quoted: A booming economy lifts peoples' spirits, and skirt length creeps up to match that feel-good vibe. But there's a virtuous circle: Economic booms can be fueled by optimism, which means that if skirts start getting shorter—evidence of good feeling—there might be good things ahead for the economy.

Anecdotal evidence seems to support Taylor's theory. The short skirts of the roaring 20s; the miniskirts of the prosperous 1960s and 1990s all argue in favor. So do the long skirts of the Great Depression, and the midi-length skirts that appeared after the stock market crash in 1987. Taylor's hypothesis got such heavy traction that the Fort Worth *Star-Telegram* once said, "If you see a guy in a three-piece suit staring out the window at female legs this autumn, don't jump to sexist conclusions . . . he could be diligently seeking clues to the financial future."

If so, though, he'd better look elsewhere, at least according to Marjolein van Baardwijk and Philip Hans Franses. Accessing almost a century's worth of the monthly French fashion magazine *L'Officiel*, they carefully measured the average hem length. Then, the duo compared the timing of skirt length changes to the NBER's official chronology of economic recessions. Frances and van Baardwijk *did* find a correlation between the two—in other words, Taylor's eyes weren't deceiving him. Their research shows that hemlines follow economic activity with about a three-year lag. That makes perfect sense to economist Bernard Baumohl, who observed that when the economy turns bad, more women have to go back to work. "They need to look more professional," Baumohl notes, "so they tend to buy dresses with a longer hemline."

Unfortunately for financial prognosticators, van Baardwijk and Franses found no evidence of a virtuous circle: While swings in the economy today were able to predict future skirt length, changes in skirt length today had no power to predict the future state of the economy. In other words, the hemline hypothesis is real, but it's of no use to Fort Worth financial professionals seeking clues about market direction—those guys really *are* only looking at legs. Instead, the hemline hypothesis turns out to be useful only to people hoping to forecast fashion trends—people like George Taylor, whose 1929 Ph.D. dissertation addressed yet another hemline theory: The usefulness of hemline length in predicting the demand for silk stockings.

See related Concept Problem 13 at the end of this chapter.

Sources: Based on Yifan Yu, "Hemline Index Actually Works! Just Not the Way You Thought," at medium.com, September 25, 2016; Marlen Komar, "Is the Hemline Index Actually Real?" InStyle.com, September 1, 2020; and Marjolein van Baardwijk and Philip Hans Franses "The Hemline and the Economy: Is There Any Match?" Econometric Institute Research Papers EI 2010-40, Erasmus University Rotterdam, Erasmus School of Economics (ESE), Econometric Institute.

Answers to Try It! Problems

1. Real GDP would decrease, as market transactions are replaced with household production. Assuming that people prefer homemade bread (and now have the time to bake it), economic well-being would increase, all else equal.

2. Real GDP would increase, but the extra expenditure in the economy was due to an increase in something "bad," so economic well-being would likely be lower.

3. No change in real GDP. For some people, economic well-being might increase and for others it might decrease, since inflation does not affect each person in the same way.

Khan Academy Link

Limitations of GDP

5.5 Review and Practice

Summary

In this chapter, we introduced the macroeconomy and explored various measures of an economy's output. Chief among them was gross domestic product, or GDP.

In looking at GDP as a measure of output, we divide it into four components: consumption, investment, government purchases, and net exports. GDP equals the sum of final values produced in each of these areas. It can also be measured as the sum of values added at each stage of production. GDP also measures income, including wages, rent, and profits.

Examining real GDP, rather than nominal GDP, over time tells us whether the economy is expanding or contracting. Real GDP in the United States shows a long upward trend, but with the economy going through phases of expansion and recession around that trend. These phases make up the business cycle. An expansion reaches a peak, and the economy falls into a recession. The recession reaches a trough and begins an expansion again.

GDP is often used as an indicator of how well off a country is. To use it for this purpose, we must be careful to use real GDP rather than nominal GDP, and to express it in per capita terms.

As a summary measure of an economy's output and income, GDP is imperfect, suffering from both measurement problems and conceptual problems. Frequent revisions in the data sometimes change our picture of the economy considerably. Accounting for the service sector is quite difficult. Conceptual problems include the omission of nonmarket production and of underground and illegal production. GDP ignores the value of leisure, and conceals the underlying income distribution. It also neglects to account for economic bads.

We cannot assert with confidence that more GDP is a good thing and that less is bad. However, real GDP remains our best single indicator of economic performance. It is used not only to indicate how any one economy is performing over time but also to compare the economic performance of different countries.

Concept Problems

1. Describe the phases of a business cycle.

2. (Related to "Case in Point: Predicting Recessions—Satisfaction (Not) Guaranteed" in Section 17.3.) On the basis of recent news reports, what phase of the business cycle do you think the economy is in now? Can you predict when the next recession might be? What factors hinder your ability to predict the next recession?

3. Suppose you compare your income this year and last year and find that your nominal income fell but your real income rose. How could this have happened?

4. GDP is used as a measure of macroeconomic performance. What, precisely, does it measure?

5. Many economists have attempted to create a set of social accounts that would come closer to measuring the economic well-being of society than does GDP. What modifications of the current approach would you recommend to them?

6. Every good produced creates income for the owners of the factors of production that created the product or service. For a recent purchase you made, try to list all the types of factors of production involved in making the product available, and try to determine who received income as a result of your purchase.

7. Explain how the sale of used textbooks in your campus bookstore affects the GDP calculation.

8. Suggest an argument for and an argument against counting in GDP all household-produced goods and services that are not sold, such as the value of child care or home-cooked meals.

9. (Related to "Try It!" in Section 17.4.) Suppose that virtually everyone in the United States decides to take life a little easier, and the length of the average workweek falls by 25%. How will that affect GDP? Per capita GDP? How will it affect economic welfare?

10. Some countries, for example the United Kingdom and Italy, have recently decided to include some illegal activities, such as drugs and prostitution, in their calculations of GDP. Other countries do not do this. Should such activities be included? What are some pros and cons?[17]

11. Name some of the services, if any, you produced at home that do get counted in GDP. Are there any goods you produce that are not counted?

12. (Related to "Case in Point: Hidden Figures—GDP Surprises in the COVID-19 Recession" in Section 17.2.) Access the FRED database and follow the links in this case's figure sources. Compare and contrast the behavior of consumption, investment, government spending, and net exports both entering and exiting the COVID-19 recession. Then, compare and contrast the behavior of those GDP components in the COVID-19 recession to how they usually behave during recessions.

13. (Related to "Case in Point: GDP, Happiness, and Hemlines" in Section 17.4.) When trying to predict recessions, economists often look at variables that change *before* real GDP starts to change. Those *leading indicators* include average weekly hours worked in manufacturing, new orders for capital goods by manufacturers, and durable goods orders by consumers. In contrast, *lagging indicators* (like corporate profits and consumer confidence) tend to change

after the economy enters a new phase of the business cycle. According to the case, do most people regard skirt length as a leading or a lagging indicator? What does the evidence suggest?

Numerical Problems

1. (Related to "Try It!" in Section 17.3.) Plot the quarterly data for real GDP for the last two years. (You can find the data online at this link. Relate recent changes in real GDP to the concept of the phases of the business cycle.)

2. Suppose a country's GDP equals $500 billion for a particular year. Economists in the country estimate that household production equals 40% of GDP.

   a. What is the value of the country's household production for that year?

   b. Counting both GDP and household production, what is the country's total output for the year?

3. Find data for each of the following countries on real GDP and population. Use the data to calculate the GDP per capita for each of the following countries:

   a. Mozambique

   b. Singapore

   c. Pakistan

   d. Colombia

   e. Russia

   f. Botswana

   g. Philippines

   h. United States

   i. Canada

4. Now construct a column graph showing your results in the previous problem, organizing the countries from the highest to the lowest GDP per capita, with countries on the horizontal axis and GDP per capita on the vertical axis.

5. Suppose you are given the following data for an economy:

Month	Real GDP ($)	Employment
1	10.0 trillion	100 million
2	10.4 trillion	104 million
3	10.5 trillion	105 million
4	10.3 trillion	103 million
5	10.2 trillion	102 million
6	10.3 trillion	103 million
7	10.6 trillion	106 million
8	10.7 trillion	107 million
9	10.6 trillion	106 million

   a. Plot the data for real GDP, with the time period on the horizontal axis and real GDP on the vertical axis.

   b. There are two peaks. When do they occur?

   c. When does the trough occur?

6. A miner extracts iron from the earth. A steel mill converts the iron to steel beams for use in construction. A construction company uses the steel beams to make a building. Assume

that the total product of these firms represents the only components of the building and that they will have no other uses. Complete the following table:

Firm	Product	Sales ($)	Value Added
Acme Mining	Iron Ore	100,000	
Fuller Mill	Steel Beams	270,000	
K&B Construction	Building	1,200,000	
Total Value Added			

7. (Related to "Try It!" in Section 17.2.) Consider the following transactions, from a small island economy. Use them to calculate GDP, broken down by category.

- Residents buy $200 of locally grown carrots.
- A local contractor builds three new houses, which sell for $800 each.
- That same contractor buys a custom crowbar from a local blacksmith for $100.
- Residents sell $300 of fish to people in South Dakota.
- Residents purchase $200 of bread flour from farmers in South Dakota.
- The government collects $400 in taxes, and then spends $100 on transfer payments and $300 building a new community center.
- The blacksmith spends $250 on a used car.

Endnotes

1. Or, for the less imaginative: "99 bottles of beer on the wall . . . "
2. Check our math just for practice!
3. There are analogues to GDP at the state, regional, and global levels. For example, the gross state product of California for 2019 was about $3 trillion, which is larger than the GDP of all but the largest ten countries on the planet.
4. An alternative measure of output, gross national product (GNP), measures the total value of final goods and services produced during a particular period with factors of production owned by the residents of a particular country. So, when a U.S. citizen makes coffeepots in a Taiwanese factory she owns, GNP will increase, but GDP will not. Likewise, when Japanese automaker Nissan builds a pickup truck at its Tennessee factory, GDP increases, but GNP does not. Ultimately, GNP and GDP are related: GNP = GDP + net income received from abroad. Both measures track one another closely; because some countries report their output as GNP, it is often used in making international comparisons.
5. Remember that many economists go back and forth between saying just "GDP" and saying "nominal GDP." Those terms are perfectly interchangeable.
6. In the base year, current and base-year prices are the same, so real GDP and nominal GDP are identical.
7. "The NBER's Recession Dating Procedure," National Bureau of Economic Research, January 7, 2008.
8. Some economists prefer to break the expansion phase into two parts. The recovery phase is said to be the period between the previous trough and the time when the economy achieves its previous peak level of real GDP. The "expansion" phase is from that point until the following peak.

9. See Pettijohn's "Tough Times, Meaningful Music, Mature Performers: Popular Billboard Songs and Performer Preferences Across Social and Economic Conditions in the USA," *Psychology of Music*, 2009.
10. Larry Swedroe, "The Smartest Things Ever Said About Market Forecasting," CBSNews.com, November 16, 2010, https://www.cbsnews.com/news/the-smartest-things-ever-said-about-market-forecasting/. Note that this quote is of uncertain origin but is often attributed to Laurence J. Peter.
11. Ameila Thomson-DeVeaux, "Economists Are Bad at Predicting Recessions," Fivethirtyeight.com, August 21, 2019.
12. You *do* remember that GDP measures both output and income, don't you?
13. Jack E. Triplett and Barry P. Bosworth, "The State of Data for Services Productivity Measurement in the United States," *International Productivity Monitor* 16 (Spring 2008): 53–70.
14. There are two exceptions to this rule. The value of food produced and consumed by farm households is counted in GDP. More important, an estimate of the rental values of owner-occupied homes is included. If a family rents a house, the rental payments are included in GDP. If a family lives in a house it owns, the Department of Commerce estimates what the house would rent for and then includes that rent in the GDP estimate, even though the house's services were not exchanged in the marketplace.
15. J. Steven Landefeld and Stephanie H. McCulla, "Accounting for Nonmarket Household Production within a National Accounts Framework," *Review of Income & Wealth 46*, no. 3 (September 2000): 289–307.
16. It's even more illuminating to see how these numbers have changed across time, as the world grew richer and richer. In 1800, even the richest countries had a mortality rate of about 500 per thousand births—four times the rate in impoverished Chad today. You can see these numbers change through time at gapminder.org.
17. Melvin Backman, "Britain, Italy include drugs and sex in GDP," CNN Money, May 30, 2014, http://money.cnn.com/2014/05/29/news/economy/uk-italy-prostitution-gdp/index.html.

CHAPTER 6
The Price Level and Inflation

6.1 Start Up: College Is More Expensive Than Ever . . . or Is It?

Read the evening newspaper for just one week straight, and you're likely to find at least one article about the growing burden of student loan debt. If you didn't know any better, you'd swear the cost of college just keeps going up, and up, and up . . . Just check out these headlines, the first five results drawn from a Google search of "student debt" the day this was written:

Why College Tuition Keeps Rising —CNBC

Why Is College So Expensive? —BusinessInsider

The Looming Student Loan Servicing Crisis —AmericanProgress.org

The Scariest Student Loan Number —The Atlantic

Student Debt Is Transforming the American Family —The New Yorker

Worried? Any truth to these statements? Well, here you are, sitting in a college classroom, studying economics. It seems natural to ask whether the headlines are accurate: Does college keep getting more expensive? Is the increasing cost of college placing you and your family at risk?

Economics students at Kansas State University wanted to find out whether these claims were justifiable or whether they were just hype. Beginning in the early 2000s, members of the university's economics club began measuring the cost of going to college, which they call the Kansas State Student Price Index, or K-State SPI for short. Their price index includes the following costs:

"What the . . . My student loan payments are going to be HOW much?"

Source: fizkes/Shutterstock.com

- Tuition
- Textbook Prices
- Housing Costs
- Gasoline
- Groceries
- Movie Prices
- Beer
- Pizza

In 2020, the cost of living for the average student decreased by the largest percentage in the nineteen-year history of the index, falling 1.5% from 2019 levels. That decrease resulted from flat tuition, as well as a 20% decrease in gas prices, a 13% drop in the cost of textbooks, and a 16% decrease in the price of that most-important-of-college-staples, beer. Brock O'Brien, senior economics major and the 2020 president of the economics club, said, "I was surprised to discover that the SPI had fallen from last year, even considering the current economic situation. I've been deeply involved with helping coordinate the SPI since 2018, and in both the past years, prices increased as we expected. These results show the powerful, disruptive impact of COVID-19 on local and national economies."[1]

Well, okay . . . college got cheaper last year, for the first time in a long time—at least in terms of dollars. But economics is about *opportunity* cost: It's not the cash we give up to go to college, it's what we could have *done* with that cash. If the prices of ordinary goods and services declined even more than the price of college, then college's opportunity cost might have actually risen.

Did that happen? In this chapter, we'll figure out how to measure those costs, and in the end-of-chapter exercises we'll find an answer. In the meantime, smile just a bit knowing that the college fund you and your parents worked so hard to build will, for at least one year, stretch a bit further than you thought it would.

6.2 Measuring Prices and Inflation

Learning Objectives

1. Define inflation and deflation, explain how their rates are determined, and articulate why price-level changes matter.
2. Explain what a price index is and outline the general steps in computing a price index.
3. Describe and compare different price indexes.
4. Explain how to convert nominal values to real values and explain why it is useful to make this calculation.
5. Discuss the biases that may arise from price indexes that employ fixed market baskets of goods and services.

Stupid price inflation—my euros don't stretch as far as they used to!

Source: Ariwasabi/Shutterstock.com

price level

The average level of prices in the economy.

Concern about changes in the **price level**, the average level of prices in the economy, has always been a hot topic both among economists ("*The dollar ain't what it used to be!*") and among ordinary people ("*My paycheck just doesn't stretch as far as it used to . . .*"). That's true, even in the relatively low-inflation environment that the United States and many other developed countries are currently experiencing. In the United States, for example, prices have risen at an average of 2.2% over the past twenty years, and only about 1.7% over the past ten.

Rising prices, or *price inflation*, is a concern today, but it was a much bigger concern in the 1970s and into the early 1980s, when prices increased by more than 10% annually. The 1970s may seem like a long time ago to you, but that kind of inflation was still a concern in 2004 when policymakers worried that rising oil prices would push up the cost of other goods and services; it was also a concern in the years following the Great Recession of 2007–2009, when the Federal Reserve pulled out all the stops in an effort to stave off an even deeper financial catastrophe. And yet, just a few years later, markets and policymakers were worried that prices wouldn't rise enough, and might actually fall—a deflation! Just what are inflation and deflation? How are they measured? What causes them? And most important, why do we care? These are some of the questions we will explore in this chapter.

Measuring the Price Level: A Moviegoer's Price Index

Inflation is an increase in the average level of prices, and **deflation** is a decrease in the average level of prices. In an economy experiencing inflation, most prices are likely to be rising; in an economy experiencing deflation, most prices are likely to be falling.

There are two key points in these definitions:

1. Inflation and deflation refer to changes in the average level of prices, not to changes in particular prices. An increase in medical costs is not inflation. A decrease in gasoline prices is not deflation. Inflation means the *average* level of prices is rising, and deflation means the *average* level of prices is falling.

2. Inflation and deflation refer to *rising* prices and *falling* prices, respectively. They have nothing to do with the *level* of prices at any particular time. "High" prices do not imply the presence of inflation, nor do "low" prices imply deflation. Inflation means a positive *rate of change* in average prices, and deflation means a negative *rate of change* in average prices.

Inflation and deflation measure the percentage change in the overall level of prices. If we want to measure the inflation rate, then, we'll first need to figure out what the price level *is*. But there are thousands and thousands of different prices in the economy, from $2.9 million Bugatti Chirons all the way down to five-cent Atomic Fireballs. Which price should we use?

The surprising answer is that we should use *all* of them! Economists typically combine prices of various goods in proportion to how big a share of the typical buyer's budget they are. The result is a single number called a *price index*. A **price index** is a single number whose movement reflects movement in the average level of prices.

A price index measures the overall level of prices. The most commonly quoted price index is probably the consumer price index, which compares how much it costs to purchase a fixed selection of consumption goods to the cost of those goods at some point in the past. To make a price index of your own like the consumer price index (and don't worry—we're going to construct one in a moment!), follow these four steps:

1. *Create a Market Basket:* Select the kinds and quantities of goods and services to be included in the index. A list of these goods and services, and the quantities of each, is the "market basket" for the index. For the consumer price index, the market basket consists of items purchased by households. Some items, like gasoline and rent, occupy a pretty large share of the basket. Bugatti Chirons occupy a very small share (not many households can afford one), as does sauerkraut juice (which many households can afford, but which few actually buy).

2. *Determine the Cost of the Basket in a Base Year:* Next, we're going to anchor the level of prices to an arbitrary point in time called the *base year* or *base period*. (All of our subsequent computations will compare the cost of the basket in some other year to what they cost in the base year.) Most often, the base period for a price index is a single year, but the consumer price index uses a three-year period from 1982–1984. Once you've chosen your base year, compute the cost of purchasing your market basket in that year. Your result should be a dollar amount.

3. *Determine the Cost of the Basket in the Current Period:* Using the same items you did when you computed the base-year cost of your market basket, figure out how much it would cost to purchase those same items today. Again, your answer will be a dollar amount.

4. *Compute the Price Index:* The price index for any period equals the cost of the market basket in that period divided by the cost of the basket in the base period. (Generally, we then convert to a more comfortable form by multiplying the result by 100.)

The basket of goods and services used to calculate the consumer price index contains a little bit of everything households buy. Somewhere in this market basket is a hot-stone massage and a tiny slice of oceangoing yacht!

Source: Africa Studio/ Shutterstock.com

EQUATION 6.1

$$\text{Price Index} = \frac{\text{Current Cost of Market Basket}}{\text{Base Year Cost of Market Basket}} \times 100$$

Let's put those steps into practice and create a price index for, say, movie fans. By surveying consumers, we determine that the typical movie buff rents four movies from Amazon Prime each month, and sees 3 movies in the theater. At the theater, the typical viewer consumes a medium-sized soft drink and one-half of a tub of popcorn; he also sneaks in a box of jujubes from a convenience store. (We're just trying to figure out how much he *spends*; we never said he played by all the rules!) Our market basket includes those items in those proportions: 4 streamed movies, 3 movie admissions, 3 medium soft drinks, and 1.5 tubs of popcorn, and 3 boxes of convenience-store jujubes.

The next step in computing our moviegoer price index is to determine the cost of the market basket in the base year. The choice of the base year is completely arbitrary—in other words, *we* get to choose it. Just because it's a nice number, let's use 2021 as our base year. How do we determine the cost of the items in the market basket? Typically, we'll survey movie theaters, convenience stores, and Amazon Prime (and possibly some other streaming services). Then, we'll use the average price of each item from various places to calculate the cost of the market basket.[2] Those hypothetical values are given in Table 6.1. At those prices, the total monthly cost of our movie market basket in 2021 was $62.96. Now suppose that in 2022, the prices of streaming rentals, movie popcorn, and jujubes rise, while soda prices remain constant and theater tickets actually decrease. The combined effect of these changes pushes the 2022 cost of the basket to $67.02.

TABLE 6.1 Pricing a Market Basket
To compute a price index, we need to define a market basket and determine its price. The table gives the composition of the movie market basket and prices for 2021 and 2022. The cost of the entire basket rises from $62.96 in the base year, 2021, to $67.02 in 2022.

Item	Quantity in Basket	2021 Price ($)	Cost in 2021 Basket ($)	2022 Price ($)	Cost in 2022 Basket ($)
Streaming rental	4	2.99	11.96	3.99	15.96
Movie admission	3	10	30	9.25	27.75
Popcorn	1.5	6	9	7.50	11.25
Jujubes	3	1.00	3.00	1.02	3.06
Soft drink	3	3.00	9.00	3.00	9.00
Total cost of basket		**2021**	62.96	**2022**	67.02

Using the data in Table 6.1, we can compute the moviegoer's price index (MPI) for each year. Let's start with 2021, which is the base year. Remember that our moviegoer's price index is the ratio of the current cost of the basket to the base-period cost:

EQUATION 6.2

$$\text{MPI}_{2021} = \frac{\text{Cost in Current Year (2021)}}{\text{Cost in Base Year (2021)}} \times 100 = \frac{\$62.96}{\$62.96} \times 100 = 100$$

That nice, round number isn't a coincidence: The value of any price index in the base period is always 100 . . . because the current year and the base year are the same. That's not particularly useful, but the tale the price index tells gets better as we move away from the base year. Let's re-compute the MPI for 2022:

$$\text{MPI}_{2022} = \frac{\text{Cost in Current Year (2022)}}{\text{Cost in Base Year (2021)}} \times 100 = \frac{\$67.02}{\$62.96} \times 100 = 106.45$$

So, the MPI for 2022 was 106.45. But what does that mean? We can interpret that number in several different ways. The most obvious is this: For every $100 spent on the movie experience in the 2021 base year, you'd have to spend $106.45 to buy the same experience in 2022. In other words, the idea of the index keeps us from dealing with odd numbers like $67.02 and $62.96 by recalibrating everything to a base year value of 100.

And why is 100 so cool? Because having an MPI value of 100 in the base year makes calculating the percentage change in prices (or . . . *inflation!*) so straightforward. Let's take a look at how to calculate a percentage change. Any percentage change can be calculated as:

$$\text{Percentage Change} = \frac{\text{New Value} - \text{Old Value}}{\text{Old Value}} \times 100 = \frac{\Delta \text{Value}}{\text{Old Value}} \times 100$$

So the percentage change in the moviegoer's price level between 2021 and 2022 is:

$$\% \text{ Change in MPI} = \frac{\text{MPI}_{2022} - \text{MPI}_{2021}}{\text{MPI}_{2021}} \times 100 = \frac{106.54 - 100}{100} \times 100 = 6.54\%$$

That means that our avid moviegoer has experienced a 6.54% increase in his cost of moviegoing between 2021 and 2022. And notice that the difference between the current and base year values is 6.54. In other words, just by looking at the value of the price index, you've got the power to say, "Prices have risen 6.54 percent since the base year." No calculator required!

That 6.54% increase is not a uniform increase; it's only an average. Even though that average increased, the cost of jujubes only increased by 2%; the cost of soda was unchanged, and the cost of theater tickets actually went down! In other words, a price index captures overall averages, but it doesn't pick up movements in everything in the basket. (That presents its own set of issues that we'll talk about a bit later.)

Very often, you'll have more than two years' worth of data to work with. Suppose, for example, that the MPI for 2023 was 110. Then, you could say that prices in 2023 had increased since the base year by 10%. You could also say that inflation between 2022 and 2023 was:

$$\% \text{ Change in MPI} = \frac{\text{MPI}_{2023} - \text{MPI}_{2022}}{\text{MPI}_{2022}} \times 100 = \frac{110 - 106.54}{106.54} \times 100 = 3.24\%$$

Notice that this calculation doesn't involve the base year at all—only the two years over which we want to measure the price increase. And because we took the trouble to get that index close to 100, it's fairly easy to estimate the percentage increase in prices just by looking at the difference: (110 − 106.54) is 3.46, which is fairly close to our calculated 3.24%.

Price Indexes

For a wide variety of reasons, it's important to keep track of how prices in the economy are behaving. Financial contracts and Social Security payments are often calibrated to keep up with inflation. Policymakers need to be aware of how prices are behaving to get a sense of whether the economy needs a kickstart or an emergency brake. There are lots of different price indexes like our moviegoer's price index. While we won't discuss them all, this section presents three of the most common and useful: the CPI, the PCE index, and the implicit price deflator.

The Consumer Price Index (CPI)

consumer price index (CPI)

A price index whose movement reflects changes in the prices of goods and services typically purchased by consumers.

The moviegoer's price index was constructed in the same way as the **consumer price index (CPI)**, a price index whose movement reflects changes in the prices of goods and services typically purchased by consumers. The CPI is a good reference point on price changes for households, since it excludes the prices of investment goods, government purchases, and intermediate goods. As we mentioned above, the CPI is the most commonly cited price index: When the media report the U.S. inflation rate, the number cited is usually a rate computed using the CPI. The CPI is also used to determine whether people's incomes are keeping up with the costs of the things they buy.

The market basket for the CPI contains thousands of goods and services. The composition of the basket is determined by the Bureau of Labor Statistics (BLS) based on Census Bureau surveys of household buying behavior. Surveyors tally the prices of the goods and services in the basket each month in cities all over the United States to determine the current cost of the basket. The major categories of items in the CPI are food and beverages, housing, apparel, transportation, medical care, recreation, education and communication, and other goods and services.

Like many other price indexes, the CPI is computed with a fixed market basket. The composition of the basket generally remains unchanged from one period to the next. Because buying patterns change, however, the basket is revised accordingly on a periodic basis. The base period, though, remains 1982–1984.

The PCE Price Index

Time for a bit of stimulus? PCE inflation must be running below 2%!

Source: Microgen/Shutterstock.com

personal consumption expenditures price index

A price index that includes durable goods, nondurable goods, and services and is provided along with estimates for prices of each component of consumption spending.

The Bureau of Economic Analysis produces a separate price index for each of the components of GDP: consumer prices, prices of investment goods, and government spending. The **personal consumption expenditures price index**, or PCE price index, measures the prices paid by households for durable goods, nondurable goods, and services.[3] There are some subtle differences between the CPI and the PCE; most notable among them is that the PCE doesn't use a fixed basket. Instead, it uses a changing basket that tracks what consumers are currently buying, rather than what they were buying in a base year.[4] The two measures—CPI and PCE—follow a very similar trend, but the CPI measure tends to produce inflation estimates that are about half a percentage point higher than those produced by the PCE.

Both the CPI and the PCE index are important for policy purposes. The CPI is used to adjust Social Security payments so seniors' payments will keep up with inflation; it's also used to adjust interest payments on the government's inflation-protection securities. On the other hand, PCE inflation is a policy target for the Federal Reserve; its behavior tells the Federal Reserve whether it should be stimulating the economy or not. That kind of policy decision is discussed in detail in later chapters.

The Implicit Price Deflator

In the previous chapter, we measured both nominal and real GDP. You might remember that:

- Nominal GDP measures the market value of today's production, valued at *current* prices.
- Real GDP measures the market value of that same bundle (today's production) valued at *base-year* prices.

That sounds very familiar! In fact, that's the same kind of difference we saw when we created the moviegoer's price index, where the only thing that changed over time were the prices used to calculate the value of the popcorn, the jujubes, and so on. So, just as the moviegoer's price index was the ratio of a basket of goods at current prices to the same basket at past prices, we can create a price index for the entire set of goods and services in GDP by calculating the ratio of all final goods and services valued at current prices (nominal GDP) to the same set of goods valued at past prices (real GDP). That measure is called the **implicit price deflator**, a price index for all final goods and services produced. The implicit price deflator is the ratio of nominal GDP to real GDP.

> **implicit price deflator**
>
> A price index for all final goods and services produced; it is the ratio of nominal GDP to real GDP.

EQUATION 6.3

$$\text{Implicit Price Deflator} = \frac{\text{Nominal GDP}}{\text{Real GDP}} \times 100$$

For example, in the second quarter of 2020, nominal GDP in the United States was $19,520.11 billion, and real GDP was $17,302.51 billion. So, the implicit price deflator for the second quarter of 2020 was:

$$\text{Implicit Price Deflator} = \frac{\$19,520.11}{\$17,302.51} \times 100 = 112.81$$

So the average prices of goods and services included in GDP had, in 2020, risen 12.81% from the base year, 2012.

Of course, this formula works in reverse, too: If you have nominal GDP and want to convert to real GDP, just divide by the implicit price deflator!

$$\text{Real GDP} = \frac{\text{Nominal GDP}}{\text{Implicit Price Deflator}}$$

What's the difference between the implicit price deflator and the other measures of price inflation we've discussed? First, the implicit price deflator (like the PCE index) uses the *current* basket of goods and services to compute inflation, which means that the basket changes from year to year. Second, and likely more important, the implicit price deflator's market basket is based on *all* domestic production—so it includes the prices of investment spending, government spending, and the prices foreigners pay for our exports; the CPI includes only consumption goods. And, unlike the CPI, the implicit price deflator *doesn't* include the prices of imported goods, because they're not produced in the United States.

How Have Prices Behaved?

We've burned a lot of real estate talking about what price indexes are, what they measure, and what they don't. That kind of information is probably fascinating to an index number theorist (yes, there really are such things!), but economists are generally more interested in what happens when the rubber hits the road. We're going to spend a lot of time talking about inflation and prices throughout the rest of this book. Let's set the stage here with a quick look at how prices have behaved over the past sixty years or so.

The data shown in Figure 6.1 show persistent increases in prices spanning over half a century. Over that time span, prices of consumer goods have risen about nine-fold, from a CPI of 29 in 1960 to a CPI of 260 in 2020.

FIGURE 6.1 Consumer Price Index: 1960-2020

The past sixty years have brought persistent increases in the prices consumers face in the marketplace. The only notable declines were during the Great Recession of 2007–2009 and the coronavirus crisis of 2020.

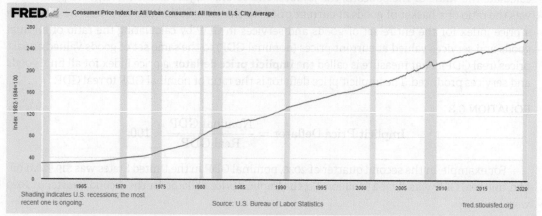

Source: U.S. Bureau of Labor Statistics, Consumer Price Index for All Urban Consumers: All Items in U.S. City Average [CPIAUCSL], retrieved from FRED, Federal Reserve Bank of St. Louis; https://fred.stlouisfed.org/series/CPIAUCSL.

So, prices have persistently increased, but how large were those increases? Let's take a look at the history of CPI price inflation, shown in Figure 6.2. Inflation, which had been low in the early 1960s, started to ratchet up in the late 1960s and through the 1970s, peaking in double-digit territory. It was such a big concern in the 1970s that President Gerald Ford ran for re-election on a campaign of "Whip Inflation Now," or "WIN." After a concerted effort by policymakers, inflation was brought under control in the 1980s; the 2000s have largely been a period of low (about 2%) and stable inflation. One noteworthy feature of this graph is that inflation has only once dipped into negative territory on a year-over-year basis. The United States has a lot of experience with inflation, but very little with deflation.

FIGURE 6.2 CPI Price Inflation: 1960–2020

Inflation was low in the 1960s, high in the 1970s, and low and stable throughout the 2000s.

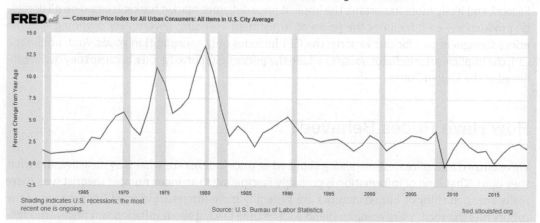

Source: U.S. Bureau of Labor Statistics, Consumer Price Index for All Urban Consumers: All Items in U.S. City Average [CPIAUCSL], retrieved from FRED, Federal Reserve Bank of St. Louis; https://fred.stlouisfed.org/series/CPIAUCSL.

Computing Real Values Using Price Indexes

Suppose your uncle started college in 2000 and had a job washing dishes that paid $7 per hour. In 2020 you went to the same college, and thanks to your uncle's connections, you landed the same glam job . . . only this time, it paid $10 per hour! At Thanksgiving time, you tease your uncle about how naive he'd been to work for such a low wage, and what a shrewd bargain you'd struck when you signed on for nearly half-again as much as he'd been paid.

But your uncle has taken a course in economics, and he understands something important: It's not how many pretty pieces of green paper you take home at the end of the week that matters . . . it's how much beer and pizza you can buy with them! You've seen how prices have been persistently increasing over time; is there a way to see whether your uncle was making more (in terms of beer and pizza) than you are?

Let's gather a bit of information that might help us figure this out. In 2000, the CPI was about 170, while in 2020, it was about 260. That means that you'd have to pay $260 today to purchase what you only paid $170 for in 2000. A dollar really doesn't go as far as it used to! Now let's take those dollar figures and convert them to hours of work for you and for your uncle.

- To buy $170 worth of beer and pizza in 2000, your uncle would have had to work just over **24** hours ($170/$7 per hour).

- To buy the same stuff today would cost you $260. At your wage of $10 per hour, that would take you **26** hours to earn.

Hoisted on your own petard! Despite being paid more *dollars* each hour, you would actually have to work *more hours* to buy the same stuff. In other words, in "real terms"—in terms of purchasing power over goods and services—your uncle was actually being paid more per hour than you!

You don't have to do all of that mathematical hoop-jumping (converting prices to hours) to compare wages across time. Instead, you can simply use dollars of equivalent purchasing power. A value expressed in units of constant purchasing power is a **real value**. A value expressed in *current* dollars is called a **nominal value**. Your uncle's $7 wage and your $10 wage are nominal wages.

To convert nominal values to real values, you can just divide by a price index (and multiply by 100 . . . we'll talk about that a bit more in a minute). That gives you a value in dollars that have the same purchasing power as a dollar in the base period. The real value of a nominal amount X at time t, X_t, is found using the price index (here, the CPI) at time t:

EQUATION 6.4

$$\text{Real Value of } X_t = \frac{X_t}{\text{CPI}_t} \times 100$$

Let's compute the real value of your uncle's $7 wage. The CPI in 2000 was 170, and the base year for the CPI was 1982–84, so in base year dollars, your uncle was being paid:

$$\text{Uncle's Real Wage} = \frac{\$7}{170} \times 100 = \$4.12$$

That means that your uncle's hourly salary in 2000 gave him the same purchasing power as a $4.12 salary would have given a worker in about 1983. And your salary?

$$\text{Your Real Wage} = \frac{\$10}{260} \times 100 = \$3.85$$

Your salary doesn't stack up. Your uncle was, indeed, making more than you in the only terms that matter, *real* terms!

Often, you may want to convert two dollar values to a common year for comparison, without taking all of them back to the base year (which, let's be honest, was probably a year long before you were born). Suppose, for example, you want to take your $10 wage in 2020 back not to the base year, but to 2000, so you can directly compare it with your uncle's wage. You can do this by applying the following formula:

$$\text{Your 2020 Wage in 2000 Dollars} = \frac{\text{Wage}_{2020}}{\text{CPI}_{2020}} \times \text{CPI}_{2000}$$

real value

A value expressed in units of constant purchasing power.

nominal value

A value expressed in dollars of the current period.

Did you remember to divide by the price index?

Source: ibreakstock/Shutterstock.com

"What don't you understand, son? It's right there in the spreadsheet—my $7 was bigger than your $10!" Less really IS more!

Source: Amorn Suriyan/ Shutterstock.com

This looks a bit different, but is really just a modification of the formula we used above to bring things back to the base year. It's got the same starting value, the current (2020) wage. It takes it back to the base year by dividing by the CPI in the current year (2020). But then it brings it *back* to 2000 by multiplying by the 2000 CPI. (In our earlier example, we kept it in the base year by multiplying by 100, the base year CPI.) So, to compare your current wage with your uncle's 2000 wage, you can first calculate:

$$\text{Your 2020 Wage in 2000 Dollars} = \frac{\$10}{260} \times 170 = \$6.53$$

In other words, your current $10 per hour wage is less in year-2000 terms ($6.53) than your uncle's $7 year-2000 wage. We knew that already, right? But it's nice to see that you can take any dollar amount back or forward in time to any year by adjusting with the CPI.

Price indexes are useful. They allow us to see how the general level of prices has changed. They allow us to estimate the rate of change in prices, which we report as the rate of inflation or deflation. And they give us a tool for converting nominal values to real values so we can make better comparisons of economic performance across time.

Are Price Indexes Accurate Measures of Price-Level Changes?

Price indexes help us understand what is happening to prices. But price indexes are a summary measure, and like all summary measures, they have problems. In our case, indexes that employ fixed market baskets (like the CPI does) are likely to overstate inflation (and understate deflation). That happens for four reasons:

1. Because the components of the market basket are fixed, the index does not incorporate consumer responses to changing relative prices.
2. A fixed basket excludes new goods and services.
3. Quality changes may not be completely accounted for in computing price-level changes.
4. The type of store in which consumers choose to shop can affect the prices they pay, and the price indexes do not reflect changes consumers have made in where they shop.

Let's see how these factors can lead to inaccurate measures of price-level changes.

Substitution Bias: Suppose, for example, that consumers really love beer and pizza. Now, suppose the price of beer rises and the price of pizza falls. The law of demand tells us that people will respond by consuming less beer and more pizza. But if we use a fixed market basket of goods and services in computing a price index, we won't make any adjustments: We'll assume that consumers keep eating the same quantities of beer and pizza as they always did.

That throws off the weights in the basket used in the index. The market will have too much of the high-priced beer, and not enough of the lower-priced pizza. As a result, the price index based on that market basket will overstate how much consumers are spending, and overstate inflation. The tendency of a fixed market basket to overstate the importance of items that rise in price and understate the importance of items that fall in price is called the *substitution bias*.

New Product Bias: A second source of bias in price indexes occurs because it takes time for new products to be incorporated into the market basket that makes up the CPI. Here's why this matters. Consider flat-screen TVs, which are commonplace for you today, but which were relatively novel just a decade or so ago. In early 2010, for example, a 46" flat-screen Samsung TV sold for a whopping $1,700. By 2015, you could buy the same TV for $450, and by 2020, it cost just $345.

That's a huge price decrease, and a very real one felt (and enjoyed) by a lot of consumers! But when we use a fixed basket to calculate inflation, a good introduced to the market after the basket has been defined will not be included in it. After all, flat-panel televisions didn't really exist in 1983.

Of course, the BLS gradually introduces new products to the market basket (flat-panel TVs, smartphones, etc.) and weeds out products that consumers don't really buy anymore. (Can anyone say "typewriter" or "camera film"?) But many new goods, once successfully introduced, tend to fall in price dramatically. If the BLS waits until 2015 to introduce 46" flat-panel televisions, it will only capture a $115 price decrease by 2020. The initial decline, from $1,700 to $450, will be missed, causing the CPI to overstate the average amount of price inflation in the economy.

Quality Change Bias: Price indexes are designed to see how the cost of the same basket of goods and services changes over time. Unfortunately, it's really hard to compare the same basket across time, even if we throw the same items in it. That's because many of the items in the basket improve in quality over time, and therefore deliver more services than earlier versions. Think about your cellphone, for example, and how its quality has changed over time. When Apple increases the price of its iPhone, which part of the price increase is just plain old price inflation, and which part goes to pay for your new phone's improved range, faster speed, clearer camera, and brighter screen?

Sometimes it's easy for the people who construct the market basket to account for quality change. When Blue Bunny shrinks the size of its ice cream from 64 oz. to 48 oz., that ice cream delivers 25% fewer services; even if the price remains stable, the size decrease will show up in inflation figures. Similarly, when the average life of a new car increases from 200,000 miles to 300,000 miles, the driver gets 50% more car for the money, and the basket can be adjusted accordingly. But what if that new car has a smoother ride, or safer crumple zones? Those kinds of quality change are more difficult to incorporate into the market basket. BLS economists faced with such changes use advanced statistical techniques called hedonic quality adjustments to try to compensate, but it's hard to measure all of the ways that quality changes. To the extent that such adjustments understate the extent of quality change, they tend to attribute price increases to plain old inflation, when in fact they're due to quality increases. That overstates the true extent of inflation.

Outlet Bias: The fourth source of bias is called outlet bias. Suppose prices start increasing rapidly. One way households can respond to rising prices is by buying less. But there's another way: Instead of shopping at the snooty grocery, households can respond by purchasing the same things at less elegant places. They shop at Walmart, TJ Maxx, and Dollar General; they scour the internet for bargains, too. This often means a bit less customer service than they would receive at traditional department stores or smaller retailers. But the reduced service must be worth the price reductions, as discount store and big-box retailers' market share (not to mention the exploding share attributed to e-commerce) has been steadily increasing. Furthermore, government data collectors do not collect price data on weekends and holidays, when many stores run sales, which further overstates inflation. Prior to 1998, the CPI didn't account for outlet bias in a timely way. Today, the BLS does quarterly surveys and updates its sample of stores much more frequently.

How much do these biases matter? In late 1996, economist Michael Boskin chaired a panel of economists appointed by the government to determine the magnitude of this problem. The panel's best estimate was that the CPI overstated inflation each year by about 1.1 percentage points. Table 6.2 shows the sources of that overstatement, with the biggest share (0.6 percentage points) being attributed to new products and quality change. Since then, the BLS has begun reporting a new consumer price index, called the *Chained Consumer Price Index* (C-CPI-U) that helps filter out the substitution bias. That effort hasn't been fully successful: Economist Robert Gordon revisited the Boskin Commission's work in 2006 and found estimates of bias that still amounted to about 0.8 percentage points per year.

Substitution Bias: When the cost of a soda at the movies rises, the moviegoer's price index keeps the same number of sodas in the market basket . . . but savvy consumers like these retirees may cut back and share, instead.

Source: Air Images/Shutterstock.com

Sometimes you get what you pay for: The family TV of the 1970s was small and lo-def. And get this: You had to get OUT OF YOUR CHAIR to change the channel.

Source: jakkapan/Shutterstock.com

TABLE 6.2 Estimates of Bias in the Consumer Price Index
The Boskin Commission reported that the CPI overstates the rate of inflation by 0.8 to 1.6 percentage points, with a best-guess estimate of 1.1. A 2006 followup by Robert Gordon estimates that the bias is still about 0.8 percentage points.

Sources of Bias	1997 Estimate	2006 Estimate
Substitution	0.4	0.4
New products and quality change	0.6	0.3
Switching to new outlets	0.1	0.1
Total	1.1	0.8
Plausible range	0.8–1.6	—

Source: Based on data from Robert J. Gordon, "The Boskin Commission Report: A Retrospective One Decade Later" (National Bureau of Economic Research Working Paper 12311, June 2006), available at http://www.nber.org/papers/w12311.

How much does this overstatement matter? A lot, actually. First, with *measured* annual inflation averaging about 1.75% over the last ten years, it means that actual inflation is likely less than 1% annually; the United States has come close to achieving true price stability over the span of an entire decade.

That's a nice goal, but there are more practical concerns with persistent overstatement of inflation. One area of concern is in measuring peoples' real incomes, which is an important metric with great significance to both households and policymakers. Overstating inflation causes us to understate real income gains. For example, average nominal hourly earnings of U.S. production workers were $18.88 in 2010, and $23.88 in 2020. Of course, we can't compare those directly, as things cost more in 2020 than they did in 2010. If we convert the 2010 earnings to 2020 dollars, though, we find that real wages in 2010 were equivalent to $22.48 in 2020. That means that measured wage growth over the decade was about 6.2% (from $22.48 to $23.88).

But, if inflation was overstated by 0.8% per year over that entire period as Gordon suggests, then the 2010 worker's equivalent wage should have been reported as $20.85 in 2020 dollars, not $22.48. That means that real wages grew 14.5% over the decade (from $20.85 to $23.88), not the recorded 6.2%. That's a big difference!

Also, because the CPI is used as the basis for calculating cost-of-living adjustments for programs such as Social Security, those payments tend to grow in real value over time due to the overstatement. The Congressional Budget Office estimates that switching to the chained CPI (which reduces substitution bias) would reduce those cost-of-living adjustments by over $200 billion in the next decade.[5]

Pop! Goes the Econ: CPI Increases in *The West Wing*

Press Secretary C.J. Cregg is getting ready for a briefing, and White House communications director Toby delivers some bad news about inflation. Which shortcomings of measured CPI inflation are highlighted in this clip from *The West Wing*? What is the approximate annualized rate of inflation they are worried about?

Key Takeaways

- Inflation is an increase in the average level of prices, and deflation is a decrease in the average level of prices. The rate of inflation or deflation is the percentage rate of change in a price index.
- The consumer price index (CPI) is the most widely used price index in the United States.

- Nominal values can be converted to real values by dividing by a price index.
- Economists generally agree that the CPI and other price indexes that employ fixed market baskets of goods and services do not accurately measure price-level changes. Biases include the substitution bias, the new-product bias, the quality-change bias, and the outlet bias.

Try It!

You've already shown, in three different ways, how your $10 per hour 2020 wage falls short of your uncle's $7 per hour year-2000 wage. Let's try a fourth. Convert your uncle's $7 per hour year-2000 wage to 2020 dollars and see if it exceeds the $10 you are currently receiving. Remember that the CPI was 170 in 2000; it was 260 in 2020.

See related Numerical Problem 8 at the end of this chapter.

Case in Point: Major League Baseball Prices Keep Increasing . . . Or Do They?

This guy may be tagged out-but you are in with the relatively low cost of a baseball game these days!

Source: © Shutterstock, Inc.

The cost of a trip to the old ball game rose 1.8% in 2019, according to *Team Marketing Report*, a Chicago-based newsletter. The report bases its estimate on its fan cost index (FCI), whose market basket includes four adult average-priced tickets, two small draft beers, four small soft drinks, four regular-sized hot dogs, parking for one car, two game programs, and two least expensive, adult-sized adjustable baseball caps. The average price of the market basket was $234.38 in 2019.

Team Marketing compiles the cost of the basket for each of Major League Baseball's teams. According to this compilation, the Chicago Cubs were the most expensive team to watch in 2019; Arizona Diamondbacks games were the cheapest, over 60% less than seeing the Cubs. That kept the Diamondbacks in the most affordable position for the eleventh straight year. The table below shows the 2019 cost of the fan price index market basket for each of the thirty MLB teams.

While spending $370 on a ball game might sound like a lot, there's good news: The price of baseball hasn't risen relative to the cost of other goods and services in the economy, at least not over the past few years. Between 2016 and 2019, the FCI increased from $219.53 to $234.38, a 6.7% increase. In percentage terms, that's almost identical to the CPI's 6.6% jump from 240 to 256. In other words, in terms of *opportunity cost* (the only real cost that matters, right? Don't make us send you back to Chapter 1!), you have to give up the same number of TVs, gasoline, movies out, and other consumer goods to attend a game today as you would have half a decade ago.

The big lesson in all this? Only an economist can claim that a 7% increase is the same as no change in cost whatsoever . . . and only a good student of economics like you can understand why!

Team	Basket Cost ($)	Team	Basket Cost ($)
Chicago Cubs	370.12	Toronto Blue Jays	216.51
Boston Red Sox	354.54	Colorado Rockies	214.64
Houston Astros	313.38	Detroit Tigers	212.22
Washington Nationals	296.48	Oakland A's	212.10
New York Yankees	293.96	Minnesota Twins	210.72
San Francisco Giants	278.20	Milwaukee Brewers	209.76
L.A. Dodgers	274.98	Cincinnati Reds	204.56
Seattle Mariners	258.06	L.A. Angels	197.66
St. Louis Cardinals	254.46	San Diego Padres	195.88
Philadelphia Phillies	250.16	Baltimore Orioles	187.80
New York Mets	247.38	Pittsburgh Pirates	182.42
Kansas City Royals	230.34	Miami Marlins	175.68
Chicago White Sox	223.50	Tampa Bay Rays	160.12
Atlanta Braves	222.74	Arizona Diamondbacks	142.42
Texas Rangers	220.98		
Cleveland Indians	219.64	**MLB Average**	**234.38**

Source: Based on data from Team Marketing Report, "TMR's Fan Cost Index Major League Baseball 2019," available at http://www.teammarketing.com.

See related Numerical Problems 1 and 2 at the end of this chapter.

Answer to Try It! Problem

You can bring any dollar value forward or backward in time by applying the principles you learned in the section above. While we used one formula, that single formula really combined two steps:

1. For a dollar value at time t, take your dollar value back to the base year by dividing by time t's CPI.

2. Bring that base-year value to the point in time you're interested in (say, time u) by multiplying by the time u's CPI.

Let's apply that here. Your uncle's $7 wage was received in 2000. Let's take that back to the base year by dividing by the 2000 CPI, 170. That give us $7/170 = 0.04117.

Now, let's bring that forward to 2020 by multiplying by the 2020 CPI, 260. That gives us 0.04117 × 260, or $10.71. We can combine those steps:

$$\text{Uncle's Salary, 2020 Dollars} = \frac{\text{2000 Salary}}{\text{2000 CPI}} \times \text{2020 CPI} = \frac{\$7}{170} \times 260 = \$10.71$$

Your uncle, for the fourth time, was right: His 2000 wage had the same purchasing power as a $10.71 hourly wage in 2020, about 7% more than your paltry $10 per hour. He really was making more!

6.3 The Causes of Inflation

Learning Objectives

1. State the equation of exchange in both levels and percentage changes.
2. Use the equation of exchange to explain the link between the quantity of money in circulation and nominal GDP.
3. Describe how money-supply changes can cause inflation.
4. Explain why governments sometimes are tempted to increase the money supply.

You've now got a good understanding of how inflation is measured, and you've taken a quick glimpse at the U.S. inflation experience. But not every country shares that experience: Over the past twenty years, as inflation in the United States was averaging a fairly calm 2.2%, inflation in Mexico was twice as high, at 4.5%. Across the Pacific, meanwhile, Japan's inflation rate has been negative in about half of those twenty years, and has averaged just 0.1%—the lowest average rate of any developed country. Meanwhile, in 2018, Venezuela's inflation rate went beyond double digits—*way beyond*—as its inflation rate topped 1,370,000 percent!

Why do some countries have low inflation, while others have high inflation? You might be surprised to learn that, even as complex as the macroeconomy can be, and even as different as the economies of Japan, the United States, Mexico, and Venezuela might be, one single factor explains the vast bulk of these countries' inflation experiences: *money*.

The Equation of Exchange

Most people are interested in money (or at least in having more of it). Economists, however, take a *special* interest in money, because it plays a key role in determining interest rates, in stimulating economic activity, and, of course, in determining prices. That interest isn't new; theories about how money and prices interact can be traced back at least as far as philosopher David Hume, who, as it turns out, was one of Adam Smith's best friends. Hume, along with John Stuart Mill (a nineteenth-century philosopher-economist) proposed a theoretical link between money and prices that was converted to an equation by early twentieth-century economist Irving Fisher.[6] That equation is called the equation of exchange:

EQUATION 6.5

$$M \times V = P \times Y$$

On the left-hand side of the equation of exchange, *M* is quantity of money circulating in the economy and *V* measures the *velocity* (or *income velocity*) of money. Velocity simply measures the number of times each dollar in the economy is spent on final goods and services each year. So, if there are 30 $1 bills in the economy, and each bill is used 4 times each year to purchase a final good or service (being passed from person to person to person to person in the process), then $M \times V$ will equal \$120.

On the right-hand side of the equation of exchange, P is the price level (you can think of it as the average price of a good or service in the economy), and Y represents the number of final goods and services produced, or real GDP. Together, $P \times Y$ represents the market value of all final goods and services sold, which we know as nominal GDP. So, if an economy produces 40 goods, and each sells for an average price of \$3, nominal GDP in the economy will be \$120.

How do we know that the left-hand side and the right-hand side are equal? We know that the right-hand side measures total spending on final goods and services in the economy. But the left-hand side *also* measures spending on final goods and services (each bill being spent on final goods and services four times). The two sides, then, must be equal, and that establishes the link between money and prices that Hume imagined and Fisher refined: To maintain the equality, if you increase the amount of money in the economy, that increase must be matched either by an equivalent *decrease* in velocity, or an equivalent *increase* in nominal GDP!

That's the link we've been looking for. If you're willing to buy for now the idea that velocity V changes relatively slowly (we can put a bar over it to show that it doesn't change much), and that real GDP Y is unlikely to grow very quickly (again, another bar), then increases in the money supply will be reflected in rising prices:

$$\uparrow M \times \overline{V} = \uparrow P \times \overline{Y}$$

This is exactly what caused Nobel Prize–winning economist Milton Friedman to observe that "inflation is always and everywhere a monetary phenomenon." High rates of inflation (large increases in P) don't just occur on their own; they're caused by large increases in the money supply!

This makes some intuitive sense. Suppose you and your archnemesis are stranded on a desert island. Every year, someone from a neighboring island comes over with a basket of 50 coconuts, and you and your foe compete for them using ten \$5 bills that get magically dropped from a helicopter each year. The seller wants to get rid of the coconuts; you want to get rid of the pretty (but otherwise useless) scraps of green paper: When all is said and done, each coconut is likely to sell for a dollar.

What will happen if the airplane happens to drop \$10 bills by accident? Now, you and your nemesis have twice the ammunition (\$!) to compete with, but still only 50 coconuts are available. Anxious to get your hands on more food, you bid up the price of coconuts to \$2 each rather than \$1. After all, what else would you do with your pile of otherwise worthless pieces of paper? Ultimately, with twice as many dollars being used to fight for the same 50 coconuts, you can expect each coconut to sell for twice as much.

Let's see if that kind of linearity holds true in the real world. Figure 6.3 plots average money growth and inflation rates over a ten-year horizon for over 160 countries around the world. The evidence in favor of a monetary explanation for inflation is strong: Countries with the highest inflation rates had the highest money growth rates; countries with low money growth rates had low inflation rates.

The dots in Figure 6.3 don't fit the line perfectly. In some countries (like Ukraine), inflation is higher than the money growth rate; in others (like Japan), it's lower. But the equation of exchange tells us that a one-arrow increase in the money supply should be matched by a one-arrow increase in prices, so why doesn't everything line up better?

Things don't line up better because we assumed earlier that velocity and real GDP were constant . . . but in the real world, they're not. Let's use a bit of mathematical wizardry on our original equation of exchange and transform it slightly, so that instead of looking at the *amount* of money, and the *level* of prices, we instead look at their growth rates, or percentage changes:[7]

$$\%\Delta M + \%\Delta V = \%\Delta P + \%\Delta Y$$

On the left-hand side, the money growth rate (%ΔM) plus the percentage change in velocity (%ΔV) can be added to get the growth rate of total spending. The same is true on the right: The inflation rate (which is just the percentage change in prices, %ΔP) plus the growth rate of real GDP (%ΔY) also equal the growth rate of total spending. The great thing about this version of the equation of exchange is that 1) you get to add things instead of multiplying, and 2) we no longer make the unrealistic assumption that velocity and real GDP don't change from year to year.

FIGURE 6.3 Money Growth and Inflation, 2009–2018
This graph plots the ten-year average growth rate of the money supply vs. the ten-year average inflation rate for 161 countries. The relationship between money and prices is clear: Countries with high money growth rates experience high rates of inflation; countries with low money growth rates experience low rates of inflation.

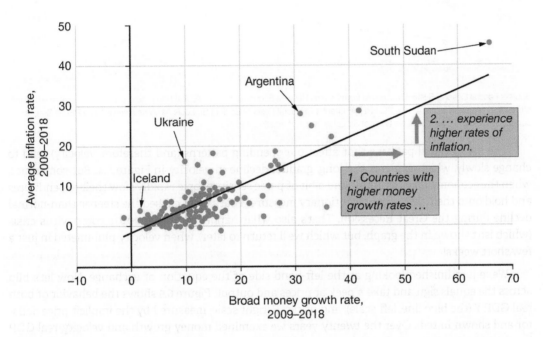

Source: Data from World Bank at https://data.worldbank.org/indicator/FP.CPI.TOTL.ZG?view=chart and https://data.worldbank.org/indicator/FM.LBL.BMNY.GD.ZS?view=chart.

Let's deal quickly with those two big (and now relaxed) assumptions. First, let's take a look at how velocity in the United States has behaved over the past few decades. Figure 6.4 charts the path of velocity (the blue line) and the path of the money supply (the red line) from 2000 to 2019. Over that time span, the money supply has increased about 5.7% annually, from roughly $4,800 billion to $14,800 billion. If velocity were constant over that time horizon, that would have led to an average increase in nominal GDP of 5.7%. But velocity didn't remain steady! Instead, it decreased relatively steadily from 2.1 to 1.4, an average decline of about 2% each year. In other words, the economy had more money, but people were spending it more slowly; the net result was an annual increase in overall spending averaging 3.7% (5.7% – 2.0%).

Velocity represents the rate at which people in the economy spend their money . . . which implies that the more we want to hold cash, the lower velocity will be. What determines our spending patterns? Generally, they're governed by institutional factors like how often we are paid (the more frequently we're paid, the less we have to hold on to to get us through the month, the higher velocity will be). Our spending patterns also depend on financial innovations like credit cards. For example, one of your authors' fellow economists uses a credit card for all of his purchases, then the minute he receives his paycheck he sends it to his credit card company to cover the last month's buying. That's a quick turnaround—his own personal velocity is very high!

FIGURE 6.4 Velocity and the Money Supply

Over the past two decades, the money supply (the red line, measured on the right-hand scale) has increased by about 5.7% per year, on average. Velocity (the blue line, measured on the left axis) has decreased by 2% each year.

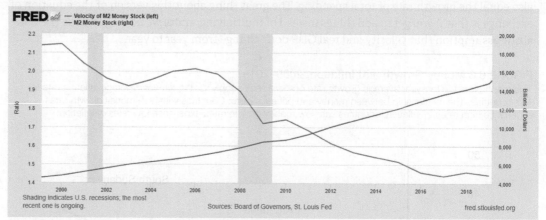

Source: Federal Reserve System, accessed from Federal Reserve Economic Data (FRED) at https://fred.stlouisfed.org/series/M2V and https://fred.stlouisfed.org/series/M2SL. FRED® Graphs ©Federal Reserve Bank of St. Louis.All rights reserved. All FRED® Graphs appear courtesy of Federal Reserve Bank of St. Louis. https://fred.stlouisfed.org/.

The institutional patterns that affect our spending patterns (and therefore, velocity) tend to change slowly, which explains the long, gradual decline in velocity in Figure 6.4. But sometimes, when the economy takes a tumble and a bit of panic sets in, people rapidly slow their expenditures and hold onto their cash as a precautionary measure. That's what caused the steeper-than-normal decline during the Great Recession. That's also what happened during 2020's coronavirus crisis (which isn't shown in the graph, but which we'll return to later), when velocity plummeted in just a few short weeks!

We've just finished looking at the left-hand side of the equation of exchange. Now let's blip across the equals sign and take a peek at prices and output. Figure 6.5 shows the behavior of both real GDP, Y (the blue line, left scale), and prices, P (right scale, measured by the implicit price deflator and shown in red). Over the twenty years we examined money growth and velocity, real GDP increased by an average of 1.9% per year, while prices increased by an average of 1.8% annually. Adding those together gives us the right-hand side of our modified equation of exchange. Not surprisingly, they add up to the same 3.7% we got when we worked with the left-hand side!

FIGURE 6.5 GDP and Prices, 2000–2019

Over two decades, real GDP (the blue line) increased by 1.9% annually, on average. Prices (the red line, right scale) increased by 1.8% annually.

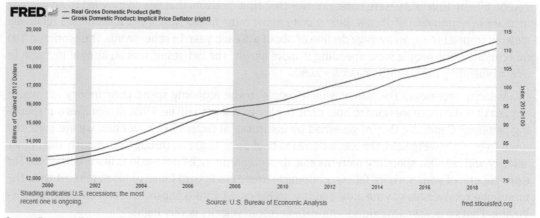

Source: Bureau of Economic Analysis, accessed through Federal Reserve Economic Data (FRED) at https://fred.stlouisfed.org/series/GDPC1 and https://fred.stlouisfed.org/series/A191RI1Q225SBEA. FRED® Graphs ©Federal Reserve Bank of St. Louis.All rights reserved. All FRED® Graphs appear courtesy of Federal Reserve Bank of St. Louis. https://fred.stlouisfed.org/.

That now gives us the intellectual ammo we need to explain why the 5.7% money growth rate in the United States hasn't caused 5.7% inflation. Part of the increase was offset by a decline in velocity (2%); another part of the new money went to purchase the new goods that were responsible for GDP growth (1.9%). The remaining 1.8% money growth did, in fact, show up in the form of higher prices:

$$\%\Delta M + \%\Delta V = \%\Delta P + \%\Delta Y$$
$$5.7\% + (-2\%) = 1.8\% + 1.9\%$$

That leaves us with just one short and practical question: Is it possible that all of the increase in net spending would show up as 3.7% growth in real GDP, with zero inflation? The answer is yes—it's possible, but only under fairly unusual circumstances. Real GDP measures output, which can only grow if 1) we find new productive resources, 2) we work those resources harder, or 3) we find new technology that lets us use those resources more efficiently. We talked about those issues earlier in the book when we discussed production possibilities; we'll return to those issues in a few chapters when we discuss economic growth. For now, experience shows that the economy's real long-run growth potential is about 2% annually.

Why Do Governments Inflate?

You've now done the critical calculations for the United States: 5.7% money growth was reflected in 1.9% inflation. But there are some countries where inflation is much higher, and others like Venezuela where inflation is much, *much* higher. That kind of inflation can only come through money growth far in excess of the potential growth in real GDP. This begs an important question: Why would a country issue so much new money?

The answer, actually, is straightforward. In many countries, the government has a hard time funding its operations (whatever those may be) through tax collections. In the United States, when tax collections fall short of expenditures, the government simply borrows the difference. But in some countries, the government doesn't have the same access to credit that the United States does, or the government doesn't *want* to borrow to fund operations. In those cases, one easy way for the government to fund its operations is to print new money and use that money to pay its bills.

Here's how it works: Suppose a government wants 80 ducats' worth of champagne for a presidential dinner (where a ducat is a unit of currency).[8] To pay for the champagne, the government prints a crisp, new 80-ducat bill and heads for the local liquor store. (Of course, most governments have larger desires than 80-ducat bottles of champagne; governments without access to taxes or credit often end up printing a *lot* of money.) From there, the new bill continues to circulate, passing from person to person throughout the economy, and driving up prices as it goes. When it's time for the next state dinner, the government discovers that it needs to print 90 ducats instead of 80.

That kind of spiral is at the heart of most big inflations. True to our story, most big inflations happen in places where the government is under a lot of fiscal stress (name your country: Zimbabwe (2008), Argentina (2020), Venezuela (2018), to mention a few). In those cases, the government often has no other option but to turn on the monetary Xerox machine.

When the government does this, the resulting inflation causes the value of the local currency to deteriorate. People who hold cash or other assets denominated in that currency often end up watching their wealth evaporate. Moneyholders lose; government wins (at least temporarily): This is why printing money is often referred to as an *inflation tax*.

If the cause of inflation is too much money, then the cure for inflation is clear: Turn off the monetary spigot. Governments who need to eradicate inflation must slow the rate of money growth, or stop using the local currency altogether

"Roll the printing presses . . . champagne for everybody! And while we're at it, son, how about a monument or two?

Source: P.Werner/Shutterstock.com

(we'll see more on this in the next section). One key to ending a big inflation (or to preventing it from happening in the first place) is to separate the process of money creation from the government. That keeps the government from treating the central bank—which is the institution responsible for issuing currency—like its own personal credit card every time it wants to buy something. It also helps prevent the government from aggressively stimulating the economy every time an election rolls around. It's no surprise to economists that the countries with the most successful experience in controlling inflation are the countries that have the greatest degree of central bank independence. We'll learn more about this in the chapter devoted to the United States' central bank, the Federal Reserve System.

Key Takeaways

- Chronic inflation has one prime cause: money growth.
- The equation of exchange relates money growth to the rate of change of prices (inflation).
- In the equation of exchange, changes in the money supply may be reflected in decreases in velocity, increases in the price level, increases in real GDP, or a combination of the three.
- Sometimes, governments print money to pay for government spending. This imposes an inflation tax on moneyholders.
- The more independent a country's central bank is from government, the less likely that country is to experience inflation.

Try It!

Last year, in the United Kingdom of Atlantis, the inflation rate was 5%, velocity fell by 3%, and real GDP decreased by 1%. What happened to the money supply?

See related Numerical Problem 6 at the end of this chapter.

Case in Point: The Equation of Exchange Meets the COVID-19 Recession

When the novel coronavirus hit American shores in January of 2020, nobody knew much about it. We weren't sure how it spread, what kind of damage it could do, how to treat it, or how widespread it might become. By early March, it still hadn't hit the United States hard, but was rolling through Europe like a runaway freight train. So many unanswered questions: Would the United States have to lock down like European countries were doing? What kind of impact would the virus have on our output and employment? What options did we have?

Here's a big secret: The Federal Reserve, the central bank of the United States and the primary agency charged with fighting economic downturns, has *zero* tools in its arsenal that can directly combat a pandemic. Really, the only tool the Fed has is printing money, and believe it or not, *the coronavirus doesn't care how many pieces of pretty green paper are floating around*!

But the Fed does what the Fed does, and in an environment of deep uncertainty, making sure there is plenty of liquidity (money!) in the economy can help ease jittery markets' nerves. So, the Federal Reserve began running the monetary printing presses triple-overtime. In a matter of weeks, they engineered a sharp increase in the money supply that injected over 2.5 *trillion* new dollars into the economy. That kind of money growth was, frankly, unprecedented, and it made some market followers wary: Would it result in runaway inflation?

The sharp increase in the money supply was the Federal Reserve's response to the coronavirus.

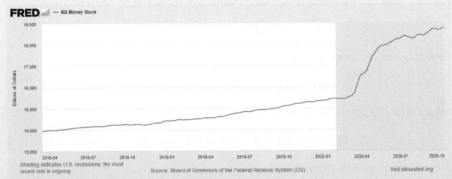

Source: Board of Governors of the Federal Reserve System (US), M2 Money Stock [M2SL], retrieved from FRED, Federal Reserve Bank of St. Louis; https://fred.stlouisfed.org/series/M2SL.

The answer to the money-inflation question can always be found in the equation of exchange. Over a few short weeks, the money supply grew by a full 7%. But remember that when the economic outlook grows uncertain, people generally respond by holding tightly to their money. Couple that tight-fistedness with a lockdown that prevented even those who *wanted* to spend money from doing so, and the result was a 12% bungee-jump of a decline in velocity in just a few weeks.

In the early days of the coronavirus crisis, velocity plummeted.

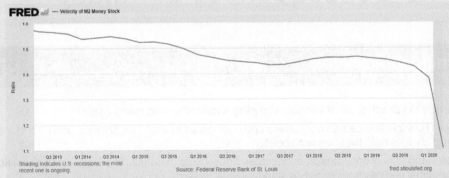

Source: Federal Reserve Bank of St. Louis, Velocity of M2 Money Stock [M2V], retrieved from FRED, Federal Reserve Bank of St. Louis; https://fred.stlouisfed.org/series/M2V.

The equation of exchange tells us that if we add up the money increase and the velocity decline, we'll get the effect on total expenditures. In the coronavirus crisis, the net of those two big changes was a 5% decline in overall spending. How did that 5% decline unfold on the right-hand side of the equation of exchange?

$$\%\Delta M + \%\Delta V = \%\Delta P + \%\Delta Y$$
$$7\% + (-12\%) = 0\% + (-5\%)$$

One thing the U.S. economy *didn't* see was inflation. In fact, real GDP plummeted by a full 5% in those early weeks (a decline sharper than the U.S. economy had ever seen in its 200+ year history, in fact). That 5% decline, as it turns out, fully absorbed the 5% decrease in spending on the left-hand side, which meant that, for all the concern about the huge increase in the money supply, the ultimate result was absolute price stability. *Inflation = 0%!*

Later in this book, we'll explore the novel use of monetary policy to combat the novel coronavirus. For now, it's worth remembering that while inflation may always be a monetary phenomenon, *money doesn't always have to be an inflationary phenomenon*!

See related Concept Problem 12 at the end of this chapter.

Answer to Try It! Problem

To answer this, write out the percentage change version of the equation of exchange:

$$\%\Delta M + \%\Delta V = \%\Delta P + \%\Delta Y$$

Then, make substitutions wherever you can:

$$\%\Delta M + (-3\%) = 5\% + (-1\%)$$

Then, just solve for the percentage change in M:

$$\%\Delta M = 5\% + (-1\%) + 3\% = +7\%$$

The money supply must have grown by 7%.

Khan Academy Link

Inflation and the quantity theory of money

6.4 The Consequences of Inflation

Learning Objectives

1. Describe the direct costs of inflation, including shoeleather and menu costs.
2. Explain how inflation causes consumers and businesses to alter their choices, and how those altered choices negatively impact society.
3. Understand how money illusion encourages households, workers, and businesses to make sub-optimal choices from society's standpoint.
4. Explain how inflation redistributes income.
5. Describe how inflation interacts with the tax system to discourage investment.
6. Explain why unanticipated inflation is more disruptive than anticipated inflation.
7. Discuss the harms of deflation.

In the previous sections of this chapter, you learned how inflation is measured and what causes it. This section addresses the most critical question: Why should we care about inflation? That probably sounds like a question with an easy answer: Because inflation makes the things we buy more expensive. But this is one of those occasions where the obvious answer turns out largely to be wrong!

Why is that? Well, remember that every transaction has a buyer and a seller; every transaction represents both expenditure and income. So, while inflation causes expenditures to increase, it also causes incomes to increase. Another way of thinking about this is to note that inflation drives up the amount received by sellers, and the most commonly sold thing in the economy is our labor. So, do wage increases fully compensate us for rising prices?

FIGURE 6.6 Wages and Prices

Inflation causes prices to increase, but wages tend to increase by just as much. Over the twelve years shown here, prices rose by 1.8% annually, and wages rose by 2.5%.

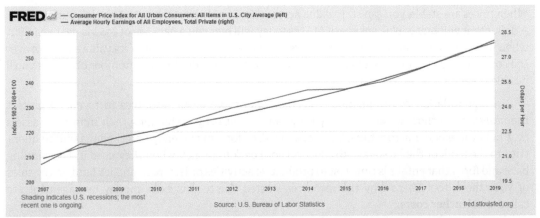

Source: Bureau of Labor Statistics, accessed via FRED: https://fred.stlouisfed.org/series/CPIAUCSL and https://fred.stlouisfed.org/series/CES0500000003. FRED® Graphs ©Federal Reserve Bank of St. Louis.All rights reserved. All FRED® Graphs appear courtesy of Federal Reserve Bank of St. Louis. https://fred.stlouisfed.org/).

Figure 6.6 shows the behavior of wages and prices over a recent twelve-year span. Wages (shown in red and measured on the right-hand scale) and prices (shown in blue and measured on the left-hand scale) track one another remarkably well. Between 2007 and 2019, inflation drove up prices by about 1.8% per year. Over the same time span, wages increased by about 2.4% annually. In other words, yes, inflation makes the things we buy more expensive in nominal terms, but because inflation also causes wages to increase, inflation generally causes little change in the *real* prices of the things we buy.

So if the obvious answer is wrong, why, then, is inflation viewed as such a harmful thing that controlling it has become job one in economies across the globe? Let's explore some of the hidden, but very real, costs of inflation.

Direct Costs

Inflation causes the purchasing power of your cash and checking account balances to decrease over time. When prices increase by 10%, each dollar you have shoved in your mattress ends up buying you 10% less than it did before. In that way, inflation amounts to an implicit tax on people who hold money.[9]

One thing is certain: Whenever the government taxes people, people will try to avoid the tax. That includes the inflation tax. So, one of the ways that inflation costs society is that it encourages individuals to take costly actions to avoid it. Those costs appear in two forms: shoeleather costs and menu costs.

Shoeleather Costs

"Good gravy, man! How bad IS inflation in your country?"

Source: Lolostock/Shutterstock.com

shoeleather costs

Resources wasted by individuals trying to avoid the effects of inflation by minimizing cash balances.

When prices are stable, you can store value across time simply by stashing money in your mattress: A dollar that will buy you a package of M&Ms today will buy you a package of M&Ms next year. But when inflation is high, every dollar you shove in your mattress loses a bit of its value each day; over the course of a year those losses can be substantial, seriously denting the number of M&Ms you'll be able to eat.

In high-inflation environments, moneyholders devote extra resources to trying to protect themselves from those losses. One way they can do that is by exchanging their money for assets that hold value better across time, like stocks, gold, or foreign currency, and then making frequent trips to the bank or the brokerage to convert those back to money when they need it. The running back and forth that entails is time lost to productive activities or leisure . . . and it's hard on the soles of your shoes, too! That's why the resources wasted due to this extra money management are called **shoeleather costs**.

Menu Costs

Menu costs at this pop-up holiday pastry sale are low!

Source: FTiare/Shutterstock.com

menu costs

The costs of changing the prices of goods and services.

Suppose you run a restaurant—maybe an upscale Chinese restaurant with a twenty-page menu. Now, suppose a large inflation rips through the economy. Everybody else is raising their prices . . . but you, you've got your prices printed on your fancy menus, and it's going to cost you a bundle to get them re-printed. The inflation continues, and with each passing day you get poorer and poorer. Eventually, you suck it up and reprint your menus. And then there's another big burst of inflation, and you have to get them reprinted *again*!

Menu costs are the costs of changing the prices of goods and services. For some businesses, menu costs are low: Your local gas station probably changes prices several times a week with little trouble. But some businesses have a harder time changing prices, like your Chinese restaurant, or catalog merchants like L.L. Bean and Land's End. The costs those merchants bear (which they wouldn't in a non-inflationary environment) are money down the drain. (Even worse, a *failure* to adjust prices can exacerbate the effects of shocks to the macroeconomy.)

Indirect Costs: Distortions & Confusion

We've just seen how rapid inflation can cause people to spend more time and money managing their financial affairs and adjusting their prices. Those direct effects are fairly simple to envision. But inflation has subtler effects that may be just as costly to society, or even worse. Inflation can cause people to change the patterns of their consumption and businesses to alter their decisions to invest. It can cause confusion and uncertainty, and it also interacts with the tax code in undesirable ways.

Consumption Distortions

Earlier, we talked about how individuals could insulate themselves from the destructive force of inflation by converting their cash into more stable assets like gold or foreign currency. But there's another way people can prevent their wealth from deteriorating when prices start rising. Instead of converting their money into shiny metals or stable dollars, they can convert their money into goods and services. After all, when everything is getting more expensive by the day, why wait for tomorrow to buy, at higher cost, what you could instead purchase now?

Not exactly how I'd pictured my retirement. Thanks, inflation.

Source: New Africa/Shutterstock. com

In that way, inflation causes people who want to store wealth to abandon their savings goals and spend their money now. That doesn't sound so bad, but remember that they were storing wealth for a reason. Saving money helps them smooth their consumption across time: They consume a bit less today so they can consume a bit more in retirement; because they do that voluntarily, we know their lifetime happiness grows. When rampant inflation erodes the future value of their money, they end up consuming more now and less later. That's a real loss—retirement on rice and beans (if they're lucky) isn't the most glamorous prospect, and it's not what they'd have chosen in a noninflationary environment.

Inflation Variability and Investment Distortions

Just as inflation can alter consumption decisions, it can also alter investment decisions. Businesses invest by spending money today in order to generate a stream of future income. When prices were stable (or even if inflation is a predictable amount each year), businesses can do a good job of estimating what those future income amounts might be. But high inflation is also more variable and less predictable, and that creates problems.

Here's an example. Suppose you're considering making an investment that will pay you a 100% certain $1,000 payment ten years in the future. Now consider what happens in each of the following cases:

1. If inflation is 0% each year, the real value of your future income will be $1,000.
2. If inflation is a steady 2% each year, the real value of your future income will be about $820.
3. If inflation averages 5% per year, but randomly swings between 2% and 8%, the real value of your future income could be as high as $820 (if inflation turns out to be 2% each year) or as low as $463 (if inflation turns out to be 8% each year).

In either of the first two cases, the real value of the future $1,000 is easy to predict. That makes it easy to evaluate whether spending money (say, $500) to make that investment today is a good idea or not. But in the third case, there's such a wide range of possibilities that it is more difficult to evaluate whether an investment will turn out to be a good deal or not. If the investment cost $500 today, *maybe* it would return $820 and end up being a pretty good deal. But *maybe* it would return only $463 and end up being a dud. Who knows? Faced with that kind of risk, a business might choose to forego the investment. So, in times of high and variable inflation, businesses tend to hold on to their cash more tightly and invest less. That keeps the production possibilities curve from shifting as far as it might, and makes the economy less productive than it could otherwise be.

Tax Distortions

Inflation can negatively influence investment in another way, too, through its interactions with the tax code. While individual income tax brackets in the United States are adjusted to account for inflation, capital gains taxes, which are the taxes you pay when something you own rises in value, are not. Let's explore the effects of the capital gains/inflation interaction with a couple of examples.

Scenario I: You buy a parcel of land in 2021 for $100,000. You hang on to it for a year, and then sell it for the same $100,000 in 2022. There is 0% inflation over the year.

Scenario II: You buy a parcel of land in 2021 for $100,000. You hang on to it for a year, and then sell it for $110,000 in 2022. Inflation is 10% over the year.

Here's the rub: In both cases, you'll be able to consume, after the sale of your land, exactly the same bundle of goods and services you started with. In the first scenario, you made no money on the land, but prices didn't rise. You were able to store 100% of your money's real value for one year. In the second scenario, you made 10% on the land, but when you cashed in, everything you wanted to buy with your money cost 10% more. Your gain on the land was just sufficient to cover the increased cost of the goods and services you buy.

Those two cases are fundamentally identical. *But!* In the first case, you experienced zero capital gains—you bought for $100,000 and sold for $100,000. As a result, you incurred zero tax liability. In the second case, you generated zero *real* capital gain but $10,000 of *nominal* capital gains, which puts you on the hook for $2,000 in capital gains taxes.[10] After you pay those taxes, you'll actually end up *worse off*.

The U.S. federal income tax is indexed to inflation—the lower limit of each tax bracket rises each year in accordance with the inflation rate. But the U.S. capital gains tax is not, which means that financial investment in businesses (via stocks and bonds) and real investment in housing and other real property is more attractive in low-inflation environments than it is in high-inflation environments. This is one great reason to either 1) reform the capital gains tax (which seems unlikely) or 2) keep inflation both low and predictable (we've had better success with this).

Money Illusion and Price Confusion

Money Illusion: Pay no attention to the smoke and mirrors, your pay raise wasn't a raise at all!

Source: Nazar Skladanyi/Shutterstock.com

There's another subtle way that inflation can lead people to make decisions that aren't good for society (or for them). People can misinterpret changes in the overall price level for changes in the prices of *their* product or *their* income.

Here's an example: You graduate, and manage to land a good $60,000 job. In your first year, you're getting in early, staying late, doing all the right things to advance in your company while keeping your expenses to a minimum—after all, those student loans won't pay *themselves* off! Unbeknownst to you, prices in the economy are rising; the inflation rate over your first year is 10%.

At your year-end performance review you get a five-star rating and your supervisor gives you a $6,000 raise. You're thrilled, and you promptly celebrate by taking your friends to dinner, signing up for a CrossFit membership, and switching your shopping from Aldi to Whole Foods.

And why not—after all, you just got a $6,000 raise! Except, of course, your raise wasn't a raise at all: Your 10% salary increase was just sufficient to cover the 10% increase in the prices of the things you were already buying. It comes as a surprise to you, in your second year of your job, that there's always a bit too much month left at the end of your money.

You've just fallen victim to what economists call *money illusion*—mistaking changes in nominal values (your paycheck) for changes in real values (your inflation-adjusted paycheck). In this case, that mistake causes you to ratchet up your consumption beyond what you otherwise would have.

In a broad general inflation, business firms might mistake the increase in the overall price level for an increase in the price for *their* product (what economists might call an increase in *relative* prices). They might interpret that rising price as an increase in demand for their product, and respond by expanding the factory floor, launching into new markets, or franchising their operation. Those changes would be unwarranted, prompted not by a real increase in demand, but merely by money illusion.

Income Redistribution

Picture this hypothetical: Your econ professor is talking about the money supply in class, and asks if anyone has a hundred-dollar bill. You've just cashed your paycheck, and you happen to have one on you. Thinking that she wants to show the bill to the rest of the class for instructional purposes, you offer it to your instructor. She takes it from you, walks all the way across the auditorium, *and gives it to some random dude wearing sweats and a baseball cap!*

What the heck?! That kind of random redistribution seems pretty unfair. Now imagine how unfair it would be if it wasn't just *your* hundred-dollar bill: What if your prof had taken a hundred bucks from *half the class* and then handed them off to the other half.

Of course, econ professors don't really do that (at least, we *hope* your econ professor doesn't do that). But inflation does! You've already seen one example of this, when we discussed how money-holders get poorer when the government prints money to pay its bills. That's a redistribution from households to the government.

But there are other ways inflation redistributes income. Here's an example: You live in Zimbabwe, and through hard work and thrift you've managed to save 100,000 Zimbabwean dollars to live on in retirement, just a few years away. Your brother-in-law the egg farmer asks to borrow it to build his dream home. You like him well enough, you suppose, but retirement is looming, so you make him sign an ironclad contract promising to repay the hundred grand within two years.

Unfortunately, within those two years the Zimbabwean government finds itself in a bit of a fiscal bind. With no other way to pay its bills, the president starts running the monetary printing presses. Inflation skyrockets, accelerates, and then skyrockets some more. Soon there are billion-dollar bills and trillion-dollar bills circulating throughout the economy; Big Macs are selling for a half-million bucks each and eggs are a hundred thousand bucks a carton.[11]

Guess what happens next? Your egg-farming brother-in-law shows up at your door with your promissory note in one hand and a dozen eggs in the other. "Paid in full," he says, and walks back to the home he built with your life savings. The rapid inflation made it easy for your brother-in-law to repay your loan—he practically chased after you to pay his debt! Meanwhile, the Zimbabwean president shows himself to be a thief of time, stealing years of your hard work from you and sentencing you to a lifetime of continued hard labor rather than the retirement you thought you'd enjoy.

It didn't have to turn out that way. If you'd properly anticipated the inflation, you could have built some compensation for it into your contract. But this inflation was unexpected—it took you by surprise, and an unpleasant surprise it was, for everyone except your brother in law . . . and anyone else in the economy who owed others money and got to pay their debts back in depreciated currency. The unanticipated inflation redistributed wealth from creditors to debtors, as arbitrary a redistribution as when your econ prof gave your hundred-dollar bill to the guy in the baseball cap.[12]

Pop! Goes the Econ: Dr. Evil Holds the World for Ransom

Poor Dr. Evil! The internationally known criminal genius has been cryogenically frozen for thirty years, and his failure to understand the consequences of inflation might lead his plan to hold the world hostage astray. Although this clip doesn't use the word "inflation," explain how it is at the source of his troubles.

View in the online reader

Hoping for High Inflation: This recent grad has scads of student loan debt.

Source: Marcos Mesa Sam Wordley/Shutterstock.com

What about Deflation?

We've taken a long journey through the costly nature of inflation. But if inflation is so bad, surely deflation must be good, right?

Not so fast! Believe it or not, deflation is actually a scarier thing for policymakers than inflation. That's because policymakers in most places are charged with keeping the economy running up to its potential, and that is hard to do when prices are falling. But if you're a consumer, and prices in the economy are falling, why buy today what you can buy at a lower price tomorrow? Because of its impact on spending, deflation can lead to a recession.

There's a second way that deflation negatively impacts the economy: It makes it very hard for borrowers to repay their loans. Suppose you run a cupcake shop where each cupcake sells for $1. To open that store, you borrowed $15,000; you planned to sell 15,000 cupcakes to repay your loan. Unfortunately, when deflation hit, the price of your cupcakes was driven down to $0.75. Now you've got to sell 20,000 cupcakes to pay your debt instead of 15,000; you'll have to work harder and sell more, and you're trying to do this at exactly the same time that your customers are trying to postpone their purchases and buy less. If you fail to sell those extra cupcakes, you'll have little choice but to default.

That kind of deflation-inspired default lay at the heart of the Great Depression, when prices fell by about one-third.[13] It was equally concerning during the Great Recession of 2007 to 2009—so concerning that policymakers pumped money into the economy at then-unprecedented rates in a successful attempt to stave it off.

So now you know: There are costs to inflation and costs to deflation. It's no great surprise, then, that price-level stability (or at least price-level predictability) is one of the most important goals of the Federal Reserve System and of central banks around the world. We'll learn more about these institutions and their goals in subsequent chapters.

Pop! Goes the Econ: The Christmas Price Index

Each year, PNC bank constructs a Christmas Price Index, which you can find at this link. What is in the market basket of the Christmas Price Index? Can you explain why the 2020 deflation might be worrisome to economic policymakers? If each of the factors in the Christmas Price Index rose in price by 10%, which would be responsible for the largest increase in the cost of Christmas?

Key Takeaways

- Shoeleather costs and menu costs are two direct costs that inflation creates in an economy.
- Consumers and businesses make different decisions about saving and investment when inflation exists than they would in a zero-inflation environment.
- Households and businesses often fall victim to money illusion, mistaking changes in the overall level of prices for changes in the prices of things they buy and sell.
- Unanticipated inflation redistributes income from moneyholders to the government and from creditors to debtors.
- Deflation imposes its own set of costs on an economy.

Try It!

You really love M&Ms, which cost $1 per package. Today, you lend your brother $100, charging him an interest rate of 5%; he pays you back $105 in a year. Over that time, M&Ms have risen in price by 10%. What is your nominal (measured in dollars) rate of return? What is your real (measured in M&Ms) rate of return?

See related Numerical Problem 7 at the end of this chapter.

hyperinflation

A period of very high and accelerating inflation.

Case in Point: *Ay Caracas!* Inflation, Venezuelan Style

It should have been one of the richest countries in the world. Thanks to its government, it became one of the poorest.

> *Nothing to smile about: In 2018, a stack of 250,000 Venezuelan bolivars had the same purchasing power as a single dollar. Today, the equivalent stack is four times higher.*

Source: sunsinger/Shutterstock.com

Venezuela, on the northern coast of South America, sits atop unspeakable wealth—a pile of oil reserves bigger than Saudi Arabia's; bigger than Canada's; bigger than Iran's and Iraq's combined. Yet through a series of more-than-questionable economic policies, Venezuela's managed to squander that wealth, becoming a hotbed of civil unrest and the home to the world's greatest economic collapse.

The most visible evidence of Venezuela's economic troubles (and there are so very many to choose from) is its inflation rate. The 1.3 *million* percent increase in prices it experienced in 2018 made it the site of the world's most recent **hyperinflation**, a period of very high and ever-accelerating inflation. That hyperinflation, like all hyperinflations, was caused by a government that ran the monetary printing presses triple overtime in order to manage a crippling debt crisis.

Well, almost: Venezuela's monetary printing presses were actually incapable of handling the volume of money the government needed. Soon, the government was importing planeloads of bolivars (their domestic currency) from printers abroad. As the inflation accelerated, however, Venezuela found itself in an odd situation: It cost more to get new bills printed than the bills were worth. The answer to that imbalance, of course, is to add more zeros to your bills, which ultimately drives inflation even higher. To economist Steven Hanke, that re-zeroing is "raising the white flag. No one wants to do it, but eventually their hand gets forced."[14]

The sheer magnitude of a hyperinflation makes it easy to see the costs ordinary inflations impose on an economy. Consider shoeleather costs. During the Venezuelan hyperinflation, workers were often paid several times a day and released to try to convert them to something more stable, like dollars . . . or rice. Office messenger Jose Marcano spent hours each week depositing stacks of his employer's bolivars into ATMs. "Carrying this amount of cash is incredibly dangerous," Marcano said. "You put your life at risk." Velocity increased as people tried to rid themselves of depreciating currency, further fueling price increases.

Shoeleather costs showed up in other ways, too. The same ATMs Marcano made his deposits into were unable to keep up with the demands of depositors who now needed stacks of currency to make even the simplest purchases. Banks resorted to filling them several times each day.

Meanwhile, merchants who had dealt with the early stages of hyperinflation by installing electronic money counters gave up on the machines as too slow; instead, they began weighing stacks of bills on scales.

Menu costs were high, too, as merchants struggled to post prices that kept up with the ever-escalating inflation. Often, sellers had to change prices several times each day. One central Caracas butcher lamented, "Sometimes I will buy a kilo of meat at 10,000 bolívars, sell it in the shop for 14,000, then go back to restock and the wholesale cost is 15,000. You can't keep going like that."[15]

Eventually, money that loses its ability to store value becomes irrelevant as a medium of exchange, as sellers refuse to accept it in favor of something more stable. In Venezuela, stores began requiring U.S dollars for purchases, a frightening prospect for those without any put aside. Other vendors circumvented cash altogether, posting signs in their shops that simply read, "Barter."

The most damaging effects of the Venezuelan hyperinflation were its impacts on the ability of Venezuelans to meet their basic needs. Store shelves quickly emptied as residents scurried to convert an ever-depreciating currency into stable food. Individuals' life savings disappeared before their very eyes; years of savings proved insufficient to purchase a weekend's worth of food. The *New York Times* reports that these persistent food shortages caused the typical Venezuelan to lose over twenty pounds.

The hyperinflation of 2018 left the Venezuelan economy in a shambles, with real wages plummeting and 35% unemployment. A series of poorly implemented monetary reforms were successful in bringing the inflation rate down to an estimated 4,000% by 2020. That was an improvement, but not enough of an improvement to keep the country from topping Bloomberg's rankings of the most economically miserable places to live for the sixth straight year.

How are ordinary Venezuelans coping? After years of civil unrest and economic strife, they've largely learned to deal with quadruple-digit inflation by ignoring the bolivar and conducting their business in dollars. Today, well over half of all transactions are conducted using U.S. currency; in some places the dollar is used almost exclusively. That *dollarization* has received the blessing of strongman President Nicolas Maduro, who relaxed rules on the use of foreign currency and who hangs on to an internationally disputed presidency by his fingertips. To Maduro, dollarization was an escape hatch, desperately needed to kickstart an economic recovery, a recovery that no amount of bolivars would ever be able to engineer.

See related Concept Problem 12 at the end of this chapter.

Sources: Based on Fabiola Zerpa and Andrew Rosati, "Venezuelans Give Up on Counting Piles of Cash and Start Weighing Them," Bloomberg.com, October 31, 2016; Tim Worstall, "Congratulations to Venezuela: Bolivar Notes Are Now Worth Less Than It Costs To Print Them," Forbes, May 4, 2016; Emma Graham-Harrison, Patricia Torres, and Joe Parkin Daniels, "Barter and Dollars the New Reality as Venezuela Battles Hyperinflation," The Guardian, March 14, 2019.

Answer to Try It! Problem

Today, you sacrifice the chance to consume 100 packages of M&Ms. In one year, you are given back $105. M&Ms now cost $1.10 per package. That means you can afford $105/$1.10 = 95.45 packages of M&Ms.

You gave up the chance to consume 100 packages of M&Ms in order to exchange $100 today for $105 tomorrow. Your nominal return is 5%. But inflation eroded your real rate of return. Because of inflation you get to consume 4.55 packages *less* in one year than you could have consumed today. You've paid someone else to postpone your consumption; your *real* rate of return is −4.55%. *Thanks, unanticipated inflation!*

Khan Academy Links

Winners and losers from inflation

Hyperinflation

6.5 Review and Practice

Summary

Inflation is an increase in the price level, and deflation is a decrease in the price level. The rate of inflation or deflation is the percentage rate of change in a price index. We looked at the calculation of the consumer price index (CPI), the personal consumption expenditures index, and the implicit price deflator. The CPI is widely used in the calculation of price-level changes. There are, however, biases in its calculation: the substitution bias, the new-product bias, the quality-change bias, and the outlet bias.

Inflation is ultimately caused by increases in the stock of money in circulation. The equation of exchange relates changes in the money supply and velocity to changes in nominal GDP. Practical experience suggests that countries with the highest rate of money growth have the highest rates of inflation.

Inflation (and deflation) is costly to society. It changes the value of money and of claims on money. It creates shoeleather costs and menu costs. It causes consumers and businesses to alter (unfavorably) the choices they'd make in a noninflationary environment. It redistributes income from creditors to debtors.

Concept Problems

1. What is the current value of the CPI? What was it a year ago? Can you calculate the inflation rate over the past year?

2. Name three items you have purchased during the past year that have increased in quality during the year. What kind of adjustment would you make in assessing their prices for the CPI?

3. Why do some people gain and other people lose from inflation and deflation?

4. Suppose that fear of a recession causes a sudden sharp drop in velocity. All else equal, what will happen to the inflation rate?

5. Explain why velocity increases during hyperinflations. What effect does the increase in velocity have on the inflation?

6. Why is deflation just as much of a problem as inflation?

7. Suppose that the price of table salt increases by 90%, and the price of gasoline increases by 20%. Which will have a larger impact on the consumer price index? Why?

8. Why are hyperinflations (a monetary problem) often caused by government budget deficits (a fiscal problem)?

9. Suppose you are ready to lend your sister $100 for a year, and wish to charge her 10% interest. If you know that prices of goods and services will increase by 20% over that year, how can you alter your contract so the inflation won't harm you?

10. Suppose that this year, running shoes increased in price by 4%, while the CPI increased by 9%. Explain why the *real* price of running shoes decreased by about 5%.

11. Why might high inflation slow a country's economic growth?

12. (Related to "Case in Point: The Equation of Exchange Meets the COVID-19 Recession" in Section 18.3 and "Case in Point: Ay Caracas! Inflation, Venezuelan Style" in Section 18.4.) Use the equation of exchange to explain why high rates of money growth resulted in inflation in Venezuela in 2018, but did not lead to inflation during the COVID-19 recession in the United States.

Numerical Problems

1. (Related to "Case in Point: Major League Baseball Prices Keep Increasing . . . Or Do They?" in Section 18.2.) The average price of going to a baseball game in 2019, based on the observations in the Case in Point, was $234.38. Using this average as the equivalent of a base year, compute fan price indexes for:

    a. The New York Yankees

    b. The Chicago Cubs

    c. The Boston Red Sox

    d. The Kansas City Royals

    e. A team of your choice

2. (Related to "Case in Point: Major League Baseball Prices Keep Increasing . . . Or Do They?" in Section 18.2.) In 2016, baseball's fan price index was 219.53. By 2019, it was 234.38. Calculate the percentage change over the three years.

3. Recompute the movie price indexes for 2021 and 2022 using 2022 as the base year. Now compute the rate of inflation for the 2021–2022 period. Compare your result to the inflation rate calculated for that same period using 2021 as the base year.

4. The Consumer Price Index in Period 1 is 107.5. It is 103.8 in Period 2. Is this a situation of inflation or deflation? What is the rate?

5. Solve these three problems:

    a. Nominal GDP for an economy is $10 trillion. Real GDP is $9 trillion. What is the value of the implicit price deflator?

    b. Nominal GDP is $20 trillion. The implicit price deflator is 130. What is real GDP?

    c. Real GDP is $12 trillion. The implicit price deflator is 120. What is nominal GDP?

6. (Related to "Try It!" in Section 18.3.) Suppose that this year, the money supply grows by 6%, velocity increases by 1%, and real GDP increases by 4%. What will the inflation rate be?

7. (Related to "Try It!" in Section 18.4.) Suppose you lend your cousin $100 for one year at 10% interest. Over the span of that year, inflation averages 7%. What is your real rate of return?

8. (Related to "Try It!" in Section 18.2.) In 2019, *Avengers: Endgame* became the highest-grossing film of all time, bringing in $2,798,000,000 at the box office worldwide. Eighty years earlier, *Gone with the Wind* grossed about a tenth that much at $202,013,000. If the CPI was 13.9 in 1939 (when *Gone with the Wind* was released), and 255 in 2019, calculate the real revenue each film received. Which grossed more in real terms? (*Hint: Convert both amounts to the 1982–84 base year.*)

9. The chapter opener introduced K-State's Student Price Index (SPI). In 2019, the SPI was 161 (the base year was 2006). Over the same horizon, the consumer price index increased from 201 to 255. Determine whether college got more expensive or less expensive in real terms between 2006 and 2019; then determine by how much.

10. The chapter opener introduced K-State's Student Price Index (SPI). Between 2015 and 2020, measured student-price inflation rates were 1.4%, 2%, 5.1%, 3.5%, 0.4% and −1.5%, respectively. Find the value of the SPI for each year (the base year is 2017).

11. Consider the table below, which outlines the prices of burger-stand items. If the monthly basket of the typical burger stand customer includes 4 burgers, 3 fries, and 5 drinks,

    a. Calculate a fixed-basket burger-stand price index, with a base year of 2021.

b. Calculate the annual inflation rate in each year.

c. Without using your calculator, indicate how much the cost of burger-standing increased between 2021 and 2023.

Year	Price of Burgers ($)	Price of Fries ($)	Price of Drinks ($)
2021	8.00	2.00	1.00
2022	8.20	2.40	1.05
2023	8.80	2.42	1.10

Endnotes

1. Kansas State University. "2020 Student Price Index Reveals Deflation for K-State Students." K-State Press Release, 13 Oct 2020. Retrieved from: https://www.k-state.edu/economics/econclub/econclub/docs/2020 Press Release FINAL.pdf

2. For the consumer price index, the fine folks at the Bureau of Labor Statistics do the survey work.

3. Because prices for food and energy can be volatile, the BEA calculates a version of this index that excludes food and energy to measure underlying, or "core," inflation.

4. For a comparison of price measures, including a comparison of the PCE price index and the consumer price index, see Brian C. Moyer, "Comparing Price Measures—The CPI and PCE Price Index" (lecture, National Association for Business Economics, 2006 Washington Economic Policy Conference, March 13–14, 2006), available at http://www.bea.gov/papers/pdf/Moyer_NABE.pdf.

5. See https://www.cbo.gov/budget-options/2018/54752

6. Our apologies for all of the name dropping . . . but these guys were serious honchos. You're likely to meet some of them again in the later chapters of this book; you're just as likely to see their names in philosophy courses or history courses . . . and possibly even after your courses are done and you're out in the real world!

7. To get from the original version to this version requires a bit of mathematical hocus pocus involving both logarithms and calculus. Don't worry about how we got from point A to point B; instead, just enjoy the simplicity in being able to add growth rates on either side of the equation of exchange.

8. The ducat was once a unit of currency—a gold or silver coin circulating through Europe that was used for trade. Here, our ducats are just a fictional paper money.

9. When we say "money" here, we mean actual money: dollar-denominated assets earning little or no interest.

10. We've simplified how the tax is calculated a little bit, but the capital gains tax code is really only slightly more complex, and the top capital gains tax rate is, in fact, 20%.

11. Zimbabwe did, in fact, have a horrible hyperinflation in 2008.

12. We're pretty sure that dude-in-cap dropped the class that afternoon and never came back. At least, that's what we would have done in his situation.

13. This theory of deflation-induced debt defaults leading to economic collapse is credited to depression-era economist Irving Fisher. He gets a big shout-out in this chapter because he's responsible for this "debt-deflation" theory, _and_ he also formalized the equation of exchange. But wait—there's more! Fisher was, in his spare time, an index number theorist (we warned you that there really such things, didn't we?); the PCE index from the first section of this chapter is a "Fisher-Ideal Index." And when he wasn't dabbling with the costs, measurement, and causes of inflation, he was out inventing things like the Rolodex that made him, at least for a while, a very wealthy man.

14. Fabiola Zerpa and Andrew Rosati, "Venezuelans Give Up on Counting Piles of Cash and Start Weighing Them," Bloomberg.com, October 31, 2016

15. Emma Graham-Harrison, Patricia Torres, and Joe Parkin Daniels, "Barter and Dollars the New Reality as Venezuela Battles Hyperinflation," _The Guardian_, March 14, 2019.

CHAPTER 7

Unemployment

7.1 Start Up: This One Was Different . . . But Was That Better or Worse?

If our goal is to produce the greatest material wealth for our people, we have to use all of our resources, and in the best possible way. Of all the resources available to us, the most valuable is people. It's people who till the soil, teach the students, and run the machines. Most important, it's people who come up with smarter ways to go about our work, which helps us squeeze more good things out of the same number of inputs. It's people who come up with new products and services that make our world richer, fuller, and happier. And it's people who step forward to dream the unimaginable and perform the impossible, like creating life-saving vaccines out of thin air in fewer weeks than you have fingers.[1]

This one was different . . . in so many ways.

Source: JeremyRichards/Shutterstock.com

One reason that economic recessions are so costly is that during recessions, we fail to use all of our people. In the COVID-19 recession of 2020, one out of every six workers suddenly found themselves out of work. Those numbers were the worst the United States had seen in almost a century. But job losses during the COVID-19 recession were notable for reasons other than their sheer magnitude. For many, job losses were exceptionally short-lived. Others returned to jobs that looked very different than the ones they'd left. And still others, having been laid off, decided not to return to work at all.

In this chapter, you'll learn why society sometimes fails to fully use all of its workers—a phenomenon that macroeconomists call unemployment. You'll also explore various types of unemployment and begin to think about the policy responses to each. But so much of the story in macroeconomics is told by data, so our first step will be to learn about how unemployment is measured . . . and then why those measurements aren't very good. Talk about your recession-proof jobs—who but an economist could convince people to pay them for producing numbers that everyone knows are wrong?[2]

7.2 Measuring Unemployment

Learning Objectives

1. Describe the labor market classifications the Bureau of Labor Statistics uses to categorize individuals' employment status.

2. Define the unemployment rate and calculate its magnitude using aggregate data on the employment status of an economy's people.

3. List three shortcomings of the measured unemployment rate and explain how each distorts our view of labor market conditions.

Nothing good about it: Unemployment can empty both your bank account and your emotional reserves.

Source: Mikateke/Shutterstock.com

unemployment

A situation that occurs when people who are willing and able to work cannot find jobs.

You're outta there! If you don't have a job and haven't looked in the past four weeks, you're not in the labor force.

Source: DarioZg/Shutterstock.com

Unemployment exists when people who are willing and able to work can't find jobs. It's not hard to figure out why economists and policymakers give unemployment so much attention. At a micro level, unemployment represents a financial setback that some people never recover from—even after regaining employment, workers often find themselves on permanently lower earnings trajectories. Not all of the costs of unemployment are measured in dollars, either. Economists Kerwin Charles and Melvin Stephens say it takes a huge toll on families, noting that the probability of a divorce rises about 15% after a spouse loses a job. It's also linked to depression, insomnia, anxiety, heart attacks, and even cancer. Those adverse health effects, coupled with a measurable increase in the risk of suicide, sharply reduce life expectancy for those suffering even a single bout of unemployment: Economists Till von Wachter and Daniel Sullivan estimate that for older male workers who were previously consistently employed, job losses increased death rates by 50% to 100%. Unemployment kills!

At the macro level, unemployment vexes policymakers for two reasons. First, for an economy to produce the greatest possible material well-being, it needs to operate on its production possibilities curve. But it can only get there if it fully utilizes all of its factors of production, and unemployment represents a failure to do that. Second, policymakers often have trouble understanding why unemployment exists at all. In a world where there's always more work to be done, and where people are willing to do that work, how is it that society somehow fails to match up the work with the workers?

Measuring Unemployment

To begin to understand unemployment, though, we'll first need to figure out exactly what unemployment is. So let's start our journey into (studying) unemployment with a look at the data. Each month, the federal government's Bureau of Labor Statistics (BLS) surveys about 60,000 households regarding their employment status. Based on the responses, each of the roughly 110,000 adults in those 60,000 households is lumped into one of three categories:

- **Employed**. The person being surveyed has a job or is self-employed.

- **Unemployed**. The person being surveyed does not have a job but is currently available for work and has taken active steps to find a job in the past four weeks.

- **Not in the labor force**. The person being surveyed does not have a job and has not taken active steps to find one in the past four weeks. (Among others, retirees, the disabled, students, and home caregivers are included in this category.)

Figure 7.1 shows the survey's results for the civilian (nonmilitary) population for November, 2020. At that time, 149.7 million adults were officially classified as employed, 10.7 million adults were unemployed, and 100.6 million adults were not in the labor force.

FIGURE 7.1 Determining Labor Status
A monthly survey of households divides the civilian adult population (261 million adults) into three groups. Those who have jobs are counted as employed; those who do not have jobs but are looking for them and are available for work are counted as unemployed; and those who are not working and are not looking for work are not counted as members of the labor force. Values are for November 2020.

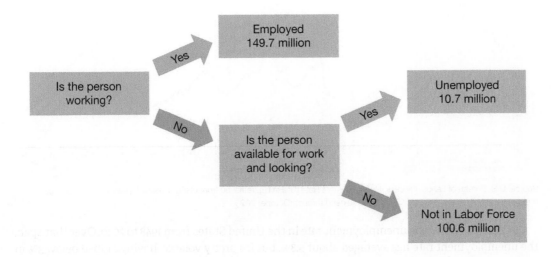

Using the data from its monthly survey, the BLS computes several statistics. First among them is the size of the **labor force** (*LF*), which is the number of people who are either employed (*E*) or who want to be working and have tried to find jobs (the unemployed, *U*):

labor force

The total number of people working or unemployed.

EQUATION 7.1

$$LF = E + U$$

In November of 2020, the labor force was 160,467,000: the 149,732,000 employed plus the 10,735,000 unemployed.

A second statistic the BLS calculates is the **labor force participation rate**, which measures the percentage of the adult population that is in the labor force. To find the labor force participation rate (*LFPR*), just divide the number in the labor force by the adult population (you can multiply by 100 if you'd like to convert to percent form):

labor force participation rate

A measurement of the percentage of the adult population that is in the labor force.

EQUATION 7.2

$$\text{Labor Force Participation Rate} = LFPR = \frac{LF}{\text{Adult Population}}$$

In November 2020, the adult population was 261,085,000, so the labor force participation rate was .615, or 61.5% (160,467,000/261,085,000).

Of all the statistics that the BLS releases, none receives more attention (and none is of greater concern to politicians!) than the **unemployment rate** which is the percentage of the labor force that is unemployed. The formula for the unemployment rate (*URATE*) is:

unemployment rate

The percentage of the labor force that is unemployed.

EQUATION 7.3

$$URATE = \frac{U}{LF} = \frac{U}{E + U}$$

In November 2020, the unemployment rate was 10,735,000/160,467,000 = .067, or 6.7%.

The unemployment rate tells us the fraction of people who would like to be working (including both those who have jobs and those who do not but who are actively seeking work) but aren't. It says nothing, however, about the fraction of people who aren't working but who don't want to work, who don't have to work, or who have quit looking for work.

FIGURE 7.2 Unemployment Rate, 1948–2020

The unemployment rate has averaged just under 6% over the past seven decades. It generally moves up during recessions and declines in expansions.

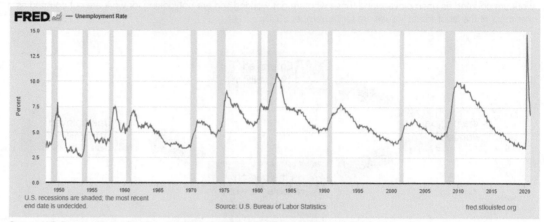

Source: U.S. Bureau of Labor Statistics, Unemployment Rate [UNRATE], retrieved from FRED, Federal Reserve Bank of St. Louis; https://fred.stlouisfed.org/series/UNRATE. Data extend through October 2020.

Figure 7.2 shows the unemployment rate in the United States from 1948 to 2020. Over that span, the unemployment rate has averaged about 5.8%, but it's pretty volatile, having dipped below 3% in the early 1950s and again in the late 2010s, while peaking at an extraordinary 14.7% at the beginning of 2020s COVID-19 recession. The unemployment rate is *countercyclical*, which means that when the economy is headed down (as it is in the shaded grey areas of recession), the unemployment rate heads up; when the economy booms, the unemployment rate generally falls.

Problems With Measured Unemployment

The unemployment rate is an imperfect measure of the true state of unemployment. Generally speaking, the figure published by the BLS understates (is a bit lower than) the "real" unemployment rate. Let's take a look at how and why the measured unemployment rate fails to capture a true picture of what's happening in the labor market.

The Unemployment Rate Doesn't Include People Who Work Part Time. When the unemployment rate is calculated, people who work part time are counted as employed, just the same as full-time workers are. Why is this a problem? Suppose, due to a raging pandemic, that restaurant chef Chloe loses her job. Worried about paying her rent, she quickly finds half-time work at another restaurant. The unemployment rate takes a quick blip upward when Chloe loses her job at the first restaurant, and then returns to its original level when she starts work at the second. That indicates that everything is just fine.

Except that everything is not fine, because the two jobs aren't equal! In the first job, society benefited from forty hours of Chloe's talents each week; in the second job, society only gets to enjoy what she produces in twenty hours. Half of her productivity has disappeared, moving society inside its production possibilities. Despite that, the unemployment numbers indicate everything is as good as ever.

The Unemployment Rate Doesn't Account for Underemployment. Dante is a precision underwater welder working on offshore oil platforms. A nasty oil spill (*not Dante's fault!*) prompts a drilling ban that lands Dante on the unemployment line. Desperate to make ends meet, Dante takes a job digging trenches for a fiber internet company.

The unemployment numbers don't change when Dante shifts from one job to another. That's problematic, because we want our employment statistics to indicate in some way how fully society is utilizing its scarce labor resources. Although Dante is still working full time, society isn't getting the full benefit of his specialized talent and training. Economists call Dante **underemployed**, which means he is performing work for which he is overqualified. That doesn't mean that digging trenches isn't honest and honorable work, and it doesn't mean that it doesn't take *any* training or talent. It simply means that Dante is trained for a far more specialized occupation, an occupation that is more valued in the marketplace.

Workin' at the Car Wash: COVID-19 cost this airline pilot his job. The measured unemployment rate doesn't account for society's opportunity loss.

Source: Nejron Photo/Shutterstock.com

The Unemployment Rate Doesn't Include Discouraged Workers. To shed light on the third major shortcoming of the unemployment rate, consider Raven, whose factory shut down months ago. Raven pursued job opening after job opening after losing her job, but nothing came through. After months of meeting with failure, Raven finally concluded that there weren't any jobs to be had, and that filling out a never-ending string of job applications was futile.

Economists call workers like Raven **discouraged workers**—people who have given up actively seeking work after an extended period of unemployment. Discouraged workers are not counted in the unemployment rate, because they're not counted as part of the labor force (see Figure 7.1). That, of course, is problematic from society's standpoint: Discouraged workers are people who *want* to work, but because they've given up looking, even if society *does* manage to create a job that is perfect for them, they'll have trouble being matched to it.

> **underemployed**
> Performing work for which a person is overqualified.
>
> **discouraged workers**
> People who have given up actively seeking work after an extended period of unemployment.

Discouraged workers distort the unemployment rate statistics in an odd way. Suppose a small town has five workers: Norm, Cliff, Diane, Carla, and Sam. If Norm, Cliff, and Diane are already working, and Carla and Sam are seeking work, then two out of the five members of the labor force are unemployed, for an unemployment rate of 40%.[3] That's pretty high--certainly high enough to concern local officials watching their approval ratings plummet.

But see what happens when Carla gets discouraged and stops looking for work. Now there are three people employed (Norm, Cliff, and Diane), one unemployed (Sam), and one not officially in the labor force (poor, discouraged Carla). Despite the fact that the labor market picture gets worse when Carla drops out of the labor force (because an able-bodied person who wants to work has stopped even looking), the unemployment rate actually improves! Now three workers of the four remaining in the labor force are employed, and the unemployment rate falls to a much more modest 25%. City leaders rejoice, sure that the improvement in the unemployment rate will guarantee them re-election!

The Unemployment Rate Doesn't Include People Who Work in the Underground Economy. Each of the potential inaccuracies we've discussed so far has tended to make the measured unemployment rate paint a picture of the employment situation that is overly rosy. There is, however, one more source of measurement error, one that makes the published unemployment rate present an artificially bleak picture of joblessness. It turns out that not everybody who is working cares to report it to the government when asked! Some work for cash to avoid paying taxes. Others make money through illicit activities like selling drugs or sex. Others are simply undocumented. These people are more likely to report being unemployed than someone with a job in the formal sector, which makes the measured unemployment rate artificially high. Most economists, however, generally agree that the effects of part-time employment, underemployment, and discouraged workers outweigh the effect that workers in the informal sector have on the unemployment rate. In other words, on net, the measured unemployment rate tends to understate the unemployment problem.

Pop! Goes the Econ: *Adam Ruins Unemployment*
In this segment of *Adam Ruins Everything*, discusses why the unemployment rate is flawed. How would Trista be classified? Charles? What shortcomings of the measured unemployment rate does this clip highlight?

View in the online reader

Why Not Fix the Shortcomings of the Unemployment Rate?

The shortcomings of the measured unemployment rate that we outlined above seem easy to fix: The BLS *could* count discouraged workers as unemployed. They *could* count someone who wants to work full time but can only find part-time work as half-unemployed. They *could* count someone who is underemployed as being partially unemployed. So why don't they?

Actually, they do—in a way. The BLS regularly publishes various alternative measures of unemployment that incorporate adjustments like these. But those alternative measures aren't relied on as heavily as the standard measure, because the survey questions used to calculate those alternative numbers are more a matter of opinion than fact. "Are you employed? Have you looked for a job in the past month?" These are the highly objective yes/no questions used to calculate the basic unemployment rate.

Inside the PPC? This econ prof feels her talents are being underutilized.

Source: Sergey Nivens/Shutterstock.com

By comparison, determining whether someone is a discouraged worker is more difficult. The BLS survey taker who is trying to count discouraged workers may have a hard time telling the difference between Julius (who really wants to work and tried unsuccessfully to find it before giving up) and his cousin George, who's not really interested in working but says he is because he doesn't want to admit (even to himself!) that he's kind of a slacker. For the same reason, its hard to distinguish between part-timers who would like to work full time and people who actually prefer to work only part time. It's even more difficult to figure out who is underemployed and who isn't: Picture an econ prof who's just sure she should be playing pro soccer and bringing in major bucks instead of teaching economics for chump change. She might think she's underemployed. Her co-workers, however, might believe that she not only is not capable of playing pro soccer, but also that her student evaluations indicate she's not really qualified to teach economics. In their minds, she is *overemployed*! So who's right, and who's wrong? Who knows?

Adjusting the unemployment rate to accurately reflect these factors is not just difficult, but likely impossible. The subjective nature of the questions used to calculate these alternative measures introduces error into the statistics. So economists usually rely on the admittedly flawed but completely objective measure of the unemployment rate that we described above.

Key Takeaways

- People who are not working but are looking and available for work at any one time are considered unemployed. The unemployment rate is the percentage of the labor force that is unemployed.
- The measured unemployment rate is an inaccurate indicator of labor market conditions because it fails to account for part-time employment, discouraged workers, workers in the underground economy, and underemployed workers.
- Attempts to alter the measured unemployment rate to correct its shortcomings introduce subjectivity and inaccuracy into the measurement process.

Try It!

Given the data in the table, compute the unemployment rate in Year 1 and in Year 2. Explain why, in this example, both the number of people employed and the unemployment rate increased.

Year	Number Employed (in millions)	Number Unemployed (in millions)
1	20	2
2	21	2.4

See related Numerical Problem 3 at the end of this chapter.

Case in Point: Good News and Bad in COVID-19 Unemployment Figures

While it may be hard to predict a recession, economists generally accept the notion that we can predict *what will happen* during a recession. Patterns in the data are so consistent over the course of the business cycle that almost half a century ago, Nobel Prize winner Robert Lucas set them down in stone as a short list of "stylized facts."

If the COVID-19 recession were music.

Source: SvetaZi/Shutterstock.com

Of course, any macroeconomist worth her mechanical pencil can describe what happens during a *typical* recession. That brings us to the COVID-19 recession, which was anything but typical in its origins, its timing, and the policy response. Throughout our macro chapters, we'll be visiting (*and revisiting, and then revisiting again*) the COVID-19 recession to see just how spectacular an economic event it really was. We've already outlined a set of COVID-19 surprises in our chapter on GDP; now let's take a brief look at just how atypically the COVID-19 recession affected employment.

It's no surprise that the unemployment rate rose during the COVID-19 recession. But that increase was notable for two big reasons. First, it reached a peak level we hadn't seen in almost a century, and half-again higher than we saw during the Great Recession, which all of a sudden wasn't looking so "great" after all. Most notable was how quickly the unemployment rate increased. During most recessions, layoffs are spread out, and as some people are thrown out of work, others are finding it. Those offsetting gains and losses cause the unemployment rate to rise slowly and steadily from the beginning of a recession and peak just as the recession ends (see Figure 7.2). Not this time! Day 1: Virus arrives. Day 2: Nonessential businesses close and people shelter in place. Day 3: The unemployment rate spikes to almost 15%. Done.

Just as quickly as the unemployment rate went up, it came down. That's not normal, either! Ordinarily, it takes *years* for the unemployment rate to gently trickle back to a level resembling normal. But during the COVID-19 recession it plummeted a full 8 percentage points (from 14.7% to 6.7%) in just seven months. That 6.7% figure was just half a percentage point higher than the average unemployment rate over the last 50 years![4]

Why did the unemployment rate return to something semi-normal so quickly? In an ordinary recession, most job losers have to search for a new employer. But in the COVID-19 recession, many of those who lost work during the early days of the pandemic simply returned to their old employer when lockdowns lifted and doors reopened. Unfortunately, millions returned to find their full-time jobs reduced to part-time. Others, reluctant to return to work in the midst of a pandemic, gave up on looking for work altogether. So while the ordinary unemployment rate was dropping into 6% territory, an alternative measure of unemployment that includes part-time and discouraged workers (called U-6) stayed well above 12%.

While most people forced out of work by the pandemic were eager to make their way back to work, many older workers, nearing the end of their careers and worried about exposure to the coronavirus, were not. During the COVID-19 recession, 42% of job losers over 55 simply declared themselves retired. That figure dwarfs even the 28% who called it quits during the Great Recession. All told, an amazing 7% of all workers over 55 left the labor force, causing a sharp drop in that age group's labor force participation rate.

Was there any good news in the COVID-19 unemployment figures? Yes—and it's news that should make you feel good about sitting in a college classroom pursuing your degree. The brunt of almost any recession, but particularly the brunt of the COVID-19 recession, is generally borne by people with less education and fewer specialized skills. Half a year into the COVID-19 recession, workers with only a high-school graduation still faced a 7.5% unemployment rate. Having a college degree cut that almost in half to a modest 4.2%. Stay in school, and you'll be in a much better position to start paying back those student loans. (For more exciting news on graduating during a recession, see "Case in Point: Is a COVID-19 Graduation an Economic Death Sentence?" in the next section.)

Compared to other recessions, the COVID-19 recession brought steep declines in employment, followed by an exceptionally rapid recovery.

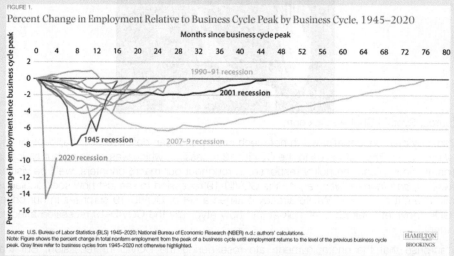

FIGURE 1.

Percent Change in Employment Relative to Business Cycle Peak by Business Cycle, 1945–2020

Source: U.S. Bureau of Labor Statistics (BLS) 1945–2020; National Bureau of Economic Research (NBER) n.d.; authors' calculations.
Note: Figure shows the percent change in total nonfarm employment from the peak of a business cycle until employment returns to the level of the previous business cycle peak. Gray lines refer to business cycles from 1945–2020 not otherwise highlighted.

Source: Brookings Institution. "Percent Change in Employment Relative to Business Cycle Peak by Business Cycle, 1945-2020 (Figure 1)." Courtesy The Hamilton Project at Brookings. Retrieved from: https://www.brookings.edu/blog/brookings-now/2020/09/11/charts-of-the-week-impacts-of-the-coronavirus-recession/. Used with permission from Brookings Institution.

In hindsight, what set the COVID-19 recession apart was not how the data behaved—the things economists *expected* to happen in the labor market *did* happen. What was different was *how* they happened, as if we'd somehow taken an ordinary recession, plugged it into a car stereo, and played it full volume at 8x speed while driving laps on a motocross track. Here's to the COVID-19 recession, providing insights for econ students (and lecture material for econ professors) for years to come.

See related Concept Problem 9 at the end of this chapter.

Answer to Try It! Problem

In Year 1 the total labor force includes 22 million workers, and so the unemployment rate is 2/22 × 100 = 9.1%. In Year 2 the total labor force numbers 23.4 million workers; therefore the unemployment rate is 2.4/23.4 × 100 = 10.3%. In this example, both the number of people employed and the unemployment rate rose, because more people (23.4 − 22 = 1.4 million) entered the labor force, of whom 1 million found jobs and 0.4 million were still looking for jobs.

Khan Academy Link

Unemployment rate primer

7.3 The Nature of Unemployment

Learning Objectives

1. Define the three different types of unemployment.
2. Illustrate graphically the natural level of employment, and relate that level of employment to the natural rate of unemployment.
3. List the causes of frictional, structural, and cyclical unemployment.

You now know how the unemployment rate is calculated and understand some of its shortcomings. Because of its shortcomings, you now know that the unemployment rate cited in the news is likely to understate the severity of the unemployment problem. But there are other questions about unemployment that remain to be asked, not least among them the big question raised earlier: If there is plenty of work to be done, and if unemployed people are genuinely interested in doing work, then why can't we place those people in jobs? Because not all unemployment is the same. Different types of unemployment occur for different reasons. In this section, we'll take a closer look at the three different types of unemployment and what causes them.

Types of Unemployment

Workers may find themselves unemployed for different reasons. To shed light on the sources of unemployment, let's take a closer look at the labor market using demand and supply as our lens.

The demand and supply model of the labor market is shown in Figure 7.3. This graph may look a bit different than the ones you've seen before: The price of labor here is not a dollar price, but is something called the *real wage*, which equals the dollar (nominal) wage workers are paid (W) divided by the price level (P). The **real wage** (represented by the Greek letter omega, ω) measures the quantity of goods and services workers can purchase for an hour's work.[5] The labor supply curve is drawn as upward sloping and steep: The quantity of labor supplied at any one time is likely to be nearly fixed. The labor demand curve shows the quantity of labor demanded by employers at each real wage. The lower the real wage, the more labor firms will want to employ.

real wage

The quantity of goods and services workers can purchase for an hour's work, measured as the nominal wage W divided by the price level, P.

**natural level of
employment**

The employment level at
which the quantity of labor
demanded equals the
quantity supplied.

Unnatural Equilibrium? The
labor market is different than
the market for apples: Even
at equilibrium, some people
remain unmatched.

Source: Denis OREA/
Shutterstock.com

**natural rate of
unemployment**

The rate of unemployment
consistent with the natural
level of employment. It
reflects both frictional and
structural unemployment.

The labor market works like any other market: Equilibrium is found at the price (in this case, the real wage) where quantity demanded equals quantity supplied. In Figure 7.3, the equilibrium real wage is ω_e and the equilibrium quantity of labor is L_e. That equilibrium level of employment is often referred to as the **natural level of employment**, or *full employment*.

Here's what's different about the labor market as opposed to, say, the market for breakfast cereal. In the demand and supply model of the market for breakfast cereal, we generally assume that at the equilibrium price, all boxes of cereal offered by sellers end up being purchased by buyers. In the labor market, however, it's possible that even at the equilibrium wage, some people willing to work can't find it, and some jobs posted by employers will be vacant. (We'll explore the reasons for that in a moment.) The rate of unemployment consistent with the natural level of employment is called the **natural rate of unemployment**. The natural rate of unemployment reflects mismatches in the labor market. Even more unemployment (not included in the natural rate) can occur during business cycles. Let's take a look at each of these types of unemployment, in turn.

FIGURE 7.3 The Natural Level of Employment

The demand for labor (D_1) represents employers who want to hire workers at various wages. The supply of labor (S_1) shows the number of workers willing to work at each real wage. The equilibrium employment level, called the natural level of employment, is found where the quantity of labor demanded equals the quantity supplied. Here, the natural level of employment is L_e, and the equilibrium real wage is ω_e. At the natural level of employment, the unemployment rate is at its natural rate, and there is no cyclical unemployment.

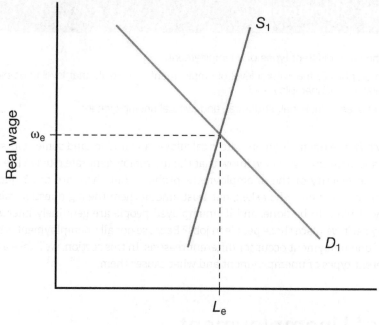

Frictional Unemployment

**frictional
unemployment**

Unemployment that occurs
because it takes time for
employers and workers to
find each other.

Even when the quantity of labor demanded equals the quantity of labor supplied, not all employers and potential workers will seamlessly find one another: Some workers will still be looking for jobs, and some employers will have unfilled vacancies. Given enough time, those employers and employees may find one another, but until they do, the workers remain unemployed. Unemployment that occurs because it takes time for employers and workers to find each other is called **frictional unemployment**.

Lots of new college graduates looking for that "just right" first job are frictionally unemployed. They may have a number of interviews scheduled, and are waiting to complete them before deciding which jobs they will choose. Or their dream job may be out there waiting, halfway across the country in Toledo, and they just haven't found out about the opening yet. Employers, too, may have many many interviews to complete before deciding who will fill their open positions. In these cases, the labor market just doesn't work as smoothly as everyone wishes it would. And what's the absence of smooth? Friction!

As strange as it sounds, a little bit of frictional unemployment isn't a terrible thing. From a social standpoint, we want to ensure that we're making the best use of our scarce (labor) resources: We want workers to find jobs that match their skills and maximize their enthusiasm. It is far better to have Neil deGrasse Tyson teaching about the cosmos than dunking fries at the nearest Burger King. If he gets thrown out of work and remains unemployed while he looks for his next job in astrophysics, that's probably a good thing. And that search time typically isn't very long: Most spells of frictional unemployment last just a few weeks.

Frictional unemployment is evidence of a dynamic economy. In a thriving market economy, new businesses are always popping up and others are dying. There will always be frictional unemployment in that kind of economy, simply because of the time it takes to shift workers from one business to another. Contrast that to the Middle Ages, when most people did they same kind of work their parents did—carpenters, masons, and farmers, for example. There was very little unemployment—very few people were between jobs waiting for the right thing to come along. But there was also very little economic progress: New industries and technologies weren't being created.

Small Price to Pay: Finding the right job is like finding the right mate—neither happens instantly, but both can be worth the wait.

Structural Unemployment

There is a second type of unemployment that we're likely to find at any given time. **Structural unemployment** is longer-term unemployment that exists because of changes in the structure of the economy or because of institutions that prevent the labor market from working as well as it might. This is a very different type of unemployment than shorter-term frictional unemployment: Structural unemployment can be persistent.

Fundamental Changes in the Economy May Cause Structural Unemployment

Like frictional unemployment, structural unemployment can exist even if there are as many workers as there are vacancies. But while frictional unemployment exists because workers and jobs just haven't found one another yet, structural unemployment exists because the skills workers have may not be the skills employers seek.

For example, in the 1980s, college students wrote their term papers on finicky typewriters that often needed repair. By the early 1990s, college students had mothballed their typewriters in favor of equally finicky computers that also often needed repair. That change in how people produced written documents was a structural change, similar in nature to the popularization of air travel in the 1950s . . . and Zoom in 2020.

structural unemployment

Longer-term unemployment due to changes in the structure of the economy or because of an economy's labor institutions.

Pop! Goes the Econ: "Video Killed the Radio Star"

This, the first video aired on the brand-new music video channel MTV, foretold the demise of radio. Many of the most popular 1970s and 1980s music stars were unable to successfully transition to video. Why do you suppose they failed? What type of unemployment did those stars face? What is now replacing television music videos?

View in the online reader

"I'm old, dammit, and no, I don't wanna learn your stupid trick."

Source: Jeff Thrower/ Shutterstock.com

As a result of the structural change in the 1980s, jobs disappeared in the typewriter industry and appeared in the computer industry. But not every typewriter repair expert had the skills and knowledge to fix a glitchy computer; there was a surplus of workers in one industry and a shortage in the other. The surplus typewriter workers were structurally unemployed. That type of structural unemployment, of course doesn't have to last any longer than the time it takes to retrain displaced workers for new jobs. But retraining takes time, and not everyone who loses their job is immediately on board with the idea of gearing up for a new career, so structural unemployment is likely to last a while.

The kind of structural unemployment that results from a skills mismatch may occur if students fail to predict how many jobs there will be available in their major field when they graduate. A similar kind of structural unemployment can also result from geographical mismatches: The economy may be booming in one region and slumping in another, and it takes time for unemployed workers to relocate and find new jobs—if they're willing to do that at all. That geographic unemployment can exist even at a micro level: Poor or costly transportation may, for example, keep some urban residents from filling an open job only a few miles away.

Labor Market Features May Create Structural Unemployment

Sometimes, long-term structural unemployment is an unfortunate consequence of the laws and institutions of an economy's labor market. This kind of structural unemployment is likely to exist as long as the institutions that created it remain in place.

Sometimes structural unemployment exists because laws designed to protect workers reduce the fluid movement into and out of jobs. One example of such a law is employment protection, which is designed to make it more difficult for businesses to lay off employees. Many European Union countries require businesses to notify the government if they dismiss a worker, and businesses are required to obtain the government's permission should they want to lay off a group of workers. Sometimes, labor protections even require firms to offer severance pay to dismissed workers.

It is admittedly comforting to know that your company can't get rid of you easily. After all, have you ever heard anyone complain about too much job security? But sometimes, employers need to let workers go, and sometimes that needs to happen quickly. Being forced to keep idle employees on payroll in a recession can drive a company into premature bankruptcy. Even worse, employment protections make it hard to get rid of employees who aren't productive, who are not a good fit for their job, or who exploit their job security by taking frequent naps in the janitor's closet.

It may be puzzling how laws that make it hard to get rid of workers cause unemployment. But workers that are hard to get rid of present a real risk to firms. Hire someone—even someone who appears to be a stellar employee—and you're stuck with her. Recession hits? Stuck. Pandemic? Stuck. She turns out to be a dud? Stuck. To avoid that risk, firms that can't fire workers may respond by not *hiring* workers . . . or by hiring fewer than they otherwise might want. The result? Structural unemployment, with firms that really *do* want more workers, and workers who really *do* want jobs, with nothing but the law standing in the way.

The evidence bears this out: Countries with greater labor protection generally have higher overall unemployment rates. Worse still, in countries with lots of labor protections, unemployment tends to last longer--one of the defining features of structural unemployment. Figure 7.4 shows the impact of labor market protections on long-term unemployment. The horizontal axis shows the degree of labor protection, as measured by the World Bank's Rigidity of Employment Index, with higher values indicating greater labor protection. The vertical axis measures the percentage of the unemployed who have been unemployed for longer than one year. In low-protection countries, about one jobless person in four has been unemployed for a year or longer. In high-protection countries, about 40% of the jobless have been unemployed for longer than a year. The pattern provides a strong testament to the impact of labor protection on structural unemployment.

I know I'm supposed to be monitoring the reactor, but I just needed some "me" time.

Source: Tim Masters/
Shutterstock.com

FIGURE 7.4 Long-Term Unemployment and Labor Protection
In countries with more labor protection (indicated by a higher labor rigidity index score), a greater proportion of unemployment is long-term unemployment.

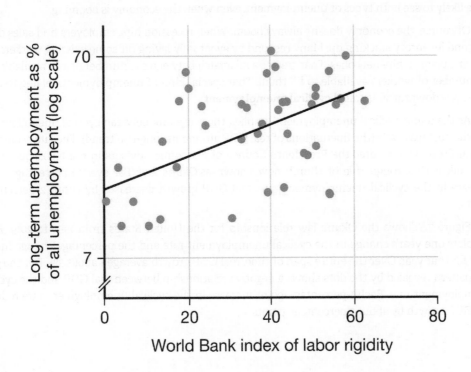

Source: Data from World Bank (2008) and OECD (2018) at https://datacatalog.worldbank.org/rigidity-employment-index-0less-rigid-100more-rigid and https://data.oecd.org/unemp/long-term-unemployment-rate.htm respectively.

There's a second way that labor market institutions may create and sustain long-term unemployment: They can prevent wages from adjusting to their equilibrium level. If law or custom holds the wage above its equilibrium level, a surplus of labor will exist . . . and a surplus of labor is just another way of saying unemployment!

Sometimes, the government is responsible for holding wages artificially high. For example, most countries have passed some form of minimum wage law. The goal of those laws is to help people at the bottom end of the income distribution be as self-sufficient as possible. Unfortunately, for the minimum wage to have any effect, it must be set above the market-clearing wage, which discourages hiring by employers and may create persistent unemployment for those at the minimum wage.

While minimum wage laws can create structural unemployment at the lower end of the wage ladder, labor unions can create structural unemployment at the other end. A labor union is a group of employees who agree to negotiate their salary and benefits and working conditions together rather than as individuals. That process, called *collective bargaining*, is based on the idea that there is strength in numbers. Over the past 150 years, unions have played a critical role in negotiating workers' rights, compensation, and safer working conditions.

Unions are less prominent today than they were half a century ago, when one worker in three was a union member. Today, only about one worker in nine belongs to a union, but despite declining membership, unions still have bargaining power: Empirical evidence suggests collective bargaining raises wages for union members by more then ten percent. Unfortunately, those above-market wages may take a toll on unemployment: Unionized industries may end up hiring fewer workers than they otherwise would; structural unemployment may result.

Cyclical Unemployment

Both frictional and structural unemployment are likely to exist at the natural level of employment, where the number of people seeking work and the number of vacancies are equal. That means that we're likely to see both types of unemployment, even when the economy is booming.

cyclical unemployment

Unemployment related to downturns in the economy during business cycles.

Of course, the economy doesn't always boom. When recession hits, employers find sales dropping and inventory stacking up. Many respond by eventually laying off some existing workers and shelving plans to hire new ones. That creates a mismatch between the number of jobs available and the number of workers available to fill them. That special kind of unemployment, related to business-cycle downturns, is called **cyclical unemployment**.

As the name "cyclical unemployment" implies, there is a link between cyclical unemployment and the business cycle (the fluctuations of real GDP around its long-run trend). The late economist Arthur Okun, who chaired the President's Council of Economic Advisors in the 1960s, quantified that link with a rough rule of thumb now known as *Okun's law*: For every 1-percentage-point increase in the cyclical unemployment rate, real GDP growth decreases by about 2 percentage points.

Figure 7.5 shows the Okun's law relationship for the United States from 1950 to 2019. Each dot plots one year's change in the cyclical unemployment rate and the percentage change in real GDP for that year. Over the entire span of time, real GDP growth averaged about 3%. But the general pattern revealed by the dots shows a negative relationship between real GDP and the cyclical unemployment rate: Each 1-percentage-point increase in the cyclical unemployment rate reduces real GDP growth by about 2 percentage points.

FIGURE 7.5 Okun's Law: 1950–2019

Each dot plots one year's measured change in the cyclical unemployment rate and the percentage change in real GDP. The general pattern indicates that each 1-percentage-point increase in the unemployment rate causes the growth rate of real GDP to decrease by about 2 percentage points.

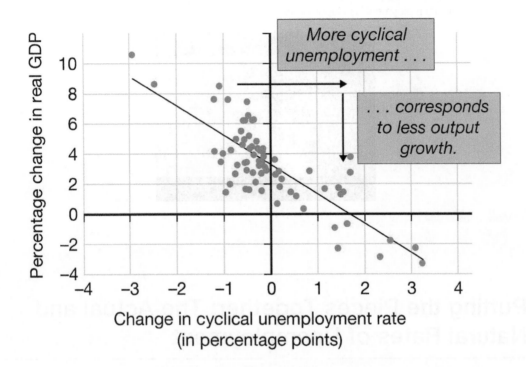

More cyclical unemployment . . .

. . . corresponds to less output growth.

Change in cyclical unemployment rate (in percentage points)

Percentage change in real GDP

Source: Data from Bureau of Labor Statistics, the Bureau of Economic Analysis, and the Congressional Budget Office, accessed through Federal Reserve Economic Data (FRED) at https://fred.stlouisfed.org/series/UNRATE; https://fred.stlouisfed.org/series/GDPC1; and https://fred.stlouisfed.org/series/NROU.

You might be wondering why the changes in GDP are larger than the changes in unemployment. After all, with 1% fewer workers, shouldn't we get 1% less output? That makes sense in theory, but the real world is messier. Some laid-off workers, for example, will become discouraged workers; the economy will lose their output, but they won't be counted among the unemployed. Also, during recessions many firms cut output but hang on to their workers because those workers were hard to find and costly to train, a practice known as *labor hoarding*. Output falls a lot, but employment doesn't decrease by as much. In both cases, the result is an increase in unemployment resulting in a larger decrease in output.

A second reason for cyclical unemployment, and one that economists find difficult to explain, is that cutting wages simply isn't part of the customary way business is done, even though it could be and, arguably, should be. In the ideal world of the economist, it would be natural for firms to immediately cut wages during economic downturns as a reflection of the decreased value those workers create for the firm. Allowing wages to fall would reduce a firm's labor costs, which would allow the firm to retain a larger fraction of its workforce and weather the recession.

Outsized strength? A 1% decrease in the cyclical unemployment rate causes a 2% increase in real GDP growth!

Source: restyler/Shutterstock.com

Pop! Goes the Econ: "Unemployment" and *Napoleon Dynamite*

Napoleon is having trouble finding a girl. If failing to pair with a girl is like failing to pair with a job, what kind of "unemployment" is Napoleon experiencing?

View in the online reader

Putting the Pieces Together: The Actual and Natural Rates of Unemployment

Workers will always be moving from one job to another. New industries will always be springing to life while others wither. And once laws have introduced wage and employment rigidities, those rigidities are hard to get rid of. That means that even when the economy is booming, there will always be frictional and structural unemployment: They naturally occur as a by-product of a dynamic economy, which is why the natural rate of unemployment is often expressed as the sum of the frictional and structural unemployment rates.

EQUATION 7.4
$$\text{Natural } URATE = \text{Frictional } URATE + \text{Structural } URATE$$

The actual rate of unemployment is the sum of the frictional, structural, and cyclical unemployment rates:

EQUATION 7.5
$$URATE = \text{Frictional } URATE + \text{Structural } URATE + \text{Cyclical } URATE$$

That means that the measured unemployment rate is the sum of the natural rate and the cyclical rate.

EQUATION 7.6
$$URATE = \text{Natural } URATE + \text{Cyclical } URATE$$

The cyclical unemployment rate, then, can be measured as the difference between the measured unemployment rate and the natural rate:

$$\text{Cyclical } URATE = URATE - \text{Natural } URATE$$

Figure 7.6 shows the actual rate of unemployment (in red) and natural rate of unemployment (in blue) from 1960 to the end of 2019. The natural rate captures the long-run trend in unemployment, changing slowly because the behaviors and institutions that cause frictional and structural unemployment tend to change slowly. The actual rate changes quickly because economic activity can be quite volatile. Because the economy is always in some phase of the business cycle or another, actual and natural unemployment rates are rarely equal.

FIGURE 7.6 The Actual and Natural Rates of Unemployment, 1960–2019

The actual rate of unemployment (in red) fluctuates around the natural rate of unemployment (blue). When the economy is in recession, the actual rate exceeds the natural rate. Near the business cycle peak, the actual rate is lower than the natural rate. These differences measure the cyclical unemployment rate.

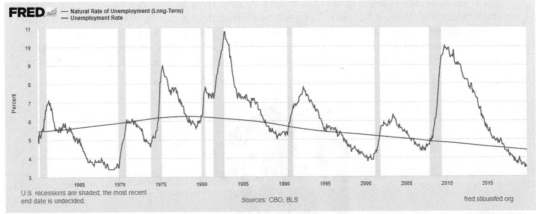

Source: Bureau of Labor Statistics and Congressional Budget Office, accessed through Federal Reserve Economic Data (FRED) at https://fred.stlouisfed.org/series/UNRATE and https://fred.stlouisfed.org/series/NROU. FRED® Graphs ©Federal Reserve Bank of St. Louis.All rights reserved. All FRED® Graphs appear courtesy of Federal Reserve Bank of St. Louis. https://fred.stlouisfed.org/).

The difference between the actual and natural unemployment rates at any point in time measures the cyclical unemployment rate. For example, in July 2009, as the Great Recession was ending, the natural rate of unemployment was 4.8%, while the actual rate of unemployment was 9.5%. The cyclical unemployment rate, then was 9.5% − 4.8% = 4.7%.

Key Takeaways

- Unemployment can be frictional, structural, or cyclical.
- Frictional unemployment exists due to difficulties matching workers with available jobs.
- Most structural unemployment exists because available workers have the wrong skills or training for the available jobs. Some also exists due to labor market institutions.
- Frictional and structural unemployment exist even at full employment. The natural rate of unemployment is the sum of the frictional and structural rates of unemployment.
- When the labor market is in equilibrium, employment is at the natural level and the unemployment rate equals the natural rate of unemployment.
- Cyclical unemployment exists because of business cycle conditions. The cyclical rate of unemployment can be measured as the difference between the actual and natural rates of unemployment. No cyclical unemployment exists at full employment.
- Okun's law says that each 1% increase in the cyclical unemployment rate is linked to a 2% decline in real output.

Try It!

Suppose that the Congressional Budget Office estimates that the frictional rate of unemployment (frictionally employed/labor force) is 1.2%, and the structural rate of unemployment is 2.8%. If we were at full employment a year ago, and today's actual unemployment rate is 5.5%,

1. What is the cyclical rate of unemployment?
2. Roughly how much has real GDP changed because of the business cycle?

See related Numerical Problem 5 at the end of this chapter.

Case in Point: Is a COVID-19 Graduation an Economic Death Sentence?

When you entered college, your future looked bright. The purposeful decision to forego work and invest in yourself looked like a good one, even if you did have to take out thousands of dollars in student loans to make it happen. The great news is that your decision was probably a great one: The college earnings premium has never been higher. People with college degrees earn over 80% more than those without. That can amount to well over one million dollars over the course of a career. Your college education will likely more than pay for itself within a decade of graduation.

Bright Future: Don't lose those shades—you're gonna need 'em . . . we think.

Source: CREATISTA/Shutterstock.com

But then . . . COVID-19. Turns out, you don't have complete control over your destiny after all. It's possible you may find yourself being both a victim of your age (which largely determines *when* you go to college) and the state of the economy when you graduate. What happens if you graduate during an economic recession? Will you be able to shrug it off, or will it permanently alter the trajectory of your career?

While the jury is still out on the impact of the COVID-19 recession on graduates, it's possible to learn from past recessions. Economists Philip Oreopoulos, Till von Wachter, and Andrew Heisz have mixed news for students graduating into a recession. The bad news: Entering the job market during a recession is rough—it's harder to find a job, because more potential workers compete for each open job, and because there are fewer jobs available. In the Great Recession of 2007–2009, for example, employers cut hiring by over 20%. That's some cyclical unemployment! Now let's add some insult to that injury: Lots of workers competing for fewer jobs causes wages to fall, with graduates joining the workforce during recessions earning about 10% less than they otherwise would have.

Oreopoulos, von Wachter, and Heisz do have some good news: The recessionary wage penalty eventually goes away, with the salaries of most "recessionary graduates" catching up to non-recessionary grads within ten or fifteen years (though graduates with poor resumes may never reach their full potential). Unfortunately, to get their earnings back on track, recessionary graduates have to change jobs more often in pursuit of higher wages. Meanwhile, the losses mount: Even the graduates who do finally catch up with their peers end up losing $60,000 to $100,000 in the process of catching up.

Here's hoping that by the time you graduate, the COVID-19 recession will be a distant memory and the economy will be strong. But even if it isn't, your decision to attend college was a good one: Recession or not, you'll be much better off than if you'd never gone to college at all. And if the economy fails to recover, or takes another tumble during your college years? You can protect yourself from the adverse effects of your graduation date by doing two simple things. First, because strong grads return to potential more quickly than weak grads, build extra skills and a strong resume to set yourself apart. *Don't be interchangeable, because interchangeable parts are both easily overlooked and easily replaced.* Second, once you've graduated, *take advantage of the mobility of youth*. The more willing you are to move from job to job and city to city, the more quickly your earnings will return to their potential.

See related Concept Problem 11 at the end of this chapter.

Sources: Based on Philip Oreopoulos, Till von Wachter, and Andrew Heisz's "The Short- and Long-Term Career Effects of Graduating in a Recession," American Economic Journal: Applied Economics, 2012; and Hannes Schwandt's "Recession Graduates: The Long-lasting Effects of an Unlucky Draw," Stanford Institute for Economic Policy Research Policy Brief, 2019.

Answers to Try It! Problems

1. The natural rate is the sum of the frictional rate (1.2%) and the structural rate (2.8%), or 4%. The actual unemployment rate (5.5%) is the sum of the natural rate and the cyclical rate. So, the cyclical rate of unemployment is the difference between today's 5.5% and the natural rate of 4%, or 1.5%.

2. We know we're in a recession because the cyclical rate has gone from 0% last year (full employment!) to 1.5% this year. Okun's law says that output declines by about 2% for every 1% increase in the cyclical unemployment rate, so output has likely fallen by 3% (2 × 1.5).

Khan Academy Link

Structural, frictional, natural, and cyclical unemployment

7.4 Policy Implications of Unemployment

Learning Objectives

1. Describe the appropriate policy recommendations to reduce frictional, structural, and cyclical unemployment. Explain how those recommendations differ.
2. Explain how policymakers might use the actual and natural unemployment rates to determine appropriate economic policy actions.
3. Explain how the inability to observe the true natural rate of unemployment might lead economic policymakers to make poor recommendations.

You may be wondering why economists bother to distinguish between the different types of unemployment. To people who have just been laid off, the distinctions probably seem immaterial. However, they matter a great deal to policymakers because the recipe for fixing an unemployment problem varies depending on what type of unemployment the economy is experiencing.

Solutions to Differing Types of Unemployment

Let's take a look at each type of unemployment, in turn, and discuss the best way to solve each.

Frictional Unemployment

Frictional unemployment exists because it takes time to match workers with available jobs. If society wants to reduce unemployment, and most of that unemployment is frictional, then the only *permanent* fix is to speed up the process of matching available workers with available jobs. Ensuring a smooth and rapid flow of information between firms and workers is the surest path to achieve that.

Decreases in frictional unemployment are responsible for a great deal of the decades-long decline in the natural rate shown in Figure 7.6, and it's largely the march of technology that's responsible. Forty years ago, the only good sources of information about job vacancies were help wanted ads in the newspaper. Finding a job out-of-state took *real* effort! Today, the internet alone provides job seekers thousands of ways to find out about new jobs across the country and around the globe. If you want to work for the European Central Bank after graduation, you can find out about employment opportunities just by visiting its website.[6] Internet enterprises like monster.com and craigslist.com are devoted to directly matching workers and jobs. Networking giant LinkedIn is a great way for college students to connect with employers, and even social networking sites like Facebook help people connect to people who know people that are related to people who might know something about employment opportunities.[7]

Reducing Friction: They say opportunity knocks, but they lie: It clicks.

Source: mstanley/Shutterstock.com

Those friction-reducing advances are largely private, but the government has done a lot to reduce frictional unemployment, too. The U.S. Department of Labor runs CareerOneStop, a one-stop shop that offers training referrals, career counseling, access to state job bank listings, and similar employment-related services. The U.S. government has also centralized its own job postings online: You can find thousands of available jobs at www.usajobs.gov. Many state and local governments also offer services similar to those offered by the federal government. In addition, many governments devote resources to improving information flow to the public; one way they do so is by improving access to libraries, computers, and the internet. To the extent that such efforts make labor-market information more readily available, they reduce frictional unemployment.

Structural Unemployment

If unemployment is mostly frictional, devise a way to do a better and faster job of matching workers with jobs, and your unemployment problem will shrink. But if most of your unemployment is structural, a job-matching program won't help much, because (1) the skills employers are looking for are different than the skills unemployed workers have, and (2) structural features that can cause unemployment, such as job protections and collective bargaining, won't disappear just because you've improved the information flow between employers and workers.

The solution to structural unemployment is addressing the underlying structural issue. Sometimes that's straightforward and unobjectionable: The United States has long had job retraining and continuing education programs for workers that have been displaced by technological progress or thrown out of work due to increasing globalization. Getting displaced workers to take advantage of those programs, however, can be difficult; more mature workers sometimes don't feel as if they can set life on hold while they return to school for retraining, because . . . bills! Solutions to other unemployment-creating structural institutions like reducing the minimum wage or reducing job protections are often met with fierce resistance. In France, where labor protections are voluminous and the unemployment rate had lingered near 9% for a decade while the rest of the developed world enjoyed unrelenting economic growth, President Emmanuel Macron's proposed labor law reforms were met with fierce political resistance, labor strikes, and nationwide protests.[8]

Cyclical Unemployment

Although government programs may reduce frictional and structural unemployment, they cannot eliminate it. Information in the labor market will always have a cost, and that cost creates frictional unemployment. In a dynamic economy with changing demands for goods and services, changing technology, and changing production costs, there will always be some sectors growing while others shrink. That makes structural unemployment inevitable. That's why the unemployment rate will always be positive even when an economy is operating at its potential.

It doesn't matter to this just-fired businesswoman whether she's frictionally, cyclically, or structurally unemployed. But it matters to policymakers.

Source: Supavadee butradee/Shutterstock.com

But cyclical unemployment is a different problem altogether. Cyclical unemployment often results from millions of people spending less than they normally do. The policy prescription for reducing cyclical unemployment, then, is to either get people to accelerate their own spending or find some way to replace the spending that evaporated. Those solutions aren't easy to implement: The government has a limited number of tools at its disposal, and at different times, those tools have varying degrees of effectiveness. The chapters that follow devote a lot of attention to examining those tools, their strengths, and their shortcomings.

Government also bumps up against limits when it tries to push unemployment permanently below its natural rate. Experience has taught economists that trying to hold unemployment unnaturally low makes undesirable things happen elsewhere in the economy. The biggest concern is that trying to push unemployment below where it naturally wants to be will cause the prices of goods and services throughout the economy to rise rapidly. The previous chapter is devoted to exploring that phenomenon, called *inflation*.

Data Quality and Policy Design

In our discussion of gross domestic product, we killed a lot of trees discussing how poor GDP data actually is. In the discussion of the consumer price index that followed, we did even more damage discussing how the consumer price index and other measures of the overall price level inaccurately capture the cost of living. And in this chapter, we've turned a rainforest into a desert talking about how unemployment numbers paint an artificially rosy view of the labor market.

Macroeconomists are often hobbled by the availability and quality of data. For policymakers, this can create real problems: Make a recommendation based on poor data and you've likely made a less-than-ideal recommendation. The quality issues regarding GDP, the price level, and unemployment surely make good decision-making difficult. But there's one more layer of complexity in the unemployment data that we need to add to the picture: *Policymakers only receive information about the <u>overall</u> unemployment rate.* They have to *estimate* how much of it is frictional, structural, and cyclical. That's hard even on a person-by-person basis: Is a recently laid-off Moroccan fusion chef frictionally unemployed because there's an opening at a Moroccan fusion restaurant in Wyoming that she doesn't know about yet? Is she structurally unemployed because Moroccan fusion is no longer popular, and she needs retraining in Hungarian cuisine? Or is she cyclically unemployed because people want to eat Moroccan fusion but can't

"Nailed that full-employment target again, Mr. President. Say, can I call you back? Daenerys Targaryen's about to unleash the dragons, and I don't want to miss it."

Source: EUStock/Shutterstock.com

afford to because of a slack economy? It's hard for her to tell, and it's hard for the BLS survey-taker who counts her as unemployed to tell. And if it's hard to tell exactly what kind of employment an individual is facing, then think how difficult it must be to determine, with no additional information, how many of the millions of unemployed people are experiencing each type of unemployment.

That uncertainty makes designing good policy difficult. Suppose the chair of the Federal Reserve System, Jerome Powell, is charged with maintaining full employment. That means that he's supposed to eliminate cyclical unemployment (there's little he can do to eliminate frictional and structural unemployment). He hops onto the BLS website and sees that the unemployment rate is 5%. What he does with this information depends on what he believes the unobserved natural rate is.

- If he thinks the natural rate of unemployment is 4.4%, then the cyclical unemployment rate must be 0.6%. That calls for some economic stimulus: Chairman Powell, as you will see in later chapters, will try to pump up the economy and stimulate spending by pumping new money into the banking system and reducing interest rates.

- If he believes that the natural rate of unemployment is 5.9%, then cyclical unemployment must be –0.9%. Powell thinks to himself, "*Hmmmm . . . there seems to be a bit of overexuberance among consumers. People are working too hard and spending too much, and businesses are overproducing. I need to lower the boom before prices start rising.*" He promptly orders his minions to pull money out of the banking system and drive up interest rates in an effort to slow down spending.

- The third and final possibility is that Fed Chair Powell believes the natural rate to be exactly 5%. In that case, Powell mixes up a dry martini, turns on *Game of Thrones*, and tells his employees to knock off early.

The difficulties in measuring the unemployment rate and its component parts make crafting policy difficult. Should Jerome Powell stimulate the economy? Should he clamp down on the economy? Or should he kick back and watch some TV? The answer depends on what the unobserved natural rate is. If he guesses wrong, he might stimulate an already-overheating economy, or he might try to slow down an economy that is already entering a recession. Even if he does the right thing, he may have trouble figuring out *how much* of the right thing to do. Because of data quality, crafting sound economic policy is an incredibly difficult (and incredibly important) guessing game—a game that is likely to be far more difficult than how it's described in your econ textbook (*yes, even this one*) or on your economics classroom whiteboard.

Key Takeaways

- Different types of unemployment demand different solutions. Frictional unemployment can be reduced through policies that make it easier to match workers and vacancies. Structural unemployment can be reduced with policies that help the unemployed train for current vacancies, or by eliminating labor-market institutions that tend to create long-term unemployment. Cyclical unemployment can be reduced through policies that stimulate spending.

- It is often difficult to tell whether any individual is frictionally, structurally, or cyclically unemployed. It's even more difficult to measure the frictional, structural, and cyclical unemployment rates for the economy as a whole. Those difficulties make it difficult to design policies to reduce unemployment.

- Attempting to hold the unemployment rate below its natural rate for long periods of time generally results in inflation.

- Because policymakers observe only the actual rate of unemployment (and not the natural rate), it is sometimes difficult to tell whether economic activity needs to be stimulated or slowed down.

Try It!

You are the chair of the Fed, one of the top brass in charge of setting the course of economic policy. Today's unemployment rate is 4.5%. You estimate that the structural rate of unemployment is 2.7%, and the frictional rate of unemployment is 1.1%.

1. Calculate the estimated cyclical unemployment rate.
2. In your role as policymaker, should you try to stimulate the economy or slow it down?
3. Suppose you have underestimated the frictional rate of unemployment, and the true rate is 2.0%. Discuss the quality of your recommendation from (2).

See related Numerical Problem 8 at the end of this chapter.

Case in Point: Unemployment Insurance—Blessing or Curse?

If you ever happen to lose your job, it's nice to know that the government has your back. The U.S. unemployment compensation system provides income stability to workers during periods of temporary unemployment. Created in the 1930s, the unemployment compensation system typically replaces about half of a worker's salary for up to a year.

Will overly generous unemployment benefits turn your hard-working roommate into . . . this?

Source: Masarik/Shutterstock.com

Unemployment insurance reduces the cost of being unemployed. That may slow the return to work: Several studies indicate that a disproportionate number of the unemployed find work just before or just after their unemployment benefits expire. That sounds like people are taking advantage of the system, but Nobel Prize winner Dale Mortensen says it's really a good thing: His research shows that unemployment insurance gives workers the freedom to look for the best work at the highest pay instead of taking early offers out of desperation. That allows the economy to make the most of its workers' training and talents, which makes the economy better rather than worse.

But if the benefits are too big, or last too long, they can backfire. As an example, compare the experience in the United States and Germany between 1980 and 2005. Over that time period, German unemployment insurance replaced at least 70% of income for up to four years. Not surprisingly, the German unemployment rate was over 3% higher than the U.S. rate, for decades. And unemployment lasted longer in Germany, too: Over half of the unemployed in Germany remained out of work for more than a year compared to just 13% in the United States. That's problematic: When you're out of work for that long, your skills deteriorate, which means that generous unemployment benefits can turn relatively painless short-term frictional unemployment into more troublesome long-term structural unemployment.

At the beginning of the COVID-19 recession, when states locked down all but essential workplaces, the U.S. federal government created programs that dramatically increased unemployment benefits and extended their duration.[9] Should we worry that those benefits will turn the United States into a country full of idlers just waiting for their checks to show up each month? Evidence from the Great Recession indicates otherwise, according to economists Henry Farber and Robert Valletta. During that historic downturn, unemployment benefits were extended to a maximum of 99 weeks. Farber and Valletta found that during the Great Recession, the unemployed found jobs just as quickly as they always did.

But the extended benefits *did* have an effect: They kept the unemployed from being discouraged and leaving the workforce entirely. That's a good thing in many ways, but perversely, it makes the numbers look worse, prolonging the average duration of unemployment by 7%, causing the unemployment rate to increase by an extra 0.4 percentage points, and contributing to about one fourth of the longer-term unemployment that followed the recession.

That evidence should ease concerns about the generosity of pandemic relief during the COVID-19 recession. One year into the pandemic, most Americans seemed not just *willing* to return to work, but *desperate* to escape their homes and return to a life resembling normal. In the meantime, unemployment compensation provided much-needed financial security to millions simultaneously thrown out of work by lockdowns, through no fault of their own.

See related Concept Problem 3 at the end of this chapter.

Sources: Based on Henry Farber and Robert Valletta's "Do Extended Unemployment Benefits Lengthen Unemployment Spells? Evidence from Recent Cycles in the U.S. Labor Market," NBER Working Paper No. 19048, 2013; Phillip Inman and Julia Kollewe, "Peter Diamond, Dale Mortensen and Christopher Pissarides Share Economics Nobel Prize for Jobs Study," The Guardian, October 11, 2010; Catherine Rampell, "Economists Share Nobel for Studying Job Market," The New York Times, October 11, 2010; and Edward L. Glaeser, "The Work Behind the Nobel Prize," The New York Times, October 11, 2010.

Answers to Try It! Problems

1. The estimated cyclical unemployment rate is the actual rate (4.5%) minus the estimated natural rate. The estimated natural rate is the estimated structural rate (2.7%) plus the estimated frictional rate (1.1%), or 3.8%. So, the estimated cyclical rate is 4.5% – 3.8% = 0.7%.
2. A positive cyclical unemployment rate calls for a shot of economic stimulus.
3. If the true frictional rate is 2.0%, then the true natural rate is 4.7%, and the cyclical rate is –0.2%. This indicates that the economy is operating beyond potential. Instead of stimulating the economy, you should have attempted to slow it down.

7.5 Review and Practice

Summary

In this chapter, we learned how individuals' labor force status is determined: They are either employed, unemployed, or not in the labor force.

The unemployment rate is measured as the percentage of the labor force not working but actively seeking work. By failing to account for discouraged workers, part-time workers, or the underemployed, the unemployment rate likely understates the true state of labor force utilization. The unemployment rate also fails to include work performed in the informal sector of the economy.

Unemployment can be frictional, resulting from ordinary difficulties matching available workers to available jobs. Unemployment can be structural, resulting from a mismatch in the skills workers possess and the skills employers desire. Unemployment can be cyclical, resulting from declining aggregate spending. Both frictional and structural employment are likely to exist, even at full employment.

The natural rate of unemployment is the sum of the frictional and structural rates of unemployment. The actual rate of unemployment is the sum of the natural rate of unemployment and the cyclical rate of unemployment.

There are different solutions to each type of unemployment. More quickly matching workers with jobs is the solution to frictional unemployment. Removing structural impediments to employment and equipping workers with desired skills is the solution to structural unemployment. Boosting overall spending is the solution to cyclical unemployment. Because the natural rate of unemployment is unobserved, crafting an appropriate policy solution to cyclical unemployment can be difficult.

Concept Problems

1. Suppose unemployed people leave one state to gain jobs in a neighboring state. What do you predict will happen to each state's unemployment rate?

2. Minority teenagers have the highest unemployment rates of any group. One reason is high transportation costs for many minority teens. What form of unemployment (frictional, structural, cyclical) do high transportation costs suggest?

3. (Related to "Case in Point: Unemployment Insurance—Blessing or Curse?" in Section 19.4.) Welfare reforms enacted in 1996 put more pressure on welfare recipients to look for work. The new law mandated cutting off benefits after a certain length of time. How do you think this provision might affect the unemployment rate?

4. American workers work more hours than their European counterparts. Should Congress legislate a shorter workweek?

5. This chapter presents information on the overall state of employment, but the BLS also publishes employment figures broken down by age, educational attainment, gender, and race. Visit the BLS website and compare the overall employment (and unemployment) numbers to the same numbers for men, women, blacks, whites, Hispanics, and Asians. Does everyone share the same employment experience?

6. On January 4, 2019, the *Denver Post* reported that the "U.S. Economy Added 312,000 jobs in December; Unemployment Rate Up to 3.9%." Explain the apparent paradox of increasing employment and the increasing unemployment rate.

7. Suppose the law required all people who go out on a first date to get married at the end of the evening. How would such a law change your dating behavior? Draw parallels between this new law and employment protection laws, focusing on the relationship between employers and workers.

8. The percentage of workers belonging to unions has declined in recent decades. Discuss the effect of this trend on the natural rate of unemployment.

9. (Related to "Case in Point: Good News and Bad in COVID-19 Unemployment Figures" in Section 19.2.) The coronavirus crisis fundamentally altered the way some business gets done. (You *are* familiar with Zoom, right?) Discuss one industry where employees are likely to find themselves structurally unemployed once the crisis is over, as a result of these structural changes. Is there an industry that's likely to have trouble finding enough trained employees?

10. Your college or university likely has a career planning and placement center. What kind of unemployment does it target?

11. (Related to "Case in Point: Is a COVID-19 Graduation an Economic Death Sentence?" in Section 19.3.) Graduating into a recession can be costly. What is the economic outlook for your anticipated graduation date? If graduation is far in the future and the outlook is uncertain, what special steps are you taking today to ensure the smoothest and most lucrative transition from school to work?

Numerical Problems

1. There are 10 million people in an economy. Seven million are employed, and 2 million are unemployed. What is the size of the labor force?

2. There are 10 million people in an economy. Seven million are employed, and 2 million are unemployed. What is the unemployment rate?

3. (Related to "Try It!" in Section 19.2.) Suppose an economy has 10,000 people who are not working but looking and available for work, and 90,000 people who are working. What is its unemployment rate? Now, suppose that 4,000 of the people looking for work get discouraged and give up their searches. What happens to the unemployment rate? Is this good news or bad news? Explain.

4. If the cyclical rate of unemployment is 2%, and the actual rate of unemployment is 6%, what is the natural rate of unemployment?

5. (Related to "Try It!" in Section 19.3.) If the frictional rate of unemployment is 5% and the structural rate of unemployment is 2%, while the actual rate is 6.7%, what is the cyclical rate of unemployment? Is the economy booming or in recession? About how far, in percentage terms, is real GDP from its potential?

6. If the labor force is 117 million, and the labor force participation rate is 62%, how many people are in the adult population?

7. If the unemployment rate is 5%, and there are 10 million unemployed, how many workers are employed?

8. (Related to "Try It!" in Section 19.4.) Suppose you're in charge of economic policy. Today's unemployment rate is 4.2%, and you estimate that the natural rate of unemployment is 4.5%. Should you stimulate the economy or work to slow it down? What will be the effect of your decision if your estimate of the natural rate is wrong, and it's really in the 3.8% range?

Endnotes

1. To read the amazing story of the first authorized COVID-19 vaccine, see "How Pfizer Delivered a Covid Vaccine in Record Time: Crazy Deadlines, a Pushy CEO," *The Wall Street Journal*, December 11, 2020. Pfizer began development of the vaccine on January 25, and the completed vaccine entered human trials in mid-April.

2. If you're thinking about changing your major to economics, this alone is a good reason!

3. $URATE = U/(E + U) = 2/(3 + 2) = 0.4$.

4. The Brookings Institute makes a striking visual comparison between unemployment during the COVID-19 recession and unemployment during other recessions. See https://www.brookings.edu/blog/brookings-now/2020/09/11/charts-of-the-week-impacts-of-the-coronavirus-recession/.

5. Suppose you're paid a nominal wage W of $20 per hour, and that you spend your money on nothing but lattes, which sell for $4 each. Then your real wage (W/P) is [($20/hour)/($4/latte)]. The dollar units cancel, leaving your real wage as 5 lattes per hour.

6. See https://talent.ecb.europa.eu/careers. Who wouldn't want to work in Frankfurt, Germany?

7. Even aged professors like your authors regularly receive unsolicited inquiries through LinkedIn, asking if they'd be interested in pursuing new job opportunities. If it works for them, it will surely work for you! And, no thanks—we love what we do too much!

8. The French labor code is over 3,000 pages long, with 170 pages devoted solely to firings!

9. The CARES Act allowed states to extend the duration of unemployment benefits by thirteen weeks, and supplemented those benefits with $600 per week of federal assistance. The Pandemic Emergency Unemployment Compensation (PEUC) extended federal compensation through the end of 2020 to those who had exhausted their state benefits, and the Pandemic Unemployment Assistance (PUA) program extended federal benefits for an extra thirty-nine weeks to those who were otherwise ineligible.

CHAPTER 8
Aggregate Demand and Aggregate Supply

8.1 Start Up: The Great Warning

The first warning came early in 1929. In its weekly newsletter, the Harvard Economic Society, an association of Harvard economists, predicted that a seven-year-old expansion was coming to an end. Recession was ahead.

Almost no one took the warning seriously. The economy, fueled by soaring investment, had experienced stunning growth. The 1920s had brought automobiles, public power, home appliances, synthetic fabrics, radio, and motion pictures to ordinary people. The decade seemed to have acquired a momentum all its own—a momentum that led celebrated Yale economist Irving Fisher to proclaim that the stock market had "reached what looks like a permanently high plateau." Prosperity was not about to end, no matter what a few *Harvard* economists might say.

Summer came, and no recession was apparent. The Harvard economists withdrew their forecast. But they lost their nerve too soon: Industrial production had already begun to fall—it just hadn't shown in the data yet. The worst downturn in U.S. history, the Great Depression, had begun.

The collapse was swift. In October 1929, just nine days after Fisher's pronouncement, the stock market crashed. The ripple effects were severe: Real GDP plunged nearly 10% by 1930, and by the time the economy hit rock-bottom in 1933, it had fallen by a staggering 30%. Unemployment, which was 3.2% in 1929, skyrocketed to 25% in 1933. Prices plunged 23% from their 1929 level. The recovery, which began in April of 1933, was long and difficult; it was not until World War II that full employment was restored.

In this chapter we go beyond descriptions of the main macroeconomic variables—output, inflation, and unemployment—to introduce a model of macroeconomic activity that incorporates and explains those variables: the model of aggregate demand and aggregate supply. We will use this model throughout our exploration of macroeconomics. In this chapter, we'll present the broad outlines of the model. Greater detail, more examples, and more-thorough explanations will follow in subsequent chapters.

We're particularly interested in the conditions under which an economy can achieve a level of real GDP consistent with the full employment of labor. **Potential output**, or *potential GDP*, or *full-employment output*, is the level of output an economy can achieve when labor is fully employed, with unemployment at its natural rate. When an economy fails to produce up to its potential, there may be actions that the government or the central bank can take to push the economy toward it. In this chapter, we'll begin to consider the pros and cons of those policies.

Irving Fisher: Yale man, inventor of the Rolodex, index number theorist, economist, and victim of the Great Depression.

Source: Prof Irving Fisher, noted economist. Bains News Service, 1927. George Grantham Bain Collection. Library of Congress, Prints & Photographs Division, reproduction number LC-USZ62-101514 (b&w film copy neg.). Retrieved from: https://www.loc.gov/pictures/item/90711700/.

potential output

The level of output an economy can achieve when labor is employed at its natural level.

8.2 Aggregate Demand

Learning Objectives

1. Define potential output, also called full-employment output or potential GDP.
2. Define aggregate demand, represent it using a hypothetical aggregate demand curve, and identify and explain the three effects that cause this curve to slope downward.
3. Distinguish between a change in the aggregate quantity of goods and services demanded and a change in aggregate demand.
4. Use examples to explain how each component of aggregate demand can be a possible aggregate demand shifter.
5. Explain what a multiplier is and how to calculate it.

aggregate demand

The relationship between the total quantity of goods and services demanded (from all the four sources of demand) and the price level, all other determinants of spending unchanged.

aggregate demand curve

A graphical representation of aggregate demand.

In our chapter about GDP, we learned that firms face four sources of demand: households (personal consumption), other firms (investment), government agencies (government purchases), and foreign markets (net exports). **Aggregate demand** is the relationship between the total quantity of goods and services demanded (from all of the four sources of demand) and the price level, holding all other determinants of spending unchanged. The **aggregate demand curve** is a graphical representation of aggregate demand.

The Slope of the Aggregate Demand Curve

The aggregate demand curve traces out the quantity of goods and services demanded in the economy at various price levels. Let's use the implicit price deflator as our measure of the price level, and real GDP as the aggregate quantity of goods and services demanded to draw an aggregate demand curve.

The table in Figure 8.1 gives values for each component of aggregate demand at each price level for a hypothetical economy. Various points on the aggregate demand curve are found by adding the values of these components at different price levels. The aggregate demand curve for the data given in the table is plotted on the graph in Figure 8.1. At point A, at a price level of 118, $11,800 billion worth of goods and services will be demanded; at point C, a reduction in the price level to 114 increases the quantity of goods and services demanded to $12,000 billion; and at point E, at a price level of 110, $12,200 billion will be demanded.

The negative slope of the aggregate demand curve suggests that it behaves just like an ordinary demand curve. But that negative slope happens for different reasons at an economy-wide level. In an individual market, like the market for chicken, falling prices encourage people to substitute more chicken for other goods (whose prices haven't fallen), like beef or pork. That's called the *substitution effect*. Lower prices in the market for chicken also cause the purchasing power of consumers' incomes to increase, which for normal goods increases quantity demanded further. That's called the *income effect*.[1]

Not that kind of "ready and willing": Aggregate demand measures the quantity of output consumers stand ready and willing to purchase at each price level.

Source: Neil Stanners/ Shutterstock.com

FIGURE 8.1 Aggregate Demand

An aggregate demand curve (AD) shows the relationship between the total quantity of output demanded (measured as real GDP) and the price level (measured as the implicit price deflator). At each price level, the total quantity of goods and services demanded is the sum of the components of real GDP, as shown in the table. There is a negative relationship between the price level and the total quantity of goods and services demanded, all other things unchanged.

Point on aggregate demand curve	Price level	C+	I+	G+	$X_n=$	Aggregate demand
A	118	8,400	1,820	2,150	−570	11,800
B	116	8,450	1,860	2,150	−560	11,900
C	114	8,500	1,900	2,150	−550	12,000
D	112	8,550	1,940	2,150	−540	12,100
E	110	8,600	1,980	2,150	−530	12,200

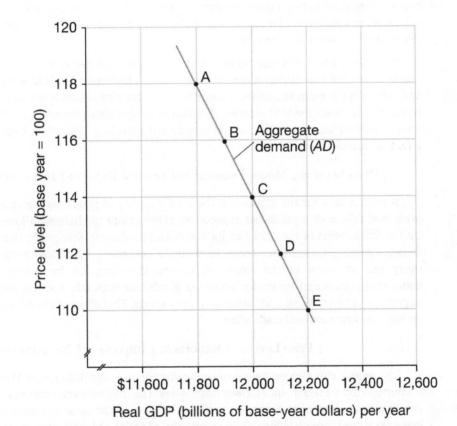

But neither of those reasons is relevant to a change in prices in the economy as a whole (or in the *aggregate*). Because a change in the overall price level implicitly assumes that all prices are falling, there is no change in the *relative* prices that should touch off the substitution effect. The price of chicken may have fallen, but the prices of pork and beef (not to mention televisions, sugar, tractors, beer, hot-stone massages, and most other goods or services produced in the economy) are likely to have fallen, too.

A decrease in the price level is also unlikely to produce the income effect that we might see in individual markets. That's because every transaction has a buyer and a seller; what's one person's expenditure is another's income. So, while the prices consumers pay are falling, so are the prices people are receiving in their roles as producers: their wages, the rents they receive as landlords, the interest rates they earn as savers, the profits they receive as entrepreneurs. If both incomes and prices fall by, say, 10%, then falling prices haven't raised the purchasing power of anyone's income; there is no income effect.

Aggregate demand's downward slope is like this car: "Porsche, there is no substitute."

wealth effect

The tendency for a change in the price level to affect real wealth and thus alter consumption.

So if the income effect doesn't explain it, and the substitution effect doesn't explain it, then why does the aggregate demand curve slope downward? First, when the price level falls, the real value of *wealth*—the stocks, bonds, and other assets that people have accumulated—increases. That gives consumers more purchasing power. For example, if the price level falls in half, then $10,000 of wealth could potentially purchase twice as many goods and services as it originally would have. When people feel wealthier, they consume more! So, as long as consumers have some wealth stored, the consumption component of aggregate demand will be greater at lower price levels than at higher price levels. The tendency for a change in the price level to affect real wealth and consumption is called the **wealth effect**. Let's summarize:

↓ Price Level ⇒↑ Purchasing Power of Wealth ⇒↑ Consumption Spending

A second reason the aggregate demand curve slopes downward lies in the relationship between interest rates and investment. A lower price level reduces the demand for money, because less money is required to buy a given quantity of goods.[2] But, as we learned in studying demand and supply, when the demand for something decreases, so does its price. In this case, the "something" is money; its price is the interest rate.

interest rate effect

The tendency for a higher price level to reduce the real quantity of money, raise interest rates, and reduce investment.

So, a lower price level reduces money demand, and that decrease in money demand reduces interest rates. But lower interest rates make borrowing by firms to build factories or buy equipment and other capital more attractive. A lower interest rate also means lower mortgage payments for homeowners, which tends to increase investment in residential houses. So, a decrease in the price level ultimately leads to an increase in investment spending. This effect, called the **interest rate effect**, is outlined here:

↓ Price Level ⇒↓ Money Demand ⇒↓ Interest Rates ⇒↑ Investment Spending

international trade effect

The tendency for a change in the price level to affect net exports.

A third reason for the increase in the total quantity of goods and services demanded as the price level falls is changes in net exports. All other things unchanged, a lower price level in the United States reduces the prices of its goods and services to foreigners; that causes exports to increase. A lower United States price level also makes foreign-produced goods and services relatively less attractive to the American buyers; they respond by substituting now-cheaper domestically produced goods for imported goods. Imports fall. Because exports increase and imports fall, the net result is an increase in net exports. This effect of the price level on net exports is called the **international trade effect**.

↓ Price Level ⇒↑ Exports & ↓ Imports ⇒↑ Net Exports

The wealth effect encourages more consumption at lower price levels. The interest rate effect encourages more investment at lower price levels. The international trade effect encourages more net exports at lower price levels. These effects all work in the same direction, which means that a lower price level corresponds to a higher quantity of goods and services demanded.[3] Any change in the price level, holding all other determinants of aggregate demand unchanged, causes a movement *along* the aggregate demand curve, which we'll call a **change in the aggregate quantity of goods and services demanded**. A movement from point A to point B on the aggregate demand curve in Figure 8.1 is an example: At a lower price level, a greater quantity of goods and services is demanded.

Anchors aweigh! A lower price level in the U.S. makes American goods look like a better deal to foreigners.

Source: Alex Kolokythas Photography/Shutterstock.com

change in the aggregate quantity of goods and services demanded

Movement along an aggregate demand curve.

Changes in Aggregate Demand

Any change in the components of aggregate demand (*C, I, G, NX*) that is caused by something *other* than a change in the price will cause the aggregate demand curve to shift. A change in the aggregate quantity of goods and services demanded at every price level is a **change in aggregate demand**. An increase in the total quantity of consumer goods and services demanded at each price level, for example, would shift the aggregate demand curve to the right—an *increase in aggregate demand*, as shown in Panel (a) of Figure 8.2. If concerns about government budget deficits cause Congress to reduce government purchases, that *decrease in aggregate demand* would shift the *AD* curve to the left, as shown in Panel (b) of Figure 8.2.

> **change in aggregate demand**
>
> Change in the aggregate quantity of goods and services demanded at every price level.

FIGURE 8.2 Changes in Aggregate Demand
An increase in consumption, investment, government purchases, or net exports shifts the aggregate demand curve AD_1 rightward to AD_2, as shown in Panel (a). A decrease in one of the components of aggregate demand shifts the aggregate demand curve to the left, as shown in Panel (b).

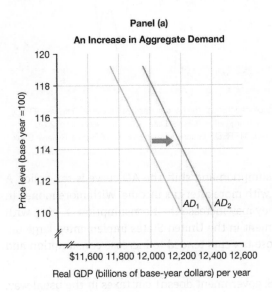

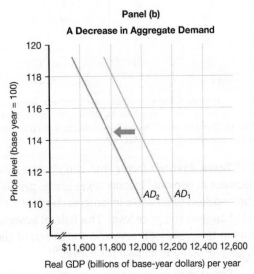

What factors might cause the aggregate demand curve to shift? Each of the components of aggregate demand is a possible aggregate demand shifter. Let's look at some of the big-ticket events that can trigger changes in these components of aggregate demand.

Changes in Consumption

Any change in consumption spending at a given price level will cause a change in aggregate demand. Let's take a look at some of the factors that can change consumption, even with prices held steady:

Consumer confidence. A great deal of consumer spending is unaffected by the current and expected future state of the economy. After all, people have to eat, right? But *some* consumer spending depends critically on what consumers think the economy will look like in the near future. If consumers expect good economic conditions and are optimistic about their own economic prospects, they're more likely to buy major items such as cars or furniture. Figure 8.3 shows the relationship between the most widely regarded measure of consumer confidence (shown in blue) and spending on consumer durable goods (shown in red). The strong correlation between them suggests that consumers are forward-looking in their major purchases: If they think the economy will be strong, they're far more likely to pull the trigger on a big-ticket item than if they think the

I'm confident I'd like to consume some more dinner. And hurry it up!

Source: Jedzura/Shutterstock. com

economy is headed south, as often happens in the months preceding a recession (shown as the shaded areas in the figure). So, an increase in consumer confidence will increase the real value of consumption at any given price level, and the aggregate demand curve will shift to the right. Declining consumer confidence causes consumers to postpone major purchases; the *AD* curve shifts to the left.

FIGURE 8.3 Consumer Confidence and Durable Goods Spending, 1959–2020
While a great deal of consumption spending is only loosely related to consumer confidence in the future state of the economy, large dives in consumer confidence like the United States sees in economic recessions (shaded) have dramatic impacts on consumer spending, especially on more optional items like durable goods.

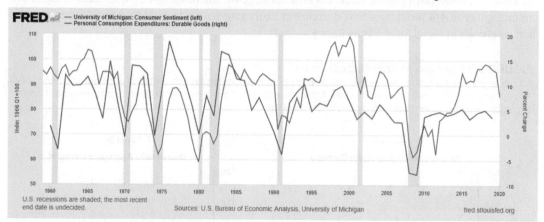

Source: University of Michigan and Bureau of Economic Analysis, accessed through the Federal Reserve Economic Database (FRED) at https://fred.stlouisfed.org/series/UMCSENT and https://fred.stlouisfed.org/series/PCEDG. Data extend through April of 2020. FRED® Graphs ©Federal Reserve Bank of St. Louis. All rights reserved. All FRED® Graphs appear courtesy of Federal Reserve Bank of St. Louis. https://fred.stlouisfed.org/).

Taxes. Another factor that can change consumption and shift the *AD* curve is tax policy. A decrease in personal income taxes leaves people with more after-tax income. With more money in their pockets (*disposable income*) each month, they may increase their consumption . . . even with no change in the price level. The federal government in the United States implemented large tax cuts in 1964, 1981, 1986, 1997, and 2003; each of those tax cuts tended to increase consumption and aggregate demand at each price level.[4]

"Here's your tax rebate. Now get out there and create some aggregate demand, for goodness' sake!"

Source: ANDREI ASKIRKA/
Shutterstock.com

Sometimes, in emergency situations, the U.S. government doesn't cut taxes in the usual way; instead, it simply sends a check to taxpayers in the form of a tax rebate. Generally, the hope is that those rebates will stimulate consumption spending and increase aggregate demand. Rebates have been used in 1975, 2001, 2008, and 2020. In each case the rebate was a one-time payment. Studies of the impact of the 2001 and 2008 rebates showed strong consumption effects, with individual households spending 12–40% of their rebates on nondurable goods in the three months after the rebate was received, and 40–60% of their rebates on durable goods during the same time period.[5] In a subsequent chapter, we'll investigate arguments about why (or why not) temporary increases in income like those produced by rebates are likely to have a significant impact on consumption.

What's true for rebates is also true for other checks sent from government to households. Transfer payments such as welfare and Social Security also affect the income people have available to spend. For a given price level, an increase in transfer payments should increase consumption and shift the *AD* curve to the right; cuts in transfer payments reduce both consumption and aggregate demand.

Changes in Investment

Any change in consumption spending at a given price level will cause a change in aggregate demand. Let's take a look at some of the factors that can change consumption, even with prices held steady:

Confidence and Expectations. Investment is the production of new capital that will be used in the future to produce goods and services. Businesses make investment choices based on what (and how much) they think they will be producing in the future, so expectations about the future play a critical role in determining investment. If firms are confident and expect their sales to increase, they're likely to increase their investment in order to meet the demand for their products. That increased investment raises the aggregate quantity of goods and services demanded at each price level, and shifts the aggregate demand curve to the right. Pessimistic firms, on the other hand, are less likely to invest today, postponing capital expenditures until they see smoother sailing ahead.

Less means more when it comes to new construction: Lower interest rates generate more interest in investment goods.

Source: ESB Professional/Shutterstock.com

Interest Rates. Because capital is often quite expensive, many firms have to borrow money in order to build new factories or install new equipment. That borrowing comes at a cost—the borrowing firm has to pay interest! (Even if they use their own money, that use comes at a cost—they could have lent that money to someone else! *The only cost that matters is opportunity cost, right?*) For a given price level, lower interest rates reduce the cost of funds firms need to invest in capital, which increases investment spending; that, in turn, increases aggregate demand. Higher interest rates do the opposite, discouraging investment and shifting the *AD* curve to the left.

Heads Up!

Warning: Technical Note! The changes in interest rates we're talking about here are interest rate changes *for a given price level*; those changes shift the position of the *AD* curve. That's different than the interest rate effect we talked about earlier, in which interest rates change *because of* a change in the price level; the investment touched off by the interest rate effect is already incorporated into the shape of the *AD* curve, and is reflected in movements *along* the aggregate demand curve.

Tax Policy. Because most investment is undertaken by firms, and because most firms pay taxes, it makes sense that tax policy has the power to affect investment spending. One way that can happen is by affecting the flow of funds to firms that they need in order to undertake large investment projects. Often, those funds are provided by investors who will end up paying taxes on any capital gains (increases in the value of their investment) they receive. The lower the tax rate the government applies to those capital gains, the more attractive those financial investments become, and the more money will flow to firms to fund their investment projects. That causes an increase in aggregate demand!

But it's not just investors who can experience capital gains. A homeowner who buys a house for $200,000 and sells it for $500,000 receives $300,000 of capital gains. A manufacturer who builds a factory for $500 million and later sells it for $700 million receives $200 million of capital gains. An increase in the capital gains tax rate reduces the rewards to building houses (residential investment) and factories (business fixed investment). Investment and aggregate demand decrease.

Really, only *one* thing is certain: High corporate taxes can be death to investment.

Source: Montri Thipsorn/ Shutterstock.com

It's not just capital gains taxes that can affect investment. When a corporation earns a profit, that profit is subject to the same kind of income tax that you pay on your wages. A high corporate income tax rate reduces the after-tax profits firms receive, and may cause them to take a pass on investment projects that *would* look attractive at lower tax rates. High corporate tax rates may have another side effect: They may encourage businesses to relocate both headquarters and production facilities overseas, a process known as corporate inversion. This is one big reason why, in 2017, the United States reduced the top corporate income tax rate from 35% (the highest in the developed world) to a more competitive 21%.

Changes in Government Purchases

The third component of aggregate demand is government purchases. We've implicitly assumed that government purchases are set by Congress in an appropriations process, and don't depend on the price level. So, if Congress decides to purchase more tanks, hire more SpaceX rockets, or buy more beans for its bureaucrats to count, that decision causes the total quantity of goods and services at any price level to increase. Aggregate demand goes up; the AD curve shifts to the right. Of course, if the congressional bean counters decide government has been playing too fast and loose with its metaphorical Visa card, they might decide to cut purchases. That will reduce the aggregate demand for goods and services and shift the AD curve to the left.

FIGURE 8.4 U.S. Defense Spending, 1981–2020
Defense spending is one of the largest categories of government purchases.

Source: U.S. Bureau of Economic Analysis, Federal Government: National Defense Consumption Expenditures and Gross Investment [FDEFX], retrieved from FRED, Federal Reserve Bank of St. Louis; https://fred.stlouisfed.org/series/FDEFX.

The impact of government purchases on GDP can be huge. Consider defense spending, a major category of government purchases, which is shown in Figure 8.4. Between the early 2000s and 2010, funding the Iraq/Afghanistan wars caused defense spending to rise from just over $400 billion per year to about $850 billion.[6] That growth added almost half a trillion dollars of aggregate demand to the economy each year, shifting the AD curve to the right. As troops were withdrawn during the Obama administration, defense spending fell and the AD curve shifted to the left, but that lost demand was replaced, and more, during the Trump presidency. All told, defense spending alone accounts for about $900 billion of aggregate demand and GDP.

Changes in Net Exports

We've now covered consumption, investment, and government purchases. The fourth and final category of spending is net exports. A change in the value of net exports at each price level shifts the aggregate demand curve. When net exports increase, so does aggregate demand; the AD curve shifts to the right. When net exports decrease, aggregate demand decreases and the AD curve shifts to the left. What can cause those changes?

Income Changes Abroad. Net exports are a country's exports minus its imports. The level of foreign demand for your country's products, then, has a huge influence on net exports. One big factor that affects foreign demand for a country's exports is the level of foreign income. For example, when your income rises, you tend to buy more goods and services, and some of those goods and services come from abroad. Likewise, when foreign incomes rise, foreigners' demand for U.S. products (our exports) tends to increase; aggregate demand rises. When foreign income falls, demand for U.S. exports tends to decrease; aggregate demand falls. Stark evidence of this was found during both the Great Recession and the coronavirus crisis, as shown in Figure 8.5. In both cases, foreign incomes plummeted, and in both cases U.S. exports to the rest of the world followed. During the Great Recession, exports fell by $400 billion. But that paled in comparison to the coronavirus crisis in early 2020 in which U.S. exports (and aggregate demand) decreased by a whopping $640 billion.

FIGURE 8.5 U.S. Exports and Global Crises, 2005–2020
During the global financial crisis of 2007–2009, and the worldwide coronavirus crisis of 2020, foreign incomes plummeted. U.S. exports to the rest of the world followed in lockstep.

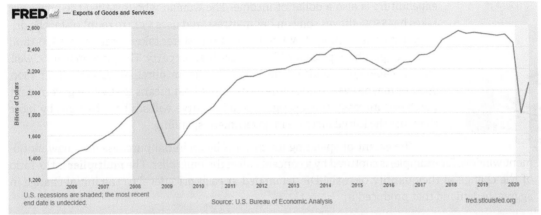

Source: U.S. Bureau of Economic Analysis, Exports of Goods and Services [EXPGS], retrieved from FRED, Federal Reserve Bank of St. Louis; https://fred.stlouisfed.org/series/EXPGS. Data extend through third quarter of 2020.

Exchange Rates. To buy a foreign product, you generally have to use the seller's home currency, which means that you have to first visit the foreign exchange market and trade some of your country's currency for the seller's currency. The rate at which one country's currency trades for another country's currency is called the **exchange rate**.[7]

Exchange rates strongly influence net exports. An increase in the U.S. exchange rate means that it takes more Japanese yen to purchase one dollar. That makes U.S. exports look more expensive to people in Japan, who have to give up more yen to buy a given U.S. product than they did before. As a result, U.S. exports to Japan decrease. An increase in the exchange rate *also* means that each dollar traded in the foreign exchange market fetches more yen. That makes Japanese goods look *less* expensive to U.S. consumers, and as a result imports from Japan increase. With exports falling and imports rising, the increase in the exchange rate causes net exports to decline; the *AD* curve shifts left. (A lower exchange rate tends to increase net exports, increasing aggregate demand.)

Foreign Price Levels. Foreign price levels can affect aggregate demand in the same way as exchange rates. When foreign price levels fall relative to the price level in the United States, U.S. goods and services become relatively more expensive. Foreigners stop importing U.S. goods in favor of their now-cheaper domestic goods. U.S. consumers start buying fewer domestically produced goods and ramp up purchases of now-cheaper imports. With exports falling and imports rising, net exports and aggregate demand decline. An increase in foreign prices relative to U.S. prices, of course, has the opposite effect: Exports rise, imports fall, and net exports and aggregate demand increase.

Trade Policy. It's not just prices and incomes that can affect net exports. The web of trade policies—tariffs, quotas, domestic content requirements, etc.—at home and abroad can have large impacts on net exports. When China banned imports of U.S. soybeans in 2018, for example, that closed off a major export market for the American farmer, reducing the demand for U.S. soybeans and reducing aggregate demand in the United States.[8]

exchange rate

The price of a currency in terms of another currency or currencies.

The Multiplier

Ripple effect: A few drops of new spending might create waves of income.

Source: Alex Staroseltsev/Shutterstock.com

multiplier

The ratio of the change in the quantity of real GDP demanded at each price level to the initial change in one or more components of aggregate demand that produced it.

Suppose that the government replaces one of the tiny little windows at the top of the Washington Monument, at a cost of $500. Government purchases rise by $500 . . . but ultimately, aggregate demand may rise by even more. That's because every transaction has a buyer and a seller, which means that every dollar of expenditure is also a dollar of income! The woman who installed the new glass takes her $500, shoves some in her mattress, and uses $300 to reupholster the driver's seat of her vintage VW Beetle. The upholsterer takes some of that $300 and uses it to purchase pizza for his son's graduation party. The pizza maker . . . well, you probably get the idea: One $500 government purchase can touch off $800, $900, or maybe even $1,000 of new spending! That means that when government purchases increase, the aggregate demand curve will shift to the right by *more* than just the initial increase in government spending.

The extent of spending touched off by an initial purchase (of a new monument window, for example) is captured by a concept called the *multiplier*. The **multiplier** is the ratio of the change in the quantity of real GDP demanded at each price level to the initial change in aggregate demand that produced it:

EQUATION 8.1

$$\text{Multiplier} = \frac{\Delta\text{Real GDP Demanded at Each Price Level}}{\text{Initial } \Delta AD}$$

We use the capital Greek letter delta (Δ) to mean "change in." In our window-glass example, let's suppose that $500 of new windows touched off $500 of additional consumption spending on upholstery, pizza parties, air fryers, and sauerkraut. The total change in spending would be $1,000, and the initial change would be the $500 window, so the multiplier would be $1,000/$500, or 2.0.[9]

We can use Equation 8.1 to solve for the change in real GDP demanded at each price level:

EQUATION 8.2

$$\Delta\text{Real GDP Demanded at Each Price Level} = \text{Multiplier} \times \text{Initial } \Delta AD$$

Let's see how this works: Suppose that a major exchange rate movement causes an initial increase in net exports of $100 billion. If the multiplier is 2.0, that change in net exports will touch off an *additional* $100 billion of consumption spending at each price level, for a total expenditure increase of $200 billion.[10] In Panel (a) of Figure 8.6, the aggregate demand curve shifts to the right by $200 billion—the amount of the initial increase in net exports times the multiplier. (Similarly, a decrease in net exports of $100 billion would lead to a *decrease* in aggregate demand of $200 billion at each price level, as shown in Panel (b).)

FIGURE 8.6 The Multiplier

A change in one component of aggregate demand shifts the aggregate demand curve by more than the initial change. In Panel (a), an initial increase of $100 billion of net exports shifts the aggregate demand curve to the right by $200 billion at each price level. In Panel (b), a decrease of net exports of $100 billion shifts the aggregate demand curve to the left by $200 billion. In this example, the multiplier is 2.

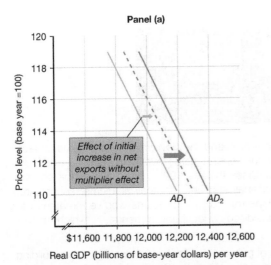

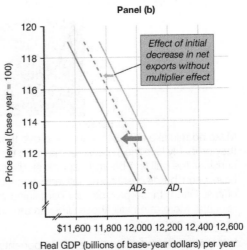

Key Takeaways

- Potential output is the level of output an economy can achieve when labor is employed at its natural level. When an economy fails to produce at its potential, the government or the central bank may try to push the economy toward its potential.

- The aggregate demand curve represents the total of consumption, investment, government purchases, and net exports at each price level in any period. It slopes downward because of the wealth effect on consumption, the interest rate effect on investment, and the international trade effect on net exports.

- The aggregate demand curve shifts when the quantity of real GDP demanded at each price level changes.

- A change in aggregate demand may ripple through the economy, touching off additional consumption spending. The multiplier tells us how much the aggregate demand ultimately shifts at each price level as a result of an initial change to one of the factors of aggregate demand.

Try It!

Explain the effect of each of the following on the aggregate demand curve for the United States:

1. A decrease in consumer optimism
2. An increase in real GDP in the countries that buy U.S. exports
3. An increase in the U.S. price level
4. A decrease in government spending on highways

See related Concept Problem 3 at the end of this chapter.

Case in Point: Taken Out to the Ball Game, or Taken for a Ride—How Big IS the Sports Stadium Multiplier?

Without the field, there can't be dreams.

Source: EFKS/Shutterstock.com

Make no mistake about it: Americans love their sports, and they love their sports teams. In fact, they probably love their sports teams more than their sports teams love them back. As evidence, consider the building boom in sports stadiums. Since the late 1990s, cities across the country have been building stadiums left and right: baseball stadiums, football stadiums, soccer stadiums. Often, those projects are bargaining chips tossed to local teams who've threatened to relocate. More often still, those projects are subsidized by local governments . . . which means, of course, taxpayers.

Is that taxpayer money well spent? Proponents of public-subsidized stadiums argue that building new stadiums boosts income in the construction sector. When the San Francisco 49ers were lobbying the city for a new stadium, their campaign slogan tugged on just those heartstrings: *"Build the Stadium—Create the Jobs!"*

But those who support building stadiums argue that the benefits don't end there. People who attend games spend money and expand local employment. Restaurants, bars, and condos tend to spring up near new stadiums, spurring neighborhood development. All the new income the stadium creates, proponents argue, ripples through the community causing still more spending and job creation. That's the multiplier effect! And because those new expenditures, those new properties, and those new incomes are taxed, it's argued that a good stadium project practically pays for itself, more than covering the cost of taxpayer subsidies.

That's a story that makes intuitive sense. Unfortunately, it's also a story that remains unsupported by data. In a 2017 survey of top economists, 70% agreed that "providing state and local subsidies to build stadiums for professional sports teams is likely to cost the relevant taxpayers more than any local economic benefits that are generated."[11][12] Survey respondent Larry Samuelson points out that the failure of a stadium to pay for itself, much less generate a multiplier effect, stems from a "fail[ure] to distinguish total economic activity from net gains in activities."

In other words, while people do spend a lot of money going to games, it isn't *new* spending. Instead, it *replaces* entertainment spending that would have occurred anyway—at restaurants, concerts, theaters, and bars. Those *unsubsidized* activities would have created the same income, the same employment, and the same ripple effect as a stadium built on the backs of taxpayers. In other words, there's an opportunity cost to building a stadium, and the stadium's true economic value isn't the *total* income it brings in, but instead is the *extra* income that wouldn't have otherwise been generated.

For a city, building a stadium has great optics, but bad mathematics. Taxpayers spend hundreds of millions of their hard-earned dollars in order to create no new net economic activity. In other words, the stadium multiplier that pro-building advocates cite so often is, in reality, zero! And while the debate about whether a stadium can spur economic development might seem trivial, it actually sheds light on a very important question: Can government spending successfully stimulate a flagging economy? We'll tackle that issue in our chapter on fiscal policy.

See related Numerical Problem 5 at the end of this chapter.

Sources: Based on "Sports Stadiums," from the Chicago Booth Initiative on Global Market survey at https://www.igmchicago.org/surveys/sports-stadiums/, 2017; Scott Wolla, "The Economics of Subsidizing Sports Stadiums," Economic Research/Federal Reserve Bank of St. Louis, Page One Economics, May 2017; Jesse Stephenson, "Letting Teams Walk: Exploring the Economic Impact of Professional Sports Franchises Leaving Cities," MPA/MPP Capstone Projects, 2014;

and Roger Noll and Andrew Zimbalist's, "Sports, Jobs, and Taxes: The Economic Impact of Sports Teams and Stadiums" (Washington, D.C.: Brookings Institution Press, 1997).

Answers to Try It! Problems

1. A decline in consumer optimism would cause the aggregate demand curve to shift to the left. If consumers are more pessimistic about the future, they are likely to cut purchases, especially of major items.

2. An increase in the real GDP of other countries would increase the demand for U.S. exports and cause the aggregate demand curve to shift to the right. Higher incomes in other countries will make consumers in those countries more willing and able to buy U.S. goods.

3. An increase in the price level corresponds to a movement up along the unchanged aggregate demand curve. At the higher price level, the consumption, investment, and net export components of aggregate demand will all fall; that is, there will be a reduction in the total quantity of goods and services demanded, but not a shift of the aggregate demand curve itself.

4. A decrease in government spending on highways means a decrease in government purchases. The aggregate demand curve would shift to the left.

Khan Academy Links

Aggregate demand

Shifts in aggregate demand

The multiplier

8.3 Aggregate Demand and Aggregate Supply: The Long Run and the Short Run

Learning Objectives

1. Distinguish between the short run and the long run in the macroeconomy.

2. Draw a hypothetical long-run aggregate supply curve and explain what it shows about the natural levels of employment and potential output at various price levels.

3. Draw a hypothetical short-run aggregate supply curve, explain why it slopes upward, and explain why it may shift.

4. Distinguish between a change in the aggregate quantity of goods and services supplied and a change in short-run aggregate supply.

5. Discuss various explanations for wage and price stickiness.

6. Explain and illustrate what is meant by equilibrium in the short run and relate the equilibrium to potential output.

In our demand and supply model of markets, our most important objective was finding equilibrium—an equilibrium price and an equilibrium quantity of output. That's useful because markets have a tendency to gravitate toward that equilibrium; it's also useful because prices and quantities are measurable variables, and we can use theory to try to explain why they behave like they do.

In macroeconomics, we have the same goal. In our model of aggregate supply and aggregate demand, we'll look for an equilibrium price level and an equilibrium level of real output. Our job as macroeconomists is more complicated, however, because there are potentially *two different equilibria*—one that we'll see the economy gravitate to in the short run, and another that we'll see the economy move toward in the long run.

In order to understand those different equilibria, we need to understand the difference between the short run and the long run. In macroeconomics, the **short run** is a time period in which wages and prices don't fully respond to changes in economic conditions. Colloquially, economists say wages and prices are *sticky*. When wages and prices are sticky, markets won't quickly adjust to their equilibrium output levels, and surpluses or shortages may persist. That keeps the economy from achieving its natural level of employment and its potential output. In contrast, the **long run** in macroeconomics is a time period in which wages and prices are flexible and can fully adjust to market conditions. With both wages and prices fully flexible in the long run, employment will move to its natural level and real GDP will move to its potential level.

We'll start our discussion with the long run, because long-run equilibrium lets us see where the macroeconomy will end up after all of the input (labor and capital) and output (goods and services) markets have time to fully adjust. After that, we'll look at what happens in the short run, when price or wage stickiness keep the economy from reaching its potential . . . at least for a while. We'll finish by discussing why that happens and what the implications are for the macroeconomy.

This marathoner-in-training knows that flexibility is the key to her long run.

Source: KieferPix/Shutterstock.com

short run

In macroeconomic analysis, a period in which wages and some other prices are sticky and do not respond to changes in economic conditions.

long run

In macroeconomic analysis, a period in which wages and prices are flexible.

The Long Run

As we saw in our chapter on unemployment, the natural level of employment is found where the real wage adjusts to eliminate cyclical unemployment. When the economy is at its natural level of employment, it's also at its potential level of output. Because all wages and prices are flexible in the long run, market forces will move the economy to the natural rate of employment and potential GDP.

Long-Run Aggregate Supply

long-run aggregate supply (LRAS) curve

A graphical representation that relates the level of output produced by firms to the price level in the long run.

In the long run, output is at its potential level and employment (and unemployment!) is at its natural rate. The **long-run aggregate supply (*LRAS*) curve** shows the level of output (potential output, or full-employment output) that corresponds to the natural rates of employment and unemployment after all prices and wages have adjusted.

Because the natural rate of unemployment doesn't depend on the price level, neither does potential output. It's the same, no matter what the price level happens to be. So, Figure 8.7 shows the long-run aggregate supply curve as a vertical line at the economy's potential level of output. No matter whether prices are P_1, P_2, P_3, or P_4, potential output, which is determined by the economy's factors of production and technology, is the same, Y_P.

FIGURE 8.7 Long-Run Aggregate Supply
When the economy is at its natural level of employment, it's also at potential output, as shown by the vertical long-run aggregate supply curve *LRAS* at Y_P.

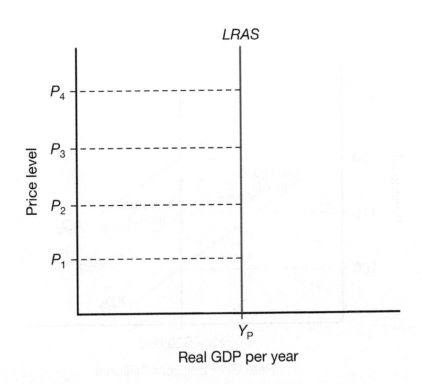

We know that Y_P is full employment output, or potential real GDP. But what does it ultimately depend on? You might remember the Chapter 2 discussion of the production possibilities frontier: Y_P depends on the same factors that affect the economy's production possibilities:

- The available productive resources (the amount of land, labor, capital, etc.).
- The extent to which those resources are employed. Are they fully used? Are any sitting idle?
- The efficiency with which those resources are used. Are we getting the greatest amount of output value from each unit of our inputs? This link between inputs and outputs is called production *technology*.

Equilibrium Price Level and Output in the Long Run

The intersection of the economy's aggregate demand curve and the long-run aggregate supply curve determines its equilibrium real GDP and price level in the long run. Figure 8.8 shows an economy in long-run equilibrium. With aggregate demand at AD_1, real GDP is \$20,000 billion per year and the price level is 110. If aggregate demand increased from AD_1 to AD_2, the long-run equilibrium quantity would stay at \$20,000 billion per year, but the extra demand for those goods and services would drive the price level up to 120. On the other hand, if aggregate demand decreased from AD_1 to AD_3, long-run *real* output would (once again!) be \$20,000, but the price level would drop to 100. In other words, because changes in demand do not alter the economy's production possibilities, they have no impact on output in the long run. Instead, changes in demand are fully reflected in changes in prices.

FIGURE 8.8 Long-Run Equilibrium

Long-run equilibrium occurs at the intersection of the aggregate demand curve and the long-run aggregate supply curve. For the three aggregate demand curves shown, long-run equilibrium occurs at three different price levels (100, 110, 120) but always at potential real output of $20,000 billion per year.

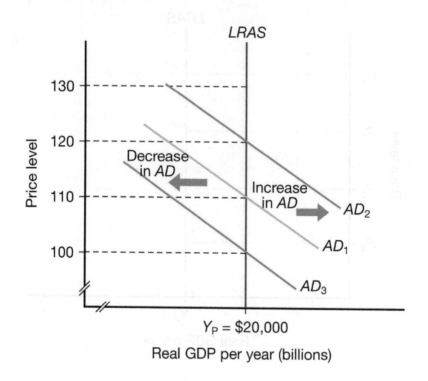

The Short Run

We've just used the *AD-AS* model to describe what we'd expect to see happen in the macroeconomy in the long run: full employment and an economy operating at its potential level. But as economist John Maynard Keynes once famously noted, "In the long run, we are all dead." In the meantime, there are short-run trials and tribulations, booms and busts that people can't simply wait out while consoling themselves with platitudes like, *"Someday, we'll be back in the long run and I can have a job to go to again."*

Those short-run economic fluctuations may pull us away from the long-run equilibrium. We need to understand both why they occur and how policymakers might want to intervene in order to nudge the economy back to its long-run equilibrium. To gather that understanding, let's take a closer look at the short-run aggregate supply curve.

Short-Run Aggregate Supply

The model of aggregate demand and long-run aggregate supply predicts that the economy will eventually move toward its potential output. To see how nominal wage and price stickiness can cause real GDP to be either above or below potential in the short run, consider the response of the economy to an increase in aggregate demand, as shown in Figure 8.9. In Panel (a), the economy is initially in long-run equilibrium at point A, where AD_1 intersects the long-run aggregate supply curve, *LRAS*. Real output is at potential ($20,000 billion); the price level is 110.

FIGURE 8.9 Deriving the Short-Run Aggregate Supply Curve

The economy shown in Panel (a) begins in long-run equilibrium at point A, where AD_1 intersects the long-run aggregate supply curve *LRAS*. If aggregate demand increases to AD_2, in the short run, the economy leaves *LRAS* and goes to point B, with output increasing past potential and prices beginning to increase. Panel (b) shows that points A and B both lie on the short-run aggregate supply curve, *SRAS*. The economy will eventually return to long-run equilibrium at point C.

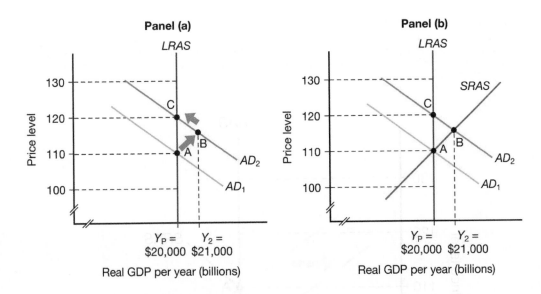

Now suppose there is an increase in aggregate demand from AD_1 to AD_2. We already know that in the long run, that change in aggregate demand will move us from point A to point C. But that move requires the price level to increase from 110 to 120, and that doesn't happen overnight, because prices (and wages) are sticky in the neighborhood of 110 and can't fully adjust. With prices held artificially low, there is some excess demand in the economy.

Excess demand means that sellers have customers lined up at their door waiting for product—an excellent situation for sellers to be in! Ally, who owns the best cupcakery in the Midwest, is pleased to find herself selling out before closing each day. Sensing a profitable opportunity, she raises the price of the Death by Chocolate (her most popular cupcake); soon, the prices of other cupcakes begin to follow. With cupcake workers' nominal wages fixed, Ally now enjoys the luxury of selling fewer cupcakes to pay each worker's hourly wage; the real wage (W/P) she pays her employees has decreased.[13] With workers cheaper in real terms to hire, Ally ramps up her employees' hours, and her store's output expands (at least temporarily) beyond potential.

"I know, I know, another Death by Chocolate."

Source: CREATISTA/Shutterstock.com

What's happening at Ally's cupcakery is also happening at car dealerships, gourmet groceries, electronics stores, and thousands of other businesses across the country. With the economy starting at full employment at point A, output expands temporarily beyond potential, moving the economy to point B (price level 115; real output $21,000 billion), where prices are just starting to adjust in response to the excess demand.

That story helps us trace out the **short-run aggregate supply (SRAS) curve**, a graphical representation of the relationship between production and the price level in the short run. In the short run, with wages and prices relatively sticky, the economy responds to an increase in aggregate demand by moving from A to B; those two points lie on a single short-run aggregate supply curve, *SRAS*, shown in Panel (b) of Figure 8.9. That curve holds the capital stock, the stock of natural resources, the level of technology, and the prices of factors of production constant.

We can also get the short-run aggregate supply by seeing what happens if aggregate demand *decreases* instead of increases. Consider a decrease in aggregate demand (perhaps due to a decrease in government spending), like the one shown in Figure 8.10. The decrease in aggregate demand from AD_1 to AD_3 creates a surplus of goods at the original price level, 110. That surplus puts downward

short-run aggregate supply (SRAS) curve

A graphical representation of the relationship between production and the price level in the short run.

pressure on prices, but because prices are sticky in the short run, they don't fully decrease to their long-run levels and return the economy to long-run equilibrium at point E. Instead, as the price level starts to fall, output also falls, and the economy finds itself at point D, with prices not yet fully adjusted, and with output temporarily below potential. Points A and D both lie on a single short-run aggregate supply curve.

FIGURE 8.10 Deriving the *SRAS*: A Decrease in Aggregate Demand

When aggregate demand decreases from AD_1 to AD_3, the economy initially moves along its short-run aggregate supply curve from point A to point D. Prices begin to decrease, causing real wages to increase; firms respond by cutting labor and producing less. Eventually, prices and wages will fully adjust and return the economy to long-run equilibrium at point E.

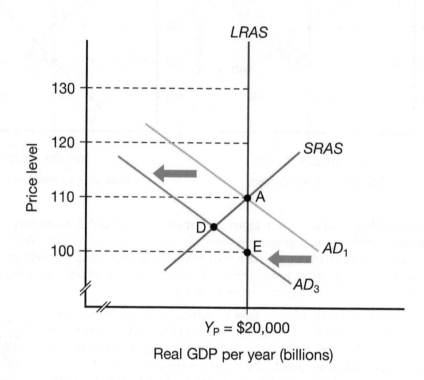

$Y_P = \$20,000$

Real GDP per year (billions)

Why does output decline? The prices firms receive are beginning to fall with the decrease in demand. Without corresponding reductions in nominal wages (because wages are sticky, especially downward), real wages increase. Facing higher (real) costs due to the wage increase, firms respond by employing less labor and producing less output.

Changes in Short-Run Aggregate Supply

change in short-run aggregate supply

A change in the aggregate quantity of goods and services supplied at every price level in the short run.

At any moment in time, the long-run aggregate supply curve is fixed at the economy's potential output.[14] But the short-run aggregate supply is not. A change in the quantity of goods and services supplied at every price level in the short run is a **change in short-run aggregate supply**. Changes in the factors held constant in drawing the short-run aggregate supply—capital stock, the stock of natural resources, the level of technology, and the prices of factors of production—will shift the *SRAS* curve.

One type of event that would shift the short-run aggregate supply curve is an increase in the price of a natural resource used in production, such as oil. That price increase raises the cost of production and leads to a decrease in short-run aggregate supply. In Panel (a) of Figure 8.11, $SRAS_1$ shifts leftward to $SRAS_2$. A decrease in the price of oil would reduce the cost of production and, other things unchanged, would shift the short-run aggregate supply curve to the right. That's shown in Panel (b) as a shift from $SRAS_1$ to $SRAS_3$.

FIGURE 8.11 Changes in Short-Run Aggregate Supply
A decrease in short-run aggregate supply shifts the *SRAS* curve leftward from *SRAS*₁ to *SRAS*₂, as shown in Panel (a). An increase in short-run aggregate supply shifts the *SRAS* curve to the right from *SRAS*₁ to *SRAS*₃, as shown in Panel (b).

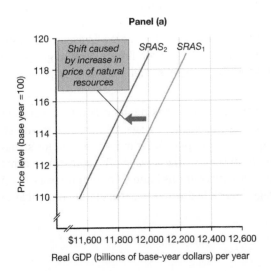
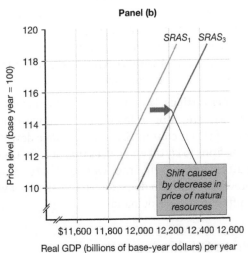

Reasons for Wage and Price Stickiness

Because of wage and price stickiness, the economy may not always be operating at potential. It may be above potential output in the short run, with the overall unemployment rate below its natural rate. Or, the economy may be operating below potential, with the overall unemployment rate above its natural rate.

Many prices in the economy adjust quickly to changes in market conditions so that equilibrium, once lost, is quickly regained. Prices for fresh produce, gasoline, and shares of common stock, for example, change by the day, and often by the hour. Other prices, though, adjust more slowly. One key price that changes very slowly is the nominal wage, which is the price of labor services. Let's take a look at why nominal wages tend to be sticky. Then, we'll look at some reasons why other prices in the economy are sometimes sticky, too.

Wage Stickiness

The ability of the economy to perform above potential for some period of time stems from the fact that nominal wages are often slow to adjust to economic conditions. Why does that happen? There are two big reasons. First, labor contracts lock in wages for some period of time. Second, wages might be sticky because of legal or cultural institutions. Let's take a look at each of these explanations in turn.

Contracts. Many workers in the economy have signed contracts with their employers. Those contracts might be as short as a week or two for temporary employees, a full year (teachers and professors often have one-year contracts), or even three years (most labor unions negotiate three-year contracts for their members). Those contracts typically fix nominal wages for the life of the contract, even though economic conditions could change while the agreement is still in force.

One reason workers and firms are willing to sign long-term contracts is that negotiating a contract is a costly, often adversarial process that soaks up both time and money. Both parties have to gather and process information about market conditions. Time spent negotiating terms of employment takes away from time spent producing goods and services. And where unions are involved, stalled wage negotiations present employers with the risk of a labor strike, an outcome that firms may try to prepare for by carrying costly extra inventories. Finally, workers may be willing to sign longer-term contracts because they simply prefer knowing that their nominal wage will be fixed for some period of time.

Some contracts *do* attempt to take into account changing economic conditions such as inflation, and may incorporate cost-of-living adjustments. But even these relatively simple contingencies are not as widespread as you might think they should be. Some firms are reluctant to build in cost-of-living adjustments because of the risk that the overall price level might go up (and carry wages with it), while the price of the good the firm sells might fail to keep pace with other prices in the economy.

Institutions. Long-term contracts can lock in nominal wages, making them slow to adjust even as prices are rising or falling. But even without long-term contracts, wages can be slow to adjust. Part of this is cultural. During economic downturns, for example, it's far more common for struggling firms to lay off employees than it is for them to cut their workers' wages. But sometimes, firms can't cut wages even if they want to. That's because legal institutions (namely, minimum wage laws) prevent them from doing so. That makes low-wage, less-skilled workers particularly vulnerable to shifts in aggregate demand.

"United We Bargain; Divided We Beg." Give these union workers the three-year contract they're asking for, or face the disruption of a labor strike.

Source: daseugen/Shutterstock.com

Price Stickiness

Rigidity of other prices becomes easier to explain in light of the arguments about nominal wage stickiness. Since wages are a major component of the overall cost of doing business, wage stickiness may lead to output price stickiness. With their wage bill locked in, some firms feel comfortable adopting a "wait and see" attitude before adjusting their prices. That gives them time to consider whether any demand changes they see are due to temporary factors (in which case they might not want to make permanent changes to their labor force) or permanent ones. It also gives them time to assess how their competitors are reacting to the change in demand (Are they raising prices? Are they matching others' price changes?). That's one explanation, but there are other reasons that prices might be sticky. Let's explore each of them in turn.

Menu Costs. Another reason for price stickiness is that it may be costly for firms to adjust prices. The costs of adjusting prices are called *menu costs*—just think of how costly it might be for your local Chinese restaurant to reprint its menus if it decides to change the price of its egg drop soup today, its kung pao tomorrow, its General Tso's chicken the day after! But it's not just restaurants that incur costs when they change prices. In many industries, firms that want to change prices have to print price lists, print new catalogs, or notify customers of price changes. That's costly in itself, but frequent changes may also alienate customers, a risk many firms would like to avoid. This is why soft-goods catalog retailers L.L. Bean and Land's End and outdoor-goods retailer REI typically change their prices just twice each year.

Frozen Prices: It takes a lot of fuel to fly from Milan to Minsk. Good thing Alitalia locks in the price of jet fuel two years in advance.

Source: Media_works/Shutterstock.com

Long-Term Contracts. Yet another explanation of price stickiness is that firms may have explicit long-term contracts to sell their products to other firms at specified prices. For example, electric utilities often lock in the price of future shipments of coal or oil by using long-term contracts with suppliers. In the same way, Southwest Airlines signs contracts to lock in the price of future deliveries of jet fuel, King Arthur Flour locks in the price of its wheat, and Anheuser-Busch locks in the price of barley and hops. Of course, once prices are locked in, they're not just sticky . . . they're frozen!

Institutions. There's one final reason that prices may not move in response to changes in the economy: Like wages, prices may be prevented from moving by law or by custom. Some prices in the economy may be set by government, like the rate your power company charges for electricity. They couldn't change if they wanted to![15] Even when the price of a product isn't locked in by the government, cultural norms may prevent prices from quickly and fully adjusting. For example, newsstand prices of magazines and vending machine soda prices change very infrequently, and sellers of steel, chemicals, and cement rarely change prices over the course of a year. That's pretty typical: In a series of interviews with price setters, economist Alan Blinder found that more than half of the firms he surveyed changed prices only once annually, with only 10% changing prices as often as once a month.

Price and Output in the Short Run

If prices and nominal wages could adjust to market conditions instantaneously, the economy might always operate at its potential, never leaving its long-run aggregate supply curve. Prices and wages *do* tend to adjust to market conditions, but for the reasons discussed above, those adjustments take some time. Until full price and wage adjustments are achieved, the economy may fail to stay at its long-run, potential level. Let's use our *AD/AS* model to look at two examples of how the economy might behave in the short run. First, let's see what happens when an increase in government purchases causes a change in aggregate demand. Then let's see what happens when there's an increase in the cost of health care. Because so many employers pay health care for their workers, that will affect the short-run aggregate supply of goods and services. Then, both of these events will, in the short run, change equilibrium real GDP and the price level.

A Change in Government Purchases

Suppose the federal government increases its spending for highway construction. This increase in government purchases causes an increase in aggregate demand. That increase is shown as a rightward shift of the aggregate demand curve from AD_1 to AD_2 in Figure 8.12. The increase in AD causes real GDP to increase from Y_1 to Y_2, and the price level to increase from P_1 to P_2. That overall inflation, with prices being pulled up by increasing demand, is known as **demand-pull inflation**.

demand-pull inflation

An overall inflation driven by increases in aggregate demand.

FIGURE 8.12 An Increase in Government Purchases
The economy is initially in short-run equilibrium at the intersection of AD_1 and $SRAS$, with price level P_1 and output level Y_1. An increase in government purchases shifts aggregate demand from AD_1 to AD_2. The new short-run equilibrium is at the intersection of AD_2 and the short-run aggregate supply curve $SRAS$. The price level rises to P_2 and real GDP rises to Y_2.

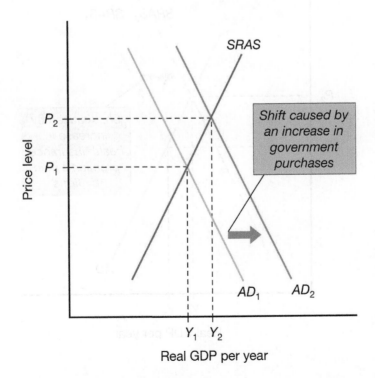

In contrast, a reduction in government purchases would reduce aggregate demand. The aggregate demand curve would shift to the left, putting pressure on both the price level and real GDP to fall.

A Change in the Cost of Health Care

In the United States, most people receive health insurance for themselves and their families through their employers. It's quite common for employers to pay a large percentage of employees' health insurance premiums. If the price of health insurance increases, that will raise firms' costs, affecting the cost of production in the same way that higher wages or higher costs for raw materials might.

cost-push inflation

An overall inflation driven by rising costs on the supply side of the economy.

Suppose the economy is initially in short-run equilibrium at the intersection of AD and $SRAS_1$, with a real GDP of Y_1 and a price level of P_1, as shown in Figure 8.13. The increase in labor costs due to rising health insurance premiums shifts the short-run aggregate supply curve leftward to $SRAS_2$. The price level rises to P_2, and the economy experiences an overall inflation driven by rising costs, which is commonly known as **cost-push inflation**. At the same time, real GDP falls to Y_2. Is that decrease in GDP reasonable? Yes! Output falls because, due to higher health insurance premiums, firms choose to employ fewer workers. Fewer inputs means fewer outputs!

Note that this inflation is, in some way, worse than demand-pull inflation. With demand-pull inflation, the economy experiences rising prices, but some of that economic pain is offset by rising employment—in fact, employment is above its natural level. With cost-push inflation, the opposite is true: The economy not only experiences inflation, but the same forces that created the inflation also create greater unemployment, with output falling below potential. This combination of economic stagnation and inflation is often referred to as *stagflation*.

FIGURE 8.13 An Increase in Health Insurance Premiums Paid by Firms
The economy is initially in short-run equilibrium at the intersection of $SRAS_1$ and AD, with price level P_1 and output Y_1. An increase in health insurance premiums paid by firms increases labor costs, reducing short-run aggregate supply from $SRAS_1$ to $SRAS_2$. The price level increases to P_2; output decreases to Y_2.

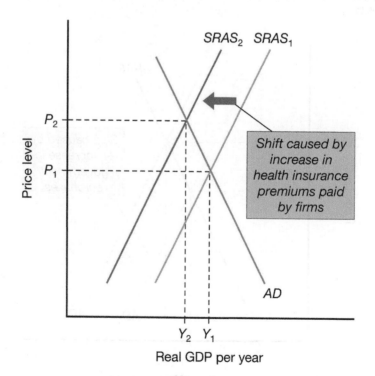

A reduction in health insurance premiums, of course, would have the opposite effect. The *SRAS* curve would shift to the right; the price level would fall and real GDP would rise.

In the short run, real GDP and the price level are determined by the intersection of the aggregate demand and short-run aggregate supply curves. Recall, however, that the short run is a period in which sticky prices and wages prevent the economy from reaching its natural level of employment and potential output. In the next section, we will see how the model adjusts to move the economy to long-run equilibrium and what, if anything, can be done to steer the economy toward its natural level of employment and potential output.

Key Takeaways

- The short run in macroeconomics is a period in which wages and some other prices are sticky. The long run is a period in which wages and prices fully adjust to changes in the economy. The full adjustment of wages and prices brings the economy to its natural level of employment and its potential output.
- The long-run aggregate supply curve is a vertical line at the potential level of output. The intersection of the economy's aggregate demand and long-run aggregate supply curves determines its equilibrium real GDP and price level in the long run.
- The short-run aggregate supply curve is an upward-sloping curve that shows the quantity of total output that will be produced at each price level in the short run. Wage and price stickiness account for the short-run aggregate supply curve's upward slope.
- Changes in prices of factors of production shift the short-run aggregate supply curve. In addition, changes in the capital stock, the stock of natural resources, and the level of technology can also cause the short-run aggregate supply curve to shift.
- In the short run, the equilibrium price level and the equilibrium level of total output are determined by the intersection of the aggregate demand and the short-run aggregate supply curves. In the short run, output can be either below or above potential output.

Try It!

The tools we have covered in this section can be used to understand the Great Depression of the 1930s. We know that investment and consumption began falling in late 1929. The reductions were reinforced by plunges in net exports and government purchases over the next four years. In addition, nominal wages plunged 26% between 1929 and 1933. We also know that real GDP in 1933 was 30% below real GDP in 1929. Use the tools of aggregate demand and short-run aggregate supply to graph and explain what happened to the economy between 1929 and 1933.

See related Concept Problem 4 at the end of this chapter.

Case in Point: Sticky Prices and the Great French Butter Shortage

Oh, yes. Yes, I can.

Source: ZikG/Shutterstock.com

The secret to great cooking isn't much of a secret at all—at least not to the French: Almost any food can be improved by throwing more butter at it. Thank goodness that butter is enjoying a renaissance. After years of being told that animal fat is unhealthy, the pendulum has returned; now carbs are the villain. *Butter's in, baby!*

And it's "in" *everywhere*. Across the United States and across Europe, demand for the creamy delight is exploding. Even the Chinese, with a developing appetite for western pastries, are buying big blocks of yellow deliciousness. But nowhere is butter more "in" than in France, where it's essential for cooking steaks and green beans, an indispensable complement to a crusty baguette, and the most important ingredient in light, flaky croissants. Heck, the French even spread it on radishes, which helps explain why the consumption of butter in France—eighteen pounds per person per year—is twice as high as the rest of Europe and triple the U.S. average!

Too bad, then, that coming into the 2017 holiday season there wasn't a bit of butter to be found—at least not in France. Price stickiness made sure of it. Elsewhere in the world, surging demand had driven up the wholesale price of butter from $1.40 per pound to $4; rising prices ensured no shortages. Not so in Paris, Nice, and Marseilles. There, shoppers found only empty shelves, while news outlets instructed French consumers how to churn their own, or suggested *gasp!* substituting margarine. *Sacré bleu!*

One of the big lessons of this section is that, in the short run, sticky prices may prevent markets from moving toward equilibrium. A second is that prices may be sticky for any number of reasons. What was the source of the price stickiness that created empty butter cases in France?

Part of the answer is legal: The French have a long history of regulating food production (and almost any other product you can name) across the board. Prices for many food items have historically been set by decree, which ensures that prices in about 1/6 of the entire French economy are slow to adjust. Quality has also been carefully regulated—it's not a baguette if it doesn't have five diagonal slashes across the top. Even summer vacations have been fair game: To ensure a steady supply of bread, bakers wanting a week off have had to apply to local authorities.

That web of economic regulations, which were viewed as stifling competition and innovation, has been slowly dismantled over the past few decades. Yet even though many of the laws are gone, the custom persists, and with that custom, price stickiness remains. In the case of butter, producers and retailers customarily negotiate prices once a year, in February. In 2017's autumn butter crisis, while worldwide prices surged, French prices remained steady, with large domestic purchasers refusing to pay more than February prices. No surprise, then, that French butter producers turned to more lucrative export markets rather than selling at home. There was plenty of French butter available . . . it just wasn't available in France!

Lucky for the 60 million residents of France, the butter shortage abated just before the holidays. That didn't happen on its own, though. Instead, equilibrium in the butter market was restored by an unprecedented emergency price renegotiation that brought French butter prices more in line with the rest of the world. Prices unstuck! And just in time for Christmas!

Yes, Genevieve, there *is* a Santa Claus. And thanks to (more) flexible prices in the French butter market, you'll be able to leave him buttery cookies on Christmas Eve.

See related Concept Problem 12 at the end of this chapter.

Sources: Based on Hugh Schofield, "Is There a Butter Crisis in France?" BBC, October 27, 2017; Eleanor Beardsley, "Sacre Beurre: France Faces a Butter Shortage," NPR, November 27, 2017; and Aurelien Breeden, "France, Land of Croissants, Finds Butter Vanishing from Shelves," The New York Times, October 30, 2017.

Answer to Try It! Problem

All components of aggregate demand (consumption, investment, government purchases, and net exports) declined between 1929 and 1933. Thus the aggregate demand curve shifted markedly to the left, moving from AD_{1929} to AD_{1933}. The reduction in nominal wages corresponds to an increase in short-run aggregate supply from $SRAS_{1929}$ to $SRAS_{1933}$. Since real GDP in 1933 was less than real GDP in 1929, we know that the movement in the aggregate demand curve was greater than that of the short-run aggregate supply curve.

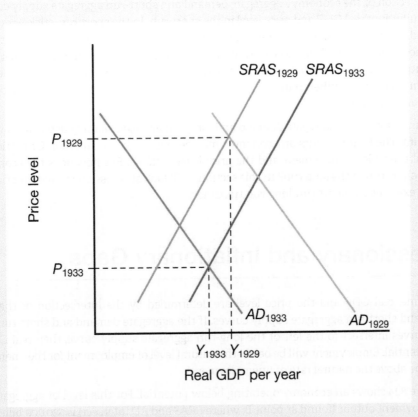

Khan Academy Links

Long-run aggregate supply

Short-run aggregate supply

Short-run changes in aggregate demand and demand pull inflation

Short-run changes in aggregate supply and cost push inflation

8.4 Recessionary and Inflationary Gaps and Long-Run Macroeconomic Equilibrium

Learning Objectives

1. Explain and illustrate graphically recessionary and inflationary gaps and relate these gaps to what is happening in the labor market.

2. Identify the various policy choices available when an economy experiences an inflationary or recessionary gap and discuss some of the pros and cons that make these choices controversial.

The intersection of the economy's aggregate demand and short-run aggregate supply curves determines equilibrium real GDP and price level in the short run. In the short run, stickiness of nominal wages and other prices can prevent the economy from achieving its potential output. Actual output may exceed or fall short of potential output. In such a situation the economy operates with a gap. When output is above potential, employment is above the natural level of employment, and an *inflationary gap* exists. When output is below potential, employment is below its natural level; a *recessionary gap* exists.

The intersection of aggregate demand and long-run aggregate supply determines its long-run equilibrium. The long run puts an economy's macroeconomic house in order: Only frictional and structural unemployment remain, and the price level is stable. But how does the economy move from the short run to the long run? In this section, we'll look at recessionary and inflationary gaps, and then examine the short run/long run transition.

Recessionary and Inflationary Gaps

At any time, real GDP and the price level are determined by the intersection of the aggregate demand and short-run aggregate supply curves. If the aggregate demand and short-run aggregate supply curves intersect to the left of the long-run aggregate supply curve, then real GDP will be below potential. Employment will be below the natural level of employment (or the unemployment rate will be above the natural rate of unemployment).

recessionary gap

The gap between the level of real GDP and potential output, when real GDP is less than potential.

Figure 8.14 shows an economy operating below potential. For this level of aggregate demand, full-employment output (found at point B, where *LRAS* and *AD* intersect) is $20,000 billion. But the economy isn't there . . . at least not yet! The economy's *current* output is found at point A, where aggregate demand intersects the short-run aggregate supply curve, *SRAS*. There, output is only $18,000 billion, well below the economy's potential output. The $2,000 billion gap between the current level of real GDP and potential output is called a **recessionary gap**.

inflationary gap

The gap between the level of real GDP and potential output, when real GDP is greater than potential.

Just as employment can fall short of its natural level, it can also exceed it. If current output is greater than its potential level, then an **inflationary gap** exists. In Figure 8.15, current output of $21,500 billion is found at the intersection of *AD* and *SRAS*, point A. This is greater than the economy's $20,000 billion long-run potential GDP (found at the intersection of *AD* and *LRAS*). This supercharged economy is operating beyond potential, with an inflationary gap of $Y_1 - Y_P$, or $1,500 billion.

FIGURE 8.14 A Recessionary Gap
The intersection of *AD* and *LRAS* at point B shows that long-run potential output Y_P in this economy is $20,000 billion. But short-run equilibrium output, found at the intersection of *AD* and *SRAS* (point A), is only $18,000 billion ($Y_1$). There is a recessionary gap of $Y_P - Y_1$, or $2,000 billion.

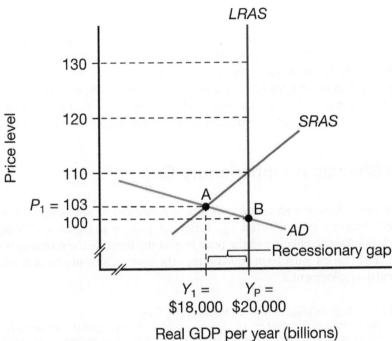

FIGURE 8.15 An Inflationary Gap
The intersection of *AD* and *LRAS* at point B shows that long-run potential output Y_P in this economy is $20,000 billion. But short-run equilibrium output Y_1, found at the intersection of *AD* and *SRAS* (point A), is greater than potential at $21,500 billion. There is an inflationary gap of $Y_1 - Y_P$, or $1,500 billion.

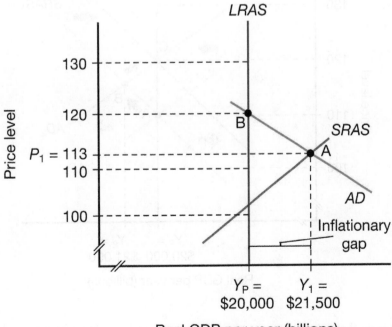

From the Short Run to the Long Run: Shocks and Adjustment

The aggregate demand curve shifts in response to changes in consumption, investment, government purchases, and net exports. The short-run aggregate supply curve shifts in response to changes in the prices of factors of production, the quantities of factors of production available, and technology. For an economy operating at potential, changes in aggregate demand or short-run aggregate supply (often called *demand shocks* and *supply shocks*, respectively) will open up inflationary or recessionary gaps. This section explores how an economy that has experienced a shock returns once again to full employment output on the long-run aggregate supply curve.

Demand Shocks: An Inflationary Gap

Let's begin by seeing how the economy responds to a demand shock. Suppose the economy is initially in both long-run and short-run equilibrium at point A in Figure 8.16.[16] Output is at its potential level, Y_P = $20,000 billion, and the price level is 110. Because the economy is operating at potential, the labor market must be in equilibrium—the unemployment rate is at its natural rate, with no cyclical unemployment.

FIGURE 8.16 Long-Run Adjustment to an Inflationary Gap
The economy begins in long-run and short-run equilibrium at point A. Rising aggregate demand (AD_1 shifts to AD_2) causes the economy to temporarily produce beyond potential at point B. As prices begin to increase, workers see their real wages fall and begin demanding nominal wage increases to restore purchasing power. Rising wages cause short-run aggregate supply to decrease from $SRAS_1$ to $SRAS_2$; output falls, and prices continue rising. Eventually, rising prices and wages return the economy to short- and long-run equilibrium at C.

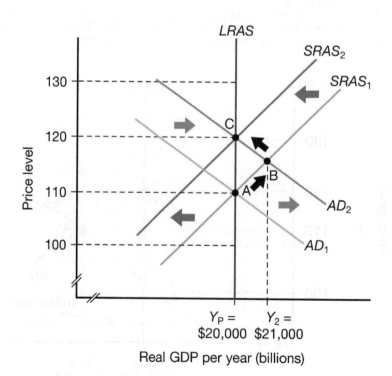

Now, suppose that rising government purchases result in an increase in aggregate demand (AD_1 to AD_2) that moves the economy temporarily beyond potential to point B.[17] The short-run effect is both higher output ($21,000 billion) and a higher price level (about 115): An inflationary gap has opened up.

The higher price level, combined with a fixed nominal wage (*wages are sticky, remember?*), reduces real wages paid by firms; those firms respond by employing the extra workers needed to supply the extra output. But operating beyond potential is like pulling an all-nighter: You might be able to do it once or twice, but sooner or later it starts to catch up with you. The same thing happens in the macroeconomy. Eventually, workers discover that while the dollar (nominal) wages they're being paid are the same, the prices of the goods and services they produce are increasing. They're working triple-overtime . . . but for lower real wages! Other workers, lured to the job market by the ease of finding work, re-evaluate that choice in the the face of rising prices and falling real wages: If they weren't working *before*, at the original real wage, they certainly don't want to work *now*, at a lower real wage.

Facing lower real wages, some workers eventually leave the labor force, reducing short-run aggregate supply. Other workers demand nominal wage increases to keep up with prices. Those wage demands increase both the nominal and real wages employers must pay, and the effect in the *AD/AS* model is the same as the effect of rising input prices in any individual market: Supply decreases. The short-run aggregate supply curve shifts from $SRAS1$ to $SRAS_2$—just enough to return the economy to short- and long-run equilibrium at point C, with the full impact of the demand shock ultimately being reflected in higher prices, and none of it showing up as a permanent increase in output.

Supply Shocks and Recessionary Gaps: An Increase in the Cost of Health Care

Now, let's see how the economy responds to a supply shock by revisiting the previous section's example of rising health care costs. Let's begin with the economy in both short- and long-run equilibrium, as shown by point A in Figure 8.17. Now suppose that there is a sudden, large increase in health care costs. Because health insurance premiums are generally paid by firms for their workers, an increase in premiums raises the cost of production, decreasing short-run aggregate supply and shifting the curve leftward from $SRAS_1$ to $SRAS_2$. The price level increases, and a recessionary gap opens up as output falls from Y_P to Y_2. This situation is particularly disagreeable—both unemployment and the price level have risen!

With real GDP below potential, though, there will eventually be pressure on the price level to fall. And in the labor market, increased unemployment also puts downward pressure on nominal wages. As wages fall, production costs follow, and the short-run aggregate supply curve begins to return to $SRAS_1$. Real GDP returns to potential at Y_P, the price level falls back to 110, and employment returns to its natural level. The recessionary gap disappears, all by itself!

An economy with a recessionary gap needs to unlock its potential. Falling real wages can make that happen!

Source: Guitarfoto/Shutterstock. com

FIGURE 8.17 Long-Run Adjustment to a Recessionary Gap

A decrease in aggregate supply from $SRAS_1$ to $SRAS_2$ reduces real GDP to Y_2, creating a recessionary gap of $Y_P - Y_2$. In the long run, as prices and nominal wages decrease, the short-run aggregate supply curve returns to $SRAS_1$ and real GDP returns to potential.

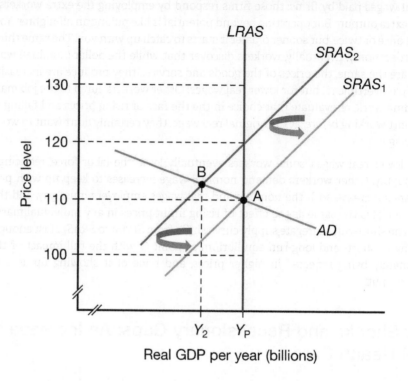

Real GDP per year (billions)

Gaps and Public Policy

stabilization policy

A policy in which the government or central bank acts to move the economy to its potential output.

We've just seen that when a shock to aggregate demand or aggregate supply causes the economy to move away from its long-run equilibrium, naturally occurring forces tend to return the economy to potential. That process of *self-correction* depends critically on how fast wages and prices adjust. Until that happens, inflationary and recessionary gaps will persist.

Gaps present us with two alternatives. First, we can do nothing, trusting that in the long run, real wages will adjust to bring employment to its natural level and real GDP back to potential. But remember the famous words of John Maynard Keynes: *In the long run, we're all dead.* In the meantime, inflationary and recessionary gaps can impose large costs on society. So, rather than waiting for the economy to self-correct, policymakers can take actions aimed at moving the economy back to potential by altering aggregate demand or short-run aggregate supply. Policy actions designed to close recessionary or inflationary gaps are referred to as **stabilization policy**.

Later chapters will explain stabilization policies in more detail, but there are essentially two types of stabilization policy: fiscal policy and monetary policy. **Fiscal policy** is the use of government purchases, transfer payments, and taxes to influence the level of economic activity. **Monetary policy** is the use of central bank policies to influence the level of economic activity.

fiscal policy

The use of government purchases, transfer payments, and taxes to influence the level of economic activity.

monetary policy

The use of central bank policies to influence the level of economic activity.

Self-Correction or Expansionary Policy?

Figure 8.18 illustrates the alternatives for closing a recessionary gap. In both panels, the economy starts with a real GDP of Y_1 and a price level of P_1. There is a recessionary gap equal to $Y_P - Y_1$. In Panel (a), policymakers do nothing: As long as employment remains below its natural level, wages and prices will fall, shifting the short-run aggregate supply curve to the right, from $SRAS_1$ to $SRAS_2$. Eventually, the economy moves to a long-run equilibrium at price level P_2 and potential output Y_P.

FIGURE 8.18 Alternatives in Closing a Recessionary Gap
Panel (a) illustrates a gradual closing of a recessionary gap. Without intervention, falling nominal and real wages return the economy to potential output by shifting the short-run aggregate supply from $SRAS_1$ to $SRAS_2$. Panel (b) shows how policymakers can speed the economy's return to potential by stimulating aggregate demand. Shifting the AD curve from AD_1 to AD_2 returns output to potential and employment to its natural level.

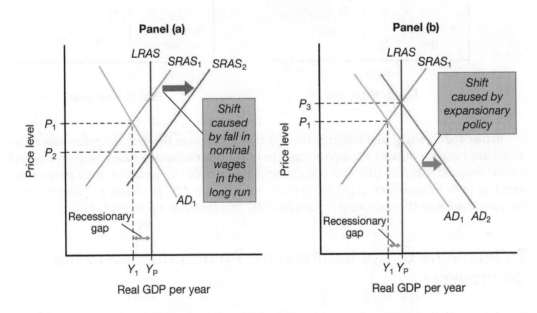

Panel (b) of Figure 8.18 illustrates how stabilization policy can close a recessionary gap. By stimulating aggregate demand, policymakers can shift the AD curve from AD_1 to AD_2. The economy returns to full-employment output Y_P, but at a higher price level, P_3. Actions taken by the government or the central bank to increase real GDP are referred to as **expansionary policy**. What kinds of actions can policymakers take to accomplish that? One option is for the government to stimulate aggregate demand directly through increases in government purchases. A second option might be for government to stimulate consumption spending by offering taxpayers a tax cut. A third option is for the central bank to stimulate consumption and investment spending by increasing the money supply and pushing interest rates downward.

expansionary policy

A stabilization policy designed to increase real GDP.

Nonintervention or Contractionary Policy?

Figure 8.19 illustrates the alternatives for closing an inflationary gap. In an economy with an inflationary gap, employment exceeds its natural level, putting upward pressure on wages. Self-correction relies on those wage increases: As wages rise, short-run aggregate supply decreases, eventually returning the economy to potential output and employment to its natural rate. That process is shown in Panel (a).

FIGURE 8.19 Alternatives in Closing an Inflationary Gap

Panel (a) illustrates the gradual closing of an inflationary gap. Self-correction shifts the short-run aggregate supply from $SRAS_1$ to $SRAS_2$, returning the economy to potential output. Panel (b) shows how contractionary policy designed to reduce aggregate demand from AD_1 to AD_2 can be used to close the gap.

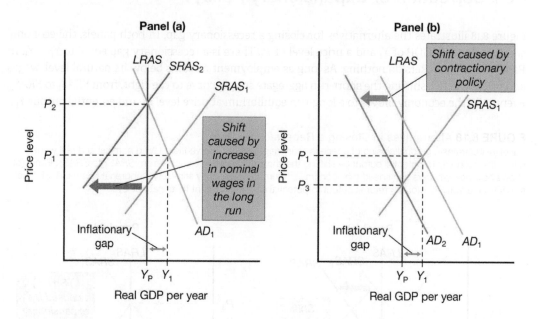

contractionary policy

A stabilization policy designed to reduce real GDP.

Rather than waiting (and suffering the effects of inflation in the process), policymakers can potentially close the inflationary gap through the use of **contractionary policy**, which consists of actions designed to reduce GDP. One straightforward way to do this would be to cut government spending in order to reduce aggregate demand from AD_1 to AD_2, as shown in Panel (b). That decrease in aggregate demand would return real GDP to potential at a price level of P_3.

To Intervene or Not to Intervene: An Introduction to the Controversy

How large are inflationary and recessionary gaps? Figure 8.20 shows potential output versus the actual level of real GDP in the United States since 1981. Actual output (in red) generally tracks potential output (in blue) quite closely. However, there are periods when actual GDP is above potential, and others where actual GDP is below potential.

FIGURE 8.20 Real GDP and Potential Output, 1981–2020

Potential output (the blue line) and actual real GDP (the red line) have trended upward through time. Potential output grows slowly and steadily; actual output is often quite near potential, but sometimes the gap between them opens up.

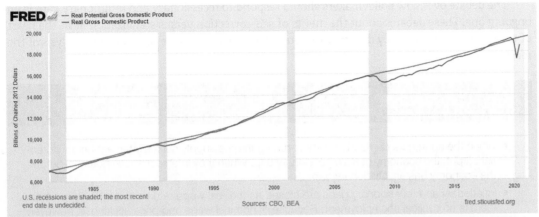

Source: Congressional Budget Office and Bureau of Economic Analysis, accessed through Federal Reserve Economic Data (FRED) at https://fred.stlouisfed.org/series/GDPPOT and https://fred.stlouisfed.org/series/GDPC1. FRED® Graphs ©Federal Reserve Bank of St. Louis.All rights reserved. All FRED® Graphs appear courtesy of Federal Reserve Bank of St. Louis. https://fred.stlouisfed.org/).

How big are those gaps? Figure 8.21 shows the size of those inflationary and recessionary gaps as a percentage of potential output. (The percentage gap is positive during periods of inflationary gaps and negative during periods of recessionary gaps.) Over the last forty years, the economy has seldom been more than 5% from its potential output. But there are exceptions: The recession of 1981 was sharp and deep, with output falling 7.5% below potential. The Great Recession of 2007–2009 wasn't quite as deep, but the recovery was slow and costly; the recessionary gap didn't fully close until ten years later, in 2017! The biggest recessionary gap, however, was the one you're probably most familiar with: In 2020, the coronavirus crisis brought with it a recessionary gap of almost 10%! That gap closed quite quickly, however—within just a few months the gap was just 3.5%.

FIGURE 8.21 Inflationary and Recessionary Gaps

This graph shows the percentage difference between actual and potential real GDP. Over the last forty years, real GDP has rarely deviated more than 5% from its potential level, indicated by the black line at 0.0.

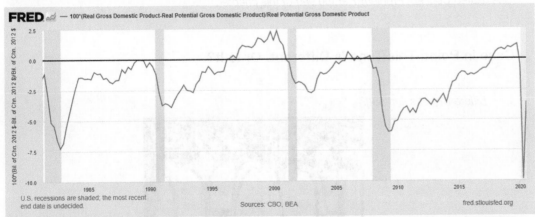

Source: Congressional Budget Office and Bureau of Economic Analysis, accessed through Federal Reserve Economic Data (FRED) at https://fred.stlouisfed.org/series/GDPPOT and https://fred.stlouisfed.org/series/GDPC1. FRED® Graphs ©Federal Reserve Bank of St. Louis.All rights reserved. All FRED® Graphs appear courtesy of Federal Reserve Bank of St. Louis. https://fred.stlouisfed.org/).

Should policymakers intervene to close inflationary and recessionary gaps? Some economists say yes, arguing that prices are sufficiently sticky that the economy's own adjustment to its potential will be a slow process—and a painful one, with inflation (in the case of inflationary gaps) or unemployment (in the case of recessionary gaps) lasting longer than it needs to.

Other economists favor relying on the economy's ability to correct itself. Those economists argue that the available policy tools might not be powerful enough to shift the *AD* curve by very much. Others argue that policy actions might not have an effect on the economy for many months, and that by the time the impact of stabilization policy is felt, the state of the economy might have already changed on its own.

The debate over how policymakers should respond to recessionary and inflationary gaps is an ongoing one. These debates about the merits of self-correction versus stabilization lie at the heart of the macroeconomic policy debate. We'll return to them often as we continue our analysis of the macroeconomy.

Key Takeaways

- When the aggregate demand and short-run aggregate supply curves intersect below potential output, the economy has a recessionary gap. When they intersect above potential output, the economy has an inflationary gap.
- Inflationary and recessionary gaps are closed as the real wage returns to equilibrium, where there is no cyclical unemployment. Because of nominal wage and price stickiness, however, such an adjustment takes time.
- When the economy has a gap, policymakers can choose to do nothing and let the economy return to potential output and the natural level of employment on its own. This process is called self-correction.
- Alternatively, policymakers can choose to try to close a gap by using stabilization policy. Stabilization policy designed to increase real GDP is called expansionary policy. Stabilization policy designed to decrease real GDP is called contractionary policy.

Try It!

Using the scenario of the Great Depression of the 1930s, as analyzed in the previous Try It!, tell what kind of gap the U.S. economy faced in 1933, assuming the economy had been at potential output in 1929. Do you think the unemployment rate was above or below the natural rate of unemployment? How could the economy have been brought back to its potential output?

See related Concept Problem 7 at the end of this chapter.

Case in Point: This Time Is Different. Or Is It?

Different? Let's find out!

Source: Brandon B/Shutterstock.com

The Great Recession of 2007–2009 was special . . . if it hadn't been, they never would have given it that name.[18] A big part of the Great Recession's uniqueness is that it was the biggest financial crisis in the modern era.

But was the Great Recession *truly* special? Economists Carmen Reinhart and Kenneth Rogoff were determined to find out. They investigated hundreds of financial crises spanning 800 years of global history, and looked at the economic bust each left in its wake. What patterns led to the crisis? What patterns characterized the recoveries?

Reinhart and Rogoff argue that looking over a long span of history is necessary because financial crises are "rare" events—not every recession involves one. Financial crises occur at varying intervals, and researchers studying a period of twenty-five years or so may not encounter the financial equivalent of a 100-year, category 5 hurricane that hits a major, low-lying city with a faulty levee system.

In general, such crises follow periods of relative economic calm. For example, the period in the United States from the mid-1980s until 2007 was often referred to as the Great Moderation. During such periods, inflationary and recessionary gaps may occur, but they are relatively small and short-lived. Societies begin to feel that they have tamed the business cycle, that policymakers have gotten smarter, and that moderation will continue.

But then it happens. The accumulation of too much debt by governments, businesses, or consumers leads to a financial meltdown. As housing prices ran up in the years before the Great Recession, for example, people found ways to justify their heavy borrowing and to rationalize rising housing prices: *Demographics have changed; mortgage terms have improved; the regulation we have put in place is better this time; it's better to buy now, before prices go up even more; housing prices won't fall.* "This time is different," they argued.

But Reinhart and Rogoff provide convincing evidence that "this time" is usually *not* different. Financial crises almost always begin with large-scale debt buildups like the housing debt buildup prior to the Great Recession. Those debt buildups eventually lead to crises of confidence that touch off legitimate financial crises. The aftermath is typically a severe and prolonged recessionary gap. On average, they find the following to be true of financial crises (though not true of ordinary recessions):

1. The collapse in asset market prices is large and long-lasting. Housing prices decline an average of 35% over 6 years, and stock prices decline an average of 56% over 3.5 years.

2. Peak-to-trough GDP falls 9% on average, and the recession averages two years in length.

3. The unemployment rate rises 7 percentage points over a four-year period.

4. Government debt swells due to bailout costs and, more important, because tax revenues fall off due to lower GDP.

5. V-shaped recoveries in stock prices are more common than V-shaped recoveries in housing prices or employment.

How well did the Great Recession fit this pattern? Let's see:

1. In the six years between 2006 and 2012, housing prices declined 37%. Stock prices declined 55% in the year and a half between June of 2007 and February of 2009.

2. Real GDP declined by 4%, peak to trough. The recession lasted nineteen months.

3. The unemployment rate rose from 4.4% to 10.0% in two years, an increase of 5.6%. Four years after unemployment began rising the unemployment rate was still 9.1%, an increase of 4.7%.

4. Government debt increased by 29% in just two years, thanks to unprecedented fiscal actions that resulted in a $1.4 trillion deficit in 2009.

5. The unemployment rate didn't return to its 2007 rate until ten years later, in 2017. Housing prices returned to 2006 levels in ten years also, in 2016. But stocks (measured by the Russell 2000 stock index) indeed had a V-shaped recovery, returning to their pre-recession values within four years.

The Great Recession was, indeed, a cataclysmic event, and taken in the context of the last ninety years of American economic history, unique. But those nintey years are only a small slice of global economic history, a history that contains hundreds of financial crises. Compared to those crises, the numbers the United States experienced were amazingly typical: The Great Recession wasn't actually great; in fact, it barely tipped the scales at ordinary. *This time, it turns out, wasn't different at all*!

See related Concept Problem 13 at the end of this chapter.

Source: Based on Carmen M. Reinhart and Kenneth S. Rogoff, This Time Is Different: Eight Centuries of Financial Folly (Princeton: Princeton University Press, 2009).

Answer to Try It! Problem

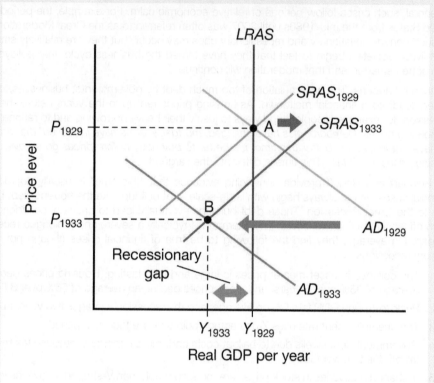

Add the long-run aggregate supply curve to show that, with the economy moving from A to B, the U.S. economy in 1933 was in a recessionary gap. The unemployment rate was above the natural rate of unemployment. Indeed, real GDP in 1933 was about 30% below what it had been in 1929, and the unemployment rate had increased from 3% to 25%. Note that during the period of the Great Depression, wages did fall. The notion of nominal wage and other price stickiness discussed in this section should not be construed to mean complete wage and price inflexibility. Rather, during this period, nominal wages and other prices were not flexible enough to restore the economy to the potential level of output.

There are two basic choices on how to close recessionary gaps. Policymakers could wait for wages (which had already fallen some) to fall further. As wages fell, the short-run aggregate supply curve would shift to the right, and the economy would self-correct, returning output to potential. The alternative would be to use some type of expansionary stabilization policy to shift the aggregate demand curve to the right. That stabilization policy could continue until the economy returned to potential.

Khan Academy Links

Recessionary and inflationary gaps

From short-run equilibrium to long-run equilibrium

8.5 Review and Practice

Summary

In this chapter, we outlined the model of aggregate demand and aggregate supply. The aggregate demand curve slopes downward: The aggregate quantity of goods and services demanded rises as the price level falls. That negative relationship results from the wealth effect on consumption, the interest rate effect on investment, and the international trade effect on net exports. The aggregate demand curve can shift as well. Due to the multiplier effect, an initial increase or decrease in *AD* will ultimately shift *AD* by a multiple of the initial change.

In the *AD/AS* model, there are two equilibria. One corresponds to the long run, in which wages and prices are fully flexible. Long-run equilibrium is found at the intersection of the aggregate demand curve and the long-run aggregate supply curve, a vertical line at the economy's potential level of output. The other equilibrium corresponds to the short run, where nominal wages and some prices are sticky. That equilibrium is found at the intersection of the aggregate demand curve and the short-run aggregate supply curve, which relates the quantity of total output produced to the price level in the short run. The short-run aggregate supply curve is upward sloping because of wage and price stickiness. In short-run equilibrium, output can be below or above potential.

If an economy is initially operating at its potential output, then a change in aggregate demand or short-run aggregate supply will induce a recessionary or inflationary gap. Such a gap will be closed in the long run by changes in the nominal wage, which will shift the short-run aggregate supply curve to the left (to close an inflationary gap) or to the right (to close a recessionary gap). Rather than relying on this self-correction, policymakers might attempt to close a recessionary or inflationary gap by using stabilization policy.

Concept Problems

1. Explain how the following changes in aggregate demand or short-run aggregate supply, other things held unchanged, are likely to affect the level of total output and the price level in the short run.

    a. An increase in aggregate demand

    b. A decrease in aggregate demand

    c. An increase in short-run aggregate supply

    d. A reduction in short-run aggregate supply

2. Explain why a change in one component of aggregate demand will cause the aggregate demand curve to shift by a multiple of the initial change.

3. (Related to "Try It!" in Section 20.2.) How will each of the events below affect aggregate demand (if at all)?

    a. An increase in government purchases

    b. A reduction in nominal wages

    c. A tax increase

    d. A reduction in net exports

4. (Related to "Try It!" in Section 20.3.) How will each of the events in Concept Problem 3 affect real GDP and the price level in the short run? (*Hint: Use the AD/AS model!*)

5. Give three reasons for the downward slope of the aggregate demand curve.

6. "When the price level falls, people's wealth increases. When wealth increases, the real volume of consumption increases. Therefore, a decrease in the price level will cause the aggregate demand curve to shift to the right." Do you agree? Explain.

7. (Related to "Try It!" in Section 20.4.) Suppose the economy has a recessionary gap. We know that if we do nothing, the economy will close the gap on its own. Alternatively, we could arrange for an increase in aggregate demand (say, by increasing government spending) to close the gap. How would your views about the degree of price stickiness in the economy influence your views on whether such a policy would be desirable?

8. The cost of hiring workers includes not only payments made directly to workers (wages), but also payments made on behalf of workers such as contributions by employers to pension plans and to health-care insurance. How would a decrease in the cost of employer-provided health insurance affect the economy (prices and output) in the short run? In the long run? (Hint: Use Figure 8.13 and Figure 8.17 for inspiration, and draw a graph to illustrate your answer.)

9. Suppose nominal wages never changed. What would be the significance of such a characteristic?

10. Suppose the minimum wage were increased sharply. How would this affect the equilibrium price level and output level in the model of aggregate demand and aggregate supply in the short run? In the long run?

11. Explain the short-run impact of each of the following.

a. A discovery that makes cold fusion a reality, greatly reducing the cost of producing energy

b. An increase in the payroll tax

12. (Related to "Case in Point: Sticky Prices and the Great French Butter Shortage" in Section 20.3.) Use the *AD/AS* framework to show how sticky prices for food contributed to an inflationary gap in France. How did the integrated nature of the global economy play a part?

13. (Related to "Case in Point: This Time Is Different. Or Is It?" in Section 20.4.) This case argues that the "Great" Recession wasn't really very different than other recessions. But what about the COVID-19 recession? Gather evidence on housing prices, stock prices, the unemployment rate, and government debt. Then, make a case either that the COVID-19 recession was ordinary, or that it was extraordinary.

Numerical Problems

1. Suppose the aggregate demand and short-run aggregate supply schedules for an economy whose potential output equals $2,500 are given by the table.

Price Level	Aggregate Quantity of Goods and Services	
	Demanded ($)	Supplied ($)
50	3,500	1,500
75	3,000	2,000
100	2,500	2,500
125	2,000	3,000
150	1,500	3,500

a. Draw the aggregate demand, short-run aggregate supply, and long-run aggregate supply curves.

b. State the short-run equilibrium level of real GDP and the price level.

c. Characterize the current economic situation. Is there an inflationary or a recessionary gap? If so, how large is it?

d. Now suppose aggregate demand increases by $500 at each price level; for example, the aggregate quantity of goods and services demanded at a price level of 50 now equals $4,000. Show the new aggregate demand curve, state the new short-run equilibrium price level and real GDP, and state whether there is an inflationary or a recessionary gap and give its size.

e. How will the economy self-correct to close the gap? What will the price level be? Output?

f. If the multiplier is 2.0, government can close the gap by changing its spending. Recommend a policy action (spend more, spend less), and specify the size of the change needed to return the economy to potential. What will the price level and output be?

2. An economy is characterized by the values in the table for aggregate demand and short-run aggregate supply. Its potential output is $1,500.

| | Aggregate Quantity of Goods and Services | |
Price Level	Demanded ($)	Supplied ($)
50	2,500	1,500
75	2,000	2,000
100	1,500	2,300
125	1,000	2,500
150	500	2,600

a. Draw the aggregate demand, short-run aggregate supply, and long-run aggregate supply curves.

b. State the equilibrium level of real GDP and the price level.

c. Characterize the current economic situation. Is there an inflationary or a recessionary gap? If so, how large is it?

d. Now suppose that nominal wages rise and that the price level required to induce a particular level of total output rises by 50. For example, a price level of 100 is now required to induce producers to produce a real GDP of $1,500. Show the new short-run aggregate supply curve, state the new equilibrium price level and real GDP, and state whether there is an inflationary or a recessionary gap and give its size. Why might such a change occur?

3. Suppose the price level in a particular economy equals 130 and that the quantity of real GDP demanded at that price level is $1,200. An increase of 10 points in the price level reduces the quantity of real GDP demanded by $220, and a reduction of 10 points increases the quantity of real GDP demanded by $220. Draw the aggregate demand curve and show the price level and quantity of real GDP demanded at three points.

4. According to Alaskan state economist Mark Edwards, the multiplier effect of Alaska's trade with Japan is such that for every $1 billion exported from Alaska to Japan another $600 million is added to the state's economy.[19] Calculate the size of the export multiplier.

5. (Related to "Case in Point: Taken Out to the Ball Game, or Taken for a Ride—How Big IS the Sports Stadium Multiplier?" in Section 20.2.) The Nottinghamshire Research Observatory in England calculated that students who attend Nottingham Technical University spend about £2,760 each in the local economy for a total of £50.45 million. In total, the impact of their spending on the local economy is £63 million.[20] Calculate the size of the student spending multiplier.

Endnotes

1. For *way* more information on this than a student of the macroeconomy might want, see Chapter 7, "The Analysis of Consumer Choice." It's a riveting dive into the demand curve, we promise!

2. You'll see much more about this in our chapter about financial markets . . . and you'll see our model of aggregate demand and aggregate supply again in that chapter, too. It's a must read!

3. What about the fourth component of aggregate spending, government purchases? For now, we're assuming that government purchases are set by a legislative process and don't respond systematically to changes in the price level. That means that government purchases will not affect the slope of the AD curve.

4. A major tax package in 2017 significantly slashed corporate tax rates, and modified parts of the household tax code, but had only modest impact on consumption.

5. See "Household Expenditure and the Income Tax Rebates of 2001," *American Economic Review*, December 2006, and "Consumer Spending and the Economic Stimulus Payments of 2008," *American Economic Review*, October 2013.

6. This is why some pundits claim that war is good for the economy. Unless, of course, you count all of the wealth destroyed and the lives lost.

7. For more on exchange rates, see our chapters on financial markets and international finance.

8. For more on trade policy, see our chapter on international trade.

9. For more on the multiplier, see our chapter on consumption and the aggregate expenditures model.

10. If the multiplier is 2, then total spending will increase by $200 billion. Because $100 billion is already accounted for by the change in net exports, the other $100 billion must be accounted for by consumption.

11. Scott Wolla, "The Economics of Subsidizing Sports Stadiums," Economic Research/Federal Reserve Bank of St. Louis, Page One Economics, May 2017.

12. Twenty-four of thirty-four economists agreed with the statement. Nine were uncertain. Only one disagreed.

13. Thinking about *real* wages instead of nominal wages may be new to you. Consider this example: If Ally's best employee, Chloe, earns $10 per hour, and cupcakes cost $1 each, then Ally must sell 10 cupcakes each hour to pay Chloe's wages. When the price of a cupcake increases to $2, Ally only has to sell 5 cupcakes each hour in order to cover Chloe's wages. The *real* wage Ally pays Chloe (W/P) declines from 10 cupcakes ($10 per hour/$1 per cupcake) to 5 cupcakes ($10 per hour/$2 per cupcake).

14. The long-run aggregate supply curve *can* move in the long run; we'll discuss the factors that make it shift in the next chapter.

15. Utility prices are generally changed each year following stakeholder testimony at a series of rate hearings. Those hearings will never, ever, be made into a Hollywood blockbuster.

16. Point A is at the intersection of all three curves: *AD*, *SRAS*, and *LRAS*. The economy is in short-run equilibrium at A because *AD* and *SRAS* intersect there. The economy is also in long-run equilibrium at A because *AD* and *LRAS* intersect there.

17. An increase like this could be caused by an increase in any of the components of GDP—consumption, investment, government spending, or net exports.

18. Whoever "they" is!

19. Matt Volz, "Trade Officials Hopeful for Japanese Recovery," *Associated Press and Local Wire*, June 22, 2004, BC cycle.

20. "University Brings in £250m to Economy," *Nottingham Evening Post*, November 4, 2004, p. 37.

CHAPTER 9
Economic Growth

9.1 Start Up: How Important Is Economic Growth?

Quick—pull out your smartphone! Now, turn it on for a moment, and think of all of the things you don't have to buy anymore because they're bundled into your phone: wristwatch, camera, alarm clock, radio, CD player, iPod, calculator, GPS navigator, TV, step counter, answering machine, video recorder, flashlight, level, compass, portable gaming device, e-reader, measuring tape, notepad, altimeter, stopwatch . . . oh—and a phone! You hold, in the palm of your hand, a collection of devices beyond the wildest imagination of the richest person of a century ago. And most of you *do* hold those devices in the palm of your hand: Survey data shows that 99% of college students have a smartphone.[1]

Elbow Room: Not so long ago, hanging out at home felt a bit like riding the A train at rush hour. Thank goodness for the march of progress.

Source: Ricardo de O. Lemos/Shutterstock.com

The fact that even the poorest college students can buy, for a couple of weeks' work at minimum wage, a collection of devices that even fifteen years ago would have cost thousands of dollars (devices that would have been completely unimaginable just a few decades before that) is a testament to the power of economic growth—the increasing ability of the economy to produce goods and services. But because college students are digital natives, many might assume that the miracles in their smartphone (not to mention all of the other miraculous things available to ordinary people today, like air travel, antibiotics, hover boards, and cronuts) have always been available and affordable. So to paint a better picture of the power of growth, let's go back in time and imagine life without the gains that growth has brought.

For starters, the average person a hundred years ago was much poorer than the average person today. How much? Divide your family's current income by six . . . and then imagine what your life would be like. For one thing, over the past century, the typical new home has grown 133%, from 1,050 square feet to 2,450. And because families in the 1920s were also larger, the typical person in 1920 had only 242 square feet of living space to claim as his own, compared to over 1,000 today—a fourfold improvement. Homes were also more primitive: Only about 10% of homes had a phone . . . and fewer than 1% had both electricity and indoor plumbing![2] *Chamber pot, anyone?*

Our lives, of course, are not just our homes. There are other material things that matter to us, too. In 1920, only about a third of households owned a car. Today, 93% of households have at least one car, and almost 60% have two or more . . . and they're much better cars, to boot! Entertainment has changed, too: In 1920, 20% of households had a radio; today, 97% of households have a TV, and 39% have more than three! Let's not forget services, either. After all, you're sitting in a college classroom, and going to college is something only about 5% of people did in 1920. Today, you're among the over 40% of people in your age group who do.

Economic growth has not only made us wealthier; it's also made us healthier. Consider life expectancy. A baby born in 1920 had a life expectancy of only fifty-eight years. Over the past century, improvements in the quality of and access to health care have added two decades to the typical lifespan, giving millions of Americans the gift of a retirement to enjoy. That 1920 baby, by the way, stood a one-in-five chance of dying before entering kindergarten; today, only one child in fifteen will fail to live to the age of five.

Economic growth has made meeting our material needs easier, and has delivered to us a prosperity that our parents and grandparents couldn't imagine, much less afford. We learned a lot about economic growth when we studied the production possibilities curve.[3] This chapter extends that analysis by relating economic growth and the previous chapter's model of aggregate demand and aggregate supply. It also introduces a new, purpose-built model to help explain the sources of economic growth. We'll begin, though, by looking at the significance of growth to the overall well-being of society.

Pop! Goes the Econ: Economic Growth at the *Superstore*

This short clip from *Superstore* explains how economic progress makes you richer by saving you money!

9.2 The Significance of Economic Growth

Learning Objectives

1. Define economic growth and explain it using the production possibilities model and the concept of potential output.
2. State the rule of 72 and use it to show how even small differences in growth rates can have major effects on a country's potential output over time.
3. Calculate the percentage rate of growth of output per capita.

Economic growth has made a huge impact on our standard of living. Let's quantify that impact by looking at how we measure economic growth—and then use those measurements to visualize how growth has improved the material well-being of even the most average person in society.

Defining Economic Growth

You'll often hear the media reporting that the economy grew at a certain rate in the last quarter, or that it is expected to grow at a particular rate during the next year. But those short-run changes in real GDP say little about economic growth. Economic growth is the long-run increase in an economy's production possibilities—in other words, in an economy's *potential* output. Those increases in potential output (which result from an outward shift of the production possibilities curve), shift the long-run aggregate supply curve to the right. In contrast, the short-run changes in *actual* output that the media focuses on are generally short-run fluctuations caused by changes in aggregate demand or short-run aggregate supply.

Figure 9.1 shows the record of economic growth for the U.S. economy over the past two centuries. The graph shows annual levels of actual real GDP (in blue) and of estimated potential output (in red). The story the figure tells is a big one: At the beginning of the 1800s, the United States was materially quite poor. Starting from that low level, total output increased fifty-fold over the next hundred years. But it was the twentieth century that really built on that momentum, as output soared another twenty-fold. Over the span of 200 years, the United States has grown from a very poor nation to the world's largest economy.

The figure also reminds us of a theme central to our analysis of macroeconomics: Real GDP fluctuates about potential output. Real GDP sagged well below its potential during the Great Depression of the 1930s, and rose well above its potential as the nation mobilized its resources to fight World War II. Since 1950, the actual level of real GDP has deviated from potential output by an average of less than 1%, but there were two big recessions: the double dip recession of the early 1980s, where actual GDP was *almost* 7% below potential, and the Great Recession of 2007–2009, where real GDP fell *more* than 7% below its potential. (The COVID-19 recession of 2020 is not yet reflected in the data shown here.)

FIGURE 9.1 Two Centuries of Economic Growth: 1820–2016
Persistent economic growth has created great rewards for society. At the start of the twenty-first century, potential output (shown in red) was nearly twenty times its level a century earlier. It grew fifty-fold in the century before that! Over the years, actual real GDP (shown in blue) fluctuated about an exponentially increasing level of potential output.

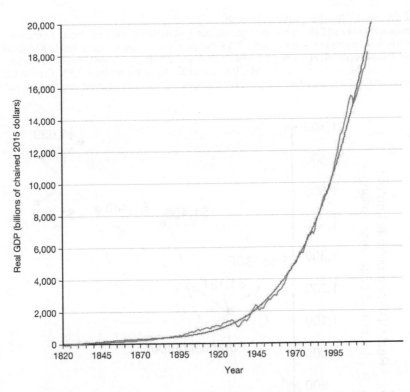

Source: Based on data from the Maddison Project at https://www.rug.nl/ggdc/historicaldevelopment/maddison/releases/maddison-project-database-2020?lang=en.

There have been some dramatic economic moments in our country's history—recessionary periods in which millions of people endured great hardship, and inflationary periods that produced dramatic increases in price levels. Those headline-grabbing fluctuations mattered. But it was the quiet, slow, steady process of economic growth—that smooth, beautiful, exponential, red arc from Figure 9.1, that continued to push living standards ever higher.

Pop! Goes the Econ: Why You'd Never Survive the Middle Ages
Economists estimate that worldwide economic growth between 1 A.D. and 1600 A.D. was essentially zero: The typical person in 1600 lived no better than the typical person of a thousand years earlier. That life was rough, one that philosopher Thomas Hobbes described as nasty, brutish, and short. This video describes the . . . romance . . . of living in the Middle Ages. Gather some stats from today to compare how far we've progressed in the last few hundred years!

View in the online reader

Take it easy, dude—the road to riches is a marathon, not a sprint!

Source: Maridav/Shutterstock.com

Why is it that we use the smooth arc of potential output to measure growth, rather than the actual real GDP numbers? Let's zoom in on a picture of the business cycle to see. Figure 9.2 shows the fluctuations of real GDP around the economy's long-run potential.

FIGURE 9.2 Cyclical Change Versus Growth

The use of actual values of real GDP to measure growth can give misleading results. Here, an economy's potential output (shown in green) grows at a steady rate of 2.5% per year, with actual values of real GDP fluctuating about that trend. If we measure growth in the first ten years as the annual rate of change between beginning and ending values of real GDP, we get a growth rate of 4.6%. The rate for the second decade is 0.5%. Growth estimates based on changes in real GDP are affected by cyclical changes that do not represent economic growth.

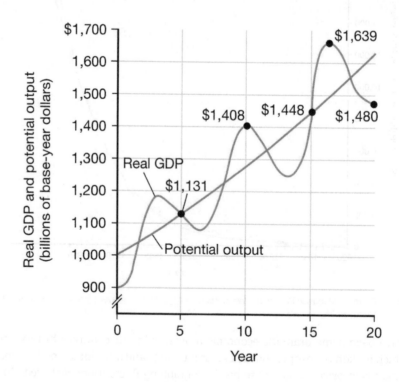

Given our definition of economic growth, we would say that the hypothetical economy depicted in Figure 9.2 grew at a 2.5% annual rate throughout the period, with potential GDP (the green line) increasing from $1,000 billion to $1,639 billion over a span of twenty years.[4] If we used actual values of real GDP, however, we might obtain quite different interpretations. Consider, for example, the first ten years, in which actual real GDP grew from $900 billion to $1,408 billion, an annual growth rate of 4.6%. Because we started measuring in the trough of a recession (temporary!), and ended at the peak of an expansion (also temporary), we paint a falsely optimistic picture of how fast the economy is capable of growing.

Now consider the second decade shown in Figure 9.2. Real GDP begins at $1,408 billion and ends at $1,480 billion, having grown at an average annual rate of only 0.5%. Because we started measuring at the business cycle peak, and ended measurement while we were in a trough, we understated the economy's long-run growth. In other words, *when you use actual real GDP to measure economic growth, your answer is very sensitive to your choice of starting and ending points.* By measuring economic growth as the rate of increase in *potential* output, we avoid such problems.

The Rule of 72 and Differences in Growth Rates

"Case in Point: Presidents and Economic Growth" later in this chapter shows that the U.S. growth rate began slowing in the 1970s, surged briefly in the mid-1990s, and slowed again in the 2000s. Those changes in growth rates, though relatively small, can make a huge difference in your standard of living. Let's see why.

When the economy grows at a given percentage rate over time, it's experiencing **exponential growth**. Exponential growth produces the same kind of smooth, rapidly growing red arc that we saw in Figure 9.1. To see where the power of exponential growth comes from, let's look at the growth in an economy with a real GDP of $1,000 that grows by 10% each year:

- At the outset, real GDP is $1,000.
- In the first year, real GDP increases by 10% to $1,100, a $100 increase. (Multiply the current value of $1,000 by the 10% growth rate (.1) to find the year's increase; then add the increase back to the original value.)
- In the second year, real GDP starts at $1,100, and grows by 10% to $1,210, an increase of $110.
- In the third year, real GDP starts at $1,210, and grows by 10% to $1,331, an increase of $121.

Notice that each year, the economy grows by an ever-increasing amount—from $100, to $110, to $121. With exponential growth, those yearly increases will continue to get bigger and bigger. Over a long span of time, they'll become positively huge!

The mathematics of exponential growth can be pretty hairy. But there is a convenient and easy rule of thumb that will offer us insight into the power of exponential growth without all of the mathematical sheep wrangling. That rule, the **rule of 72**, says that the number of years required for something growing exponentially to double in size is approximately 72 divided by the growth rate (expressed in percent). So, if real GDP was growing at a 9% rate, it would double every 72/9, or eight years.[5]

$$\text{Years to Double} \approx \frac{72}{\text{Growth Rate (\%)}}$$

Let's see what the rule of 72 can tell us about why small differences in growth rates—like the ones politicians often argue about—matter so much. Suppose two economies (A and B) have equal populations and the same level of real GDP—what we might call one dollar sign's worth of output, $. If Economy A grows at a rate of 2%, and Economy B grows at a rate of 1%, after a year, the difference in A's and B's real GDP will hardly be noticeable. But over longer periods, the seemingly tiny 1% difference in growth rates produces dramatic differences in output, as shown in Table 9.1. In seventy-two years, output in Economy A will be *twice* as big as output in Economy B. In the space of a couple of centuries (like the two centuries shown in Figure 9.1), output and the standard of living in Economy A grows by a factor of 64, while output in Economy B grows only by a factor of 8, leaving A's residents with a standard of living not twice that in B (as the 2% v. 1% figure might lead you to believe), but *eight times higher!* In other words, *over time, small differences in growth rates create large differences in output and the standard of living.* This is why alarm bells ring in the Oval Office every time growth slows from 3% to 2%!

exponential growth

When a quantity grows at a given percentage rate.

Exponential growth, like Newton's cradle, relies on momentum. But Newton's cradle *conserves* momentum; exponential growth *builds* it!

Source: TAGSTOCK1/ Shutterstock.com

rule of 72

A variable's approximate doubling time equals 72 divided by the growth rate, stated as a whole number.

TABLE 9.1 Economic Growth Over Long Time Horizons
Modest differences in growth, sustained over long periods of time, result in tremendous differences in standard of living. Starting with identical standards of living, if Country A grows at 2% per year and Country B grows at 1% per year, over two centuries, Country A will become eight times richer than Country B.

Date	Economy A's Real GDP, Growing at 2%	Economy B's Real GDP, Growing at 1%
Today	$	$
In 36 years . . .	$$	$
In 72 years . . .	$$$$	$$
In 108 years . . .	$$$$ $$$$	$$$
In 144 years . . .	$$$$ $$$$ $$$$ $$$$	$$$$
In 180 years . . .	$$$$ $$$$ $$$$ $$$$ $$$$ $$$$ $$$$ $$$$	$$$$ $$
In 216 years . . .	$$$$ $$$$ $$$$ $$$$ $$$$ $$$$ $$$$ $$$$ $$$$ $$$$ $$$$ $$$$ $$$$ $$$$ $$$$ $$$$	$$$$ $$$$

 Pop! Goes the Econ: Economic Growth in *The Pajama Game*

In this clip from *The Pajama Game*, workers protest for a meager seven-and-a-half cent raise. Draw a link between this small change in pay and a large change in these worker's well-being. How does this parallel the ideas behind long-run economic growth? And what is the importance of saving in the video?

View in the online reader

Growth in Output per Capita

output per capita

Real GDP per person.

Of course, it is not just how fast potential output grows that determines how fast the average person's material standard of living rises. If the extra output is the result of more people working, then the bigger economic pie ends up being divided more ways. That makes it possible that the typical person is getting poorer rather than richer! For that reason, economists often measure economic progress on a per capita basis. An economy's **output per capita** equals real GDP per person. If N represents the population, then

EQUATION 9.1

$$\text{Output per Capita} = \frac{\text{Real GDP}}{N}$$

In the United States in 2020, for example, real GDP was about $19 trillion, and the U.S. population was 328 million.[6] Using those numbers, real GDP per capita was about $58,000.

Because GDP measures both output *and* income, output per capita (which measures the typical person's income) is a decent gauge of an economy's material standard of living. If the economy's population is growing (making the denominator in Equation 9.1 larger), then output (in the numerator) must rise at least as rapidly to prevent the standard of living from falling. That may be hard to visualize, so with a little mathemagic, we can transform the variables in Equation 9.1 from levels (level of real GDP, level of population) into rates of change:[7]

EQUATION 9.2

$$\%\Delta\text{Output per Capita} = \%\Delta\text{Real GDP} - \%\Delta N$$

The left-hand side of Equation 9.2 measures the percentage change in the standard of living. If, for example, the population increases by 2%, and real GDP rises by 2%, too, then the standard of living for the typical person won't change. If real GDP grows faster than the population, living standards will rise; if real GDP grows more slowly than the population, living standards will fall. From 1970 to 2004, for example, Sierra Leone's population grew at an annual rate of 2.1% per year, while its real GDP grew at an annual rate of 1.4%; its output per capita and standard of living fell at a rate of 0.7% per year. Over the same period, Singapore's population grew at an annual rate of 2.1% per year, while its real GDP grew 7.4% per year. The resulting 5.3% annual growth in output per capita transformed Singapore from a relatively poor country to a country with the one of the highest per capita incomes in the world.

Crazy Rich Asians: At the end of World War II, Singapore was little more than a malaria-infested swamp. Today, it's a glistening jewel. Thanks, economic growth!

Source: anek.soowannaphoom/Shutterstock.com

Key Takeaways

- Economic growth is the process through which an economy's production possibilities curve shifts outward. We measure it as the rate at which the economy's potential level of output increases.
- Measuring economic growth as the rate of increase of the actual level of real GDP can lead to misleading results due to the business cycle.

- Growth of a quantity at a particular percentage rate implies exponential growth. When something grows exponentially, it doubles over fixed intervals of time; these intervals may be computed using the rule of 72.

- Small differences in rates of economic growth can lead to large differences in levels of potential output over long periods of time.

- To assess changes in average standards of living, we subtract the percentage rate of growth of population from the percentage rate of growth of output to get the percentage rate of growth of output per capita.

Try It!

Suppose an economy's potential output and real GDP is $5 million in 2020 and its rate of economic growth is 3% per year. Also suppose that its population is 5,000 in 2020, and that its population grows at a rate of 1% per year. Compute GDP per capita in 2020. Now estimate GDP and GDP per capita in 2092, using the rule of 72. At what rate does GDP per capita grow? What is its doubling time? Is this result consistent with your findings for GDP per capita in 2020 and in 2092?

See related Numerical Problem 4 at the end of this chapter.

Case in Point: Presidents and Economic Growth

Sources: U. S. Navy. "Portrait Photo of President Truman, Seated in Chair." December 14, 1952. Harry S. Truman Library & Museum, Accession Number 75-01. Reproduced via Wikimedia: https://commons.wikimedia.org/wiki/File:Harry_S._Truman_1952. jpg; Craighead, Shealah, photographer. Official portrait of President Donald J. Trump, 2017. October 6. Photograph. https://www.loc.gov/item/2017656484/.

President	Average Annual Increase in Real GDP (%)	Average Growth Rate (%)
Truman 1949–1952	5.9	5.2
Eisenhower 1953–1960	2.5	2.8
Kennedy-Johnson 1961–1968	4.2	3.8
Nixon-Ford 1969–1976	2.3	2.9
Carter 1977–1980	2.9	2.9

President	Average Annual Increase in Real GDP (%)	Average Growth Rate (%)
Reagan 1981–1988	2.9	3.0
G. H. W. Bush 1989–1992	2.0	2.5
Clinton 1993–2000	3.5	2.9
G. W. Bush 2001–2008	2.1	2.2
Obama 2009–2016	1.9	1.3
Trump 2017–2020	0.8	1.6

Source: Based on data from Bureau of Economic Analysis and the Congressional Budget Office, accessed through Federal Reserve Economic Data (FRED).

Presidents are often judged by the rate at which the economy grew while they were in office. That test is unfair on two counts. First, a president often has little to do with the forces that determine growth. Second, simply computing the annual rate of growth in real GDP over the course of a presidential term paints an inaccurate picture of the economy's true economic growth: A president who takes office when the economy is down and leaves with the economy up will look like an economic rock star; a president with the bad luck to inherit a strong economy and leave in a recession will look like a loser.

Here are annual rates of change in actual real GDP for each of the post-WWII presidents, along with rates of economic growth, measured as the annual percent change in *potential* output. These figures show that presidents' economic records are clearly affected by luck.

- Presidents Truman, Kennedy, Reagan, Clinton, and Obama for example, began their terms when the economy had a recessionary gap and ended them with an inflationary gap or at about potential output. As a result, real GDP generally rose faster than potential output during their presidencies.

- The Eisenhower, Nixon-Ford, G. H. W. Bush, and G. W. Bush administrations each started with an inflationary gap or at potential and ended with a recessionary gap. They recorded rates of real GDP increase below the rate of gain in potential output.

- Jimmy Carter, who both came to office and left office with recessionary gaps, ended up with equal increases in both actual and potential real GDP.

The big loser in the presidential economic lottery, however, is clearly President Trump. Trump very badly wanted to be a rock star, promising 4% annual growth during his presidential campaign. That kind of long-run growth number wasn't very realistic in the first place—potential GDP just doesn't rise that quickly. But timing is everything, and because Trump entered office with a strong economy and left office right in the middle of the very sharp, very deep COVID-19 recession, he had the misfortune to log the worst economic record of any president in the last eighty years, with actual real GDP rising only 0.8% per year, on average. That unfortunate artifact of timing will likely change Trump's economic legacy from champ to chump.

See related Concept Problem 6 at the end of this chapter.

Answer to Try It! Problem

GDP per capita in 2020 equals $1,000 ($5,000,000/5,000). If GDP rises 3% per year, it doubles every 24 years (= 72/3), so GDP will be $10,000,000 in 2044, $20,000,000 in 2068, and $40,000,000 in 2092. Growing at a rate of 1% per year, population will have doubled once by 2092 to 10,000, which means that GDP per capita will be $4,000 ($40,000,000/10,000).

GDP ultimately increases eight-fold. The increase in GDP *per capita* is four-fold, which implies growth in output per capita of 2% per year. (Run the rule of 72 backwards!) At that rate, the doubling time is thirty-six years, giving us two doublings in GDP per capita between 2020 and 2092, a four-fold increase.

Khan Academy Link

Understanding economic growth

9.3 Growth and the Long-Run Aggregate Supply Curve

Learning Objectives

1. Explain and illustrate graphically the concept of the aggregate production function. Explain how its shape relates to the concept of diminishing marginal returns.
2. Derive the long-run aggregate supply curve from the model of the labor market and the aggregate production function.
3. Explain how the long-run aggregate supply curve shifts in response to shifts in the aggregate production function, and distinguish between catching-up growth and cutting-edge growth.
4. Explain how the long-run aggregate supply curve shifts in response to shifts in the demand for or supply of labor.

Economic growth means that the economy's potential output is rising. In our aggregate demand/aggregate supply model, potential output is reflected in the vertical long-run aggregate supply curve. Economic growth shifts that long-run aggregate supply curve to the right.

Figure 9.3 illustrates economic growth in the *AD/AS* model of the macroeconomy. The economy begins at potential output Y_1, on $LRAS_1$. Growth increases potential output—first to Y_2, then Y_3, then Y_4. Those increases shift the long-run aggregate supply, in turn, to $LRAS_2$, $LRAS_3$, and $LRAS_4$. If the economy is growing at a particular percentage rate, and if the levels shown represent successive years, then each year's increase will be larger than the once before—as if the economy is ramping up the red arc of exponential growth in the previous section's Figure 9.1.

That explanation may make sense, but it leaves a big question unanswered: *How do we know where potential output is?* To answer that question, let's take a closer look at where the long-run aggregate supply (*LRAS*) comes from, and what factors cause it to shift. We shall begin our work by defining an aggregate production function.

FIGURE 9.3 Economic Growth and the Long-Run Aggregate Supply Curve
Economic growth raises the economy's potential output. In the *AD/AS* model, we can depict economic growth as a series of rightward shifts in the long-run aggregate supply curve, *LRAS*. With exponential growth, each successive shift in LRAS gets larger and larger.

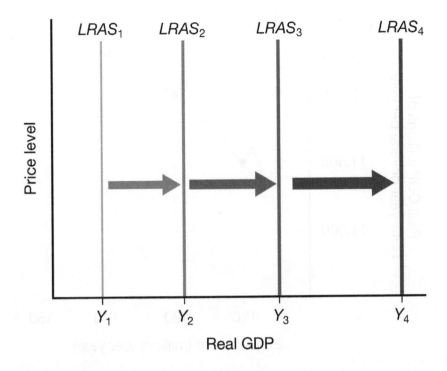

The Aggregate Production Function

Potential output, reflected in the position of the *LRAS* curve, measures the economy's ability to produce goods and services. For that reason, the first step in understanding the nature of the *LRAS* curve is to look at an aggregate production function. An **aggregate production function** relates the total output of an economy to the total amount of an input used—more inputs means more output. An economy operating on its aggregate production function is producing its potential level of output.

Of course, there are lots of inputs used in production—capital, natural resources, and labor are three big ones. In this section, we'll look at the relationship between output and the quantity of labor employed in the economy; we'll leave all other inputs unchanged. (In the next one, we'll use *capital* as our input and hold *labor* constant. Exciting, right?)

Figure 9.4 shows an aggregate production function (*PF*). It shows output levels for a range of employment between 120 million and 140 million workers, holding all other factors of production fixed. When the level of employment is 120 million, the economy produces a real GDP of $11,500 billion (point A). A level of employment of 130 million produces a real GDP of $12,000 billion (point B), and when 140 million workers are employed, a real GDP of $12,300 billion is produced (point C).

aggregate production function

Function that relates the total output of an economy to the total amount of labor employed in the economy, all other determinants of production (capital, natural resources, and technology) being unchanged.

All a production function does is show how many outputs you'll get if you you use a certain number of inputs.

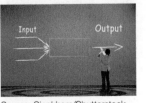

Source: Singkham/Shutterstock. com

FIGURE 9.4 The Aggregate Production Function

An aggregate production function (*PF*) relates total output to total employment, assuming all other factors of production and technology are fixed. Increases in employment lead to increases in output, but successively *smaller* increases in output.

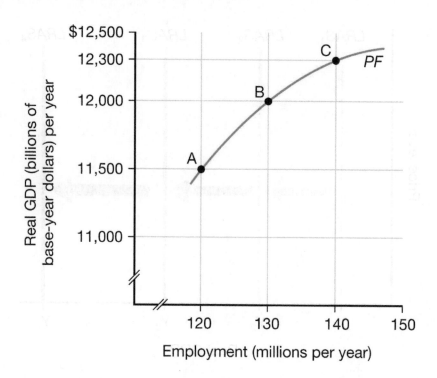

diminishing marginal returns

Situation that occurs when additional units of a variable factor add less and less to total output, given constant quantities of other factors.

Diminishing Returns: Too many cooks spoil the lip balm . . . as if the onions hadn't already done the job.

Source: Robert Adrian Hillman/Shutterstock.com

The shape of the aggregate production function shows that as employment increases, output increases—in other words, more inputs equals more output. But those increases get smaller and smaller as more labor is employed. Increasing employment from 120 million to 130 million moves the economy to point B, an increase in output of $500 billion. The next 10 million workers increase production by $300 billion, at point C. Those successively smaller increases in output illustrate **diminishing marginal returns**, which means that additional units of an input add less and less to total output, holding other factors constant.

It is easy to picture the problem of diminishing marginal returns in the context of a single firm—say, one producing designer lip balm. The firm can always increase output by adding workers—that gives them the power to divide labor and specialize. The easiest gains come first—one mixes ingredients and the other melts and pours into molds. Then, one mixes, one melts, and one pours. But the firm has a set number of lip balm melting kettles, which limits its total production, and the gains from division start to get smaller and smaller—you can only divide one big job into so many little tasks before you've got an entire factory full of workers employed in thousands of ways to make a few boxes of Chap-Stick. Each new worker may help the factory produce more lip balm, but the last workers don't provide the same gains as the early division into mixing, melting, and pouring did. That's diminishing returns.

The Aggregate Production Function, the Market for Labor, and Long-Run Aggregate Supply

To derive the long-run aggregate supply curve, let's bring together a model of the labor market and the aggregate production function.

The labor market is in equilibrium at the natural level of employment—there is no cyclical unemployment there, and for those who are unemployed, there is a vacancy waiting out there for them, somewhere. (Finding it might be hard, though—that's the nature of frictional unemployment.) The demand and supply curves for labor intersect at a real wage where the economy achieves its natural level of employment (and its natural rate of unemployment). Panel (a) of Figure 9.5 shows that the equilibrium real wage in a hypothetical economy is ω_1, and the natural level of employment is L_1. Panel (b) takes that level of employment and plugs it into the production function to show that with employment of L_1, the economy can produce a real GDP of Y_P. That output equals the economy's *potential* output—the level of output that determines the position of the long-run aggregate supply curve in Panel (c).

FIGURE 9.5 Deriving the Long-Run Aggregate Supply Curve
Panel (a) shows that the equilibrium real wage is ω_1, and the natural level of employment is L_1. Panel (b) shows that with employment of L_1, the economy can produce a real GDP of Y_P. That output equals the economy's potential output. That is the level of potential output where we draw the long-run aggregate supply curve in Panel (c).

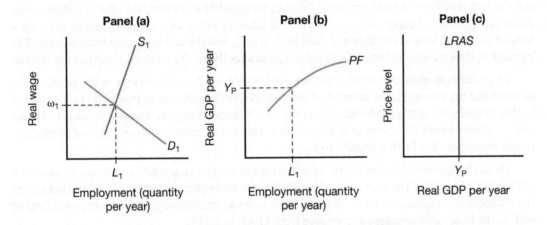

Changes in Long-Run Aggregate Supply

We've just seen that the position of the long-run aggregate supply curve is determined by both the aggregate production function and the demand and supply curves for labor. A change in any of these will shift the long-run aggregate supply curve. Let's take a look at both.

A Shift in the Aggregate Production Function

Figure 9.6 shows one possible shifter of long-run aggregate supply: a change in the production function. Suppose, for example, that an improvement in technology shifts the aggregate production function in Panel (b) from PF_1 to PF_2. Other developments that could produce an upward shift in the curve include an increase in the capital stock or in the availability of natural resources.

FIGURE 9.6 A Shift in the Aggregate Production Function

An improvement in technology shifts the aggregate production function upward in Panel (b). Because labor is more productive, the demand for labor shifts to the right in Panel (a), and the natural level of employment increases to L_2. In Panel (c) the long-run aggregate supply curve shifts to the right to Y_3.

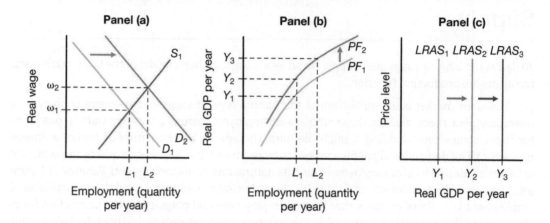

productivity

The amount of output per worker.

The shift in the production function to PF_2 means that labor is now more productive than before. This has two effects: First, each unit of labor employed will produce more stuff. Second, because each unit of labor is more productive than before, more units of labor will be employed. This is a double dose of good news: more labor, and better!

Those two effects are shown in Panels (b) and (a). First, in Panel (b), the production function shifts upward. Each unit of labor employed (L_1) makes more stuff—output increases from Y_1 to Y_2. But the fact that labor is more productive makes hiring labor more desirable. For any given wage, employers get more output! So, the demand for labor in Panel (a) increases from D_1 to D_2. As a result, the natural level of employment rises from L_1 to L_2, and the real wage rises from ω_1 to ω_2. The increase in the real wage reflects labor's enhanced **productivity**, the amount of output per worker.

To see how potential output changes, we need to evaluate *both* the change in the productivity of labor and the change in the amount of labor employed. The change in productivity is captured in the vertical shift of the production function, which causes output to increase from Y_1 to Y_2. But wait ... there's more! The increase in labor L_1 to L_2 moves the economy *along* the new production function; output rises further from Y_2 to Y_3.

Those changes feed forward into the position of the long-run aggregate supply curve, as shown in Panel (c). The shift of the production function causes an increase in potential output that moves the economy from $LRAS_1$ to $LRAS_2$. The new labor hired as productivity increases causes a further shift in the long-run aggregate supply curve from $LRAS_2$ to $LRAS_3$.

This dispels a common misconception about the impact of improvements in technology or increases in the capital stock on employment. Some people believe that technological gains or increases in the stock of capital reduce the demand for labor, reduce employment, and reduce real wages. Actual evidence suggests otherwise. Between 1995 (when computerization and the internet began to explode) and 2020, the U.S. capital stock and the level of technology increased dramatically. Over the same period, both employment and real wages rose. That suggests that even as capital was accumulating, it was making workers more productive, causing the demand for labor to increase. Of course, as some firms add capital or incorporate new technologies, some workers at those firms may lose their jobs. But for the economy as a whole, new jobs become available *and* they generally offer higher wages.

One natural question to ask is whether it's better to spur growth through capital accumulation or through technological innovation. After all, each shifts the production function upward ... so is there any difference between growing one way or growing the other?

The answer, of course, is that both capital-driven growth and technological innovation have their places in the growth recipe. For countries that are developing, the quickest, surest recipe for growth is to reduce consumption of consumer goods in favor of producing more capital goods. Because it's comparatively easier to, say, double the capital stock in a country that doesn't have much capital (compared to doubling the capital stock in a country that already has lots), developing countries can make large economic gains by investing in capital goods. The growth that is fueled by such investment is called *catching-up growth*.

But it's hard to maintain huge increases in a country's capital stock year after year. A country that has a lot of capital already will find it very costly to try to double its capital stock ... and because of diminishing returns, even if it does increase its capital substantially over time, the gains in output and consumption will tend to taper off at the margin. Once those gains begin to dwindle, the only reliable means for a country to continue to improve its standard of living is to improve its production technology. That growth is called *cutting-edge growth*; our appendix on the Solow growth model explores the distinction between catching-up and cutting-edge growth in depth.

A Change in Labor Supply

Another event that can shift the long-run aggregate supply curve is an increase in the supply of labor, as shown in Figure 9.7. The increase in the supply of labor could result from immigration, an increase in the population, or increased participation in the labor force. Increased labor force participation by women over the past few decades, for example, has increased the supply of labor.

FIGURE 9.7 An Increase in the Supply of Labor and the Long-Run Aggregate Supply Curve
An increase in the supply of labor shifts the labor supply curve in Panel (a) to S_2, and the natural level of employment rises to L_2. The real wage falls to ω_2. The increase in employment moves the economy along the aggregate production function in Panel (b); output increases to Y_2. The long-run aggregate supply curve in Panel (c) shifts to $LRAS_2$.

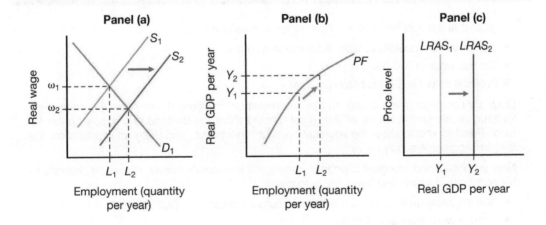

Do machines make labor better off or worse? This section's Case In Point explores the evidence.

Source: Everett Collection/Shutterstock.com

In Panel (a), an increase in the labor supply shifts the supply curve to S_2. The real wage falls from ω_1 to ω_2, and the natural level of employment rises from L_1 to L_2. (Because there is no change in the stock of capital, natural resources, or technology, there is no change in the aggregate production function or labor demand.) Panel (b) shows that the increase in employment from L_1 to L_2 causes output to increase from Y_1 to Y_2. That causes the long-run aggregate supply curve to shift to $LRAS_2$ (corresponding to Y_2) in Panel (c).

Of course, the aggregate production function and the supply curve of labor *can* shift together. If the demand for labor increases more than the labor supply, you'll see more people working at higher real wages. That's been the experience of most industrialized nations. The increase in real wages in the United States between 1995 and 2020, for example, was accompanied by an increase in the labor force from 132 million to 165 million--more workers, higher wages! This section's "Case in Point: Is It Time for a Robot Tax?" takes a data-driven look at a current policy proposal that has roots in the economy of two centuries ago.

Key Takeaways

- The aggregate production function relates the level of employment to the level of real GDP produced per period.
- The real wage and the natural level of employment are determined by the intersection of the demand and supply curves for labor. Potential output is given by the point on the aggregate production function corresponding to the natural level of employment. This output level is the same as that shown by the long-run aggregate supply curve.
- Economic growth can be shown as a series of shifts to the right in *LRAS*. Such shifts require either upward shifts in the production function or increases in demand for or supply of labor.

Try It!

Suppose that the economy is currently in long-run equilibrium:

- The equilibrium quantity of labor is 50 million workers.
- The real wage is $20,000 per year.
- Potential output is $2,000 billion per year.

Draw a three-panel graph similar to the one presented in Figure 9.5 to show the economy's long-run equilibrium. Panel (a) of your graph should show the demand and supply curves for labor, Panel (b) should show the aggregate production function, and Panel (c) should show the long-run aggregate supply curve.

Now suppose a technological change increases the economy's output. Show the changes to the economy, incorporating these key outcomes:

- *With the same quantity of labor as before*, output increases to $2,200 billion.
- The real wage rises to $21,500.
- Employment increases to 51 million workers.
- Long-run potential output rises to $2,250 billion.

Explain, using your diagram, these changes. Make sure your new numbers are consistent with the story told above.

See related Numerical Problem 7 at the end of this chapter.

Case in Point: Is It Time for a Robot Tax?

"Hasta la vista, baby—you've been terminated."

Source: RichartPhotos/Shutterstock.com

My friend John refuses to throw out his own trash when we eat at McDonalds: "I'm creating jobs for college students," he tells me. After all, someone has to dump that trash; John doesn't want to replace college students' *paid* labor with his *unpaid* labor![8]

John's sentiment echoes centuries of economic lament about the origins of economic progress. Two hundred years earlier, at the dawn of the Industrial Revolution, a group of weavers called the Luddites set out to destroy the newly invented looming equipment that threatened to throw them out of work. Across the English Midlands, they smashed factories, threatened magistrates, and ultimately found themselves skirmishing with the British army. Defeated, tried, and sometimes even executed, the Luddites were ultimately crushed by legislation that made industrial sabotage a capital crime (see "Pop! Goes the Econ: The Luddites and Technology Today—Is This Time Different?" above).

Today, many people feel similar resistance to technology that just seems to be taking over everywhere. McDonald's has ordering kiosks, Walmart has self-checkout, banks have ATMs, and automobile factories are largely staffed by high-tech industrial robots. These innovations have made life simpler, easier, and cheaper for millions, yet they have all replaced workers with machines. Economists Claudia Goldin and Lawrence Katz believe that this kind of technological change is responsible for the widening income inequality that has become a focal point of politicians in recent years: With capital replacing lower-skilled workers, laborers need to acquire more and more education and training just to remain employable . . . and many haven't.

That leaves society with a big question about its obligation to people with strong backs but few skills. During the 2020 presidential campaign, an interesting solution emerged, one popularized by Microsoft icon Bill Gates: How about discouraging firms from replacing humans with machines by placing a tax on robots? Such a tax would encourage firms to retain labor while raising revenue for the government in the process: That sounds like a win-win!

Except, of course, that it's not: It's a win-win-lose, with labor and the government better off, and consumers worse off. After all, the reason firms want to replace workers with machines is because machines give the business a better bang for their buck.[9] Try to reverse that with a robot tax and you'll find consumers paying higher prices because of less efficient production . . . and then higher prices still because of the added tax!

And, of course, there are logistical issues, foremost among them the question of what exactly a robot is—because if we can't draw a clear line, we'll end up taxing *every* machine. If a robot automates tasks that could be done by humans, we'll have to tax spreadsheet programs that do jobs once performed by mathematicians and accountants, the internet (which has undoubtedly replaced thousands of librarians), and even vacuum cleaners (think of the unemployed house-keepers vacuums have created!).

Another concern is that most companies investing in capital don't buy a machine and then immediately lay off a worker that machine replaces. Typically, they'll buy a machine, see how it works, and then lay off people who aren't needed any more while hiring others—perhaps one to run the machine and a few more because the robot has improved overall productivity. In other words, machinery may replace some workers, but create opportunities for others.

There's strong evidence to support that. Economists Ian Stewart, Debrapratim De, and Alex Cole looked at census data from industrializing Wales and found that mechanization in agriculture during the late 1800s was "a great job-creating machine . . . [with lost jobs] being more than offset by rapid growth in the caring, creative, technology, and business services sectors."[10] That growth in employment, plus rising real wages, is exactly what our *AD/AS* model predicts!

Machines have been replacing humans for hundreds of years, with largely positive effects. The big question is, "*Is this time different?*" Ultimately, the innovation-stifling, efficiency-reducing effects of the robot tax are unlikely to meet much favor as a practical solution to the broader problem of how to ensure those at the bottom of the income distribution aren't entirely left behind by progress. That's a problem without an easy and immediate solution, one worth mulling over while your self-driving Tesla chauffeurs you to McDonald's for a breakfast biscuit you ordered in advance online. But for goodness sake, let's not carry things too far: When you're finished eating, the rules of polite society still demand that you *pick up your trash and throw it away*!

See related Concept Problem 2 at the end of this chapter.

Sources: Based on Claudia Goldin and Lawrence Katz, The Race Between Education and Technology (Cambridge: Belknap Press, 2008); and Ian Stewart, Debrapratim De, and Alex Cole, "Technology and People: The Great Job Creating Machine," Deloitte, 2015.

Answer to Try It! Problem

The changes are shown in the diagram below:

- First, the production function in Panel (b) shifts up to PF_2. Note that at 50 million workers, output is now $2,200 billion.
- Because labor is more productive, the demand for labor increases in Panel (a) to D_2. Employment increases to 51 million; the real wage increases to $21,500.
- Because employment has increased, we move *along* the production function PF_2 in Panel (b). Output increases to $2,250 billion.
- The technological change initially shifts the long-run aggregate supply curve to the right from $2,000 billion ($LRAS_1$) to $2,200 billion ($LRAS_2$). Then, the subsequent increase in employment causes a second shift from $LRAS_2$ to $LRAS_3$ ($2,250 billion), as shown in Panel (c).

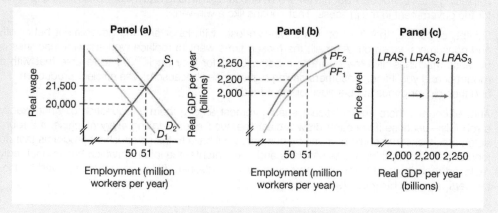

9.4 A Recipe for Economic Growth

Learning Objectives

1. Explain why capital accumulation and technology improvements do not happen equally everywhere.
2. List and describe three political factors that can foster the accumulation of capital.
3. Explain the importance of a high savings rate in an economy.
4. Explain the importance of a sound education system to long-term economic growth.

We now know that economic growth is important—it's the force behind an improving standard of living that brings all kinds of benefits both to you and to society as a whole. We also know that small differences in growth rates can lead to large differences in the standard of living. The big question for an economy, then, is how to foster and encourage economic growth. Let's begin by listing a few potential engines of growth:

- One path to growth is for an economy to discover or utilize previously untapped resources. That could mean discovering a natural resource like the Alberta tar sands, or it could mean greater labor force participation—which might be fostered by policies guaranteeing equal opportunity, or that encourage moving from home to work.

- A second path to growth is to build a larger capital stock. More rapid accumulation of capital can be achieved by pursuing policies that encourage less consumption and more saving.

- A final path to growth is technological improvement. Those innovations can spring from government directly (witness global positioning systems, or NASA), or they can be fostered by creating a competitive marketplace that encourages and fosters innovation by firms.

The Sources of Economic Growth

It appears that there is no single path to growth. Even worse, there's no single magic formula: The countries that have grown most rapidly over the past few hundred years have each chosen various items from a menu of practices and institutions that have been shown to promote growth. It would be impossible to list everything on that menu, but just as a restaurant menu has different pages for starters, entrees, and desserts, the growth menu has a few broad categories that deserve general discussion:

Honesty and the Rule of Law. Economic growth is measured by changes in the value of market transactions. If buyers and sellers don't trust one another, they'll avoid those transactions (they might get cheated!) in favor of self-sufficiency. That stunts economic activity and growth. Honesty is also important at a macro level. Generally speaking, the more corrupt the government is, the slower that country's growth and development. That's because corrupt public officials often make decisions based on what's best for their own pocketbooks, not on what's best for the economy.

Countries with legal institutions designed to encourage honesty tend to grow more sustainably; countries with poor legal systems and lots of public corruption may not grow at all. The evidence is strong: According to non-profit think tank Transparency International, in 2019, the least corrupt nations were Denmark, New Zealand, Finland, Singapore, and Sweden—five countries with track records of sustained economic growth. In contrast, the five most corrupt countries—Venezuela, Yemen, Syria, South Sudan, and Somalia—have had little, zero, or even negative economic growth over a period of several decades.

Competition and International Trade. Competition disciplines producers, encouraging them to specialize, to minimize wastefulness in production, and to think outside the box to come up with new ways to serve consumers and accomplish the ordinary. At the macro level, countries that engage in lots of international trade expose themselves to competition with the rest of the world and simultaneously gain access to larger markets. Those countries tend to grow more rapidly than countries that wall themselves off. The fastest-growing countries of the past few decades include a disproportionate number of open traders, including the rapidly growing Asian economies of South Korea, Taiwan, Singapore, China, and Hong Kong.

Property Rights. Over several centuries, the countries that have grown most consistently have almost invariably been countries with market economies. The basic function of a market economy is to facilitate transfers of property from one party to another. Well-defined and well-protected property rights encourage those transactions: When you buy a new car, it's nice to know a neighbor or a government official won't take it from you. Otherwise, you'd likely never buy a car in the first place.

Property rights are also a critical component of the market system because people work smarter, harder, and more creatively when they get to keep the rewards of their efforts for themselves. Property rights—namely, the right to own and operate a business—provide an incentive (the profit motive) for entrepreneurs to create new goods and services, explore new ideas, and produce more efficiently. To that end, institutions that create and protect property rights—patents, trademarks, copyrights, and the right to own a business—are key ingredients in the formula for economic growth.

Produce all the goods you want—but you'll need a way to get them to market. Good infrastructure helps producers spend less time *moving* goods and more time *making* goods.

Source: Avigator Fortuner/Shutterstock.com

Physical Capital. The accumulation of physical capital is the engine behind catching-up growth. Physical capital, of course, comes in many different forms. It encompasses investment goods, such as factories, tools, and other equipment used to produce other goods; infrastructure, such as the roads, bridges, and railroads necessary to move goods from place to place; and communications networks, such as the telephone system and the internet, that help facilitate the buying and selling of goods and services.

Physical capital makes workers more productive, so an expanding capital stock helps the economy grow. This is why policymakers emphasize the public investment in infrastructure and policies that encourage greater private investment in businesses. Of course, business owners don't generally pay for factories out of their own pockets; instead, they typically borrow money from banks or sell shares in their business to people—investors—who have some savings set aside that they'd like to earn a return on.[11] So, a high savings rate and a well-functioning financial system that helps businesses access households' accumulated savings are important prerequisites for a large and growing stock of physical capital.

 Pop! Goes the Econ: Hans Rosling and the Magic Washing Machine

Global health expert Hans Rosling tells the story of his family's first washing machine. How does this video highlight the importance of accumulating capital, the link between saving and investment, and the link between physical capital and human capital?

View in the online reader

human capital

The knowledge and skills people accumulate through experience, education, and training.

Human Capital. If investing in machinery and infrastructure can spur growth, so can investing in people. The knowledge and skills that people accumulate through experience, education, and training is called **human capital**. The more human capital a country's labor force has, the more likely sustained economic growth will be. Basic literacy makes workers more productive by making it easier for them to read and follow instructions. Mathematical training helps them with basic job tasks and helps them analyze problems: *If I've got a five-acre plot and can grow one coffee plant per square yard, how many pounds of coffee beans will I be able to sell in August?* But most important, education and training help workers develop critical reasoning skills, learn construction methods, understand essential business practices, and figure out innovative ways to do the previously unimaginable. In other words, *human capital is the source of the technological improvements that can sustain cutting-edge growth even after capital accumulation ceases!* Not surprisingly, countries that have educated and literate labor forces tend to have stronger and more sustained growth than countries that don't.

Political Stability. One of the most important ingredients in fostering economic growth is political stability—a peaceful, orderly transition of power between governments that preserves existing institutions. It's hard to convince people to invest in businesses, houses, consumer goods, and farms when you don't know when a new government might take over, and whether that new government might seize them. It's even harder convince multinational corporations to build factories in your country if the next government might confiscate those factories.

We also know that growth and saving are related. But it's hard to convince people to save money if the next government might appropriate that savings, devalue that savings by creating rapid inflation, or replace the country's currency entirely. In other words, political instability creates uncertainty about honesty and property rights that discourages economic growth. Not surprisingly, over longer time horizons, the world's slowest-growing economies are often found in countries that have experienced significant civil unrest.

Pop! Goes the Econ: *Adam Ruins* Economic Growth

Why was American economic growth so high in the Golden Age of Manufacturing? This clip from *Adam Ruins Everything* explores the sources of economic growth. Identify examples of catching-up growth and cutting-edge growth. What does Adam suggest is the importance of human capital to sustaining American economic growth? What policies might encourage that growth?

Extra credit! What principle from Chapter 2 explains the Chinese edge in manufacturing?

Double top-secret bonus: What kind of unemployment is Hank experiencing?

Key Takeaways

- The primary engines for growth are the discovery or accumulation of productive resources, improvements in technology, and labor force growth.
- Capital accumulation and technological improvements lead to higher standards of living. Each may not happen if the environment is not favorable.
- Factors that improve a country's odds of accumulating capital and becoming a technological innovator are a culture of honesty, a market system based on competition and trade, well-defined property rights, a high savings rate, an educated labor force, and political stability.

Try It!

YOLO! After emerging from a deadly pandemic, consumers celebrate by reducing their saving and spending more on all the things they'd been missing: travel, dining out, clubbing, and lavish holiday parties. Discuss the immediate and long-term implications of this change in behavior on the capital stock, output, and consumption.

See related Concept Problem 1 at the end of this chapter.

Case in Point: Tortoise and the Hare—How Did China Catch the United States?

Will the Chinese hare sprint away from the American tortoise?

Source: James Steidl/Shutterstock.com

When it was founded, the United States was just about as poor as any other place on Earth. Until recently, it had the world's largest economy. The rags-to-riches recipe for building that economy was simple: Grow at 2% or 3% per year for a couple of centuries, and then sit back and enjoy one of the highest standards of living on the planet.

Americans enjoyed that number one position since about 1890, when they overtook China for the lead. But after a century and a quarter of global economic dominance, China began taking action to reclaim the title, overtaking Japan for the number two spot in about 2010, and then outpacing the U.S. in purchasing power parity terms in 2017.[12] That's some kind of progress, given that less than half a century ago, China's economy was only about one-tenth the size of the U.S. economy. How did they accomplish this economic miracle?

The secret to China's rise to preeminence was simple: extremely rapid growth, year after year, for four straight decades. In contrast to the United States, which has averaged about 3% growth, the Chinese economy has increased at an astonishing average of 9.45% per year since 1980. Holy moly—*that's* progress! If China can keep that up, it will not just have passed the United States . . . it will have left it in the dust!

But can China keep that up? Probably not. China's phenomenal growth began just after a 1978 economic liberalization that opened markets, reduced the poor incentives created by communism, and made the accumulation of private capital possible. Over the next forty years, China's capital stock exploded, and it was that increased access to capital that fueled the Chinese economic miracle. In other words, the vast portion of Chinese economic growth has been catching-up growth that put more tools in the hands of what was already the world's largest labor force.

China's catching-up growth is by no means done. Today, the typical American worker still has access to three times the capital that the typical Chinese worker does. That means China has some capital accumulation still ahead of it that will likely propel it even further past the United States in the race for the world's largest economy.

The unfortunate thing about catching-up growth, however, is that sooner or later an economy runs out of it. China's economy is already displaying signals that capital accumulation and capital productivity are beginning to slow as China gets closer to its steady state: Its growth declined steadily over the five years before the coronavirus crisis, averaging not 9.45%, but only 6.5%.

That may mean that while China may indeed have surpassed the United States for the number one spot, it may have trouble holding onto it. Despite its enormous reservoir of labor power, China has yet to become the hotbed of innovation that's been the primary driver of the United States' cutting-edge growth. But the steady state is a long-run idea, and the capital accumulation needed to get there happens over long spans of time. Put a reminder on your smartphone calendar to buy an updated copy of this book in the year 2060; we'll be sure to let you know exactly how this race between the innovative tortoise and the ambitious hare played out.

See related Concept Problem 3 at the end of this chapter.

Answer to Try It! Problem

Emerging from the pandemic, consumers splurge on consumption goods at the expense of investment in capital. This will slow the accumulation of capital, and slow growth in the standard of living in the country. In the short run, consumers will enjoy increased consumption; in the long run, their consumption may well decrease.

9.5 Review and Practice

Summary

Economic growth can be measured by the rate of increase in potential output. Measuring the rate of increase in *actual* real GDP can confuse growth statistics by introducing elements of cyclical variation.

Growth is an exponential process. A variable increasing at a fixed percentage rate doubles over fixed intervals. The doubling time is approximated by the rule of 72. The exponential nature of growth means that small differences in growth rates have large effects over long periods of time. Per capita rates of increase in real GDP are found by subtracting the growth rate of the population from the growth rate of GDP.

Growth can be shown in the model of aggregate demand and aggregate supply as a series of rightward shifts in the long-run aggregate supply curve. The position of the *LRAS* is determined by the aggregate production function and by the demand and supply curves for labor. A rightward shift in *LRAS* results either from an upward shift in the production function, due to increases in factors of production other than labor or to improvements in technology, or from an increase in the demand for or the supply of labor.

Institutions important for fostering capital accumulation and growth include honesty, competition, property rights, human capital, and political stability.

Concept Problems

1. (Related to "Try It!" in Section 21.4.) Suppose that residents of a small nation save a very large fraction of their income. What are the implications of the high savings rate for today's consumption and standard of living? What are the implications for long-run growth and the future standard of living?

2. (Related to "Case in Point: Is It Time for a Robot Tax?" in Section 21.3.) Some people worry that increases in the capital stock will bring about an economy in which everything is done by machines, with no jobs left for people. What does the model of economic growth presented in this chapter predict?

3. (Related to "Case in Point: Tortoise and the Hare—How Did China Catch the United States?" in Section 21.4.) China's annual rate of population growth was 1.2% from 1975 to 2003 and has fallen to about 0.6% since then. How do you think this will affect the rate of increase in China's real GDP? How will this affect the rate of increase in per capita real GDP?

4. Suppose technology stops changing. Explain the impact on economic growth. Draw on the *AD/AS* model in your explanation.

5. Suppose a series of terrorist attacks destroys half the capital in the United States but does not affect the population. Use the *AD/AS* model to determine what will happen to potential output and to the real wage.

6. (Related to "Case in Point: Presidents and Economic Growth" in Section 21.2.) Suppose real GDP increases during President Biden's first term in office at a 5% rate. Would that imply that his policies were successful in "growing the economy"?

7. Suppose that for some country it was found that its economic growth was based almost entirely on increases in quantities of factors of production. Why might such growth be difficult to sustain?

Numerical Problems

1. In 2020, the world population was 7.8 billion, having grown at a 1.2% rate since 2000. If the population continues to grow at the same rate:

   a. Calculate the doubling time.

   b. Calculate the population in 2080.

   c. Calculate the population in 2140.

2. With a world population in 2020 of 7.8 billion and a projected population growth rate of 0.5% instead (which is the United Nations' projection for the period 2020 to 2100):

   a. Compute the doubling time.

   b. State the year in which the world's population would be 11 billion.

3. Suppose a country's population grows at the rate of 2% per year and its output grows at the rate of 3% per year.

    a. Calculate its rate of growth of per capita output.

    b. If instead its population grows at 3% per year and its output grows at 2% per year, calculate its rate of growth of per capita output.

4. (Related to "Try It!" in Section 21.2.) The rate of economic growth per capita in France from 2000 to 2020 was 0.7% per year, while in Korea over the same period it was 3.1%. Per capita real GDP was $44,317 in France in 2020, and $28,675 in Korea. Assume the growth rates for each country remain the same.

    a. Compute the doubling time for France's per capita real GDP.

    b. Compute the doubling time for Korea's per capita real GDP.

    c. What will France's per capita real GDP be in 2070?

    d. What will Korea's per capita real GDP be in 2070?

5. Suppose real GDPs in country A and country B are identical at $10 trillion dollars in 2020. Suppose country A's economic growth rate is 2% and country B's is 4% and both growth rates remain constant over time.

    a. On a graph, show country A's potential output until 2056.

    b. On the same graph, show country B's potential output.

    c. Calculate the percentage difference in their levels of potential output in 2056.

Suppose country A's population grows 1% per year and country B's population grows 3% per year.

    a. On a graph, show country A's potential output per capita in 2056.

    b. On the same graph, show country B's potential output per capita in 2056.

    c. Calculate the percentage difference in their levels of potential output per capita in 2056.

6. Two countries, A and B, have identical levels of real GDP per capita. In country A, an increase in the capital stock increases the potential output by 10%. Country B also experiences a 10% increase in its potential output, but this increase is the result of an increase in its labor force. Using aggregate production functions and labor-market analyses for the two countries, illustrate and explain how these events are likely to affect living standards in the two economies.

7. (Related to "Try It!" in Section 21.3.) Suppose the information below characterizes an economy:

Employment (in Millions)	Real GDP (in Billions $)
1	200
2	700
3	1,100
4	1,400
5	1,650
6	1,850
7	2,000
8	2,100
9	2,170
10	2,200

    a. Construct the aggregate production function for this economy.

    b. What kind of returns does this economy experience? How do you know?

    c. Assuming that total available employment is 7 million, draw the economy's long-run aggregate supply curve.

Suppose that improvement in technology means that real GDP at each level of employment rises by $200 billion.

d. Construct the new aggregate production function for this economy.

e. Construct the new long-run aggregate supply curve for the economy.

Endnotes

1. See Ryan Seilhamer, Baiyun Chen, Sue Bauer, Ashley Salter, and Luke Bennett's "Changing Mobile Learning Practices: A Multiyear Study 2012–2016," at https://er.educause.edu/articles/2018/4/changing-mobile-learning-practices-a-multiyear-study-2012-2016.

2. See, "Lest We Forget, A Short History of Housing in the United States," at https://www.aceee.org/files/proceedings/2004/data/papers/SS04_Panel1_Paper17.pdf

3. You did read Chapter 2, right? If not, don't wait for the movie—go scan it now!

4. You can multiply anything that grows by (1 + Growth Rate) to find its value in the next period. If, for example, your savings account has $100 in it today, and earns 7% (or 0.07), then multiply $100 by (1 + 0.07) to find out that next year you'll have $107. In our twenty-year growth problem, take the starting value of $1,000 billion, and multiply it 20 times (once for each year's growth) by (1 + 0.025) to get the ending value of $1,639 billion.

5. The Rule of 72 is an approximation. For example, if real GDP started at $1,000 and grew at a 9% rate, after eight years, it would grow to $1,992.56—just about, but not exactly, what the Rule of 72 predicts.

6. Real GDP in 2020 was measured in 2012 dollars.

7. The mathemagic here involves logarithms and a bit of calculus, which most students find daunting. If you're willing to trust, we're willing to do the heavy mathematical lifting.

8. John should have recognized that all labor is paid in one way or another—by refusing to bus his own table, he drove up the cost of every Big Mac he ate. That cost, of course, was borne by thousands of diners; if he'd bussed his own table, he'd have borne that cost all by himself. Perhaps John was a game theorist in training?

9. See our microeconomics chapter on production and cost for more on the choice between man and machine.

10. Ian Stewart, Debrapratim De, and Alex Cole, "Technology and People: The Great Job Creating Machine," Deloitte, 2015.

11. You'll learn more about this in our chapter on the financial system.

12. In terms of real purchasing power, China has surpassed the U.S. by most estimates. In nominal terms, the U.S. economy is still larger than China's.

CHAPTER 10
The Nature and Creation of Money

10.1 Start Up: Holy Mackerel—This Fish Story Is True!

Larry Levine helped a client prepare divorce papers a few years ago. He got paid . . . in fish. Mackerel, to be precise.

"It's the coin of the realm," his client, Mark Bailey, told the *Wall Street Journal*. The two men were prisoners at the time at the federal penitentiary at Lompoc, California.

Holy Mackerel: You can eat this oily fish . . . or you can spend it!

Source: Kirill Zakabluk/
Shutterstock.com

The somewhat oily fish emerged as the currency of choice in many federal prisons in 1994 when cigarettes, which had long been used as money in the prison system, were banned. Money, as you'll see in this chapter, is a useful thing: It greases the wheels of commerce by helping facilitate exchange; it provides a convenient yardstick for valuing goods and services; and it helps people store value across time.

Mackerel served all of these functions. With the use of cash forbidden in prison and cigarettes now off the table, prisoners quickly transitioned to using foil pouches of mackerel fillets, referred to as "macks," to facilitate exchange. Prisoners can use them to purchase almost anything, legal or not: food, tattoos, coffee, drugs, sex, and more. The pouches, which sell for about $1.50 in prison commissaries, are a convenient yardstick for valuing other goods and services: Want a joint? Three macks. Phone call? One mack.

Prisoners use outside funds to purchase macks at the prison commissary, which receives a steady supply of macks each week. That adds new macks to the prison economy, but because some macks are consumed (they feature prominently in prison cookbooks; you can find bunches of those on Amazon), the "money supply" remains relatively stable. That keeps prices from swinging wildly from week to week, and makes the mack a good yardstick for measuring value.

Finally, macks are a good store of value. In fact, pouches of mackerel continue to circulate long past their expiration date, and long after time and handling having reduced the contents to watery mush. These "money macks" are generally worth 75% of the unexpired "edible macks," or EMAKS. [1]

We've already seen (in our chapter on inflation) how money affects the price level. In this chapter, we'll focus on the nature of money and the process through which it is created. We will also introduce the largest financial institution in the world, the Federal Reserve System of the United States. The Fed, as it's commonly called, plays a key role in determining the quantity of money in the United States. We'll see how the Fed operates and how it attempts to control the supply of money. Let's begin with a closer look at the functions and evolution of money.

10.2 What Is Money?

Learning Objectives

1. Define money and discuss its three basic functions.
2. Distinguish between commodity money and fiat money, giving examples of each.
3. Define what is meant by the money supply and discuss what is included in the Federal Reserve System's two definitions of it (M1 and M2).

money

Anything that serves as a medium of exchange.

medium of exchange

Anything that is widely accepted as a means of payment.

Earlier in the book, we took an in-depth look at the role money plays in causing inflation. Now, we're about to launch into a study of the financial system, and there's no better way to start than to take a closer look at money. But what *is* money—after all, in some places it's cigarettes, in others it's fish, and in still others it's pretty green pieces of paper and shiny silver coins. Honestly, any of those things, and more, can serve as money. **Money** is anything that is commonly acceptable as payment for goods and services. In economist-speak, it serves as a **medium of exchange**.

Pop! Goes the Econ: Alligator Money

If mackerel can serve as money, why not alligators? This clip describes a failure of society to glom on to an alligator currency. Read ahead in the Section 2 section to find out what condition a gator likely fails to satisfy!

Money, ultimately, is defined by people and what they do. If people were to begin accepting basketballs as payment for most goods and services, basketballs would become money. We'll learn in this chapter that changes in the way people use money have created new types of money, and have changed the way money is measured.

The Functions of Money

Money serves three basic functions. By definition, it is a medium of exchange. It also serves as a unit of account and as a store of value—just like the mack did in Lompoc.

A Medium of Exchange

In 1776, Adam Smith observed a characteristic of humanity not found in other animals, "*a certain propensity . . . to truck, barter, and exchange one thing for another.*" The exchange of goods and services in markets is among the most universal activities of human life, and money makes it easier. That's why, in even the most primitive societies, people almost spontaneously settle on something that will serve as a medium of exchange—they *select* something to be money.

barter

When goods are exchanged directly for other goods.

We can understand the usefulness of having a medium of exchange by considering what would happen if we didn't. In that case, we would have to trade the things we have for the things we want, or barter. **Barter** is a system of exchange where goods are directly traded for other goods.

Imagine how miserable your economics professor would be in such a system. Every time she wanted a loaf of bread, she'd have to scour the state in search of a baker who wanted to listen to a short lecture about Adam Smith, index numbers, or the quantity theory of money. If she wanted to buy something really valuable, like a car, she'd have to find someone willing to listen to an entire *series* of lectures. Yep, good luck with that. Economists call this "has what I want and wants what I have" requirement for trade the *double coincidence of wants*.

That double coincidence of wants makes barter a horribly inefficient system, as people who live in barter economies can attest.[2] Satisfying that double coincidence of wants requires a search for a suitable trading partner. In simple economies, searches aren't too costly: *I'll trade you one ear of corn for two of your carrots, Bob.* But costs escalate with an economy's complexity: *I really need my Lexus aligned—any mechanics itching to watch an interpretive dance of the aurora borealis?* That's horribly wasteful, as people often end up spending more time searching for trading partners than they do producing goods and services to trade.

Money solves the double coincidence of wants problem. Your econ professor sells lectures for money to college students who love econ but haven't the slightest clue how to bake a loaf of bread. Then, she uses the money from her lectures to buy bread from someone who makes an amazing marble rye, but who's never had even the slightest desire to set foot on a college campus. Search costs, slashed; productivity, up!

A Unit of Account

Ask someone in the United States what he paid for something, and he'll reply, "I paid $75 for this Kanken backpack," or "I paid $15 for this pizza." You never hear them say, "I paid five pizzas for this backpack," or the even more abstract, "I gave up two hours of work for this pizza."

Those statements might be literally true (*the only real cost is opportunity cost, right?*). But we don't report prices that way for two reasons. One is that Urban Outfitters is seldom willing to accept five pizzas in trade for their backpacks. The second reason is that such information wouldn't be very useful, because not everyone thinks of values in pizza terms or work hours (which vary, of course, depending on your wage). Instead, money gives us all a common denominator: When we report the value of things in terms of dollars, everyone understands what that means.[3]

In econ-speak, that service as a common denominator is called money's **unit of account** function; this is often also referred to as it's *standard of value* function. That just means that money is a consistent means of measuring the value of things. Money serves as a unit of account largely because it's also our medium of exchange: When we report the value of a good or service in units of money, we're reporting what another person is likely to have to pay to obtain that good or service.

Money's use as a means of measuring value is, however, slightly different than using a ruler to measure length.[4] That's because the value of money changes from year to year (see Chapter 6). It's like measuring your height with a 12" ruler one year, and an 11" ruler the next! But, at any given point in time, that common denominator allows us to quickly evaluate the trade-offs between any two goods, no matter how diverse or unrelated: At today's prices, I can give up one car detailing ($150) for two hot yoga sessions ($75 each).

A Store of Value

The third function of money is to serve as a **store of value**; that is, an item that holds value over time. Ever find a $20 bill that you accidentally left in a coat pocket last winter? How happy were you? We're guessing the joy you felt wasn't because you like pretty green paper . . . it's because you knew you could buy something nice (and unexpected) with it! Value, purchasing power, was "stored" in that little piece of paper.

Money, of course, is not the only thing that stores value. Houses, office buildings, gold, Bitcoin, works of art—they all store wealth and value to a greater or lesser degree. But not all of them are

Pop! Goes the Econ: *Schoolhouse Rock!* **and Barter**
A good money should be relatively scarce, stable in supply, durable, and divisible into convenient units. Explain why yaks and cows were replaced by shells and metal coins. Why do you suppose the paper money from China failed as money?

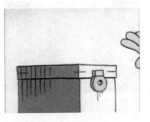

View in the online reader

No Accountant Required: Money helps us measure the value of one good relative to another.

Source: Yuganov Konstantin/ Shutterstock.com

unit of account

A consistent means of measuring the value of things.

store of value

An item that holds value over time.

readily exchangeable for other commodities. Money's role as a medium of exchange makes it special, and money's role as a store of value makes it a convenient medium of exchange.

Why is that important? Because when money stores value, it allows us to separate our purchases across time, so that we aren't forced to spend our money when we happen to receive it. Think about what your working life might look like if it didn't. On the first of each month, you'd receive your pay. Then, you (and everyone else with the same payday) would have a mad scramble to convert that paycheck to goods and services before its value ran out. You'd buy a month's worth of groceries, an oil change for your car, and maybe do all of your holiday shopping, all within hours—because if you didn't spend it right away . . . *poof!* its value would disappear.

Money's ability to store value is important for our transactions in goods and services, but it's also important for our financial transactions. When you borrow money, for example, you generally sign a contract pledging to make a series of future payments, in money, to settle the debt. It's only because money stores value that the lender is willing to accept those future payments in exchange for giving you use of his money today.

Money's ability to store value is linked to the behavior of prices. When prices are stable, money holds its value. When prices are falling, money does an even better job. But when prices are *rising*, money loses its value in proportion; the faster the price increase, the faster money's value deteriorates. That's why, in periods of high inflation, people often try to rid themselves of rapidly depreciating cash in favor of assets that are better stores of value, like commodities, metals, shares of stock, or even a different country's currency.

Go ahead—bury it. When you dig it up, all the bills will still be there. But their purchasing power might not be.

Source: Kelly Tippett/
Shutterstock.com

Types of Money

Although money has taken an extraordinary variety of forms over the ages, there are really only two types of money: money that has intrinsic value and money that does not have intrinsic value.

commodity money

Money that has value apart from its use as money.

Commodity money is money that has value apart from its use as money—what economists call "value in use and value in exchange." You've already seen one example of commodity money—the mack, which can be used to buy laundry service or can be eaten with ramen. Throughout history, many substances have served as money—shells, woodpecker scalps, tobacco, and, of course, gold and silver.[5] Even today, some politicians advocate a return to gold as the basis for money in the United States.[6]

"Recession looming. Must. Find. Gold."

Source: Ollyy/Shutterstock.com

But commodity monies have drawbacks. One particular disadvantage is that the supply of many of the commodities that have historically served as money can fluctuate erratically. The money supply increased dramatically, for example, during the California and Alaskan gold rushes; those increases proved to be highly inflationary. The problem exists in reverse, too: When a country's money supply depends on how many shiny rocks you can dig out of the ground, sometimes there won't be enough. Suppose, for example, that the economy starts to slide into recession. Today, the Federal Reserve would fight that with an injection of new money in hopes of jumpstarting a bit of commerce (you'll see more on this in a couple of chapters). But under a gold standard, increasing the money supply is difficult—it's hard to imagine the central bank handing each of its employees a shovel accompanied by this message: *"Get out there and dig, troops—the economy depends on you!"*

Commodity monies have also proven costly to use, because sellers have to take the time to verify the quality of the money they accept. Why pay with an ounce of your tastiest tobacco, after all, when an ounce of your nastiest stuff weighs the same? Merchants also have to verify the *quantity* they receive. In the gold and silver era, for example, it was common to shave a bit off the outside of gold coins before you spent them (a practice called *clipping*). Government's answer was to mill the edges of its most valuable coins, a tradition that has carried over to today's dimes, quarters, and half-dollars.[7] The tendency for buyers to use the lowest-quality (or quantity) commodity in exchange, while saving the best for use in consumption was noted by Tudor-era financier Sir Thomas Gresham, and formalized as *Gresham's Law*: Bad money drives good money out of circulation.

Commodity monies, especially metallic monies, are socially inefficient for one other important reason: opportunity cost. If society's goal is to make the greatest possible use of its scarce resources, it should put its people to work making things that people enjoy—guitars and televisions and delicious restaurant meals. But in a country with a commodity money, some of its productive people (and some of its productive capital) are devoted to a completely nonproductive yet highly costly activity: Digging holes in the ground merely in hopes of finding money—*money that could have been printed on fancy paper for next to nothing!*

Opportunity Loss: These prospectors could have spent their adult years producing things people would find useful. Instead, they spent years digging holes in the ground in search of shiny things.

Source: Everett Collection/Shutterstock.com

That's right . . . money doesn't have to be an intrinsically valuable substance. Nor does it need to be backed by an intrinsically valuable substance. It just needs to be something commonly acceptable in exchange. While sometimes intrinsically useless items spring to life as money on their own (see this section's "Case in Point: Is Bitcoin Money?"), it is usually the case that the common acceptability that money requires springs from governmental decree: **Fiat money** is money that some authority, generally a government, has ordered to be accepted as a medium of exchange. The **currency**—paper money and coins—used in the United States today is fiat money; those bills and coins have very little use other than money. You'll also notice the decree that makes those pieces of fancy green paper money; it's printed on each bill: "*This note is legal tender for all debts, public and private.*"

Checkable deposits, which are balances in checking accounts, are another form of money that has no intrinsic value. So are traveler's checks. Each can be converted to currency, but generally they are not; they simply serve, themselves, as a medium of exchange. If you want to buy something, you can often pay with a check or a debit card. (A **check** is a written order to a bank to transfer ownership of a checkable deposit. A debit card is the electronic equivalent of a check.) Suppose, for example, that you have $100 in your checking account and you use your debit card to buy a set of juggling balls from a local toy store. When you swipe your card, $30 will be "juggled" from your checking account to the toy store's checking account. *Notice that it is the checkable deposit, not the check or debit card, that is money.* The check or debit card just facilitates the transfer.

Fiat money, as we mentioned, often exists due to government decree. But sometimes that decree is, in and of itself, insufficient to create money that serves all its functions. If the government prints too much fiat money, too quickly, it may lose its common acceptability. That's happened in many countries over the years, including Zimbabwe, Russia, Ecuador, and Venezuela, as we noted in Chapter 6. In each case, too-rapid money growth caused the domestic currency to lose value so quickly that that people refused to accept it in payment. Instead, they reverted to a different fiat money with a more stable value—the U.S. dollar.[8]

fiat money

Money that some authority, generally a government, has ordered to be accepted as a medium of exchange.

currency

Paper money and coins.

checkable deposits

Balances in checking accounts.

check

A written order to a bank to transfer ownership of a checkable deposit.

Measuring Money

money supply

The total quantity of money in the economy at any one time.

The total quantity of money in the economy at any given time is called the **money supply**, or *money stock*. Economists measure the money supply because it affects economic activity. But what should be included in the money supply? Currency seems like an obvious choice—after all, we use bills and coins to complete transactions, and they're commonly acceptable as payment. But so are checkable deposits, even though they are not issued by government or officially declared legal tender. In reality, checkable deposits are a financial asset that happen to be denominated in dollars. So, too, are traveler's checks, which, though little used, have broad acceptability.[9]

M1

The narrowest of the Fed's money supply definitions that includes currency in circulation, checkable deposits, and traveler's checks.

The Federal Reserve System (the United States' central bank) includes all of these financial assets in what it calls the M1 measure of the money supply. **M1** includes currency in circulation, but as we noted, it also includes some financial assets (checkable deposits and traveler's checks) that are not themselves legal tender, but which can easily be *converted* into legal tender. And if we're willing to include those "near monies" in our measurement of money, why not include some other things that aren't currency, but which are easy to change into currency? That's exactly the motivation behind a broader definition of the money supply, **M2**, which includes everything in M1, but then adds other financial assets commonly held by households, such as savings accounts and small certificates of deposit (less than $100,000), as well as personal money market deposit accounts and money market mutual funds (MMMFs).[10]

M2

A broader measure of the money supply than M1 that includes M1 and other deposits.

liquidity

The ease with which an asset can be converted into currency.

The M2 measure of the money supply includes some financial assets that are a bit more difficult to convert to cash than the items included in M1. The ease with which an asset can be converted into currency is called **liquidity**. The assets in M1 are highly liquid (currency itself is perfectly liquid; you can always change two $5 bills for a $10 bill; checkable deposits are almost perfectly liquid, as you can easily cash a check or visit an ATM). The extra assets in M2 are slightly less liquid, but often pay the holder interest: M2 tends to place increasing emphasis on money's store-of-value function. Figure 10.1 shows the components of M1 and M2 as of October 2020.

Heads Up!

Is your credit card money? A credit card identifies you as a person who has a special arrangement with a card issuer, in which the issuer will lend you money and transfer the proceeds to someone else when you want. If you use your Visa to pay for a $3,000 engagement ring, the transaction transfers some of Visa's (existing and already counted) money to the jeweler. Like your debit card or a personal check, the card *facilitates* the transfer of money, but is not money in and of itself.

With two different definitions of money available (M1 and M2), which one should we use? Economists generally answer that question by asking another: Which measure of money is most closely related to real GDP and the price level?[11] As that changes, so should policymakers' choice of money definition. For example, in 1980, the Fed decided that changes in the ways people were managing their money made M1 useless for policy choices—the link between M1 and the ultimate goals of policy had been broken. Today the Fed doesn't even pay much attention to M2. In fact, it has largely given up tracking a particular measure of the money supply, recognizing that there are other policy goals (say, the price level or level of interest rates) that are more meaningful than the number of dollars in circulation. Nevertheless, the amount of money in circulation *does* affect both the price level and interest rates, so the Fed continues to publish these money supply measures.

FIGURE 10.1 M1 and M2: October 2020

M1, the narrowest definition of the money supply, includes highly liquid assets commonly used in exchange. In October 2020, M1 was $5,603 billion, with checkable deposits accounting for about 2/3 of the total and currency accounting for the other third (traveler's checks are negligible). M2 totaled $18,795 billion, with M1 constituting about 30% of the total, savings deposits 62%, and money market mutual funds about 6%. (Amounts represent money supply data in billions of dollars for October 2020, seasonally adjusted.

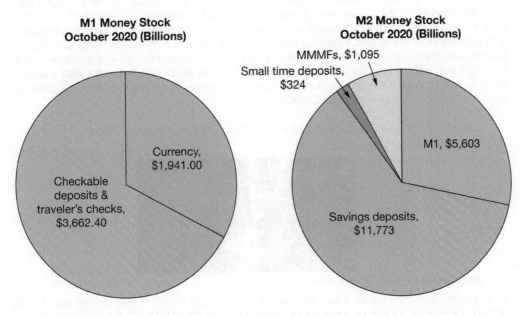

Source: Based on data from Federal Reserve *Statistical Release* H.6, Tables 3 and 4 (November 4, 2020). Amounts are in billions of dollars for October 2020, seasonally adjusted.

Key Takeaways

- Money is anything that serves as a medium of exchange. Other functions of money are to serve as a unit of account and as a store of value.
- Money may or may not have intrinsic value. Commodity money has intrinsic value because it has other uses besides being a medium of exchange. Fiat money serves only as a medium of exchange because its use as such is authorized by the government and because it has common acceptability. Fiat money has no intrinsic value.
- The Fed reports several different measures of money, including M1 and M2; the Fed's goal is to find a measure of money that is linked to the performance of the economy.

Try It!

Which of the following are money in the United States today and which are not? Explain your reasoning in terms of the functions of money.

1. Gold
2. A Van Gogh painting
3. A dime
4. Your savings account balance

See related Concept Problem 1 at the end of this chapter.

Case in Point: Is Bitcoin Money?

You may have never used one. For sure, you haven't seen one. But it's highly unlikely that you haven't heard of the world's newest kind of currency, Bitcoin. Bitcoin is an encrypted digital currency invented in 2008 by a mysterious figure who called himself Satoshi Nakamoto. Bitcoin is based on blockchain technology, which stores linked sets of ownership records across a decentralized network of computers. One important feature for users of Bitcoin is that transactions are anonymous; coins can be sent from user to user on the blockchain network without government oversight and without passing through a bank. That makes Bitcoin appealing for illicit transactions . . . but you can also use it to buy a sandwich at Subway, see a Dallas Mavericks game, or pay for a flight into space with Virgin Galactic.

Cleanest Mine Ever: Bitcoin mines often have thousands of computers "digging" for the elusive cryptocurrency.

Source: Mark Agnor/Shutterstock.com

Well, alright, you can spend them. But where do you get them? Each Bitcoin has to be "mined." But instead of digging them out of a hole in the ground, Bitcoin miners use computers to solve difficult mathematical puzzles. Each miner competes with hundreds of thousands of other computers around the world; the first to solve each puzzle is awarded 12.5 Bitcoins. The supply of Bitcoins is finite: Nakamoto pledged to create only 21 million digital coins, with the puzzles needed to mine them becoming increasingly difficult as the total in circulation increases.

There's good news if you hate math and don't understand computers: You don't have to mine them to own them. Anyone can buy Bitcoins for dollars on Bitcoin exchanges, and then use them, in turn, to buy things they want, or just hold them for speculative purposes. In 2011, Bitcoins sold for about $5 apiece. By 2018, the price had risen to almost $20,000 per Bitcoin, only to plummet to around $3,000 by the year's end, and then rebound to $38,000 in the days following 2021's Capitol insurrection.

The Economist reports that Bitcoins have three properties desirable in a currency. Bitcoins are limited in supply, they're easy to verify for transactions, and they're hard to earn. But while Bitcoins may have qualities that are desirable in a money, the question remains: *Are Bitcoins money?* Scott Wolla, an economist at the Federal Reserve Bank of St. Louis, answers with a resounding no: Bitcoin may have some desirable properties, but it fails, spectacularly, to fulfill the three functions of money.

First, Wolla notes, Bitcoin is not commonly acceptable in exchange. There are, of course, places where you can use your Bitcoins to fund purchases, but most merchants and individuals don't accept them. That's because most people don't really understand how the Bitcoin payments system works, and most don't have the hardware and software needed to carry out transactions.

The real problem, though, lies in capacity: The network of mining computers that hold records of transactions can only process, at a maximum, about seven transactions per second (credit card issuer Visa, in contrast, can process twenty-four *thousand*). That makes Bitcoin slow: Individual transactions often take an hour to complete, a time that will increase as Bitcoin's blockchain network grows.

Second, a good money should serve as a unit of account, a common denominator people can use when valuing goods and services. Bitcoin scores poorly on this criterion as well. Because its dollar price fluctuates so wildly, merchants must frequently recalculate the Bitcoin prices of their products. And because of Bitcoin's high dollar value, prices for low-cost goods like peanut butter or clothing are often quoted out to many decimal places instead of the customary two. That's confusing to buyers who, in order to figure out how expensive a product really is, must distinguish between 0.00005 Bitcoin and 0.000005 Bitcoin. A good standard of value? *Nope!*

Third, a good money should serve as a store of value. Wolla notes that "stable value is an important aspect of store of value." But stable value and Bitcoin are rarely used in the same sentence: The dollar value of Bitcoin has fluctuated wildly over its short history, which makes it both a poor store of value and less desirable as a medium of exchange. After all, who wants to sell a $200,000 condominium for Bitcoin in 2018, only to see that $200,000 worth of Bitcoin plummet to less than $40,000 before the year ends?

Finally, while being inexpensive to produce isn't one of the three major functions of money, it's certainly desirable to minimize how many resources get chewed up producing money that could be printed almost for free. Blockchain mining for Bitcoin, however, is quite costly, the modern-day equivalent of digging holes in the ground. In its infancy, the math problems were simple and individuals mined Bitcoins on home computers. But like honey draws flies, the profits that could be earned mining Bitcoins drew capital. Today, small-scale miners have been shunted aside by corporate Bitcoin-mining farms, warehouses full of computers cranking 24/7 to solve made-up puzzles in hopes of finding imaginary money. The combined power consumption of those computers is equivalent to the output of seven Dungeness nuclear power plants, enough to power the entirety of Switzerland. Opportunity cost matters!

Bitcoin is new, it's flashy, it's sexy. And it *does* have some desirable characteristics—anonymity and security foremost among them. But it is decidedly *not* money, lacking the three essential elements of a good currency, and being enormously costly to produce, besides. Nobel Prize winner Paul Krugman summed up the consensus of the economics community—including at least seven other Nobel Prize winners who have denounced the crypto-currency—in a *New York Times* op-ed piece: "[Bitcoin is] a bubble wrapped in techno-mysticism inside a cocoon of libertarian ideology."

See related Concept Problem 10 at the end of this chapter.

Sources: Based on Paul Krugman's "Bubble, Bubble, Fraud and Trouble," The New York Times, January 29, 2018; "The Magic of Mining," The Economist, January 8, 2015; and Scott Wolla's "Bitcoin: Money or Financial Investment?" Page One Economics, March 2018.

Answers to Try It! Problems

1. Gold is not money because it is not used as a medium of exchange. In addition, it does not serve as a unit of account. It may, however, serve as a store of value.

2. A Van Gogh painting is not money. It serves as a store of value. It is highly illiquid but could eventually be converted to money. It is neither a medium of exchange nor a unit of account.

3. A dime is money and serves all three functions of money. It is perfectly liquid.

4. Your savings account balance cannot generally be used as a medium of exchange; it is not part of M1 money. But because it is a highly liquid store of value, it is included in M2. It is not "money" but it has "money-ness."

10.3 The Banking System and Money Creation

Learning Objectives

1. Explain what banks are, what their balance sheets look like, and what is meant by a fractional reserve banking system.
2. Describe the process of money creation and destruction using the concept of the deposit multiplier.
3. Describe how and why banks are regulated and insured.

If you've read the introductory chapter on inflation or the previous section in this chapter, you might be under the impression that today, our money is created and then injected into the economy by a government's central bank. That's partially true . . . but not *completely* true! This section explores the role that ordinary, everyday banks play in the process of money creation. One surprising takeaway is that the Federal Reserve (the United States' central bank) has only partial control over the supply of money in the U.S. economy. To help us understand why that is, let's take a closer look at the commercial banking system.

Banks and Other Financial Intermediaries

financial intermediary

An institution that amasses funds from one group and makes them available to another.

You probably have some experience with a bank. A bank is just one type of **financial intermediary**, which is an institution that gathers funds from one group and makes them available to another group. A bank isn't the only kind of financial intermediary, though. One example is a pension fund, where workers place money into a fund for retirement, and until those workers retire, the fund lends those funds out to firms to earn interest or invests in corporations' stock. Insurance companies are also financial intermediaries; they lend some of the premiums paid by their customers to firms for investment.

While there are several types of financial intermediaries, commercial banks are both the largest and perhaps the most important. Three key functions define a commercial bank (what we'll just call a *bank*): First, a bank accepts deposits. Second, a bank allows depositors to withdraw their deposits on short notice; often those deposits are *checkable* deposits, meaning they can be transferred to someone else by check or by debit card. Finally, a bank makes loans to borrowers. With the interest banks earn on their loans, they're able to pay interest to their depositors, cover their own operating costs, and earn a profit, all the while maintaining the ability of the original depositors to spend the funds when they desire to do so. These functions define a **bank**, a financial intermediary that accepts deposits, makes loans, and offers checking accounts.[12]

A bank accepts deposits and makes loans. This little piggy? Not a bank!

Source: NAR studio/Shutterstock. com

Bank Finance and a Fractional Reserve System

Commercial banks play an integral role in the process of creating money. To understand that role, we need to dig into the basics of the business of banking. That deep dive involves some principles of finance and accounting that are applicable to every kind of business. Let's take a closer look.

Banks accept deposits of money from their depositors. They then use that money to extend loans to borrowers. It's important for a bank to keep track of how much money has come into the bank through deposits and how much has been sent out in the form of loans. To help give bankers a bird's-eye view of the bank's financial position, they use a **balance sheet**, a financial statement that shows the bank's assets, liabilities, and net worth. **Assets** are items of value to the bank, including the bank's equipment, real estate holdings, and, most important, the loans it has made to borrowers. Those loans will be repaid over time, representing a bunch of future "incoming cash" transactions for the bank. **Liabilities** are financial obligations to other parties. Banks' biggest liabilities are often their deposits: When you put money in your checking account, the bank owes you that money and is obliged to pay it to you whenever you demand it back. (This is why those checkable deposits are often called *demand deposits*.)

We've now got a measure of what a bank has (its assets), and what a bank owes (its liabilities). The bank's **net worth** equals its assets minus its liabilities. (Often in the general world of business, net worth is called *owner's equity*; in banking it's generally referred to as *capital accounts*.) Imagine that a banker decides to close her bank's doors and go out of business. After she's sold off all of the bank's assets, and used the proceeds to pay off the bank's liabilities, anything left over (the net worth) goes into her pocket to keep. So,

$$\text{Assets} - \text{Liabilities} = \text{Net Worth}$$

The bank's balance sheet, which summarizes all of these accounts, often rearranges this slightly:

$$\text{Assets} = \text{Liabilities} + \text{Net Worth}$$

bank

A financial intermediary that accepts deposits, makes loans, and offers checking accounts.

balance sheet

A financial statement showing assets, liabilities, and net worth.

assets

Anything of value.

liabilities

Obligations to other parties.

net worth

Assets less liabilities.

This frustrated woman knows why they're called demand deposits: "Give. Me. My. Money!"

Source: Federico Marsicano/Shutterstock.com

That rearrangement happens for a reason. Everything on the right represents the bank's sources of funds, including 1) things that it's borrowed and its deposits (liabilities) and 2) any financial capital contributed by the owners or any profits that were plowed back into the business (net worth). Everything on the left represents the bank's uses of those funds: "*Last year, we installed a new computer system, purchased a new building, and made $80 million worth of loans.*"

Table 10.1 shows the balance sheet for the entire commercial banking system as of mid-2020. That balance sheet is just a graphical version of the equation above. The left side of the balance sheet summarizes the banking system's assets; the right side summarizes its liabilities and net worth. Down the middle of the balance sheet is a vertical bar; you can think of that vertical bar as representing the equals sign. Let's take a look at both sides of that balance sheet.

TABLE 10.1 The Consolidated Balance Sheet for U.S. Commercial Banks, 2020

The balance sheet for all commercial banks in the United States shows their financial situation, in billions of dollars, as of the second quarter of 2020.

Assets			Liabilities and Net Worth		
Reserves	$	2,761.0	Checkable deposits	$	3,733.5
Securities	$	4,923.8	Time and savings deposits	$	13,152.5
Loans	$	10,795.1	Borrowings	$	358.4
Other assets	$	2,581.8	Other liabilities	$	1,669.3
Total assets	**$**	**21,061.7**	**Total liabilities**	**$**	**18,913.7**
			Net worth	**$**	**2,148.0**

Source: Based on data from Federal Reserve Statistical Release H.8 (July 2, 2020).

Let's take a quick peek at that balance sheet, which summarizes the bulk of bank activities. The right-hand side summarizes how the banking system raises the cash it needs for its operations. Its biggest source of funds is its customers' time and savings deposits, followed by its customers' checking account balances. As strange as it may sound, banks also borrow money to fund their operations—from the Fed, from one another, from investors, and from corporate bank holding companies. All told, the banks that form our banking system have about $19 trillion in liabilities.

reserves

Bank assets held as cash in vaults and in deposits with the Federal Reserve.

fractional reserve banking system

System in which banks hold a fraction of their deposits as reserves.

The left-hand side of the balance sheet summarizes how banks use the funds they've raised. The biggest use of funds is to extend loans, like commercial loans to businesses, consumer loans for cars and appliances, and real estate mortgage loans. Banks also use the funds they raise to purchase interest-earning securities. Finally, banks hold substantial money "in reserve" to meet the needs of their depositors. Those **reserves** can be held either in a bank's vault or in that bank's account at the Federal Reserve. (In other words, the Fed acts like a bank for banks!) In fact, banks are *required* by the Fed to hold a certain fraction of their checkable deposits as reserves, which is why the U.S. banking system is called a **fractional reserve banking system**.

Money Creation

We realize you didn't sign up for an economics course expecting a crash course in accounting.[13] But our purpose is to describe the process of money creation, and a bare-bones acquaintance with accounting will help us do that.

To begin that exploration, let's create a tiny banking system, like one that might exist on a small, tropical island. Our miniature banking system has three banks: Acme Bank, Bellville Bank, and Clarkston Bank. As is generally true in the United States, these banks will be required by the central bank to hold reserves equal to 10% of their checkable deposits. Those reserves are called **required reserves**. As we did above, the reserve requirement is generally expressed as a **required reserve ratio** that specifies the fraction of checkable deposits that a bank has to hold as reserves. Banks can, if they want, hold more reserves than the central bank requires; those extra reserves are called **excess reserves**. So a bank's total reserves are the sum of its required and excess reserves.

Let's make some assumptions to help keep things simple. First, let's assume that our three island banks' only liabilities are checkable deposits. Second, let's assume that the only assets banks want to hold besides reserves are loans. Finally, let's assume that banks don't want to hold any excess reserves. (That's not unreasonable—banks earn zero interest on cash in their vault, and pretty low interest on their reserve deposits at the Fed. It makes good financial sense to lend them, at a higher rate of interest, to a creditworthy borrower.) When a bank's excess reserves equal zero, it's said to be **loaned up**. Finally, let's not worry about keeping track of our banks' net worth; let's just assume their assets are equal to their liabilities.

Let's suppose that every bank in our imaginary system begins with $1,000 in reserves, $9,000 in loans outstanding, and $10,000 in checkable deposit balances held by customers. The balance sheet for one of these banks, Acme Bank, is shown in Table 10.2. Remember that our reserve requirement is 10%; Acme bank is just meeting that requirement, with $1,000 of reserves being held against $10,000 of deposits. It's currently holding no excess reserves.

TABLE 10.2 A Balance Sheet for Acme Bank

We assume that all banks in a hypothetical system of banks have $1,000 in reserves, $10,000 in checkable deposits, and $9,000 in loans. With a 10% reserve requirement, each bank is loaned up, holding zero excess reserves.

Acme Bank			
Assets		**Liabilities**	
Reserves	$ 1,000	Deposits	$ 10,000
Loans	$ 9,000		

Acme Bank, like every other bank in our hypothetical system, initially holds reserves equal to the level of required reserves. Now suppose that Manuel, one of Acme Bank's customers, deposits $1,000 in cash into a checking account. (We'll think later about where that cash might have come from!) That money goes into the bank's vault, where it adds $1,000 to Acme's reserves. But one of the principles of accounting is that *every transaction is always recorded with two entries*. In fact, our modern system of accounting is often referred to as *double-entry accounting*.

Let's see why two entries are required for this transaction. On the right-hand side of the balance sheet, Manuel now has an additional $1,000 in his account. That's a liability to Acme Bank—they have to pay him back if he asks. Note also that it is a source of funds to the bank—they've got some new money to play with. How will they use it? For now, let's assume they want to stash it in the vault and just hold it as reserves. Those reserves are an asset to Acme Bank; we'll mark up their reserve account on the left-hand side of the balance sheet.

Table 10.3 shows the impact of Manuel's deposit in two different ways. The left (light blue) side shows the *changes* to the bank's balance sheet caused by Manuel's deposit: Reserves and checkable deposits each increase by $1,000. The right (light green) side shows how these changes affect Acme's *total* balances: Reserves now equal $2,000 and checkable deposits equal $11,000. With checkable deposits of $11,000 and a 10% reserve requirement, Acme is *required* to hold reserves of only $1,100. Because Acme's *actual* reserves are $2,000, Acme Bank has $900 of excess reserves.

required reserves

The quantity of reserves banks are required to hold.

required reserve ratio

The ratio of reserves to checkable deposits a bank must maintain.

excess reserves

Reserves in excess of the required level.

loaned up

When a bank's excess reserves equal zero.

In accounting, every entry has an offsetting entry somewhere else.

Source: My Ocean Production/ Shutterstock.com

TABLE 10.3 Impact of Manuel's Deposit on Acme Bank

Changes to Acme Bank's Balance Sheet				Acme Bank's Balance Sheet			
Assets		Liabilities		Assets		Liabilities	
Reserves	+ $1,000	Deposits	+ $1,000	Reserves	$2,000	Deposits	$11,000
				Loans	$9,000		
				(Excess Reserves = $900)			

Remember that the money supply is the sum of currency in circulation and checkable deposits. At this point, there has been no change in the money supply. When Manuel brought in the $1,000 and Acme put the money in the vault, currency in circulation fell by $1,000. At the same time, the $1,000 was added to Manuel's checking account balance, so the money supply did not change.

Now Acme Bank has $900 of excess reserves. But idle excess reserves don't bring Acme profits! The way to put them to work earning Acme money is to loan them out. Lucky for Acme, Mariah wants a $900 loan to purchase a matching washer/dryer set. She's got great credit, and Acme approves the loan.

Here's how Acme administers the loan: It credits Mariah's checking account with $900, the amount of the loan. At the same time (and because every accounting entry has two pieces) it marks up its loan assets by $900—after all, Mariah *will* have to pay that $900 back! Acme's loans rise to $9,900; its deposits rise to $11,900.

Back the truck up! Look at what's happened to the money supply! Manuel deposited $1,000, but traded it for $1,000 in checkable deposits, with no impact on the money supply. But when Acme bank loaned out part of Manuel's deposit to Mariah, checkable deposits rose again . . . with no corresponding reduction in circulating currency. The money supply *grew* when Acme loaned Mariah money! (If in doubt, net out the totality of these transactions: Currency in circulation fell by $1,000; checkable deposits grew by $1,900, so M1, the sum of currency in circulation and checkable deposits, grew by exactly $900 when Acme Bank extended the $900 loan!)

TABLE 10.4 Impact of Mariah's Loan on Acme Bank

Changes to Acme Bank's Balance Sheet				Acme Bank's Balance Sheet			
Assets		Liabilities		Assets		Liabilities	
Loans	+ $900	Deposits	+ $900	Reserves	$2,000	Deposits	$11,900
				Loans	$9,900		

But Mariah didn't take out a $900 loan so she could enjoy looking at a high checking account balance—she took out a loan so she could spend it! Let's suppose the appliance store she buys her washer/dryer set from (Stoneback Appliance) banks at Bellville Bank. When Mariah writes a check (or uses her debit card) to buy the washer/dryer set, Acme's checkable deposits fall by $900. Through the payments system run by the Federal Reserve (an automatic system that is fascinating, but which doesn't need to be explored here) Stoneback Appliance's account at Bellville Bank gets credited with that $900, and $900 of reserves are transferred from Acme Bank to Bellville Bank to cover the transfer between their depositors, Mariah and Stoneback Appliance.

FIGURE 10.2 Impact of Mariah's Loan and Subsequent Spending on Acme Bank and Bellville Bank

Changes to Acme Bank's Balance Sheet				Acme Bank's Balance Sheet			
Assets		**Liabilities**		**Assets**		**Liabilities**	
Reserves	−$900	Deposits	−$900	Reserves	$1,100	Deposits	$11,000
				Loans	$9,900		

Changes to Bellville Bank's Balance Sheet				Bellville Bank's Balance Sheet			
Assets		**Liabilities**		**Assets**		**Liabilities**	
Reserves	+$900	Deposits	+$900	Reserves	$1,900	Deposits	$10,900
				Loans	$9,000		
				(Excess reserves = $810)			

After Mariah's check clears, Acme Bank finds itself with $11,000 in checkable deposits and $1,100 in reserves—just enough to meet its reserve requirement. It has eliminated its excess reserves by issuing the loan for $900. But the $900 in new money Acme created when it issued Mariah's loan didn't vanish—it was just transferred to an account in Bellville Bank.

Against that $900 deposit, Bellville Bank will have to hold $90 in required reserves, but remains free to lend out the remaining $810 of excess reserves. When Bellville makes that loan—say, to Elizabeth, who wants to buy a vintage VW Beetle, the money supply rises by *another* $810, for a total increase of $1,710.

Of course, Elizabeth's not borrowing money for fun—she's going to spend it. The next thing you know, she is the proud owner of a slightly sketchy looking Beetle and the seller has deposited Elizabeth's $810 check in his own bank, Clarkston Bank. The process continues: Because Clarkston's deposits rise by $810, its required reserves increase by $81, leaving $729 of excess reserves. When Clarkston bank lends out those excess reserves, the money supply will increase yet again . . . and that new money will find its way to yet some other bank, which will then have excess reserves—and create still more money.

When will that cycle of money creation end? That process will keep going as long as there are excess reserves to pass through the banking system in the form of loans. To answer that question, let's make a quick observation. Notice that Manuel's deposit supplied the banking system with $1,000 of new reserves, and in the process of making loans, those reserves got passed from bank to bank, but never increased. As checkable deposits grew, more and more of Manuel's new reserves became required, and fewer remained excess.

That gives us the answer we're looking for: The process of deposit creation will stop when all of the $1,000 in new reserves that Manuel brought into the banking system are required reserves, and no excess reserves remain. That $1,000 is just sufficient to back $10,000 of checkable deposits, so in the banking system, checkable deposits will increase by $10,000. Subtracting the original $1,000 that *had* been a part of currency in circulation, we see that Manuel's deposit of cash could cause the money supply to grow by as much as $9,000.

Whenever your bank makes a loan, the money supply rises. But when mobster Al Capone makes a loan, it doesn't. Can you figure out why?

Source: Anton_Ivanov/ Shutterstock.com

The Deposit Multiplier

deposit multiplier

The ratio of the maximum possible change in checkable deposits (ΔD) to the change in reserves (ΔR).

We can relate the potential increase in the money supply to the change in reserves that created it using the **deposit multiplier** (m_d), which equals the ratio of the maximum possible change in checkable deposits (ΔD) to the change in reserves (ΔR). The deposit multiplier shows us, potentially, how much checkable deposits will grow for each dollar of new reserves in the banking system. In our example, the deposit multiplier was 10:

EQUATION 10.1

$$m_d = \frac{\Delta D}{\Delta R} = \frac{\$10,000}{\$1,000} = 10$$

To see how the deposit multiplier m_d is related to the required reserve ratio, we use the fact that if banks in the economy are loaned up, then all reserves are required reserves. That means that reserves, R, must equal the required reserve ratio (rrr) times the total amount of checkable deposits, D:

EQUATION 10.2

$$R = rrr \times D$$

An increase in reserves will create the opportunity to extend loans, which will cause checkable deposits to grow. Once banks are fully loaned up, the change in reserves, ΔR, will equal the required reserve ratio times the change in deposits, ΔD:

EQUATION 10.3

$$\Delta R = rrr \times \Delta D$$

In our example, the change in reserves was $1,000; that equaled the 10% reserve requirement times the $10,000 change in deposits. Remember that our goal is to find the multiplier, $\Delta D / \Delta R$. Let's take one step in that direction and solve for ΔD:

EQUATION 10.4

$$\frac{1}{rrr} \Delta R = \Delta D$$

If we divide both sides by ΔR, we'll get our deposit multiplier, $\Delta D / \Delta R$. That deposit multiplier, abbreviated m_d, is $1/rrr$:

EQUATION 10.5

$$\frac{1}{rrr} = \frac{\Delta D}{\Delta R} = m_d$$

The deposit multiplier is simply one over the required reserve ratio. With a required reserve ratio of 0.1, the deposit multiplier is 10: Each new dollar of reserves provided to the banking system can create $10 of new deposits. The higher the required reserve ratio, the lower the deposit multiplier: If the reserve requirement were 20%, the deposit multiplier would be 1/0.2, or 5. Each new dollar of reserves would only create five dollars of new deposits.

In the real world, each dollar of new reserves actually produces fewer deposits than this money multiplier predicts. To understand why, remember that deposits are created when banks extend loans. If a bank decides to hold on to some excess reserves rather than using those excess reserves to make loans, then fewer new deposits will be created than is possible. It's also true that sometimes not every dollar of new reserves necessarily gets passed from bank to bank: If Stoneback Appliance decides to cash Mariah's check rather than deposit it in its own account, then the process of deposit creation will come to a dead stop; no more loans will be made, no more deposits created. Nevertheless, the basic mechanism works as described in our example, and the conclusion is interesting: *While the Federal Reserve is in part responsible for creating money (it provided the bills that Manuel deposited), the banking system created a good chunk of the money supply all on its own!*

Deposit (and Money) Contraction

The process of money creation can also work in reverse. When you withdraw cash from your bank, you reduce the bank's reserves. Just as a deposit at Acme Bank increases the money supply by a multiple of the original deposit, your withdrawal reduces the money supply by a multiple of the amount you withdrew. Let's think about why.

Suppose your bank is loaned up, with zero excess reserves. You decide to withdraw $100 from your checking account. Where does your bank get the $100 bill you ask for? From its vault! But cash in the vault is part of your bank's reserves, so total reserves fall by $100.

It's true that your bank's required reserves have fallen—they no longer need to hold $10 in reserve against your $100 deposit. But because your bank lost a full hundred in reserves, it actually has *negative* excess reserves of $90. The bank is failing to meet its reserve requirement, which is bad mojo that can potentially bring down the wrath of the Fed. In order to find the $90 of excess reserves it needs, the bank may have to call in loans or sell some securities; as people write checks for those loan payments or securities, deposits in the banking system will decrease. Ultimately, your $100 withdrawal will result in $1,000 of deposit contraction:

$$\Delta D = \frac{\Delta R}{rrr} = \frac{-\$100}{0.10} = -\$1,000$$

Checkable deposits fall by $1,000, but currency in circulation increases by $100 (money that was locked in your bank's vault is now in your pocket). The money supply, which is the sum of checkable deposits and currency, will fall by $900.

The Regulation of Banks

Banks are among the most heavily regulated financial institutions. They are regulated, in part, to protect individual depositors against corrupt business practices. But banks are also very susceptible to crises of confidence: The very nature of their business involves using short-term, volatile deposits to make long-term, stable loans, holding only a fraction of their total deposit liabilities in the form of cash. If customers line up to withdraw all of their cash from a bank—called a *bank run*—they could cause it to fail. And if a few poorly managed banks experienced runs at the same time, it could lead nervous depositors to try withdrawing funds even from well-managed banks, an event known as a bank *panic*.

You can bet these depositors weren't the only ones fretting during the Panic of 1914. If there'd been Xanax then, bank owner L.W. Schwenk would surely have been a preferred customer.

Source: Depositors at failed bank, [L.W. Schwenk], 7th St. & Ave. A, [New York City]. Bains News Service, 1914. George Grantham Bain Collection. Derived from Library of Congress, Prints & Photographs Division, reproduction number LC-USZ62-78694 (b&w film copy neg.) via Wikimedia: https://commons.wikimedia.org/wiki/File:Schwenk-bank-failure-1914.jpg.

Pop! Goes the Econ: Bart Simpson Starts a Bank Run
This spoof of the classic movie *It's a Wonderful Life* shows how easily a bank run can get started. What does the banker mean when he says, "I don't have your money here—it's in Bill's house, and Fred's house"? Revisit bank runs by watching the original in our next section on the Federal Reserve!

View in the online reader

The repercussions of bank panics can be severe. Not least among them is the impact on the money supply, which collapses as bank deposits shrink. Because troubles in the financial sector can spill over into the rest of the economy, the Treasury, the FDIC, and the Fed regulate banks closely both to stabilize the money stock and to prevent situations that might give rise to panics.

Deposit Insurance

From a customer's point of view, the most important form of regulation comes in the form of deposit insurance. For commercial banks, this insurance is provided by the Federal Deposit Insurance Corporation (FDIC). Insurance funds are maintained through a premium assessed on banks for every $100 of bank deposits.

If a commercial bank fails, the FDIC guarantees to reimburse depositors up to $250,000 (raised from $100,000 during the financial crisis of 2008) per insured bank, for each account ownership category. From a depositor's point of view, therefore, it's not necessary to worry about a bank's safety.

Deposit insurance is great for depositors. But knowing its depositors won't lose their money no matter what they do, bank managers can sometimes be tempted to take on more lucrative, but more risky, opportunities. That's a problem of *moral hazard*, the tendency to take on extra risk after insuring against it.

With federal deposit insurance, bank officers are more free to extend riskier loans and invest in riskier securities. That makes failure more likely. To add insult to injury, depositors, knowing that their deposits are insured, may not scrutinize the banks' lending activities as carefully as they would if they felt that unwise loans could result in their losing their deposits.

In the end, banks present us with a fundamental dilemma. A fractional reserve system means that banks can operate only if depositors are confident in the financial security of their bank. If they lose confidence, a bank run or a panic is possible. To prevent that, regulators created the deposit insurance system. But the deposit insurance system encourages banks to take more risks, which makes failure more likely and can erode confidence. The only solution to this dilemma? Tight supervision and regulation.

No Virtue Here: Bank risk led to bank runs; bank runs led to deposit insurance; deposit insurance fueled more bank risk!

Regulation to Prevent Bank Failure

To reduce the number of bank failures, banks are limited in what they can do. Banks are required to maintain a minimum level of net worth as a fraction of total assets. Regulators from the FDIC regularly perform audits and other checks of individual banks to ensure they are operating safely.

The FDIC has the power to close a bank whose net worth has fallen below the required level. In practice, it typically acts to close a bank when it becomes *insolvent*—when its net worth becomes negative, with liabilities exceeding assets.

When the FDIC closes a bank, it arranges for depositors to receive their funds. When the bank's funds are insufficient to return customers' deposits, the FDIC uses money from the insurance fund for this purpose. Alternatively, the FDIC may arrange for another bank to purchase the failed bank. The FDIC, however, continues to guarantee that depositors will not lose any money.

Regulation in Response to Financial Crises

Deposit insurance and bank regulation were both responses to an otherworldly banking crisis during the Great Depression. In four turbulent years, 1929–1933, fully one-third of the country's banks failed, taking with them the life savings of millions of Americans, and causing a collapse of the money supply that turned what would have been an ordinary downturn into the largest economic calamity in the United States, either before or since.

In the aftermath of those events, laws were passed to try to make the banking system safer. The Glass-Steagall Act created the FDIC and separated commercial banks from riskier investment banks. Over time, the financial system in the United States and in other countries began to change, and in 1999, a law was passed in the United States that reversed that separation between commercial and investment banking. Proponents of eliminating the separation between the two types of banks argued that banks could better diversify their investments if they were allowed invest in other assets; they pointed to an early-1980s crisis in the savings and loan (S&L) industry as evidence: Savings and loan associations were required to hold most of their assets in long-term mortgage loans; when interest rates skyrocketed in the early 1980s they found themselves paying more interest to their depositors than they were receiving from their long-term mortgage loans. About 1/3 of the S&Ls failed as a result.

The financial crisis of 2008 and the Great Recession again led to calls for financial market reform. The result was the Dodd-Frank Wall Street Reform and Consumer Protection Act, usually referred to as the Dodd-Frank Act, which passed in July 2010. More than 2,000 pages in length, this act created the Consumer Financial Protection Agency to oversee and regulate various aspects of consumer credit markets, such as credit card and bank fees and mortgage contracts. It also created the Financial Stability Oversight Council (FSOC) to assess risks for the entire financial industry. The FSOC can recommend that a nonbank financial firm, such as a hedge fund that is perhaps threatening the stability of the financial system (i.e., getting "too big to fail") become regulated by the Federal Reserve. If such firms do become insolvent, they can be liquidated just like when the FDIC takes over a bank. The Dodd-Frank Act also calls for implementation of the Volcker rule, which was named after the former chair of the Fed who argued the case. The Volcker rule is meant to ban banks from using depositors' funds to engage in certain types of speculative investments to try to enhance the profits of the bank, at least partly reinstating the separation between commercial and investment banking that the Glass-Steagall Act had created.

Key Takeaways

- Banks are financial intermediaries that accept deposits, make loans, and provide checking accounts for their customers.
- Money is created within the banking system when banks issue loans; it is destroyed when the loans are repaid.
- An increase (decrease) in reserves in the banking system can increase (decrease) the money supply. The maximum amount of the increase (decrease) is equal to the deposit multiplier times the change in reserves; the deposit multiplier equals the reciprocal of the required reserve ratio.
- Bank deposits are insured and banks are heavily regulated.
- Similar to the passage of the Glass-Steagall Act during the Great Depression, the Dodd-Frank Act was the comprehensive financial reform legislation passed in response to the financial crisis in 2008 and the Great Recession.

Try It!

1. Suppose Acme Bank initially has $10,000 in deposits, reserves of $2,000, and loans of $8,000. At a required reserve ratio of 0.2, is Acme loaned up? Show the balance sheet of Acme Bank at present.

2. Now suppose that an Acme Bank customer, planning to take cash on an extended college graduation trip to India, withdraws $1,000 from her account. Show the changes to Acme Bank's balance sheet and Acme's balance sheet after the withdrawal. By how much are its reserves now deficient?

3. Acme would probably replenish its reserves by reducing loans. This action would cause a multiplied contraction of checkable deposits as other banks lose deposits because their customers would be paying off loans to Acme. How large would the contraction be?

See related Numerical Problem 3 at the end of this chapter.

Case in Point: A Big Bank Goes Under

Washington Mutual was a big bank . . . and a big failure.

Source: Westonmr at English Wikipedia. "Seattle Washington Mutual Tower 2004-08-30."
Public domain via Wikimedia Commons; https:// commons.wikimedia.org/wiki/File:Seattle_
Washington_Mutual_Tower_2004-08-30.jpg.

It was the darling of Wall Street—it showed rapid growth and made big profits. Washington Mutual, a savings and loan based in the state of Washington, was a relatively small institution whose CEO, Kerry K. Killinger, had big plans. He wanted to transform his little Seattle S&L into the Walmart of banks.

Killinger began pursuing a relatively straightforward expansion strategy. He acquired banks in large cities such as Chicago and Los Angeles. He acquired banks up and down the east and west coasts. He aggressively extended credit to low-income individuals and families—credit cards, car loans, and especially home mortgages. In a very short period of time, Washington Mutual's assets grew to a whopping $300 billion.

In making mortgage loans to low-income families, WaMu, as the bank was known, quickly became very profitable. But those profits came at the cost of increasing risk. Between 1997 and 2007, housing prices in the United States more than doubled, and during that time loans to even low-income households were profitable. But housing prices crashed in 2007, and homeowners began walking away from their properties: Why continue to pay your $600,000 mortgage when the home's value has plummeted to just $200,000?

To a bank, that's a crisis in the making. When loans go bad, the bank has to mark down the value of its assets, but the bank's liabilities don't change—the bank still has to honor its deposits. That means loan defaults have a negative dollar-for-dollar impact on the bank's net worth:

$$\downarrow \text{Assets} = \overline{\text{Liabilities}} + \downarrow \text{Net Worth}$$

As loan defaults mounted, WaMu began losing money. Its earnings, which had been $3.6 billion in 2006, swung to losses of $67 billion in 2007. As bad as 2007 was, 2008 was worse. Already-nervous depositors learning of the failure of investment bank Lehman Brothers began lining up to pull their deposits from WaMu. Over the space of ten days, they withdrew $16.7 billion, fully 9% of WaMu's total deposits.

That bank run ended it for the bank: With no cash on hand and highly negative net worth, it was seized by the FDIC and sold to banking firm JPMorgan Chase for the bargain-basement price of $1.9 billion. JPMorgan Chase, which had already been interested in acquiring WaMu's customer base and physical facilities, quickly wrote down the bank's nonperforming loans and gave the bank an injection of $8 billion in new capital. WaMu's facilities were rebranded with the Chase name.

The WaMu failure came at great cost. Investors who had bought WaMu bonds and WaMu's shareholders lost virtually all of their investments. But the WaMu failure gave regulators new insight into the importance of a bank's net worth; in the years following the Great Recession those regulators shored up net worth requirements and tightened lending standards in order to prevent a recurrence of what turned out to be the largest bank failure in U.S. history.

See related Numerical Problem 6 at the end of this chapter.

Sources: Based on Eric Dash and Andrew Ross Sorkin, "Government Seizes WaMu and Sells Some Assets," The New York Times, September 25, 2008, p. A1; Kirsten Grind, "Insiders Detail Reasons for WaMu's Failure," Puget Sound Business Journal, January 23, 2009; and FDIC website at https://www.fdic.gov/edie/fdic_info.html.

Answers to Try It! Problems

1. Acme Bank is loaned up, since $2,000/$10,000 = 0.2, which is the required reserve ratio. Acme's balance sheet is:

Assets		Liabilities Plus Net Worth	
Reserves	$2,000	Deposits	$10,000
Loans	$8,000		

2. Acme Bank's balance sheet after losing $1,000 in deposits:

Changes to Acme Bank's Balance Sheet				Acme Bank's Balance Sheet			
Assets		Liabilities		Assets		Liabilities	
Reserves	– $1,000	Deposits	– $1,000	Reserves	$1,000	Deposits	$9,000
				Loans	$8,000		

Required reserves are deficient by $800. Acme must hold 20% of its deposits, in this case $1,800 $(0.2 \times \$9,000 = \$1,800)$, as reserves, but it has only $1,000 in reserves at the moment.

3. The contraction in checkable deposits would be $\Delta D = (1/0.2) * (-\$1,000) = -\$5,000$

Khan Academy Links

Bank balance sheets in a fractional reserve system

Money creation in a fractional reserve system

10.4 The Federal Reserve System

Learning Objectives

1. Explain the primary functions of central banks.
2. Describe how the Federal Reserve System is structured and governed.
3. Identify and explain the tools of monetary policy.
4. Describe how the Fed creates and destroys money when it buys and sells federal government bonds.

Earlier in this chapter, and in Chapter 6 on inflation, you were introduced to a special institution called a central bank. Most countries have a central bank: The Federal Reserve System of the United States, or the Fed, is the U.S. central bank; Japan's central bank is the Bank of Japan; the European Union has established the European Central Bank. A **central bank** performs five primary functions: (1) it acts as a banker to the central government, (2) it acts as a banker to banks, (3) it acts as a regulator of banks, (4) it conducts monetary policy, and (5) it supports the stability of the financial system.

Just because most countries today have a central bank doesn't mean that it's an absolute *requirement*, however. For the first 137 years of its history, the United States didn't have a true central bank. While a central bank was often proposed (going back to the days of Hamilton the man rather than *Hamilton* the musical), there was resistance to creating an institution with such enormous power. A series of bank panics slowly increased support for the creation of a central bank. The bank panic of 1907 proved to be the final straw. Bank failures were so widespread, and depositor losses so heavy, that concerns about centralization of power gave way to a desire for an institution that would provide a stabilizing force in the banking industry. Congress passed the Federal Reserve Act in 1913, creating the Fed and giving it all the powers of a central bank.

A country doesn't have to have a central bank . . . and a central bank doesn't have to serve a particular country. The European Central Bank in Frankfurt, Germany, serves as the central bank for (almost) all member countries of the European Union.

Source: Pradeep Thomas Thundiyil/Shutterstock.com

> **central bank**
>
> A bank that acts as a banker to the central government, acts as a banker to banks, acts as a regulator of banks, conducts monetary policy, and supports the stability of the financial system.

Structure of the Fed

In creating the Fed, Congress determined that a central bank should be as independent of the government as possible. It also sought to avoid too much centralization of power in a single institution. These potentially contradictory goals of independence and decentralized power are evident in the Fed's structure and in the continuing struggles between Congress and the Fed over possible changes in that structure.

In an effort to decentralize power, Congress designed the Fed as a system of twelve regional banks, as shown in Figure 10.3. Each of these banks operates as a kind of bankers' cooperative; the regional banks are owned by the commercial banks in their districts that have chosen to be members of the Fed.[14] The owners of each Federal Reserve bank select the board of directors of that bank; the board selects the bank's president.

FIGURE 10.3 The Twelve Federal Reserve Districts and the Cities Where Each Bank Is Located

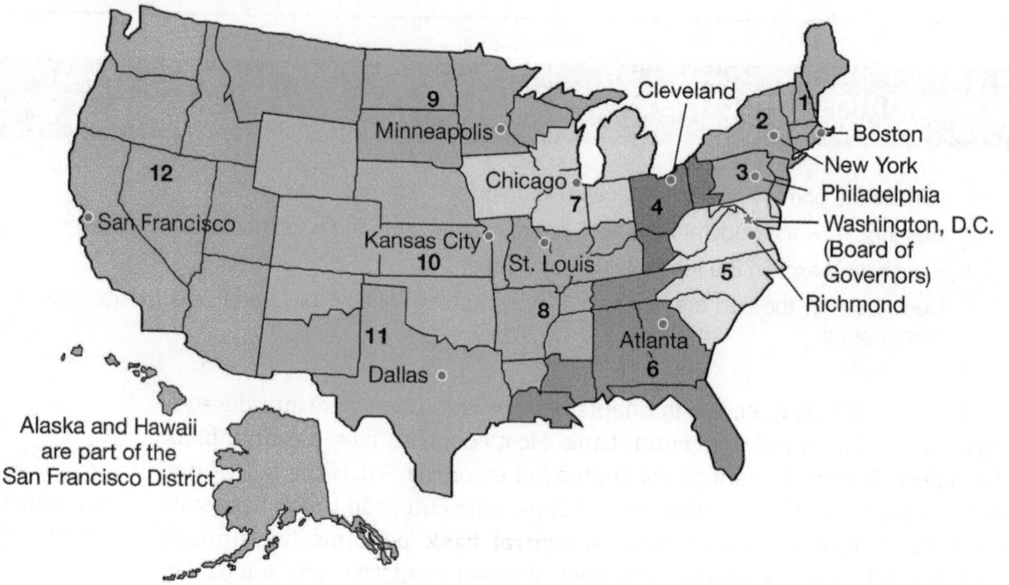

Source: Federal Reserve System; https://www.federalreserve.gov/aboutthefed/federal-reserve-system.htm

Several provisions of the Federal Reserve Act seek to maintain the Fed's independence. The board of directors for the entire Federal Reserve System is called the Board of Governors. The seven members of the board are appointed by the president of the United States and confirmed by the Senate. To ensure a large measure of independence from any one president, the members of the Board of Governors have staggered fourteen-year terms. One member of the board is selected by the president of the United States to serve as chairman for a four-year term.

As a further means of ensuring the independence of the Fed, Congress authorized it to buy and sell federal government bonds. Those bonds pay interest, making bond purchases a profitable enterprise that allows the Fed to pay its own bills. That means that the Fed doesn't have to depend on Congress for its funding, and removes a potential conflict of interest from the conduct of monetary policy.[15]

Despite its official-sounding name, the Fed is technically *not* part of the federal government. Members of the Board of Governors do not legally have to bend to the will of Congress, the president, or anyone else. (The president and members of Congress can certainly try to *influence* the Fed, but they can't *order* it to do anything, under today's laws, at least.) Congress, however, created the Fed. Congress (in the Employment Act of 1946 and the Humphrey–Hawkins Act of 1978) established its charge: maintain full employment, economic growth, price stability, and some form of international equilibrium. The Humphrey–Hawkins Act also requires the chairman of the Fed to give Congress a bi-annual report on the Fed's monetary policies.

Ultimately, the Fed operates independently. But it is clear that the Fed must be responsive to the wishes of Congress, because Congress, through acts of legislation, can force the Fed to do things it otherwise might not want to. Should the Fed choose not to comply, it remains in Congress's power to pass a law abolishing the Fed's independence, or eliminating the Fed altogether.

Powers of the Fed

The Fed's principal powers stem from its authority to conduct monetary policy—adjusting the supply of money and credit to influence the economy's economic performance. It has four main policy tools at its disposal: setting reserve requirements, operating the discount window and other credit facilities, conducting open-market operations, and setting the interest rate payable to banks on their reserve holdings.

Reserve Requirements

The Fed sets the percentage reserve requirement that determines how many reserves banks must hold against their deposit liabilities. In theory, the Fed could use this power as an instrument of monetary policy. It could reduce reserve requirements when it wanted to increase the money supply—that would change some required reserves into excess reserves and free up funds for banks to make loans. The Fed could increase reserve requirements when it wants to reduce the money supply, forcing banks to scramble to bring in circulating cash and lock it away in their vaults. In practice, however, the Fed doesn't use its power to set reserve requirements in this way, as changes in the reserve requirement have proven to be too blunt and to make life difficult for bankers. For decades, the reserve requirement was a flat 10% of checkable deposits, with no adjustment. But as we'll see in this section's "Case in Point: Practice Meets Crisis—Fed Policy Tools in the Time of COVID-19", that's no longer true.

The Discount Window (and Other Credit Facilities)

The Fed's primary responsibility at its creation was to serve as a "lender of last resort" to commercial banks experiencing unexpected withdrawals. Banks that found themselves strapped for cash and unable to meet depositors' demands could borrow reserves from the Fed through its *discount window*.[16] The **discount rate** is the interest rate charged by the Fed when it lends reserves to banks. Each Federal Reserve district bank has the power to set its own discount rate, but in practice they all generally set a uniform rate with guidance from Board of Governors.

> **discount rate**
>
> The interest rate charged by the Fed when it lends reserves to banks.

Reducing the discount rate makes funds cheaper for banks to acquire. A lower discount rate can, then, place downward pressure on the *overall* level of interest rates in the economy by making money more plentiful. However, when financial markets are operating normally, banks rarely borrow from the Fed, reserving use of the discount window only for emergencies.

Instead of borrowing from the Fed when they need reserves, banks typically rely on the federal funds market to obtain reserves. Despite its official-sounding name, the **federal funds market** is a market in which privately owned banks lend excess reserves to one another (the only reason for the word "federal" in the title is because transfers of funds between banks are coordinated through the Fed's payment system). The **federal funds rate** is the interest rate charged for such loans; it's determined by banks' demand for and supply of these reserves.

> **federal funds market**
>
> A market in which banks lend reserves to one another.

> **federal funds rate**
>
> The interest rate charged when one bank lends reserves to another.

The Federal Reserve does not directly set the federal funds rate. But it does have the power to strongly influence it. If it wants to force the federal funds rate down, it can pump new reserves into the banking system. Like all things, the more plentiful something is, the cheaper it gets; when the Fed makes funds plentiful, their price (the interest rate) falls. Of course, this process works in reverse: If the Fed wants the federal funds rate to rise, it can suck reserves out of the banking system, making them both more scarce and more valuable.

The discount window used to be a real window, like this one at the Federal Reserve Bank of St. Louis. Today, bankers obtain their discount loans electronically.

Source: Credit Discount Window at the St. Louis Fed [Photograph] . https://fraser.stlouisfed.org/ archival/5182/item/527398.

The Fed's control over the fed funds rate makes the discount rate less relevant for implementing Federal Reserve policy. In the late 1990s, the Federal Reserve System abandoned explicit control of the discount rate as a policy target, pegging it to the fed funds rate plus half a percentage point. But, as we'll see in this section's "Case in Point: Practice Meets Crisis—Fed Policy Tools in the Time of COVID-19", the Fed has revisited that decision during periods of crisis.

Pop! Goes the Econ: Lender of Last Resort in *It's a Wonderful Life*

A bank run, once started, is hard to stop unless the bank can acquire an infusion of cash from the outside. Today, that outside source, the lender of last resort, is the Fed. Who was the lender of last resort in this clip?

View in the online reader

Open-Market Operations

bond

A promise by the issuer of the bond to pay the owner of the bond a payment or a series of payments on a specific date or dates.

open-market operations

The buying and selling of federal government bonds by the Fed.

The Fed's ability to buy and sell federal government bonds has proven to be its most potent policy tool. A **bond** is a promise by the issuer of the bond (in this case the federal government) to pay the owner of the bond a payment or a series of payments on a specific date or dates. The buying and selling of federal government bonds by the Fed is called **open-market operations**. When the Fed buys or sells government bonds, it adds or subtracts reserves from the banking system. Those changes, in turn, affect the money supply.

Let's see how that works. Suppose the Fed buys a bond for $1,000 from Chloe, who banks at Acme Bank. The Fed prints a check and gives it to Chloe in exchange for the bond. When Chloe deposits that check, Acme's checkable deposits (a liability to Acme) will rise by $1,000. Acme, of course, needs funds to cover that liability, so it sends the check to the Fed's payments center for processing.

The check the Fed printed came out of thin air, but that doesn't mean the Fed won't honor it! When Acme presents the check to the Fed for payment, the Fed simply pushes a button and *poof!* credits Acme Bank's reserve account with the $1,000 it needs to cover Chloe's new deposits. $100 of those reserves are required (assuming a 10% reserve requirement for consistency); $900 are excess reserves. The Fed's purchase of a bond created new reserves with the stroke of a pen!

TABLE 10.5 Impact of an Open-Market Purchase by the Fed

Changes to Acme Bank's Balance Sheet			
Assets		**Liabilities Plus Net Worth**	
Reserves	+ $1,000	Deposits	+ $1,000

So, the Fed has created $1,000 of reserves out of thin air (and received a nice interest-paying bond in exchange for them!). The Fed could just as easily have printed $1,000 of new bills and used those to pay for the bond. Either way, once that $1,000 finds its way into the banking system, those new reserves touch off deposit expansion: With a 10% reserve requirement, the $1,000 of new reserves can ultimately support $10,000 of new deposits. The money supply grows by the full $10,000![17]

That process works in reverse, too. When the Fed sells a bond, it gives the buyer a federal government bond that it had previously purchased. In exchange, it accepts a check that it passes through the Fed's check-clearing system. When the check clears, the bank on which the check was written will find its deposit with the Fed (its reserves) reduced by the amount of the check. Those reserves simply disappear, whisked away with the touch of a button. Ultimately, the money supply decreases by that reduction in reserves times the multiplier. So, the Fed *increases* the money supply by buying bonds, paying for them with new money; it *reduces* the money supply by selling bonds in exchange for money that will be withdrawn from circulation and sucked into the darkest corners of the Fed, there to be locked away for good.

When the Fed wants more money to circulate, it metaphorically prints some new bills, then gets them into circulation by purchasing government bonds. It could just as easily use them to buy cars, toilet paper, or cheese!

Source: Jherbstman. "1979 $10,000 Treasury Bond ." Via Wikimedia: https://commons.wikimedia.org/wiki/File:1979_$10,000_Treasury_Bond_.jpg.

How does the Fed make the decision about how much to buy or sell? And how are these actions implemented? The decisions are made by a special group of leaders at the Federal Reserve called the Federal Open Market Committee (FOMC). The FOMC consists of the seven members of the Board of Governors plus five regional bank presidents. The president of the New York Federal Reserve Bank serves as a permanent member of the FOMC; the other eleven bank presidents take turns filling the remaining four seats.

The FOMC meets eight times per year to chart the Fed's monetary policies. At the end of each meeting, the FOMC issues a *directive* outlining policy actions that the Fed plans to take. In the past, FOMC meetings were closed, with no report of the committee's action until the release of the minutes six weeks after the meeting. Faced with pressure to open its proceedings, the Fed began, in 1994, issuing a report of the decisions of the FOMC immediately after each meeting.

The Fed's purchase or sale of bonds is conducted by the Open Market Desk at the Federal Reserve Bank of New York, one of the twelve district banks. Traditionally, the Fed has bought and sold short-term government securities; however, during the Great Recession, interest rates on short-term government securities (and in the fed funds market) approached zero, so the Fed also began buying longer-term government securities in hopes of influencing longer-term interest rates like the home mortgage rate.

FOMC meetings are somber and serious affairs. These few people direct policy that affects millions.

Source: Federalreserve, Public domain, via Wikimedia Commons; https://commons.wikimedia.org/wiki/File:FOMC_042616_00071_(26605969282).jpg

While our discussion to this point has made it sound like the Fed explicitly targets the amount of money in circulation, in practice, the Fed's real policy goal is the federal funds rate. To force the federal funds rate downward, the Fed buys bonds, pumping new reserves into the banking system. Those new reserves can be traded between banks in the fed funds market; the abundance of new reserves lowers their value (the fed funds rate). So, rather than saying, "The FOMC recommends a 12% increase in the money supply this year," the Fed directive actually says something like, "The FOMC will buy bonds until the federal funds rate falls to 2.7%."

Of course, the opposite is true, too: When the Fed sells bonds, it sucks reserves out of the banking system, and the money supply falls. With fewer reserves available for banks to lend one another, the value of those reserves (the fed funds rate) rises.

Paying Interest on Reserves

Historically, commercial banks have received zero interest for their reserve holdings. Even though the Fed required them to set money aside against their deposits, that money sat idle, earning banks nothing.

That changed during the Great Recession, when the Federal Reserve began paying commercial banks interest not only on their required reserve holdings, but also on any *excess* reserves they held. And in that magic moment, the Fed discovered a brand-new policy tool that was both easy to implement and highly effective.

Doubly Blessed: First, the Fed pumps a bunch of money into your bank; then it pays interest on that money. What do you have to do to earn it? Nothing!

Source: Dean Drobot/ Shutterstock.com

Consider this scenario: The economy is overheating, and banks are extending too much credit to customers to buy cars, washing machines, and she-sheds. Anxious to clamp down on that lending, the Fed raises the interest payable on excess reserves above the interest rate markets had set for consumer loans. Instantly, lending disappears . . . *poof!* After all, if you're a banker, why lend your excess reserves to a customer who might default at 3% interest when the Fed will pay you 3.5% for nothing more than locking them away in your vault and letting them sit?

This policy tool works in the other direction, too: By dropping the interest rate payable on reserves below market interest rates, the Fed can encourage banks to extend more credit to customers and hold less cash in reserve.

The Fed has been using this tool with increasing frequency since its "discovery" in 2008. In this section's "Case in Point: Practice Meets Crisis—Fed Policy Tools in the Time of COVID-19", we'll see how the Fed adjusted interest payable on reserves in response to the coronavirus crisis of 2020.

Key Takeaways

- The Fed, the central bank of the United States, acts as a bank for other banks and for the federal government. It also regulates banks, sets monetary policy, and maintains the stability of the financial system.
- The Fed sets reserve requirements and the discount rate and conducts open-market operations. The Fed also adjusts the interest rate payable on reserves. Of these tools of monetary policy, open-market operations are the most important.
- The Fed creates new reserves and new money when it purchases bonds; that puts downward pressure on interest rates. It destroys reserves and reduces the money supply when it sells bonds; that puts upward pressure on interest rates.
- By reducing the interest payable on reserves, the Fed can encourage banks to lend those reserves to customers at higher market rates. By raising the interest payable on reserves, the Fed can encourage banks to hold onto excess reserves rather than lending them to customers.

Try It!

Suppose the Fed sells $8 million worth of bonds.

1. How do bank reserves change?
2. Will the money supply increase or decrease?
3. What is the maximum possible change in the money supply if the required reserve ratio is 0.2?

See related Numerical Problems 3 and 9 at the end of this chapter.

Case in Point: Practice Meets Crisis—Fed Policy Tools in the Time of COVID-19

Source: © Shutterstock, Inc.

Fighting viruses is usually the job of doctors and nurses. In 2020, it became the job of the Federal Reserve.

You might think that Fed economists, with their silly little money stories, might not have much to contribute to fighting the coronavirus. You'd be wrong, though. The efforts of the Fed were crucial in preventing the economy from imploding in a time of great uncertainty. Let's take a closer look at how the Fed was instrumental in combating this mysterious, microscopic scourge.

When the coronavirus hit, nobody knew exactly how it was transmitted, exactly what its health impacts were, or how contagious it would be. With that uncertainty looming, governments were quick to lock down all but essential businesses. That was hard on wage earners, hard on students, and certainly hard on small businesses ordered to shutter their doors or reduce their capacity in the name of social distancing.

That uncertainty was hard on financial markets, too: It sent stocks into a downward spiral, with stocks losing a third of their value in just a few short days. Fears of furloughed workers unable to pay their mortgages and car payments cost bank CEOs and finance company execs sleepless night after sleepless night.

But the Fed was quick to respond, and quick and coordinated Fed action likely staved off a financial catastrophe. Let's take a look at the Fed's response through the lens of its four tools of policy.

Reserve Requirements: In the early 1990s, the Federal Reserve abandoned reserve requirements on checking accounts and set a uniform 10% rate for checkable deposits. They stayed at that level for decades, largely because changing reserve requirements is such a blunt policy instrument: Changes can potentially free up or tie up huge quantities of reserves at the stroke of a pen. But if there were ever the time for a blunt policy instrument, the early days of the coronavirus qualified. And so, in those first few uncertain days, the Fed completely eliminated the reserve requirement for all deposits, checkable or otherwise. $214 billion of reserves that were required reserves on March 25th became excess reserves on March 26th, available for extending credit to businesses, governments, and households.

Discount Window Policy: Historically, banks have been discouraged from using the Fed's discount window—the Fed has wanted its use to be a genuine last resort. That's why the Fed pegged the discount rate higher than the fed funds rate, a practice known as a *penalty discount rate*. The difference between those rates encourages banks to make use of lower-cost interbank loans rather than higher-cost discount loans from the Fed.

While the Fed continued to maintain a penalty discount rate during the coronavirus crisis, it *did* reduce the penalty. Since 2010, the discount rate had been set at about .66% above the fed funds rate, but during the coronavirus crisis that spread narrowed to just .1%, bringing the two rates into nearly equal alignment.

More important than the rate adjustment was the Fed's attitude toward discount window borrowing. Instead of messaging that the discount window should be a last resort, the Fed actually *encouraged* banks that needed rapid injections of funds to come to the discount window.

The Fed also took unusual steps in its role as a lender of last resort to ensure credit flowed to strained businesses and households during the crisis. It pledged financial support to banks participating in the Main Street Lending Program, which provided emergency loans to smaller businesses suffering because of the crisis. The Fed also established the Municipal Liquidity Facility to keep money flowing to state and local governments experiencing tax shortfalls due to reduced sales and postponement of the income tax filing date. Finally, the Fed supported the Payroll Protection Program, which provided emergency loans to businesses that kept their employees on the payroll through the crisis. All told, these actions by the Fed supported $2.7 trillion in loans.

Open-Market Operations: In an economic crisis, the Fed's #1 job is to pump new reserves into the banking system, a mission it largely carries out by purchasing government bonds in the open market. In early March, 2020, the Fed's holdings of government bonds was a historically high $2.5 trillion. Then the crisis hit, and the Fed responded: By late April, aggressive bond purchases by the Fed had increased that total to $3.9 trillion. As the summer wore on, bond purchases continued, totaling $4.5 trillion by November. Every dollar of bonds added to the Fed's balance sheet injected new reserves into the banking system: Between March and May, bank excess reserves more than doubled, from $1.5 trillion to $3.2 trillion.

Those aggressive purchases had a dramatic impact on interest rates. As the Fed flooded the banking system, the federal funds rate (which is the interest rate banks charge one another for loans of excess reserves) plummeted from 1.6% to 0.1%. In other words, banks had access to essentially unlimited funds, at almost zero cost!

Interest on Reserves: You've probably heard the old adage, "*You can lead a horse to water, but you can't make him drink.*" The Fed has its own version: "*You can fill banks with excess reserves, but you can't make them lend.*" Aggressive bond purchases had pumped tons of new reserves into the banking system, but those new reserves would only help stabilize the economy if banks used them to extend credit. But what a lousy time to lend someone money—anyone might lose their job, their business, at any time, and find themselves unable to make the payments on their loan. Far better for a bank to keep those new reserves locked away in their Fed account earning safe, stable interest.

Don't think the Fed didn't know that! To encourage bankers to take money out of their reserve accounts and put it to work on the street, the Fed dropped the interest payable on reserves from 1.5% to 0.1%, literally overnight. That move, combined with a reduction in the fed funds rate that made obtaining money historically cheap, encouraged banks to pursue new opportunities in consumer and mortgage lending. Within the short period of time, the interest rate charged on thirty-year mortgages declined from 3.5% to an all-time-low rate of just 2.8%. The housing market responded, staying remarkably robust through most of the crisis.

A tale of four indicators: During the coronavirus crisis, the Fed reduced the discount rate to zero (top), eliminated reserve requirements entirely (second), and engaged in massive bond purchases (third). These actions, unprecedented in scale, ensured liquidity and calmed nerves by flooding the financial system with excess reserves (bottom).

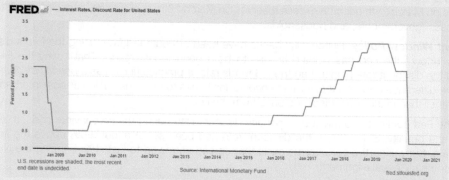

Source: International Monetary Fund, Interest Rates, Discount Rate for United States [INTDSRUSM193N], retrieved from FRED, Federal Reserve Bank of St. Louis; https://fred. stlouisfed.org/series/INTDSRUSM193N.

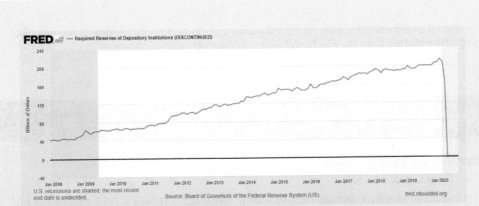

Source: Board of Governors of the Federal Reserve System (US), Required Reserves of Depository Institutions (DISCONTINUED) [REQRESNS], retrieved from FRED, Federal Reserve Bank of St. Louis; https://fred.stlouisfed.org/series/REQRESNS.

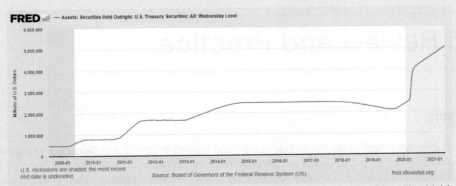

Source: Board of Governors of the Federal Reserve System (US), Assets: Securities Held Outright: U.S. Treasury Securities: All: Wednesday Level [TREAST], retrieved from FRED, Federal Reserve Bank of St. Louis; https://fred.stlouisfed.org/series/TREAST.

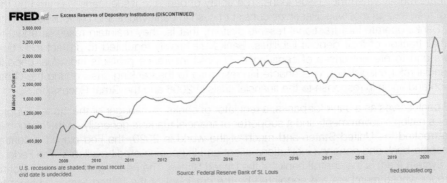

Source: Federal Reserve Bank of St. Louis, Excess Reserves of Depository Institutions (DISCONTINUED) [EXCSRESNW], retrieved from FRED, Federal Reserve Bank of St. Louis; https://fred.stlouisfed.org/series/EXCSRESNW.

The coronavirus recession was the sharpest recession in the country's history—far more dramatic even than what happened in the weeks following the Crash of '29. Yet the coronavirus recession also witnessed the sharpest recovery. The Fed's aggressive use of its four tools of policy—reserve requirement adjustments, discount window policy, open-market operations, and adjusting the interest payable on reserves—deserves a great deal of credit both for keeping the recession from turning into something much worse, and for the speed of that subsequent recovery.

See related Concept Problem 9 at the end of this chapter.

Source: Based on information obtained from the Board of Governors of the Federal Reserve System and data obtained from the FRED, the St. Louis Fed's economic database.

Answers to Try It! Problems

1. Bank reserves fall by $8 million.
2. The money supply decreases.
3. The maximum possible decrease is $40 million, since $\Delta D = (1/0.2) \times (-\$8 \text{ million}) = -\$40$ million.

10.5 Review and Practice

Summary

In this chapter we investigated the money supply and looked at how it is determined. Money is anything that serves as a medium of exchange. Whatever serves as money also functions as a unit of account and as a store of value. Money may or may not have intrinsic value. In the United States, the total of currency in circulation, traveler's checks, and checkable deposits equals M1. A broader measure of the money supply is M2, which includes M1 plus assets that are highly liquid, but less liquid than those in M1.

Banks create money when they issue loans. The ability of banks to issue loans is limited by the amount of their excess reserves. Reserves consist of cash in bank vaults and bank deposits with the Fed. Banks operate in a fractional reserve system; that is, they maintain reserves equal to only a small fraction of their deposit liabilities. Banks are heavily regulated to protect individual depositors and to prevent crises of confidence. Deposit insurance protects individual depositors. Financial reform legislation was enacted in response to the banking crisis during the Great Depression and again in response to the financial crisis in 2008 and the Great Recession.

A central bank serves as a bank for banks, a regulator of banks, a manager of the money supply, a bank for a nation's government, and a supporter of financial markets generally. In the economic crisis that rocked the United States and much of the world in 2020, the Fed played a central role in keeping bank and nonbank institutions afloat and in keeping credit available. The Federal Reserve System (Fed) is the central bank for the United States. The Fed is governed by a Board of Governors whose members are appointed by the president of the United States, subject to confirmation by the Senate.

The Fed has four tools of policy. It can lend to banks and other institutions through the discount window and other credit facilities; it can change reserve requirements; it can engage in purchases and sales of federal government bonds in the open market; and it can adjust the interest payable to banks on reserves. Decisions to buy or sell bonds are made by the Federal Open Market Committee (FOMC); the Fed's open-market operations represent its primary tool for influencing the money supply. Purchases of bonds by the Fed initially increase the reserves of banks. With excess reserves on hand, banks can increase their loans, and in the process, the money supply will change by an amount less than or equal to the deposit multiplier times the change in reserves. Similarly, the Fed can reduce the money supply by selling bonds.

Concept Problems

1. (Related to "Try It!" in Section 22.2.) Airlines have "frequent flier" clubs in which customers accumulate miles according to the number of miles they have flown with the airline. Frequent flier miles can then be used to purchase other flights, to rent cars, or to stay in some hotels. Are frequent flier miles money?

2. Debit cards allow an individual to transfer funds directly from a checkable account to a merchant without writing a check. How is this different from the way credit cards work? Are either credit cards or debit cards money? Explain.

3. Many colleges sell special cards that students can use to purchase everything from textbooks or meals in the cafeteria to the use of washing machines in the dorm. Students deposit money in their cards; as they use their cards for purchases, electronic scanners remove money from the cards. To replenish a card's money, a student makes a cash deposit that is credited to the card. Would these cards count as part of the money supply?

4. Which of the following items is part of M1? M2?

    a. $0.27 cents that has accumulated under a couch cushion.

    b. Your $2,000 line of credit with your Visa account.

    c. The $210 balance in your checking account.

    d. $417 in your savings account.

    e. 10 shares of stock your uncle gave you on your eighteenth birthday, which are now worth $520.

    f. $200 in traveler's checks you have purchased for your spring-break trip.

5. In the Middle Ages, goldsmiths took in customers' deposits (gold coins) and issued receipts that functioned much like checks do today. People used the receipts as a medium of exchange. Goldsmiths also issued loans by writing additional receipts against which they were holding no gold to borrowers. Were goldsmiths engaging in fractional reserve banking? Why do you think that customers turned their gold over to goldsmiths? Who benefited from the goldsmiths' actions? Why did such a system generally work? When would it have been likely to fail?

6. A $1,000 deposit in Acme Bank has increased reserves by $1,000. A loan officer at Acme reasons as follows: "The reserve requirement is 10%. That means that the $1,000 in new reserves can back $10,000 in checkable deposits. Therefore I'll loan an additional $10,000." Is there any problem with the loan officer's reasoning? Explain.

7. When the Fed buys and sells bonds through open-market operations, the money supply changes, but there is no effect on the money supply when individuals buy and sell bonds. Explain.

8. Suppose that the Fed wants to stimulate the economy. Through aggressive bond purchases, it forces the federal funds rate down a full percentage point; it also reduces the interest payable on reserves by one-half of a percentage point. Will the Fed be successful in stimulating the economy? Why or why not?

9. (Related to "Case in Point: Practice Meets Crisis—Fed Policy Tools in the Time of COVID-19" in Section 22.4.) Suppose that the economy is overheating and the Fed would like to slow things down by reducing the money supply. Recommend actions for each of the Fed's four tools of policy.

10. (Related to "Case in Point: Is Bitcoin Money?" in Section 22.2.) Does Bitcoin more closely resemble commodity money, representative commodity money, or fiat money?

Numerical Problems

1. Consider the following example of bartering:

1 10-ounce T-bone steak can be traded for 5 soft drinks.
1 soft drink can be traded for 10 apples.
100 apples can be traded for a T-shirt.
5 T-shirts can be exchanged for 1 textbook.

a. How many 10-ounce T-bone steaks could you exchange for 1 textbook? How many soft drinks? How many apples?

b. State the price of T-shirts in terms of apples, textbooks, and soft drinks.

c. Why do you think we use money as a unit of account?

2. (Related to "Try It!" in Section 22.4.) Assume that the banking system is loaned up and that any open-market purchase by the Fed directly increases reserves in the banks. If the required reserve ratio is 0.2, by how much could the money supply expand if the Fed purchased $2 billion worth of bonds?

3. (Related to "Try It!" in Section 22.3.) Suppose the Fed sells $5 million worth of bonds to Econobank.

a. What happens to the reserves of the bank?

b. What happens to the money supply in the economy as a whole if the reserve requirement is 10%, all payments are made by check, and individuals keep all of their money in their checking account (rather than pulling some out in cash)?

c. How would your answer in part b be affected if you knew that some people involved in the money creation process kept some of their funds as cash?

4. Suppose that the reserve requirement against deposits is 0%, but that cautious banks voluntarily hold 5% of their deposits in reserve, just in case. If the Federal Reserve buys $1,000 of bonds, how many new deposits could that $1,000 of new reserves create? Does this scenario differ from one in which banks desire to hold no excess reserves but the Fed has a 5% reserve requirement?

5. Suppose a bank with a 10% reserve requirement has $10 million in reserves and $100 million in checkable deposits, and a major corporation makes a deposit of $1 million.

a. Explain how the deposit affects the bank's reserves and checkable deposits.

b. By how much can the bank increase its lending?

c. What will be the ultimate effect on total checkable deposits in the banking system? On loans in the banking system?

d. What will be the ultimate effect on the M1 money supply?

6. (Related to "Case in Point: A Big Bank Goes Under" in Section 22.3.) Suppose that the only items on Washington Mutual's balance sheet are $187 billion in deposits, $18.7 billion in reserves, and $168.3 billion in loans. Draw WAMU's balance sheet.

a. Over a ten-day period, rumors of insolvency caused depositors to withdraw $16.7 billion of deposits. Show the effect of these withdrawals on WAMU's balance sheet. What options did WAMU have to raise the money its depositors wanted to withdraw? How big a reserve deficiency did it face?

b. WAMU had $11 billion of nonperforming loans listed as assets on its balance sheet. Show the impact on the balance sheet of writing these loans off. What happens to WAMU's net worth?

7. Consider an economy in which the central bank has just purchased $8 billion worth of government bonds from banks in the economy. What would be the effect of this purchase on the money supply in the country, assuming reserve requirements of:

a. 10%.

b. 15%.

c. 20%.

d. 25%.

8. (Related to "Try It!" in Section 22.4.) Consider the same economy from Numerical Problem 8. If the central bank *sells* $8 billion worth of government bonds to local banks. state the likely effects on the money supply under reserve requirements of:

a. 10%.

b. 15%.

c. 20%.

d. 25%.

9. How would the purchase of $8 billion of bonds by the central bank from local banks be likely to affect interest rates? How about the effect on interest rates of the sale of $8 billion worth of bonds? Explain your answers carefully.

Endnotes

1. Justin Scheck, "Mackerel Economics in Prison Leads to Appreciation for Oily Fish," *Wall Street Journal*, October 2, 2008, p. A1, and https://bit-coinist.com/charlie-shrems-mackerel-prison-currency-bitcoins-evolution-money/, February 4, 2017.

2. Economies often revert to barter when a country's monetary system collapses. See the inflation chapter's Case in Point about the Venezuelan hyperinflation for more on this.

3. At least in the U.S. In other countries, of course, the currency differs: Brits use pounds, Germans use euros, Japanese use yen, and so on. But most transactions take place between countrymen, and a common currency puts all parties to those transactions on the same page.

4. In truth, even the definition of a foot was ambiguous until a short time ago. See https://oceanservice.noaa.gov/geodesy/international-foot.html for more detail. Who knew?!

5. Paul Einzig's *Primitive Money* is a fascinating journey through the history and evolution of money. A must read!

6. In more modern times, commodity money often took the form of paper that could be redeemed for a fixed amount of a valuable commodity. That money is called *representative commodity money*. Even though the money that circulated was paper, the basic principle is still the same: It was backed by some substance with intrinsic value.

7. Government isn't concerned about somebody shaving today's dimes, quarters, and half-dollars—they're now made of nickel and copper. Milled edges are just tradition today, a throwback to the early 1960s, when those coins were made of silver.

8. For more on the relationship between money and prices, see our chapter on inflation. In it, you'll find a Case in Point on the Venezuelan hyperinflation of 2018, one of many episodes of hyperinflation in the twentieth and twenty-first centuries.

9. You're unlikely to ever come across a traveler's check—in this age of globally integrated financial systems, you're much more likely to conduct transactions by simply using your debit card. But before the electronic era, traveler's checks were an internationally acceptable form of payment. Today, only a tiny volume of traveler's checks continue to circulate.

10. Those money market accounts generally include limited check-writing privileges.

11. There are many possible definitions of money; M1 and M2 are just the most common. Economist and index-number theorist (in the chapter on inflation we told you there were such things, didn't we?!) William Barnett argues that a money index that weights alternative assets by their "moneyness" has a much stronger link to real economic activity. See his terrific book, *"Getting It Wrong: How Faulty Monetary Statistics Undermine the Fed, the Financial System, and the Economy,"* for more on his *divisia* measure of the money supply.

12. Over time, some nonbank financial intermediaries have become more and more like banks. For example, brokerage firms usually offer customers interest-earning checkable accounts and make loans. But they do not participate in the money supply process in the same way or to the same extent as commercial banks.

13. An old joke told in business-school hallways goes something like this: *An economist is someone who wanted to be an accountant, but didn't have enough charisma.* No wonder accountants are so much fun at parties . . . right?

14. All nationally chartered banks (like "1st National Bank") are required to be members. State-chartered banks may become members provided they meet certain requirements.

15. The Fed is limited in the profits it is allowed to earn; its "excess" profits are returned to the Treasury.

16. Before the computer age, there really was a discount window at regional Fed facilities that bankers would visit when they needed short-term loans of reserves. Today, the discount window is electronic.

17. You may be wondering why, in the previous section, Manuel's $1,000 deposit only created $9,000 of money. As is the case here, Manuel's deposit of $1,000 created $10,000 of total checkable deposits. But in Manuel's case, the bank took in his $1,000 cash and locked it away, so the net change in the money stock was $9,000. No such thing happens here: The Fed's injection of $1,000 was completed by "printing" brand new reserves.

CHAPTER 11

Financial Markets and the Economy

11.1 Start Up: Who Wants to Be a Millionaire?

Champagne nights, caviar dreams. A Beemer in the driveway; a condo in Aspen. This is the lifestyle so many of us like to daydream about! Yet for so many of us, it seems beyond reach.

Financial markets make it possible for this thrifty fry cook to live out his caviar dreams.

Source: AS Inc/Shutterstock.com

What would you say if we told you that not only can you have this kind of lifestyle, but also that you won't have to become a viral social influencer, Silicon Valley entrepreneur, or NBA star to get it? As long as you're willing to put in a little bit of effort over a long period of time, the millionaire lifestyle is within your reach. We promise!

Let's shine a spotlight on your future by doing some fun math. Those words—fun and math—don't always go well together, but when we're talking about the mathematics of becoming a millionaire, they seem to blend quite nicely. If you're a typical college student, you'll graduate at about age 22. That will leave you forty years to work before you retire a millionaire at 62 (we really do want an early retirement, don't we?). Over those forty years, if you shove just $2,083 into a slit in your mattress each month, you'll hit the million-dollar mark just as your retirement party begins. *Gold watch, anyone?*

What's that? You need that $2,083 for *other* things, like housing and food? Ok, so maybe those basic needs will prevent you from becoming a mattress millionaire. (Besides, who wants to sleep on a mattress that gets lumpier with every passing month?) But don't let that prevent you from dreaming, because by letting your money *work* for you instead of sitting idle in your mattress, you can still become a millionaire, and you can enjoy a decent apartment, healthy food, and a perfectly serviceable car along the way.

And just how do you get your money to work for you? You let other people use your savings while you're counting down to retirement—people who want to build businesses, build roads, or build social media empires. Those people will pay you for the temporary use of your money! One way to do this is to lend your money to other people and charge them interest. If you charge them just 5.4% interest annually, you'll reach your retirement million by setting aside just $625 each month.[1] That may seem like a lot of money, but it's *way* less than $2,083, and low enough to almost sound manageable.

But we can go you one better. Instead of lending your savings at interest, you can use your money to buy into existing businesses and share in their profits. By owning a company . . . or a bunch of companies . . . you can reach your million by saving not $2,083 each month, not $625 each month, but a mere $248![2] That kind of savings seems very reasonable, and is unlikely to negatively impact your current lifestyle. In fact, it's so affordable that you might even be able to get an early start while you're still a college student![3]

You might be wondering how to find creditworthy people to borrow your money . . . or how to prevent them from running off with it once they've gotten their grubby mitts on it. You might also be wondering how to purchase an ownership stake in a company, and worrying about what might happen to your millionaire dreams if that company were to go under. The answers to all of these perfectly reasonable questions are found in financial markets. In financial markets, even the smallest saver can lend money to governments and businesses around the globe. In financial markets, ordinary people like us can acquire ownership stakes in the world's largest corporations. *Move over, Jeff Bezos!*

Financial markets give you the power to become a millionaire not through a brilliant idea, not through a scintillating persona, not through a 48" vertical leap, but through a tiny bit of sacrifice accumulated over a large number of months. Financial markets will help you build wealth, and they'll help you protect it from deadbeats who don't pay their debts and from managers' poor decisions.

This chapter provides the building blocks for understanding financial markets. It begins with an overview of financial markets and the securities and financial instruments that get traded there. The second section digs deeper into two important financial markets, the bond market and the foreign exchange market, that have a strong and direct bearing on real GDP and the price level. The final section draws on the workings of the bond market to develop a more comprehensive model of the money market. That model will help us understand how Federal Reserve policy can bring about changes in the interest rate and potentially affect output, employment, and prices in the macroeconomy.

Get ready to pop the cork on those champagne nights; our study of financial markets is about to begin!

11.2 The Functions of Financial Instruments

Learning Objectives

1. List the four functions of financial instruments.
2. Explain how businesses can use stocks or bonds to raise money.
3. Compare financial instruments to cash as a means of storing wealth.
4. List and explain one way that financial instruments can be used to reduce risk.
5. Contrast destabilizing speculation with stabilizing speculation.

You've just learned about the nuts and bolts of the banking system. That system plays a critical role in the macroeconomy. But there are other financial institutions besides banks, and those institutions are just as important to the functioning of a modern, integrated economy as commercial banks. Nonbank financial institutions produce a wide and bewildering array of financial products and services: *stocks, bonds, options, futures, swaps, straddles, repos, forex* . . . the list just goes on and on.

We're about to begin exploring the inner workings of **financial markets**—the markets where **financial instruments**—documents that represent agreements between two or more parties about rights to payments of money—are traded. We're going to focus on only two of the most common financial instruments: bonds and foreign exchange. Don't let the fact that we're ignoring all of the other interesting financial products bother you, though. While each financial instrument works a bit differently under the hood, all financial instruments tend to perform the same few jobs:

- Some people use financial instruments to raise the funds they need to open or expand a business.

- Other people use financial instruments to sock money away for their kids' educations, or to save for retirement.

- Many businesses use financial instruments to reduce their exposure to risk.

- Other people, called *speculators*, use financial instruments to increase their exposure to risk, in hopes of earning large profits.

Those four scenarios describe the four functions of financial instruments: raising capital, storing wealth, reducing risk, enabling speculation. Let's take a closer look at each.

financial markets

The markets where financial instruments are traded.

financial instruments

Documents that represent agreements between two or more parties about rights to payments of money.

Raising Capital

The first thing financial instruments are used for is to raise money to fund business ventures. That money is often referred to as *financial capital*. Financial capital is different than the capital economists generally talk about, the tools and equipment firms use to produce other products or services. But building factories and conducting R&D can be very expensive, so business owners often need to raise money to pay for them. Financial instruments help make that happen.

Suppose that Zoom founder Eric Yuan wants to install a new supercomputer at Zoom headquarters, and he needs a hundred million dollars to do it. Yuan can turn to financial markets to raise the funds. There, Zoom can request money from people all over the world in order to amass the financial capital it takes to crush competing videoconferencing platforms like Cisco's Webex and Microsoft's Teams.

Stocks. One way that Zoom can raise funds is by selling stock. *Stock* is a financial asset that represents partial ownership of a corporation. That ownership can be easily transferred from person to person because stock can be easily bought and sold at *exchanges*—centralized trading places—like the New York Stock Exchange and the NASDAQ. There, people buy and sell small ownership stakes in existing companies like General Electric and Tesla. If you purchase stock in Zoom, and Zoom does well, you (as partial owner) will share in those profits. If Zoom does poorly, so will you.[4]

When you buy a twenty-year-old Camry from your neighbor down the block, Toyota doesn't receive a dime. In the same way, when you buy a share of Zoom from someone else, neither Zoom nor Eric Yuan gets a cut of the money—that share was a used share just like your Camry was a used car. Zoom only receives money from selling a share of stock the very first time it's sold. A special financial institution called an *investment bank* helps companies like Zoom sell newly created shares of stock to the public. Often, the investment bank will purchase a large number of shares for itself and then gradually resell those shares to individuals or mutual fund managers (more on this later!). By doing so, investment banks help make raising the money entrepreneurs need to start or expand their business both easier and faster.

Thornbridge's Jaipur IPA hit the English brewing scene like a sledgehammer. When skyrocketing sales pushed Thornbridge to expand its operation, they raised the millions they needed in financial markets.

Source: barinart/Shutterstock.com

A bond is just a fancy IOU that represents a debt of the issuer. Unlike the IOUs you may have given your siblings, bonds have a definite "pay me back by" date!

Source: Mega Pixel/Shutterstock. com

interest

The price a borrower must pay for the use of other peoples' money.

interest rate

Interest expressed as a percentage of the amount borrowed.

Bonds. Instead of selling off ownership of his company by issuing stock, Eric Yuan might borrow the money he needs. He could take out a loan at a bank, or he could print up a bunch of legally-binding IOUs and sell them to people who are willing to lend Zoom money. Those IOUs come in many forms, the most common of which is called a *bond*. A bond is a financial instrument that represents a debt contract. It is essentially an IOU that, in exchange for using a person's money today, obligates the borrower to pay back a specified amount of money at a particular point in the future. From Zoom's standpoint, the advantage of using bonds to raise funds instead of stock is that Zoom only has to pay back what's specified in the contract; if a pandemic causes Zoom's earnings to skyrocket, its owners don't share those increased earnings with bondholders. On the other hand, if Zoom has a terrible year, its bondholders are still entitled to their contractual payment; people who own Zoom stock may not receive a dime.

Bonds come in all shapes and sizes. Some *mature*, or come due (require full repayment), in a year or less; others mature in twenty or thirty years. Some require the borrower to make periodic payments to the lender; others simply require a single lump-sum payment at maturity.[5] Like stocks, existing bonds can be bought and sold on organized exchanges: If you buy one of Zoom's bonds and then later decide you'd rather not wait twenty years for the bond to mature, you can sell your (used!) bond to someone else for cash today.

No matter whether Zoom borrows money from a bank or borrows by issuing bonds, it will always have to pay back more money than it borrowed. The difference is called **interest**, and it represents the price a borrower must pay for the use of other peoples' money. It's also the reward to the people who postponed spending money on things that *they* wanted in order to let Zoom spend their money on the things *it* wanted. Often, interest is expressed as a percentage of the amount borrowed, which is called the **interest rate**.

Businesses often borrow money by issuing and selling bonds, and again, investment banks help bring those new bonds to market for sale.[6] Governments rely on bond financing, too. When the federal government spends more on its programs than it takes in from taxes, it uses bonds to make up the difference. State and local governments do the same, and often turn to the bond market to fund special projects like new roads, new schools, and new parks.

Small Loan, Large Impact: Across Asia, Latin America, and Africa women like this one are using microcredit to open stores and fund cottage industries.

Source: Dishant Shrivastava/Shutterstock.com

The large-scale credit we've been talking about in our discussion of stocks and bonds is essential for the development and functioning of both businesses and government. But loans don't have to be measured in trillions, billions, or even millions to be useful. In fact, some of the most useful loans are the smallest. In *microcredit* programs, people lend budding entrepreneurs in developing countries $25 or $50 at a time. Those loans help small businesswomen put together the few hundred or few thousand dollars necessary to launch their own enterprises.[7] Microcredit, which originated in Bangladesh's Grameen Bank, has been instrumental in promoting economic development and empowering women in countries in which they are often considered second-class citizens. Its impact has been so notable that its originator, Muhammad Yunus, was awarded the 2006 Nobel Peace Prize.

Storing Wealth

Financial markets make it easy for Zoom to borrow other peoples' money for its own use. But why do people want to lend Zoom their money in the first place? Part of the answer is that people wish to trade the opportunity to buy some things today for the opportunity to buy even more things tomorrow. But even if you're a minimalist who's not motivated by the lure of "more," you might still want to consume less than you earn now and put the difference to work in financial markets. That's because financial instruments can help you store your wealth across time.

Consider Graciela, who wants to buy a nice used car. She plans to set aside some of her earnings each month until she has enough to buy one. She could store that money in a coffee can buried in her backyard, but that's not a great system. Because the prices of the things people buy generally increase each year (that's called *inflation*, and we've got an entire chapter devoted to it), Graciela will find that the dollars she's buried today will buy fewer things when she digs them up.

Financial markets can help Graciela preserve the purchasing power of her savings. In fact, financial instruments can help her savings grow instead of shrinking. Graciela can use her money to buy shares of stock in Apple, or she might buy bonds issued by Microsoft if she's seeing more PCs and fewer Macs. With even less effort, she can visit her local bank and tuck her money away in a savings account or purchase a certificate of deposit (CD). Any of those options is likely better than tucking her money in a coffee can, because the interest or profits those financial instruments generate can help offset the adverse effects of inflation.

When it's time for Graciela to purchase the car she's been saving for, she'll need to convert her financial instrument to cash. That could be easy—if she just opened a savings account, she'll just need to visit her bank and make a withdrawal. But it can be hard: If Graciela stored her wealth by buying superhero action figures, she might have trouble finding the right person willing to purchase her collection for the right price. Savings accounts, collectibles, and other assets have different degrees of *liquidity*, the ease with which they can be converted to cash. From a saver's standpoint, liquidity is very desirable: It makes it easy to get into desirable investments, and then to get out if a better opportunity comes along. (It also makes it easy to convert your savings to cash if you're ready to buy a nice used car!)

Even if you're not saving for anything big, you might still want to store wealth in order to smooth your consumption of goods and services over time. Few people want to consume exorbitantly during their high-earning years and then go on a starvation diet the instant they retire. You can prevent that from happening to you by using financial markets. When you're young and bringing in money hand over fist, you can buy stocks and bonds and CDs and whatnot; when you're old and the only money coming is your Social Security check, you can sell off those financial instruments and use the proceeds for that trip around the world you've always dreamed of, to pay for your grandkids' college . . . or to keep your now sixty-year-old Camry on the road.

It's not just old people who want to smooth their consumption across time. Young people do, too, and financial markets help them. Take for example, Jasmine, a typical college student, who has little income but who wants to live in a decent place, drive a decent car, and maybe even study abroad. If Jasmine had to live on her current income, her life might be pretty bleak (or she'd be working so many hours her college would put her on the ten-year plan). Instead, Jasmine takes out student loans that let her borrow against her future earnings to finance a better life today. Student loans are just as much financial instruments as stocks and bonds are!

You'll be solid if you stay liquid . . . at least if you're concerned about being able to access your wealth.

Source: Sahara Prince/ Shutterstock.com

Reducing Risk

If you're one of the people who watched stock prices plunge during the coronavirus crisis of 2020, it might not be intuitively obvious that one of the major functions of financial markets is to help people reduce risk.[8] Nevertheless, that's *exactly* what some of the most volatile financial instruments are actually designed to do.

Consider Ted, a wheat farmer in western Kansas. Each September, Ted plants wheat that he won't harvest until the following July. Without financial markets, the decision about how much wheat to plant in September would depend on Ted's guess about the price of wheat ten months into the future. If the price turns out to be lower than expected, Ted might have trouble paying back the money he borrowed for seeds, fuel, and fertilizer . . . or he might have trouble putting enough rice and beans on his table to feed his family.

Worried the price of that barley will plummet before harvest? Sell it in advance with a futures contract and lock in its value today!

Source: ankit1992200/Shutterstock.com

Yep, that's right—baskets. Plural. Lots of them.

Source: batjaket/Shutterstock.com

Ted can turn to financial markets to prevent that from happening. A financial instrument called a **futures contract** allows Ted to sell some of his wheat at the time it's planted, with the promise to deliver that wheat and receive payment in July. That promise, which locks in a future price and quantity, is a financial instrument. Futures contracts are especially well-suited for commodities with uniform quality, like wheat.

Suppose Ted sells some wheat to King Arthur Flour in September for delivery in July at $6 per bushel. If the price of wheat ends up being $10, then locking in the price in September will have caused Ted to miss a lucrative opportunity. But if the July price of wheat turns out to be $2 per bushel, Ted's futures contract will have helped him avoid a financial disaster. Either way, the contract stabilizes Ted's income, and as long as he is willing to forgo the possibility that the price might rise to eliminate the risk of its falling, it will help him smooth his consumption and soothe his anxiety. King Arthur Flour benefits, too: By using the futures market, it's eliminated the chance of paying $10 for wheat by forgoing the chance to buy $2 wheat.

Another way financial markets help investors reduce their exposure to risk is by helping them diversify. **Diversification** is the practice of spreading your wealth across multiple investments. That's simply good investment practice: It was for his work on diversification that economist James Tobin won the Nobel Prize. He formalized mathematically what rural housewives have known for centuries: *"Don't put all your eggs in one basket."*[9]

Here's why diversification is so wise. Suppose you have $10,000 buried in a coffee can in your back yard. You're anxious to put that money to work, so you use it to buy stock in Zoom. But when you do that, you put your life savings in the hands of Eric Yuan. One bad headache, one foggy morning, and he can make your savings disappear. But if you divide your savings between Zoom and the General Dynamics corporation, you'll substantially reduce your risk of losing it all. If Zoom tanks, you've still got your General Dynamics holdings. If General Dynamics tanks, you've still got your Zoom holdings. You're much safer holding two companies rather than one, because the chance of *both* companies going under at the same time is much smaller than the chance of just one company or the other going under.[10]

Financial markets make it easy to spread your savings across ten, or one hundred, or even one thousand different companies by purchasing shares of a financial instrument called a mutual fund. A **mutual fund** is a financial asset that pools the savings of investors and uses those funds to buy stock, bonds, or other financial assets issued by firms and governments. When you buy shares of a mutual fund, you are entitled to a proportionate share of the earnings generated by each asset the fund invests in. One great thing about mutual funds is that there's one to satisfy every taste: If you want to invest in Bitcoin, or green technology, or companies that don't use child labor, there's a fund for each.

Enabling Speculation

Financial markets fill one final need, and it's a need that not everyone looks on favorably: Financial markets make it easy for people to speculate. Just like a gambler might feel like the next hand of cards will come up four aces, a speculator might feel that the price of wheat (or the value of Bitcoin, or silver, or even the price of hand sanitizer) will go up or down. Financial markets help those speculators put your money where their hunch is.

Suppose you believe the price of wheat will rise from $3 per bushel today to $10 per bushel by July. Here's one way to act on that hunch: Buy 5,000 bushels of wheat today for $3 per bushel and have it delivered to your home. Store it in your basement over the winter. Then, in July, shovel the wheat out of your basement into a truck, deliver it to a nearby flour mill for $10 per bushel, and earn a nice $35,000 profit.

But there's an easier way to make money, and it's one that won't attract mice! For a small fee, buy a futures contract for 5,000 bushels of wheat, priced at $3, to be delivered and paid for in July. On June 30, if wheat is selling for the $10 you guessed it would, your futures contract will be worth a net of $35,000. You don't have to accept delivery of the wheat, though—instead, you can sell your contract for $33,000 to a flour mill and let them deal with the logistics. The next day the contract expires: The flour mill receives the wheat from the farmer and pays him the $15,000 specified in the futures contract. With this arrangement, the mill gets its wheat for $48,000 ($2,000 less than it would otherwise have to pay), the farmer gets $15,000 (which is what he originally wanted for his wheat), and you make $33,000 without ever having to lift a shovel.

Of course, you could be wrong. If wheat turns out to be $1 a bushel in July, you'll lose $10,000, regardless of whether you stored the wheat in your basement or used a futures contract. But win or lose, it's worth remembering that the person on the other end of your contract may not be speculating at all: The same financial instrument you are using to indulge your risk might be used by a farmer or baker or miller to *reduce* his!

Speculators are often criticized for their ability to destabilize markets. For example, in 1600s Holland, speculators began buying up tulip bulbs on the belief that their prices would rise in the future. Speculators' hoarding drove bulb prices higher, which sustained their belief in ever-increasing tulip prices and created more hoarding at ever-higher prices. At the height of the tulip craze, a single bulb sold for ten times the annual salary of a skilled worker.

When prices are driven not by the intrinsic value of an item but rather by such a speculative spiral, a *speculative bubble* or an *asset bubble* is said to exist.[11] The problem with bubbles is that they pop, and when they do, prices plummet and wealth evaporates. If large numbers of people are involved, those wealth effects can plunge an entire economy into recession.

Despite some spectacular historical episodes of destabilizing speculation, on a day-to-day basis, speculators actually *help* stabilize prices. For example, suppose that pecans are plentiful and cheap today, but you and a few others believe that a drought will drive next year's prices skyward. You can profit from that belief by buying lots of pecans today, storing them, and then selling them next year.

That's speculative, but it does a service for society by pulling pecans off the market at a time when they have relatively low value (today), and returning them to the market at a time when they'll be particularly scarce (next year). That helps society get more happiness out of each pecan. Your speculative gamble also helps stabilize pecan prices. Buying up pecans when pecans are cheap drives up their price a bit; making them available next year when pecans are scarce helps hold their price down. Because of speculation, price swings in the pecan market are smaller than they would otherwise be.

Speculation helps stabilize prices in the pecan market. Financial instruments like futures contracts make it easier for speculators to perform this valuable function. In addition, speculation may help stabilize prices in financial markets themselves: Speculating in Apple stock is easier than speculating in real apples!

In 1637, a speculative frenzy drove the price of a single tulip bulb to more than ten times the annual income of a skilled craftsman. Then, of course, the tulip bubble popped . . . because that's what bubbles do.

Source: Alex_An_Der/ Shutterstock.com

I'd hate to speculate whether this COVID-19 TP hoarder is an opportunist or a public servant.

Source: Koldunova Anna/ Shutterstock.com

Pop! Goes the Econ: Kramer Makes (Blood) Bank
In this clip from *Seinfeld*, Kramer makes use of the (blood) banking system. What are his motives for using the blood bank? What function does this quasi-financial market play at the end of the clip?

View in the online reader

Key Takeaways

- Financial markets are where claims on future payments, called financial instruments, are traded.
- Financial instruments help businesses and individuals raise financial capital to fund purchases like machinery, factories, and homes.
- Financial instruments store value over time, which helps individuals smooth consumption over their lifetime.
- Financial instruments help people reduce risk by locking in prices for future transactions and making it easy to diversify.

- Financial instruments help speculators gamble on future price movements.
- Speculation can be stabilizing or destabilizing.

Try It!

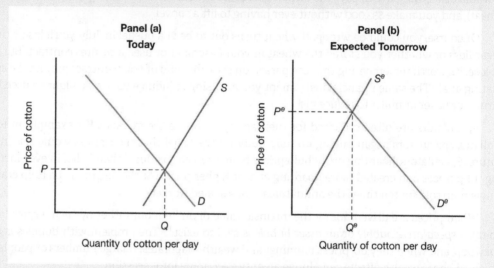

Panel (a)
Today

Panel (b)
Expected Tomorrow

Panel (a) above shows the state of the cotton market today. Panel (b) shows the expected state tomorrow. Suppose you are a professional cotton speculator.

a. How can you make money speculating in cotton? (Assume your beliefs about conditions in the cotton market are accurate.)

b. Show, by shifting the demand or supply curve in each panel, how your speculative activity helps stabilize prices and quantities in the cotton market.

c. What if your guess about tomorrow's price of cotton is wrong, and tomorrow's price turns out to be lower than today's? How will your speculative gamble affect the market?

See related Concept Problem 1 at the end of this chapter.

Case in Point: Not-So-Great Financial Instruments Touch Off Great Recession

The housing boom of the early 2000s was built on a financial house of cards. When one card slipped, the pyramid collapsed.

Source: Syda Productions/Shutterstock.com

No two recessions are exactly alike. Some are short, others long. Some are deep, others barely a blip. Some appear to happen spontaneously, without rhyme or reason. Others, like the COVID-19 recession of 2020, have a clear and observable cause. Of the dozen recessions since the end of World War II, the COVID-19 recession was the sharpest, with unemployment hitting 14.7% in April of 2020. But the COVID-19 recession was quick and dirty; the recovery began almost as fast as the virus had arrived. In contrast, the most painful of all the postwar recessions was surely the one now referred to as the Great Recession. Although unemployment "only" nudged 10% in the Great Recession, the recovery was so long and drawn out that it is now widely regarded as the worst economic downturn since the Great Depression of 1929–1933.

Both pundits and economists often blame the housing market collapse of 2007 for touching off the Great Recession. But in truth, the potential for such a calamity began a decade earlier, when the perfect storm of *financial innovation* (the development of new financial instruments), a relaxed regulatory environment, and an economic boom fueled by low interest rates made such a housing collapse possible.

Not long ago, someone who borrowed money to buy a house would have made monthly payments to the bank that made the loan. But about thirty-five years ago, banks began making loans and then selling the stream of future loan repayments to third parties in exchange for lump sums of cash. Many of those loans were sold to investment banks; even more were sold to two quasi-governmental corporations created to encourage home ownership: the Federal National Mortgage Association (Fannie Mae, created in 1938) and the Federal Home Loan Mortgage Corporation (Freddie Mac, created in 1970). Both Fannie Mae and Freddie Mac repackaged large blocks of the mortgages they'd purchased into special bonds called "mortgage-backed securities," using the stream of mortgage interest payments to pay the regular interest payments specified in the bond contract. Each bond, backed by a small slice of many home loans, was diversified and presumably low risk. Then Fannie Mae and Freddie Mac sold those bonds to large investors like mutual funds and pension funds.

If diversifying once is good, diversifying twice must surely be better, right? In the 1990s, investment bankers began combining payments from multiple mortgage-backed securities into yet another financial instrument called a collateralized debt obligation (CDO). Because they were double-diversified, they were believed to be extremely safe. That made them wildly popular with large investors, including foreign governments and investment banks.

The housing financial system was now three layers deep: mortgages combined into mortgage-backed securities combined into CDOs. Why not add another layer? The investors and investment banks who bought CDOs wanted to insure them against default; Wall Street responded by creating yet another financial instrument called a *credit default swap* that would compensate CDO holders if their investment went sour.

As we entered the 2000s, interest rates, low by historical standards, encouraged homeowners to take out more and larger loans. Banks were happy to play along—the financial innovations of the 1990s gave them the power to make loans and then sell the proceeds without bearing any repayment risk themselves. Their lending fueled a housing boom that sent prices spiraling upward, touching off a speculative flipping craze in which people would buy houses at very high prices in hopes of reselling shortly afterward at even higher prices. Tulip bulbs, anyone?

The government played its part, too. Under direction from the federal government, Fannie Mae and Freddie Mac increased purchases of mortgage loans that had been extended to less credit-worthy borrowers. (Those loans are referred to as subprime loans.) Banks and other mortgage lenders were happy to play along. They chased after high-risk borrowers with handfuls of cash, offering them adjustable-interest-rate mortgages with low introductory rates, knowing that those mortgages, which would be quickly resold and converted to CDOs, exposed them to no risk whatsoever. Those same lenders encouraged existing homeowners to refinance their existing mortgages, often offering new loans for more than a house was actually worth and letting the homeowner take the difference in cash.

The unprecedented housing boom soon gave credit default swaps a life of their own. Prescient speculators who owned no CDOs whatsoever were buying credit default swaps, gambling that the housing market itself and CDOs that financed it would go sour. Betting that the market will take a nosedive is called *shorting* the market; the negative bets these speculators took were so large and consequential that they eventually spawned an Oscar-winning movie starring Brad Pitt called *The Big Short*.

Those speculators saw something coming that the government and Wall Street did not. A booming economy led the Federal Reserve to begin raising interest rates, which increased from 2% in 2004 to 5% by May 2006. That was the beginning of the fall of the house of cards. Homeowners with adjustable-rate mortgages saw their monthly payments ratchet upward, and millions of them, subprime and otherwise, suddenly found themselves unable to make their payments. At the worst of the crisis, more than 10% of all mortgage holders nationwide had failed to make all of their scheduled house payments.

The effects of those defaults were quick and disastrous. With no mortgage revenue coming in, issuers of mortgage-backed securities and CDOs couldn't make their scheduled interest payments. Three renowned Wall Street investment banks with major CDO holdings collapsed, nearly dragging the entire U.S. financial system with them. The world's largest insurance company, American International Group (AIG), which had issued $400 billion of credit default swaps to insure CDOs against loss, could only pay its claims with the help of an enormous government bailout. With millions of homes in foreclosure, housing values plummeted. Worried about the tidal wave of foreclosures and the fragility of the financial system, banks quickly choked off lending to even the most credit-worthy homeowners and businesses. New construction disappeared, and consumption and business investment spending plummeted. Fueled by financial innovation, the Great Recession had begun.

See related Concept Problem 2 at the end of this chapter.

Source: Based on Lloyd B. Thomas's The Financial Crisis and Federal Reserve Policy (Palgrave-Macmillan, 2013).

Answers to Try It! Problems

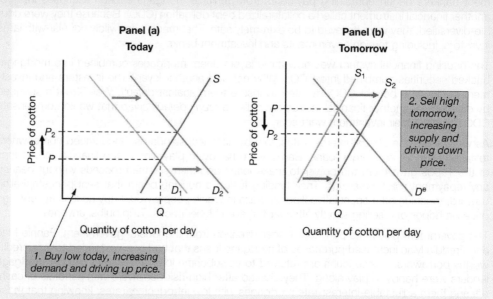

Panel (a) Today

Panel (b) Tomorrow

2. Sell high tomorrow, increasing supply and driving down price.

1. Buy low today, increasing demand and driving up price.

a. You can try to buy cotton today at a low price and sell it tomorrow at the high price you expect.

b. When you (and other speculators) try to buy cotton today, the demand for cotton increases, driving up the price. When you and others try to sell it tomorrow (to take advantage of the high price you expect), tomorrow's supply increases, driving down tomorrow's price. In this way, you reduce the variability of prices (see figure).

c. If your guess is wrong, and in the absence of speculation tomorrow's price turns out to be less than today's, then your actions will be destabilizing. Buying cotton today will drive up its price; selling it tomorrow will drive down its price even further. Speculation will widen the gap between today's and tomorrow's prices.

11.3 The Bond and Foreign Exchange Markets

Learning Objectives

1. Explain and illustrate how the bond market works and discuss the relationship between the price of a bond and that bond's interest rate.
2. Explain and illustrate the relationship between a change in the demand for or supply of bonds and macroeconomic activity.
3. Explain and illustrate how the foreign exchange market works and how a change in demand for a country's currency or a change in its supply affects macroeconomic activity.

All financial instruments may do the same four things, but not all financial instruments are created equal. In this section, we'll look at two financial instruments that play a more prominent role in the macroeconomy: bonds and foreign exchange. Events in these markets can have large macroeconomic effects; we'll briefly explore those effects in this section.

The Bond Market

The previous section introduced us to bonds, which are used by business firms and governments to raise funds for special projects and operations. When an institution first sells a bond, it receives the price paid for the bond as a kind of loan. The issuer then makes future payments to the buyer of the bond that exceed its price at issue. The difference between the value of those future payments and the price is interest, which means that the interest *rate* is determined both by the size of the future payments and by the price of the bond.

Bond Prices and Interest Rates

Let's take a closer look at a bond to see how it works. While the future payments that bond issuers make are structured in all kinds of different ways, the basic features can all be explored by looking at the simplest type of bond, a *discount bond*, which promises the purchaser a single payment at a specified future date.

Suppose you're the manager of a firm that makes flux capacitors, and you want to borrow money to install a robotic welder. To raise those funds, you print, say, 500 pieces of paper, each promising to pay the bearer (whoever it is that holds it when it's time for repayment) $1,000 in one year. Those papers are bonds! You then offer these bonds for sale to whoever bids the most.[12] Let's suppose that all of the bonds get snapped up for a price of $950 each. That means that you'll end up paying the buyers of the bonds $50 interest in exchange for a year's use of their money.[13]

face value of a bond

The amount the issuer of a bond will have to pay on the maturity date.

maturity date

The date when a bond matures, or comes due.

The $1,000 printed on each bond is the **face value of the bond**; it's the amount the issuer will have to pay on the date the loan comes due, which is called the **maturity date** of the bond. Finally, the price of each bond was $950.

The interest rate expresses the payment you make for the use of the bondholders' money, expressed as a percentage of the amount borrowed. That payment is the difference between the face value and the bond price, so the interest rate (multiplying by 100 to convert the decimal to a percentage) is:

EQUATION 11.1

$$\text{Interest Rate} = \frac{\text{Face Value} - \text{Bond Price}}{\text{Bond Price}} \times 100$$

$$\text{Interest Rate} = \frac{\$1,000 - \$950}{\$950} \times 100 = 5.3\%$$

At a price of $950, the interest rate is 5.3%. That means that the people who bought your bonds get all of their investment back, plus 5.3% more for delaying the use of their funds for themselves.

The interest rate on any bond is determined by its price. As the price falls, the total amount of interest earned by bondholders increases, and the interest rate rises. Suppose, for example, that the best price you can get for your company's bonds is $900. Now the interest rate is 11.1%:

$$\text{Interest Rate} = \frac{\$1,000 - \$900}{\$900} \times 100 = 11.1\%$$

A price of $800 would mean an interest rate of 25%; $750 would mean an interest rate of 33.3%. The lower the price of a bond relative to its face value, the higher the interest rate. The fundamental lesson is that bond prices and interest rates are inversely related: *When bond prices fall, interest rates rise. When interest rates fall, bond prices rise!*

Here's a reminder: The original buyer of a bond doesn't have to hold it until maturity! She can sell it halfway through the year for, say, $975. She will have earned $25 for half a year's use of her money; the new buyer will earn $25 for half a year's use of his money. [14]

In our example, the bonds your company issued sold for $950. Bonds are like apples—their prices are determined in the market by the forces of demand and supply. Figure 11.1 illustrates the bond market. The supply of bonds comes from firms like your flux capacitor company that want to sell bonds in order to raise cash. The supply of bonds is upward-sloping. At low prices (and high implied interest rates) borrowing is expensive to firms; few bonds will be issued. At high prices (and relatively low rates of interest) borrowing is cheaper; more firms will issue bonds and offer them for sale in the market.

The demand for bonds comes from people with money sitting idle who want to earn some return by lending it out. The demand for bonds is downward sloping. At high prices, savers don't earn a high rate of return. (Think about lending someone $999, and getting back $1,000 in a year. You're not making much money!) So, at high prices, fewer savers will lend their money by purchasing bonds. At low prices, investors receive a high implied rate of interest; that convinces more savers to offer up their money for loans by purchasing bonds.

Bond prices are very flexible, and they will quickly adjust to ensure that the quantity of bonds demanded equals the quantity supplied. Suppose, for example, that the initial price of bonds is $950, as shown by the intersection of the demand and supply curves in Figure 11.1. If surging optimism convinces firms to increase their borrowing by offering more bonds for sale at each interest rate, the supply of bonds will increase from S_1 to S_2. The equilibrium price of bonds will fall to $900, driving the interest rate up to 11.1%.

It's easy to get turned around backwards when the same market contains two "prices," like the bond market does: the price of bonds and the price of using someone else's money (the interest rate). But notice how the result we just got makes intuitive sense. Business firms wanted access to

Because math.

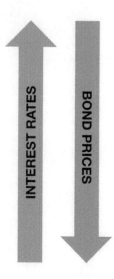

INTEREST RATES   BOND PRICES

more money, and in competing for that scarce resource with one another, drove up the interest rate, its price.

FIGURE 11.1 The Bond Market

The equilibrium price of bonds is determined by the demand for bonds and the supply of bonds. The initial price of $950 and the implied interest rate, 5.3%, is determined by D_1 and S_1. An increase in the desire to borrow increases the supply of bonds to S_2 and forces the price of bonds down to $900. The interest rate rises to 11.1%.

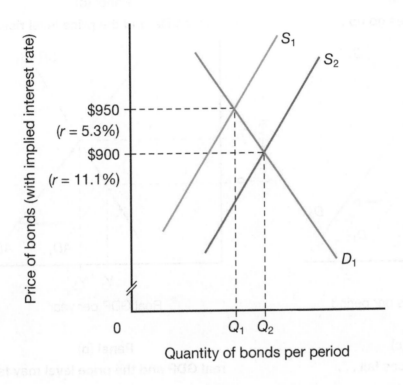

The Bond Market and Macroeconomic Performance

You might be wondering why, out of all the financial instruments we *could* be studying, we chose the bond market. We're particularly interested in the bond market because it's there that interest rates are determined (as we just saw in Figure 11.1), and interest rates have a strong influence on aggregate demand. Investment, for example, is one component of aggregate demand that is sensitive to the interest rate. If interest rates are high, borrowing the money needed to fund new capital is costly, so firms are likely to spend less on investment goods. Those same firms are more likely to add capital if interest rates are low.[15]

That links the bond market, bond prices, and aggregate demand. If bond prices fall, driving interest rates up, that will discourage investment and aggregate demand will decrease. A fall in aggregate demand, other things unchanged, will mean fewer jobs and less total output than would have been the case at a lower interest rate. It works in the other direction, too: An increase in the price of bonds reduces interest rates and makes investment in new capital more attractive. The increase in investment causes an increase in aggregate demand.

Figure 11.2 shows how an event in the bond market can stimulate changes in the economy's output and price level (which measures the average level of prices in the economy). In Panel (a), an increase in the demand for bonds raises bond prices and forces interest rates downward. Lower interest rates make investment more attractive; aggregate demand shifts to the right, from AD_1 to AD_2 in Panel (b). Real GDP rises from Y_1 to Y_2; the price level rises from P_1 to P_2.

This pipeline factory seems far removed from the canyons of Wall Street. But the interest rates that are determined in New York City can make or break this company.

Source: Gorodenkoff/Shutterstock.com

FIGURE 11.2 Bond Prices and Macroeconomic Activity

An increase in the demand for bonds from D_1 to D_2 in Panel (a) raises the price of bonds and reduces interest rates, boosting investment. Increased investment increases aggregate demand from AD_1 to AD_2 in Panel (b); real GDP rises from Y_1 to Y_2 and the price level increases from P_1 to P_2. An increase in the supply of bonds from S_1 to S_2 is shown in Panel (c). The increased supply forces bond prices downward and raises interest rates. Higher interest rates cause reduced investment; as a result, aggregate demand decreases from AD_1 to AD_2, as shown in Panel (d). Real GDP falls from Y_1 to Y_2, and the price level falls from P_1 to P_2.

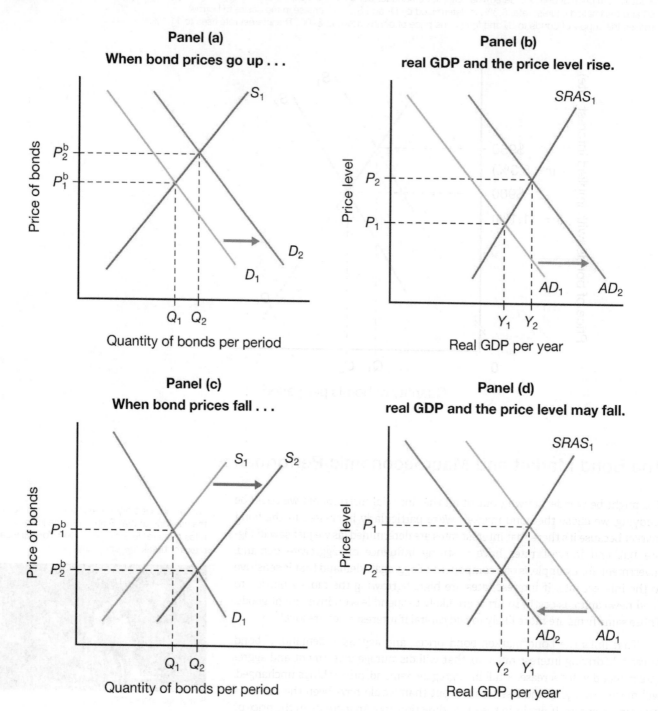

Panels (c) and (d) in Figure 11.2 explore an increase in the supply of bonds. In Panel (c), an increase in the supply of bonds pushes bond prices down and drives interest rates upward. The increase in interest rates discourages some investment and shifts aggregate demand to the left, from AD_1 to AD_2 in Panel (d). Output and the price level fall from Y_1 to Y_2 and from P_1 to P_2, respectively.

These two markets—the bond market and the market for goods and services—are interrelated. We've been focused on how changes in financial markets can cause changes in aggregate demand. But causation can flow in both directions: Some events that change aggregate demand can affect interest rates. We'll take a closer look at those events in the chapters to come.

Foreign Exchange Markets

Another financial market that wields a strong influence over macroeconomic variables is the **foreign exchange market**, a market where currencies of different countries are traded for one another. Because changes in exports and imports affect aggregate demand, real GDP, and the price level, the foreign exchange market has tremendous importance.

Foreigners who want to purchase goods, services, or assets in the United States generally have to pay for them with dollars. An Egyptian family visiting Disney, for example, has to exchange Egyptian pounds for U.S. dollars in order to pay for admission; a German financial investor who wants to buy shares in Tesla first has to trade some of his euros for the dollars he needs to buy the stock.

> **foreign exchange market**
>
> A market in which currencies of different countries are traded for one another.

The foreign exchange market works in both directions: People in the United States who want to buy foreign goods generally have to make payment in the seller's currency. A family from the United States visiting India needs to obtain Indian rupees in order to make purchases there. A U.S. bank wanting to purchase real estate in Mexico City must first purchase pesos. These transactions are accomplished in the foreign exchange market.

The foreign exchange market isn't a single location. Instead it's an entire array of institutions through which people buy and sell currencies—from hotel desk clerks who change guests' pounds into dollars, to brokers who arrange billion-dollar transactions for multinational corporations, to governments and central banks that exchange currencies between one another.

This mom-and-pop currency exchange in Florence, Italy, is as much a part of the foreign exchange market as the biggest banks in London, Tokyo, and New York.

Source: Nataly Reinch/Shutterstock.com

The Exchange Rate

When you go to the foreign exchange market to buy Swiss francs, you'll discover that francs, like coffee and like the bonds we just learned about, have a price. A country's **exchange rate** is the price of its currency in terms of another currency. On November 11, 2020, for example, an American who wants to purchase a British 1-pound (£) coin would have to pay \$1.32. That's a price—the dollar price of a British pound—but it's generally expressed as an exchange rate: 1.32 dollars per pound, or using E to represent the exchange rate, $E_{\$/£} = 1.32$.

> **exchange rate**
>
> The price of one country's currency in terms of another country's currency.

Out of all the prices in the economy, exchange rates are special, because they're really two prices in one. Consider, for example, the dollar–pound exchange rate we just discussed. That exchange rate tells us how many dollars it takes to buy a pound, but it *also* tells us how many pounds it will take a Brit to buy a dollar. A little algebra shows us why: If \$1.32 = £1, then dividing both sides by 1.32 tells us that \$1 = £(1/1.32) = £0.76. So, the pound–dollar exchange rate, 0.76 pounds per dollar, is the reciprocal of the dollar–pound exchange rate we calculated above, or $E_{£/\$} = 1/E_{\$/£}$.

We've just shown that each exchange rate contains two different prices (the price of the pound in dollars and the price of the dollar in pounds, for example). That makes it really important to keep track of units: Dollars per pound is not the same as pounds per dollar!

Don't get turned upside down—keep track of your units when you're doing foreign exchange calculations! (You'll make your algebra teacher proud, too!)

Source: ESB Professional/Shutterstock.com

There are lots of exchange rates—hundreds in fact. On the same day that a dollar could be traded for 0.76 British pounds, it could have just as easily been traded for 0.85 euros, 105.4 Japanese yen, 3.81 Polish zloty, or 20.5 Mexican pesos. There are as many exchange rates for the dollar as there are currencies . . . and each of those currencies trades for one another in foreign exchange markets, too.

Determining Exchange Rates

The rates at which most currencies exchange for one another are determined by the forces of demand and supply.[16] How does the model of demand and supply operate in the foreign exchange market?

Let's look at the market for U.S. dollars.[17] The demand curve for dollars stems from foreigners' desire to acquire dollars to purchase goods, services, and assets. The demand for dollars shows the number of dollars foreigners want to buy at any given exchange rate, with the exchange rate is quoted in units of foreign currency (FC) per dollar, $E_{FC/\$}$. Quoted in that way, a higher exchange rate means it takes more foreign currency to buy a dollar, so a higher exchange rate makes U.S. goods and services more expensive for foreign buyers. That reduces the quantity of goods and services they'll demand. So, at higher exchange rates, fewer dollars are likely to be demanded, and the demand for dollars slopes downward, as shown in Figure 11.3.

FIGURE 11.3 Determining an Exchange Rate
The equilibrium exchange rate is the rate at which the quantity of dollars demanded equals the quantity supplied. Here, equilibrium occurs at exchange rate $E_{FC/\$}$, and Q dollars are exchanged per period.

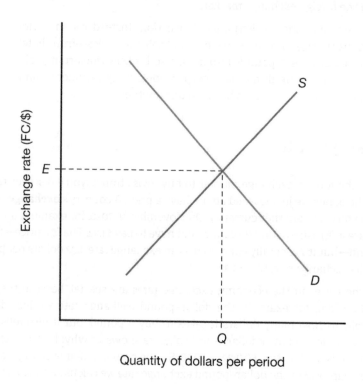

Where does the supply curve for dollars come from? It helps to picture a bunch of Americans, walking into the foreign exchange market with wads of dollar bills in their outstretched hands. Those Americans are anxious to use those dollars to buy the foreign currency needed to buy foreign-produced goods and services.

Without trying to make things confusing, we hope it's clear from this example that *the supply of dollars is the same thing as the demand for foreign currency . . . and the demand for dollars is like-*

wise the supply of foreign currency! In other words, the market for dollars presented in Figure 11.3 is nothing more than a mirror image of the market for foreign currency.

A higher exchange rate $E_{FC/\$}$ means that one dollar will fetch more foreign currency. So, higher exchange rates make foreign goods and services cheaper to U.S. buyers. At higher exchange rates, then, U.S. consumers will want to purchase more foreign goods and services, and will require more foreign currency to do so. Because of this, we expect U.S. consumers to supply more dollars at a higher exchange rates than they do at lower exchange rates, and the supply curve for dollars will slope upward, as shown in Figure 11.3.

The forces of demand and supply determine the price of a dollar (in units of foreign currency) in the same way they determine the price of wheat.[18] Exchange rates, which are generally quite free to move up and down, quickly adjust to equate quantity demanded and quantity supplied. In Figure 11.3 that happens at the exchange rate, E, with Q dollars being traded for foreign currency in the market.

Wanna slide behind the wheel of this curvylicious Italian beast? Then buy some euros, because Enzo Ferrari has no use for dollars!

Source: Kevin Tichenor/Shutterstock.com

Exchange Rates and Macroeconomic Performance

People purchase a country's currency for two different reasons: to purchase goods or services in that country, or to purchase the assets of that country—its capital, its stocks, its bonds, or its real estate. Both of these motives must be considered to understand why demand and supply in the foreign exchange market may change.

One thing that can cause the price of the dollar to rise, for example, is a decrease in bond prices in American markets. Figure 11.4 illustrates the effect of this change. Suppose the supply of bonds in the U.S. bond market increases from S_1 to S_2 in Panel (a). Bond prices will decrease, and because bond prices and interest rates are inversely related, interest rates will rise.

An increase in interest rates attracts investors both at home and abroad. Foreign financial investors interested in taking advantage of high returns in the United States increase their demand for dollars in order to purchase U.S. bonds. Panel (b) shows that the demand curve for dollars shifts from D_1 to D_2. U.S. financial investors are also now finding U.S. bonds more attractive. That causes them to make fewer financial investments abroad, and reduces their need to acquire foreign currency to purchase those foreign financial assets. The supply of dollars to the foreign exchange market decreases from S_1 to S_2. The increase in the demand for dollars, coupled with a decrease in the supply of dollars, forces the exchange rate upward from E_1 to E_2.

FIGURE 11.4 Shifts in Demand and Supply for Dollars on the Foreign Exchange Market
In Panel (a), an increase in the supply of bonds forces bond prices downward and interest rates upward. Higher interest rates boost the demand for, and reduce the supply of dollars, increasing the exchange rate in Panel (b) from E_1 to E_2. Higher interest rates lead to less domestic investment; higher exchange rates make imports less expensive and exports less attractive to foreigners, driving down net exports. Aggregate demand decreases from AD_1 to AD_2 in Panel (c). The price level in the economy falls to P_2, and real GDP falls from Y_1 to Y_2.

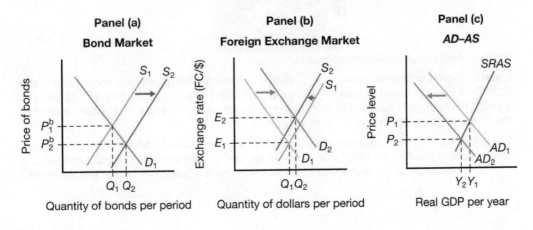

The higher exchange rate makes U.S. goods and services more expensive to foreigners, so it reduces exports. It makes foreign goods cheaper for U.S. buyers, so it increases imports. Net exports decrease, reducing aggregate demand. Panel (c) shows that output falls from Y_1 to Y_2; the price level falls from P_1 to P_2. This development in the foreign exchange market reinforces the impact of higher interest rates we observed in Figure 11.2, Panels (c) and (d). They not only reduce investment—they reduce net exports as well.

Key Takeaways

- A bond represents a borrower's debt; bond prices are determined by demand and supply.
- The interest rate on a bond is negatively related to the price of the bond. As the price of a bond increases, the interest rate falls.
- An increase in the interest rate tends to decrease the quantity of investment demanded and, hence, to decrease aggregate demand. A decrease in the interest rate increases the quantity of investment demanded and aggregate demand.
- The demand for dollars on foreign exchange markets represents foreign demand for U.S. goods, services, and assets. The supply of dollars on foreign exchange markets represents U.S. demand for foreign goods, services, and assets. The demand for and the supply of dollars determine the exchange rate.
- A rise in U.S. interest rates will increase the demand for dollars and decrease the supply of dollars on foreign exchange markets. As a result, the exchange rate will increase and aggregate demand will decrease. A fall in U.S. interest rates will have the opposite effect.

Try It!

Suppose the supply of bonds in the U.S. market decreases. Show and explain the effects on the bond and foreign exchange markets. Use the aggregate demand/aggregate supply framework to show and explain the effects on investment, net exports, real GDP, and the price level.

See related Concept Problem 11 at the end of this chapter.

Case in Point: Wouldn't You Think a COVID-19 Vaccine Would Be Good News?

COVID-19 vaccine: Great for humans; lousy for bonds.

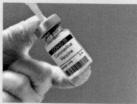

Source: Maria Kaminska/Shutterstock.com

On the morning of Monday, November 5, 2020, pharmaceutical giant Pfizer announced that a COVID-19 vaccine it had developed in conjunction with German firm BioNTech had breezed through the third and final stage of testing and would become available to the public as soon as the Food and Drug Administration granted approval.

It was the news teachers, children, grandparents, health care workers, and politicians across the globe had been waiting the better part of a year for, and it came just as a huge autumn surge in COVID-19 cases began to overwhelm hospitals once again. Pfizer's third-stage results showed that the vaccine could prevent more than 90% of recipients from getting COVID-19, and BioNTech founder Ugur Sahin added that the vaccine could potentially halve transmission of the virus, suggesting that life might return to something approaching normal by the following winter.

The announcement immediately touched off a huge wave of financial optimism, which sent stock futures soaring in pre-hours trading. When markets opened, stocks rallied, finishing the day strongly upward by 3%. And why not? With a safe, highly effective vaccine on tap, the promise of returning to some semblance of normalcy was a strong positive omen for health care professionals, students, and the businesses that form the core of the global economy. You'd think everyone would be feeling optimistic, right?

Everyone, that is, except bond traders. Within minutes of the announcement, Citigroup's head of Rates Strategy, Jabaz Mathai, said the development was "unambiguously bearish" for long-term government-issued Treasury bonds. Mathia was right: While stock prices surged, bond prices crumbled. What on earth?

The most straightforward answer is that with a solution on the horizon, prospects for higher corporate earnings increased and drove up the demand for stocks. But the money used to pay for those stocks had to come from somewhere, and that somewhere was bonds. As trading continued through the day, investors moved money *en masse* from the safe, secure government bonds they'd parked so much money in at the beginning of the crisis back into the riskier stocks they'd abandoned.

The second answer to the "why bonds tanked" question draws on our knowledge of both expectations and the inverse relationship between bond prices and interest rates. The coronavirus crisis and the accompanying Federal Reserve response had pushed interest rates to all-time lows. With the prospect of a healthy economy once again on the table, investors began to anticipate the Fed's usual response to a boom: an increase in interest rates designed to keep price inflation under control. *The vaccine hadn't even been approved yet, and already investors were anticipating not only its effects on the economy, but also the policy response. That's foresight!*

The mere prospect of higher long-term interest rates in the future caused long-term rates to jump sharply at the opening bell on November 9, 2020. Why did this happen? Remember this mantra about interest rates and bond prices: *When interest rates rise, bond prices fall.* Investors, seeing interest rates at historical lows, anticipated a future increase . . . an increase that would cause the value of bonds to plummet. To avoid losing money as bond prices fell, bond traders "took their gains" by quickly selling off their bond holdings. It was that increase in the supply of bonds that caused bond prices to plummet, exactly as expected. *Prophecy, self-fulfilled!*

There are a couple of big lessons in the events of November 9, 2020. First, the old saying that "One man's trash is another man's treasure," was proven correct: While most of the world celebrated the good news, bondholders suffered. Second, November 9 serves as a good reminder that the macroeconomy is a complex place, with lots of interconnected moving parts: For every part that turns forward, another turns backward. Part of the joy of economics is understanding those interconnections and not being surprised when something unexpected occurs.

See related Concept Problem 13 at the end of this chapter.

Sources: Based on "Covid-19: Normal Life Back Next Winter, Says Vaccine Creator," BBC News, November 15, 2020; Sunny Oh, "Here's Why the Biggest Bond Market Selloff Since March May Run Out of Steam," MarketWatch.com, November 10, 2020; and Colby Smith, "Covid Vaccine News Sends Tremors Through Bond Market," Financial Times, November 12, 2020.

Answer to Try It! Problem

If the supply of bonds decreases from S_1 to S_2, bond prices will rise from P^b_1 to P^b_2, as shown in Panel (a). Higher bond prices mean lower interest rates, which will make financial investments in the United States less attractive to foreigners. As a result, their demand for dollars will decrease from D_1 to D_2, as shown in Panel (b). Similarly, U.S. financial investors will look abroad for higher returns and thus supply more dollars to foreign exchange markets, shifting the supply curve from S_1 to S_2. The exchange rate decreases from E_1 to E_2.

The quantity of investment rises due to lower interest rates. Net exports rise because the lower exchange rate makes U.S. goods and services more attractive to foreigners (increasing exports), and makes foreign goods less attractive to U.S. buyers (reducing imports). Increases in investment and net exports imply a rightward shift in the aggregate demand curve from AD_1 to AD_2. Real GDP and the price level increase.

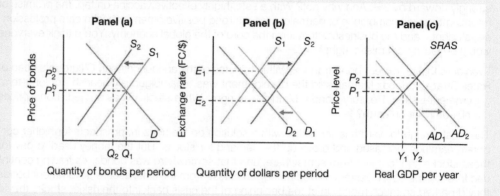

Khan Academy Links

Introduction to bonds

Relationship between bond prices and interest rates

Exchange rate primer

Currency exchange introduction

Supply and demand for foreign exchange

11.4 Demand, Supply, and Equilibrium in the Money Market

Learning Objectives

1. Explain the motives for holding money and relate them to the interest rate that could be earned from holding alternative assets, such as bonds.
2. Draw a money demand curve and explain how changes in other variables may lead to shifts in the money demand curve.
3. Illustrate and explain the notion of equilibrium in the money market.
4. Use graphs to explain how changes in money demand or money supply are related to changes in the bond market, in interest rates, in aggregate demand, and in real GDP and the price level.

We're about to begin learning about stabilization policy—how the government and the central bank can attempt to guide the economy toward the full employment of its scarce resources. In the previous chapter, you learned how the central bank can engineer changes in the money supply.

During that discussion, we made passing mention that changes in the money supply ultimately cause changes in interest rates, but we never really explored how that happens.

This section closes the loop by developing a demand and supply model for money. We'll start by looking at the demand for money, which shows the relationship between the "price" of money (which, we'll see, is the interest rate) and the quantity of money demanded. Then we'll combine money demand with the supply of money we developed in the last chapter to determine the equilibrium rate of interest. Finally, we'll show how changes in interest rates can affect the macro-economy.

The Demand for Money

People with wealth have to decide how they'd like to hold it.[19] "Should I store my wealth in hundred dollar bills shoved into a slit in my matress? Should I buy stock in Tesla? Or should I buy that collectible Porsche I've always lusted after?" The answer to those questions depends on the relative costs and benefits of holding money instead of some other asset. The **demand for money** is the relationship between the quantity of money people want to hold and the factors that determine that quantity.

> **demand for money**
>
> The relationship between the quantity of money people want to hold and the factors that determine that quantity.

Let's build a simple model of money demand. Let's start by assuming that there are only two ways to hold wealth: as money in a checking account, or in shares of a mutual fund that purchases long-term bonds on behalf of its subscribers. These two options have relative pros and cons: Checking accounts earn little or no interest (we'll assume no interest in our example); bond funds likely do. But checking accounts are highly liquid; bond funds are less so. Limiting our options to these two lets us picture the demand for money as a curve illustrating the trade-off between the greater liquidity of money deposits and the higher interest rates that can be earned in a bond fund.

Motives for Holding Money

Why would we want to hold money when we could hold a higher-yielding bond fund instead? One reason people hold their assets in the form of money is that they'll need that money to purchase goods and services—buying groceries, paying tuition, going to the movies, making the mortgage payment . . . and let's not forget essentials like beer and pizza! The **transactions demand for money** is money people hold to pay for goods and services they anticipate buying. An individual's transactions demand for money often depends on their income: People with higher incomes tend to buy more (and more expensive) things; they need more money to finance those purchases.

Gotta pay the piper . . . or, you know, the pizza guy. The more you eat, the more money you'll need: That's transactions demand.

Source: Serhii Bobyk/Shutterstock.com

The transactions demand for money exists because people have ordinary purchases and recurring transactions that they plan to spend money on. But sometimes, life throws a curveball, and people find themselves facing unexpected expenditures: A bat gets into an AC unit and short-circuits your home's cooling system; you take a bad fall and end up with your leg in a cast; a pipe bursts and turns your basement into an indoor swimming pool. Lots of people create an emergency fund just for unexpected events like these. The money they set aside represents their **precautionary demand for money**.

> **transactions demand for money**
>
> Money people hold to pay for goods and services they anticipate buying.

> **precautionary demand for money**
>
> The money people hold for contingencies.

People also hold money to take advantage of financial market opportunities . . . or to avoid financial catastrophe. For example, we know that bond prices fluctuate constantly, and as a result, bondholders will not only earn interest but may also experience gains or losses in the value of their bonds. Economist John Maynard Keynes (who was an enormously successful speculator in bond markets himself), suggested that bondholders who anticipate a drop in bond prices will try to sell their bonds for cash ahead of the price drop. On the other hand, investors may sit on a pile of cash waiting for a time when they believe bond prices have bottomed out and will begin turning around, and then plunge that cash into bonds once that point is reached. Keynes referred to the cash that investors sit on while waiting for a good investment opportunity as the **speculative demand for money**.

Of course, money is money—it all looks alike. That makes it hard to sort through someone's checking account and determine which funds are held for transactions, which are "just in case" money, and which are there because the owner of the account is worried about a drop in bond prices. We distinguish money held for different motives in order to understand how the quantity of money demanded will be affected by a key determinant of the demand for money: the interest rate.

Can't Be Too Careful: "Wish I'd had some some emergency cash set aside during the coronavirus TP shortage . . ."

Source: Hung Chung Chih/ Shutterstock.com

Interest Rates and the Demand for Money

The quantity of money people hold to pay for transactions and to satisfy their precautionary and speculative demand is likely to depend, in part, on the interest rates available to them from investing in alternative assets like bonds. When interest rates rise, the opportunity cost of holding money increases and people will try to reduce their money holdings. When interest rates are low, there's not much of an opportunity cost to holding money; piles of cash (or checking account balances) tend to grow. The logic of these conclusions about the money people hold and interest rates depends on the different motives for holding money.

Time Is Money: "I reduced my money demand and put my money to work . . . but I've doubled my trips to the bank."

Source: wavebreakmedia/ Shutterstock.com

Transactions and Precautionary Demand. Let's consider the transactions demand for money. The quantity of money households want to hold for transactions purposes depends, as we mentioned, on their income: People with higher incomes tend to buy more goods and services. But the transactions demand can also depend on the interest rate. To see why, let's consider Andre, who makes $3000 on the first of each month and spends it evenly, $100 per day, until the next payday. One way Andre could manage his spending would be to deposit his paycheck in his checking account and leave it there, drawing it out as needed. He'd have $3,000 on payday morning, $2,900 at the end of the first day, $2,800 at the end of the second, $1,500 halfway through the month, and he would just hit zero in the last minute of the last hour of the last day of the month. Andre's average daily balances, his average transactions demand, would be $1,500. This approach to money management, which we'll call the "cash approach," is simple, but it comes at a cost: Andre earns no interest.

Is there a way Andre can maintain the same spending pattern but earn a bit of interest? Of course! Consider this approach: At the beginning of the month, he deposits $1,500 in his checking account and puts the other $1,500 in a bond fund that pays 1% interest per month. Halfway through the month, Andre's checking account is exhausted, so he pulls $1,500 out of his bond fund and resumes spending as usual. With this strategy, Andre has an average daily money (checking account) balance of $750 rather than $1,500. Let's call this money management strategy the "bond fund approach."

Both approaches allow Andre to spend $100 per day, $3,000 per month. But the bond fund approach generates some interest income for Andre.[20] However, those earnings come at a cost—Andre must arrange two additional transactions (the deposit into the bond fund and the withdrawal from the bond fund), and pay any fees associated with those transactions. The higher the interest rate available through the bond fund, the more likely that the benefits—interest earnings—outweigh those costs, and the more likely Andre is to use the bond fund approach.[21] Additionally, the lower the costs associated with money management are, the more likely Andre is to use the bond fund approach. The creation of savings plans in the 1980s that allowed easy transfer of funds between interest-earning assets and checkable deposits reduced the demand for money; so did the rise of low-cost, one-click internet investment accounts in the 1990s and early 2000s.

Speculative Demand. We've just seen how the transactions demand for money depends on the interest rate (and by the same token, precautionary balances are more likely to be tucked into a bond fund when interest rates are high). How is the speculative demand for money related to interest rates?

When financial investors believe that the prices of bonds and other assets will fall, their speculative demand for money goes up—they convert out of bonds and back into cash. But when bond prices are high (and therefore likely to fall), interest rates are low. So, at low interest rates, the speculative demand for money will be high.

What if interest rates are high? When interest rates are high, they're more likely to decrease in the future. As interest rates fall, bond prices will rise and financial investors will enjoy capital gains. So at high interest rates, financial investors are likely to minimize their cash holdings and buy lots of bonds, instead. That means that the speculative demand for money, like the transactions and precautionary demands for money, is inversely related to the level of interest rates.

The Demand Curve for Money

The transactions, precautionary, and speculative demands for money are all likely to be negatively related to the interest rate. Putting those three sources of money demand together, we can draw a **demand curve for money** that shows the quantity of money demanded at each interest rate, all other things unchanged. Figure 11.5 shows that an increase in the interest rate reduces the quantity of money demanded; a decrease in the interest rate increases the quantity of money demanded.

demand curve for money

Curve that shows the quantity of money demanded at each interest rate, all other things unchanged.

FIGURE 11.5 The Demand Curve for Money
The demand curve for money shows the quantity of money demanded at each interest rate. Its downward slope expresses the negative relationship between the quantity of money demanded and the interest rate.

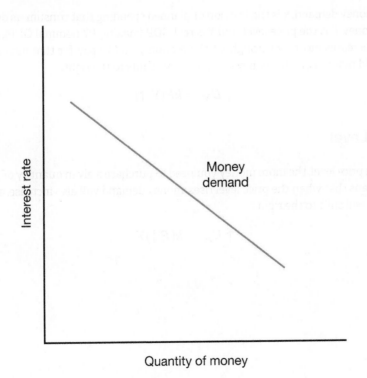

The relationship between interest rates and the quantity of money demanded is just an application of the law of demand, where the price of holding money is foregone interest, a price that grows with the interest rate. As is the case with pickles, duct tape, tea, and just about any other good or service you could name, an increase in price reduces the quantity demanded.

Money Demand Shifters

The money demand curve shows the quantity of money people want to hold at various interest rates, all other things held constant. But just like the demand for peanut butter depends on factors other than just its price, money demand depends on factors in addition to the interest rate.[22] Instead of moving us up and down *along* the money demand curve, a change in those other factors will *shift* the money demand curve to the left (a decrease in money demand) or the right (an increase in money demand). What are those factors? Among the most important are the level of income (or real GDP), the price level, expectations about the future, transfer costs, and preferences. Let's look at each one in turn.

Real GDP

When you're buying more bling, you're needing more green!

Source: More Than Production/ Shutterstock.com

A household with an income of $10,000 per month is likely to demand more money at any given interest rate than a household with an income of $1,000 per month. The difference mainly stems from differences in the two households' transactions demands: Households that make more spend more, and need more money on hand to finance that spending.

Let's scale that up to the entire economy. Economists at Cambridge in the early 1900s theorized that desired money holdings at a given interest rate were proportional to the economy's total spending. But remember that an economy's total spending is just nominal GDP! So,

$$D_M = kPY$$

where D_M is money demand, k is the fraction of planned spending that consumers desire to hold in the form of money, P is the price level, and Y is real GDP (making PY nominal GDP). An increase in real GDP (Y) increases incomes throughout the economy, and to pay for that increased spending, consumers hold more cash. The money demand curve shifts to the right.

$$\uparrow D_M = kP(Y \uparrow)$$

The Price Level

The higher the price level, the more money you need to purchase a given quantity of goods and services. That means that when the price level rises, money demand will also increase, and the money demand curve will shift to the right.

$$\uparrow D_M = k(P \uparrow)Y$$

FIGURE 11.6 An Increase in Money Demand
An increase in real GDP or the price level will increase the quantity of money demanded at any interest rate r. Money demand increases (shifts right) from D_1 to D_2. The quantity of money demanded at interest rate r rises from M to M'. A fall in the price level or real GDP would reduce the quantity of money demanded at every interest rate, shifting the money demand curve to the left.

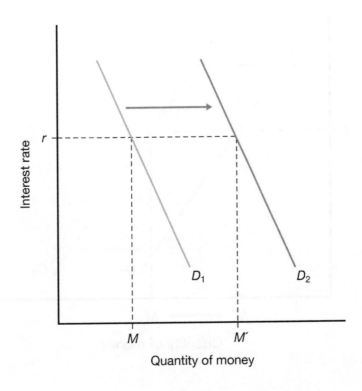

Expectations

The speculative demand for money is based on expectations about bond prices. All other things unchanged, if people expect bond prices to fall, they will increase their demand for money (the money demand curve will shift right). If they expect bond prices to rise, they will reduce their demand for money (the money demand curve will shift left).

Expectations about future price levels also affect the demand for money. An increase in the expected future price level means that people expect the money they are holding to fall in value. To avoid that loss, people try to reduce their money holdings, both at any given interest rate and for any given level of income. Money demand decreases, caused by a decrease in k.

$$\downarrow D_M = (\downarrow k)PY$$

That reaction to prices becomes particularly noticeable in periods of hyperinflation, when prices keep rising faster and faster. In hyperinflations, people try to get rid of cash as fast as it comes in, quickly converting their paychecks into goods and services. For more on this, see "Case in Point: Ay Caracas! Inflation, Venezuelan Style".

FIGURE 11.7 A Decrease in Money Demand

An increase in expected inflation will nudge consumers to reduce their money demand from D_1 to D_2. At every level of the interest rate, consumers will hold less money. For example, at interest rate r, consumers will reduce money holdings from M to M'.

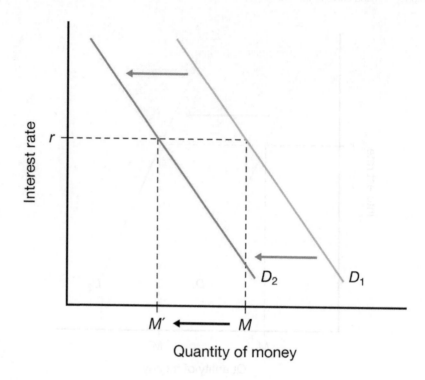

Transfer Costs

Our representative money demander, Andre, had to choose between the cash approach to money management and the bond fund approach. One factor that might affect his decision besides the level of interest rates is how easy it is to implement the bond fund approach. If moving wealth from money into bonds is costly (maybe because of commissions, or maybe because it requires a trip to the bank), Andre will be less interested in taking that approach and will have high money demand. If the costs of adopting the bond fund approach fall, Andre will take advantage of that lower cost by putting more of his wealth in bonds and holding less as money; money demand will decrease (shift leftward).

Preferences

Preferences also play a role in determining the demand for money. Some people place a high value on having a considerable amount of money on hand. For others, this may not be important.

Household attitudes toward risk are another aspect of preferences that affect money demand. As we have seen, bonds pay higher interest rates than money deposits, but holding bonds entails a risk that bond prices might fall. There is also a chance that the issuer of a bond will default, that is, will not pay the amount specified on the bond to bondholders; indeed, bond issuers may end up paying nothing at all. A money deposit, such as a savings deposit, might earn a lower yield, but it is a safe yield. People's attitudes about the trade-off between risk and yields affect the degree to which they hold their wealth as money. Heightened concerns about risk in the last half of 2008, for example, led many households to increase their demand for money.

The Supply of Money

The **supply curve of money** shows the relationship between the quantity of money supplied and the market interest rate. In the previous chapter, we saw that the Fed can set the money supply to any level it desires, regardless of the interest rate. In Figure 11.8, then, we show the money supply curve as a vertical line: At any rate of interest, the Fed can use open-market operations and its other tools of policy to peg the money stock at M.

FIGURE 11.8 The Supply Curve of Money
We assume that the quantity of money supplied in the economy is determined by, and completely controllable by, the Fed. Because the money supply doesn't depend on the interest rate, the money supply curve is vertical at the Fed's chosen level of the money stock, M.

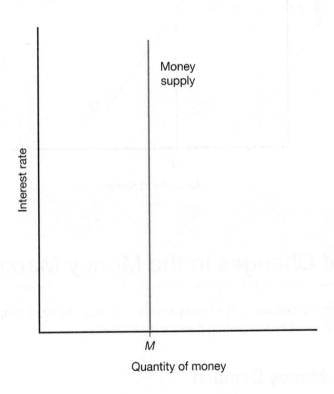

Equilibrium in the Market for Money

The **money market** consists of the institutions through which money is supplied to individuals, firms, and other institutions that demand money. In the money market, the interest rate adjusts to equate the quantity of money supplied and the quantity of money demanded, or **money market equilibrium**. Figure 11.9 combines demand and supply curves for money to illustrate money market equilibrium. With a stock of money (M), the equilibrium interest rate is r.

supply curve of money

Curve that shows the relationship between the quantity of money supplied and the market interest rate, all other determinants of supply unchanged.

money market

The institutions through which money is supplied to individuals, firms, and other institutions that demand money.

money market equilibrium

The interest rate at which the quantity of money demanded is equal to the quantity of money supplied.

FIGURE 11.9 Money Market Equilibrium

The market for money is in equilibrium if the quantity of money demanded is equal to the quantity of money supplied. Here, equilibrium occurs at interest rate *r*.

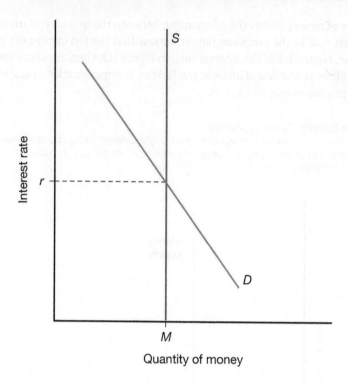

Effects of Changes in the Money Market

A shift in either money demand or the money supply will cause the equilibrium interest rate to change. Let's look at the effects of such changes on the economy.

Changes in Money Demand

Suppose that the money market is initially in equilibrium at r_1 with money supply curve *S* and a money demand curve D_1, as shown in Panel (a) of Figure 11.10. Now suppose that money demand decreases from D_1 to D_2. That decrease could result from a decrease in the cost of transferring between money and nonmoney deposits, from a change in expectations, or from a change in preferences.[23] At the current interest rate *r*, there is more money circulating than people want to hold, which puts downward pressure on interest rates. As interest rates decrease, people become more willing to hold money (its opportunity cost decreases); interest rates will continue to decrease until the quantity of money demanded once again equals the quantity of money supplied.

FIGURE 11.10 A Decrease in the Demand for Money

A decrease in the demand for money due to a change in transactions costs, preferences, or expectations, as shown in Panel (a), will be accompanied by an increase in the demand for bonds as shown in Panel (b), and a fall in the interest rate. The fall in the interest rate will cause a rightward shift in the aggregate demand curve from AD_1 to AD_2, as shown in Panel (c). As a result, real GDP and the price level rise.

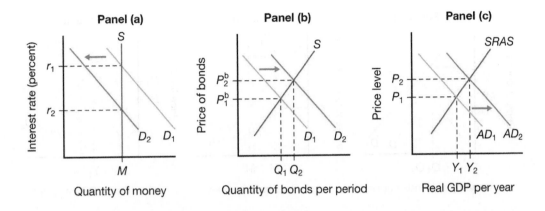

An alternative way to explain the change in interest rates is to think about what happens in the bond market. The decrease in money demand means that people like Andre in our example above are abandoning the cash management approach in favor of the bond fund approach. The demand for bonds increases, as shown in Panel (b); the price of bonds increases, and their implied interest rate decreases.

The changes in the money market have macroeconomic effects. The decrease in interest rates causes an increase in investment spending. It also stimulates net exports because lower interest rates lead to a lower exchange rate.[24] Both the change in investment and the change in net exports cause aggregate demand to increase; the AD curve shifts to the right, as shown in Panel (c), from AD_1 to AD_2, causing an increase in real GDP and an increase in the price level.

That process, of course, works in reverse, too. An increase in money demand due to a change in expectations, preferences, or transactions costs will make people want to hold more money at each interest rate. The money demand curve will shift to the right (and the demand for bonds will shift to the left). The resulting higher interest rate will cause investment and net exports to decrease, reducing aggregate demand, real GDP, and the price level.

Changes in the Money Supply

Now suppose the market for money is in equilibrium and the Fed changes the money supply. All other things unchanged, how will this change in the money supply affect the equilibrium interest rate and aggregate demand, real GDP, and the price level?

Suppose the Fed increases the money supply through the open-market purchase of bonds.[25] The impact of Fed bond purchases is illustrated in Panel (a) of Figure 11.11. The Fed's purchase of bonds shifts the demand curve for bonds to the right; bond prices rise, and the implied interest rate falls. Of course, when the Fed buys bonds, the supply of money increases. Panel (b) of Figure 11.11 shows the money market, initially in equilibrium with money supply M and interest rate of r_1. The bond purchases by the Fed shown in Panel (a) result in an increase in the money supply to M'; that policy change shifts the supply curve for money to the right to S_2. At the original interest rate r_1, people don't want to hold the newly supplied money; they would prefer to hold bonds. To reestablish equilibrium in the money market, the interest rate must fall to r_2, increasing the quantity of money demanded until it equals the new money supply, M'.

FIGURE 11.11 An Increase in the Money Supply

The Fed increases the money supply by buying bonds, increasing the demand for bonds in Panel (a) from D_1 to D_2 and the price of bonds to P^b_2. This corresponds to an increase in the money supply to M' in Panel (b). The interest rate must fall to r_2 to achieve equilibrium. The lower interest rate leads to an increase in investment and net exports, which shifts the aggregate demand curve from AD_1 to AD_2 in Panel (c). Real GDP and the price level rise.

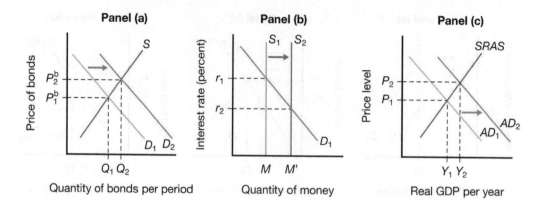

The increase in the money supply and the corresponding decrease in interest rates have macroeconomic effects. Lower interest rates will stimulate both investment and net exports, causing the aggregate demand curve to shift to the right, as shown in Panel (c), from AD_1 to AD_2. Given the short-run aggregate supply curve $SRAS$, real GDP increases from Y_1 to Y_2, and the price level rises from P_1 to P_2.

Open-market operations in which the Fed sells bonds—that is, a contractionary monetary policy—will have the opposite effect. When the Fed sells bonds, the supply curve of bonds shifts to the right and the price of bonds falls, driving interest rates upward. The bond sales lead to a reduction in the money supply, causing the money supply curve to shift to the left and raising the equilibrium interest rate. Higher interest rates cause a reduction in investment and net exports, shifting the aggregate demand curve to the left.

In the previous section, interest rates were determined in the bond market. In this section, we used a different model—a model of the money market—to show the same thing. That may seem confusing, but the good news is that our results are both consistent and compatible: The money market works in tandem with the bond market to arrive at an interest rate where *both* markets are in equilibrium.

As economists, we don't generally recommend throwing money at your problems. But when you're the Fed and the problem is a recession, we'll make an exception.

Source: LightField Studios/Shutterstock.com

Pop! Goes the Econ: Monetary Stimulus in *Living It Up*

Rat Pack icon Dean Martin gives a lecture on the power of money to increase spending.

View in the online reader

Key Takeaways

- People hold money in order to buy goods and services (transactions demand), to have it available for contingencies (precautionary demand), and in order to avoid possible drops in the value of other assets such as bonds (speculative demand).
- The higher the interest rate, the lower the quantities of money demanded for transactions, precautionary, and speculative purposes. The lower the interest rate, the higher the quantities of money demanded for these purposes.
- The demand for money will change as a result of a change in real GDP, the price level, transfer costs, expectations, or preferences.
- The supply of money is determined by the Fed, which can choose any level it wants without regard to the interest rate. The supply curve for money, therefore, is a vertical line.
- Money market equilibrium occurs at the interest rate where the quantity of money demanded equals the quantity of money supplied.
- All other things unchanged, a shift in money demand or supply will lead to a change in the equilibrium interest rate, and therefore to changes in aggregate demand, real GDP, and the price level.

Try It!

Suppose that the Fed is concerned about the possibility that the United States is moving into an inflationary gap, and decides to fight inflation by implementing contractionary monetary policy (a decrease in the money supply). Draw a four-panel graph showing this policy and its expected results. In Panel (a), use the model of aggregate demand and aggregate supply to illustrate an economy with an inflationary gap. In Panel (b), show how the Fed's policy will affect the market for bonds. In Panel (c), show how it will affect the demand for and supply of money. In Panel (d), show how it will affect the exchange rate. Finally, return to Panel (a) and incorporate these developments into your analysis of aggregate demand and aggregate supply, and show how the Fed's policy will affect real GDP and the price level in the short run.

See related Numerical Problem 7 at the end of this chapter.

Case in Point: Hold On Tight—Money Demand in the Coronavirus Crisis

Source: © Shutterstock, Inc.

The early days of the COVID-19 pandemic shine interesting light on peoples' motives for holding money and the large-scale effects of their actions. As news of the coronavirus began to trickle in and the potential seriousness became known, individuals made dramatic changes in their money management. Let's look at the three motives for holding money and then peek at the data to uncover what really happened in the early weeks of the crisis.

Transaction Demand for Money. With the impact of the virus and its degree of transmissibility unknown, state and local governments locked down a large chunk of commercial society. At the same time, individuals holed up in their homes to "flatten the curve." Many businesses shuttered their doors entirely. Other essential businesses (big box stores, groceries, gas stations, carryout restaurants, and liquor stores, for example) remained open, but even then, consumers often cut back considerably on their buying.[26] While internet shopping and sales of some items like flour, toilet paper, and laptop computers boomed, that extra spending wasn't enough to outweigh declines elsewhere in the economy. Overall spending, as measured by nominal GDP, declined by an astounding 9.5% in just one quarter, dragging the transactions demand for money right along with it.

Speculative Demand for Money. In March and April of the coronavirus crisis, lockdowns and uncertainty took a huge toll in financial markets. Stocks tumbled as fearful investors fled the market, anxious to get rid of struggling stocks before their prices declined even further. At the same time, the Federal Reserve went on a bond-buying binge, driving interest rates down to near zero. With nowhere for interest rates to go in the future but up, even the safe, sane U.S. Treasury bond market looked unappealing to investors, because *when interest rates rise, bond prices fall*. In the end, financial investors felt they had few good options: Stocks were too dangerous; bonds were both risky and low-yielding. Many of those investors, having sold off their risky stocks and bonds, chose to sit on piles of dependable cash instead. Money was in high speculative demand!

Precautionary Demand for Money. The early days of the coronavirus crisis left Americans with lots of questions. *"When will the company I work for reopen? Will I be able to return to work full-time? Will I have to stay home with my kids while they learn remotely?"* Those are big, hard questions that many people were asking themselves for the first time in their lives. What's the best way to deal with that kind of uncertainty? Not by purchasing a new boat or by signing up the family for a Caribbean cruise, that's for sure! Instead, Americans did something they're not really well known for: They cashed their paychecks and their pandemic assistance checks, and instead of spending them, they saved them, just in case! The personal saving rate, which measures the percentage of income Americans save, skyrocketed from its long-run 6.5% average to 33.6% in March alone, and about 20% over the rest of the year. With financial markets shaky, most of that savings was simply shoved into checking accounts, readily accessible for whatever lean times lay ahead.

What was the ultimate impact of these wild swings in the demand for money? Currency in circulation, which had grown steadily at about 6.4% per year since the end of the Great Recession in 2009, shot upward by 14% in the six months following the virus's arrival. That dramatic change was dwarfed, however, by balances in checking accounts. Checkable deposits increased 22% in March alone, and another 12% in April. By September, those deposits had grown at ten times the average annual rate in the decade before, rising an astonishing 64%. People were almost literally sitting on piles of money!

During the COVID-19 recession, checkable deposits skyrocketed as money demand soared.

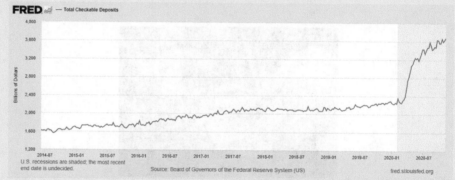

Source: Board of Governors of the Federal Reserve System (US), Total Checkable Deposits (DISCONTINUED) [TCD], retrieved from FRED, Federal Reserve Bank of St. Louis; https://fred.stlouisfed.org/series/TCD.

Of course, money that's being sat on isn't being spent. The combined actions of millions of tightfisted consumers and financial investors and hundreds of thousands of businesses putting investment plans on hold created an extremely sharp and sudden recession that, in spite of a rapid bounce back, continued throughout the year.

See related Concept Problem 9 at the end of this chapter.

Source: Data provided by Federal Reserve System and Bureau of Economic Analysis.

Answer to Try It! Problem

In Panel (a), with the aggregate demand curve AD_1, short-run aggregate supply curve *SRAS*, and long-run aggregate supply curve *LRAS*, the economy has an inflationary gap of $Y_1 - Y_P$. The contractionary monetary policy means that the Fed sells bonds—a rightward shift of the bond supply curve in Panel (b), which decreases the money supply—as shown by a leftward shift in the money supply curve in Panel (c). In Panel (b), we see that the price of bonds falls, and in Panel (c) that the interest rate rises. A higher interest rate will reduce the quantity of investment demanded. The higher interest rate also leads to a higher exchange rate, as shown in Panel (d), as the demand for dollars increases and the supply decreases. The higher exchange rate will lead to a decrease in net exports. As a result of these changes in financial markets, the aggregate demand curve shifts to the left to AD_2 in Panel (a). If all goes according to plan (and we will learn in the next chapter that it may not!), the new aggregate demand curve will intersect *SRAS* and *LRAS* at Y_P.

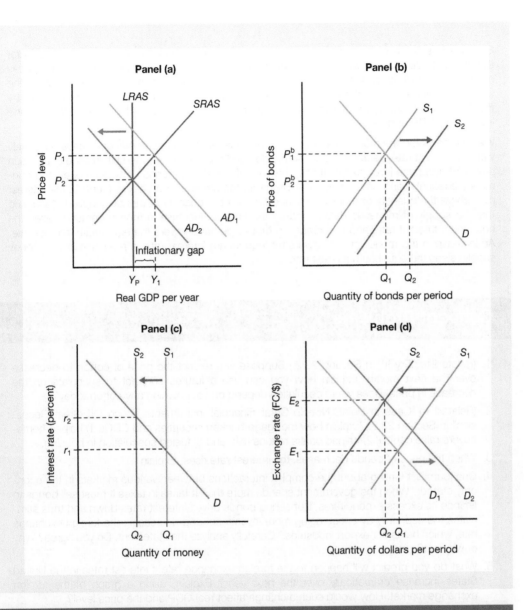

Panel (a)

Inflationary gap

Y_P Y_1

Real GDP per year

Panel (b)

Quantity of bonds per period

Panel (c)

Quantity of money

Panel (d)

Quantity of dollars per period

Khan Academy Links

Demand for money

Equilibrium nominal interest rates in the money market

11.5 Review and Practice

Summary

We began this chapter by looking at the purposes and functions of financial instruments in general—raising capital, storing wealth, reducing risk, and speculation. Then, we looked at two special financial markets, the bond and foreign exchange markets.

Bonds represent the obligation of the seller to repay the buyer the face value by the maturity date; their interest rate is determined by the demand and supply for bonds. An increase in bond prices means a drop in interest rates. A reduction in bond prices means interest rates have risen. In the foreign exchange market, the price of the dollar, known as the exchange rate, is determined by the demand and supply for dollars. We showed how both of those markets were related to the level of real GDP and the price level.

We then saw how the money market works. The quantity of money demanded varies negatively with the interest rate. Factors that cause the demand curve for money to shift include changes in real GDP, the price level, expectations, the cost of transferring funds between money and non-money accounts, and preferences. Equilibrium in the market for money is found at the interest rate where the quantity of money demanded equals the quantity of money supplied. Assuming that the supply of money is determined by the Fed, an increase in money demand raises the equilibrium interest rate, and a decrease in money demand lowers the equilibrium interest rate. An increase in the money supply lowers the equilibrium interest rate; a reduction in the money supply raises the equilibrium interest rate.

Concept Problems

1. (Related to "Try It!" in Section 23.2.) Suppose you expect the price of cotton to decrease over the next month. Explain how you can use a futures contract to speculate on the decrease in price. Does your speculation depend on your owning any cotton today?

2. (Related to "Case in Point: Not-So-Great Financial Instruments Touch Off Great Recession" in Section 23.2.) Explain how mortgage-backed securities and CDOs 1) helped homebuyers raise capital, 2) helped banks reduce risk, and 3) fueled speculation in housing.

3. When the price of bonds decreases, the interest rate rises. Explain.

4. One journalist writing about the complex interactions between various markets in the economy stated: "When the government spends more than it takes in taxes it must sell bonds to finance its excess expenditures. But selling bonds drives interest rates down and thus stimulates the economy by encouraging more investment and decreasing the foreign exchange rate, which helps our export industries." Carefully analyze the statement. Do you agree? Why or why not?

5. What do you predict will happen to the foreign exchange rate if interest rates in the United States increase dramatically over the next year? Explain, using a graph of the foreign exchange market. How would such a change affect real GDP and the price level?

6. Suppose the government were to increase its purchases, issuing bonds to finance these purchases. Use your knowledge of the bond and foreign exchange markets to explain how this would affect investment and net exports.

7. How would each of the following affect the demand for money?

    a. A tax on bonds held by individuals

    b. A forecast by the Fed that interest rates will rise sharply in the next quarter

    c. A wave of muggings

    d. An announcement of an agreement between Congress and the president that, beginning in the next fiscal year, government spending will be reduced by an amount sufficient to eliminate all future borrowing

8. Some low-income countries do not have a bond market. In such countries, what substitutes for money do you think people would hold?

9. (Related to "Case in Point: Hold On Tight—Money Demand in the Coronavirus Crisis" in Section 23.4.) Illustrate the effects of rising money demand on the part of consumers in the money market. Then, illustrate the impact of that increased money demand in the bond market. Does your analysis predict an increase or a decrease in interest rates? Did interest rates behave as you predict? If not, explain why not.

10. Explain how the Fed's sale of government bonds shifts the supply curve for money.

11. (Related to "Try It!" in Section 23.3.) Trace the impact of a sale of government bonds by the Fed on bond prices, interest rates, investment, net exports, aggregate demand, real GDP, and the price level.

12. Beginning in the money market, determine the impact of the following events on money demand, money supply, interest rates, bond prices, and aggregate demand.

   a. A government spending program increases real GDP.

   b. Fears of high future inflation begin to mount.

   c. There is an increase in the price level.

   d. As the economy heads into recession, investors begin to worry about bond defaults.

13. (Related to "Case in Point: Wouldn't You Think a COVID-19 Vaccine Would Be Good News?" in Section 23.3.) The Pfizer announcement was good news for stocks, but bad news for bonds. Illustrate the impact of the announcement on the bond market, separating 1) the change in the opportunity cost of holding bonds, and 2) the change in expectations of future interest rates. Indicate the impact of the two events on bond prices. What was the (implied) impact on interest rates?

Numerical Problems

1. Compute the rate of interest associated with each of these bonds that matures in one year:

	Face Value ($)	Selling Price ($)
a.	100	80
b.	100	90
c.	100	95
d.	200	180
e.	200	190
f.	200	195
g.	Describe the relationship between the selling price of a bond and the interest rate.	

2. Suppose that the demand and supply schedules for bonds that have a face value of $100 and a maturity date one year in the future are as follows:

Price ($)	Quantity Demanded	Quantity Supplied
100	0	600
95	100	500
90	200	400
85	300	300
80	400	200
75	500	100
70	600	0

   a. Draw the demand and supply curves for these bonds, find the equilibrium price, and determine the interest rate.

   b. Now suppose the quantity demanded increases by 200 bonds at each price. Draw the new demand curve and find the new equilibrium price. What has happened to the interest rate?

3. Compute the dollar price of a German car that sells for 40,000 euros at each of the following exchange rates:

    a. $1 = 1 euro

    b. $1 = 0.8 euro

    c. $1 = 0.75 euro

4. Consider Japan and the eurozone of the European Union (the countries that use the euro as currency). The demand and supply curves for euros are given by the following table (prices for the euro are given in Japanese yen; quantities of euros are in millions):

Price (in Yen)	Euros Demanded	Euros Supplied
75	0	600
70	100	500
65	200	400
60	300	300
55	400	200
50	500	100
45	600	0

    a. Draw the demand and supply curves for euros and state the equilibrium exchange rate (in yen) for the euro. How many euros are required to purchase one yen?

    b. Suppose an increase in interest rates in the European Union increases the demand for euros by 100 million at each price. At the same time, it reduces the supply by 100 million at each price. Draw the new demand and supply curves and state the new equilibrium exchange rate for the euro. How many euros are now required to purchase one yen?

    c. How will the event in (b) affect net exports in the European Union?

    d. How will the event in (b) affect aggregate demand in the European Union?

    e. How will the event in (b) affect net exports in Japan?

    f. How will the event in (b) affect aggregate demand in Japan?

5. Suppose you earn $6,000 per month and spend $200 in each of the month's 30 days. Compute your average quantity of money demanded if:

    a. You deposit your entire earnings in your checking account at the beginning of the month.

    b. You deposit $2,000 into your checking account on the 1st, 11th, and 21st days of the month.

    c. You deposit $1,000 into your checking account on the 1st, 6th, 11th, 16th, 21st, and 26th days of the month.

    d. How would you expect the interest rate to affect your decision to opt for strategy (a), (b), or (c)?

6. Suppose the quantity demanded of money at an interest rate of 5% is $2 billion per day, at an interest rate of 3% is $3 billion per day, and at an interest rate of 1% is $4 billion per day. Suppose the money supply is $3 billion per day.

    a. Draw a graph of the money market and find the equilibrium interest rate.

    b. Suppose the quantity of money demanded decreases by $1 billion per day at each interest rate. Graph this situation and find the new equilibrium interest rate. Explain the process of achieving the new equilibrium in the money market.

    c. Suppose instead that the money supply decreases by $1 billion per day. Explain the process of achieving the new equilibrium in the money market.

7. (Related to "Try It!" in Section 23.4.) We know that the U.S. economy faced a recessionary gap during the coronavirus crisis of 2020, and that the Fed responded with an expansionary monetary policy. Present the results of the Fed's action in a four-panel graph. In Panel (a), show the initial situation in the money market, and then show how the Fed's actions changed it. In Panel (b), show how the Fed's policy affects the bond market, bond prices, and interest rates. In Panel (c), show how the market for U.S. dollars and the exchange rate will be affected. In Panel (d), incorporate these developments into your analysis of aggregate

demand and aggregate supply, and show how the Fed's policy will affect real GDP and the price level in the short run.

Endnotes

1. That number is based on historical bond market returns over the past few decades.

2. That number is based on historical stock market returns over the past few decades.

3. And what happens if you decide to go all in and save the entire $2083 each month while investing in businesses this way? You won't retire with $1 million; you'll retire with almost $10 million!

4. We spend a bit more time talking about stock in Chapter 4.

5. In the next section, we'll explore the simplest type of bond, the *discount bond*, which will do everything we need it to do while keeping the math as simple as possible. If you're interested in seeing how other types of bonds work, we encourage you to take an introductory course in corporate finance.

6. For all of the attention paid to the stock market, it's the bond market businesses most often turn to to raise money. There is a huge difference between the value of outstanding bonds at any time (about $100 trillion in 2020) and the total value of stock (about $36 trillion).

7. While microcredit facilities can potentially provide loans to anyone, many of the most prominent microlending programs focus on funneling funds to women.

8. Stocks lost a full third of their value in a matter of days. Yikes!

9. Your authors are anxiously awaiting their nomination for, "*A penny saved is a penny earned*." Maybe next year.

10. Holding stock in companies that tend to swing in opposite directions, like Walmart and Whole Foods, is a great strategy to reduce the variability of your earnings. For more on this, a first course in corporate finance is highly recommended!

11. Asset bubbles often result from what we call the "bigger fool theory": "*A tulip bulb priced at a hundred thousand dollars is a great buy, because I believe an even bigger fool will be willing to pay two hundred thousand tomorrow*."

12. In the real world, it's most likely that an investment bank would handle the nuts and bolts of this initial sale of bonds, and would auction those bonds off as described here.

13. This type of bond is called a discount bond because the buyers purchase them at a discount from face value. That discount ultimately becomes the buyers' interest earnings. Some bonds provide their buyers periodic interest payments as well; those bonds don't have to sell at a discount, and may, in fact, actually sell for *more* than face value!

14. The original buyer only earns $25 in interest . . . but she only gives up the use of her $950 for half a year. Calculating her interest rate is slightly more complex (it involves an adjustment to the formula and an exponent—more than we need here, but great material for an introductory course in finance), but the *annualized* result is the same 5.33%.

15. Consumption may also be affected by changes in interest rates. For example, if interest rates fall, consumers can more easily obtain credit and thus are more likely to purchase cars and other durable goods. To simplify, we ignore this effect.

16. Sometimes, however, those rates are controlled or managed by the government. We'll see more about this in our chapter on international finance.

17. We could just as easily look at the market for foreign currency—as we'll see, the market for foreign currency is essentially a mirror image of the market for dollars.

18. Some governments carefully intervene in foreign exchange markets to prop up or force down the value of their currency. This is discussed in our chapter on international finance, but honestly, the world of currency intervention is a complex one that can easily fill a semester-long course all by itself.

19. "People with wealth" isn't the same thing as "wealthy people." Anyone with some assets and a desire to store value over time qualifies as a person with wealth.

20. Andre has $1,500 in the bond fund for half a month. At a 1% monthly interest rate, his interest earnings will be $1,500 × (1/2) × (.01) = $7.50, enough for a slice of pizza and a cold beer!

21. In fact, if interest rates were really high, Andre could put the entire $3,000 in the bond fund at the beginning of the month, and make 30 separate $100 transfers to checking throughout the month. That might be costly, but his average bond-fund balance would be $1,500, and his interest earnings would climb to $15 per month—enough to fund pizza and beer both for himself *and* a date!

22. The demand for peanut butter can be affected by changes in the price of substitute goods (Nutella), complementary goods (jelly), income, information, and expectations about future availability. See Chapter 3 for a review!

23. In this chapter we are looking only at changes that originate in financial markets to see their impact on aggregate demand and aggregate supply. Changes in the price level and in real GDP also shift the money demand curve, but these changes are the result of changes in aggregate demand or aggregate supply and are considered in more advanced courses in macroeconomics.

24. See the previous section for more on this. The exchange rate here is quoted in units of foreign currency per dollar.

25. You can review the nuts and bolts of this process with a quick peek back to the previous chapter.

26. See Chapter 4's Case in Point on negative oil prices ("The Topsy Turvy World of 2020 Oil Prices"), which resulted in part because of declining gasoline consumption.

CHAPTER 12

Monetary Policy and the Fed

12.1 Start Up: The Fed Goes to War

It's not every day that the Fed goes to war. It's even less often that the Fed goes to war against an unseen enemy, one so small that it can only be detected in a laboratory.

Yet that's the challenge the Fed was faced with in early 2020, as a new and microscopic virus swept the globe. With so much unknown about the virus, the Fed was left to anticipate what its effects on the economy would be, and also had to determine which policy tools it could possibly bring to bear during a public health crisis. In easier times, the Fed had fought against known, identifiable enemies: inflation, unstable financial markets, unemployment. The policy responses to those types of crisis are relatively straightforward. But how effective could printing more fancy green paper be against a pandemic?

Look Out, Virus: Fed Chairman Jerome Powell is prepared to use every weapon in his arsenal against you . . . and even a few than haven't been invented yet.

Source: MilanTomazin/Shutterstock.com

Nevertheless, the Fed acted both decisively and publicly. On March 15, 2020, just as the first few cases of COVID-19 were appearing, and as state governments were beginning to lock down residents and businesses, the Federal Open Market Committee released a statement reiterating its determination to combat the virus in every way. *"Consistent with its statutory mandate, the Committee seeks to foster maximum employment and price stability. The effects of the coronavirus will weigh on economic activity in the near term and pose risks to the economic outlook. In light of these developments the Committee decided to lower the target range for the federal funds rate to 0 to 1/4 percent. The Committee expects to maintain this target range until it is confident that the economy has weathered recent events . . . The Federal Reserve is prepared to use its full range of tools to support the flow of credit to households and businesses and thereby promote its maximum employment and price stability goals."*[1]

We've already explored the Fed's use of policy tools during the coronavirus crisis in "Case in Point: Practice Meets Crisis—Fed Policy Tools in the Time of COVID-19". In this chapter we'll examines in greater detail the challenges of using monetary policy to fight even ordinary downturns . . . much less global pandemics. We'll also take some notice of how modern Fed policy has stretched, to the economy's benefit, beyond the limits of what was previously imaginable.

12.2 Monetary Policy in the United States

Learning Objectives

1. Discuss the Fed's primary and secondary goals and relate these goals to the legislation that created the Fed as well as to subsequent legislation that affects the Fed.
2. State and show graphically how expansionary and contractionary monetary policy can be used to close gaps.

When it comes to setting and implementing policy, the Fed is a true powerhouse. But even the strongest face challenges: The power of that policy to make a real impact is sometimes in question.

Source: Maksim Toome/ Shutterstock.com

Both fiscal policy (using the government's power to tax and spend) and monetary policy (the central bank's use of changes to the supply of money and credit) can be used to fight recessionary or inflationary gaps. But fiscal policy can be tough to implement: Congress can pass laws, but the president must execute them; the president can propose laws, but only Congress can pass them. The Fed, however, both sets monetary policy *and* carries it out. While deliberations regarding fiscal policy can drag on for months (or even years!), the Federal Open Market Committee (FOMC) can, behind closed doors, set monetary policy in a day—and see that policy implemented within hours. And the impact of those policies can be quite dramatic: By pushing interest rates up or down, the Fed can promote a recession or an expansion, or cause the inflation rate to rise or fall. Those impacts are very real, and are felt directly by millions of people across the country. The Fed wields enormous power!

That power can be used to improve the performance of the macroeconomy. It also has the potential, if not used correctly, to cause great harm. With that in mind, let's look at the major goals of monetary policy, and some of the difficulties that can stand in the way of achieving those goals.

Goals of Monetary Policy

Poor Fed: Always getting tugged in different directions.

Source: absolutimages/ Shutterstock.com

When we think of the goals of monetary policy, we naturally think of standards of macroeconomic performance that seem desirable—a low unemployment rate, a stable price level, and economic growth. It's perfectly reasonable to conclude that the goals of monetary policy should include maintaining full employment, avoiding excessive inflation or deflation, and encouraging growth in potential GDP.

Each of these goals is desirable in itself. But each may find itself in conflict with the others. A monetary policy action that helps to close a recessionary gap and promotes full employment may cause inflation to accelerate. A policy action to reduce inflation may increase unemployment and slow growth. You might expect that in such cases, monetary authorities would receive guidance from legislation spelling out goals for the Fed to pursue and specifying what to do when achieving one goal means not achieving another. Unfortunately, that kind of guidance doesn't exist.

The Federal Reserve Act

When Congress established the Federal Reserve System in 1913, it said little about the policy goals the Fed should seek. The closest it came to spelling out the goals of monetary policy was in the first paragraph of the Federal Reserve Act, the legislation that created the Fed:

An Act to provide for the establishment of Federal reserve banks, to furnish an elastic currency, [to make loans to banks], to establish a more effective supervision of banking in the United States, and for other purposes.[2]

We are used to a Fed that "leans against the wind" to close recessionary or inflationary gaps, that tries to spur economic growth, and that works to keep the price level steady. Unfortunately, the legislation that created the Fed offered zero guidance as to what the Fed should do when those goals conflict with one another. In fact, the legislation that created the Fed didn't charge it with working to stabilize overall economic activity at all!

"No, no, no, lady! The only way to get past this is to lean *into* it!"

Source: Rainer Fuhrmann/ Shutterstock.com

The Employment Act of 1946

The first U.S. effort to specify macroeconomic goals came after World War II. The Great Depression of the 1930s left both ordinary people and policymakers with a deep desire to prevent similar calamities in the future. That desire, coupled with the 1936 publication of John Maynard Keynes's prescription for avoiding such problems through government policy (*The General Theory of Employment, Interest and Money*), led to the passage of the Employment Act of 1946, which charged the federal government with using "*all practical means . . . to promote maximum employment, production and purchasing power.*" That same act also created the Council of Economic Advisers (CEA) to advise the president on economic matters.

Unfortunately, the Employment Act of 1946 offers no guidance as to what should be done if the goals of achieving full employment and maximum purchasing power conflict. Add to that the fact that the Fed was specifically chartered to be independent from the government, which means that the Fed isn't bound to adopt the same goals set out by the government.

The Full Employment and Balanced Growth Act of 1978

The clearest, and most specific, statement of federal economic goals came in the Full Employment and Balanced Growth Act of 1978. This act, generally known as the *Humphrey–Hawkins Act*, specified that by 1983 the federal government should achieve an unemployment rate among adults of 3% or less, a civilian unemployment rate of 4% or less, and an inflation rate of 3% or less. Although these goals have the virtue of specificity, they offer little in terms of practical policy guidance. For the vast majority of the time since the Humphrey–Hawkins Act's passage, for example, the unemployment rate has been well above 4%. That's changed in the last decade or so, as the unemployment rate right before the coronavirus crisis stood at 3.6% (a level it hadn't seen since the 1950s), while inflation ran at a subdued 1.3%. In other words, forty-plus years after the Humphrey–Hawkins Act passed, its goals had finally been met!

How does the Humphrey–Hawkins Act impact the Fed? Perhaps most notably, the Act requires the chairman of the Fed's Board of Governors to report twice each year to Congress about the Fed's monetary policy. Those sessions provide an opportunity for members of the House and Senate to express their views on monetary policy.

The Humphrey–Hawkins goals are like artisanal ketchup poured from a glass bottle: Each takes forever to deliver on a promise that is really, really good.

Source: Akemaster/Shutterstock. com

Federal Reserve Policy and Goals

With no explicit goals binding the Fed externally, perhaps the clearest way to see what the Fed deems important is to observe the policy choices it makes. Since 1979 (following a bout of double-digit inflation), its actions have suggested that the Fed's primary goal is to keep inflation under control. In fact, the very passage quoted in the chapter opener also referred explicitly to maintaining the Fed's "symmetric 2% inflation objective." Provided that the inflation rate falls within acceptable limits, however, the Fed stands ready to use stimulative measures to attempt to close recessionary gaps.

In the early 1980s, Fed Chairman Paul Volcker's job one was wringing inflation (and expectations of inflation) out of the economy.

Source: Alextype/Shutterstock.com

Real-world evidence supports this "inflation first" objective. Following the double-digit inflation of the 1970s, new Fed Chairman Paul Volcker launched a deliberate program of reducing the inflation rate by contracting the money supply. The Fed stuck to that program through the early 1980s, even in the face of a major recession. The effort achieved its goal: The annual inflation rate fell from 13.3% in 1979 to 3.8% in 1982. The cost, however, was great. Unemployment soared to an astonishing 10.8%—a level higher than the economy experienced in what is commonly termed the "Great Recession." By 1983, with the inflation rate below 4%, the Fed shifted to a stimulative policy to close that recessionary gap.

Fast forward to the late 1990s: By March 1997 the inflation rate had fallen to 2.4%, and the economy was booming. Concerned that inflationary pressures were starting to mount, the Fed, under Chairman Alan Greenspan, tightened monetary policy, raising the goal for the federal funds interest rate to 5.5%. That kept inflation well below 2.0% throughout the rest of 1997 and 1998. But in the fall of 1998, with inflation low, economic crisis in Asia had the Fed concerned that the economic recession abroad would reduce growth in the United States.[3] In quarter-point steps, the Fed reduced the goal for the federal funds rate to 4.75%. But inflation is the Fed's Grim Reaper, and with real GDP growing briskly in the first half of 1999, the Fed became concerned that inflation would once again rear its ugly head—never mind that the inflation rate at the time was about 2%. Those fears drove the Fed to gradually raise its goal for the federal funds rate, which eventually reached 6.5% in May 2000.

And then came the Goldilocks years. With inflation under control, the Fed began to reduce the fed funds rate and stimulate the economy. After eleven rate cuts in 2001 and a few further cuts in 2002 and 2003, the fed funds rate stood at a modest 1.0%. Those low interest rates fueled an unprecedented housing boom and, with the economy heating up, the Greenspan Fed tightened policy and began raising interest rates once again in 2005 and 2006.

The dream economy of the early 2000s turned into a nightmare; while interest rates went on a wild ride, falling, rising, and falling again.

Source: Jacob Lund/Shutterstock.com

Those rate increases led to increases in the rates charged to homeowners who'd taken out adjustable rate mortgages, touching off a string of mortgage defaults that proved troubling (to say the least). Starting in September 2007, the Fed (now under the leadership of Ben Bernanke), shifted gears and began reducing the federal funds rate, mostly in larger steps of 0.5 to 0.75 percentage points. Even with the financial sector crumbling, inflation remained a concern—though inflation was more a worry than a reality. By the time the extent of the crisis was understood, the Fed knew that inflation would not be an immediate problem; unemployment became more pressing. The Bernanke Fed moved aggressively to lower rates over the course of the next fifteen months, and by the end of 2008, the rate was targeted at between 0% and 0.25%. In fact, inflationary pressure turned out to be so nonexistent that for a period of time between 2008 and 2013, the Fed was actually more concerned about the very real and very troubling threat of *deflation*. In January 2014 the Fed went on record to say that it intended to keep the federal funds rate at extremely low levels so long as the unemployment rate stayed above 6.5%, and possibly even if it went below that, provided inflation remained in check.

Over the next couple of years, the economy continued to recover. With the inflation rate still very low and the unemployment rate at about 5%, the Fed, now led by Janet Yellen, finally raised the federal funds rate by a quarter point to the 0.25 to 0.50 range in December 2015. This ended a rather extraordinary, nearly decade-long period of no change in the federal funds target rate. But, due to a rocky economic start in 2016, it would be another year before the Fed raised the rate by another quarter point. By then, the unemployment rate had fallen to 4.6% and inflation had picked up a little but was still below 2%.

What do these episodes tell us? It seems clear that the Fed is determined to not allow the high inflation rates of the 1970s to occur again. When the inflation rate is within acceptable limits, the Fed will undertake stimulative measures in response to a recessionary gap, or even in response to the possibility of a growth slowdown. Those limits seem to have tightened over time. In the late 1990s and early 2000s, it appeared that an inflation rate above 3%—or any indication that inflation might rise above 3%—would lead the Fed to adopt a contractionary policy.

Yellen made clear in a speech in January 2017 that the Fed now sees 2% as the appropriate desired rate of inflation, a policy that current Fed Chairman Jerome Powell continues to follow. In 2020, after nearly a decade of actual inflation falling *below* that target, the Powell Fed announced that its policy stance had changed slightly: Just as the Fed would work to keep inflation from rising *above* 2%, it would actively work to keep inflation from falling *below* 2%. *"The persistent undershoot of inflation from our 2 percent longer-run objective is a cause for concern. Many find it counterintuitive that the Fed would want to push up inflation. After all, low and stable inflation is essential for a well-functioning economy . . . [I]nflation that is persistently too low can pose serious risks to the economy. Inflation that runs below its desired level can lead to an unwelcome fall in longer-term inflation expectations, which, in turn, can pull actual inflation even lower, resulting in an adverse cycle of ever-lower inflation and inflation expectations."*[4] The rationale for that change in policy stance is discussed in "Case in Point: Two-Front War—COVID-19 and the Zero Lower Bound".[5]

In the eyes of the Powell Fed, underinflation can be just as problematic as overinflation.

Source: Andrey_Popov/Shutterstock.com

Monetary Policy and Macroeconomic Variables

In our chapter on the nature of money, we looked at the four tools the Fed can use to influence the level of economic activity. It can buy or sell federal government bonds through open-market operations; it can change the discount rate; it can change reserve requirements; it can change the interest payable to banks on reserve holdings. It can, and does, use these tools in combination.

Most economists agree that these tools of monetary policy affect the economy, but they sometimes disagree on the precise mechanisms through which this occurs, on the strength of those mechanisms, and on the ways in which monetary policy should be used. We'll look at those issues in this chapter, but before we do, let's review the basics of how monetary policy affects the economy in the context of our model of aggregate demand and aggregate supply. While our focus will be on open-market operations, the purchase or sale of government bonds by the Fed, other policy measures tend to stimulate or reduce economic activity in similar ways.

Expansionary Monetary Policy

Let's suppose the economy has faltered, as shown in Panel (a) of Figure 12.1., where an economy with a potential output of Y_P is operating below potential at Y_1. Policymakers could, if they wanted, adopt a "hurry up and wait" policy that allows the economy to self-correct through decreases in nominal wages and other prices. (To review how that happens, revisit our chapter on aggregate demand and aggregate supply.) An alternative to waiting for that to happen on its own is for the Fed to adopt stimulative measures to increase aggregate demand. A shift from AD_1 to AD_2 would close the recessionary gap and restore full employment.

How does the Fed increase aggregate demand? The typical recipe is for the Fed to buy bonds in the open market. That accomplishes two things:

- When the Fed buys bonds, that new demand for bonds bids up their price, as illustrated in Panel (b), where bond prices rise from P^b_1 to P^b_2. That price increase reduces the interest rate.[6]
- Those changes in the bond market are consistent with the changes in the money market, where the Fed's bond purchases cause the money supply to increase as the Fed "prints" more money to pay for those bonds.[7] The increase in the money supply, shown in Panel (c), leads to a fall in the interest rate from r_1 to r_2.

The lower interest rate reduces the cost of borrowing by firms and households and stimulates investment and interest-sensitive consumption purchases like cars and other consumer durables.[8] That shifts the aggregate demand curve to the right by an amount equal to the multiplier times the sum of the initial changes in investment and consumption. In Panel (a), this is shown as a shift from AD_1 to AD_2, just enough to close the recessionary gap.

FIGURE 12.1 Expansionary Monetary Policy to Close a Recessionary Gap

In Panel (a), the economy begins with a recessionary gap $Y_P - Y_1$. Expansionary monetary policy closes this gap by shifting the aggregate demand curve from AD_1 to AD_2. In Panel (b), the Fed buys bonds, shifting the demand curve for bonds from D^{bonds}_1 to D^{bonds}_2 and increasing the price of bonds from P^b_1 to P^b_2. By buying bonds, the Fed increases the money supply from Q^m_1 to Q^m_2, which causes interest rates to decrease from r_1 to r_2, as shown in Panel (c). Falling interest rates stimulate consumption and investment, shifting the aggregate demand curve as shown in Panel (a).

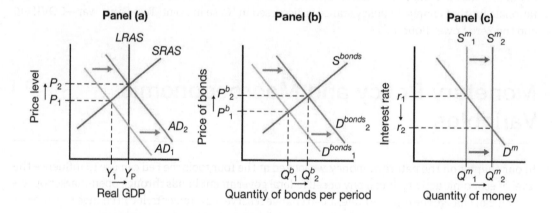

Contractionary Monetary Policy

The Fed pursues contractionary monetary policy when it considers inflation a threat. Suppose, for example, that the economy faces an inflationary gap; the aggregate demand and short-run aggregate supply curves intersect to the right of the long-run aggregate supply curve, as shown in Panel (a) of Figure 12.2.

FIGURE 12.2 A Contractionary Monetary Policy to Close an Inflationary Gap

In Panel (a), the economy has an inflationary gap $Y_1 - Y_P$. Contractionary monetary policy could close this gap by shifting the aggregate demand curve to AD_2. In Panel (b), the Fed sells bonds, shifting the supply curve for bonds to S_2 and lowering the price of bonds to P^b_2. The lower price of bonds means a higher interest rate, r_2, as shown in Panel (c). Higher interest rates lead to less investment and consumption, which are responsible for the decrease in aggregate demand shown in Panel (a).

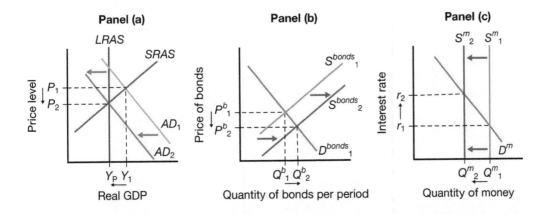

To implement contractionary policy, the Fed sells bonds. In the bond market, shown in Panel (b) of Figure 12.2, the supply curve for bonds shifts to the right, lowering the price of bonds and increasing the interest rate. In the money market, shown in Panel (c), the Fed's bond sales reduce the money supply and raise the interest rate. The higher interest rate reduces investment and some consumption spending. Contractionary monetary policy ends up shifting aggregate demand to the left by an amount equal to the multiplier times the combined initial changes in investment and consumption, as shown in Panel (a).

Key Takeaways

- The Federal Reserve Board and the Federal Open Market Committee are among the most powerful institutions in the United States.
- The Fed's primary goal appears to be the control of inflation. Provided that inflation is under control, the Fed will act to close recessionary gaps.
- Expansionary policy, such as a purchase of government securities by the Fed, tends to push bond prices up and interest rates down, increasing investment and aggregate demand. Contractionary policy, such as a sale of government securities by the Fed, pushes bond prices down, interest rates up, investment down, and aggregate demand shifts to the left.

Try It!

The figure shows an economy operating at a real GDP of Y_1 and a price level of P_1, at the intersection of AD_1 and $SRAS_1$.

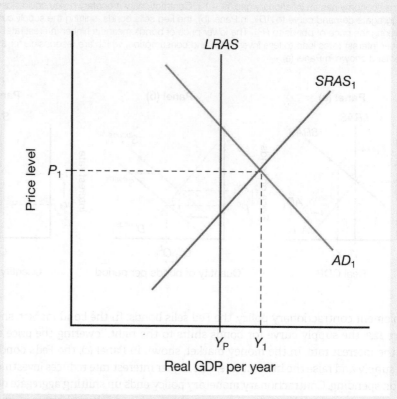

1. What kind of gap is the economy experiencing?
2. What type of monetary policy (expansionary or contractionary) would be appropriate for closing the gap?
3. If the Fed decided to pursue this policy, what type of open-market operations would it conduct?
4. How would bond prices and interest rates change?
5. How would investment and consumption change?
6. How would the aggregate demand curve shift?

See related Concept Problem 12 at the end of this chapter.

Case in Point: The Fed's Job May Be Easing, but It Isn't Easy

Poor Jerome Powell.

It's not, of course, that's he's actually poor. In fact, before he became chair of the Fed, his work on Wall Street set him up for life. And it's not that he's incapable: He's served as undersecretary of the Treasury, and has a tenure on the Fed's Board of Governors that goes back to the Obama administration.

And it's not that he's done a bad job as the chair of the Fed, either. In fact, in the face of the coronavirus crisis, the mild-mannered man unleashed the Fed's power on a scale larger than anything the world has ever seen. Ever. He's made former Fed Chair Ben Bernanke's response during the Great Recession look positively timid.

Why, then, should we pity Jerome Powell? Because he was saddled with someone else's ill-thought-out promises, and took a beating every time he refused to keep them.

Those promises came from the very man who appointed him to be chair, former President Donald J. Trump. Even before he was elected, Trump was promising voters that he'd deliver 4% growth. Of course, a president can't single-handedly make the economy grow. And the 4% figure was so outlandish, so outsized, that there was never really any way to make it happen even *with* the cooperation of the Fed and the Treasury.

Making economic policy is like making sausage: The end result might be terrific, but the process can be messy and unappetizing.

Source: CCat82/Shutterstock.com

But Donald Trump, for all of his qualities, never let something as trivial as facts get in the way of his words. Even before the coronavirus was a thing, Trump made a practice of pressuring Powell to stimulate, stimulate, stimulate. In September of 2019, with the economy booming, Trump launched a series of attacks on the Federal Reserve, demanding that it slash interest rates to zero or even push them into negative territory. Those demands, driven by a desire to fulfill his growth promise in the face of an upcoming election cycle and a desire to refinance the federal debt, which had ballooned in his first term of office, went unheeded. "The USA should always be paying the lowest rate," Trump tweeted. "It is only the naivete of Jay Powell and the Federal Reserve that doesn't allow us to do what other countries are already doing. A once in a lifetime opportunity that we are missing because of 'Boneheads.'"

Against impossible odds, Jerome Powell proved himself worthy against both the coronavirus and intense political pressure.

Source: Official portrait of Governor Jerome H. Powell, Chair. Federalreserve via Wikimedia: https://commons.wikimedia.org/wiki/File:Jerome_H._Powell.jpg.

That kind of ill-advised policy recommendation didn't sit well with economists like David Wessel of the Hutchins Center on Fiscal and Monetary Policy. "The President is calling for what essentially are emergency monetary policy measures at a time when unemployment is at a 50-year low . . . and [the economy] is still growing."[9]

Powell would not be swayed, and within a month delivered a set of thoughtful and pointed comments while introducing a film about former Fed Chair Marriner Eccles. "He is responsible more than any other person, for the fact that the United States today has an independent central bank . . . able to make decisions in the long-term best interest of the economy, without regard to . . . political pressures."[10]

By March, the coronavirus had arrived, and Jerome Powell had responded forcefully. But not forcefully enough, apparently, as whispers of talk to remove Powell from office began trickling out of the Oval Office. Ultimately, of course, that didn't happen: Powell turned out to be a hero, and Trump failed in his bid for re-election.

Fed chairs are often brilliant, though not every Fed chair makes that cut. No matter how capable, though, they're almost always slow to get credit and quick to get blame. That's never been more true than in the case of the Powell Fed under Trump, where the most brilliant recipe for monetary policy had to be baked in the hottest of kitchens.

See related Concept Problem 14 at the end of this chapter.

Answers to Try It! Problems

1. Inflationary gap
2. Contractionary
3. Open-market sales of bonds
4. The price of bonds would fall. The interest rate would rise.
5. Investment and consumption would fall.
6. The aggregate demand curve would shift to the left.

12.3 Problems and Controversies of Monetary Policy

Learning Objectives

1. Identify the macroeconomic targets at which the Fed can aim in managing the economy, and discuss the difficulties inherent in using each of them as a target.
2. Explain the three kinds of lags that can influence the effectiveness of monetary policy.
3. Discuss how political pressures can influence a central bank's ability to achieve its policy goals, the degree of impact on the economy (including the situation of a liquidity trap), and the rational expectations hypothesis.
4. Describe the liquidity trap, and explain how a liquidity trap can keep a central bank from achieving its objectives.
5. Illustrate how rational expectations can potentially render monetary policy ineffective.

From the outside, it looks like the Fed ought to have an easy time conducting monetary policy. The two policymaking bodies—the Board of Governors and the Federal Open Market Committee (FOMC)—are small and largely independent from other political institutions. Their small size enables them to reach decisions quickly and implement them immediately. Their relative independence allows them to operate in the best interest of the nation, without regard to prevailing political winds.

Nevertheless, the Fed still faces difficulties in its efforts to stabilize the economy. We'll examine some of the problems and uncertainties associated with monetary policy in this section. Let's begin by discussing the targets of policy.

Targets of Policy

In its attempts to manage the economy, the Fed doesn't just start printing money and then stop when everything looks good. Instead, it relies on a set of targets that it wants to achieve. If the economy pushes the Fed's objectives away from its targets, then the Fed intervenes with monetary policy to head the economy back toward its targets.

But what should the Fed's targets be? We've already mentioned a few over the last few chapters, including interest rates, money growth rates, and the price level or expected changes in the price level. Let's take a look at each, in turn.

Interest Rates

Today, interest rates (especially the federal funds rate) play a key role in Fed policy. When the FOMC sets monetary policy, it doesn't specify a quantity of money. Instead, it directs the New York Federal Reserve to buy or sell bonds until the fed funds rate hits its target:

- To stimulate the economy, the Fed buys bonds, which pumps new reserves into the banking system. As banks make those new reserves available for interbank loans, the interest rate on those loans (the fed funds rate) declines.

- To slow an overheating economy, the Fed sells bonds. The funds received in payment for those bonds are drained from the banking system and are essentially locked away, out of circulation. With fewer reserves available in the fed funds market, the fed funds rate rises.

While the Fed has a number of target objectives, the current operating procedures of the Fed focus explicitly on interest rates. At each of its eight meetings during the year, the FOMC sets a specific target or target range for the federal funds rate, and then carries out action to achieve that rate. While changes in the fed funds rate only directly affect the banks that borrow and lend excess reserves to one another, those changes typically lead to similar changes in other short-term lending rates that affect the flow of credit to households, firms, and units of government.

Money Growth Rates

In 1979, following a decade of high and costly inflation, new Fed Chairman Paul Volcker announced that the Fed would begin wringing inflation out of the system by adhering to strict money growth targets. That new policy stance was highly effective at reducing inflation, but came at great cost, touching off a sharp double-dip recession. In response to the recession, Volcker quickly abandoned strict monetary targeting, concluding in short order what was termed the "monetarist experiment."[11]

Despite abandoning money growth as an explicit target of policy, the Fed was still required to announce its target for money growth to Congress each year. The Fed dutifully fulfilled that requirement until 2000, when it was phased out. At the same time, the Fed report always mentioned that its money growth targets were benchmarks based on historical relationships rather than guides for policy. As soon as the legal requirement to report targets for money growth ended, the Fed stopped reporting on them. Because the Fed now places more importance on the federal funds rate, it simply adjusts the money supply to whatever it needs to be in order to nudge the fed funds rate toward its target. Whether that requires a 2% increase in the money supply or a 15% decrease is immaterial.

Price Level or Expected Changes in the Price Level

In the 1980s and 1990s, many countries struggled with inflation problems—problems with the potential to wreck an economy.[12] Observing the success of Japan's and Germany's low-inflation economies, some nations' central banks began targeting inflation as not just *a* target of policy, but *the* target of policy. In many cases, central bankers in inflation-targeting countries face sanctions if they fail to achieve their goals.

Those efforts have been highly successful in reducing inflation and promoting economic stability. As time has elapsed, more countries have begun formally or informally targeting inflation, often alongside other shorter-term policy targets like the interbank lending rate. Today, central banks of about thirty developed or developing countries have adopted inflation targeting as a primary goal of policy. Those inflation targeters include Australia, Brazil, Canada, Great Britain, New Zealand, and South Korea. The Fed began informally targeting inflation under Ben Bernanke in 2012; today, that practice continues, with Fed Chairman Jerome Powell targeting a "symmetric 2% goal." If average inflation rises above 2%, then the Fed can shift to a contractionary stance to bring inflation back to target. If average inflation dips below goal, it gives the Fed room to stimulate. (If it seems odd for the Fed to want a higher inflation rate, see this section's "Case in Point: Two-Front War—COVID-19 and the Zero Lower Bound" for an explanation as to why.)

One difficulty with an inflation-targeting policy is that the Fed is put in the position of responding to past economic conditions with policies that are not likely to affect the economy for a year or more. Another difficulty is that an adverse supply shock can cause inflation to rise and output to fall: In other words, we can experience both inflation and recession. This is exactly what happened in 1990, when inflation increased due to a seemingly temporary increase in oil prices following Iraq's invasion of Kuwait. It happened again in the first half of 2008, when a huge spike in oil prices threatened to nudge inflation upward just when the full force of the Great Recession was starting to be felt.

Adverse supply shocks like these put inflation targeters in an awkward position: Fight the inflation with contractionary monetary policy, and that policy change makes the recession worse. Fight the recession with expansionary policy, and it makes the inflation worse. One very imperfect solution to this problem is for the central bank to focus not on the past rate of inflation or even the current rate of inflation, but on the expected rate of inflation, as revealed by various indicators, over a period of say six months or a year.

The global experience with inflation targeting has been, by and large, a good one. Inflation targeting has helped many high-inflation countries bring prices under control, and that, in turn, has paid dividends elsewhere in the economy. Economist Carl Walsh has found that inflationary experiences among developed countries have been similar, regardless of whether their central banks had explicit or more flexible inflation targets. In developing countries, he found that strict inflation targeting enhanced macroeconomic performance, both in terms of lower inflation and in terms of greater overall stability.[13]

Pop! Goes the Econ: Jamaica Extols the Virtues of Inflation Targeting

This film, from the Bank of Jamaica, is designed to bring transparency to the conduct of monetary policy. As you read this section, evaluate whether that transparency may help or hinder the central bank's ability to stabilize the economy.

View in the online reader

The Challenges of Monetary Policy

Our analysis to this point makes the use of monetary policy look as simple as following a recipe in a cookbook: *When this happens, respond by doing that; when that happens, respond by doing this.* In the real world, however, implementing effective monetary policy is a much messier endeavor. For one, as we've mentioned, the goals of policy sometimes conflict with one another. But even when all indicators point to "stimulate," using monetary policy to achieve policy objectives can be difficult. Those difficulties largely stem from three issues: timing, magnitude, and effectiveness.

The Lags of Policy

Perhaps the greatest obstacle facing the Fed (or any other central bank) is time. It's easy enough to show a recessionary gap on a graph and then to show how monetary policy can shift aggregate demand to close that gap. In the real world, however, it may take several months before anyone even realizes that a particular macroeconomic problem is occurring. When monetary authorities become aware of a problem, they can act quickly to inject reserves into the system or to withdraw reserves from it. Once that's done, however, it may be a year or more before those new reserves exert any noticeable effect on aggregate demand.

Fed policy, like synchronized swimming, depends on precise timing!

Source: UzFoto/Shutterstock.com

The delay between the time a macroeconomic problem arises and the time at which policymakers become aware of it is called a **recognition lag**. The 1990–1991 recession, for example, began in July 1990. It wasn't until late October that members of the FOMC noticed a slowing in economic activity, and there wasn't enough evidence to officially declare the economy in recession until April 1991—*a month after the recession had ended!*

Recognition lags stem largely from problems in collecting economic data. First, data are available only after the conclusion of a particular period. Preliminary estimates of real GDP, for example, are released about a month after the end of a quarter, so a change that occurs early in a quarter won't show up in the data until several months later. Second, estimates of economic indicators are subject to revision. The first estimates of real GDP in the third quarter of 1990, for example, showed it increasing. Not until several months had passed did revised estimates show that a recession had begun. And finally, different indicators can lead to different interpretations. Consider the COVID-19 recession, in which data on employment and retail sales pointed to an economy in serious trouble, while data on housing starts and business investment suggested everything was not just back on track, but better than ever. (For more on this, see "Case in Point: Investment in a COVID-19 Recovery".) It's one thing to look back after a few years have passed and determine whether the economy was expanding or contracting. It's a much harder thing to decipher changes in the macroeconomy at the time. Even in a world overrun with computer-generated data on every aspect of the economy, recognition lags can be substantial.

It's only after policymakers *recognize* there's a problem that they can begin to *deal* with it. The time between when a problem is recognized and when a policy is implemented to fix it is called the **implementation lag**. For monetary policy changes, the implementation lag is quite short. The FOMC meets regularly eight times per year, and its members may confer between meetings through conference calls. Once the FOMC determines that a policy change is in order, the required open-market operations to buy or sell bonds can be put into effect immediately.

That doesn't mean the problem is solved however! It may take time for the Fed's action to trickle into the economy and affect aggregate demand. In other words, policymakers at the Fed still have to contend with the **impact lag**, the delay between the time a policy is enacted and the time that policy has its impact on the economy.

Monetary policy's impact lag exists for several reasons. First, it takes some time for the deposit multiplier process to work itself out. The Fed can inject new reserves into the economy immediately, but the deposit expansion process of bank lending takes time to have its full effect on the money supply. Interest rates are affected right away (the Fed's purchases of bonds immediately drive up bond prices and drive down interest rates), but the money supply grows more slowly. Second, firms and households need some time to respond to expansionary monetary policy with new spending—if they respond at all. Just because the Fed makes new money available doesn't mean that consumers are ready to buy new cars, or that firms have shovel-ready projects ready to go. That means that an initial change in aggregate demand may take a while to unfold . . . and then the economy might have to wait even longer for the multiplier process to kick in and shift aggregate demand the rest of the way.

recognition lag

The delay between the time a macroeconomic problem arises and the time at which policymakers become aware of it.

implementation lag

The delay between the time at which a problem is recognized and the time at which a policy to deal with it is enacted.

impact lag

The delay between the time a policy is enacted and the time that policy has its impact on the economy.

The problem of lags suggests that monetary policy should respond not to statistical reports of economic conditions in the recent past, but to conditions expected to exist in the future. In justifying the imposition of a contractionary monetary policy early in 1994, when the economy still had a recessionary gap, then-Fed-chair Alan Greenspan indicated that the Fed expected a one-year impact lag. The policy initiated in 1994 was a response not to the economic conditions thought to exist at the time, but to conditions *expected* to exist in 1995. That kind of foresight became even more clear during the early days of the coronavirus crisis, when Jerome Powell announced unprecedented stimulative measures just as the first few cases were showing up. Had Powell looked backward instead of forward he'd have announced, "*The data shows that everything is A-OK; let's knock off early, and I'll see you in eight weeks!*" The hard part about looking forward, however, is that it's easy to guess wrong about what the future holds: Relying on imperfect information and imperfect forecasts can lead policymakers to make imperfect decisions.

Like jet lag, the lags of Fed policy have the potential to create a nasty little hangover.

Source: interstid/Shutterstock.com

Estimates of the length of time required for the impact lag to work itself out range from six months to two years. Worse, the length of the lag can vary—when they take action, policymakers can't know whether their choices will affect the economy within a few months or within a few years. Because of the uncertain length of the impact lag, efforts to stabilize the economy through monetary policy could potentially be destabilizing: Suppose, for example, that the Fed responds to a recessionary gap with an expansionary policy, but that by the time the policy begins to affect aggregate demand, the economy has already returned to potential GDP. Instead of correcting a recessionary gap, the Fed's stimulus could create an inflationary gap. Likewise, a shift to a contractionary policy in response to an inflationary gap might not affect aggregate demand until after the economy has already self-corrected on its own. In that case, the policy could plunge the economy into a recession.

Political Pressures

The institutional relationship between the leaders of the Fed and the executive and legislative branches of the federal government is structured to provide for the Fed's independence. There's a reason for that: When the government, which *spends* money to please its own desires or the desires of its constituents, also has the power to *print* money (either literally or electronically), it can become very tempting to spend elaborately at the expense of existing moneyholders.[14]

To insulate sound monetary policy from the potential excesses of government, the creators of the Federal Reserve Act incorporated a number of measures to ensure its independence. Members of the Board of Governors are appointed by the president, with confirmation by the Senate, but the fourteen-year terms of office provide a considerable degree of insulation from political pressure—no appointee needs to worry about being re-elected within a short period of time.[15] Furthermore, those fourteen-year terms are nonrenewable, which means that even if an appointed governor were interested in appeasing a forceful president, there would be no point: Can't be fired; can't be re-elected.

Like the musk ox, the Fed gets much of its power from its insulation.

Source: Martin Hejzlar/ Shutterstock.com

At a slightly (but not much!) lower level, neither the president nor Congress has any direct say over the selection of the presidents of Federal Reserve district banks. They are chosen by their individual boards of directors, with the approval of the Board of Governors. That may not sound like a big deal—after all, the Board of Governors sits in D.C., while the chair of the Cleveland Fed sits in, well, Cleveland. But because district Fed presidents each occupy a position on the Fed's main policymaking body (the FOMC), even those district Fed presidents wield an enormous amount of power, and wield it insulated from any capriciousness from the White House or the Capitol.

While independence is the norm in the United States, the degree of independence that central banks around the world enjoy varies. A central bank is considered to be more independent if it is insulated from the government by such factors as longer term appointments of its governors and fewer requirements to finance government budget deficits. Studies in the 1980s and early 1990s showed that, in general, greater central bank independence was associated with lower average inflation, and that there was no systematic relationship between central bank independence and other indicators of economic performance, such as real GDP growth or unemployment.[16] By the rankings used in those studies, the Fed was considered quite independent, second only to Switzerland and the German *Bundesbank* at the time. Perhaps as a result of such findings, a number of countries have granted greater independence to their central banks in the last decade. The charter for the European Central Bank, which began operations in 1998, was modeled after the German *Bundesbank*. Its charter states explicitly that its primary objective is to maintain price stability. Also, since 1998, central bank independence has increased in the United Kingdom, Canada, Japan, and New Zealand.

While the Fed is formally insulated from the political process, the men and women who serve on the Board of Governors and the FOMC are human beings . . . and human beings under enormous pressure to deliver on very important goals. They are not immune to the pressures that can be placed on them by members of Congress and by the president. The chairman of the Board of Governors meets regularly with the president and the executive staff and also reports to and meets with congressional committees that deal with economic matters. Add to that the fact that the Fed, created by the Congress, could have its charter altered or even revoked by that same body, and you've got a Fed that walks a delicate line between the economic interests of the country and the political interests of elected officials. That puts the Fed in the somewhat paradoxical situation of having to cooperate with the legislative and executive branches in order to preserve its independence. (For more on this, see "Case in Point: The Fed's Job May Be Easing, but It Isn't Easy".)

The Degree of Impact on the Economy

The problem of lags suggests that the Fed does not know with certainty *when* its policies will work their way through the financial system to have an impact on macroeconomic performance. The Fed is also in the dark about *how much* of an impact its decisions will have on the macroeconomy.

For example, investment can be particularly volatile. An effort by the Fed to reduce aggregate demand to close an inflationary gap could be partially offset by rising investment demand spurred by growing business confidence. But, generally, contractionary policies *do* tend to slow down the economy as if the Fed were "pulling on a rope."

That may not be the case with expansionary policies. Since investment depends crucially on expectations about the future, business leaders must be optimistic about economic conditions in order to expand production facilities and buy new equipment. That kind of optimism might not exist in a recession . . . even if expansionary actions by the Fed push interest rates to very low levels. In short, the Fed can flood the economy with money, but if firms don't want to invest, then there's little the Fed can do to make economic activity happen. In other words, conducting monetary policy in such an environment isn't like pulling on a rope; instead, it's like pushing on a string!

A second complication exists when the Fed finds it difficult to bring about changes in interest rates—a situation economists refer to as a **liquidity trap** . The liquidity trap exists when the money demand curve becomes horizontal, as shown in Figure 12.3. If a change in the money supply from M to M' cannot change interest rates, then, unless there is some other change in the economy, there is no reason for investment or any other component of aggregate demand to change. Monetary policy in those circumstances is rendered totally ineffective.

Unconvinced: "I won't drink, dammit—I won't!"

Source: Willyam Bradberry/Shutterstock.com

liquidity trap

Situation that exists when a change in monetary policy has no effect on interest rates.

FIGURE 12.3 A Liquidity Trap
When a change in the money supply has no effect on the interest rate, the economy is said to be in a liquidity trap.

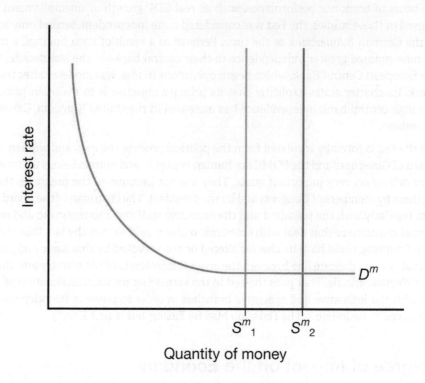

With the federal funds rate in the United States close to zero at the end of 2008, the possibility that the country was in or nearly in a liquidity trap could not be dismissed. As Figure 12.4 shows, the Fed, pumping reserves into the banking system at an unprecedented scale, saw those reserves accumulate in banks' vaults and reserve accounts rather than being fed into circulation in the form of loans.

FIGURE 12.4 Liquidity Trap? Bank Holdings of Excess Reserves, 2005–2020
Until the summer of 2008, banks made a practice of minimizing excess reserves. As the Fed pumped reserves into the banking system during the Great Recession and coronavirus crisis, those new reserves simply accumulated in bank vaults and in banks' accounts at the Fed.

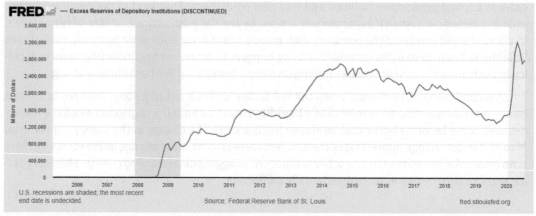

Source: Federal Reserve Bank of St. Louis, Excess Reserves of Depository Institutions (DISCONTINUED) [EXCSRESNS], retrieved from FRED, Federal Reserve Bank of St. Louis; https://fred.stlouisfed.org/series/EXCSRESNS.

To combat the "wait-and-see" mentality that kept businesses from borrowing and banks from lending, the Fed tried to build confidence that it would maintain its stimulative stance into the distant future. When the Fed lowered the rate to between 0% and 0.25% in December 2008, it added that "the committee anticipates that weak economic conditions are likely to warrant exceptionally low levels of the federal funds rate for some time."[17] That transparency, called *forward guidance*, is designed to build confidence in a recovery and confidence in the funds necessary to make that recovery happen. During the COVID-19 recession of 2020, for example, Fed Chairman Jerome Powell indicated that the Fed stood ready to keep interest rates at zero at least until 2023—a promise that cheap money would be available not only at the trough of the recession, but during the recovery that would follow.

Rational Expectations

Another challenge the Fed faces in trying to achieve objectives has to do with how well the public anticipates the Fed's actions and then acts on those expectations. It's possible, under the right circumstances, that monetary policy may only be able to affect the price level, and is (almost) powerless to influence real GDP. That unfortunate prediction stems from the **rational expectations hypothesis**, which states that people use all available information to make forecasts about future economic activity and the price level, and they adjust their behavior to these forecasts.

Figure 12.5 uses the model of aggregate demand and aggregate supply to show the implications of the rational expectations argument for monetary policy. Suppose the economy is operating at Y_P, as illustrated by point A, and that an increase in the money supply increases aggregate demand from AD_1 to AD_2. In the analysis we have explored until this point, that shift in aggregate demand would move the economy to a higher level of real GDP and create an inflationary gap. That, in turn, would put upward pressure on wages and other prices, shifting the short-run aggregate supply curve to $SRAS_2$ and moving the economy to point B. After that long-run self correction, the inflationary gap would be eliminated.

FIGURE 12.5 Monetary Policy and Rational Expectations
Suppose the economy is operating at point A and that individuals have rational expectations. They calculate that an expansionary monetary policy undertaken at price level P_1 will raise prices to P_2. They adjust their expectations—and wage demands—accordingly, quickly shifting the short-run aggregate supply curve to $SRAS_2$. The result is a movement along the long-run aggregate supply curve *LRAS* to point B, with no change in real GDP.

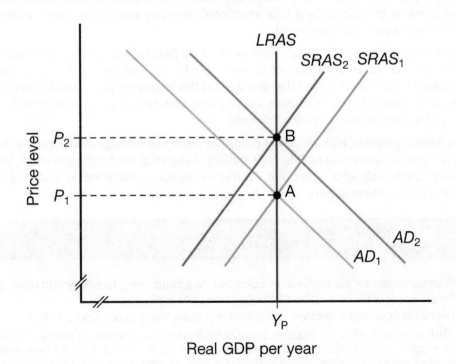

rational expectations hypothesis

Individuals form expectations about the future based on the information available to them, and they act on those expectations.

The rational expectations hypothesis, however, suggests a quite different interpretation. Suppose people observe the initial monetary policy change undertaken when the economy is at point A, and those people calculate that the increase in the money supply will ultimately drive the price level up to point B. Anticipating this change in prices, people adjust their behavior. For example, if the increase in the price level from P_1 to P_2 is a 10% change, workers will anticipate that the prices they pay will rise 10%, and they will demand 10% higher wages. Their employers, anticipating that the prices they will receive will also rise, will agree to pay those higher wages. As nominal wages increase, the short-run aggregate supply curve *immediately* shifts to $SRAS_2$. The result is an upward movement along the long-run aggregate supply curve, *LRAS*. There is no change in real GDP, and the monetary action has no effect other than its impact on the price level. This rational expectations argument relies on wages and prices' being sufficiently flexible—not sticky, as described in an earlier chapter—so that the change in expectations will allow the short-run aggregate supply curve to shift quickly to $SRAS_2$.

One important implication of the rational expectations argument is that a contractionary monetary policy could be painless. Suppose the economy is at point B in Figure 12.5, and the Fed reduces the money supply in order to decrease aggregate demand from AD_2 to AD_1. In the model of aggregate demand and aggregate supply, the result would be a recession. But in a rational expectations world, people's expectations change: Anticipating the coming disinflation, the short-run aggregate supply immediately shifts to the right (from $SRAS_2$ to $SRAS_1$), and the economy moves painlessly down its long-run aggregate supply curve *LRAS* to point A. It should come as no surprise that those who support the rational expectations hypothesis believe that monetary policy should not be used as a tool of stabilization policy—in their eyes, there's no point!

The rational expectations school of thinking reached its peak in the 1970s. In 1979 President Jimmy Carter appointed Paul Volcker as chairman of the Federal Reserve and pledged his full support for whatever the Fed might do to contain inflation. Volcker made it clear that the Fed was going to slow money growth and boost interest rates. He acknowledged that this policy would have costs but said that the Fed would stick to it as long as necessary to control inflation. Here was a monetary policy that was clearly announced and carried out as advertised. But the policy brought on the most severe recession the country had seen since the Great Depression—a recession that saw unemployment rates climb higher than they did in the subsequent Great Recession. That outcome—a recession brought on by a fully announced monetary contraction, seems inconsistent with the rational expectations argument.

Others, however, argue that people were aware of the Fed's pronouncements but were skeptical about whether the anti-inflation effort would persist, because the Fed had not vigorously fought inflation in the late 1960s and the 1970s. Against this history, people adjusted their estimates of inflation downward slowly. In essence, the recession occurred because people were surprised that the Fed was serious about fighting inflation.

The 1980s experiment with monetary policy has made one message clear: Once the Fed has proven it is serious about maintaining price stability, doing so in the future gets easier. Volcker's fight made Greenspan's work easier, and Greenspan's legacy of low inflation made Bernanke's, Yellen's, and Powell's easier in turn.

Worst-Case Scenario: Forward-looking people render stabilization policy ineffective.

Source: Andrey_Popov/ Shutterstock.com

Key Takeaways

- Potential targets for macroeconomic policy include interest rates, money growth rates, and the price level or expected rates of change in the price level.
- The recognition, implementation, and impact lags make timing policy actions difficult.
- When a central bank is not independent of political pressure, disagreements may arise over the magnitude of an appropriate policy response to economic events. Even if a central bank is structured to be independent of political pressure, its officers are likely to be affected by such pressure.

- To counteract liquidity traps or the possibility thereof, central banks have used quantitative-easing and credit-easing strategies.
- No central bank can know in advance how its policies will affect the economy; the rational expectations hypothesis predicts that central bank actions will affect the money supply and the price level but not the real level of economic activity.

Try It!

The scenarios below describe the U.S. recession and recovery in the early 1990s. Identify the lag that may have contributed to the difficulty in using monetary policy as a tool of economic stabilization.

1. The U.S. economy entered into a recession in July 1990. The Fed countered with expansionary monetary policy in October 1990, ultimately lowering the federal funds rate from 8% to 3% in 1992.
2. Investment began to increase, although slowly, in early 1992, and surged in 1993.

See related Concept Problem 4 at the end of this chapter.

Case in Point: Two-Front War—COVID-19 and the Zero Lower Bound

Mind = Blown: Everything I thought I knew about interest rates just got turned trunk over teakettle!

Source: michaeljung/Shutterstock.com

For the better part of the last forty years, the Fed has been satisfied when inflation runs below target. The target's 2% and actual inflation is 1%? *Exceeding expectations—time to knock off and head for the golf course!*

That perspective, however, has recently changed: Actual inflation below target is no longer a good thing, it's something requiring attention. The impetus for that shift in perspective was the well-observed relationship between interest rates and expected inflation: When lenders expect high inflation, they demand more interest, knowing that the loans they make will be paid back in depreciated dollars.[18]

The problem, then, with *low* inflation is that people come to expect it to *remain* low . . . with interest rates following in lockstep. That's exactly the problem Fed Chairman Jerome Powell found himself in during the COVID-19 recession: With interest rates hovering just above zero and a lot of crisis still in front of him, Powell found himself handcuffed by what is referred to as the *zero lower bound*—the inability to push interest rates lower in order to stimulate the economy. After all, interest rates can't go below zero, right?

Or can they? Imagine a world with interest rates below zero, one where lenders pay borrowers for letting them use their money! That kind of world runs counter to every bit of conventional wisdom we've accumulated . . . and it's exactly the kind of world that exists in Japan and a host of European countries, including economic powerhouses Sweden, France, Germany, and Italy. On the heels of the Great Recession, with their economies stagnating, those countries found that filling the banking system with reserves simply wasn't stimulating lending. Instead, commercial banks were content to sit on piles of excess reserves rather than using them to extend credit. This is the impact lag writ large: You can pump banks full of reserves, but you can't make them lend.

And so, to escape that liquidity trap and get commercial bankers to put those excess reserves to work, central bankers began charging commercial banks interest on their excess reserve deposits—making the commercial bankers essentially pay the central bank a storage fee. The only way to avoid paying that fee? Lend those excess reserves to the public for car loans and business loans and home loans.

As originally implemented, negative interest rates were only supposed to be binding on banks' reserve deposits. But interest rates tend to move together, and soon many commercial rates dipped into negative territory, too. On the lending side, that encouraged more consumption: Why lend money and get less back next year, when you could just spend it now instead? And on the borrowers' side, there's a big potential impact. Forget zero-percent financing—when interest rates are negative people actually pay you to use their money!

Negative interest rates are now a normal state of affairs in low-inflation Europe and Japan, but Fed officials have resisted the urge to follow. Chairman Powell's 2020 move to nudge inflation upward in order to drive interest rates away from the zero lower bound is just one more sign of that reluctance. Nevertheless, with the seal broken on negative interest rates, U.S. policymakers are prepared, at least, to *consider* the possibility should future conditions warrant. In the words of former Fed chairman Alan Greenspan, it's "only a matter of time."

See related Concept Problem 8 at the end of this chapter.

Answers to Try It! Problems

1. The recognition lag: the Fed did not seem to "recognize" that the economy was in a recession until several months after the recession began.
2. The impact lag: investment did not pick up quickly after interest rates were reduced. Alternatively, it could be attributed to the expansionary monetary policy's not having its desired effect, at least initially, on investment.

12.4 The Trade-Off Between Inflation and Unemployment

Learning Objectives

1. Draw a short-run Phillips curve and describe the relationship between inflation and unemployment that it expresses.
2. Describe the other relationships or phases that have been observed between inflation and unemployment.

Our model of aggregate demand and aggregate supply suggests that, in the short run, there may be a trade-off between inflation and real GDP: Stimulative actions by the Fed may increase real output at the cost of higher inflation. Because output doesn't just *appear*—instead, it's produced by inputs. More output implies fuller utilization of the economy's productive resources—especially labor resources. That means that there's an implied trade-off between inflation and unemployment.

Inflation and unemployment are the macroeconomy's two main nemeses. Unemployment represents a lost opportunity for workers to engage in productive effort—and to earn income. Inflation erodes the value of money people hold, and more important, the threat of inflation adds to uncertainty and makes people less willing to save and firms less willing to invest. If there were a trade-off between the two, we could reduce the rate of inflation or the rate of unemployment, but not both.

The fact that the United States has made steady progress against both unemployment and inflation over the last forty years represents a genuine macroeconomic triumph, one that appeared impossible in the 1960s and 1970s. To understand that triumph, we need to take a step back in time to take a closer look at an argument that once dominated macroeconomic thought—that a simple trade-off between inflation and unemployment did, indeed, exist.

Macro Villains: Inflation and Unemployment, inextricably linked.

Source: Vladimir Gappov/Shutterstock.com

The Phillips Curve in the Short Run

In 1958, economist A.W. Phillips published an analysis of British wage and unemployment data spanning an entire century. That data suggested an inverse relationship between rates of increase in wages and British unemployment.[19] Economists were quick to incorporate this idea into their thinking, extending the relationship to the rate of price-level changes—inflation—and unemployment. The notion that there is a trade-off between the two is expressed by a **short-run Phillips curve**, a curve that suggests a negative relationship between inflation and unemployment. Figure 12.6 shows a short-run Phillips curve.

short-run Phillips curve

A curve that suggests a negative relationship between inflation and unemployment.

FIGURE 12.6 The Short-Run Phillips Curve
The relationship between inflation and unemployment suggested by the work of A.W. Phillips is shown by a short-run Phillips curve.

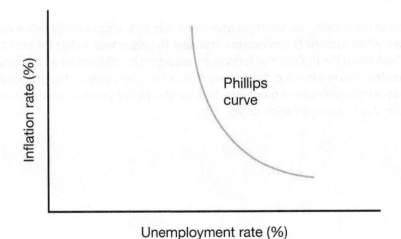

The short-run Phillips curve seemed to make good theoretical sense: An economy with a recessionary gap would have high unemployment and little or no inflation. An economy with an inflationary gap would have very little unemployment and a higher rate of inflation. The Phillips curve suggested a smooth transition between the two. As expansionary policies were undertaken to move the economy out of a recessionary gap, unemployment would fall and inflation would rise. Policies to correct an inflationary gap would bring down the inflation rate, but at a cost of higher unemployment.

The experience of the 1960s supported precisely the kind of trade-off the Phillips curve implied. Figure 12.7 shows annual rates of inflation plotted against annual rates of unemployment from 1961 to 1969. The points appear to follow a path quite similar to a Phillips curve relationship, and suggest that for the decade as a whole, a reduction in unemployment had been "traded" for an increase in inflation.

FIGURE 12.7 The Short-Run Phillips Curve in the 1960s

Values of U.S. inflation and unemployment rates during the 1960s generally conformed to the trade-off implied by the short-run Phillips curve. The points for each year lie close to a curve with the shape that Phillips's analysis predicted.

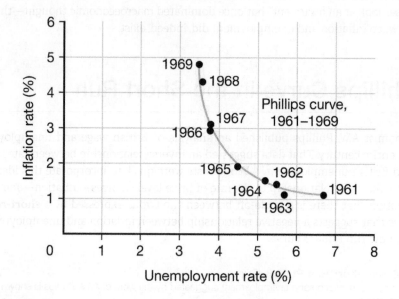

Source: Based on data from Economic Report of the President: 2011, (Washington, DC: U.S. Government Printing Office, 2011), Tables B-3 and B-42.

By the end of the decade, the unemployment rate was 3.5%, substantially below estimates of its natural level. When Richard Nixon became president in 1969, it was widely believed that it was time to move back down the Phillips curve, trading a reduction in inflation for an increase in unemployment. President Nixon moved to do precisely that, serving up a contractionary fiscal policy by ordering cuts in federal government purchases. Meanwhile, the Fed pursued a contractionary monetary policy aimed at bringing inflation down.

The Short-Run Phillips Curve Goes Awry

The effort to nudge the economy back down the Phillips curve to an unemployment rate closer to the natural level and a lower rate of inflation met with an unhappy surprise in 1970. Unemployment increased as expected. But inflation rose—from 4.8% in 1969 to 5.3% in 1970. The tidy relationship between inflation and unemployment that existed in the 1960s continued to disintegrate through the 1970s. By the end of the decade, the unemployment rate stood at 6%, and inflation had hit double digits. With inflation and unemployment both rising in tandem, the Phillips curve trade-off appeared to be broken.

Everything I learned in Professor Phillips' class is apparently useless. Thanks, 1970s.

Source: StoryTime Studio/Shutterstock.com

Indeed, a look at annual rates of inflation and unemployment since 1961 suggests that the 1960s were quite atypical. Figure 12.8 shows inflation and unemployment from 1960 to 2020. It is hard to see a negatively sloped Phillips curve lurking within that seemingly random scatter of points. That begs the question . . . exactly where did the Phillips curve go?

FIGURE 12.8 Inflation and Unemployment, 1960–2020
Annual observations of inflation and unemployment in the United States from 1960 to 2020 do not seem consistent with a Phillips curve.

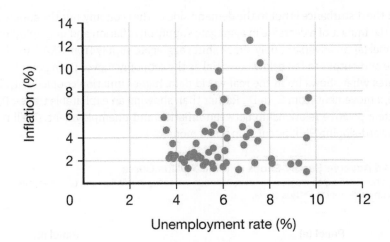

Sources: Data from Bureau of Labor Statistics, accessed through Federal Reserve Economic Data (FRED) at https://fred.stlouisfed.org/series/CPIAUCSL and https://fred.stlouisfed.org/series/UNRATE.

The Phillips Curve and Supply Shocks

The notion of a trade-off between inflation and unemployment presumes that shocks to the economy originate on the demand side of the economy. As an example consider the economy, depicted by the *AD/AS* model, in Panel (a) of Figure 12.9. An increase in aggregate demand moves the economy from A to B, putting upward pressure on prices and moving output past potential. Panel (b) shows the short-run Phillips curve that the change in aggregate demand produces: Originally at point A′, unemployment falls from U_1 to U_2, because producing more output requires more inputs. At the same time, the upward price pressure gives a nudge to the inflation rate, pushing it up from INF_1 to INF_2. The end result is a move to point B′, along a Phillips curve with the expected downward-sloping shape.

FIGURE 12.9 Demand Shocks Produce a Short-Run Phillips Curve

An increase in aggregate demand from AD_1 to AD_2 moves the economy from A to B in Panel (a), driving up output (which reduces unemployment) and increasing the price level. In Panel (b), which relates unemployment and inflation, there is a movement along the short-run Phillips curve from A' to B'.

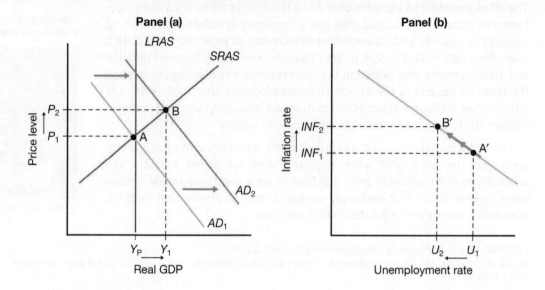

But what if the disturbance is not to the demand side of the economy, but the supply side? Figure 12.10 shows the impact of a decrease in aggregate supply on inflation and unemployment in the short run. In Panel (a), an adverse supply shock shifts aggregate supply from $SRAS_1$ to $SRAS_2$, causing prices to rise and output to fall below potential as the economy moves from point C to point D. Panel (b) indicates what shows up in the real-world data: higher inflation coupled with increased unemployment, a movement from C' to D'. Rather than showing an exploitable trade-off, the data *seems* to indicate a positive relationship between inflation and unemployment. (We'll revisit this notion of an upward-sloping Phillips curve in just a moment.)

FIGURE 12.10 An Adverse Supply Shock and the Phillips Curve

An adverse supply shock produces stagflation—simultaneous increases in inflation and unemployment. Stagflation seems to imply an upward-sloping Phillips curve.

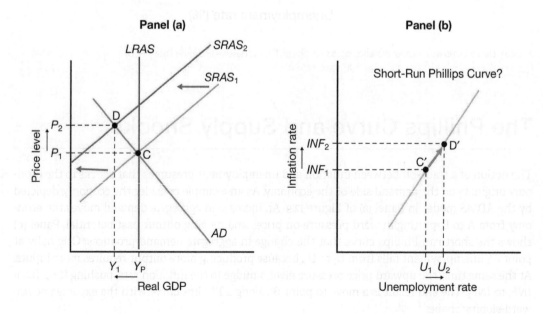

This is exactly the scenario that unraveled the trusty, dependable Phillips curve of the 1960s. A series of OPEC oil price hikes during the 1970s sent oil prices up tenfold. That both plunged the economy into a recessionary gap and fueled a high inflation that endured throughout the decade.

Inflation and Unemployment in the Long Run: The Importance of Expectations

To shed further light on the lack of an observed trade-off between inflation and unemployment over the past few decades, it's worth making the leap from the short run to the long run. After all, it's been fifty years since the Phillips curve relationship seemed to go haywire; five decades is a *long* time!

Extending our analysis from the short run to the long run is easier if we first note these two things:[20]

1. Inflation is everywhere and always a monetary phenomenon.

2. Putting more fancy pieces of paper (money!) in circulation doesn't fundamentally alter the ability of the economy to produce goods and services.

Taken together, this tells us that the amount of money in circulation *does* have the power to alter the inflation rate, but *does not* have the power to affect the economy's long-run potential output, nor the economy's natural rate of unemployment. In other words, full employment is the norm in the long run, and is compatible with any number of different inflation rates: The long-run Phillips curve, shown in Figure 12.11. is vertical at the natural rate of unemployment.

FIGURE 12.11 The Long-Run Phillips Curve
In the long run, any number of different inflation rates are compatible with full employment; the long-run Phillips curve is vertical.

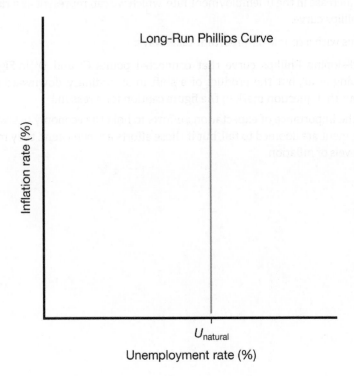

This begs the question as to how, exactly, we move from the downward-sloping short-run Phillips curve of the 1960s (or the seemingly upward-sloping curve from the 1970s) to the vertical long-run Phillips curve. The answer came from famed economist Milton Friedman, who, in his presidential address to the American Economic Association, asserted that policymakers could not permanently hold unemployment below its natural rate.

> *To state this conclusion differently, there is always a temporary trade-off between inflation and unemployment; there is no permanent trade-off. The temporary trade-off comes not from inflation per se, but from unanticipated inflation, which generally means, from a rising rate of inflation.*[21]

"He shouldn't have tried to hold unemployment below its natural rate."

Source: Romariolen/Shutterstock.com

Friedman acknowledges that there is always an exploitable trade-off in the short run: The Fed can, by printing money, create an inflation that stimulates production and reduces unemployment. In other words, the short-run Phillips curve slopes downward. But as soon as that inflation becomes expected, workers will build that expected inflation into their contracts by asking for higher wages, merchants will build that expected inflation into their prices, lenders will build that expected inflation into their interest calculations. The economy will return to full employment and potential output through the self-correcting mechanism we explored in our chapter on aggregate supply and aggregate demand: An adverse shift in short-run aggregate supply that increases both unemployment and inflation.

Figure 12.12 shows Freidman's view of the Phillips curve economy. Beginning at point B', the Fed temporarily stimulates the economy by pumping in money and forcing down interest rates. Unemployment decreases and inflation rises as the economy moves along short-run Phillips curve PC_1 to point C'. But that's only temporary. In the long run, workers and merchants are starting to build the new, higher rate of inflation into their wage demands and prices; in the *AD/AS* model, the short-run aggregate supply curve is starting to shift to the left, producing both rising inflation and an increase in the unemployment rate, which we can represent as a rightward shift in the short-run Phillips curve.

That leaves us with a couple of important takeaways:

1. The upward-sloping Phillips curve that connected points C' and D' in Figure 12.10 wasn't upward-sloping at all, but the product of a shift in an ordinary, downward-sloping Phillips curve. (We put that question mark in the figure caption for a reason!)

2. Because of the importance of expectations, efforts to hold the economy below its natural rate of unemployment are doomed to fail, but if those efforts are persistent, they may lead to ever-increasing levels of inflation.

FIGURE 12.12 The Expectations-Augmented Phillips Curve
In the short run, policymakers can stimulate aggregate demand to reduce unemployment at the cost of higher inflation. That's shown as a move from B' to C' along the original short-run Phillips curve PC_1. As people become used to the inflation, workers ask for higher wages and firms charge higher prices. Aggregate supply decreases, causing both more unemployment and higher prices, a move from C' to D'. There, the central bank faces a new, exploitable Phillips curve trade-off, PC_2, where it can reduce unemployment once again at the cost of ever-higher inflation.

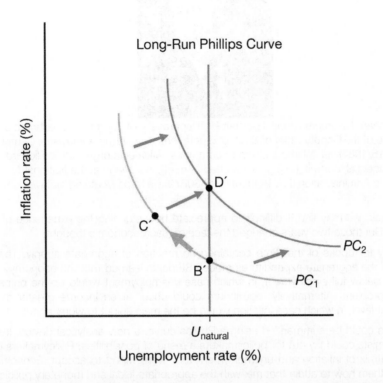

Key Takeaways

- The view that there is a trade-off between inflation and unemployment is expressed by a short-run Phillips curve.
- While there are periods in which a trade-off between inflation and unemployment appears to exist, the actual relationship indicated by data show differing episodes in which inflation and unemployment have been positively related and negatively related.
- Shifts in aggregate supply tend to shift the short-run Phillips curve in the opposite direction.
- The observed positive correlation between inflation and unemployment during the 1970s may well have been the result of a shifting Phillips curve.

Try It!

Suppose an economy receives a series of virtuous (positive) short-run supply shocks. Show the impact on the short-run Phillips curve. Then show the impact in the long run. Does your answer depend on the nature of the return to full employment and potential output?

See related Concept Problem 13 at the end of this chapter.

Case in Point: Some Reflections on the 1970s

Source: Richard Nixon presidential portrait (1). Department of Defense. Department of the Army. Office of the Deputy Chief of Staff for Operations. U.S. Army Audiovisual Center.(ca. 1974 - 05/15/1984) via Wikimedia: https://commons. wikimedia.org/wiki/File:Richard_Nixon_presidential_portrait_(1).jpg. Retouched from original image at the National Archives and Records Administration (NARA Identifier: 530679) via https://catalog.archives.gov/id/530679.

Looking back, we may find it difficult to appreciate how stunning the experience of 1970 and 1971 was. But those two years changed the face of macroeconomic thought.

Introductory textbooks of that time contained no mention of aggregate supply. The model of choice was the aggregate expenditures model. Students learned that the economy could be in equilibrium below full employment, in which case unemployment would be the primary macroeconomic problem. Alternatively, equilibrium could occur at an income greater than the full employment level, in which case inflation would be the main culprit to worry about.

These ideas could be summarized using a Phillips curve, a new analytical device. It suggested that economists could lay out for policymakers a menu of possibilities. Policymakers could then choose the mix of inflation and unemployment they were willing to accept. Economists would then show them how to attain that mix with the appropriate fiscal and monetary policies.

Then 1970 and 1971 came crashing in on this well-ordered fantasy. President Richard Nixon had come to office with a pledge to bring down inflation. The consumer price index had risen 4.7% during 1968, the highest rate since 1951. Nixon cut government purchases in 1969, and the Fed produced a sharp slowing in money growth. The president's economic advisers predicted at the beginning of 1970 that inflation and unemployment would both fall. Appraising the 1970 debacle early in 1971, the president's economists said that the experience had not been consistent with what standard models would predict. The economists suggested, however, that this was probably due to a number of transitory factors. Their forecast that inflation and unemployment would improve in 1971 proved wide of the mark—the unemployment rate rose from 4.9% to 5.9% (an increase of 20%), while the rate of inflation measured by the change in the implicit price deflator barely changed from 5.3% to 5.2%.

As we've seen, the experience can be readily explained using the model of aggregate demand and aggregate supply. But this tool was not well developed then. The experience of the 1970s forced economists back to their analytical drawing boards and spawned dramatic advances in our understanding of macroeconomic events.

Related to Numerical Problem 2 at the end of this chapter.

Source: Based on United States. President and Council of Economic Advisers (U.S.). "1971," Economic Report of the President (1971). United States Government Printing Office (Washington: 1971).

Answer to Try It! Problem

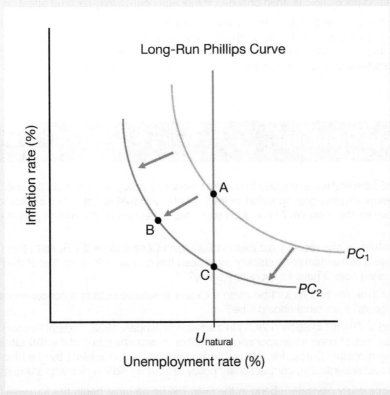

The positive supply shock, which you can show using *AD/AS*, reduces the price level and pushes output beyond potential. In the Phillips curve diagram, inflation decreases and unemployment dips, a move from A on PC_1 to B on a new Phillips curve PC_2.

If the economy is allowed to self-correct, aggregate supply will decrease as workers begin demanding higher wages and sellers charge higher prices. The Phillips curve will shift back to PC_1 and the economy will return to A. If the Fed introduces contractionary policy to reduce the inflationary gap and bring the economy back to potential output, that action will reduce inflation and increase unemployment; the economy will move along PC_2 to point C.

12.5 Review and Practice

Summary

Part of the Fed's power stems from the fact that it has no legislative mandate to seek particular goals. That leaves the Fed free to set its own goals. In recent years, its primary goal has seemed to be the maintenance of an inflation rate below 2% to 3%. Given its success in meeting that goal, the Fed has used its tools to stimulate the economy to close recessionary gaps. Once the Fed has made a choice to undertake an expansionary or contractionary policy, we can trace the impact of that policy on the economy.

There are a number of problems in the use of monetary policy. These include various types of lags, the issue of the choice of targets in conducting monetary policy, political pressures placed on the process of policy setting, and uncertainty as to how great an impact the Fed's policy decisions have on macroeconomic variables. We highlighted the difficulties for monetary policy if the economy is in or near a liquidity trap and discussed the use of quantitative easing and credit easing in such situations. If people have rational expectations and respond to those expectations in their wage and price choices, then changes in monetary policy may have no effect on real GDP.

We saw in this chapter that there is an exploitable trade-off between inflation and unemployment called the Phillips curve relationship. The Phillips curve, however, has the power to shift when expectations about inflation change. That makes using monetary policy to keep an economy perpetually stimulated undesirable, as the stimulus needed would produce ever-increasing levels of inflation.

Concept Problems

1. Suppose the Fed were required to conduct monetary policy so as to hold the unemployment rate below 4%, the goal specified in the Humphrey–Hawkins Act. What implications would this have for the economy? How does your answer depend on the natural rate of unemployment?

2. The statutes of the recently established European Central Bank (ECB) state that its primary objective is to maintain price stability. How does this charter differ from that of the Fed? What significance does it have for monetary policy?

3. Do you think the Fed should be given a clearer legislative mandate concerning macroeconomic goals? If so, what should it be?

4. (Related to "Try It!" in Section 24.3.) In a speech in January 1995, Federal Reserve Chairman Alan Greenspan used a transportation metaphor to describe some of the difficulties of implementing monetary policy. He referred to the criticism levied against the Fed for shifting in 1994 to an anti-inflation, contractionary policy when the inflation rate was still quite low:

   "To successfully navigate a bend in the river, the barge must begin the turn well before the bend is reached. Even so, currents are always changing and even an experienced crew cannot foresee all the events that might occur as the river is being navigated. A year ago, the Fed began its turn (a shift toward contractionary monetary policy), and we do not yet know if it has been successful."[22]

   Mr. Greenspan was referring, of course, to the problem of lags. What kind of lag do you think he had in mind? What do you suppose the reference to changing currents means?

5. In a speech in August 1999, Mr. Greenspan said,

   "We no longer have the luxury to look primarily to the flow of goods and services, as conventionally estimated, when evaluating the macroeconomic environment in which monetary policy must function. There are important—but extremely difficult—questions surrounding the behavior of asset prices and the implications of this behavior for the decisions of households and businesses."[23]

   The asset price that Mr. Greenspan was referring to was the U.S. stock market, which had been rising sharply in the weeks and months preceding this speech. Inflation and unemployment were both low at that time. What issues concerning the conduct of monetary policy was Mr. Greenspan raising?

6. Suppose we observed an economy in which changes in the money supply produce no changes whatever in interest rates. What could we conclude about money demand?

7. How is it possible that stimulative Fed policy that reduces interest rates ends up having no real effect on output?

8. (Related to "Case in Point: Two-Front War—COVID-19 and the Zero Lower Bound" in Section 24.3.) Explain how a decrease in the interest payable on reserves leads to a decrease in the interest rates bankers charge for loans. Then, explain how reducing interest below zero on reserve balances encourages bankers to lend to the public . . . even at rates below 0%.

9. Four meetings at which the Fed changed the target for the federal funds rate are shown below.

January 30, 2008	June 30, 2004
September 18, 2007	March 15, 2020

Pick one of these dates and find out why it chose to change its target for the federal funds rate on that date.

10. Trace the impact of an expansionary monetary policy on bond prices, interest rates, investment, real GDP, and the price level. Illustrate your analysis graphically.

11. Trace the impact of an expansionary monetary policy on inflation and unemployment. What does the policy imply for the position of the Phillips curve?

12. (Related to "Try It!" in Section 24.2.) Trace the impact of a contractionary monetary policy on bond prices, interest rates, investment, real GDP, and the price level. Illustrate your analysis graphically.

13. (Related to "Try It!" in Section 24.4.) Trace the impact of a contractionary monetary policy on inflation and unemployment. What does the policy imply for the position of the Phillips curve in the short run? The long run?

14. (Related to "Case in Point: The Fed's Job May Be Easing, but It Isn't Easy" in Section 24.2.) After reading the case, review Section 22.4 on the Federal Reserve System. What protections built into the Fed's structure helped Powell resist the pressure to stimulate an already robust economy during the fall of 2019?

Numerical Problems

1. Use the following data to construct two Phillips curves, one for June and July, the other for August and September. indicate which changes are due to supply shifts, and which may be due to demand shifts.

	Inflation Rate (%)	Unemployment Rate (%)
June	5	7
July	4	9
August	4	4
September	5	3

2. (Related to "Case in Point: Some Reflections on the 1970s" in Section 24.4.) Using the long-run model of the Phillips curve and the *AD/AS* model of the economy, illustrate what happened in the U.S. economy between 1970 and 1971. Integrate data from the case into your illustration.

Endnotes

1. Federal Open Market Committee. "Federal Reserve issues FOMC statement." Board of Governors of the Federal Reserve System, March 15, 2020. Retrieved from: https://www.federalreserve.gov/newsevents/press-releases/monetary20200315a.htm.

2. Federal Reserve Press Release, 12/16/2008. https://www.federalreserve.gov/newsevents/press/monetary/20081216b.htm.

3. For more on this, see the opener to our chapter on international finance.

4. Jerome H. Powell, "New Economic Challenges and the Fed's Monetary Policy Review." Board of Governors of the Federal Reserve System, August 27, 2020. Retrieved from: https://www.federalreserve.gov/newsevents/speech/powell20200827a.htm.

5. You can read the entirety of Powell's speech, delivered at the Kansas City Fed's annual conference on monetary policy, at https://www.federalreserve.gov/newsevents/speech/powell20200827a.htm

6. Remember the mantra regarding the inverse relationship between interest rates and bond prices from our chapter on financial markets: "When interest rates rise, bond prices fall." Or, in this case, "When bond prices rise, interest rates fall."

7. In reality, the Fed buys bonds from a securities dealer, and credits that dealer's bank account with the necessary funds. That means the new money created is electronic, rather than paper.

8. For more on this, see our positively riveting chapter on investment, which contains a dandy primer on one of the most important tools of finance, present and future value. The decrease in the interest rate is *also* likely to cause the dollar to depreciate in foreign exchange markets, which can lead to an increase in net exports. Our chapter on international finance discusses this in greater detail.

9. David J. Lynch and Taylor Telford, "Trump says 'Boneheads' at Fed should cut interest rates to zero—or even set negative rates." *The Washington Post*, September 11, 2019. Retrieved from: https://www.washingtonpost.com/business/2019/09/11/trump-says-boneheads-fed-should-cut-interest-rates-zero-or-even-set-negative-rates/.

10. Jerome H. Powell, "Brief Remarks (At the premiere of 'Marriner Eccles: Father of the Modern Federal Reserve,' Salt Lake City, Utah)." Board of Governors of the Federal Reserve System, October 7, 2019. Retrieved from: https://www.federalreserve.gov/newsevents/speech/powell20191007a.htm.

11. For more on the philosophy of monetarism, see our chapter on the history of macroeconomic thought.

12. For more on this, see our chapter on inflation. It's an eye-opener how much damage rising prices can do!

13. Carl E. Walsh, "Inflation Targeting: What Have We Learned?," *International Finance* 12, no. 2 (2009): 195–233.

14. For more on this, see our chapter on inflation, which discusses the ins and outs of inflationary finance in riveting detail!

15. Contrast that to members of the House of Representatives, who are up for reelection every two years. They have zero choice but to bow to the political winds: Their re-election campaigns begin about two days after they're elected!

16. See, for example, Alberto Alesina and Lawrence H. Summers, "Central Bank Independence and Macroeconomic Performance: Some Comparative Evidence," *Journal of Money, Credit, and Banking* 25, no. 2 (May 1993): 151–62.

17. Federal Open Market Committee. "FOMC statement." Board of Governors of the Federal Reserve System, December 16, 2008. Retrieved from: https://www.federalreserve.gov/newsevents/pressreleases/monetary20081216b.htm.

18. That observation is attributed to the famed economist Irving Fisher, and is known as the *Fisher effect.*

19. Alban W. Phillips, "The Relation between Unemployment and the Rate of Change of Money Wage Rates in the United Kingdom, 1861–1957," *Economica* 25 (November 1958): 283–99.

20. The first item in the list is attributable to Milton Friedman, who revolutionized thinking about the Phillips curve by incorporating expectations.

21. Milton Friedman, "The Role of Monetary Policy," *The American Economic Review,* Vol. 58, No. 1, 1968, pp. 1–17. JSTOR, www.jstor.org/stable/1831652.

22. Board of Governors of the Federal Reserve System (U.S.) and Greenspan, Alan. "Remarks before the Board of Directors of the National Association of Home Builders, Houston, Texas." January 28, 1995, https://fraser.stlouisfed.org/title/452/item/8527.

23. Alan Greenspan, "New challenges for monetary policy," speech delivered before a symposium sponsored by the Federal Reserve Bank of Kansas City in Jackson Hole, Wyoming, on August 27, 1999. Mr. Greenspan was famous for his convoluted speech, which listeners often found difficult to understand. CBS correspondent Andrea Mitchell, to whom Mr. Greenspan is married, once joked that he had proposed to her three times and that she had not understood what he was talking about on his first two efforts. Retrieved from: https://www.federalreserve.gov/boarddocs/speeches/1999/19990827.htm.

CHAPTER 13
Government and Fiscal Policy

13.1 Start Up: A Massive Stimulus

In late 2019, the economy was dialed in: Inflation was subdued, interest rates were low, and the unemployment rate was near an all-time low. By March of 2020, the coronavirus had arrived, the unemployment rate had reached a ninety-year high, and the stock market had lost 40% of its value in a matter of days. Policymakers trembled in fear, faced with the daunting challenge of shutting down the economy to prevent a pandemic while keeping money in peoples' pockets.

Those policymakers, however, had learned some big lessons from the Great Recession a decade before: In a genuine crisis, there's no value in being timid. And so, within a matter of weeks, the federal government hurled the largest fiscal stimulus package ever right into the face of the coronavirus. The $3 trillion package, three times as large as the response to the Great Recession, included a number of targeted programs designed specifically to fight the challenge posed by COVID-19.

D.C. policymakers took this message to heart during the early days of the coronavirus.

Source: Ivelin Radkov/Shutterstock.com

On March 18, 2020, the Families First Coronavirus Response Act enhanced and extended unemployment benefits for workers who lost jobs as a result of shutdowns, as well as increased federal Medicaid benefits and food-security spending. By March 27, Congress had passed the CARES Act, a $2 trillion relief package that included economic support for small businesses to help them avoid laying off employees, a second extension and expansion of unemployment benefits, a payroll tax deferral for businesses, and direct payments of up to $1200 (officially, a tax rebate) to taxpayers. Less than a month later, Congress followed up this legislation with the Paycheck Protection Program, which provided more economic support for small businesses and further funding for hospitals and coronavirus testing.

These acts made use of all of the usual fiscal policy suspects. They contained discretionary fiscal policy measures designed to increase aggregate demand, such as increases in spending and tax cuts. They also gave greater power to automatic stabilizers by liberalizing unemployment eligibility and benefits. On the one-year anniversary of the coronavirus's arrival, the tab was at $3 trillion and counting—over half of what government normally spends in a year, and about a seventh of a year's gross domestic product for the country as a whole.

Prudent use of fiscal policy raises a lot of important questions: How do government tax and expenditure policies affect real GDP and the price level? Why do economists differ so sharply in assessing the likely impact of such policies? Can fiscal policy be used to stabilize the economy in the short run? What are the long-run effects of government spending and taxing?

Let's dig in to some of these questions. We'll begin with a look at the government's budget to see how it spends the tax revenue it collects. Clearly, the government's budget is not always in balance, so we'll also look at government deficits and debt. Then we'll look at how fiscal policy works to stabilize the economy, distinguishing between built-in stabilization methods and discretionary measures. Finally, we'll end the chapter with a discussion of why fiscal policy is so controversial.

13.2 Government and the Economy

Learning Objectives

1. Identify the major components of U.S. government spending and sources of government revenues.
2. Define the terms *budget surplus*, *budget deficit*, *balanced budget*, and *national debt*, and discuss their trends over time in the United States.

Fiscal policy is one of the two main types of stabilization policy used to steer the economy to its potential output. We saw in the previous chapter that monetary policy is carried out by the central bank. In contrast, fiscal policy uses the government's taxing and spending powers to close recessionary or inflationary gaps. Let's start our analysis of fiscal policy by examining the nature of government's revenues and expenditures.

Government Purchases

Kansas City's magnificent public library was included in government purchases. So are the salaries paid to the shushers.

Source: PhotoTrippingAmerica/Shutterstock.com

The government purchases component of aggregate demand includes purchases by governments of goods and services produced by firms, as well as goods and services that are directly produced by governments (or government agencies) themselves. When the federal government buys staples and staplers, the transaction is part of government purchases. When a professor at a state college delivers a sparkling course on the effectiveness of monetary and fiscal policy, that professor's compensation is also included in government purchases.

Government purchases, like the economy, have grown over time. But as a *share* of total spending (GDP), government purchases have been generally declining. Figure 13.1 shows both federal and state and local government purchases as a percentage of GDP from 1960 to 2020. The general decline in overall government purchases over that time has been driven by an almost 50% decrease in federal government purchases. State and local purchases, on the other hand, have risen relative to GDP.

FIGURE 13.1 Federal, State, and Local Purchases Relative to GDP, 1960–2020
Government purchases were generally above 20% of GDP from 1960 until the early 1990s, and then below 20% of GDP except during the 2007–2009 recession. State and local government purchases in 2020 were about 11% of GDP; federal government purchases were about 7%.

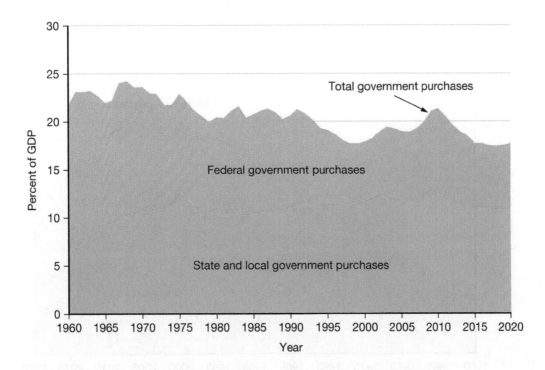

Source: Data from Bureau of Economic Analysis, accessed through Federal Reserve Economic Data (FRED) at https://fred.stlouisfed.org/series/FGCE, https://fred.stlouisfed.org/series/SLCE, and https://fred.stlouisfed.org/series/GDP.

Transfer Payments

Transfer payments are payments made by the government that do not require the recipients to produce a good or service in order to receive the payment. For example, to receive Social Security benefits, you only need to meet the Social Security Administration's eligibility criteria; most of those receiving benefits are retirees who produce nothing for sale in the greater economy. Transfer payments also include various welfare benefits.

Transfer payments increased rapidly during the late 1960s and early 1970s. This was the period in which federal programs such as Medicare (health insurance for the elderly) and Medicaid (health insurance for the poor) were created and other programs were expanded.

Figure 13.2 shows that transfer payment spending by the federal government and by state and local governments has risen as a percentage of GDP. In 1960, such spending totaled about 6% of GDP; in recent years, it has been above 16%. The federal government accounts for the bulk of transfer payment spending in the United States.

FIGURE 13.2 Federal, State, and Local Transfer Payments as a Percentage of GDP, 1960–2020

As a percentage of GDP, transfer payments rose dramatically during the late 1960s and the 1970s as federal programs expanded. More recently, rising health-care costs have driven the spending for transfer payment programs such as Medicare and Medicaid upward. Transfer payments fluctuate with the business cycle, rising in times of recession and falling during times of expansion: Notice the sharp increase during the 2007–2009 recession.

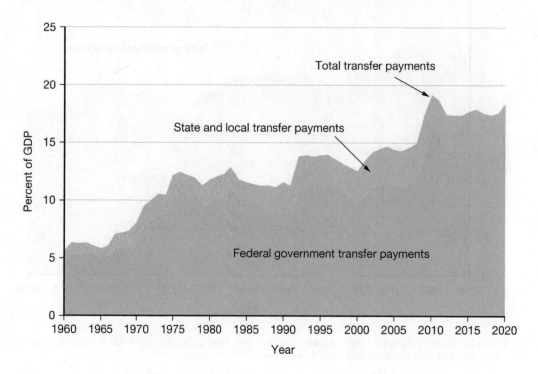

Source: Data from Bureau of Economic Analysis, accessed via Federal Reserve Economic Data (FRED) at https://fred.stlouisfed.org/series/W014RC1Q027SBEA, https://fred.stlouisfed.org/series/LA0000171A027NBEA, and https://fred.stlouisfed.org/series/GDP.

Transfer payment spending relative to GDP tends to fluctuate with the business cycle. Transfer payments fell during the late 1980s, a period of rapid expansion, but then rose sharply as the economy slipped into recession in 1990. Similar sharp increases occurred during the recession of 2001 and the Great Recession of 2007; each increase was followed by a period of decline as the economy recovered and began to expand.

Why do transfers increase during recessions? Generally, welfare benefits are extended on the basis of eligibility. People qualify to receive welfare benefits, such as cash, food stamps, or Medicaid, only if their income falls below a certain level. They qualify for unemployment compensation by losing their jobs. When economic activity falls, incomes fall, people lose jobs, and more people qualify for aid. When the economy expands, incomes and employment rise, and fewer people qualify for welfare or unemployment benefits. Spending for those programs therefore tends to fall during an expansion.

Figure 13.3 summarizes trends in total government spending (including government purchases, transfer payments, and net interest on its debt obligations and transfer payments) since 1960. Relative to GDP, total government spending has risen over time, from about 26% in 1960 to 34% in 2019, just before the COVID-19 recession. The bulk of that growth has been driven by growth in transfer payments . . . especially during the COVID-19 recession, where shrinking GDP was met with an unprecedented government fiscal response.

Before WWII, the economically vulnerable, like these men lined up outside Al Capone's soup kitchen, had to rely on private charity for assistance. Today, these men would be able to count on a host of federally run transfer payment programs, instead of depending on the questionable kindness of Capone.

Source: Everett Collection/Shutterstock.com

FIGURE 13.3 Government Spending as a Percentage of GDP, 1960–2020

Relative to income, government spending tends to rise in recessions and fall during expansions. Before the coronavirus crisis, government spending was about one-third of GDP; it spiked briefly to 55% early in the crisis as GDP plummeted and spending skyrocketed.

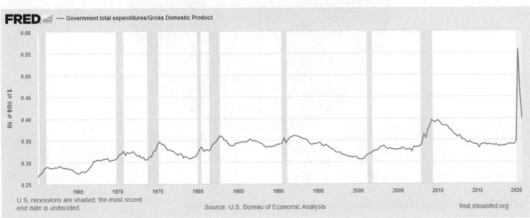

Source: Bureau of Economic Analysis, accessed through Federal Reserve Economic Data (FRED) at https://fred.stlouisfed.org/series/W068RCQ027SBEA and https://fred.stlouisfed.org/series/GDP. FRED® Graphs ©Federal Reserve Bank of St. Louis. All rights reserved. All FRED® Graphs appear courtesy of Federal Reserve Bank of St. Louis. https://fred.stlouisfed.org/.

Taxes

Taxes affect the relationship between real GDP and personal disposable income; disposable income, in turn, affects the level of consumption. Taxes imposed on firms affect the profitability of investment decisions, and therefore affect the levels of investment firms will choose. Payroll taxes imposed on firms affect the costs of hiring workers; they therefore have an impact on employment and on the real wages earned by workers.

As shown in Figure 13.4, the bulk of federal receipts come from the personal income tax and from payroll taxes. In contrast, state and local governments rely less on income and payroll taxes, and more on sales and property taxes. Fees are also a major source of revenue at the state and local level, as are grants from the federal government to administer programs. State and local government revenue sources are shown in Figure 13.5.

FIGURE 13.4 The Composition of Federal Revenues, 2020

About half of the federal government's $3.4 trillion in 2020 revenues came from individual income taxes. Payroll taxes and corporate income taxes made up the bulk of the remaining receipts.

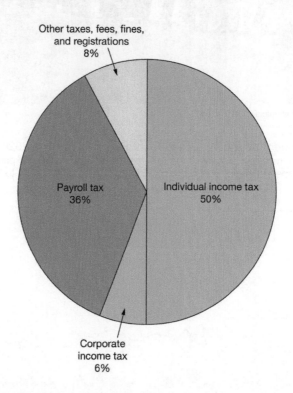

Source: Data from Bureau of Economic Analysis Table 3.1 at https://www.bea.gov/tools/.

FIGURE 13.5 Sources of State and Local Government Revenue, 2020
In contrast to the federal government, which is largely funded by income and payroll taxes, state governments, shown in Panel (a), tend to rely more heavily on sales taxes; local governments, shown in Panel (b), are more dependent on property taxes.

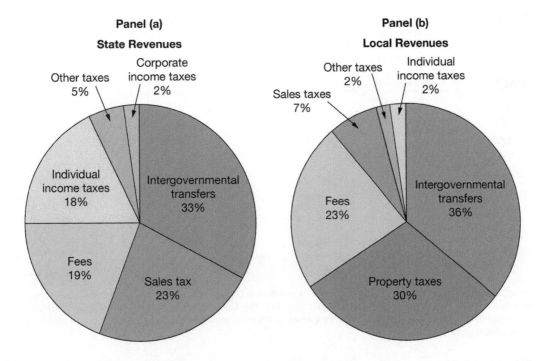

Source: Data from Bureau of Economic Analysis Tables 3.20 and 3.21 at https://www.bea.gov/tools/.

The Government's Budget Balance

The government's budget balance is the difference between the government's revenues and its expenditures. If revenues are greater than expenditures, the government runs a **budget surplus**. If, however, the government spends more than it takes in, it runs a **budget deficit**. If receipts equal expenditures, the government has a **balanced budget**.

Figure 13.6 compares federal, state, and local government revenues to expenditures relative to GDP since 1960. The government's budget has been generally in deficit since the 1960s, a brief period between 1998 and 2001 being the lone exception.

In Figure 13.6 the deficit can be measured as the size of the gap between spending (in blue) and revenues (in red). Deficits tend to widen after tax cuts, driven by declining government revenue. That's true for the Reagan tax cuts in the early 1980s, the Bush tax cuts in 2001, and the Trump tax cuts in 2017. Deficits also widen in response to increased spending. That's particularly evident in the early years of the George W. Bush presidency, as the post-9/11 war effort drove a large military expansion. Rising spending is also partially responsible for the sharp increases in deficits during the Great Recession and the COVID-19 recession.

The United States is used to seeing government operate with a deficit. That doesn't necessarily mean, however, that government deficits are the norm in other places. Figure 13.7 compares the recent deficit experience in the United States with forty-one other developed countries, with deficits hanging below the zero line and budget surpluses rising above. The figure reveals two striking facts:

budget surplus

Situation that occurs if government revenues exceed expenditures.

budget deficit

Situation that occurs if government expenditures exceed revenues.

balanced budget

Situation that occurs if the budget surplus equals zero.

1. Not all countries operate perpetually in deficit. About half of these forty-two developed countries had budget surpluses.

2. Among the deficit spenders, the U.S. deficit is notably large as a percentage of GDP.

FIGURE 13.6 Government Revenue and Expenditure as a Percentage of GDP, 1960–2020

The government's budget has generally been in deficit since the 1960s, with expenditures (blue) exceeding receipts (red). Budget deficits, measured as the distance between the blue and red lines at any particular date, tend to widen in recessions and narrow during expansions.

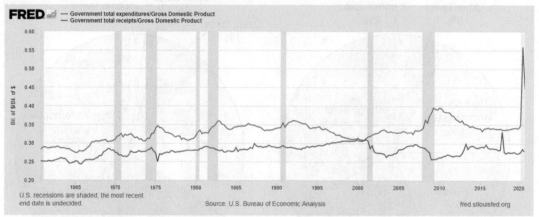

Source: Bureau of Economic Analysis, accessed through Federal Reserve Economic Data (FRED) at https://fred.stlouisfed.org/series/ W068RCQ027SBEA, https://fred.stlouisfed.org/series/W066RC1Q027SBEA, and https://fred.stlouisfed.org/series/GDP. FRED® Graphs ©Federal Reserve Bank of St. Louis. All rights reserved. All FRED® Graphs appear courtesy of Federal Reserve Bank of St. Louis. https://fred.stlouisfed.org/.

FIGURE 13.7 Deficits as a Percentage of GDP in Forty-Two Countries, 2019

In this figure, negative values indicate deficits and positive values surpluses. The United States (far left) had a 2019 deficit greater than 6% of GDP. Most developed countries' deficits are smaller than that, and many run large budget surpluses. Norway (far right) at the other extreme had a surplus of over 6%.

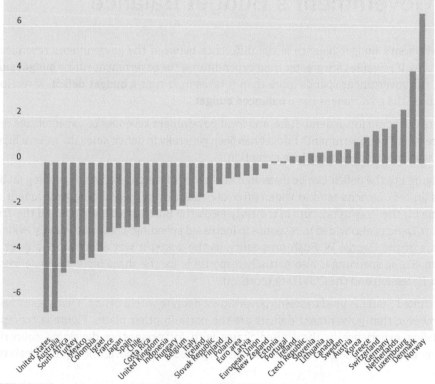

Source: OECD (2021), General government deficit (indicator). doi: 10.1787/77079edb-en.

The National Debt

Because governments must borrow money to pay for any spending beyond revenue, the **national debt** represents the sum of all past federal deficits, minus any surpluses. Figure 13.8 shows the national debt as a percentage of GDP. The debt, which peaked near the end of World War II, declined steadily as a fraction of income until 1980. The debt rose from 1981 to 1996, fell during the surplus years of the Clinton administration, and has risen substantially ever since. Today, the relative size of the debt is approaching post-WWII levels.

national debt

The sum of all past federal deficits, minus any surpluses.

FIGURE 13.8 The National Debt and the Economy, 1939–2019
Relative to GDP, the national debt was at its peak during World War II. It fell dramatically over the next few decades, then began to rise during the 1980s and 1990s. It rose markedly during the Great Recession, and it has continued to increase since then. It has since spiked again in response to the coronavirus crisis (data not available at time of publication).

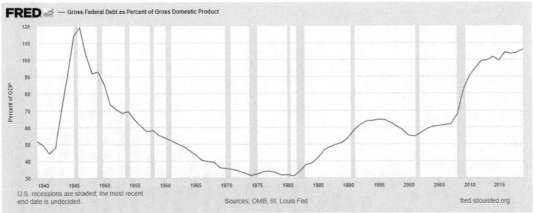

Source: U.S. Office of Management and Budget and Federal Reserve Bank of St. Louis, Gross Federal Debt as Percent of Gross Domestic Product [GFDGDPA188S], retrieved from FRED, Federal Reserve Bank of St. Louis; https://fred.stlouisfed.org/series/GFDGDPA188S.

Judged by international standards, the U.S. national debt relative to its GDP is above average. Figure 13.9 shows national debt as a percentage of GDP for thirty-four countries in 2020. While the U.S. debt is high relative to its income, it's not the highest: The troubled economies of Greece and Japan are carrying even higher debt burdens.

In the United States, Congress authorizes the maximum amount of federal government borrowing. That process is often messy at best, and has resulted in several government shutdowns during times of disagreement. Most recently, the federal government shut down for thirty-five straight days between December 2018 and January 2019. The shutdown, which affected some 800,000 federal employees, occurred because of President Donald Trump's refusal to sign any appropriations bill that didn't include $5.7 billion in federal funds for construction of a border wall. Without approval to borrow in order to continue operations, nonessential government spending had to cease. In late January, Trump ended the shutdown by endorsing a stopgap bill to allow for negotiating a more favorable appropriations bill. Ultimately, Trump bypassed the usual appropriations process by declaring a federal emergency at the border; that declaration empowered Trump to spend outside the budget in order to fund wall construction.

"Politics is a messy business, mister!"

Source: Natalia Deriabina/ Shutterstock.com

That shutdown was the longest shutdown, but there have been others. One intense struggle in the summer of 2011 between the Republican-majority U.S. House of Representatives and the Obama administration and the Democratic-majority U.S. Senate almost resulted in a government shutdown, as the debt ceiling had been reached. In an effort to avoid the shutdown, Congress passed the Budget Control Act of 2011, raising the borrowing limit but calling for a $1 trillion deficit reduction over ten years with additional reductions to follow. The Act provided for across-the-board (with only a few exceptions) spending cuts, called sequestration, if Congress failed to agree on those further deficit-reducing measures. In the fall of 2013 with another debt ceiling breach looming, a sixteen-day government shutdown did occur when the Republican-majority House of Representatives would only agree to pass a general budget resolution if it included provisions to defund the Patient Protection and Affordable Care Act (Obamacare). When the Senate refused to go along with this, the shutdown ended with legislation—opposed by most Republicans—to raise the debt ceiling and allow government spending to resume temporarily while the actual spending bill was worked out. In late 2013, Congress finally agreed on a bipartisan two-year budget that reduced sequestration, and in early 2014 it agreed to raise the debt ceiling. Another similar two-year budget deal was reached in November 2015. These deals put these issues aside until after the U.S. presidential election in November 2016.

FIGURE 13.9 General Government Debt as a Percentage of GDP in Thirty-Four Countries, 2020

As a percentage of GDP, the U.S. general government debt (shown third from right) is high relative to many other developed countries. Greece and Japan are higher; at the far left, Estonia, Luxembourg, and Turkey are lowest.

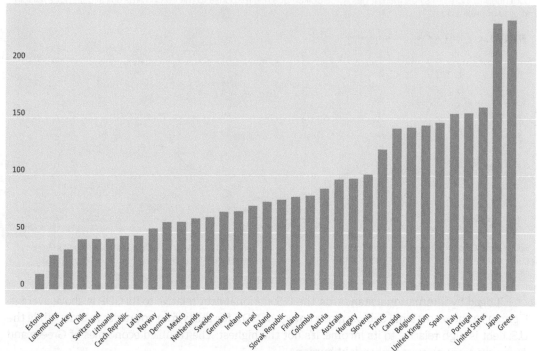

Source: OECD (2021), General government debt (indicator). doi: 10.1787/a0528cc2-en.

Key Takeaways

- Over the last fifty years, government purchases fell from about 20% of U.S. GDP to below 20%, except for a brief period around the time of the Great Recession.
- Transfer payment spending has risen sharply, both in absolute terms and as a percentage of real GDP since 1960.
- The bulk of federal revenues comes from income and payroll taxes. State and local revenues consist primarily of sales and property taxes.
- The government budget balance is the difference between government revenues and government expenditures.
- The national debt is the sum of all past federal deficits minus any surpluses.

Try It!

What happens to the national debt when there is a budget surplus? What happens to it when there is a budget deficit? What happens to the national debt if there is a decrease in a surplus? What happens to it if the deficit falls?

See related Numerical Problem 3 at the end of this chapter.

Case in Point: Options for Reducing the U.S. Federal Budget Deficit

Source: © Leonard Zhukovsky / Shutterstock.com

The Congressional Budget Office (CBO) is a federal agency within the legislative branch of the U.S. government. The CBO was created in 1974 to provide nonpartisan and objective information to Congress on budgetary and economic matters. Its periodic report, *Options for Reducing the Deficit*, typically examines about a hundred options for raising revenues or reducing expenditures. *Options* estimates the budgetary impacts of these options over ten-year time horizons and enumerates advantages and disadvantages of each option, but does not make recommendations.

The December 2020 report provides eighty-three options divided into three categories: mandatory spending options, discretionary spending options, and revenue options. The report begins by noting the daunting budgetary situation presented by the coronavirus, which drove the deficit-to-GDP ratio to 14.5%, the largest it has been since World War II. That large deficit is likely to drive the ratio of the publicly held debt to GDP to over 100% in 2021, and to an all-time high of 107% by 2023.[1]

What can we do to stave off the debt collectors and move our budget back toward balance? Let's take a look at the top money-savers in each of the report's three categories, along with the anticipated ten-year savings provided for each.

Mandatory Spending. The CBO lists thirty-two options for reducing mandatory spending, ranging from limiting enrollment in the Ag Department's conservations programs and reducing student loan benefits at the low end to these big-ticket items at the high end:

- Increasing premiums for Medicare Parts B and D: $462 billion
- Reducing Medicaid (a joint federal-state health care program for low-income households) matching rates: $529 billion
- Establishing caps on federal spending for Medicaid: $959 billion

It's no coincidence that programs generating the biggest savings are all health care programs: Together, Medicare and Medicaid are about the same size as our Social Security program, and those three programs together make up the bulk of mandatory spending. With an increasingly aging population, coupled with increases in life expectancy and the rising cost of end-of-life care, the United States will be spending more and more on health care in coming years. Unfortunately, the Medicare Trust fund is in dire condition; the program is rapidly approaching insolvency.

Discretionary Spending. Unlike mandatory expenditures, discretionary expenditures require annual authorization from Congress. The CBO report lists twenty options for reducing discretionary spending. At the low end, it evaluates ceasing production of Ford-class aircraft carriers (a savings of $3 billion over ten years). At the top end, the CBO lists these three options:

- Reducing the Department of Defense's budget: $607 billion
- Reducing the Department of Defense's operations and maintenance appropriation: $168 billion
- Reducing funding for international affairs programs: $117 billion

It's no surprise that defense options occupy an outsized portion of this list—in fact, eleven of the twenty options involve some cuts to defense overall or to specific defense programs. That's because defense is, by far, the largest discretionary program the government funds. You can't eliminate trillions of dollars of budget deficits by cutting million-dollar programs!

Revenue Options. If you can't close a deficit by cutting spending, you've no other choice but to enhance revenues—which is general D.C.-speak for raising taxes! There are some big-ticket items in this category, but two of the three biggest are focused on the revenues needed to fund the government's big entitlement programs, Social Security and Medicare. Those programs' trust funds are nearly exhausted, and funding benefits over the next half-century presents a daunting challenge. Here are the biggest options for closing the deficit in the revenue category:

- Impose a 5% value added tax (the rough equivalent of a national sales tax): $2,830 billion
- Increase the payroll tax rate for Medicare hospital insurance: $1,736 billion
- Increase the payroll tax rate for Social Security: $1,406 billion

The CBO report cites the risks of rising debt and deficits: increased spending as interest payments rise with projected increases in interest rates; a lower capital stock as government borrowing diverts the nation's savings toward servicing the debt; less flexibility to respond to national challenges that may arise; and the increased likelihood of a fiscal crisis if the government's creditors become less willing to lend. Returning to a sustainable path requires less spending or greater revenues—it's not rocket science! The devil, of course, is in the details: How will we return to that path? As lawmakers and the public consider changes, they might ask:

- What are acceptable levels for the debt and deficit as percentages of GDP?
- What types of policy changes might enhance long-term economic growth?
- Who would bear the burdens of various changes and who would benefit?
- At what speed should policy changes be implemented?

As a member of the public, take a look at this report and come up with your own assessments of the options. Are there any that you absolutely wouldn't want to implement? Are there any that you'd consider low-hanging fruit?[2]

 Pop! Goes the Econ: *The Onion* Solves the Deficit

In this tongue-in-cheek, slightly risqué video, *The Onion* makes a modest proposal to help Social Security pay for itself.

View in the online reader

See related Concept Problem 10 at the end of this chapter.

Answer to Try It! Problem

A budget surplus leads to a decline in national debt; a budget deficit causes the national debt to grow. If there is a decrease in a budget surplus, national debt still declines but by less than it would have had the surplus not gotten smaller. If there is a decrease in the budget deficit, the national debt still grows, but by less than it would have if the deficit had not gotten smaller.

13.3 The Use of Fiscal Policy to Stabilize the Economy

Learning Objectives

1. Define automatic stabilizers and explain how they work.
2. Explain and illustrate graphically how discretionary fiscal policy works and compare the changes in aggregate demand that result from changes in government purchases, income taxes, and transfer payments.

Fiscal policy—the use of government expenditures and taxes to influence the level of economic activity—is the government counterpart to monetary policy. Like monetary policy, it can be used in an effort to close a recessionary or an inflationary gap.

Some tax and expenditure programs change automatically with the level of economic activity. We'll look at those first, and then we'll look at *discretionary* fiscal policies—targeted measures to steer the economy. Discretionary fiscal policy has become a go-to in times of economic crisis, from the tax cuts of the Kennedy, Reagan, and George W. Bush administrations to the huge spending bills passed during the Great Recession and the coronavirus crisis.

Automatic Stabilizers

Some government expenditure and taxation policies automatically work to insulate individuals from the impact of shocks to the economy. Transfer payments have this effect: Because more people become eligible for income supplements when income is falling, transfer payments reduce the effect of a change in real GDP on disposable personal income, and help to insulate households from the impact of a recession. Income taxes also have this effect: As incomes fall, people pay less in income taxes.

Transfer payments and the tax system stabilize the economy like shock absorbers stabilize your car: Automatically.

Source: Iaroslav Neliubov/
Shutterstock.com

automatic stabilizer

Any government program that tends to reduce fluctuations in GDP automatically.

Any government program that tends to reduce fluctuations in GDP automatically is called an **automatic stabilizer**. Automatic stabilizers tend to increase GDP when it is falling and reduce GDP when it is rising.

To see how automatic stabilizers work, consider the decline in real GDP that occurred during the recession of 1990–1991. Real GDP fell 1.6% from the peak to the trough of that recession. The reduction in economic activity automatically reduced tax payments, diminishing the impact of the downturn on disposable personal income. Furthermore, the reduction in incomes increased transfer payment spending, boosting disposable personal income further. Real disposable personal income ended up falling by only 0.9% during the 1990–1991 recession, a much smaller percentage than the decrease in real GDP. Rising transfer payments and falling tax collections helped cushion households from the impact of the recession and kept real GDP from falling as much as it would have otherwise.

Automatic stabilizers have emerged as key elements of fiscal policy. The expansion of unemployment benefits and the introduction in the 1960s and 1970s of means-tested federal transfer payments (in which individuals qualify depending on their income) have added to the nation's arsenal of automatic stabilizers. The advantage of automatic stabilizers is suggested by their name: As soon as income starts to change, they go to work. Because they affect disposable personal income directly, and because changes in disposable personal income are closely linked to changes in consumption, automatic stabilizers act swiftly to reduce the degree of changes in real GDP.

Discretionary Fiscal Policy Tools

The Swiss Army Knife of Stabilization Policy: The Fed has really just one way to combat recessions with monetary policy. But the government has lots of fiscal policy tools at its fingertips.

Source: infocus/Shutterstock.com

Discretionary fiscal policy is a deliberate government effort to stabilize the economy through fiscal policy actions. Of course, most of the government's taxing and spending is for purposes other than economic stabilization. For example, increases in defense spending in the early 1980s under President Ronald Reagan and in the George W. Bush administration were undertaken primarily to promote national security; that the increased spending affected real GDP and employment was a by-product. Those effects can't be ignored, but our focus here is on discretionary fiscal policy that is undertaken with the intention of stabilizing the economy.

Discretionary government spending and tax policies can be used to shift aggregate demand. Expansionary fiscal policy might consist of an increase in government purchases or transfer payments, a decrease in taxes, or a combination of both to shift the aggregate demand curve to the right. Contractionary fiscal policy might involve reducing government purchases and transfer payments, increasing taxes, or a combination of them all to shift the aggregate demand curve to the left.

Figure 13.10 illustrates the use of fiscal policy to shift aggregate demand in response to both recessionary and inflationary gaps. In Panel (a), the economy produces a real GDP of Y_1, which is below its potential level of Y_p. Expansionary fiscal policy (increases in spending or cuts in taxes) can close the recessionary gap by shifting aggregate demand to AD_2. In Panel (b), the economy initially has an inflationary gap, with real GDP greater than potential GDP at Y_1. Contractionary fiscal policy (spending cuts or tax increases) can close the gap by reducing aggregate demand to AD_2.

FIGURE 13.10 Expansionary and Contractionary Fiscal Policies to Shift Aggregate Demand
With aggregate demand at AD_1, the economy in Panel (a) faces a recessionary gap ($Y_P - Y_1$). Expansionary fiscal policy attempts to shift aggregate demand to AD_2 to close the gap. In Panel (b), the economy faces an inflationary gap ($Y_1 - Y_P$). Contractionary fiscal policy attempts to reduce aggregate demand from AD_1 to AD_2 to close the gap.

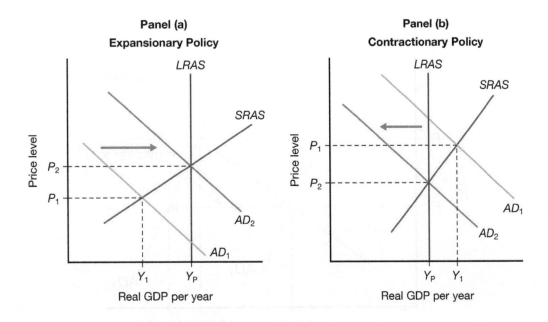

Changes in Government Purchases

Now let's look at how specific fiscal policy options work.[3] One policy the government can use to shift aggregate demand is a change in government purchases. For example, an increase in government spending will shift the aggregate demand curve to the right by an amount equal to the initial change in government purchases times the multiplier. This multiplied effect of a change in government purchases occurs because the increase in government purchases drives up income, and higher income in turn drives up consumption (increasing income even further). As income rises, however, part of the impact of the increase in aggregate demand is absorbed by higher prices. That prevents GDP from rising by the full amount of the change in aggregate demand at each price level.

Figure 13.11 illustrates this with an increase in government purchases of $200 billion. The initial price level is P_1 and the initial equilibrium for real GDP is $12,000 billion. Suppose the multiplier is 2. The $200 billion increase in government purchases increases the total quantity of goods and services demanded (holding the price level constant at P_1) by $400 billion—the $200 billion increase in government purchases times the multiplier. If the price level remained at P_1, real GDP would increase to $12,400 billion. But upward pressure on prices forces the price level to P_2, and real GDP ends up rising only to $12,300 billion.

FIGURE 13.11 An Increase in Government Purchases

The economy shown here is initially in equilibrium at a real GDP of $12,000 billion and a price level of P_1. If the fiscal multiplier is 2.0, an increase in government purchases (ΔG) of $200 billion would shift the aggregate demand curve to the right by $400 billion to AD_2. The equilibrium level of real GDP would rise to $12,300 billion, while the price level would rise to P_2.

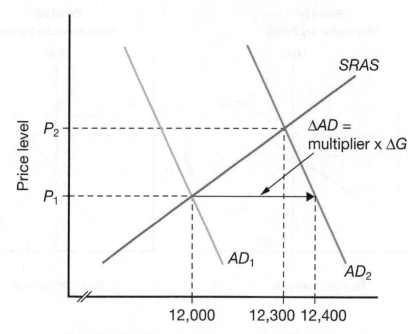

A decrease in government purchases would have the opposite effect. The aggregate demand curve would shift to the left by an amount equal to the initial change in government purchases times the multiplier. Real GDP and the price level would fall.

Changes in Business Taxes

Investment Tax Credit: These robots build cars, and cut taxes better than an accountant!

Source: Jenson/Shutterstock.com

One way to stimulate spending is to leave more money in spenders' pockets. Government can do that by cutting taxes in various ways. For example, one of the first fiscal policy measures undertaken by the Kennedy administration was an investment tax credit that allowed firms to reduce their tax liability if they'd undertaken investment during the previous tax year. With an investment tax credit of 10%, for example, a firm that purchased a new $1 million robotic welder would be able to reduce its overall tax liability for that year by $100,000. The investment tax credit introduced by the Kennedy administration was later repealed, but it returned for five years during the Reagan administration, and again during the Bush years.

An investment tax credit is intended, of course, to stimulate additional private sector investment. A reduction in the tax rate on corporate profits—a key element of the Trump administration's 2017 tax bill—would be likely to have a similar effect. Conversely, an increase in the corporate income tax rate or a reduction in an investment tax credit could be expected to reduce investment.

A change in investment affects the aggregate demand curve in precisely the same manner as a change in government purchases. It shifts the aggregate demand curve by an amount equal to the initial change in investment times the multiplier. An increase in the investment tax credit, or a reduction in corporate income tax rates, will increase investment and shift the aggregate demand curve to the right. Real GDP and the price level will rise. A decrease in the investment tax credit or an increase in corporate income tax rates will reduce investment and shift the aggregate demand curve to the left; real GDP and the price level will fall.[4]

Changes in Income Taxes

Income taxes affect the consumption component of aggregate demand. An increase in income taxes reduces disposable personal income. That, in turn, causes households to cut their their consumption spending (but by less than the change in disposable personal income). The decrease in consumption spending shifts the aggregate demand curve leftward by an amount equal to the initial change in consumption times the multiplier.[5]

"Read my lips: Cut. My. Taxes . . . Please!"

Source: Red Confidential/ Shutterstock.com

The process works in reverse, too. A decrease in income taxes increases disposable personal income, increases consumption (but by less than the change in disposable personal income), and increases aggregate demand. Suppose, for example, that the government reduces income taxes by $200 billion. Only some of the increase in disposable personal income (say, $180 billion) will be used for consumption; and the rest ($20 billion) will be saved. If the multiplier is 2, then aggregate demand will shift to the right by $360 billion (2 × $180 billion). So, compared to the $200 billion increase in government purchases that we saw in Figure 13.11, the shift in the aggregate demand curve due to an income tax cut is somewhat less, as is its effect on real GDP and the price level.

> **Pop! Goes the Econ: Fiscal Policy in *South Park***
>
> Watch this clip from *South Park*, then draw parallels between it and the government's response to the coronavirus pandemic, in which it borrowed $2 trillion in order to send tax rebate checks of $1,200 to every adult. How are these policies likely to affect disposable income and spending?

Changes in Transfer Payments

Changes in transfer payments, like changes in income taxes, alter the disposable personal income of households. That, in turn, affects their consumption and aggregate demand. Because people tend to save part of any increase in their income, if the government ramps up transfer payments to fight a recession, consumption will change by a bit less than the increase in transfer payments. For example, if households save 10% of any income increases, a $200 billion increase in transfer payments will shift the aggregate demand curve to the right by $180 billion—that's less than the $200 billion increase in government purchases that we saw in Figure 13.11.

Table 13.1 summarizes U.S. fiscal policies undertaken to shift aggregate demand since the 1964 tax cuts. It shows that expansionary policies have been chosen in response to recessionary gaps and that contractionary policies have been chosen in response to inflationary gaps. Changes in government purchases and in taxes have been the primary tools of fiscal policy in the United States.

TABLE 13.1 Fiscal Policy in the United States Since 1964
The table lists the major proposed uses of discretionary policy over a period of more than five decades.

Year	Situation	Policy Response
1968	Inflationary gap	A temporary tax increase, first recommended by President Johnson's Council of Economic Advisers in 1965, goes into effect. This one-time surcharge of 10% is added to individual income tax liabilities.
1969	Inflationary gap	President Nixon, facing a continued inflationary gap, orders cuts in government purchases.
1975	Recessionary gap	President Ford, facing a recession induced by an OPEC oil-price increase, proposes a temporary 10% tax cut. It is passed almost immediately and goes into effect within two months.
1981	Recessionary gap	President Reagan had campaigned on a platform of increased defense spending and a sharp cut in income taxes. The tax cuts are approved in 1981 and are implemented over a period of three years. The increased defense spending begins in 1981. While the Reagan administration rejects the use of fiscal policy as a stabilization tool, its policies tend to increase aggregate demand early in the 1980s.
1992	Recessionary gap	President George H.W. Bush had rejected the use of expansionary fiscal policy during the recession of 1990–1991. Indeed, he agreed late in 1990 to a cut in government purchases and a tax increase. In a campaign year, however, he orders a cut in withholding rates designed to increase disposable personal income in 1992 and to boost consumption.
1993	Recessionary gap	President Clinton calls for a $16 billion jobs package consisting of increased government purchases and tax cuts aimed at stimulating investment. The president says the plan will create 500,000 new jobs. The measure is rejected by Congress.
2001	Recessionary gap	President George W. Bush campaigned to reduce taxes in order to reduce the size of government and encourage long-term growth. When he took office in 2001, the economy was weak and the $1.35 billion tax cut was aimed at both long-term tax relief and stimulating the economy in the short term, including a personal income tax rebate of $300 to $600 per household. With unemployment still high a couple of years into the expansion, another tax cut is passed in 2003.
2008	Recessionary gap	At the end of his presidency, George W. Bush signs into law a $150 billion fiscal stimulus package to spur the economy. It includes $100 billion in tax rebates and $50 billion in tax cuts for businesses.
2009	Recessionary gap	Just a month after taking office, President Obama signs the American Recovery and Reinvestment Act to help end the Great Recession with a fiscal stimulus package of $784 billion. It includes tax rebates and increased government spending.
2010–2012	Recessionary gap	Extensions of the payroll tax reduction and unemployment insurance benefits continue through Obama's presidency.
2020	Recessionary Gap	A $2.2 trillion economic stimulus bill (the Coronavirus Aid, Relief, and Economic Security Act) is passed by Congress and signed by President Trump in March 2020 to respond to the economic fallout of the COVID-19 pandemic. It includes direct checks to individuals and increased unemployment benefits as well as a loan forgiveness program for small businesses. Trump signs a second relief bill authorizing a second set of direct payments to individuals just before leaving office.
2021	Recessionary Gap	In his first days in office, President Biden signs the American Rescue Plan, authorizing direct payments to individuals, expanded child care credits, emergency funding to state and local governments, increased funding for vaccine distribution, and extensions of many existing COVID-19 relief measures.

Key Takeaways

- Discretionary fiscal policy may be either expansionary or contractionary.

- A change in government purchases shifts the aggregate demand curve at a given price level by an amount equal to the initial change in government purchases times the multiplier. The change in real GDP, however, will be reduced by the fact that the price level will change.

- A change in income taxes or government transfer payments shifts the aggregate demand curve by a multiple of the initial change in consumption (which is less than the change in personal disposable income) that the change in income taxes or transfer payments causes. Then, the change in real GDP will be reduced by the fact that the price level will change.

- A change in government purchases has a larger impact on the aggregate demand curve than does an equal change in income taxes or transfers.

- Changes in business tax rates, including an investment tax credit, can be used to influence the level of investment and thus the level of aggregate demand.

Try It!

Suppose the economy has an inflationary gap. What fiscal policies might be used to close the gap? Using the model of aggregate demand and aggregate supply, illustrate the effect of these policies.

See related Concept Problem 6 at the end of this chapter.

Case in Point: How Large *Is* the Fiscal Multiplier?

Source: © Shutterstock, Inc.

There is a wide range of opinions among economists regarding the size of the fiscal multiplier. In 2011, the American Economic Association's *Journal of Economic Literature* published three papers on this topic in a special section titled "Forum: The Multiplier." The papers provide at least two-and-a-half different answers!

In her paper titled "Can Government Purchases Stimulate the Economy?" Valerie Ramey concludes that the size of the government purchases multiplier depends on many factors but that, when the increase in government purchases is temporary and financed by government borrowing, the multiplier "is probably between 0.8 and 1.5. Reasonable people can argue, however, that the data do not reject 0.5 to 2."[6] That's a wide range . . . and a confusing one at the low end, which suggests that $100 billion of government spending might only create $50 billion of real income. How about a hand for the efficiency of government?

In "An Empirical Analysis of the Revival of Fiscal Activism in the 2000s," John Taylor argues that the various components of the recent fiscal packages (tax cuts, aid to states, and increased government purchases) had little effect on the economy—implying a multiplier of zero or nearly so. Using aggregate quarterly data simulations for the 2000s, he argues (1) that transfers and tax cuts were used by households to increase savings, (2) that the increase in government purchases was too small to have made much of a difference, and (3) that state and local governments used their stimulus dollars for transfers or to reduce their borrowing.

In "On Measuring the Effects of Fiscal Policy in Recessions," Jonathan Parker essentially argues that the statistical models built to date are ultimately inadequate, and that we will only be able to get at the answer as better and more refined studies are conducted. Noting that the multiplier effect of fiscal policy is likely to depend on the state of the economy, he concludes that "an important difficulty with further investigation is the limited macroeconomic data available on the effects of policy in recessions (or deep recessions)."[7] Perhaps we need a few more Great Recessions and COVID-19 recessions in order to figure this out.

Does that mean fiscal policy is worthless? In another American Economic Association publication, the *Journal of Economic Perspectives*, Alan Auerbach, William Gale, and Benjamin Harris provide an extensive review of the variety in multiplier estimates, which they acknowledge is "embarrassingly large" after so many years of trying to measure it. Concerning the 2009 American Recovery and Reinvestment Act, though, they write, "If a fiscal stimulus were ever to be considered appropriate, the beginning of 2009 was such a time. . . . In these circumstances, our judgment is that a fiscal expansion carried much smaller risks than the lack of one would have."[8]

See related Concept Problem 3 at the end of this chapter.

Sources: Based on Alan J. Auerbach, William G. Gale, and Benjamin H. Harris, "Activist Fiscal Policy," Journal of Economic Perspectives 24, no. 4 (Fall 2010): 141–64; Jonathan A. Parker, "On Measuring the Effects of Fiscal Policy in Recessions," Journal of Economic Literature 49, no. 3 (September 2011): 703–18; Valerie A. Ramey, "Can Government Purchases Stimulate the Economy?," Journal of Economic Literature 49, no. 3 (September 2011): 673–85; John B. Taylor, "An Empirical Analysis of the Revival of Fiscal Activism in the 2000s," Journal of Economic Literature 49, no. 3 (September 2011): 686–702.

Answer to Try It! Problem

Fiscal policies that could be used to close an inflationary gap include reductions in government purchases and transfer payments and increases in taxes. As shown in Panel (b) of Figure 13.10, the goal would be to shift the aggregate demand curve to the left so that it will intersect the short-run aggregate supply curve at Y_P.

13.4 Fiscal Policy in Practice

Learning Objectives

1. Explain how the various kinds of lags influence the effectiveness of discretionary fiscal policy.
2. Explain and illustrate graphically how crowding out (and its reverse) influences the impact of expansionary or contractionary fiscal policy.
3. Discuss the controversy concerning which types of fiscal policies to use, including the arguments from supply-side economics.

Now we know that it's possible to use the government's taxing and spending power to close gaps. But just because it's possible doesn't mean that it's necessarily easy. As we discovered with monetary policy in the previous chapter, using fiscal policy to stabilize the economy can be a difficult and frustrating undertaking.

Possible does not equal easy.

Source: RFarrarons/Shutterstock. com

Lags

One big problem with using fiscal policy to lean against the economic wind is that discretionary fiscal policy is subject to the same lags that exist for monetary policy. First, it takes some time for policymakers to realize that a recessionary or an inflationary gap exists—the *recognition lag*. Recognition lags stem largely from the difficulty of collecting economic data in a timely and accurate fashion. Then, once a problem has been recognized, it takes still more time to put together and implement a plan to combat the problem. That's the *implementation lag*. But even once the problem's been recognized and the plan's been put into effect, it can take still *more* time for the full effects of the policy change to be felt. That's the *impact lag*.

Compared to monetary policy, changes in fiscal policy are likely to involve a particularly long implementation lag. For example, consider the famous Kennedy tax cuts. Those cuts were proposed to Kennedy in 1960, while he was still a presidential candidate, as a means of ending the recession that year. He recommended the tax cuts to Congress in 1962, but they were not passed until 1964, months after Kennedy had been killed, and three years after the recession had ended.

Congress: Flexible, responsive, and working together to make things better since . . . uh . . .

Source: mark reinstein/Shutterstock.com

In today's polarized political climate, stonewalling is a political tool and gridlock is a fact of life. This can contribute to an even longer implementation lag, which has caused more than one economist to question the value of discretionary fiscal policy as a stabilization tool. But even if discretionary policy is only useful in dire emergencies like the coronavirus crisis, that doesn't mean fiscal policy is completely useless in combatting milder business cycle swings: Automatic stabilizers respond *automatically* to changes in the economy, avoiding both the recognition lag and the some-times-frustratingly-long implementation lag.

It's also a mistake to attribute all of the implementation lag to gridlock in Congress. At least part of the implementation lag results from the nature of bureaucracy itself. Consider, for example, the Obama administration's hopes for fiscal policy in combatting the Great Recession. President Obama, anxious to metaphorically "get ahead of the pain," announced that there was federal money available for "shovel ready" infrastructure projects. The only problem? A bureaucratic process of applications and approvals that ultimately delivered billions of dollars worth of new infrastructure . . . but at an agonizingly slow crawl.

Crowding Out

The government's pistachio plan is a stimulating one.

Source: Volodymyr_Shtun/ Shutterstock.com

crowding out

The tendency for an expansionary fiscal policy to reduce other components of aggregate demand.

Even if there were no policy lags, fiscal policy still might have a hard time reviving a troubled econ-omy. To see why, suppose the government decides that aggregate demand is too low; there's an recessionary gap, and the government wants to close it by purchasing $1 million worth of pista-chios. But where will government get the million dollars that it needs to pay for its nuts?

The government can't simply print the money it needs—that's the Fed's job, and at least in the United States, the Fed is independent of the government. It is, however, possible to raise the money by increasing taxes by $1 million. Then, the government can use that money to buy the pistachios it believes are vital to the recovery. This plan, however, raises an important question: If government hadn't increased taxes by $1 million, what would consumers have done with that money?

If consumers would have spent that million dollars anyway, then the government hasn't *cre-ated* any new spending, it's simply *replaced* consumer spending with government spending, an outcome that economists refer to as **crowding out**. Because of crowding out, the government's pis-tachio plan has resulted in zero net stimulus, a situation referred to as *complete crowding out*.

Of course, consumers generally save some part of their income and spend the rest. Let's sup-pose that in the short run, consumers spend about 75 cents of each dollar they receive in income. This means that if consumers paid $1 million in taxes to fund the government's pistachio plan, they were probably only planning on spending $750,000 of that money anyway. The net impact of the government program, then, is a $250,000 increase in spending: not zero, but also not the $1 million shot of stimulus that pistachio-loving politicians are likely to advertise. In other words, the fiscal policy worked, but it didn't work very well.

Of course, even politicians recognize that if stimulating the economy is the goal, raising taxes is a poor way to do it (not to mention politically unpopular). Suppose instead that the government decides to fund its million-dollar pistachio plan by *borrowing* the money it needs instead of raising taxes. That way the government's expenditure won't crowd out spending elsewhere in the economy . . . or will it?

Crowded out by great power: "There ain't room enough in this town for the two of us, Pilgrim."

Source: Anton_Ivanov/ Shutterstock.com

Unfortunately, the government spending may *still* crowd out spending elsewhere in the econ-omy. Here's how that happens: The government goes to the bond market and borrows the $1 million it needs. But it's not likely that bond purchasers who've just lent the government $1 million were planning on just letting their money sit idle in a pile: Ultimately, the government may prevent that $1 million from being borrowed by someone else—perhaps a business looking to install a robotic welder, or a homeowner planning to add on a sunroom. In this case, government spending has crowded out investment spending.

A more sophisticated way to envision government's crowding out of investment spending is to picture a pool of available cash, waiting to be lent to creditworthy borrowers. Ordinarily, that money would be borrowed by consumers and businesses. When government suddenly decides it wants a big share of that pool to finance its pistachio program, the demand for those funds increases and the price of those funds—the interest rate—rises. That increases the cost of borrowing by firms and households, and makes some investment projects look less profitable (see our investment chapter for more on this). Firms abandon those projects, and some investment spending doesn't occur—investment spending that would have occurred had government not driven up interest rates.

Figure 13.12 shows the impact of government borrowing in greater detail. To facilitate its borrowing, the Treasury sells new bonds, shifting the supply curve for bonds to the right in Panel (a). That reduces the price of bonds and causes the interest rate to increase.[9]

- The increase in the interest rate reduces the quantity of private investment demanded. (Note that the expansionary fiscal policy *could* take the form of an increase in the investment component of government purchases, such as roads and schools. In that case, government investment may crowd out private investment.)

- The higher interest rate increases the demand for and reduces the supply of dollars in the foreign exchange market, raising the exchange rate in Panel (b). A higher exchange rate reduces net exports (see more on this in Chapter 11, which is devoted to financial markets and the economy).

FIGURE 13.12 Expansionary Fiscal Policy and Crowding Out

In Panel (a), increased government purchases are financed through the sale of bonds, lowering their price from P^b_1 to P^b_2, and driving up interest rates, which reduces investment demand. In Panel (b), the higher interest rate causes the exchange rate to rise, reducing net exports. If there were no crowding out, the increased government purchases would shift the aggregate demand curve from AD_1 to AD_2 in Panel (c). Because of the crowding out of investment and net exports, aggregate demand only shifts to AD_3.

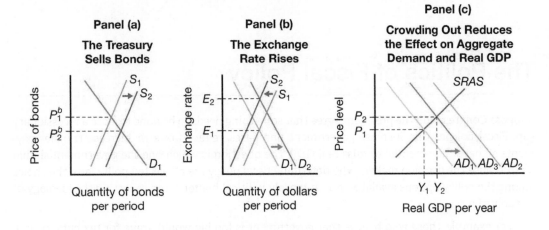

Panel (c) shows the effects of all these changes on the aggregate demand curve. Before the change in government purchases, the economy is in equilibrium at a real GDP of Y_1, determined by the intersection of AD_1 and the short-run aggregate supply curve. The increase in government expenditures would shift the curve outward to AD_2 if there were no adverse impact on investment and net exports. But the reduction in investment and net exports partially offsets this increase. Taking the reduction in investment and net exports into account means that the aggregate demand curve shifts only to AD_3. In the case of bond-financed fiscal expansion, the expansion of government spending crowds out investment spending and net exports. Those declines partially offset the impact of the fiscal expansion.

The effectiveness of fiscal policy ultimately hinges on the strength of the crowding-out effect. If spending was likely to have occurred anyway, the government expenditures merely replace other forms of spending and provide no net stimulus to the economy. On the other hand, if the funds government acquires through taxes or borrowing wouldn't have been spent, then the government spending provides a boost to GDP. That means that fiscal policy is most likely to be effective when consumers and businesses are, on a large scale, cautiously holding onto cash instead of spending it—exactly the situation the United States found itself in during the early days of the coronavirus, when the U.S. savings rate skyrocketed. Alternatively, fiscal policy may be effective if consumers and businesses are reluctant to borrow in credit markets or if financial institutions like banks are reluctant to make loans to them, as was the case during the Great Recession, when financial risk created a genuine credit crunch.

 Pop! Goes the Econ: Crowding Out in Shawshank Prison

Shawshank Prison Warden Norton is hiring out his prisoners to do construction work. How does this illustrate the notion of government activity crowding out private activity?

View in the online reader

The Politics of Fiscal Policy

Suppose Congress and the president agree that something needs to be done to close a recessionary gap. Fiscal policies that increase government purchases, reduce taxes, or increase transfer payments all have the potential to raise real GDP. The question is which one the government should use. Because the decision makers who determine fiscal policy are all elected politicians, the choice among the policy options available is an intensely political matter, often reflecting the ideology of the politicians.

For example, those who believe that government is too big would argue for tax cuts to close recessionary gaps and for spending cuts to close inflationary gaps. In contrast, people who believe that the private sector has failed to provide adequately a host of services that would benefit society—maybe better education, or public transportation—tend to advocate for increases in government purchases to close recessionary gaps and tax increases to close inflationary gaps.

supply-side economics

The school of thought that promotes the use of fiscal policy to stimulate long-run aggregate supply.

Another area of contention comes from those who believe that fiscal policy can be used as a tool to promote long-term growth. **Supply-side economics** is the school of thought that promotes the use of fiscal policy to stimulate long-run aggregate supply. Supply-side economists argue for reducing tax rates in order to encourage people to work more (or more individuals to work). They also argue for policies that stimulate capital creation, such as investment tax credits.

While there is considerable debate over how strong the supply-side effects are in relation to the demand-side effects, such considerations may affect the choice of policies. Supply-siders tend to favor tax cuts over increases in government purchases or increases in transfer payments. President Reagan advocated tax cuts in 1981 on the basis of their supply-side effects. Coupled with increased defense spending in the early 1980s, fiscal policy under Reagan clearly stimulated aggregate demand by increasing both consumption and investment. Falling inflation and accelerated growth are signs that supply-side factors may also have been at work during that period. While the Reagan administration popularized the supply-side argument for tax cuts, presidents since have continued to promote tax cuts on a supply-side basis. For example, President George W. Bush's chief economic adviser, N. Gregory Mankiw, argued that the Bush tax cuts would encourage economic growth, a supply-side argument. The most recent tax overhaul in 2017 was also argued for on a supply-side basis: After receiving pushback on the tax cut's effect on the deficit, Trump administration Treasury Secretary Stephen Mnuchin argued, *"On a static basis our plan will increase the deficit by a trillion and a half. Having said that, you have to look at the economic impact. There's 500 billion that's the difference between policy and baseline that takes it down to a trillion dollars, and there's two trillion dollars of growth. So with our plan we actually pay down the deficit by a trillion dollars and we think that's very fiscally responsible."*[10]

Finally, even when there *is* agreement to stimulate the economy—say, through increasing government expenditures on highways—the *how* question remains. How should the expenditures be allocated? Specifically, which states should the highways run through? Each member of Congress has a political stake in the outcome. These types of considerations make the implementation lag particularly long for fiscal policy.

Key Takeaways

- Discretionary fiscal policy involves the same kind of lags as monetary policy. However, the implementation lag in fiscal policy is likely to be more pronounced, while the impact lag is likely to be less pronounced.
- Expansionary fiscal policy may result in the crowding out of private investment and net exports, reducing the impact of the policy. Similarly, contractionary policy may "crowd in" additional investment and net exports, reducing the contractionary impact of the policy.
- Supply-side economics stresses the use of fiscal policy to stimulate economic growth. Advocates of supply-side economics generally favor tax cuts to stimulate economic growth.

Try It!

Do the following hypothetical situations tend to enhance or make more difficult the use of fiscal policy as a stabilization tool?

1. Better and more speedily available data on the state of the economy
2. A finding that private sector investment spending is not much affected by interest rate changes
3. A finding that the supply-side effects of a tax cut are substantial

See related Concept Problem 2 at the end of this chapter.

Case in Point: An Oprah Stimulus

Everybody loves Oprah, especially around the holidays, when her iconic TV show featured Christmas gift giveaways that were nothing short of spectacular: "*You* get a car . . . and *YOU* get a car!"

And then, there was the coronavirus, which hit the United States like a bolt of lightning: powerful, deadly, and unpredictable. Nobody in government knew much about it, but they decided it was better to be safe than sorry, initiating lockdowns and issuing shelter-in-place orders. But how can you order people not to go to work without giving them the means to survive while they're homebound?

"You want a car, too? Well, of COURSE you're getting a car!"

Source: Kathy Hutchins/Shutterstock.com

That's why, in those first early weeks of the coronavirus crisis, the Treasury began cutting $1,200 stimulus checks to every taxpayer in America. And it wasn't just taxpayers—the Treasury issued checks to people long-deceased; even foreign nationals who had once worked in the United States were surprised to find checks in their Aukland and Oslo mailboxes. It really was an Oprah stimulus: *"You* get a check . . . and *YOU* get a check!"

That money was supposed to be a lifeline for families in need, and was also supposed to provide a general stimulus to the economy. It was a quick reaction to an impossible situation. But with the benefit of hindsight (and ignoring anecdotal accounts of checks being sent to people in Sierra Leone) we now know that a good chunk of that money was put to good use . . . and another big chunk wasn't put to use at all.

That insight is due to economists Raj Chetty, John Friedman, and Michael Stepner, who analyzed credit and debit card spending data in the early days of the COVID-19 recession. Chetty, Friedman, and Stepner found a marked uptick in spending for households earning less than $50,000 in the days immediately after those households received their stimulus checks. That's exactly what the checks were supposed to do—help lower-income people weather the lockdowns and generate spending for the economy.

But the numbers tell a different story for households earning over $75,000. Those households were, by and large, insulated from the COVID-19 recession.[11] With money in the bank and jobs still in hand, what did those higher-income households do with their checks? According to Chetty, Freidman, and Stepner, about 93 cents of each dollar went straight to savings or to pay off credit card debt; only 7 cents was spent. That's a textbook example of almost-complete crowding out, with the government borrowing money from someone who wasn't using it in order to give it to someone *else* who wouldn't use it!

The data back that up: During the coronavirus crisis, the U.S. savings rate skyrocketed to a historic high of 33%. But almost all of that increase can be attributed to the top 20% of earners. In that bracket, the typical household managed to sock away $50,000 in the first year after the pandemic, with $1,200 (or $2,400 for couples) coming straight from the coffers of the Treasury. As the new Biden administration prepared the country's third round of stimulus payments in a year, the pointlessness of those pure transfers was not only noticed, but acted on. The Biden proposal eliminated checks for individuals earning more than $80,000, an amount largely in sync with Chetty, Friedman, and Stepner's research. After all, even in a pandemic, there's no reason for the general American taxpayer to be funding the retirement savings of the already well-to-do.

See related Concept Problem 5 at the end of this chapter.

Source: Based on Chetty, Friedman, and Stepner, "Effects of January 2021 Stimulus Payments on Consumer Spending," Opportunity Insights, February 4, 2021; https://opportunityinsights.org/ wp-content/uploads/2021/01/Oi_Secondstimulus_analysis.pdf.

Answers to Try It! Problems

1. Data on the economy that are more accurate and more speedily available should enhance the use of fiscal policy by reducing the length of the recognition lag.

2. If private sector investment does not respond much to interest rate changes, then there will be less crowding out when expansionary policies are undertaken. That is, the rising interest rates that accompany expansionary fiscal policy will not reduce investment spending much, making the shift in the aggregate demand curve to the right greater than it would be otherwise. Also, the use of contractionary fiscal policy would be more effective, since the fall in interest rates would "invite in" less investment spending, making the shift in the aggregate demand curve to the left greater than it would otherwise be.

3. Large supply-side effects enhance the impact of tax cuts. For a given expansionary policy, without the supply-side effects, GDP would advance only to the point where the aggregate demand curve intersects the short-run aggregate supply curve. With the supply-side effects, both the short-run and long-run aggregate supply curves shift to the right. The intersection of the *AD* curve with the now increased short-run aggregate supply curve will be farther to the right than it would have been in the absence of the supply-side effects. The potential level of real GDP will also increase.

13.5 Review and Practice

Summary

The government sector plays a major role in the economy. The spending, tax, and transfer policies of local, state, and federal agencies affect aggregate demand and aggregate supply and thus affect the level of real GDP and the price level. An expansionary policy tends to increase real GDP. Such a policy could be used to close a recessionary gap. A contractionary fiscal policy tends to reduce real GDP. A contractionary policy could be used to close an inflationary gap.

Government purchases of goods and services have a direct impact on aggregate demand. An increase in government purchases shifts the aggregate demand curve by the amount of the initial change in government purchases times the multiplier. Changes in personal income taxes or in the level of transfer payments affect disposable personal income. They change consumption, though initially by less than the amount of the change in taxes or transfers. They thus cause somewhat smaller shifts in the aggregate demand curve than do equal changes in government purchases.

There are several issues in the use of fiscal policies for stabilization purposes. They include lags associated with fiscal policy, crowding out, the choice of which fiscal policy tool to use (often based on political considerations), and the possible burdens of accumulating additional national debt.

Concept Problems

1. What is the difference between government expenditures and government purchases? How do the two variables differ in terms of their effect on GDP?

2. (Related to "Try It!" in Section 25.4.) If investment and consumer spending are very sensitive to small changes in interest rates, will fiscal actions (tax cuts or spending increases) be crowded out? What are the implications for the effectiveness of fiscal policy? Explain your answer.

3. (Related to "Case in Point: How Large Is the Fiscal Multiplier?" in Section 25.3.) Why is it important to try to determine the size of the fiscal policy multiplier? How is the size of the multiplier related to the strength of the crowding-out effect?

4. Suppose an economy has an inflationary gap. How does the government's actual budget deficit or surplus compare to the deficit or surplus it would have at potential output?

5. (Related to "Case in Point: An Oprah Stimulus" in Section 25.4.) Suppose the government wants to close an inflationary gap by increasing income taxes. Based on the data in the case, should the government increase income taxes on high-income households or on low-income households? Why might such a policy be hard to sell on Capitol Hill?

6. (Related to "Try It!" in Section 25.3.) Suppose the government increases purchases in an economy with a recessionary gap. How would this policy affect bond prices, interest rates, investment, net exports, real GDP, and the price level? Show your results graphically.

7. Suppose the government cuts transfer payments in an economy with an inflationary gap. How would this policy affect bond prices, interest rates, investment, the exchange rate, net exports, real GDP, and the price level? Show your results graphically.

8. Suppose that at the same time the government undertakes expansionary fiscal policy, such as a cut in taxes, the Fed undertakes contractionary monetary policy. How would this policy affect bond prices, interest rates, investment, net exports, real GDP, and the price level? Show your results graphically.

9. Given the nature of the implementation lag discussed in the text, discuss possible measures that might reduce the lag.

10. (Related to "Case in Point: Options for Reducing the U.S. Federal Budget Deficit" in Section 25.2.) Suppose you've been charged with reducing the budget deficit by $3 trillion over the next ten years. Based on the options presented in the case, how will you go about your task? Are there other options you'd like to consider? How might your administration's political philosophy influence your answer?

Numerical Problems

1. Look up the table on Federal Receipts and Outlays, by Major Category, in the most recent *Economic Report of the President* available in your library or on the internet.

   a. Complete the following table:

Category	Total Outlays	Percentage of Total Outlays
National defense		
International affairs		
Health		
Medicare		
Income security		
Social security		
Net interest		
Other		

   b. Construct a pie chart showing the percentages of spending for each category in the total.

2. Look up the table on ownership of U.S. Treasury securities in the most recent *Economic Report of the President* available on the internet.

   a. Make a pie chart showing the percentage owned by various groups in the earliest year shown in the table.

b. Make a pie chart showing the percentage owned by various groups in the most recent year shown in the table.

c. What are some of the major changes in ownership of U.S. government debt over the period?

3. (Related to "Try It!" in Section 25.2.) Suppose a country has a national debt of $5,000 billion, a GDP of $10,000 billion, and a budget deficit of $100 billion.

a. How much will its new national debt be?

b. Compute its debt/GDP ratio.

c. Suppose its GDP grows by 1% in the next year and the budget deficit is again $100 billion. Compute its new level of national debt and its new debt-GDP ratio.

4. Suppose a country's debt rises by 10% and its GDP rises by 12%.

a. What happens to the debt-GDP ratio?

b. Does the relative level of the initial values affect your answer?

5. The data below show a country's national debt and its prime lending rate.

Year	National Debt (Billions of $)	Lending Rate (%)
1992	4,064	6.0
1993	4,411	6.0
1994	4,692	8.5
1995	4,973	8.7
1996	5,224	8.3
1997	5,413	8.5

a. Plot the relationship between national debt and the lending rate.

b. Based on your graph, does crowding out appear to be a problem?

6. Suppose a country increases government purchases by $100 billion. Suppose the multiplier is 1.5 and the economy's real GDP is $5,000 billion.

a. In which direction will the aggregate demand curve shift and by how much?

b. Explain using a graph why the change in real GDP is likely to be smaller than the shift in the aggregate demand curve.

7. Suppose a country decreases government purchases by $100 billion. Suppose the multiplier is 1.5 and the economy's real GDP is $5,000 billion.

a. In which direction will the aggregate demand curve shift and by how much?

b. Explain using a graph why the change in real GDP is likely to be smaller than the shift in the aggregate demand curve.

8. Suppose a country decreases income taxes by $100 billion, and this leads to an increase in consumption spending of $90 billion. Suppose the multiplier is 1.5 and the economy's real GDP is $5,000 billion.

a. In which direction will the aggregate demand curve shift and by how much?

b. Explain using a graph why the change in real GDP is likely to be smaller than the shift in the aggregate demand curve.

9. Suppose a country increases income taxes by $100 billion, and this leads to a decrease in consumption spending of $90 billion. Suppose the multiplier is 1.5 and the economy's real GDP is $5,000 billion.

a. In which direction will the aggregate demand curve shift and by how much?

b. Explain using a graph why the change in real GDP is likely to be smaller than the shift in the aggregate demand curve.

10. Suppose a country institutes an investment tax credit, and this leads to an increase in investment spending of $100 billion. Suppose the multiplier is 1.5 and the economy's real GDP is $5,000 billion.

a. In which direction will the aggregate demand curve shift and by how much?

b. Explain using a graph why the change in real GDP is likely to be smaller than the shift in the aggregate demand curve.

11. Suppose a country repeals an investment tax credit, and this leads to a decrease in investment spending of $100 billion. Suppose the multiplier is 1.5 and the economy's real GDP is $5,000 billion.

a. In which direction will the aggregate demand curve shift and by how much?

b. Explain using a graph why the change in real GDP is likely to be smaller than the shift in the aggregate demand curve.

12. Explain why the shifts in the aggregate demand curves in questions 7 through 11 above are the same or different in absolute value.

Endnotes

1. The debt-to-GDP figures in the text are based on the gross debt. But some of that debt is internally held—one government agency borrows from another. The publicly held debt cited here excludes that interagency borrowing and lending.

2. Source: Congressional Budget Office, Options for Reducing the Deficit, 2021 to 2030, available at https://www.cbo.gov/publication/56783

3. In this preliminary analysis of the effects of fiscal policy, we'll assume that these policies have no effect on interest rates or exchange rates. We'll relax that assumption later in the chapter.

4. Investment also affects the long-run aggregate supply curve, since a change in the capital stock changes the potential level of real GDP. We examined this earlier in the chapter on economic growth.

5. A change in tax rates will change the value of the multiplier. The reason is explained in our chapter on consumption.

6. Valerie A. Ramey, "Can Government Purchases Stimulate the Economy?," Journal of Economic Literature 49, no. 3 (September 2011).

7. Jonathan A. Parker, "On Measuring the Effects of Fiscal Policy in Recessions," Journal of Economic Literature 49, no. 3 (September 2011): 703–18.

8. Alan J. Auerbach, William G. Gale, and Benjamin H. Harris, "Activist Fiscal Policy," Journal of Economic Perspectives 24, no. 4 (Fall 2010): 141–64.

9. For a refresher on the inverse relationship between bond prices and interest rates, see our chapter on financial markets.

10. Kailani Koenig, "Mnuchin Says FEMA Doing 'A Terrific Job' in Puerto Rico. NBCNews.com, October 1, 2017. Retrieved from: https://www.nbcnews.com/politics/politics-news/mnuchin-says-fema-doing-terrific-job-puerto-rico-n806356.

11. A year after COVID-19 hit, life for the upper-middle class had largely returned to normal, while the unemployment rate among low-income households still lingered near 20%.

CHAPTER 14
Consumption and the Aggregate Expenditures Model

14.1 Start Up: Consumption Spending Plummets as the COVID-19 Recession Begins

2020 might well be called the "Year of the Big Surprise." In January and February, consumer confidence was high, and financial markets agreed, with stock prices hitting all-time highs coming into the last week of February.

Then, in an instant, the bottom dropped out. Word of a novel coronavirus had reached the United States in early January, but in the last week of February cases began to appear and deaths began to mount. So much was unknown about this new plague that fear and uncertainty began to take hold. Financial markets tumbled, losing a third of their value over the course of a few weeks; business confidence plummeted and investment spending dried up. Imports and exports evaporated as countries began closing borders. Consumer confidence took its sharpest nosedive ever, and consumption spending, ordinarily very stable, plummeted for just about every item except toilet paper, hand sanitizer, and flour as families sheltered in place. With every private component of spending declining sharply, real GDP tumbled at a –30% annual rate.

GDP Not Allowed: The city that never sleeps took one hellacious nap during the COVID-19 lockdown, as this photo of Times Square attests.

Source: GetCoulson/Shutterstock.com

Consumption accounts for the bulk of aggregate demand in the United States and in other countries. In this chapter, we will examine the determinants of consumption and introduce a new model, the aggregate expenditures model, which will give insights into the aggregate demand curve. Any change in aggregate demand causes a change in income, and a change in income causes a change in consumption—which changes aggregate demand, income, and consumption. The aggregate expenditures model will help us to unravel the important relationship between consumption and real GDP.

14.2 Determining the Level of Consumption

We work so hard, we study so hard, we invest and produce so much. Ultimately, all of this is done so you, and I, and this cute little girl can consume the things we love.

Source: antoniodiaz/Shutterstock. com

J. R. McCulloch, an economist of the early nineteenth century, wrote, "Consumption . . . is, in fact, the object of industry."[1] Our economy doesn't produce goods and services just for the satisfaction of a job well done—they're produced so that people can use them! The factors that determine consumption thus determine how successful an economy is in fulfilling its ultimate purpose: providing goods and services for people. So consumption is not just important because it is such a large component of economic activity. It is important because, as McCulloch said, consumption is at the heart of the economy's fundamental purpose.

Consumption and Disposable Personal Income

It seems reasonable to expect that consumption spending by households will be closely related to their disposable personal income. Disposable personal income and GDP are not the same thing: GDP is a measure of an economy's *total* income, no matter where it's received; disposable personal income is the income households have available to spend during a specified period. That's equal to the income households receive less the taxes they pay:

$$Y_d = Y - T$$

where Y_d is disposable personal income, Y is income, and T represents taxes. Real values of disposable personal income and consumption per year from 1980 through 2020 are plotted as a line graph in Figure 14.1. The data suggest a strong association between consumption and disposable income: Increases in income are generally matched by increases in consumption. (You may notice that disposable income sometimes spikes; that's generally in response to a tax change. Consumption changes much more smoothly, with the exception of the first quarter of 2020, when it plummeted during the coronavirus lockdown.)

FIGURE 14.1 The Relationship between Consumption and Disposable Personal Income, 1980–2020

Plots of consumption and disposable personal income over time suggest that consumption increases as disposable personal income increases. One large and surprising exception to this rule was the behavior of consumption during the coronavirus crisis of 2020.

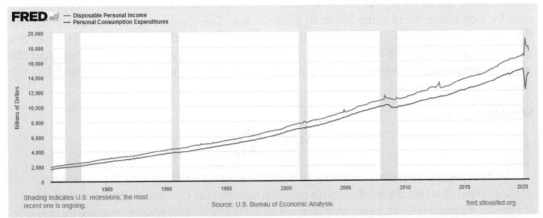

Shading indicates U.S. recessions; the most recent one is ongoing.

Source: U.S. Bureau of Economic Analysis

fred.stlouisfed.org

Source: Bureau of Economic Analysis, accessed through Federal Reserve Economic Data (FRED) at https://fred.stlouisfed.org/series/ DSPI and https://fred.stlouisfed.org/series/PCE. FRED® Graphs ©Federal Reserve Bank of St. Louis. All rights reserved. All FRED® Graphs appear courtesy of Federal Reserve Bank of St. Louis. https://fred.stlouisfed.org/.

The data suggests that consumption depends on disposable income. That relationship is called the **consumption function**. The consumption function can be represented algebraically as an equation, as a schedule in a table, or as a curve on a graph. Let's work with a hypothetical consumption function (Equation 14.1) that shows how consumption depends on disposable income:

consumption function

The relationship between consumption and disposable personal income.

EQUATION 14.1

$$C = \$300 \text{ billion} + 0.8Y_d$$

FIGURE 14.2 Plotting a Consumption Function

The consumption function relates consumption C to disposable personal income Y_d. The equation for the consumption function shown here in tabular and graphical form is $C = \$300$ billion $+ 0.8Y_d$.

Point on curve	A	B	C	D	E
Y_d (billions)	$ 0	500	1,000	1,500	2,000
C (billions)	$300	700	1,100	1,500	1,900

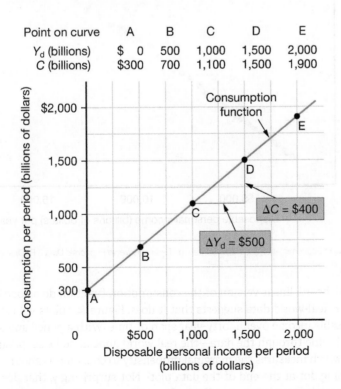

Figure 14.2 illustrates our hypothetical consumption function, plotting disposable income as the independent variable and consumption as the dependent variable. In both the table and the graph, consumption in any period increases as disposable personal income increases in that period; the *slope* of the consumption function tells us by how much. Consider points C and D. When disposable personal income (Y_d) rises by $500 billion (from $1,000 billion to $1,500 billion), consumption rises by $400 billion (from $1,100 billion to $1,500 billion). The slope of the consumption function between points C and D is the ratio of the change in consumption (ΔC) to the change in disposable personal income (ΔY_d). The slope of this particular relationship has a special name; it's called the **marginal propensity to consume** (*MPC*), and is shown in Equation 14.2. (The Greek letter delta (Δ) is used to denote "change in.")

EQUATION 14.2

$$MPC = \frac{\Delta C}{\Delta Y_d}$$

In this case, the marginal propensity to consume equals $400/$500 = 0.8. It can be interpreted as the fraction of an extra $1 of disposable personal income that people spend on consumption. So, if a person with an *MPC* of 0.8 suddenly received an extra $1,200 of disposable personal income (perhaps due to an unexpected tax rebate offered by the government in a time of crisis), that person's consumption would rise by $0.80 for each extra $1 of disposable personal income, or $960.

FIGURE 14.3 The Consumption Function and Real-World Data: 1980–2020

Real-world data supports the notion of the consumption function we've described. A plot of actual values of disposable income and consumption over the past forty years shows a remarkably linear relationship, with a marginal propensity to consume of 0.88. The data point not on the line, not surprisingly, come from mid-2020, when the coronaviris crisis caused consumption to plummet relative to income.

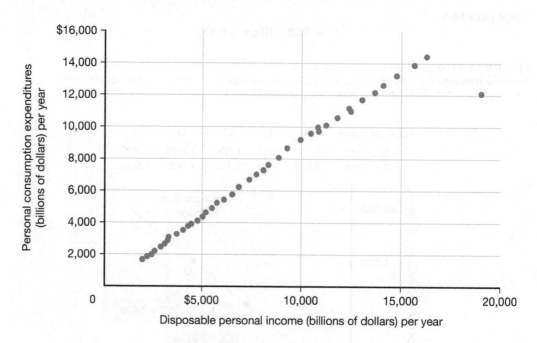

Source: Data from Bureau of Economic Analysis, accessed through Federal Reserve Economic Data (FRED) at https://fred.stlouisfed.org/series/DSPI and https://fred.stlouisfed.org/series/PCE.

Does this whiteboard, linear version of the consumption function do a good job of representing the real world? Real-world data suggests that it does. Figure 14.3 plots values of consumption vs. personal disposable income over a forty-year span of time. With a pencil and a ruler, you could draw a very straight line through the data—the real world appears to be surprisingly linear![2] The slope of that line, which measures the marginal propensity to consume, is about 0.88. What can we make of the dangling dot at the end of the data plot? Not surprisingly, that dot is from the first months of the coronavirus crisis, when individuals were hoarding their paychecks, and lockdowns prevented them from spending their money even when they wanted to. During those months, consumption fell far below what would ordinarily be predicted, so the dot falls below the hypothetical line of the consumption function.

Heads Up!

It is important to note carefully the definition of the marginal propensity to consume. It is the change in consumption divided by the change in disposable personal income. It is not the level of consumption divided by the level of disposable personal income. Using Equation 14.1, at a level of disposable personal income of $500 billion, for example, the level of consumption will be $700 billion so that the ratio of consumption to disposable personal income will be 1.4, while the marginal propensity to consume remains 0.8. The marginal propensity to consume is, as its name implies, a marginal concept: It tells us what will happen to an *additional* dollar of personal disposable income.

Notice in Figure 14.2 that the vertical intercept of the consumption function is $300 billion. That $300 billion figure is called *autonomous consumption*, and it's consumption that would take place (perhaps by drawing down previous savings) even if there were no income. Then, because our consumption function is linear with slope 0.8, for every $500 billion increase in disposable personal income, consumption rises by $400 billion.

We can use the consumption function to show the relationship between personal saving and disposable personal income. **Personal saving** is disposable personal income *not* spent on consumption during a particular period, and can be found by subtracting consumption from disposable personal income for that period:

personal saving

Disposable personal income not spent on consumption during a particular period.

EQUATION 14.3

$$\text{Personal Saving} = \text{Disposable Personal Income} - \text{Consumption}$$

In the United States, the personal savings rate (the percent of disposable personal income that is saved) averages about 7%, as shown in Figure 14.4. But during the coronavirus crisis, spending decreased dramatically, and the personal savings rate rose to an all-time high.

FIGURE 14.4 The Personal Savings Rate, 1998–2020
In the early days of the coronavirus crisis, consumption plummeted . . . but when consumption plummets, the savings rate skyrockets. In 2020, it hit an all-time high!

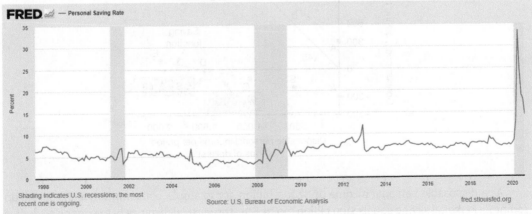

Source: U.S. Bureau of Economic Analysis, Personal Saving Rate [PSAVERT], retrieved from FRED, Federal Reserve Bank of St. Louis; https://fred.stlouisfed.org/series/PSAVERT.

saving function

The relationship between personal saving in any period and disposable personal income in that period.

The **saving function** relates personal saving in any period to disposable personal income in that period. Personal saving is not the only form of saving—firms and government agencies may save as well. In this chapter, however, our focus is on the choice households make between using disposable personal income for consumption or for personal saving.

Figure 14.5 shows how the consumption function and the saving function are related. Personal saving is calculated by subtracting values for consumption from values for disposable personal income, as shown in the table. The values for personal saving are then plotted in the graph. Notice that a 45-degree line has been added to the graph. At every point on the 45-degree line, the value on the vertical axis equals that on the horizontal axis—in other words, if we were on the 45-degree line, consumption and disposable income would be equal.

That actually happens at one point on the consumption function, where it intersects the 45-degree line at point D. There, both disposable income and consumption are $1,500 billion—consumers spend everything they take in, and personal saving equals zero (point D' on the graph of personal saving). Using the graph to find personal saving at other levels of disposable personal income, we subtract the value of consumption, given by the consumption function, from disposable personal income, given by the 45-degree line.

FIGURE 14.5 Consumption and Personal Saving

Personal saving equals disposable personal income minus consumption. The table gives hypothetical values for these variables. The consumption function (in blue) is plotted in the upper part of the graph. At points along the 45-degree line, the values on the two axes are equal; we can measure personal saving as the distance between the 45-degree line and consumption. The saving function (in yellow) is in the lower portion of the graph.

Point on curve	A	B	C	D	E
Y_d (billions)	$ 0	500	1,000	1,500	2,000
C (billions)	$300	700	1,100	1,500	1,900
S (billions)	–$300	–200	–100	0	100

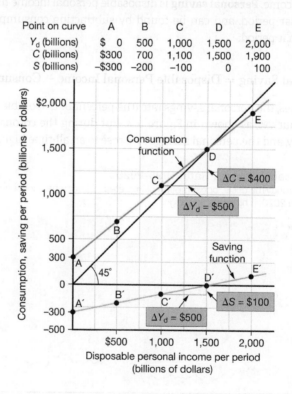

At a disposable personal income of $2,000 billion, for example, consumption is $1,900 billion (point E). Personal saving equals $100 billion (point E')—the vertical distance between the 45-degree line and the consumption function. At an income of $500 billion, consumption totals $700 billion (point B). The consumption function lies above the 45-degree line at this point; personal saving is –$200 billion (point B'). A negative value for saving means that consumption exceeds disposable personal income; it must have come from saving accumulated in the past, from selling assets, or from borrowing.

Notice that for every $500 billion increase in disposable personal income, personal saving rises by $100 billion, just as we see between points C' and D' in Figure 14.5. The slope of the saving function is the ratio of those changes; more generally, it is calculated as the change in personal saving (ΔS) to the change in disposable personal income (ΔY_d). The slope of the saving function has a special name; it measures the **marginal propensity to save** (*MPS*).

EQUATION 14.4

$$MPS = \frac{\Delta S}{\Delta Y_d}$$

The marginal propensity to save measures the fraction of an extra $1 of disposable personal income that people save. In this case, the marginal propensity to save equals $100/$500 = 0.2. So, if a person with an *MPS* of 0.2 received an extra $1,200 of disposable personal income, that person's saving would rise by $0.20 for each extra $1 of disposable personal income, or $240.

Because people have only two choices of what to do with additional disposable personal income—either use it for consumption or save it—the fraction of disposable personal income that people consume (*MPC*) plus the fraction of disposable personal income that people save (*MPS*) must add to 1:

EQUATION 14.5

$$MPC + MPS = 1$$

Current versus Permanent Income

The discussion so far has related consumption in a particular period to income in that same period. The **current income hypothesis** says that consumption in any one period depends on income during that period, or current income.

Although it seems obvious that consumption should be related to disposable personal income, it's not so obvious that consumers base their consumption in any one period on the income they receive during that same period. In buying a new car, for example, consumers might base their decision not only on their current income but on the income they expect to receive during the three or four years they'll be making payments on the car. Parents who purchase a college education for their children might base their decision on their own expected lifetime incomes.

It seems reasonable that most consumption choices could be affected by expectations of income over a long period of time. After all, people choose to save (read: consume less) for their retirement, even when they're in their twenties! Others save to build an estate they can leave to their heirs. The amount people save today depends on their distant future goals, but it also depends on the income they expect to receive for the rest of their lives—after all, why struggle to save now, while you're working minimum wage; saving will be so much easier when you're 50 and pulling down high six figures. For these and other reasons, then, consumption and personal saving are likely influenced by your **permanent income**, the average annual income people expect to receive for the rest of their lives.

People who have the same *current* income but different *permanent* incomes might make very different saving decisions. Someone with a relatively low current income but a high permanent income, like a college student planning to go to medical school, might save little or nothing now, but plan to save for retirement and for bequests later. A person with the same low income but no expectation of higher income later might try to save some money now to provide for retirement or bequests later.

The difference between permanent and current income is the difference between a raise and a bonus.

Source: fizkes/Shutterstock.com

permanent income hypothesis

Consumption in any period depends on permanent income.

Because saving and consumption are two sides of the same (disposable income) coin, an alternative approach to explaining consumption behavior is the **permanent income hypothesis**, which assumes that consumption in any period depends not on current income, but on permanent income. An important implication of the permanent income hypothesis is that a change in income regarded as temporary will not affect consumption much, since it will have little effect on average lifetime income; a change regarded as permanent will have a larger effect. In contrast, the current income hypothesis predicts that it does not matter whether consumers view a change in disposable personal income as permanent or temporary; *any* change in income will move them along the consumption function and change consumption accordingly.

Other Determinants of Consumption

The consumption function graphed in Figure 14.2 and Figure 14.5 relates consumption spending to the level of disposable personal income. Changes in disposable personal income cause movements *along* this curve, from left to right. But there are other things that may affect consumption besides disposable income, things like increased confidence about the future, or changes in wealth (perhaps due to a boom in the stock market). Those kinds of changes won't move us along the consumption function; they'll shift the entire curve upward or downward, as shown in Figure 14.6.

FIGURE 14.6 Shifts in the Consumption Function

An increase in the level of consumption at each level of disposable personal income shifts the consumption function upward in Panel (a). Among the events that would shift the curve upward are an increase in real wealth and an increase in consumer confidence. A reduction in the level of consumption at each level of disposable personal income shifts the curve downward in Panel (b). The events that could shift the curve downward include a reduction in real wealth and a decline in consumer confidence.

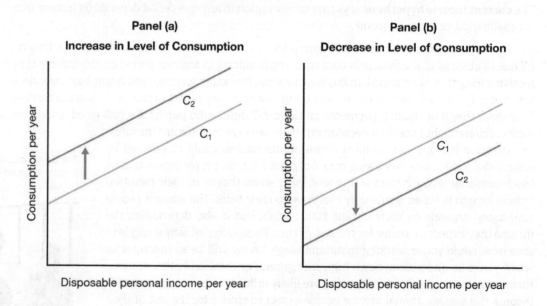

Changes in Real Wealth

An increase in stock and bond prices, for example, would make holders of these assets wealthier, and as a result, they would be likely to increase their consumption . . . even if their current disposable income remained unchanged. An increase in real wealth will shift the consumption function upward, as illustrated in Panel (a) of Figure 14.6. A reduction in real wealth (due to a decline in the stock market, for example, as happened during the early weeks of the coronavirus crisis) shifts it downward, as shown in Panel (b).

One big factor that affects real wealth is the price level. If your life savings is in hundred dollar bills carefully concealed in your mattress, inflation that causes prices to double will cut the purchasing power of your savings in half. That's true for your cash, and it's true for others who have their savings in stable-valued assets that may not keep up with inflation. We learned in an earlier chapter that the relationship among the price level, real wealth, and consumption is called the *wealth effect*. A reduction in the price level increases real wealth and shifts the consumption function upward, as shown in Panel (a). An increase in the price level shifts the curve downward, as shown in Panel (b).

Changes in Expectations

Consumers are likely to be more willing to spend money when they are optimistic about the future. Surveyors attempt to gauge this optimism using "consumer confidence" surveys that ask respondents to report whether they are optimistic or pessimistic about their own economic situation and about the prospects for the economy as a whole. An increase in consumer optimism tends to shift the consumption function upward as in Panel (a) of Figure 14.6; an increase in pessimism tends to shift it downward as in Panel (b). The sharp reductions in consumer confidence during the coronavirus crisis of early 2020 (shown in Figure 14.7) contributed to a sharp downward shift in the consumption function, resulting in the largest and fastest decline in consumption in the U.S. economy's history.

FIGURE 14.7 Consumer Confidence and Economic Activity
Consumer confidence is closely linked to economic activity, plummeting sharply just before, or at the beginning of, the shaded areas of economic recession.

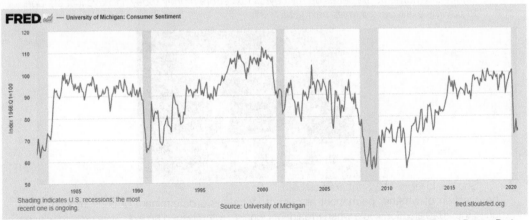

Source: University of Michigan, University of Michigan: Consumer Sentiment [UMCSENT], retrieved from FRED, Federal Reserve Bank of St. Louis; https://fred.stlouisfed.org/series/UMCSENT.

The relationship between consumption and consumer expectations concerning future economic conditions tends to be a form of self-fulfilling prophecy. If consumers expect economic conditions to worsen, they will cut their consumption—and economic conditions will worsen! Political leaders often try to persuade people that economic prospects are good. In part, such efforts are an attempt to increase economic activity by boosting consumption.

Key Takeaways

- Consumption is closely related to disposable personal income and is represented by the consumption function, which can be presented in a table, in a graph, or in an equation.
- Personal saving is disposable personal income not spent on consumption.
- The marginal propensity to consume is $MPC = \Delta C/\Delta Y_d$ and the marginal propensity to save is $MPS = \Delta S/\Delta Y_d$. The sum of the MPC and MPS is 1.

- The current income hypothesis holds that consumption is a function of current disposable personal income, whereas the permanent income hypothesis holds that consumption is a function of permanent income, which is the income households expect to receive annually during their lifetime. The permanent income hypothesis predicts that a temporary change in income will have a smaller effect on consumption than is predicted by the current income hypothesis.
- Other factors that affect consumption include real wealth and expectations.

Try It!

For each of the following events, draw a curve representing the consumption function and show how the event would affect the curve.

1. A sharp increase in stock prices increases the real wealth of most households.
2. Consumers decide that a recession is ahead and that their incomes are likely to fall.
3. The price level falls.

See related Concept Problem 4 at the end of this chapter.

Case in Point: Permanent Income and the Trump Tax Shuffle

Light Bulb Moment: "If I set aside my payroll tax rebate money today, I'll have just enough to pay my extra payroll taxes next year."

Source: lovelyday12/Shutterstock.com

The question of whether permanent or current income is a determinant of consumption arose during the 2020 election cycle when President Donald Trump issued an executive order declaring a temporary payroll tax holiday. That order eliminated Social Security tax collections for workers earning less than $104,000 per year, amounting to a 6.2% raise.

Those Social Security tax reductions would last from September 1 through December, after which payroll taxes collections would return to their usual level. But there was a twist! Every dollar not collected in the fall would be collected in full later, between January and April of 2021! That made the extra $70–$80 the typical worker would find in her paycheck during fall 2020 truly temporary, with exactly zero change in permanent income. The implications of such a change for consumption are interesting:

- If the current income hypothesis is true, consumers should react to the payroll tax cut by spending more in the fall (when disposable income increases) and less in the spring, when double-taxes kicked in.
- If the permanent income hypothesis is true, consumers would not change consumption at all. Every penny of the tax cut would be saved in the fall to cover repayments in the spring.

The tax reshuffling was designed to stimulate demand (and, perhaps more cynically, to win some votes in a contentious election cycle). And to some households, struggling after eight months of pandemic-related financial stress, those few dollars might well have been spent. It left many concerned, including one military constituent of Congressperson Donald Beyer, who wrote, "Many of these men and women are fresh out of high school and earning the first paychecks of their lives. The sudden influx of money, unexplained, will likely be spent very quickly by many of them, with little regard for later consequences. Many of the soldiers within the ranks live paycheck to paycheck, and if they are not aware that all of this money must be paid back next year, it could be ruinous to their financial health."[3]

That tacit support for the current income hypothesis is backed by good research. Economists Sumit Agarwal, Chunlin Liu, and Nicholas Souleles studied the effects of a 2001 tax rebate on consumption. They found that while consumers initially saved much of the rebate, spending eventually increased, leveling off at about 40% of the rebate. Not surprisingly, consumers who were most liquidity constrained (for example, those close to their credit card debt limits) spent more of their rebate than consumers who were in better shape financially. Their results showed that financially stressed consumers *do* respond to "lumpy" changes in disposable income like the Trump tax shuffle created—in other words, current income does seem to matter. But they also showed that more financially secure consumers—consumers with access to savings and credit, were less responsive to the rebate—to them, changes in permanent income seem to be more important.

Ultimately the transparent nature of the stimulus program's non-effect on permanent income ("I'll put a dollar in your pocket now, but you'll have to pay it all back tomorrow") made the program largely appear akin to rearranging deck chairs on the *Titanic*, a costly reshuffling that drew attention away from both a much more serious problem and from a much better solution. One defense department employee commented, "As far as I can see, it is really idiotic, costs a lot of money to the government, and doesn't help anyone. It is an unnecessary hassle."[4]

Due to legal concerns, the program was ultimately made voluntary, at the employer's discretion. Concerned that their workers might have difficulty coping with double taxation during the payback period, and also concerned they, themselves, would end up paying the back taxes should an employee leave the company, few employers—not even the U.S. Postal Service—elected to participate. The sole large employer that opted in was the U.S. federal government, but buy-in was even spotty there: The administrators of the House of Representatives opted out of the plan, saying that "the deferral would not be in the best interests of the House or our employees."

See related Concept Problem 3 at the end of this chapter.

Sources: Based on Sumit Agarwal, Chunlin Liu, and Nicholas S. Souleles, "The Reaction of Consumer Spending and Debt to Tax Rebates—Evidence from Consumer Credit Data," NBER Working Paper No. 13694, December 2007; David S. Johnson, Jonathan A. Parker, and Nicholas S. Souleles, "Household Expenditure and the Income Tax Rebates of 2001," American Economic Review 96, no. 5 (December 2006): 1589–1610; Jim Tankersley, "Trump's Payroll Tax 'Cut' Fizzles," The New York Times, September 11, 2020; and Michelle Singletary, "The president's payroll tax cut is really a loan that workers have to pay back. Let's call it what it is," Washington Post, September 8, 2020.

Answers to Try It! Problems

1. A sharp increase in stock prices makes people wealthier and shifts the consumption function upward, as in Panel (a) of Figure 14.6.

2. This would be reported as a reduction in consumer confidence. Consumers are likely to respond by reducing their purchases, particularly of durable items such as cars and washing machines. The consumption function will shift downward, as in Panel (b) of Figure 14.6.

3. A reduction in the price level increases real wealth and thus boosts consumption. The consumption function will shift upward, as in Panel (a) of Figure 14.6.

14.3 The Aggregate Expenditures Model

Learning Objectives

1. Explain and illustrate the aggregate expenditures model and the concept of equilibrium real GDP.
2. Distinguish between autonomous and induced aggregate expenditures and explain why a small change in autonomous expenditures leads to a larger change in equilibrium real GDP.
3. Discuss how adding taxes, government purchases, and net exports to a simplified aggregate expenditures model affects the multiplier and the impact on real GDP arising from a change in autonomous expenditures.

aggregate expenditures model

Model that relates aggregate expenditures to the level of real GDP.

aggregate expenditures

The sum of planned levels of consumption, investment, government purchases, and net exports at a given price level.

The consumption function relates the level of consumption in a period to the level of disposable personal income in that period. In this section, we'll incorporate other components of aggregate demand—investment, government purchases, and net exports—into a new model of real GDP, the **aggregate expenditures model**. This model relates **aggregate expenditures**, the sum of planned levels of consumption, investment, government purchases, and net exports at a given price level, to the level of real GDP. In this model, we'll find that people, firms, and government agencies may not always spend what they had planned to spend. In that case, actual real GDP will not be the same as aggregate expenditures, and the economy will not be at the equilibrium level of real GDP.

That seems like a lot of hard work! What will we gain from it? The biggest takeaway is a deeper understanding of the "ripple effects" from a change in one or more components of aggregate demand. As we saw in the chapter that introduced the aggregate demand and aggregate supply model, a change in investment, government purchases, or net exports leads to greater production; that creates additional income for households, which spurs additional consumption, which in turn leads to still more production, more income, and more consumption. That spiral of economic activity eventually has to wind itself down—if it didn't we'd all be infinitely rich, and have an infinite amount of stuff! The aggregate expenditures model is going to help us figure out exactly how that winding down happens. As a side benefit, the aggregate expenditures model can ultimately be used to derive the aggregate demand curve for our model of aggregate demand and aggregate supply.

To see how the aggregate expenditures model works, we'll begin with a very simplified model in which there is neither a government sector nor a foreign sector. Eliminating those sectors will keep our mathematics simple and let us figure out how things work. Then, once we know how the simplified economy works, we'll add back in government and international trade.

The Aggregate Expenditures Model: A Simplified View

In our simple model, there are only two components of aggregate expenditures: consumption and investment. There are no government purchases, no taxes, and no trade, so in our model, disposable personal income and real GDP are identical.

Finally, we'll assume that the only component of aggregate expenditures that may not be at its planned level is investment. In our model of aggregate expenditures, firms determine a level of investment they intend to make in each period, called **planned investment**. But some investment may be unplanned. Suppose, for example, that firms produce and expect to sell more goods during a period than they actually sell. The unsold goods will be added to the firms' inventories. You might remember that additions to inventories are included in the investment category of GDP. In our model, these unplanned additions to inventory are called *unplanned investment*. **Unplanned investment** is investment during a period that firms did not intend to make. Both planned and unplanned investment will play key roles in the aggregate expenditures model.

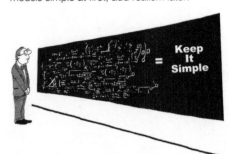

Don't learn this lesson the hard way: Keep your models simple at first; add realism later.

Source: Cartoon Resource/Shutterstock.com

It is also possible that firms may sell more than they had expected. In that case, inventories will fall below what firms had planned to maintain, and unplanned investment would be negative. Regardless of whether unplanned investment is negative or positive, total investment (I) will be the sum of planned investment (I_P) and unplanned investment (I_U).

EQUATION 14.6

$$I = I_P + I_U$$

Autonomous and Induced Aggregate Expenditures

Economists distinguish two types of expenditures. Expenditures that don't vary with the level of real GDP are called **autonomous expenditures**. In our example, planned investment expenditures are autonomous. But some expenditures do vary with real GDP. We looked at one example of that, consumption, in the previous section. Expenditures that vary with real GDP are called **induced expenditures**.

Figure 14.8 illustrates the difference between autonomous and induced aggregate expenditures. With real GDP on the horizontal axis and aggregate expenditures on the vertical axis, autonomous aggregate expenditures are shown as the line in Panel (a). That line is flat: The level of expenditure is the same regardless of income.

Panel (b) of Figure 14.8 shows induced expenditures. It starts at the origin: No income, no induced expenditures. It's also positively sloped: As real GDP rises, so does induced spending.

planned investment

The level of investment firms intend to make in a period.

unplanned investment

Investment during a period that firms did not intend to make.

autonomous expenditures

Expenditures that do not vary with the level of real GDP.

induced expenditures

Expenditures that vary with real GDP.

FIGURE 14.8 Autonomous and Induced Aggregate Expenditures

Autonomous expenditures do not vary with the level of real GDP; induced expenditures do. Autonomous expenditures are shown by the horizontal line in Panel (a). Induced expenditures rise with real GDP, as in Panel (b).

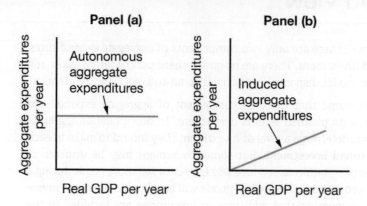

Autonomous and Induced Consumption

The consumption function we looked at in the previous section assumed that consumption had both autonomous and induced components. Consider the consumption function we used in deriving the schedule and curve illustrated in Figure 14.2:

$$C = \$300 \text{ billion} + 0.8Y$$

In this slightly modified version, we've omitted the subscript on disposable personal income, because with no government sector, there are no taxes. That means that Y represents both disposable personal income and GDP. We can take it one step further if we assume that the price level is constant; in that case, GDP will equal real GDP.

At every level of real GDP, consumption includes $300 billion in autonomous aggregate expenditures. It also includes expenditures "induced" by the level of real GDP. At a level of real GDP of $2,000 billion, for example, consumption equals $1,900 billion: $300 billion in autonomous aggregate expenditures and $1,600 billion in consumption induced by the $2,000 billion level of real GDP.

Figure 14.9 illustrates these two components of consumption. Autonomous consumption, C_a, which is always $300 billion, is shown in Panel (a); its equation is

EQUATION 14.7

$$C_a = \$300 \text{ billion}$$

Induced consumption C_i, is shown in Panel (b); its equation is

EQUATION 14.8

$$C_i = 0.8Y$$

The consumption function given by the sum of Equation 14.7 and Equation 14.8 is shown in Panel (c) of Figure 14.9.

FIGURE 14.9 Autonomous and Induced Consumption

Consumption has an autonomous component and an induced component. In Panel (a), autonomous consumption C_a equals $300 billion at every level of real GDP. Panel (b) shows induced consumption C_i. Total consumption C is shown in Panel (c).

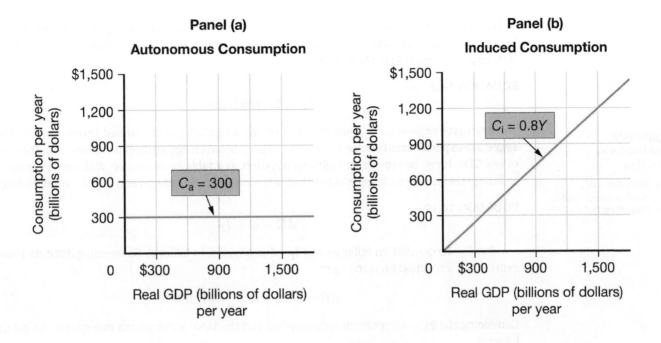

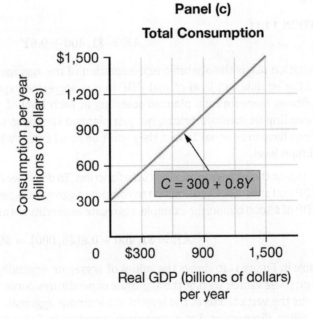

Plotting the Aggregate Expenditures Curve

In this simplified economy, investment is the only other component of aggregate expenditures. Let's assume that investment is completely autonomous, and is unaffected by the level of real GDP. If firms plan to invest $1,100 billion per year:

EQUATION 14.9

$$I_P = \$1,100 \text{ billion}$$

aggregate expenditures function

The relationship of aggregate expenditures to the value of real GDP.

Aggregate expenditures equal the sum of consumption C and planned investment I_P. The **aggregate expenditures function** is the relationship between aggregate expenditures and the level of real GDP. It can be represented with an equation, as a table, or as a curve. With no government or foreign sector, aggregate expenditures AE is the sum of consumption and investment spending:

EQUATION 14.10

$$AE = C + I_P$$

But C = $300 + 0.8Y (in billions), and I_P = $1,100 (again, in billions). So we can substitute those expressions into Equation 14.10 to get:

$$AE = \$300 + 0.8Y + \$1,100$$

Combining the $300 autonomous consumption and the $1,100 autonomous investment, we get (in billions)

EQUATION 14.11

$$AE = \$1,400 + 0.8Y$$

Equation 14.11 is the algebraic representation of the aggregate expenditures function we'll use to find the equilibrium level of real GDP in our aggregate expenditures model. These aggregate expenditures measure total *planned* spending at each level of real GDP. But real GDP measures total spending (at constant prices), not just planned spending, so aggregate expenditures and real GDP don't have to be equal. In fact, they won't be equal *except* when the economy is operating at its equilibrium level.

Let's plot the aggregate expenditures function. To do so, we'll arbitrarily select various levels of real GDP and then use Equation 14.11 to compute aggregate expenditures at each level. At a level of real GDP of $6,000 billion, for example, aggregate expenditures are $6,200 billion:

$$AE = \$1,400 + 0.8(\$6,000) = \$6,200$$

The table in Figure 14.10 shows the values of aggregate expenditures at various levels of real GDP. Based on these values, we plot the aggregate expenditures curve. The aggregate expenditures curve intersects the vertical axis at the level of autonomous aggregate expenditures—in our example, at $1,400 billion. (Remember that autonomous spending includes $1,100 billion in planned investment and $300 billion in autonomous consumption.)

FIGURE 14.10 Plotting the Aggregate Expenditures Curve

Values for aggregate expenditures *AE* are computed by inserting values for real GDP into the formula for aggregate expenditures. These are given in the aggregate expenditures schedule. The point at which the aggregate expenditures curve intersects the vertical axis is the value of autonomous aggregate expenditures, here $1,400 billion. The slope of this aggregate expenditures curve is 0.8.

Point on curve	A	B	C	D	E	F
Y (billions)	$ 0	2,000	4,000	6,000	8,000	10,000
AE (billions)	$1,400	3,000	4,600	6,200	7,800	9,400

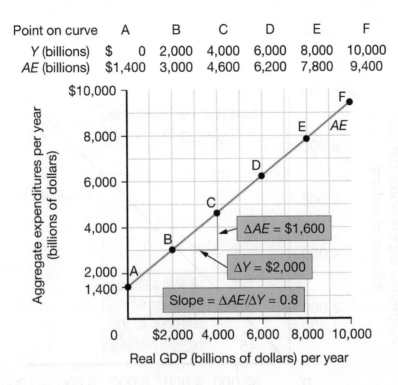

The Slope of the Aggregate Expenditures Curve

The slope of the aggregate expenditures curve, given by the change in aggregate expenditures divided by the change in real GDP between any two points, measures the additional expenditures induced by increases in real GDP. The slope for the aggregate expenditures curve in Figure 14.10 is shown for points B and C: It is 0.8.

In Figure 14.10, the slope of the aggregate expenditures curve equals the marginal propensity to consume. That's because we assumed that all investment was autonomous; only consumption spending has an induced component. For every dollar of additional income, consumption rises by $0.80, the *MPC*.

Equilibrium in the Aggregate Expenditures Model

Real GDP is a measure of the total output of firms. Aggregate expenditures equal total planned spending on that output. In this model, equilibrium is found where aggregate expenditures equal real GDP. One way to think about equilibrium is to recognize that firms, except for some inventory that they plan to hold, produce goods and services with the intention of selling them. Aggregate expenditures consist of what people, firms, and government agencies plan to spend. If the economy is at its equilibrium real GDP, then firms are producing and selling what they plan to sell (that is, there are no unplanned changes in inventories).

Figure 14.11 illustrates the concept of equilibrium in the aggregate expenditures model. A 45-degree line connects all the points at which the values on the two axes are equal. In this case, any point on the 45-degree line is a point where aggregate expenditures equal real GDP. That means that equilibrium must occur at some point along this 45-degree line. Specifically, it's found where the aggregate expenditures curve crosses the 45-degree line; here, that's at a real GDP of $7,000 billion.

FIGURE 14.11 Determining Equilibrium in the Aggregate Expenditures Model

The 45-degree line shows all the points at which aggregate expenditures AE equal real GDP, as required for equilibrium. The equilibrium solution occurs where the AE curve crosses the 45-degree line, at a real GDP of $7,000 billion.

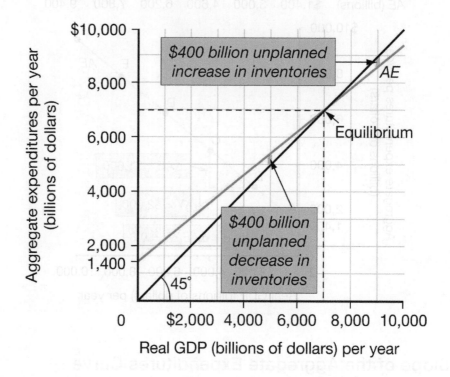

Equation 14.11 tells us that at a real GDP of $7,000 billion, the sum of consumption and planned investment is $7,000 billion—precisely the level of output firms produced. At that level of output, firms sell what they planned to sell and keep inventories that they planned to keep. A real GDP of $7,000 billion represents equilibrium in the sense that it generates an equal level of aggregate expenditures.

If firms were to produce a real GDP greater than $7,000 billion per year, aggregate expenditures would fall short of real GDP. At a level of real GDP of $9,000 billion per year, for example, aggregate expenditures equal $8,600 billion. Firms are left with $400 billion worth of goods they intended to sell but didn't; and their actual level of investment would be $400 billion greater than their planned level of investment because of these unexpected additions to inventory. In the next year, those firms would be likely to cut their output (why produce as much when you've already got so much stowed away in inventory?), moving the economy toward its equilibrium GDP of $7,000 billion.

On the other hand, if firms were to produce goods worth $5,000 billion, aggregate expenditures would be $5,400 billion. Consumers and firms would demand more goods and services than were being produced. To satisfy that demand, firms would draw down their existing inventories, which would drop below the planned level. In the next year, they would increase output in an attempt to restore those inventories and satisfy their customers' demand. That would move the economy toward its equilibrium real GDP of $7,000 billion.

Table 14.1 shows possible levels of real GDP in the economy for the aggregate expenditures function illustrated in Figure 14.11. It shows the level of aggregate expenditures at various levels of real GDP and the direction in which real GDP will change whenever AE does not equal real GDP. At any level of real GDP other than the equilibrium level, there is unplanned investment (or disinvestment).

TABLE 14.1 Adjusting to Equilibrium Real GDP

Each level of real GDP will result in a particular amount of aggregate expenditures. If aggregate expenditures are less than the level of real GDP, firms will reduce their output and real GDP will fall. If aggregate expenditures exceed real GDP, then firms will increase their output and real GDP will rise. If aggregate expenditures equal real GDP, then firms will leave their output unchanged; we have achieved equilibrium in the aggregate expenditures model. At equilibrium, there is no unplanned investment. Here, that occurs at a real GDP of $7,000 billion.

If real GDP is ($)	Consumption expenditures will be ($)	Planned investment will be ($)	Aggregate expenditures will equal ($)	Unplanned investment will be ($)	Real GDP will
9,000	7,500	1,100	8,600	400	Fall ↓
8,000	6,700	1,100	7,800	200	Fall ↓
7,000	5,900	1,100	7,000	0	Remain unchanged
6,000	5,100	1,100	6,200	−200	Rise ↑
5,000	4,300	1,100	5,400	−400	Rise ↑

Changes in Aggregate Expenditures: The Multiplier

In the aggregate expenditures model, equilibrium is found at the level of real GDP at which the aggregate expenditures curve crosses the 45-degree line. Any shift in the *AE* curve will change equilibrium real GDP. Let's look at the magnitude of such changes.

Figure 14.12 begins with the aggregate expenditures curve shown in Figure 14.11. Now suppose that planned investment increases from the original value of $1,100 billion to a new value of $1,400 billion—an increase of $300 billion. This increase in planned investment shifts the aggregate expenditures curve vertically upward by $300 billion, all other things unchanged. The new aggregate expenditures curve intersects the 45-degree line at a real GDP of $8,500 billion, so the $300 billion increase in planned investment has produced an increase in equilibrium real GDP of $1,500 billion ($8,500 billion – $7,000 billion).

How could an increase in aggregate expenditures of $300 billion produce an increase in equilibrium real GDP of $1,500 billion? Because firms have increased their demand for investment goods (that is, for capital) by $300 billion, the firms that produce those capital goods will have $300 billion in additional orders. They will produce $300 billion in additional real GDP and, given our simplifying assumption, $300 billion in additional disposable personal income.

But in this economy, each $1 of additional real GDP induces $0.80 in additional consumption. The $300 billion increase in autonomous aggregate expenditures touches off $240 billion (= 0.8 × $300 billion) in new consumption. But wait . . . there's more! The $240 billion in additional consumption *also* boosts production, creating another $240 billion in real GDP. And that increase induces even *more* consumption—specifically $192 billion (= 0.8 × $240) worth.

That cycle of new consumption touching off more new consumption touching off even more new consumption continues. But each new round of consumption spending is smaller than the one before, so eventually, after many additional rounds of increases in induced consumption, the process limits out, with the initial $300 billion increase in aggregate expenditures causing a $1,500 billion increase in equilibrium real GDP.[5]

Not a drop in the bucket: One small splash of autonomous spending ripples through the economy, creating more income as it goes.

Source: WhiteJack/Shutterstock.com

FIGURE 14.12 A Change in Autonomous Aggregate Expenditures Changes Equilibrium Real GDP

An increase of $300 billion in planned investment raises the aggregate expenditures curve by $300 billion. The $300 billion increase in planned investment results in an increase in equilibrium real GDP of $1,500 billion.

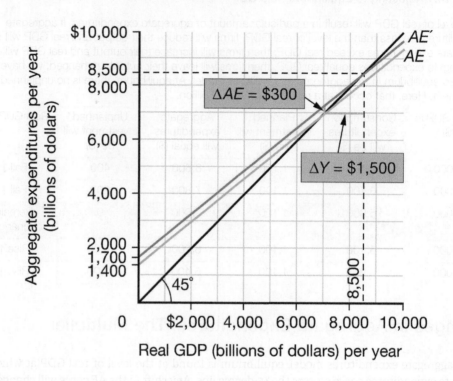

Table 14.2 shows the multiplied effect of a $300 billion increase in autonomous aggregate expenditures, assuming each $1 of additional real GDP induces $0.80 in additional consumption.

TABLE 14.2 The Multiplied Effect of an Increase in Autonomous Aggregate Expenditures

A $300 billion increase in autonomous aggregate expenditures initially increases real GDP and income by that amount. This is shown in the first round of spending. The increased income leads to additional consumption, which boosts production and leads to even higher real GDP, touching off additional rounds of consumption. Assuming each $1 of additional real GDP induces $0.80 in additional consumption, the multiplied effect of a $300 billion increase in autonomous aggregate expenditures leads to additional rounds of spending that ultimately create a $1,500 billion increase in real GDP.

Round of Spending	Increase in Real GDP (Billions of $)
1	300
2	240
3	192
4	154
5	123
6	98
7	79
8	63
9	50
10	40
11	32
12	26

Round of Spending	Increase in Real GDP (Billions of $)
Subsequent rounds	+103
Total increase in real GDP	$1,500

The size of the additional rounds of expenditure is based on the slope of the aggregate expenditures function, which in this example is simply the marginal propensity to consume. Had the marginal propensity to consume been lower (making the slope flatter), the additional rounds of spending would have been smaller. A steeper slope would mean that the additional rounds of spending would have been larger.

This process also works in reverse—a decrease in planned investment leads to a multiplied decrease in real GDP. Such a decrease in planned investment would reduce the incomes of some households, who would, in turn, reduce their consumption by the *MPC* times the reduction in their income. The cycle of reductions would continue, with the reduction in planned investment ultimately causing a much larger decrease in GDP.

Computation of the Multiplier

We've just learned that a small increase in planned investment spending can lead to a large increase in real GDP. But *how* large? In our simple model, the $300 billion increase in planned investment was multiplied by a factor of five: GDP increased by $500 billion. In this case, the multiplier is:

EQUATION 14.12

$$\text{Multiplier} = \frac{\Delta Y_{eq}}{\Delta A} = \frac{\$1,500}{\$300} = 5$$

where ΔY_{eq} is the change in equilibrium real GDP ($1,500 billion) and ΔA is the $300 billion change in autonomous spending. With $300 billion of spending causing a $1,500 increase in GDP, the value of the multiplier therefore is $1,500/$300 = 5.

Does the multiplier always equal five? It certainly doesn't have to! It depends on how much additional spending an extra dollar of income induces, which is captured in the slope of the expenditure function. In the example we've been working with, GDP creation in each successive round of spending depended on the size of the marginal propensity to consume. (The slope of the expenditure function equaled the *MPC*, in fact.) If the marginal propensity to consume were higher, consumption in each round of spending wouldn't drop off so quickly and overall growth (and the multiplier) would be larger. But how much larger? Let's see exactly how the multiplier and the *MPC* are related.

The Marginal Propensity to Consume and the Multiplier

We can compute the multiplier for this simplified economy from the marginal propensity to consume. We know that the amount by which equilibrium real GDP will change as a result of a change in aggregate expenditures consists of two parts: the change in autonomous aggregate expenditures itself, ΔA, and the induced change in spending. The induced change in spending is the additional consumption spending caused by rising income, and is measured as the *MPC* times the additional income, ΔY_{eq}. So,

$$\Delta Y_{eq} = \Delta A + MPC\Delta Y_{eq}$$

Subtract the $MPC\Delta Y_{eq}$ term from both sides of the equation:

$$\Delta Y_{eq} - MPC\Delta Y_{eq} = \Delta A$$

Factor out the ΔY_{eq} term on the left:

$$\Delta Y_{eq}(1 - MPC) = \Delta A$$

Finally, solve for the multiplier by dividing both sides of the equation above by ΔA and by dividing both sides by $(1 - MPC)$:

EQUATION 14.13

$$\frac{\Delta Y_{eq}}{\Delta A} = \frac{1}{(1 - MPC)}$$

The left-hand side is the multiplier—it tells you how much equilibrium income changes for each additional dollar of autonomous spending. Just as we suspected, the right-hand side shows that the multiplier depends on the MPC. The bigger the MPC, the smaller the denominator will be, and the larger the multiplier. In our example, the marginal propensity to consume is 0.8; so the multiplier will be

$$\text{Multiplier} = \frac{1}{(1 - 0.8)} = \frac{1}{0.2} = 5$$

which matches our answer from before: $300 of additional autonomous investment spending led to $1,500 of additional income.

Since the sum of the marginal propensity to consume and the marginal propensity to save is 1, the denominator on the right-hand side of Equation 14.13 is equivalent to the MPS, and the multiplier could also be expressed as 1/MPS.

EQUATION 14.14

$$\text{Multiplier} = \frac{1}{MPS}$$

We can rearrange terms in Equation 14.13 to use the multiplier to compute the impact of a change in autonomous aggregate expenditures. Just multiply both sides of the equation by ΔA to obtain the following:

EQUATION 14.15

$$\Delta Y_{eq} = \frac{1}{(1 - MPC)} \times \Delta A$$

The change in the equilibrium level of income in the aggregate expenditures model (remember that the model assumes a constant price level) equals the change in autonomous aggregate expenditures times the multiplier. The greater the multiplier, the greater the impact on income stemming from a change in autonomous aggregate expenditures.

The Aggregate Expenditures Model in a More Realistic Economy

Let's recap what we've learned from our simple model of aggregate expenditures:

1. The aggregate expenditures function relates aggregate expenditures to real GDP. The intercept of the aggregate expenditures curve shows the level of autonomous spending. The slope of the aggregate expenditures curve shows how much increases in real GDP induce additional aggregate expenditures.
2. Equilibrium real GDP occurs where aggregate expenditures equal real GDP.

3. A change in autonomous aggregate expenditures changes equilibrium real GDP by a multiple of the change in autonomous aggregate expenditures.

4. The size of the multiplier depends on the slope of the aggregate expenditures curve. The steeper the aggregate expenditures curve, the larger the multiplier; the flatter the aggregate expenditures curve, the smaller the multiplier.

We've been dealing with a highly simplified model. But these four points will still hold as we add a bit more realism (and a bit more complexity) to our model. Let's start by incorporating taxes, and then add back the two other components of aggregate expenditures—government purchases and net exports.

Taxes and the Aggregate Expenditure Function

Suppose that the only difference between real GDP and disposable personal income is personal income taxes. Let us see what happens to the slope of the aggregate expenditures function. We'll continue to assume that the marginal propensity to consume is 0.8, but let's add the assumption that ¼ of real GDP is captured as income taxes. That means that for every additional $1 of real GDP, disposable personal income rises by $0.75 and, in turn, consumption rises by $0.60 (= 0.8 × $0.75). That flattens the slope of the aggregate expenditures curve from 0.8 to 0.6.

The wedge between disposable personal income and real GDP created by taxes means that the additional rounds of spending induced by a change in autonomous aggregate expenditures will be smaller than if there were no taxes. Now, $300 of autonomous spending creates $180 of spending in the first round (instead of $240); $108 in the second round (instead of $192), and so on. The multiplier shrinks—in fact, the 25% tax rate causes the multiplier to fall in half, from 5 to 2.5.

It's not just you who's feeling blue about taxes—they depress the value of the multiplier, too.

Source: Andrei_R/Shutterstock. com

The Addition of Government Purchases and Net Exports

Suppose that government purchases and net exports are autonomous. If so, they enter the aggregate expenditures function in the same way that investment did. Compared to the simplified aggregate expenditures model, the aggregate expenditures curve shifts up by the amount of government purchases and net exports.[6]

Figure 14.13 shows the difference between the aggregate expenditures model of the simplified economy in Figure 14.11 and a more realistic view of the economy. Panel (a) shows an *AE* curve for an economy with only consumption and investment expenditures. In Panel (b), the *AE* curve includes all four components of aggregate expenditures.

There are two major differences between the aggregate expenditures curves shown in the two panels. Notice first that the intercept of the *AE* curve in Panel (b) is higher than that of the *AE* curve in Panel (a). The reason is that, in addition to the autonomous part of consumption and planned investment, there are two other components of aggregate expenditures—government purchases and net exports—that we have also assumed are autonomous. Thus, the intercept of the aggregate expenditures curve in Panel (b) is the sum of the four autonomous aggregate expenditures components: consumption (C_a), planned investment (I_P), government purchases (G), and net exports (X_n). In Panel (a), the intercept includes only the first two components.

Second, the slope of the aggregate expenditures curve is flatter for the more realistic economy in Panel (b) than it is for the simplified economy in Panel (a). This can be seen by comparing the slope of the aggregate expenditures curve between points A and B in Panel (a) to the slope of the aggregate expenditures curve between points A′ and B′ in Panel (b). Between both sets of points, real GDP changes by the same amount, $1,000 billion. In Panel (a), consumption rises by $800 billion, whereas in Panel (b) consumption rises by only $600 billion. This difference occurs because, in the more realistic view of the economy, households have only a fraction of real GDP available as disposable personal income. Thus, for a given change in real GDP, consumption rises by a smaller amount.

FIGURE 14.13 The Aggregate Expenditures Function: Comparison of a Simplified Economy and a More Realistic Economy

Panel (a) shows an aggregate expenditures curve for a simplified view of the economy; Panel (b) shows an aggregate expenditures curve for a more realistic model. The *AE* curve in Panel (b) has a higher intercept than the *AE* curve in Panel (a) because of the additional components of autonomous aggregate expenditures in a more realistic view of the economy. The slope of the *AE* curve in Panel (b) is flatter than the slope of the *AE* curve in Panel (a). In a simplified economy, the slope of the *AE* curve is the marginal propensity to consume (*MPC*). In a more realistic view of the economy, it is less than the *MPC* because of the difference between real GDP and disposable personal income.

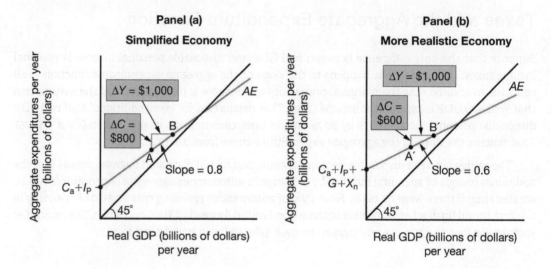

Let's see what happens to equilibrium real GDP in each case if there is a shift in autonomous aggregate expenditures, such as an increase in planned investment, as shown in Figure 14.14. In both panels, the initial level of equilibrium real GDP is the same, Y_1. Equilibrium real GDP occurs where the given aggregate expenditures curve intersects the 45-degree line. The aggregate expenditures curve shifts up by the same amount—ΔA is the same in both panels. The new level of equilibrium real GDP occurs where the new *AE* curve intersects the 45-degree line. In Panel (a), we see that the new level of equilibrium real GDP rises to Y_2, but in Panel (b) it rises only to Y_3. Since the same change in autonomous aggregate expenditures led to a greater increase in equilibrium real GDP in Panel (a) than in Panel (b), the multiplier for the more realistic model of the economy must be smaller. The multiplier is smaller, of course, because the slope of the aggregate expenditures curve is flatter.

FIGURE 14.14 A Change in Autonomous Aggregate Expenditures: Comparison of a Simplified Economy and a More Realistic Economy

In Panels (a) and (b), equilibrium real GDP is initially Y_1. Then autonomous aggregate expenditures rise by the same amount, ΔI_P. In Panel (a), the upward shift in the AE curve leads to a new level of equilibrium real GDP of Y_2; in Panel (b) equilibrium real GDP rises to Y_3. Because equilibrium real GDP rises by more in Panel (a) than in Panel (b), the multiplier in the simplified economy is greater than in the more realistic one.

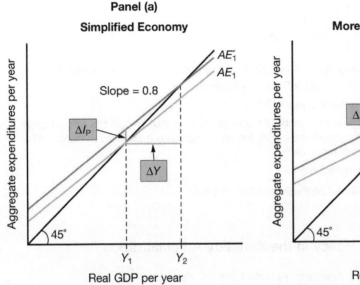
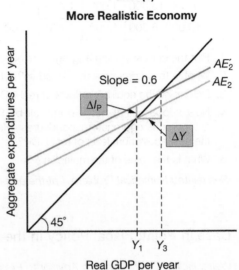

Key Takeaways

- The aggregate expenditures model relates aggregate expenditures to real GDP. Equilibrium in the model occurs where aggregate expenditures equal real GDP and is found graphically at the intersection of the aggregate expenditures curve and the 45-degree line.

- Economists distinguish between autonomous and induced aggregate expenditures. The former do not vary with GDP; the latter do.

- Equilibrium in the aggregate expenditures model implies that unintended investment equals zero.

- A change in autonomous aggregate expenditures leads to a change in equilibrium real GDP, which is a multiple of the change in autonomous aggregate expenditures.

- The size of the multiplier depends on the slope of the aggregate expenditures curve. In general, the steeper the aggregate expenditures curve, the greater the multiplier. The flatter the aggregate expenditures curve, the smaller the multiplier.

- Income taxes tend to flatten the aggregate expenditures curve.

Try It!

Suppose you are given the following data for an economy. All data are in billions of dollars. Y is actual real GDP, and C, I_P, G, and X_n are the consumption, planned investment, government purchases, and net exports components of aggregate expenditures, respectively.

Y	C	I_p	G	X_n
$0	$800	$1,000	$1,400	–$200
2,500	2,300	1,000	1,400	–200
5,000	3,800	1,000	1,400	–200
7,500	5,300	1,000	1,400	–200
10,000	6,800	1,000	1,400	–200

1. Plot the corresponding aggregate expenditures curve and draw in the 45-degree line.
2. What is the intercept of the *AE* curve? What is its slope?
3. Determine the equilibrium level of real GDP.
4. Now suppose that net exports fall by $1,000 billion and that this is the only change in autonomous aggregate expenditures. Plot the new aggregate expenditures curve. What is the new equilibrium level of real GDP?
5. What is the value of the multiplier?

See related Numerical Problem 4 at the end of this chapter.

Case in Point: Fiscal Policy in the Kennedy Administration

Walter Heller, Chief Economic Advisor to President John F. Kennedy

Source: Robert Knudsen. White House Photographs."Walter Heller 1962." Derived from image KN-C23016 at John F. Kennedy Presidential Library and Museum, Boston. Reproduced via Wikimedia: https://commons.wikimedia.org/wiki/File:Walter_Heller_1962. jpg.

It was the first time expansionary fiscal policy had ever been proposed. The economy had slipped into a recession in 1960. Presidential candidate John Kennedy received proposals from several economists that year for a tax cut aimed at stimulating the economy. As a candidate, he was unconvinced. But, as president he proposed the tax cut in 1962. His chief economic adviser, Walter Heller, defended the tax cut idea before Congress and introduced what was politically a novel concept: the multiplier.

In testimony to the Senate Subcommittee on Employment and Manpower, Mr. Heller predicted that a $10 billion cut in personal income taxes would boost consumption "by over $9 billion."

To assess the ultimate impact of the tax cut, Mr. Heller applied the aggregate expenditures model. He rounded the increased consumption off to $9 billion and explained,

This is far from the end of the matter. The higher production of consumer goods to meet this extra spending would mean extra employment, higher payrolls, higher profits, and higher farm and professional and service incomes. This added purchasing power would generate still further increases in spending and incomes. . . . The initial rise of $9 billion, plus this extra consumption spending and extra output of consumer goods, would add over $18 billion to our annual GDP.[7]

In other words, $9 billion of initial spending ultimately creates $18 billion of GDP: Heller was assuming a multiplier of 2!

Heller also predicted that proposed cuts in corporate income tax rates would increase autonomous investment by about $6 billion. The total change in autonomous aggregate expenditures would thus be $15 billion: $9 billion in consumption and $6 billion in investment. Using his multiplier of 2, Heller predicted that the total increase in equilibrium GDP would be $30 billion, the amount the Council of Economic Advisers had estimated would be necessary to reach full employment.

In the end, the tax cut was not passed until 1964, after President Kennedy's assassination in 1963. While the Council of Economic Advisers ultimately concluded that the tax cut had worked as advertised, it came long after the economy had recovered and tended to push the economy into an inflationary gap. As we will see in later chapters, the tax cut helped push the economy into a period of rising inflation.

See related Concept Problem 12 at the end of this chapter.

Source: Based on Economic Report of the President 1964 (Washington, DC: U.S. Government Printing Office, 1964), 172–73.

Answers to Try It! Problems

1. The aggregate expenditures curve is plotted in the accompanying chart as AE_1.

2. The intercept of the AE_1 curve is $3,000. It is the amount of aggregate expenditures ($C + I_P + G + X_n$) when real GDP is zero. The slope of the AE_1 curve is 0.6. It can be found by determining the amount of aggregate expenditures for any two levels of real GDP and then by dividing the change in aggregate expenditures by the change in real GDP over the interval. For example, between real GDP of $2,500 and $5,000, aggregate expenditures go from $4,500 to $6,000. Thus,

$$\frac{\Delta AE_1}{\Delta Y} = \frac{\$6,000 - \$4,500}{\$5,000 - \$2,500} = \frac{\$1,500}{\$2,500} = 0.6$$

3. The equilibrium level of real GDP is $7,500. It can be found by determining the intersection of AE_1 and the 45-degree line. At $Y = \$7,500$, $AE_1 = \$5,300 + 1,000 + 1,400 - 200 = \$7,500$.

4. A reduction of net exports of $1,000 shifts the aggregate expenditures curve down by $1,000 to AE_2. The equilibrium real GDP falls from $7,500 to $5,000. The new aggregate expenditures curve, AE_2, intersects the 45-degree line at real GDP of $5,000.

5. The multiplier is 2.5 [= (−$2,500)/(−$1,000)].

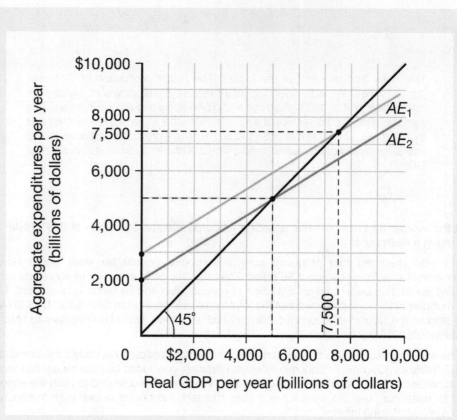

14.4 Aggregate Expenditures and Aggregate Demand

Learning Objectives

1. Explain and illustrate how a change in the price level affects the aggregate expenditures curve.
2. Explain and illustrate how to derive an aggregate demand curve from the aggregate expenditures curve for different price levels.
3. Explain and illustrate how an increase or decrease in autonomous aggregate expenditures affects the aggregate demand curve.

Until this point, we've been holding the price level in the economy constant. In this section, we'll allow it to change, and see how those changes affect the equilibrium level of real GDP. By matching up various price levels with their associated level of output, we'll end up with the two components of the aggregate demand curve. Our goal in this section, then, is to use the aggregate expenditures model to derive aggregate demand.

Aggregate Expenditures Curves and Price Levels

An aggregate expenditures curve assumes a fixed price level. When the price level changes, the levels of consumption, investment, and net exports change in response. That shifts the position of the aggregate expenditures curve and moves the economy to a new equilibrium.

Consumption. How exactly does a change in the price level alter consumption, investment, and net exports? Let's dig into each, in turn, beginning with consumption. You may remember that one of the factors besides disposable income that impacts individuals' willingness to spend is their wealth. A change in the price level changes people's real wealth: Increases in the price level tend to reduce wealth; decreases increase wealth. Suppose, for example, that your wealth includes $10,000 cash. An increase in the price level would reduce the purchasing power of that money, reducing your real wealth. In response, you're likely to be more careful about what you spend in the marketplace. Similarly, a *reduction* in the price level would increase the real value of your money holdings. With that added financial security, you (and others) might feel compelled to go on that dream vacation you've always wanted, or buy a new car. When you do, consumption increases. The tendency for price level changes to change real wealth and consumption is called the **wealth effect**.

Investment. Because changes in the price level affect the real quantity of money circulating in the economy, we can expect changes in the price level to change the interest rate. A decrease in the price level will increase the real quantity of money in circulation and push down interest rates. Lower interest rates, in turn, cause firms to increase investment spending. (See the chapter on monetary policy, or the next chapter on investment for more detail.) Similarly, a *higher* price level reduces the real quantity of money in circulation, raises interest rates, and reduces investment. This is called the **interest rate effect**.

Net Exports. Finally, a change in the domestic price level will affect exports and imports. A higher domestic price level makes foreign-produced goods look more attractive to home country consumers, so imports tend to increase. At the same time, higher domestic prices make home-produced goods look less attractive to foreigners, so exports decrease.[8] Because a country's net exports are the sum of its exports (which are falling here) minus the sum of its imports (which are rising), net exports decrease as the price level increases. The impact of changing price levels on net exports is called the **international trade effect**.

Now we know that an increase in the price level has three big effects:

- A higher price level causes real consumption spending to decrease.
- A higher price level causes real investment spending to decrease.
- A higher price level causes net exports to decrease.

Let's incorporate the price level into our aggregate expenditures model. Panel (a) of Figure 14.15 shows three possible aggregate expenditures curves for three different price levels.

- The aggregate expenditures curve labeled $AE_{P=50}$ is the aggregate expenditures curve for an economy with a price level of 50. At that price level, equilibrium real GDP is $10,000 billion (point C).
- The aggregate expenditures curve labeled $AE_{P=100}$ is the aggregate expenditures curve for an economy with a price level of 100. At that price level, equilibrium real GDP is $6,000 billion (point B).
- The aggregate expenditures curve labeled $AE_{P=150}$ is the aggregate expenditures curve for an economy with a price level of 150. At that price level, equilibrium real GDP is $2,000 billion (point A).

Generally speaking, there is a different level of equilibrium real GDP for each price level; the higher the price level, the lower the equilibrium value of real GDP.

"Honey . . . my 401(k) just hit seven figures. You know what that means? It's time to go test-drive convertibles!"

Source: fizkes/Shutterstock.com

wealth effect

The tendency for price level changes to change real wealth and consumption.

interest rate effect

The tendency for a higher price level to reduce the real quantity of money, raise interest rates, and reduce investment.

international trade effect

The tendency for a change in the price level to affect net exports.

FIGURE 14.15 From Aggregate Expenditures to Aggregate Demand

Because there is a different aggregate expenditures curve for each price level, there is a different equilibrium real GDP for each price level. Panel (a) shows aggregate expenditures curves for three different price levels. Panel (b) shows the aggregate demand curve derived from the aggregate expenditures model. The aggregate expenditures curve for a price level of 100, for example, intersects the 45-degree line in Panel (a) at point B, producing an equilibrium real GDP of $6,000 billion. Point B′ on the aggregate demand curve in Panel (b) plots a point at that price level and level of real GDP. Adding additional points to the lower panel to correspond to points A and C in the AE model gives us the aggregate demand curve for the economy.

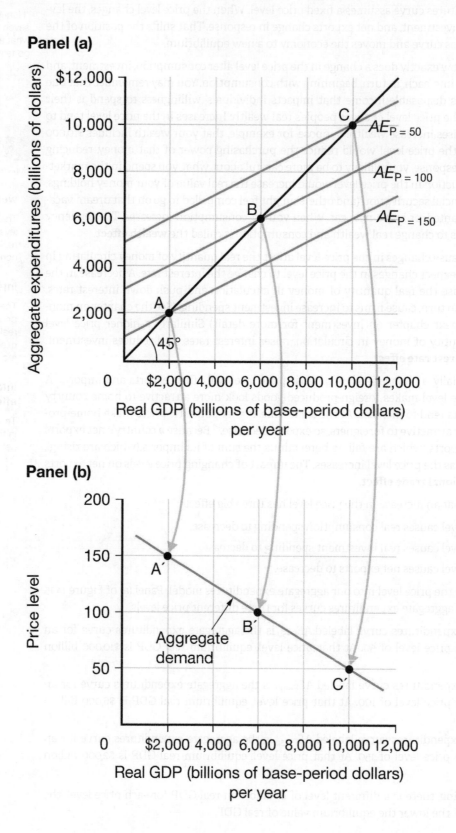

Panel (b) of Figure 14.15 shows how the aggregate demand curve is derived from the aggregate expenditures curves for different price levels. The equilibrium real GDP associated with each price level in the *AE* model in Panel (a) is plotted as a single point on the aggregate demand curve in Panel (b). At a price level of 100, for example, the equilibrium level of real GDP in the aggregate expenditures model in Panel (a) is $6,000 billion at point B. Point B' in the lower panel plots the price/quantity pair from the top panel: At a price level of 100, real GDP demanded is $6,000 billion. Similarly, at a price level of 50 the equilibrium GDP demanded is $10,000 billion (point C'), and at a price level of 150 the equilibrium real GDP demanded is $2,000 billion (point A'). Connecting the dots gives us the aggregate demand curve showing real GDP demanded at each price level.

The Multiplier and Changes in Aggregate Demand

In the aggregate expenditures model, a change in autonomous aggregate expenditures changes equilibrium real GDP by the multiplier times the change in autonomous aggregate expenditures. That model, however, assumes a constant price level. How can we incorporate the multiplier into our model of aggregate demand and aggregate supply?

Consider the aggregate expenditures curves given in Panel (a) of Figure 14.16, each of which corresponds to a particular price level. Suppose net exports rise by $1,000 billion. Such a change increases aggregate expenditures at each price level by $1,000 billion (the *AE* curve shifts vertically upward by $1,000).

A $1,000 billion increase in net exports shifts each of the aggregate expenditures curves up by $1,000 billion, to $AE'_{P=100}$ and $AE'_{P=150}$. That changes the equilibrium real GDP associated with each price level. For example, at a price level of 100, equilibrium real GDP increases from $6,000 billion to $8,000 billion. (The multiplier in this model is 2.0, right?)

FIGURE 14.16 Changes in Aggregate Demand
The aggregate expenditures curves for price levels of 100 and 150 are the same as in Figure 14.15, as is the aggregate demand curve. Now suppose a $1,000 billion increase in net exports shifts each of the aggregate expenditures curves up; $AE_{P=100}$, for example, rises to $AE'_{P=100}$. The aggregate demand curve thus shifts to the right by $2,000 billion, the change in aggregate expenditures times the multiplier, assumed to be 2 in this example.

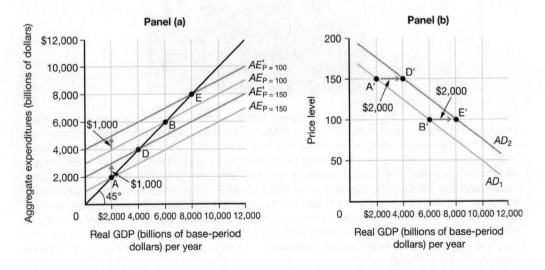

So, at a price level of 100, aggregate demand increases by $2,000 billion. That is shown as the rightward shift in aggregate demand from AD_1 to AD_2 in Panel (b). In other words, aggregate demand shifts rightward by the amount of the shift times the multiplier! Should the initial change in autonomous spending have been negative, aggregate demand would have decreased (shifted left) by the amount of the change times the multiplier.

Key Takeaways

- There will be a different aggregate expenditures curve for each price level.
- Aggregate expenditures will vary with the price level because of the wealth effect, the interest rate effect, and the international trade effect. The higher the price level, the lower the aggregate expenditures curve and the lower the equilibrium level of real GDP. The lower the price level, the higher the aggregate expenditures curve and the higher the equilibrium level of real GDP.
- A change in autonomous aggregate expenditures shifts the aggregate expenditures curve for each price level by the change in autonomous aggregate expenditures times the multiplier.

Try It!

Sketch three aggregate expenditures curves for price levels of P_1, P_2, and P_3, where P_1 is the lowest price level and P_3 the highest (you do not have numbers for this exercise; simply sketch curves of the appropriate shape). Label the equilibrium levels of real GDP Y_1, Y_2, and Y_3. Now draw the aggregate demand curve implied by your analysis, labeling points that correspond to P_1, P_2, and P_3 and Y_1, Y_2, and Y_3. You can use Figure 14.15 as a model for your work.

See related Numerical Problem 10 at the end of this chapter.

Case in Point: Not All Fiscal Policy Is Created Equal

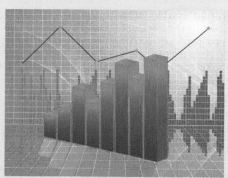

Source: © Shutterstock, Inc.

Using a large-scale model of the U.S. economy to simulate the effects of government policies, Princeton University professor Alan Blinder and Moody Analytics chief economist Mark Zandi concluded that the expansionary fiscal, monetary, and other policies (such as the Troubled Asset Relief Program, or TARP) aimed at relieving the financial crisis worked together from 2008 onward to effectively combat the Great Recession and probably kept it from turning into the Great Depression 2.0. Specifically, they estimated that U.S. GDP would have fallen about 12% peak-to-trough and that the unemployment rate would have hit 16.5% without these policies, instead of GDP declining about 4% and the unemployment rate reaching about 10%. While they attribute the bulk of the improvement to monetary and other financial policies, they found that fiscal policies also played a substantial role. For example, they concluded that fiscal stimulus added more than 3% to real GDP in 2010.

How much did the different components of the fiscal policies contribute? The following table provides estimates for the multiplied effects of various stimulus measures that were considered. In general, they estimate a stronger "bang for the buck," or multiplier, from spending increases than from tax cuts.

Tax Cuts	Bang for the Buck
Nonrefundable lump-sum tax rebate	1.01
Refundable lump-sum tax rebate	1.22
Temporary tax cuts	
Payroll tax holiday	1.24
Across-the-board tax cut	1.02
Accelerated depreciation	0.25
Permanent tax cuts	
Extend alternative minimum tax patch	0.51
Make Bush income tax cuts permanent	0.32
Make dividend and capital gains tax cuts permanent	0.32
Spending Increases	
Extending UI benefits	1.61
Temporary increase in food stamps	1.74
General aid to state governments	1.41
Increased infrastructure spending	1.57

While Blinder and Zandi acknowledge that no one can know for sure what would have happened without the policy responses and that not all aspects of the programs were perfectly designed or implemented, they feel strongly that the aggressive policies were, overall, appropriate and worth taking.

See related Concept Problem 11 at the end of this chapter.

Source: Based on Alan S. Blinder and Mark Zandi, "How the Great Recession Was Brought to an End," Moody's Economy.com, July 27, 2010.

Answer to Try It! Problem

The lowest price level, P_1, corresponds to the highest AE curve, $AE_{P = P_1}$, as shown. This suggests a downward-sloping aggregate demand curve. Points A, B, and C on the AE curve correspond to points A′, B′, and C′ on the AD curve, respectively.

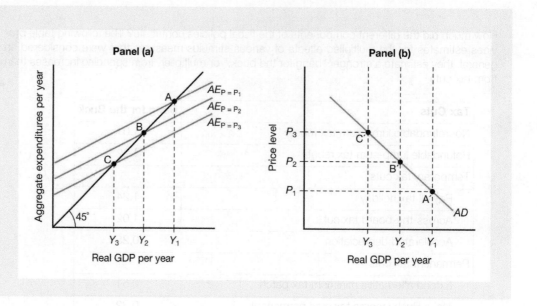

Panel (a)

Panel (b)

14.5 Review and Practice

Summary

This chapter presented the aggregate expenditures model. Aggregate expenditures are the sum of planned levels of consumption, investment, government purchases, and net exports at a given price level. The aggregate expenditures model relates aggregate expenditures to the level of real GDP.

We began by observing the close relationship between consumption and disposable personal income. A consumption function shows this relationship. The saving function can be derived from the consumption function.

The time period over which income is considered to be a determinant of consumption is important. The current income hypothesis holds that consumption in one period is a function of income in that same period. The permanent income hypothesis holds that consumption in a period is a function of permanent income. An important implication of the permanent income hypothesis is that the marginal propensity to consume will be smaller for temporary than for permanent changes in disposable personal income.

Changes in real wealth and consumer expectations can affect the consumption function. Such changes shift the curve relating consumption to disposable personal income, the graphical representation of the consumption function; changes in disposable personal income do not shift the curve but cause movements along it.

An aggregate expenditures curve shows total planned expenditures at each level of real GDP. This curve is used in the aggregate expenditures model to determine the equilibrium real GDP (at a given price level). A change in autonomous aggregate expenditures produces a multiplier effect that leads to a larger change in equilibrium real GDP. In a simplified economy, with only consumption and investment expenditures, in which the slope of the aggregate expenditures curve is the marginal propensity to consume (MPC), the multiplier is equal to $1/(1 - MPC)$. Because the sum of the marginal propensity to consume and the marginal propensity to save (MPS) is 1, the multiplier in this simplified model is also equal to $1/MPS$.

Finally, we derived the aggregate demand curve from the aggregate expenditures model. Each point on the aggregate demand curve corresponds to the equilibrium level of real GDP as derived in the aggregate expenditures model for each price level. The downward slope of the aggregate demand curve (and the shifting of the aggregate expenditures curve at each price level) reflects the wealth effect, the interest rate effect, and the international trade effect. A change in autonomous aggregate expenditures shifts the aggregate demand curve by an amount equal to the change in autonomous aggregate expenditures times the multiplier.

In a more realistic aggregate expenditures model that includes all four components of aggregate expenditures (consumption, investment, government purchases, and net exports), the slope of the aggregate expenditures curve shows the additional aggregate expenditures induced by increases in real GDP, and the size of the multiplier depends on the slope of the aggregate expenditures curve. The steeper the aggregate expenditures curve, the larger the multiplier; the flatter the aggregate expenditures curve, the smaller the multiplier.

Concept Problems

1. Explain the difference between autonomous and induced expenditures. Give examples of each.

2. The consumption function we studied in the chapter predicted that consumption would sometimes exceed disposable personal income. How could this be?

3. (Related to "Case in Point: Permanent Income and the Trump Tax Shuffle" in Section 26.2.) You're an analyst with the Treasury Department, and have been asked to evaluate two proposals to stimulate a flagging economy: A temporary tax rebate (in the form of a check mailed to taxpayers) or a lasting reduction in income tax rates that would go into effect next year. Which policy is likely to be most effective in reducing the recessionary gap if consumers make spending decisions based on their permanent income?

4. (Related to "Try It!" in Section 26.2.)The introduction to this chapter described the behavior of consumer spending at the beginning of the coronavirus crisis of 2020. Using the terms of analysis in this chapter, explain the factors that led to decreased consumption, and the impact of reduced consumption on GDP.

5. Explain the role played by the 45-degree line in the aggregate expenditures model.

6. Your college or university, if it does what many others do, occasionally releases a news story claiming that its impact on the total employment in the local economy is understated by its own employment statistics. If the institution keeps accurate statistics, is that possible?

7. Suppose the level of investment in a certain economy changes when the level of real GDP changes; an increase in real GDP induces an increase in investment, while a reduction in real GDP causes investment to fall. How do you think such behavior would affect the slope of the aggregate expenditures curve? The multiplier?

8. Give an intuitive explanation for how the multiplier works on a reduction in autonomous aggregate expenditures. Why does equilibrium real GDP fall by more than the change in autonomous aggregate expenditures?

9. Explain why the marginal propensity to consume out of a temporary tax rebate would be lower than that for a permanent rebate.

10. You are a member of the Council of Economic Advisers. The coronavirus has just hit, and you are trying to persuade the members of the House Appropriations Committee to purchase $100 billion worth of new materials, in part to stimulate the economy. Explain to the members why the purchase is necessary and how the multiplier process will work.

11. (Related to "Case in Point: Not All Fiscal Policy Is Created Equal" in Section 26.4.) The coronavirus crisis has just hit, and real GDP is tumbling. You, as a member of the Council of Economic Advisers, are asked to endorse either a $200 billion spending increase or a $200 billion tax cut. If the goal is to stimulate the economy, which do you recommend and why?

12. (Related to "Case in Point: Fiscal Policy in the Kennedy Administration" in Section 26.3.) The Kennedy tax cuts were designed to stimulate an economy in recession, yet ended up over-stimulating an economy that had already begun self-correcting. Review the lags of policy in Chapter 12 and Chapter 13, then determine which lags of policy played a role in this mis-timed policy. Which lag of policy is likely related to the multiplier effect that Walter Heller referred to in the case?

Numerical Problems

1. Suppose the following information describes a simple economy. Figures are in billions of dollars.

Disposable Personal Income (Billions of Dollars)	Consumption (Billions of Dollars)
0	100
100	120
200	140
300	160

   a. What is the marginal propensity to consume?
   b. What is the marginal propensity to save?
   c. Write an equation that describes consumption.
   d. Write an equation that describes saving.

2. The graph below shows a consumption function.

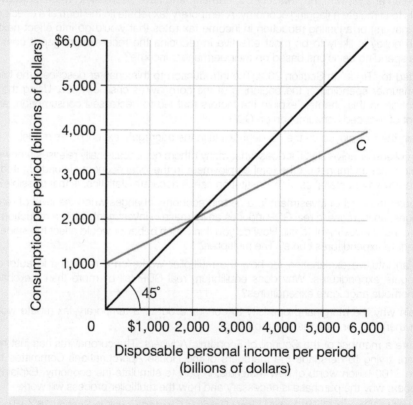

   a. When disposable personal income is equal to zero, how much is consumption?
   b. When disposable personal income is equal to $4,000 billion, how much is consumption?
   c. At what level of personal disposable income are consumption and disposable personal income equal?
   d. How much is personal saving when consumption is $2,500 billion?
   e. How much is personal saving when consumption is $5,000 billion?
   f. What is the marginal propensity to consume?
   g. What is the marginal propensity to save?
   h. Draw the saving function implied by the consumption function above.

3. For the purpose of this exercise, assume that the consumption function is given by $C = \$500$ billion $+ 0.8Y_d$. Construct a consumption and saving table showing how income is divided between consumption and personal saving when disposable personal income (in billions) is $0, $500, $1,000, $1,500, $2,000, $2,500, $3,000, and $3,500.

   a. Graph your results, placing disposable personal income on the horizontal axis and consumption on the vertical axis.

   b. What is the value of the marginal propensity to consume?

   c. What is the value of the marginal propensity to save?

4. (Related to "Try It!" in Section 26.3.) The graph below characterizes a simple economy with only two components of aggregate expenditures: consumption and investment.

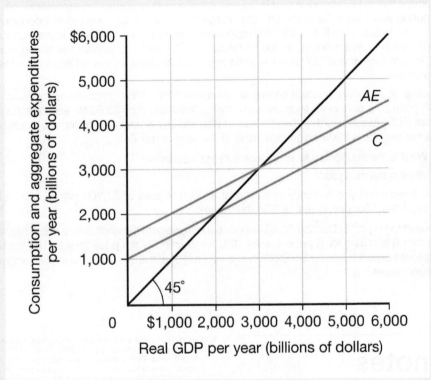

   a. How much is planned investment? How do you know?

   b. Is planned investment autonomous or induced? How do you know?

   c. How much is autonomous aggregate expenditures?

   d. What is the value of equilibrium real GDP?

   e. If real GDP were $2,000 billion, how much would unplanned investment be? How would you expect firms to respond?

   f. If real GDP were $4,000 billion, how much would unplanned investment be? How would you expect firms to respond?

   g. Write an equation for aggregate expenditures based on the graph above.

   h. What is the value of the multiplier in this example?

5. Explain and illustrate graphically how each of the following events affects aggregate expenditures and equilibrium real GDP. In each case, state the nature of the change in aggregate expenditures, and state the relationship between the change in AE and the change in equilibrium real GDP.

   a. Investment falls.

   b. Government purchases go up.

   c. The government sends $1,000 to every person in the United States.

   d. An exchange rate change causes imports to decrease by $500 million and exports to increase by $200 million.

6. Mary Smith, whose marginal propensity to consume is 0.75, is faced with an unexpected increase in taxes of $1,000. Will she cut back her consumption expenditures by the full $1,000? How will she pay for the higher tax? Explain.

7. The equations below give consumption functions for economies in which planned investment is autonomous and is the only other component of GDP. Compute the marginal propensity to consume and the multiplier for each economy.

   a. $C = \$650 + 0.33Y$

   b. $C = \$180 + 0.9Y$

   c. $C = \$1,500$

   d. $C = \$700 + 0.8Y$

8. Suppose that in Economies A and B the only components of aggregate expenditure are consumption and planned investment. The marginal propensity to consume in Economy A is 0.9, while in Economy B it is 0.7. Both economies experience an increase in planned investment, which is assumed to be autonomous, of $100 billion. Compare the changes in the equilibrium level of real GDP and the shifts in aggregate demand this will produce in the two economies.

9. Assume an economy in which people would spend $200 billion on consumption even if real GDP were zero and, in addition, increase their consumption by $0.50 for each additional $1 of real GDP. Assume further that the sum of planned investment plus government purchases plus net exports is $200 billion regardless of the level of real GDP.

   a. What is the equilibrium level of income in this economy?

   b. What is the multiplier?

   c. If the economy is currently operating at an output level of $1,200 billion, what do you predict will happen to real GDP in the future?

10. (Related to "Try It!" in Section 26.4.) Suppose the aggregate expenditures curve in Numerical Problem 9 is drawn for a price level of 120. A reduction in the price level to 100 increases aggregate expenditures by $400 billion at each level of real GDP. Draw the implied aggregate demand curve.

Endnotes

1. J. R. McCulloch, *A Discourse on the Rise, Progress, Peculiar Objects, and Importance, of Political Economy: Containing the Outline of a Course of Lectures on the Principles and Doctrines of That Science* (Edinburgh: Archibald Constable, 1824), 103.

2. If you really want to try this, we recommend printing the graph out on paper, first . . . or having a nice bottle of spray cleaner on hand.

3. Jim Tankersley, "Trump's Payroll Tax 'Cut' Fizzles," *The New York Times*, September 11, 2020.

4. Michelle Singletary, "The president's payroll tax cut is really a loan that workers have to pay back. Let's call it what it is," Washington Post, September 8, 2020.

5. You may have a hard time understanding how adding thousands of rounds of consumption spending to the economy fails to give GDP more than a $1,500 boost. That happens because each step in the chain of GDP increases is smaller than the one before. Here's an analogue: Stand 6 feet from a wall. Now, take a step and cover half the distance to the wall. Now do it again, and again, and again. Because each step is smaller than the one before, you will never reach the wall . . . *even if you take an infinite number of steps!* The same things happens here with consumption—even if there are an infinite number of rounds of consumption causing consumption causing consumption, GDP will never rise more than $1,500. *Mind = Blown!*

6. An even more realistic view of the economy might assume that imports are induced, since as a country's real GDP rises it will buy more goods and services, some of which will be imports. In that case, the slope of the aggregate expenditures curve would change.

7. United States. President and Council of Economic Advisers (U.S.). "1964." Economic Report of the President (1964). United States Government Printing Office, Washington: 1964, p.172. Retrieved from: https://fraser.stlouisfed.org/title/45/item/8135?start_page=2.

8. The relative attractiveness of imports and exports discussed here depends critically on how the exchange rate changes in response to changing prices. That topic is discussed further in this book's chapter on international finance, but a full understanding likely requires *gasp* an *entire course* in international macroeconomics. Wouldn't that be fun?

CHAPTER 15
Investment and Economic Activity

15.1 Start Up: Jittery Firms Slash Investment as Great Recession Unfolds

The Great Recession of 2007–2009 was a doozy—the biggest downturn since the Great Depression of the 1930s, and a downturn with such prolonged staying power that it made the COVID-19 recession look like a blip on the radar (albeit, a *big* blip!). As the Great Recession began, the first component of GDP to take a turn for the worse was investment. The biggest declines were seen in investment in housing (or, as economists call them, residential structures). Housing investment started falling as housing prices began trending downward in 2006; by 2008, the housing sector had shrunk by more than 40%.

It wasn't just the housing part of investment that faltered. In 2008, the part of investment that reflects business spending on equipment ranging from computers to machines to trucks also reversed course. In late 2008, firms around the world seemed to be trying to outdo each other in announcing cutbacks. The only major part of investment left standing was business spending on commercial structures such as factories, hospitals, and office buildings.

During the Great Recession, the housing sector shrank like a wool sweater in a hot dryer.

Source: Irk Boockhoff/Shutterstock.com

The big three U.S. automakers were in trouble. Two of them—General Motors and Chrysler—ended up taking government bailouts, with only Ford refusing. And it wasn't just U.S. automakers retrenching: Toyota announced an indefinite delay in building a Prius plant in Mississippi.[1] Meanwhile, Walgreen's, which had been increasing drugstore locations by about 8% a year, said it would expand by only about 4% in 2009 and by less than 3% in 2010.[2] Package carrier FedEx announced a 20% decline in capital spending, on top of suspending pension contributions and cutting salaries.[3] Even hospitals began scaling back on construction.[4]

The Great Recession, which started in the United States, became global. Consumer electronics maker Sony announced it was not only not moving forward with constructing an LCD television plant in Slovakia, but also shuttering existing plants.[5] Oil prices, which had plummeted, touched off a wave of canceled projects with oil companies.[6]

Choices about how much to invest are always made in circumstances of uncertainty; firms cannot know what the market has in store. That makes investment a calculated gamble; firms that make the gamble hope for a profitable payoff. When they find themselves concerned that their investment might not pay off, they're quick to slash investment spending.

Those decisions have big implications for the macroeconomy. In the short run, private investment plays an important role in determining aggregate demand. But as a component of GDP, investment spending is truly special, because only investment causes a nation's future production possibilities (and therefore, its potential output) to increase. In other words, investment has important implications for short-run aggregate demand, but it also has important implications for *long-run* aggregate supply.

In this chapter, we'll examine factors that determine investment by firms and investment's relationship to output in the short run and in the long run. Our focus will be on investment by private firms. Of course, those firms aren't the only source of investment: Government agencies engage in investment as well—building things that make the economy more productive, like roads and bridges, schools, and GPS networks. For now, we'll focus on investment carried out in the private sector. The impact of the public sector on macroeconomic performance is covered in our chapter on fiscal policy.

Do all recessions begin and end with shocks to investment? The Great Recession surely did. And yet, it may well be investment spending that kept the coronavirus crisis of 2020 from turning a health crisis into an enduring economic crisis. We'll close our chapter with a look at why.

Dream big and replace this factory? Not in the middle of a recession, I won't!

Source: Zorro12/Shutterstock.com

15.2 The Role and Nature of Investment

Learning Objectives

1. Discuss the components of the investment spending category of GDP and distinguish between gross and net investment.
2. Discuss the relationship between consumption, saving, and investment, and explain the relationship using the production possibilities model.

How important is investment? Think about a job you might have worked at: Your productivity in that job was largely determined by the investment choices that had been made before you arrived. If you worked as a clerk in a store, the equipment used in collecting money from customers affected your productivity. It may have been a simple cash register, or it may have been a sophisticated computer terminal that scanned purchases and was linked to the store's computer, which computed the store's inventory and did an analysis of the store's sales every time you served a new customer. Or maybe you've worked for a lawn maintenance firm. There, the kind of equipment you had to work with made a huge difference in what you could accomplish: A riding mower with hydrostatic drive that cuts a 60" swath makes you far more productive than an 18" reel mower with no motor at all. Whatever the work you might have done, the kind and quality of capital you had to work with strongly influenced your productivity. That capital was available because investment choices had provided it.

Only twelve more acres, kid. I'll have lemonade waiting for you when you're finished.

Source: blaine linton/Shutterstock.com

Components of Investment

As we saw in the chapter on aggregate demand and aggregate supply, investment is a component of aggregate demand. Changes in investment shift the aggregate demand curve: An increase in investment shifts the aggregate demand curve to the right; a reduction shifts it to the left. That can cause both GDP and the price level to change in the short run. But, just as investment is one of several components of aggregate demand, investment itself has its *own* components. Let's take a look.

Investment goods add to the stock of private capital. Those additions are referred to as gross private domestic investment (GPDI). GPDI includes four categories:

1. Nonresidential Structures. This category of investment includes the construction of business structures such as private office buildings, warehouses, factories, private hospitals and universities, and other structures in which the production of goods and services takes place.

2. Nonresidential Equipment and Intellectual Property (IP). Producers' equipment includes computers and software, machinery, trucks, cars, and desks; that is, any business equipment that is expected to last more than a year. This category of investment also includes intellectual property development, including software development and R&D.

3. Residential Investment. This category includes all forms of residential construction, whether apartment houses or single-family homes, as well as residential equipment such as computers and software.

4. Change in Private Inventories. Private inventories are considered part of the nation's capital stock because, like equipment, those inventories will produce benefits (namely, sales revenue) in the future. The sum of all private inventories is included in capital; additions to private inventories in any given year, then, represent investment spending. When private inventories fall, that is recorded as negative investment, or *disinvestment*.

Figure 15.1 shows the components of gross private domestic investment from 2002 through 2020. Producers' equipment and intellectual property investment constitutes the largest component of GPDI in the United States. Residential investment was the second largest component of GPDI for most of the period shown, but it shrank considerably during the 2007–2009 recession and has only recently returned to a level nearing its pre–Great Recession high.

FIGURE 15.1 Components of Gross Private Domestic Investment, 2002–2020
This chart shows the levels of each of the four components of gross private domestic investment from 2002 through 2020. Nonresidential equipment and IP is the largest component of GPDI and has shown the most substantial growth over the period.

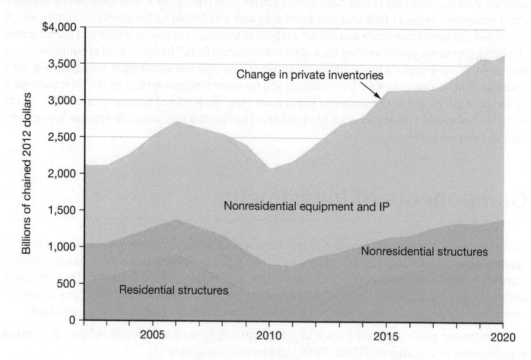

Source: Data from Bureau of Economic Analysis, accessed through Federal Reserve Economic Data (FRED) at https://fred.stlouisfed.org/series/PRFIC1, https://fred.stlouisfed.org/series/B009RX1Q020SBEA, https://fred.stlouisfed.org/series/Y033RX1Q020SBEA, https://fred.stlouisfed.org/series/Y001RX1Q020SBEA, https://fred.stlouisfed.org/series/Y033RX1Q020SBEA, and https://fred.stlouisfed.org/series/CBIC1.

Gross and Net Investment

Anyone who's ever owned an older car likely understands the nature of investment and depreciation: Keep pumping money in; stuff keeps wearing out.

Source: ronstik/Shutterstock.com

New additions to the capital stock are referred to as gross investment. But as capital is used, some of it wears out or becomes obsolete. In the language of economics and accounting, it *depreciates*.[7] So overall changes in the capital stock reflect both additions (investment, or *gross investment*) and subtractions (depreciation). If gross investment is greater than depreciation in any period, then *net investment*—the combined influence of new investment and depreciation—is positive and the capital stock increases. If gross investment is less than depreciation in any period, then net investment is negative and the capital stock declines.

In the official estimates of total output, gross investment (GPDI) minus depreciation equals net private domestic investment (NPDI). The value for NPDI in any period gives the amount by which the privately held stock of physical capital changed during that period.

Figure 15.2 shows the real (inflation-adjusted) values of GPDI, depreciation, and NPDI from 1970 to 2020. The bulk of new investment spending (GPDI) replaces capital that has been depreciated. Notice the sharp reductions in NPDI during the recessions of 1990–1991, 2001, and especially 2007–2009.

FIGURE 15.2 Gross Private Domestic Investment, Depreciation, and Net Private Domestic Investment, 1970–2020

In most years, gross investment (red line) exceeds depreciation (purple line), though the bulk of new investment is devoted to replacing capital that has depreciated. Net new additions to the capital stock (the difference between gross investment and depreciation), shown in green, are almost always positive.

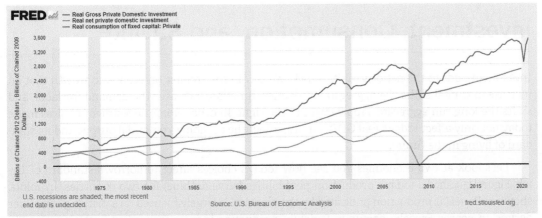

Source: Bureau of Economic Analysis, accessed through Federal Reserve Economic Data (FRED) at https://fred.stlouisfed.org/series/GPDIC1, https://fred.stlouisfed.org/series/A557RX1A020NBEA, and https://fred.stlouisfed.org/series/A024RX1Q020SBEA. FRED® Graphs ©Federal Reserve Bank of St. Louis. All rights reserved. All FRED® Graphs appear courtesy of Federal Reserve Bank of St. Louis. https://fred.stlouisfed.org/.

The Volatility of Investment

Investment, measured as GPDI, is among the most volatile components of GDP. In percentage terms, year-to-year changes in GPDI are far greater than the year-to-year changes in consumption or government purchases. (Net exports are also quite volatile, but they represent a much smaller share of GDP.) Figure 15.3 compares annual percentage changes in GPDI, personal consumption, and government purchases. Of course, a dollar change in investment will be a much larger change in percentage terms than a dollar change in consumption, which is the largest component of GDP. But compare investment and government purchases: Their shares of GDP are comparable, yet investment is clearly more volatile.

FIGURE 15.3 The Volatility of Investment, 1960–2020

Swings in investment spending (shown as year-over-year percentage changes, in green) are much larger than similarly measured percentage changes in consumption (in blue) or government purchases (in red).

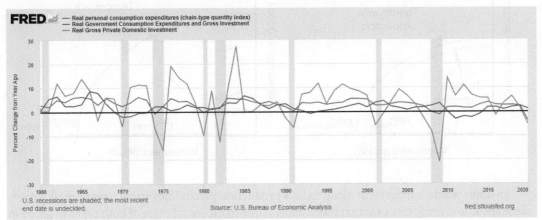

Source: Bureau of Economic Analysis, accessed through Federal Reserve Economic Data (FRED) at https://fred.stlouisfed.org/series/PCEC96, https://fred.stlouisfed.org/series/GCEC1, and https://fred.stlouisfed.org/series/GPDIC1. FRED® Graphs ©Federal Reserve Bank of St. Louis. All rights reserved. All FRED® Graphs appear courtesy of Federal Reserve Bank of St. Louis. https://fred.stlouisfed.org/.

Changes in investment, of course, cause changes in aggregate demand, changes made larger because of the multiplier. Investment's volatility, then, can cause relatively large changes in GDP in the short run, and downturns in investment can be large enough to trigger recessions.

Investment, Consumption, and Saving

Investment adds to the nation's capital stock. We saw in the chapter on economic growth that an increase in capital shifts the aggregate production function, increases the demand for labor, and shifts the long-run aggregate supply curve to the right. In other words, investment choices made today not only affect today's real GDP, but also affect the economy's potential output and its standard of living in the future.

Let's look at two economies and see how today's choices affect tomorrow's standard of living. Figure 15.4 shows today's production possibilities curve (in blue) for two countries. In Yoloia, shown in Panel (a), production (indicated by the blue dot) is largely focused on satisfying consumer desires. In nearby Frugalia, shown in Panel (b), production is more focused on investment goods, leaving Frugalians a slightly lower standard of living today.

But investment, remember, is the production *today* of goods that will be used to produce other goods *tomorrow*. With its relatively low investment, Yoloia's production possibilities don't grow much over time—tomorrow's PPC (shown in red) is close to today's PPC (in blue). On the other hand, in Frugalia, the shift in the PPC is dramatic. That large shift is the result of Frugalians' decision to expend their energy today producing investment goods that will produce still more goods in the future. And not just any goods! Because of Frugalians' small sacrifice today, they'll get to enjoy more consumption goods in the future than consumers in Yoloia.

FIGURE 15.4 The Choice between Consumption and Investment
In Yoloia, the economy produces lots of consumer goods and not many investment goods. Low investment leads to a relatively small outward shift in Yoloia's PPC, limiting tomorrow's production and consumption. Frugalia, however, produces lots of investment goods (and relatively fewer consumption goods) today, which leads to a large shift in the PPC over time. By sacrificing a little bit of consumption today, Frugalia gets to enjoy greatly expanded consumption in the future.

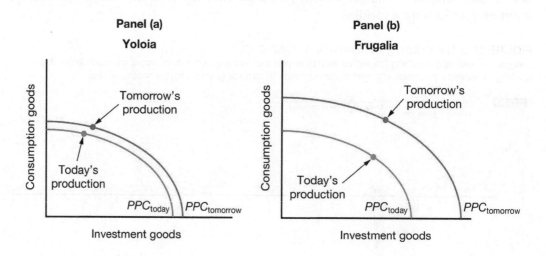

In other words, a movement along today's production possibilities curve toward more investment goods and fewer consumption goods allows the production of more of *both* types of goods in the future.

Key Takeaways

- Investment adds to the nation's capital stock.
- Gross private domestic investment includes the construction of nonresidential structures, the production of equipment and software, private residential construction, and changes in inventories.
- The bulk of gross private domestic investment goes to the replacement of depreciated capital.
- Investment is the most volatile component of GDP.
- Investment represents a choice to postpone consumption—it requires saving.

Try It!

Which of the following would be counted as gross private domestic investment?

1. Millie hires a contractor to build a new garage for her home.
2. Millie buys a new car for her teenage son.
3. Grandpa buys Tommy a savings bond.
4. General Motors builds a new automobile assembly plant.

See related Concept Problem 1 at the end of this chapter.

Pop! Goes the Econ: Investment in Training in *A Knight's Tale*
William Thatcher (Heath Ledger) convinces his friends that they should take their winnings and invest it in better training. What does this increased investment imply for current consumption? For future consumption?

View in the online reader

Case in Point: The Reduction of Private Capital in the Depression and in the Great Recession

Thanks, depreciation: Even though gross investment was positive during the Great Depression, equipment wore out faster than it was replaced. The U.S. capital stock shrunk as a result.

Source: Delmas Lehman/Shutterstock.com

Net private domestic investment (NPDI) has been negative during only three periods in the last hundred years. During one period, World War II, massive defense spending forced cutbacks in private-sector spending. (Recall that government investment is not counted as part of net private domestic investment in the official accounts; production of defense capital is not reflected in these figures.) NPDI was also negative during the Great Depression.

As shown in the graph below, aggregate demand plunged during the first four years of the Depression. As firms cut their output in response to reductions in demand, their need for capital fell as well. They reduced capital by holding gross private domestic investment (shown in green in the figure below) below depreciation beginning in 1931. That produced negative net private domestic investment (shown in orange). NPDI remained negative until 1936 and became negative again in 1938. In all, firms reduced the private capital stock by more than $529.5 billion (in 2009 dollars) during the period.

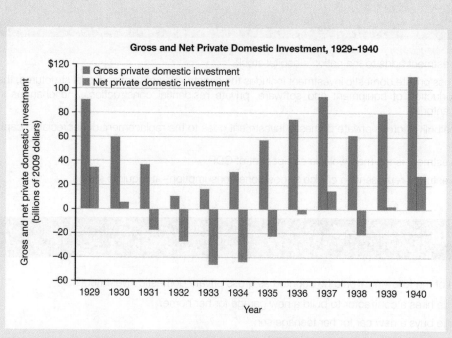

A third, brief, and very small encounter with negative net private domestic investment occurred during the Great Recession, as shown below. In 2009, as the downturn was ending, net investment fell by $47 billion—which sounds like a lot, but in the context of the largest economy in the world, amounts to almost nothing.

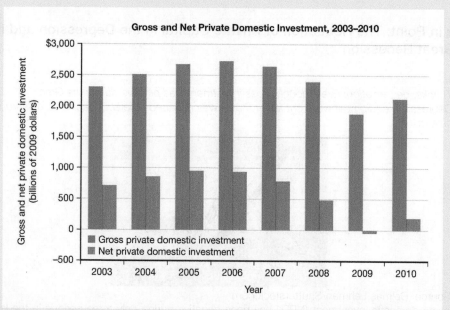

Sources: Based on data from U.S. Bureau of Economic Analysis, NIPA Table 5.2.6 (revised February 28, 2014).

There are many reasons why one downturn was called the Great *Depression* and the other was merely a Great *Recession*. Among those reasons was the behavior of investment spending. Investment spending during the Great Depression fell by much more than it did during the Great Recession, and the decline in the country's capital stock, with depreciation outpacing new additions, limited the economy's ability to produce its way back to prosperity. In contrast, the capital stock largely continued to grow during the Great Recession and subsequent recovery (the small decline in 2009 amounting to a minor exception), leaving the economy with higher potential productivity after it exited the recession than it had as it entered it. These two graphs, then, present just one contrast between the Great Depression and the Great Recession. The Great Recession was a genuinely bad downturn in so many dimensions, but in almost all of those dimensions, including the overall impact on the capital stock, the Great Depression was ever so much worse.

See related Concept Problem 7 at the end of this chapter.

Answers to Try It! Problems

1. A new garage would be part of residential construction and thus part of GPDI.

2. Consumer purchases of cars are part of the consumption component of the GDP accounts and thus not part of GPDI.

3. The purchase of a savings bond is an example of a financial investment. Since it is not an addition to the nation's capital stock, it is not part of GPDI.

4. The construction of a new factory is counted in the nonresidential structures component of GPDI.

15.3 Determinants of Investment

Learning Objectives

1. Draw a hypothetical investment demand curve, and explain what it shows about the relationship between investment and the interest rate.

2. Discuss the factors that can cause an investment demand curve to shift.

Time, the saying goes, is nature's way of keeping everything from happening all at once. And the fact that everything *doesn't* happen at once introduces an important complication in economic analysis—especially where investment is concerned.

When a company decides to use funds to install capital that won't begin to produce income for several years, it needs a way to compare the magnitude of funds spent on capital *today* to the income that capital will create *later*. How can payments that occur at different points in time be compared? The answer lies in interest rates, which can effectively link the past, the present, and the future . . . at least where cash is concerned.

Unusual Business Model: The distiller hopes the resources invested in making this fine bourbon *won't* begin to pay rewards for another eighteen years.

Source: GolubSergei/Shutterstock.com

The Nature of Interest Rates

Here's a nice problem to have: Your Aunt Carmen has just offered to give you $10,000 now, or $10,000 in one year. Which do you choose? If you're like us, you'd likely take that payment now. One reason why is that the average level of prices is likely to rise over the next year. That means that you'll be able to buy more goods and services with today's $10,000 than with tomorrow's. There is also a question of whether you can count on receiving the payment. Who knows what might happen to your Aunt Carmen if you decide to wait—if her circumstances change over the next year (say, she gets hit by a bus), her offer may be off the table.

But let's assume away both of those problems. Suppose that you're 100% confident that the average level of prices won't change in the next year, and you're absolutely certain that Aunt Carmen will come through. Even with those guarantees, chances are you'd still want to take the payment now. Maybe there's something you'd like to purchase with it, and you'd like it sooner rather than later. Even if that's not the case, it's nice to have the *option* of sooner: Taking the cash now and stashing it away gives you that choice.

But what if, instead, Aunt Carmen offers you the choice of $10,000 now or *$11,000* in one year. The $1,000 bonus Aunt Carmen is offering if you will wait a year for her payment is *interest*, which, generally speaking, is a payment made to people who agree to postpone their use of wealth. Very often, interest is expressed as an annual percentage, known as the *interest rate*. Aunt Carmen is offering you $1,000 if you will forgo using the $10,000 today, so she is offering you an interest rate of $1,000/$10,000, or 10%. The more Aunt Carmen pays you for waiting, the higher the implicit interest rate.

You're probably familiar with the role of interest rates in loans, where a borrower receives a payment now in exchange for the promise to repay the lender in the future. To convince lenders to postpone the use of their money until later, borrowers repay more than they borrowed—in other words, they offer up some interest. Borrowers are willing to pay that interest because it allows them to use the money they've borrowed today, rather than having to save it up themselves over time for use in the future.

Interest Rates, Future Value, and Present Value

The interest rate, which allows us to link past, present, and future payments to one another, plays a critical role in investment decisions. To understand that role, let's dig into the the role of interest rates in turning an amount of money today (which we'll call a *present value*) into a different (hopefully bigger!) amount of money in the future (which we'll call a *future value*).

Suppose, for example, that you take $1,000 of your hard-earned dollars and deposit them in the bank, where they earn interest at a rate of 10% per year. How much will you have in your bank account at the end of one year?

- You will have the original $1,000.

- Added to that, you'll have interest earnings of 10% of $1,000, or $0.1 \times \$1,000 = \$100$.

So, your balance in one year will be:

$$\text{Balance in One Year} = \$1,000 + 0.1 \times \$1,000 = \$1,100$$

Let's draw a timeline of just what you've done. Today, you sacrifice the use of $1,000. In one year, you receive $1,100. Visually, that looks like Figure 15.5, where *t* indicates the time of a cash flow, the downward-pointing red arrow indicates cash flowing out, and the green upward-pointing arrow indicates cash coming in.

FIGURE 15.5 The Timing of Cash Flows

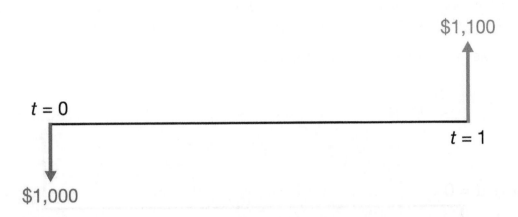

There's a "$1,000" in each term on the left-hand-side of that equation. It may feel a bit strange, but let's factor it out:

$$\text{Balance in One Year} = \$1,000(1+0.1) = \$1,100$$

That factoring gives us just what we need to generalize this example:

- $1,000 is the amount you set aside today, or the *present value*. Let's denote present value with a *PV*.
- 0.1 (the same as 10%) is the interest rate, which we'll call *r*.
- $1,100 is the future value of the amount saved. Let's call that FV_1, where *FV* means it's a future value, and the "1" subscript means it will be received in a year.

So, the calculation we've just done can be restated as:

EQUATION 15.1

$$FV_1 = PV(1+r)$$

How much will your savings account grow if you decide to leave your money in the bank for a second year? Essentially, you're taking the $1,100 you'll have at the end of the first year and re-investing it for a second year at the same interest rate. So the future value at the end of year 2, FV_2, will be

$$\text{Future Value in Two Years} = \$1,100(1+0.1)$$
$$FV_2 = FV_1(1+r)$$

But FV_1 was just your initial investment of $1,000 and its first-year interest earnings, $1000(1 + 0.1), so

$$\text{Future Value in Two Years} = [\$1,000(1+0.1)](1+0.1)$$
$$\text{Future Value in Two Years} = \$1,000(1+0.1)^2$$
$$FV_2 = PV(1+r)^2$$

This gives us a general formula we can use to calculate the future value of any investment today (*PV*) for any number of years (*n*) at an interest rate of *r*:

$$FV_n = PV(1+r)^n$$

So, for example, if you (a 20-year-old economics student) set Aunt Carmen's $1,000 aside in a 5%-earning savings account until you were 65 old, you'd end up at retirement (in 45 years) with:

$$FV_{45} = PV(1+r)^n = \$1,000(1+.05)^{45} = \$8,985$$

Not bad! Let's draw a diagram of what you've just done. Figure 15.6 shows that with a small sacrifice of $1,000 today, you'll have $8,985 to spend forty-five years from now in retirement.

FIGURE 15.6 Cash Flows Over Long Time Horizons

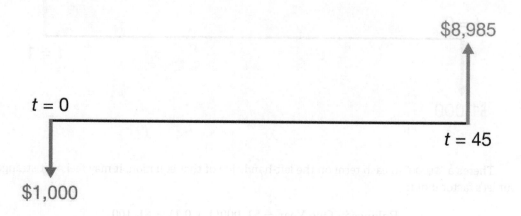

Knowing the interest rate allows you to see far into your financial future. Your success in romance may not be quite so predictable.

Source: Chad Zuber/Shutterstock.com

Equation 15.1 shows how to determine the future value of a payment or deposit made today. But firms deciding whether or not to invest in capital often need to turn that question around: How much would cash received in the distant future be worth today?

U-Turn: Present Values from Future Values

You already know how, given a present value and an interest rate, to figure out how much you'll have in the future. In our example, your $1,000 today would generate a future value in 45 years of $8,985.

But what if you didn't have any money today, but knew you were to receive $8,985 in 45 years? (Perhaps you're the recipient of a trust that promises to give you that upon your retirement!) Clearly, $8,985 received in 45 years isn't as valuable as $8,985 received today. So, how much *is* it worth today? One very objective answer is that *it's worth as much as you'd have to put in savings today in order to enjoy that amount in the future . . . exactly $1,000!* In other words, instead of solving the problem forwards (using present value to figure out future value), you can solve exactly the same problem backwards (using future value to figure out today's present value)! If

$$FV_n = PV(1+r)^n$$

then

EQUATION 15.2

$$PV = \frac{FV_n}{(1+r)^n}$$

Suppose, for example, that your Aunt Carmen offers you the option of $1,000 now or $6,700 in 30 years. We can use Equation 15.2 to help you decide which sum to take. The present value of $6,700 to be received in 30 years, assuming an interest rate of 5%, is:

$$PV = \frac{\$6,700}{(1+0.05)^{30}} = \$1,550$$

What does this mean for decision-making purposes? If your Aunt Carmen offers you the choice of $1,000 today, or $6,700 in 30 years, you should take the $6,700: It would take *more* than $1,000 today (specifically, it would take $1,550), invested for 30 years, to generate the same $6,700 by the time you reach 65!

Let's double-check to make sure that's right: If you set aside the $1,000 today, at an interest rate of 5%, it would grow to $1,000(1 + .05)^{30} = $4,322 in 30 years. You really *are* better off taking the future $6,700 than the present $1,000. In essence, your aunt is offering you two equivalent choices:

- $6,700 in 30 years by waiting, or $4,322 in 30 years by taking the cash today
- $1,550 today by waiting, or $1,000 today by taking the cash now

Whether we evaluate the value of the gift today or 30 years in the future, we get the same answer: Pass up the immediate gratification and wait for a bigger reward than you could generate for yourself at current interest rates!

The general present value formula, $PV = FV/(1 + r)^n$, can give us some useful insights about the nature of present value:

1. *Today's present value depends on the size of the future payment.* The more you receive in the future, the larger the present value today.

2. *Today's present value depends on how long you have to wait for it.* The longer the time until you receive it, the lower the present value. For example, the present value of $15,000 in 30 years at 10% is $859.63. The same sum, if paid in 20 years, has a present value of $2,229.65.

3. *Today's present value depends on the interest rate.* The higher the interest rate, the less you'd have to set aside today to generate a future amount, so the lower the present value. The present value of a payment of $15,000 to be made in 20 years is $5,653.34 at an interest rate of 5%, but only $2,229.65 at an interest rate of 10%.

"Not today, Aunt Carmen: I'll take the three in the bush."

Source: NCAimages/Shutterstock.com

Evaluating Multiple Cash Flows

Our purpose in converting future payments into present values is to explain how companies that shell out cash on investment today compare those expenditures to income received in the future. But often, that future income flows in over a number of years. How can we evaluate a *stream* of future payments in order to compare to a current investment expenditure?

The short and simple answer (and yes, this one really does have a short and simple answer!) is that you can compute the present value of each cash flow separately, and simply add your answer together. In other words, *the present value of a sum is the sum of the present values!*

FIGURE 15.7 The Present Value of a Stream of Future Payments
The present value of a stream of future payments is simply the sum of the present values. At an interest rate of 5%, three years' worth of $1,000 payments are worth $2,723.

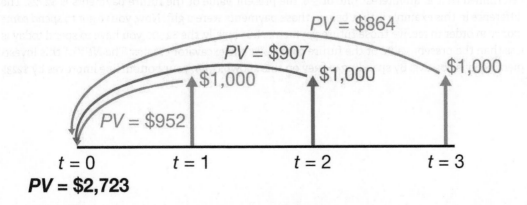

Let's look at an simple example to show how this works. Suppose you've been promised $1,000 at the end of each of the next 3 years. You're interested in calculating the present value of this promise. Let's break those three payments up and handle each individually. At an interest rate of 5%, the first $1,000, received in one year, has a present value of $952. That translation, from future $1,000 to present $952, is shown in blue in Figure 15.7. The second $1,000 payment, received in two years, is worth $907—less than the first payment, because you had to wait longer to receive it. The final $1,000 payment, shown in green, is worth less still: Its present value is only $864.[8] The present value of all of the payments taken together is the sum of the individual present values: $952 + $907 + $864, or $2,723.

Interest Rates, Net Present Value, and Investment Demand

We often hear reports that low interest rates have stimulated housing construction, or that high rates have reduced it. Those reports imply a negative relationship between interest rates and investment in residential structures. That relationship applies to all forms of investment—not just housing: Higher interest rates tend to reduce the quantity of investment, while lower interest rates increase it. The tools of present value can help us explain why.

Investment (by firms or by homeowners) involves spending money today (incurring costs) in hopes of getting something even more valuable back at a point in the future (receiving benefits). In the case of a business, that "something more valuable" might be sales revenue; in the case of someone building a new home, that "something more valuable" might be housing services or rental income.

The great news is that the tools of present value allow decision-makers to compare the costs and the benefits of investment decisions. That allows them to use the marginal decision rule: If the benefits outweigh the costs, then the investment decision is worth pursuing; if the costs outweigh the benefits, there's a better use for the cash than the project you're considering.

net present value

The present value of the benefits of an investment project less the present value of its costs.

The tool most often used when considering investment decisions is called net present value, or NPV. **Net present value** is the present value of the benefits of an investment project $PV_{Benefits}$, less the present value of its costs, PV_{Costs}.

$$NPV = PV_{Benefits} - PV_{Costs}$$

If the NPV for an investment project is greater than zero, then in present value terms, benefits must be greater than costs; this investment project is worth undertaking. On the other hand, if the NPV of a project is less than zero, then in present value terms, costs must be greater than benefits; the project isn't worth doing.

Let's apply the NPV tool to look at an example: Suppose you run a landscaping company, and you've got the chance to buy a new snowblower for $2,500 that will increase your revenues by $1,000 in each of the next three years. A diagram of the cash flows is shown in Figure 15.8. We've already determined that at an interest rate of 5%, the present value of the future payments is $2,723. The difference in this example is that before, those payments were a gift. Now, you've got to *spend some money* in order to receive those future payments. But luckily, the $2,500 you have to spend today is less than the present value of the future cash flows the excavator creates: The NPV of this investment good is positive. By spending money on this snowblower, your bottom line improves by $223!

FIGURE 15.8 Positive *NPV*
The present value of the future benefits is $2,723; the present value of the costs is $2,500. With *NPV* = +$223, this project is a go!

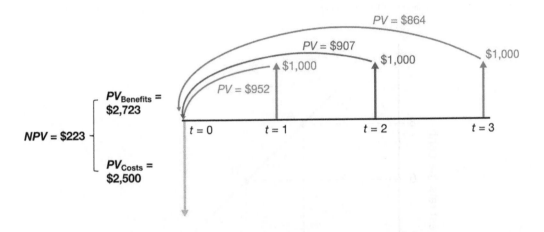

What if the snowblower costs $2,900? Then today's payment (cash out) would be greater than the value of the future cash flows it creates (cash in), and the net present value would be negative (specifically, –$177: Check your work to see if you're following along ok). Simply put, *you'd generate more future cash by putting your $2,900 into a 5% savings account than you would if you bought the snowblower*. In other words, *NPV is based on the notion of opportunity cost!*

Glad I waited, Aunt Carmen—the aviary had a positive *NPV!*

Source: Impact Photography/Shutterstock.com

The Role of Interest Rates

Let's reconsider the net present value problem we just looked at to see how interest rates affect investment decisions. Recall that you were considering how to spend a spare $2,500: You could put it in the bank at 5% . . . or you could generate even more cash ($223, in present value terms) by buying the snowblower.

Would you have made the same decision if interest rates were 10%? Let's find out, by writing out our *NPV* expression, which calculates the future value of benefits (three years of $1,000 revenues) minus the present value of costs ($2,500 today):

$$NPV = -\$2,500 + \frac{\$1,000}{(1+.10)^1} + \frac{\$1,000}{(1+.10)^2} + \frac{\$1,000}{(1+.10)^3} = -\$13.14$$

At a 10% interest rate, you'll make $13.14 more by putting your money into the bank at 10% than you would buying the snowblower. With a *NPV* less than zero, you should forego buying the equipment and park your cash in savings instead. In other words, *when interest rates increase, firms are less likely to purchase investment goods*. On the other hand, the lower the interest rate, the greater the number of investments that will be justified on the basis of positive *NPV*. That gives us a downward-sloping investment demand curve, like the one shown in Figure 15.9. That **investment demand curve** shows the quantity of investment goods demanded at each interest rate, with all other determinants of investment unchanged. At an interest rate of 8%, the level of investment is $950 billion per year, at point A. At a lower interest rate of 6%, the investment demand curve shows that the quantity of investment demanded will rise to $1,000 billion per year at point B. A decrease in the interest rate, then, causes a movement along the investment demand curve.

investment demand curve

A curve that shows the quantity of investment demanded at each interest rate, with all other determinants of investment unchanged.

FIGURE 15.9 The Investment Demand Curve

The investment demand curve (*ID*) shows the volume of investment spending per year at each interest rate, assuming all other determinants of investment are unchanged. The curve shows that as the interest rate falls, the level of investment per year rises. A reduction in the interest rate from 8% to 6%, for example, would increase investment from $950 billion to $1,000 billion per year, all other determinants of investment unchanged.

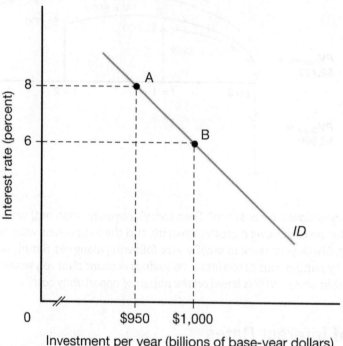

Heads Up!

It's easy to fall into the following kind of error: "Higher interest rates mean a greater return on investment, so higher interest rates lead to greater investment." But that confuses the more colloquial *financial* investment (say, buying bonds) with *economic* investment (purchasing real capital that will increase your future productivity). Higher interest rates increase the opportunity cost of using funds for economic investment (the kind that really can increase a nation's productivity), so higher interest rates *reduce* economic investment.

Other Determinants of Investment Demand

Perhaps the most important characteristic of the investment demand curve is not its negative slope, but rather the fact that it shifts often. Although the quantity of investment certainly depends on interest rates, changes in other factors also play important roles in driving investment choices.

This section examines eight additional determinants of investment demand: expectations, the level of economic activity, the stock of capital, capacity utilization, the cost of capital goods, other factor costs, technological change, and public policy. A change in any of these can shift the investment demand curve.

Expectations

A firm's *NPV* calculations depend critically on that firm's estimates of future cash flows. If expectations of future cash flows increase, then *NPV* will increase in lockstep; more projects will look profitable at any given interest rate. That shifts the investment demand curve to the right. On the other hand, expectations of *reduced* future profitability decrease *NPV*; fewer projects will appear to be cost-justified; the investment demand curve will shift to the left.

 Pop! Goes the Econ: Preston Tucker Chases the American Dream

In this movie adaptation of a real-life story, entrepreneur Preston Tucker has been waiting for this moment to give Americans the car of their dreams—a car more forward-looking than anything Detroit has ever produced. How do expectations play into Tucker's decision? Explain how this unique moment in history led to greater investment.

View in the online reader

The Level of Economic Activity

Firms need capital to produce goods and services. An increase in the overall level of production is likely to boost demand for capital and lead to greater investment. Therefore, an increase in GDP is likely to shift the investment demand curve to the right.

"The new Amazon fulfillment center has our lunchtime business booming—time to add a second truck!"

Source: Blulz60/Shutterstock.com

To the extent that an increase in GDP boosts investment, the multiplier effect of an initial change in one or more components of aggregate demand will be enhanced. We've already seen that the increase in production that occurs with an initial increase in aggregate demand will increase household incomes; that, in turn, increases consumption and produces a further increase in aggregate demand. If the initial increase also spurs firms to increase their investment, that multiplier effect will be even stronger.

The Stock of Capital

The quantity of capital already in use affects the level of investment in two ways. First, because most investment replaces capital that has depreciated, a greater capital stock is likely to lead to more (gross) investment; there will be more capital to replace. But it's also true that a greater capital stock might tend to *reduce* investment. That's because investment occurs to adjust the stock of capital to its desired level. Given that desired level, the amount of investment needed to reach it will be lower when the current capital stock is higher.

Suppose, for example, that real estate analysts expect that 100,000 homes will be needed in a particular community by 2030. That will create a boom in construction—and thus in investment—if the current number of houses is 50,000. But it will create hardly a ripple if there are now 99,980 homes.

How will these conflicting effects of a larger capital stock sort themselves out? Because most investment occurs to replace existing capital, a larger capital stock is likely to increase investment. But the more capital already in place, the less new capital will be required to reach a given level of desired capital. The ultimate net impact depends on the sizes of these two effects.

Capacity Utilization

capacity utilization rate

A measure of the percentage of the capital stock in use.

The **capacity utilization rate** measures the percentage of the capital stock in use. Because capital generally requires downtime for maintenance and repairs, the measured capacity utilization rate typically falls below 100%. For example, the average manufacturing capacity utilization rate was 79% for the period from 1980 to 2020. But the trend has been downward: Even before the coronavirus crisis, it was only 77%; by December 2020, in the depths of the COVID-19 recession, it was only 73%.

If a large percentage of the current capital stock is being utilized, firms are more likely to increase investment than they would be if a large percentage of the capital stock were sitting idle. During recessions, the capacity utilization rate tends to fall. The fact that firms have more idle capacity then depresses investment even further. During expansions, as the capacity utilization rate rises, firms wanting to produce more often have to increase investment spending in order to do so.

The Cost of Capital Goods

The demand curve for investment stems from the collective *NPV* calculations of thousands of firms. Net present value, remember, compares future benefits (+) to present costs (–). If investment goods become more expensive (as when the price of the snowblower rose to $2,900), then more projects will have negative net present values, and less investment spending will occur.

Other Factor Costs

"There ain't room enough in this town for the two of us, pilgrim." A company's investment in robotics depends critically on how much an equivalent amount of labor costs.

Source: PHOTOCREO Michal Bednarek/Shutterstock.com

Firms have a range of choices concerning how particular goods can be produced. A factory, for example, might use a sophisticated capital facility and relatively few workers, or it might use more workers and relatively less capital. The choice to use capital will be affected by the cost of the capital goods and the interest rate, but it will also be affected by the cost of labor. As labor costs rise, the demand for capital is likely to increase.

Other factor costs may influence the demand for capital as well. A firm considering investing in solar panels, for example, must base that decision on the prices of fuel oil, natural gas, and electricity. The higher those prices are, the greater the savings from installing solar power, and the higher the investment demand for solar panels will be.

Technological Change

The implementation of new technology often requires new capital. Changes in technology can thus increase the demand for capital. Advances in computer technology have encouraged massive investments in computers. The development of fiber-optic technology for transmitting signals has stimulated huge investments by telephone and cable television companies.

Public Policy

Public policy can have significant effects on the demand for capital. Consider two big policies, for example, from the Kennedy administration of the early 1960s. One strategy, accelerated depreciation, allowed firms to claim the cost of new equipment as an expense in the first few years after it was purchased, even if the equipment was expected to remain in service for decades. That acceleration of expenses reduced reported profits in those early years, and made investment in new equipment more attractive.

The second strategy was the investment tax credit, which permitted a firm to reduce its tax liability by a percentage of its investment during a period. That means that in addition to expensing the cost of the asset by claiming depreciation, a firm acquiring new capital could *also* subtract a fraction of its cost—10% under the Kennedy administration's plan—from the taxes it owed the government. Buy a $1 million robot, and your tax bill immediately falls by $100,000! In effect, the government paid 10% of the cost of any new capital, an implicit subsidy that shifted investment demand to the right.

There are, of course, other ways that public policy affects investment demand. A less direct (but still highly effective) strategy for stimulating investment is reducing taxes on corporate profits (called the *corporate income tax*). Greater after-tax profits mean that firms can retain a greater portion of any return on an investment. This strategy was adopted by the Trump administration in 2017 following a wave of corporate inversions that saw U.S. corporations re-domiciling in countries with lower income-tax rates. The Trump tax bill reduced the top corporate income tax rate from 35% (the highest in the developed world) to a much more internationally competitive 21%.

A fourth measure to encourage greater capital accumulation is a capital gains tax rate that allows gains on assets held during a certain period to be taxed at a different rate than other income. When an asset such as a building is sold for more than its purchase price, the seller of the asset is said to have realized a capital gain. Such a gain could be taxed as income under the personal income tax. Alternatively, it could be taxed at a lower rate reserved exclusively for such gains. A lower capital gains tax rate makes assets subject to the tax more attractive and increases the demand for capital. Congress reduced the capital gains tax rate from 28% to 20% in 1996 and reduced the required holding period in 1998. The Jobs and Growth Tax Relief Reconciliation Act of 2003 reduced the capital gains tax further to 15% and also reduced the tax rate on dividends from 38% to 15%. A proposal to eliminate capital gains taxation for smaller firms was considered but dropped before the stimulus bill of 2009 was enacted.

Accelerated depreciation, the investment tax credit, and lower taxes on corporate profits and capital gains all increase the demand for private physical capital. Public policy can also affect the demands for other forms of capital. The federal government subsidizes state and local government production of transportation, education, and many other facilities to encourage greater investment in public sector capital. For example, the federal government pays 90% of the cost of investment by local government in new buses for public transportation.

Said Nobody, Not Even a Stoner: "The government just jacked up the tax on something I enjoy; I think I'll do more of it."

Source: DisobeyArt/Shutterstock.com

Key Takeaways

- A dollar received in the future is worth less than a dollar today.
- Present value allows us to value future payments in today's terms.
- Net present value compares future benefits with present costs. A positive net present value means an economic investment is cost-effective.
- The quantity of investment demanded in any period (as well as that investment's *NPV*) is negatively related to the interest rate. This relationship is illustrated by the investment demand curve.
- A change in the interest rate causes a movement along the investment demand curve. A change in any other determinant of investment causes a shift of the curve.
- The other determinants of investment include expectations, the level of economic activity, the stock of capital, the capacity utilization rate, the cost of capital goods, other factor costs, technological change, and public policy.

Try It!

Show how the investment demand curve would be affected by each of the following:

1. A sharp increase in taxes on profits earned by firms
2. An increase in the minimum wage
3. The expectation that there will be a sharp upsurge in the level of economic activity
4. An increase in the cost of new capital goods
5. An increase in interest rates
6. An increase in the level of economic activity
7. A natural disaster that destroys a significant fraction of the capital stock

See related Concept Problem 2 at the end of this chapter.

Case in Point: Assessing the Impact of a One-Year Tax Break on Investment

Source: FxJ. "ICC 2008 Poland Silicon Wafer 2 edit" Public domain dedication via Wikimedia: https://commons.wikimedia.org/wiki/File:ICC_2008_Poland_Silicon_Wafer_2_edit.png.

The U.S. economy was expanding in 2004, but there was a feeling that it still was not functioning as well as it could, as job growth was rather sluggish. To try to spur growth, Congress, supported by President George W. Bush, passed a law in 2004 called the American Jobs Creation Act that gave businesses a one-year special tax break on any profits accumulating overseas that were transferred to the United States. Such profits are called repatriated profits and were estimated at the time to be about $800 billion. For 2005, the tax rate on repatriated profits essentially fell from 25% to 5.25%.

Did the tax break have the desired effect on the economy? To some extent yes, though businesses also found other uses for the repatriated funds. There were 843 companies that repatriated $312 billion that qualified for the tax break. The Act thus generated about $18 billion in tax revenue, a higher level than had been expected. Some companies announced they were repatriating profits and continuing to downsize. For example, Colgate-Palmolive brought back $800 million and made known it was closing a third of its factories and eliminating 12% of its workforce. However, other companies' plans seemed more in line with the objectives of the special tax break—to create jobs and spur investment.

For example, the *Wall Street Journal* reported that spokesman Chuck Mulloy of Intel, which repatriated over $6 billion, said the company was building a $3 billion microchip fabrication facility and spending $345 million on expanding existing facilities. "I can't say dollar-for-dollar how much of the funding for those comes from off-shore cash," but he felt that the repatriated funds were contributing to Intel's overall investments.[9] Spokeswoman Margaret Graham of Bausch and Lomb, which makes eye-care products and repatriated $805 million, said, "We plan to use that cash for capital expenditures, investment in research and development, and paying nonofficer compensation."

Analysts are skeptical, though, that the repatriated profits really contributed to investment. The *New York Times* reported on one study that suggested it had not. Rather, the repatriated funds were used for other purposes, such as stock repurchases. The argument is that the companies made investments that they were planning to make and the repatriated funds essentially freed up funding for other purposes.

See related Concept Problem 8 at the end of this chapter.

Sources: Based on Timothy Aeppel, "Tax Break Brings Billion to U.S., But Impact on Hiring Is Unclear," Wall Street Journal, October 5, 2005, p. A1; Lynnley Browning, "A One-Time Tax Break Saved 843 U.S. Corporations $265 Billion," The New York Times, June 24, 2008, p. C3.

Answers to Try It! Problems

1. The investment demand curve shifts to the left: Panel (b).

2. A higher minimum wage makes labor more expensive. Firms are likely to shift to greater use of capital, so the investment demand curve shifts to the right: Panel (a).

3. The investment demand curve shifts to the right: Panel (a).

4. The investment demand curve shifts to the left: Panel (b).

5. An increase in interest rates causes a movement along the investment demand curve: Panel (c).

6. The investment demand curve shifts to the right: Panel (a).

7. The need to replace capital shifts the investment demand curve to the right: Panel (a).

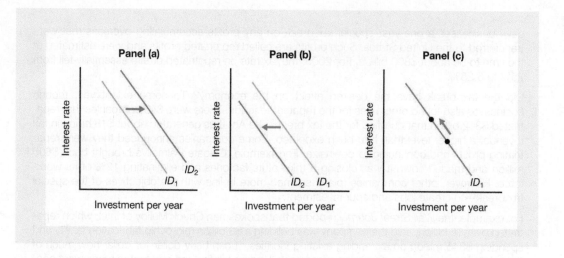

15.4 Investment and the Economy

Learning Objectives

1. Explain how investment affects aggregate demand.
2. Explain how investment affects long-run aggregate supply.
3. Explain how investment affects economic growth.

A shot of consumption spending satisfies your appetite today; the same amount of investment spending gives you more power tomorrow.

Source: Paradise studio/ Shutterstock.com

You now know what investment is, what influences it, and how today's investment can affect the economy in the long run. Let's take a look at how investment spending affects the economy today, by using our model of aggregate demand and aggregate supply. You'll remember, of course, that investment—along with consumption, government spending, and net exports—is a component of aggregate demand. In the world of $C + I + G + X_n$, investment's I is just as important, dollar for dollar, as consumption's C, or any other category of spending, for that matter. So, in the short run, changes in investment demand will shift the aggregate demand curve. In the long run, we've already seen that investment may arguably be the *most* important component of aggregate demand. That's because increases in investment change the capital stock, and growth of capital favorably shifts the economy's production possibilities curve, the economy's aggregate production function, and the economy's long-run aggregate supply.

Investment and Aggregate Demand

In the short run, changes in investment cause aggregate demand to change. Consider, for example, the impact of a reduction in the interest rate, given the investment demand curve (*ID*). In Figure 15.10, Panel (a), which uses the investment demand curve introduced in Figure 15.9, a decrease in interest rates from 8% to 6% increases investment by $50 billion per year. If the aggregate expenditures multiplier is 2.0, that $50 billion increase in investment will lead to a total increase in aggregate demand of $100 billion. That increase is represented by the $100 billion rightward shift in aggregate demand from AD_1 to AD_2 in Panel (b). At a price level of 100, for example, the quantity of real GDP demanded rises from $8,000 billion to $8,100 billion per year. A reduction in investment would shift the aggregate demand curve to the left by an amount equal to the multiplier times the change in investment.

FIGURE 15.10 A Change in Investment and Aggregate Demand
A decrease in the interest rate from 8% to 6% increases the level of investment by $50 billion per year in Panel (a). With a multiplier of 2, the aggregate demand curve shifts to the right by $100 billion in Panel (b). The total quantity of real GDP demanded increases at each price level. Here, for example, the quantity of real GDP demanded at a price level of 100 rises from $8,000 billion per year at point C to $8,100 billion per year at point D.

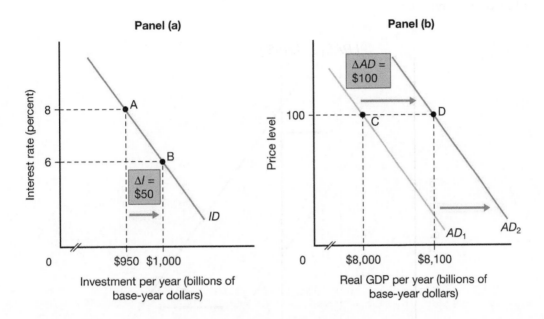

The relationship between investment and interest rates is one key to the effectiveness of monetary policy in the economy. When the Fed wants to stimulate aggregate demand, it buys bonds in the open market. That increases bond prices and reduces interest rates. The decrease in interest rates, in turn, stimulates investment and aggregate demand, as illustrated in Figure 15.10. When the Fed wants to slow the economy, it sells off some of its existing bond holdings. That pushes bond prices lower, raises interest rates, and reduces investment and aggregate demand. The aggregate demand curve shifts to the left rather than the right.

The extent to which investment responds to a change in interest rates is a crucial factor in how effective monetary policy is. If investment isn't very sensitive to interest rates, it will take a huge push from the Fed to stimulate spending: lots of bond purchases and large changes in interest rates. That may happen in an environment where business confidence is very low; even if money is extremely cheap, firms may be reluctant to undertake new investment projects, because they don't see good prospects for selling the products those investment goods would eventually make. On the other hand, if investment is very sensitive to changes in interest rates, even a small nudge by the Fed—small bond purchases and relatively small changes in interest rates—can touch off a lot of new investment spending.

Excess Capacity: When the economy has lots of resources sitting idle, a decrease in interest rates is unlikely to convince firms to invest more.

Source: LuckyPhoto/Shutterstock.com

Investment, Supply, and Economic Growth

Investment adds to the stock of capital, and the quantity of capital available to an economy is a crucial determinant of its productivity—the more capital an economy has, all else equal, the more productive the economy will be. We saw in Figure 15.4 that an increase in an economy's stock of capital shifts its production possibilities curve outward.[10] That also shifts its long-run aggregate supply curve to the right. At the same time, of course, an increase in investment affects aggregate demand, as we saw in Figure 15.10.

FIGURE 15.11 The Long-Run Impact of Increased Investment
An increase in investment today shifts aggregate demand from AD_1 to AD_2. Because the large investment this year leads to a series of smaller returns each year in the future, LRAS shifts from $LRAS_1$ to $LRAS_2$, but the shift is likely to be proportionately smaller.

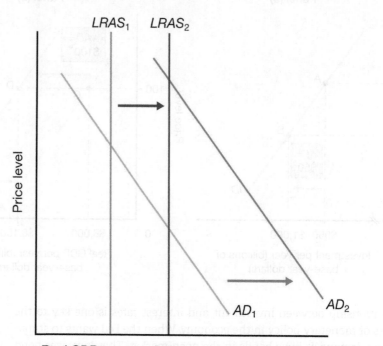

Let's combine the two effects. The long-run impact of a *one-time* increase in investment demand is illustrated in Figure 15.11. The increase today in investment demand causes the aggregate demand curve to shift rightward from AD_1 to AD_2. The increase in investment also builds capital that expands the economy's production possibilities; that increase shifts the LRAS curve from $LRAS_1$ to $LRAS_2$.

The size of that shift depends on the nature of the investment undertaken. If the new investment spending was a one-time increase, the shift in LRAS is likely to be relatively small; aggregate demand will soon return to AD_1 and the economy will find its new long-run equilibrium where the new LRAS curve intersects AD_1. If, on the other hand, the change in investment was permanent—in other words, an increase in spending that will be sustained into the future—then the aggregate demand curve may remain at AD_2, with higher output but an indeterminate effect on the price level (depending on the magnitude of the shifts in AD and LRAS). In either case, the impact of greater investment spending is greater output, the result of increased production possibilities that neither consumption spending nor net exports has the power to generate. It's no wonder, then, that both businesses and policymakers pay so much attention to investment and the capital stock!

Key Takeaways

- Changes in investment shift the aggregate demand curve to the right or left by an amount equal to the initial change in investment times the multiplier.
- Investment adds to the capital stock; it therefore contributes to economic growth.

Try It!

Use the *AD/AS* framework to show all of the possible ways a permanent increase in investment spending could impact the economy in the long run. (*Hint: There are three different possible impacts on the price level.*)

See related Concept Problem 9 at the end of this chapter.

Case in Point: Investment in a COVID-19 Recovery

Mixed Messages: During the COVID-19 recession, investment in housing didn't slow . . . it skyrocketed!

Source: Brandon Bourdages/Shutterstock.com

We've already seen in the chapter opener how investment spending declined during the Great Recession. And then, in this chapter's earlier "Case in Point: The Reduction of Private Capital in the Depression and in the Great Recession", we saw how investment positively plummeted during the Great Depression. That's a pattern that generally repeats itself during downturns—after all, what business wants to build a factory when the economy's headed south and people are slowing their spending?

And then there's the coronavirus crisis and the subsequent COVID-19 recession, which took everything we thought we knew about economics and turned it on its head. That downturn began in March and April of 2020 with a sharp, steep drop in aggregate spending, followed by a rapid, but incomplete, bounce back toward normal in the summer months and through the fall of 2020. That bounce was driven in part by consumption spending, though a year after the crisis began consumption had failed to return to pre-COVID-19 levels. In and of itself, that wasn't normal: During most recessions, consumption declines a bit, but generally it recovers to pre-recession levels before the recession ends. Not this time!

Instead, much of the strength of the COVID-19 recovery can be attributed, oddly, to investment spending. That spending was driven in part by business investment among firms that recognized the temporary nature of the pandemic and who rallied each time there was good news about a vaccine or a reopening.

What the . . . !?!?! In the depths of the COVID-19 recession, business confidence reached a level it hadn't seen in the ten years since the end of the Great Recession.

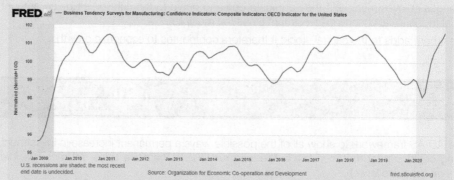

Source: Organization for Economic Co-operation and Development, Business Tendency Surveys for Manufacturing: Confidence Indicators: Composite Indicators: OECD Indicator for the United States [BSCICP03USM665S], retrieved from FRED, Federal Reserve Bank of St. Louis; https://fred.stlouisfed.org/series/BSCICP03USM665S.

But the real story of the COVID-19 recession was its impact on the housing market. Within weeks of the pandemic's beginning, housing markets started heating up, driven in large part by workers who discovered that Zooming from the front-hall closet eight hours a day was no fun, and that kids forced to school from home needed a bit of space and an up-to-date Wi-Fi connection. Private residential investment in both new homes and home improvements soared. Daryl Fairweather, chief economist at Redfin, remarks that housing's performance "has more to do with the pandemic itself: how everyone is stuck at home, working from home, teaching their kids at home. The home has just become so much more important."[11]

During the COVID-19 recession, the number of new houses under construction (red line, right axis) soared, as did private residential investment (blue line, left axis).

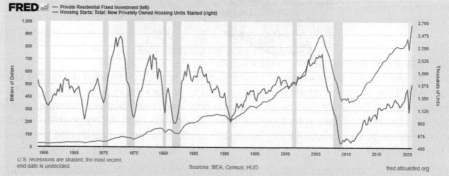

Source: Bureau of Economic Analysis, Bureau of the Census, Department of Housing and Urban Development, accessed through Federal Reserve Economic Data (FRED) at https://fred.stlouisfed.org/series/PRFI and https://fred.stlouisfed.org/series/HOUST. FRED® Graphs ©Federal Reserve Bank of St. Louis. All rights reserved. All FRED® Graphs appear courtesy of Federal Reserve Bank of St. Louis. https://fred.stlouisfed.org/.

Usually, the housing market is driven by existing homeowners looking to relocate, which keeps the market somewhere near equilibrium: Every buyer is also a seller. But the COVID-19 recession saw millions of first-time buyers anxious to leave crowded city apartments in favor of larger, more comfortable suburban single-family homes. A Realtor.com survey published in October 2020 revealed that over 60% of millennials planned to buy a home within the next year. That new housing demand dried up inventories of housing to levels not seen since the 1960s, a scarcity that sent prices soaring with houses across the country being sold in bidding wars at prices half again as much as the asking price.

During the COVID-19 recession, the thirty-year mortgage rate, already low by historical standards, was pushed lower by the Fed's response to the coronavirus. Fueled by low interest rates, investment boomed!

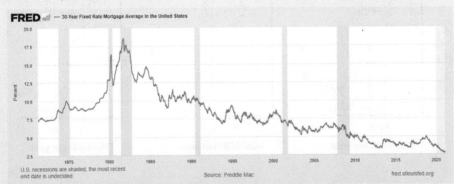

Source: Freddie Mac, 30-Year Fixed Rate Mortgage Average in the United States [MORTGAGE30US], retrieved from FRED, Federal Reserve Bank of St. Louis; https://fred.stlouisfed.org/series/MORTGAGE30US.

There's no doubt that there was a fundamental shift in investment demand during the COVID-19 recession. But there was also a movement *along* the investment demand curve driven by the Fed's reaction to the pandemic. Even in the earliest days of the pandemic, when cases numbered in the hundreds and thousands rather than the tens of millions, Fed Chair Jerome Powell made it clear that the Fed stood ready to take unprecedented action to keep money flowing. Powell's action pushed short-term interest rates to near zero, flooding banks with liquidity that dragged down the crucially important long-term mortgage rate, as well as the lending rates faced by businesses, to all-time lows. Those low rates made bigger and better houses more affordable to consumers, and they made more business investments profitable.

In an ordinary recession, anxious householders and businesses typically postpone plans for investment. But because of the unusual nature of the COVID-19 recession and the strength of the Fed's response, the U.S. economy got *more* investment spending rather than less. That investment spending accounted for a major slice of the rapid initial rebound: Had investment spending behaved the way it *usually* does during downturns, a recession that has already been one of the defining moments in American economic history would have undoubtedly been deeper, longer, and much, much more painful.

See related Concept Problem 10 at the end of this chapter.

Sources: Based on Daria, Solovieva, "Behind Real Estate's Surprise 2020 Boom and What Comes Next," Fortune, October 20, 2020; and Chris Arnold, "More Space, Please: Home Sales Booming Despite Pandemic," Recession, NPR, August 28, 2020.

Answer to Try It! Problem

Panel (a) shows *AD* shifting by more than *LRAS*; the price level will rise in the long run.

Panel (b) shows *AD* and *LRAS* shifting by equal amounts; the price level will remain unchanged in the long run.

Panel (c) shows *LRAS* shifting by more than *AD*; the price level falls in the long run.

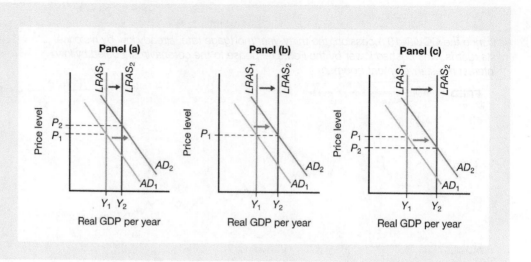

15.5 Review and Practice

Summary

Investment is an addition to the capital stock. Investment may occur as a net addition to capital or as a replacement of depreciated capital. The bulk of investment spending in the United States falls into the latter category. Investment is a highly volatile component of GDP.

The decision to save is linked directly to the decision to invest. If a nation is to devote a larger share of its production to investment, then it must devote a smaller share to consumption, all other things unchanged. And that requires people to save more.

Investment is affected by the interest rate; the negative relationship between investment and the interest rate is illustrated by the investment demand curve. The position of this curve is affected by expectations, the level of economic activity, the stock of capital, capacity utilization, the price of capital, the prices of other factors, technology, and public policy.

Because investment is a component of aggregate demand, a change in investment shifts the aggregate demand curve to the right or left. The amount of the shift will equal the initial change in investment times the multiplier.

In addition to its impact on aggregate demand, investment can also affect economic growth. Investment shifts the production possibilities curve outward, shifts the economy's aggregate production function upward, and shifts the long-run aggregate supply curve to the right.

Concept Problems

1. (Related to "Try It!" in Section 27.2.) Which of the following would be counted as gross private domestic investment?

   a. General Motors issues 1 million shares of stock.

   b. Consolidated Construction purchases 1,000 acres of land for a regional shopping center it plans to build in a few years.

   c. A K-Mart store adds 1,000 T-shirts to its inventory.

   d. Crew buys computers for its office staff.

   e. Your family buys a house.

2. (Related to "Try It!" in Section 27.3.) What would happen to investment demand if

   a. interest rates decreased sharply

   b. local governments throughout the United States increased their tax on business inventories

   c. the government announced it would pay for half of any new investment undertaken by firms

   d. the economy entered a recession

   e. the government increased the corporate income tax rate

3. White House officials often exude more confidence than they actually feel about future prospects for the economy. Why might this be a good strategy? Are there any dangers inherent in it?

4. Suppose everyone expects investment to rise sharply in three months. How would this expectation be likely to affect bond prices?

5. Suppose that every increase of $1 in real GDP automatically stimulates $0.20 in additional investment spending. How would this affect the multiplier?

6. If environmental resources were counted as part of the capital stock, how would a major forest fire affect net investment?

7. (Related to "Case in Point: The Reduction of Private Capital in the Depression and in the Great Recession" in Section 27.2.) In this case, we saw that net investment was negative during the Great Depression. Could gross investment ever be negative? Explain.

8. (Related to "Case in Point: Assessing the Impact of a One-Year Tax Break on Investment" in Section 27.3.) This case discussed reducing the tax rate for one year for companies that repatriated profits. The case showed that investment did not increase, even though company representatives maintained they were using the repatriated profits for investment. Explain this seeming contradiction.

9. (Related to "Try It!" in Section 27.4.) Use the model of aggregate demand and aggregate supply to evaluate the argument that an increase in investment would raise the standard of living.

10. (Related to "Case in Point: Investment in a COVID-19 Recovery" in Section 27.4.) Use a graph of the investment demand curve to illustrate the factors that led to rising investment during the COVID-19 recession. Be sure that your analysis shows both a shift in the curve and a shift along the curve. Then, illustrate the impact of the change in investment demand in the *AD/AS* framework.

Numerical Problems

1. Suppose a construction company is trying to decide whether to buy a new nail gun. The table below shows the hypothetical costs for the nail gun and the amount the gun will save the company each year. Assume the gun will last forever. In each case, determine the highest interest rate the company should pay for a loan that makes purchase of the nail gun possible.

	Cost ($)	Savings ($)
a.	1,000	100
b.	1,000	200
c.	1,000	300

2. A car company currently has capital stock of $100 million and desires a capital stock of $110 million.

   a. If it experiences no depreciation, how much will it need to invest to get to its desired level of capital stock?

b. If its annual depreciation is 5%, how much will it need to invest to get to its desired level?

c. If its annual depreciation is 10%, how much will it need to invest to get to its desired level?

3. Suppose your college education costs $100,000, paid up front. (Assume that covers the full opportunity cost), but raises your income in the six years following by $20,000. Assuming your employer pays you at the beginning of the year, draw a timeline of cash flows.

4. You save $10,000 today.

a. What will that $10,000 grow to in 40 years, if the interest rate is 8%?

b. What will your $10,000 grow to in 40 years if the interest rate is only 6%?

5. Your mother has promised you a $100,000 trust fund payment in ten years. If the interest rate is 5%, what is it worth today?

6. Your mother has promised you a $100,000 trust fund payment in ten years, and a $200,000 payment in 20 years. Draw a timeline of cash flows, and calculate the present value of these promises.

7. Consider the cost of college described above in question 3. If the interest rate is 10%, what is the NPV of your college education? Is college worth it?

8. Consider the cost of college described in the previous question. If the cost of college can be spread into four equal payments of $25,000, will college have a positive NPV?

9. Burger World is contemplating installing an automated ordering system. The ordering system will allow Burger World to permanently replace five employees for an annual (and permanent) cost savings of $100,000.

a. If the automated system cost $1,000,000, what would be the rate of return on the investment?

b. If the system cost $2,000,000, what would be its rate of return?

c. If the government were to introduce an investment tax credit that allowed firms to deduct 10% of their investments from their tax liability, what would happen to the rate of return if the system were to cost $1,000,000?

d. If Burger World has to pay 8% to borrow the funds to purchase the system, what is the most it should pay for the system? Assume that there is no investment tax credit.

10. The table below shows a number of investment projects and their effective earned interest rates or returns. Given the market interest rates shown below, identify which projects will be undertaken and the total amount of investment spending that will ensue.

Project	Return on Project (%)	Cost ($)
A	30	1,000
B	28	500
C	22	2,500
D	17	1,000
E	8	750
F	4	1,200

a. 20%

b. 15%

c. 10%

d. 5%

e. 3%

f. Sketch out the investment demand curve implied by these data.

11. The table below describes the amounts of investment for different interest rates.

Interest Rate (%)	Amount of Investment (billions of $)
25	5
20	10
15	15
10	20
5	25

   a. Draw the investment demand curve for this economy.

   b. Show the effect you would expect a decrease in the cost of capital goods to have on this investment demand curve.

   c. Show the effect you would expect an investment tax credit to have on this investment demand curve.

   d. Show the effect you would expect a recession to have on this investment demand curve.

12. Suppose real GDP in an economy equals its potential output of $2,000 billion, the multiplier is 2.5, investment is raised by $200 billion, and the increased investment does not affect the economy's potential.

   a. Show the short- and long-run effects of the change upon real GDP and the price level, using the graphical framework for the model of aggregate demand and aggregate supply.

   b. Would real GDP rise by the multiplier times the change in investment in the short run? In the long run? Explain.

Endnotes

1. Kate Linebaugh, "Toyota Delays Mississippi Prius Factory Amid Slump," *Wall Street Journal*, December 16, 2008, p. B1.

2. Amy Merrick, "Walgreen to Cut Back on Opening New Stores," *Wall Street Journal*, December 23, 2008, p. B1.

3. Darren Shannon, "FedEx Takes More Measures to Offset Fiscal Uncertainty," *Aviation Daily*, December 19, 2008, p. 6.

4. Reed Abelson, "Hurting for Business," *New York Times*, November 7, 2008, p. B1.

5. Bettina Wassener, "Sony to Cut 8,000 Workers and Shut Plants," *New York Times*, December 10, 2008, p. B8.

6. Steve LeVine, "Pullback in the Oil Patch," *Business Week*, December 8, 2008, p. 60.

7. The Commerce Department reports depreciation as "consumption of fixed capital."

8. We encourage you to check our math by calculating the present value of these individual cash flows for yourself!

9. Timothy Aeppel, "Tax Break Brings Billion to U.S., But Impact on Hiring Is Unclear," *The Wall Street Journal*, October 5, 2005, p. A1.

10. For a more in-depth look at the role of investment, capital, and the economy's long-run potential, see the discussion of the Solow model in our chapter on economic growth.

11. Daria, Solovieva, "Behind Real Estate's Surprise 2020 Boom and What Comes Next," *Fortune*, October 20, 2020.

CHAPTER 16
Net Exports and International Finance

16.1 Start Up: Currency Crises Shake the World

It became known as the "Asian Contagion," and it swept the world as the twentieth century came to a close.

Japan, crippled by the threat of collapse of many of its banks, seemed stuck in a recessionary gap for most of the decade. Because Japan was a major market for the exports of economies throughout East Asia, the slump in Japan translated into falling exports in neighboring economies. Slowed growth in a host of economies that had grown accustomed to phenomenal growth set the stage for trouble throughout the world.

The first crack appeared in Thailand, whose central bank had successfully maintained a stable exchange rate between the baht, Thailand's currency, and the U.S. dollar. But weakened demand for Thai exports, along with concerns about the stability of Thai banks, put downward pressure on the baht. Thailand's effort to shore up its currency ultimately failed, and the country's central bank gave up the effort in July of 1997. The baht's value dropped nearly 20% in a single day.

Is your currency on solid ground? Or is it in danger of collapse?

Source: Pictrider/Shutterstock.com

Holders of other currencies became worried about their stability and began selling. Central banks that, like Thailand's, had held their currencies stable relative to the dollar, gave up their efforts as well. Malaysia quit propping up the ringgit less than two weeks after the baht's fall. Indonesia's central bank gave up trying to hold the rupiah's dollar value a month later. South Korea let the won fall in November.

Currency crises continued to spread in 1998, capped by a spectacular plunge in the Russian ruble. As speculators sold other currencies, they bought dollars, driving the U.S. exchange rate steadily upward.

What was behind the currency crises that shook the world? How do changes in a country's exchange rate affect its economy? How can events such as the fall of the baht and the ringgit spread to other countries?

We will explore the answers to these questions by looking again at how changes in a country's exchange rate can affect its economy—and how changes in one economy can spread to others. We will be engaged in a study of **international finance**, the field that examines the macroeconomic consequences of the financial flows associated with international trade.

We will begin by reviewing the reasons nations trade. International trade has the potential to increase the availability of goods and services to everyone. We will look at the effects of trade on the welfare of people and then turn to the macroeconomic implications of financing trade.

international finance

The field that examines the macroeconomic consequences of the financial flows associated with international trade.

16.2 The International Sector: An Introduction

In the river markets of Bangkok, you can find a stunning array of fruits and vegetables for sale. Thanks to globalization, you can also find them at the nearest Piggly Wiggly.

Source: Juriah Mosin/ Shutterstock.com

Take a look at the labels on some of your clothing. You are likely to find that the clothes in your closet came from all over the globe. Look around any parking lot. You may find cars from Japan, Korea, Sweden, Britain, Germany, France, Italy—and even the United States! Do you use a computer? Even if it is an American computer (perhaps a Dell or an HP), its components are likely to have been assembled in Indonesia or in some other country. Are you a fan of fruits and veggies? Much of the produce you enjoy may come from Latin America and Asia.

The international market is important not just in terms of the goods and services it provides *to* a country but also as a market *for* that country's goods and services. Foreign demand for U.S. exports is a large component of aggregate demand, and it can be very important in terms of growth: An increase in exports in 2011, for example, accounted for about half of the gain in U.S. real GDP in that year.

The Case for Trade

International trade increases the quantity of goods and services available to the world's consumers. Trade allows countries to specialize in goods and services they're good at producing, and then swap for the goods and services they're not so good at producing. When countries specialize like this, world production increases, allowing trading nations to consume outside their production possibilities.

What defines what a country is "good at" producing? A country is good at producing a good or service if it can produce it at lower cost than a trading partner. Of course, this is an econ course, and so cost, rather than being measured in dollars and cents, is measured in terms of opportunity cost. A country that can produce a good at a lower opportunity cost than other countries has a comparative advantage in that good's production. If each country specializes in the production of goods in which it has a comparative advantage and trades those goods for things in which other countries have a comparative advantage, global production of all goods and services will be increased. The result can be higher levels of consumption for all.

If the specialization necessary for international trade expands global production of goods and services, then *restrictions* on trade will *reduce* world production. That, in a nutshell, is the economic case for free trade. It suggests that restrictions on trade, such as a **tariff**, a tax imposed on imported goods and services, or a **quota**, a ceiling on the quantity of specific goods and services that can be imported, reduce world living standards.

The conceptual argument for free trade is compelling: Virtually all economists support policies that reduce barriers to trade. Economists were among the most outspoken advocates for the 1993 ratification of the North American Free Trade Agreement (NAFTA), which virtually eliminated trade restrictions between Mexico, the United States, and Canada.[1] Likewise, economists strongly supported the 2004 Central American Free Trade Agreement (CAFTA), which did the same for trade between the United States, Central America, and the Dominican Republic. They supported a 2007 free trade agreement with Peru and the 2011 agreements with Colombia, Panama, and South Korea. Most economists have also been strong supporters of worldwide reductions in trade barriers, including the 1994 ratification of the General Agreement on Tariffs and Trade (GATT), a pact slashing tariffs and easing quotas among 117 nations, including the United States, and the Doha round of World Trade Organization negotiations, named after the site of the first meeting in Doha, Qatar, in 2001 and still continuing. In Europe, member nations of the European Union (EU) have virtually eliminated trade barriers among themselves, and nineteen EU nations now have a common currency, the euro, and a single central bank, the European Central Bank. Trade barriers have also been slashed among the economies of Latin America and of Southeast Asia, including via a 2018 agreement among eleven major Pacific Rim countries to reduce tariffs and move toward free trade.

The global embrace of the idea of free trade demonstrates the triumph of economic ideas over powerful forces that oppose free trade. One source of opposition to free trade comes from the owners of factors of production used in industries in which a nation lacks a comparative advantage. It's often argued that when trade opens, domestic jobs are stolen by foreigners, reducing employment not only in specific sectors of the economy, but also in the economy as a whole. In the long run, this argument is clearly wrong. The economy's natural level of employment is determined by forces unrelated to trade policy, and employment moves to its natural level in the long run. In the short run, trade does affect aggregate demand. Net exports are one component of aggregate demand; a change in net exports shifts the aggregate demand curve and affects real GDP in the short run. All other things unchanged, a reduction in net exports reduces aggregate demand, and an increase in net exports increases it.

Protectionist sentiment always rises during recessions. During the Great Depression of the 1930s, political pressure from ailing businesses resulted in the Hawley–Smoot Tariff, a disastrous policy that ratcheted the average import tariff to 60% and brought the bulk of global trade to a halt. While there was a lot of talk during the Great Recession about trade protection, most countries avoided new trade restrictions.

However, in 2016, two events rocked both world trade and international diplomacy. The first was the vote in the United Kingdom, commonly referred to as *Brexit*, to leave the European Union.[2] While the main reason a majority of voters voted to leave was concern over immigration, there is a great deal of uncertainty regarding how trade will look in the near future. For now, the United Kingdom retains free trade with the EU, but it has gained the power to increase protection and to negotiate its own trade deals outside the EU.

tariff

A tax imposed on imported goods and services.

quota

A ceiling on the quantity of specific goods and services that can be imported, which reduces world living standards.

Advocates of free trade have stood steadfast against a strong tide of protectionism.

Source: lassedesignen/Shutterstock.com

Pop! Goes the Econ:
Protection in _Ferris Bueller_
Real-life economist, lawyer, and actor Ben Stein delivers an important lesson: Economic downturns often prompt a call for protection that only makes the downturn worse.

View in the online reader

The other major shock to globalization that 2016 brought was the election of Donald Trump as U.S. president. A self-proclaimed economic nationalist, Trump withdrew the United States from the Obama-negotiated Trans-Pacific Partnership on his first day in office, declaring an end to the era of multinational trade agreements. By 2018, he had imposed high tariffs on steel and aluminum and then ratcheted up tariffs on a wide variety of imports from China and the EU, proclaiming, "Trade wars are good, and easy to win." As Trump exited office, he left behind a political base energized by his economic nationalism and an economy damaged by a contraction in exports, fueled in part by retaliatory tariffs imposed by U.S. trading partners.

The Rising Importance of International Trade

International trade is important, and its importance is increasing. From 1990 to 2010, world output growth was about 3% per year on average, but world _export_ growth averaged twice that, about 6% per year.

International trade is playing a more significant role in the United States as well. In 1960, exports represented only about 4% of real GDP; by 2020, exports accounted for almost 12% of GDP, and imports even more than that. Figure 16.1 shows the growth in exports and imports as a percentage of real GDP in the United States from 1947 to 2020.

FIGURE 16.1 U.S. Exports and Imports Relative to U.S. Real GDP, 1947–2020
The chart shows exports (in red) and imports (in blue) as a percentage of real GDP from 1947 through 2020. Both imports and exports have risen in importance over the past half-century.

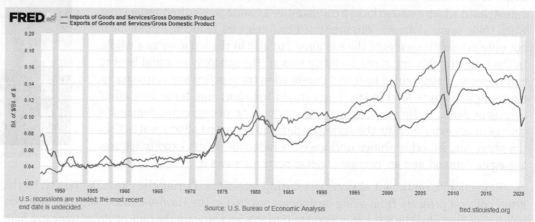

Source: Bureau of Economic Analysis, accessed through Federal Reserve Economic Data (FRED) at https://fred.stlouisfed.org/series/IEAMGSN, https://fred.stlouisfed.org/series/EXPGS, and https://fred.stlouisfed.org/series/GDP. FRED® Graphs ©Federal Reserve Bank of St. Louis. All rights reserved. All FRED® Graphs appear courtesy of Federal Reserve Bank of St. Louis. https://fred.stlouisfed.org/.

Why has world trade risen so spectacularly? Two factors have been important. First, advances in transportation and communication have dramatically reduced the cost of moving goods around the globe. The development of shipping containerization that allows cargo to be moved seamlessly from trucks or trains to ships, which began in 1956, reduced the cost of moving goods around the world by as much as 90%. As a result, the numbers of container ships and their capacities have markedly increased.[3] Second, on a global basis, trade barriers between countries have decreased, and are likely to fall further in the future.

 Pop! Goes the Econ: The Story of Containerization

In this TedEd video, Sir Harold Evans describes how frustration drove Malcom McLean, a small-town truck driver, to invent the shipping container.

View in the online reader

Container ships like the *Ever Given* make world trade go around; when this behemoth got stuck sideways in the Suez Canal in 2021, the resulting traffic jam disrupted billions of dollars of global trade.

Source: Robert Schwemmer for NOAA's National Ocean Service. "Ever Given container ship (cropped)." Via Wikimedia: https://commons.wikimedia.org/wiki/File:Ever_Given_container_ship_(cropped).jpg. Reproduced via Creative Commons Attribution 2.0 Generic (CC BY 2.0) license: https://creativecommons.org/licenses/by/2.0/.

Net Exports and the Economy

We have already discussed the increased shares of U.S. real GDP represented by exports and by imports. As trade has become more important worldwide, exports and imports have assumed increased importance in nearly every country on the planet. We will find in this section that the economy both influences and is influenced by net exports. First, we will examine the determinants of net exports, and then we will discuss the ways in which net exports affect aggregate demand.

Determinants of Net Exports

Net exports (X_n) equal exports (X) minus imports (M):

EQUATION 16.1

$$X_n = X - M$$

Many of the same forces affect both exports and imports, albeit in different ways. Let's take a look at each, in turn.

Income

A nation's level of income affects its imports the same way it affects consumption. For example, as income in the United States increases, consumers respond by purchasing more goods and services. Because some of those goods and services are produced in other nations, imports increase. An increase in GDP, then, increases imports; a decrease in GDP reduces imports. Figure 16.2 shows the relationship between GDP and the level of import spending in the United States from 1947 through 2020. Each dot in the figure plots one year's level of GDP (on the horizontal axis) and imports (on the vertical axis). Those points all lie close to the straight black trend line, which indicates that on average, each additional dollar of income (GDP) leads to a sixteen-cent increase in imports.

FIGURE 16.2 U.S. Real GDP and Imports, 1947–2020
The chart shows annual values of U.S. real imports and real GDP from 1947 through 2020. The observations lie quite close to a straight line: Each dollar's increase in GDP causes a sixteen-cent increase in imports.

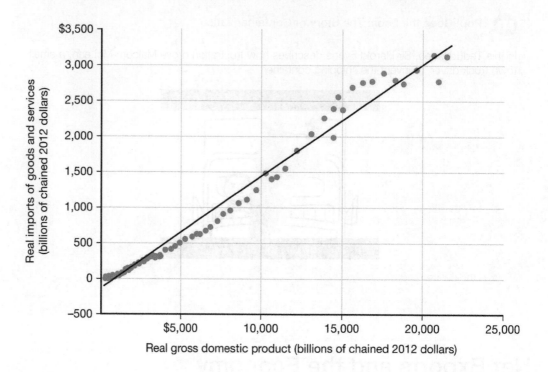

Source: Data from Bureau of Economic Analysis, accessed through Federal Reserve Economic Data (FRED) at https://fred.stlouisfed.org/series/IMPGSC1 and https://fred.stlouisfed.org/series/GDPC1.

Of course, trade flows in two directions: As incomes in other nations rise, the people of those nations will be able to buy more goods and services, including imports. But the imports of one country are the exports of another: As foreign incomes increase, then, we can expect U.S. exports to those foreign countries to increase. If foreign incomes were to decrease, our exports would likely fall.

Relative Prices

A change in the price level within a nation affects exports and imports. For example, when the price level increases in the United States (P_{us}), that makes U.S. exports more expensive for foreigners, so exports tend to decrease. At the same time, higher prices in the United States make foreign goods and services look relatively more price-attractive to U.S. buyers. Imports into the United States increase. A higher price level, by reducing exports and increasing imports, reduces net exports.

$$\uparrow P_{us} \Longrightarrow \downarrow X_{us} - \uparrow M_{us} = \downarrow\downarrow X_{n_{us}}$$

A lower price level in the United States does the opposite: It encourages exports and reduces imports, increasing net exports. As we saw in the chapter that introduced the aggregate demand and supply model, the negative relationship between net exports and the price level is called the *international trade effect* and is one reason for the negative slope of the aggregate demand curve.

Of course, trade is bilateral: One country's exports are another's imports. That means that the same analysis holds for changes in the foreign price level, P_f: An increase in the foreign price level will cause U.S. net exports to increase, while a decrease in the foreign price level will cause U.S. net exports to decrease.

$$\uparrow P_f \Longrightarrow \uparrow X_{us} - \downarrow M_{us} = \uparrow\uparrow X_{n_{us}}$$

The Exchange Rate

Because U.S. suppliers want to be paid in their own currency, the purchase of U.S. goods and services by foreign buyers generally first requires the purchase of dollars. Similarly, foreign sellers want to be paid in their own country's money, so purchases of foreign goods and services by U.S. buyers generally first require the purchase of foreign currencies.

The foreign exchange market is where the currency from one country is traded for the currency of another. The exchange rate tells us how big the bags are.

Source: vchal/Shutterstock.com

The rate at which dollars trade for foreign currencies is called the *exchange rate*. The exchange rate can be quoted in two different ways—either foreign currency per dollar, or dollars per unit of foreign currency. For example the exchange rate between the U.S. dollar and the Malaysian ringgit might be expressed as:

$$E_{\$/ringgit} = \frac{\$0.25}{ringgit}$$

So, each ringgit costs one quarter. If that's that case, you should be able to buy four ringgit for a dollar, which can be expressed as:

$$E_{ringgit/\$} = \frac{4 \; ringgit}{\$} = \frac{1}{E_{\$/ringgit}}$$

In other words, the two exchange rates we can use to quote the rate at which ringgit and dollars trade for one another are simply reciprocals of one another. Which way to quote the exchange rate is right? They both are! But it *is* easy to get turned around, which can lead to miscalculations. We recommend 1) keeping track of your units, and 2) choosing one way and sticking with it. *Our convention will be to quote the exchange rate in terms of foreign currency per dollar*: 4 ring-git/$; 110 Japanese yen/$, etc.

A little appreciation is always a nice thing . . . unless, of course, you're an exporter.

Source: ESB Professional/Shutterstock.com

Taken that way, an increase in the exchange rate means that foreigners must give up more of their own currency to obtain each dollar . . . or that each dollar taken to foreign exchange markets will fetch more foreign currency. This is generally referred to as an *appreciation* (or strengthening) of the dollar; the flip side of that coin is that the foreign currency has weakened, or *depreciated*.

Let's use a quick example to show how an appreciation of the dollar can impact U.S. net exports. Suppose a Malaysian is interested in importing the latest Miley Cyrus tell-all book, which sells in the United States for $10. At an exchange rate of 4 ringgit/$, our Malaysian bookworm will have to part with 40 ringgit. But if the exchange rate increases to 5 ringgit/$, he'll have to come up with 50 ringgit.

In other words, an increase in the exchange rate (quoted in foreign currency per dollar) makes U.S. products look more expensive to Malaysians, so U.S. exports decrease. At the same time, the stronger dollar makes Malaysian goods look *more* price attractive to Americans: They now get 5 ringgit for each dollar instead of just 4. So, U.S. imports increase. The net effect on U.S. net exports is unambiguous: They decrease.

$$\uparrow E_{ringgit/\$} \Longrightarrow \downarrow X_{us} - \uparrow M_{us} = \downarrow\downarrow X_{n_{us}}$$

The opposite happens if the exchange rate decreases: U.S. exports to Malaysia would increase, imports would decrease, and net exports would rise.

The link between exchange rate movements and net exports is strong, as shown in Figure 16.3. In the figure, the blue line shows net exports' share of GDP from 1973 to 2020. The red line shows the real weighted dollar exchange rate with the rest of the world (we use the reciprocal, which has units of $/foreign currency, so that the relationship between exchange rates and net exports is easier to see). In the figure, an increase in the exchange rate means that it takes more dollars to buy a unit of foreign currency, making U.S. exports more attractive and foreign imports less attractive. That's exactly what happens: During periods when it takes more dollars to buy foreign currency, net exports rise; when it takes fewer, net exports fall.

FIGURE 16.3 Exchange Rates and Net Exports, 1973–2020
The value of the dollar is strongly linked to the behavior of net exports. Here, the inflation-adjusted exchange rate (shown in red) is quoted in terms of dollars per foreign currency; an increase in the exchange rate represents a depreciation of the dollar that is associated with fewer imports, more exports, and increased net exports (shown in blue as a percentage of GDP).

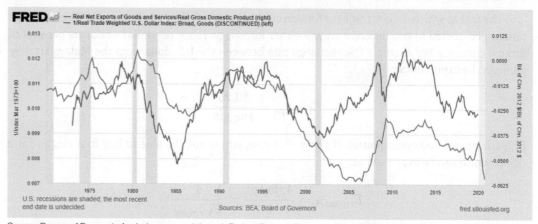

Source: Bureau of Economic Analysis, accessed through Federal Reserve Economic Data (FRED) at https://fred.stlouisfed.org/series/GDPC1, https://fred.stlouisfed.org/series/NETEXC, and https://fred.stlouisfed.org/series/RTWEXBGS. FRED® Graphs ©Federal Reserve Bank of St. Louis. All rights reserved. All FRED® Graphs appear courtesy of Federal Reserve Bank of St. Louis. https://fred.stlouisfed.org/.

Trade Policies

A country's exports depend on its own trade policies as well as the trade policies of other countries. A country may be able to increase its exports by providing some form of government assistance (such as special tax considerations for companies that export goods and services, government promotional efforts, assistance with research, or subsidies). A country's exports are also affected by the degree to which other countries restrict or encourage imports. The United States, for example, has sought changes in Japanese policies toward products such as U.S.-grown rice. Japan banned rice imports in the past, arguing it needed to protect its own producers. That has been a costly strategy; consumers in Japan typically pay as much as ten times the price consumers in the United States pay for rice. Japan has given in to pressure from the United States and other nations to end its ban on foreign rice as part of the GATT accord. That will increase U.S. exports and lower rice prices in Japan.

Similarly, a country's imports are affected by its trade policies and by the policies of its trading partners. A country can limit its imports of some goods and services by imposing tariffs or quotas on them—it may even ban the importation of some items. If foreign governments subsidize the manufacture of a particular good, then domestic imports of the good might increase. For example, if the governments of countries trading with the United States were to subsidize the production of steel, then U.S. companies would find it cheaper to purchase steel from abroad than at home, increasing U.S. imports of steel.

Preferences and Technology

Consumer preferences are one determinant of the consumption of any good or service; a shift in preferences for a foreign-produced good will affect the level of imports of that good. The preference among the French for movies and music produced in the United States has increased French imports of these services. Indeed, the shift in French preferences has been so strong that the government of France, claiming a threat to its cultural heritage, has restricted the showing of films produced in the United States. French radio stations are fined if more than 40% of the music they play is from "foreign" (in most cases, U.S.) rock groups.

Changes in technology can affect the kinds of capital firms import. Technological changes have changed production worldwide toward the application of computers to manufacturing processes, for example. This has led to increased demand for high-tech capital equipment, a sector in which the United States has a comparative advantage and tends to dominate world production. This has increased U.S. net exports.

It's common knowledge that the quality of a wine is directly related to the number of kangaroos on the label. Serve this excellent Australian merlot in France, however, and you might earn a date with the magistrate.

Source: Mihai_Andritoiu/ Shutterstock.com

Net Exports and Aggregate Demand

Net exports affect both the slope and the position of the aggregate demand curve. A change in the price level causes a change in net exports that moves the economy along its aggregate demand curve. That is the international trade effect described in our chapter on aggregate demand. A change in net exports produced by one of the *other* determinants of net exports listed above (incomes and price levels in other nations, the exchange rate, trade policies, and preferences and technology) will *shift* the aggregate demand curve. The magnitude of this shift equals the change in net exports times the multiplier, as shown in Figure 16.4. Panel (a) shows an increase in net exports; Panel (b) shows a decrease. In both cases, the aggregate demand curve shifts by the multiplier times the initial change in net exports, provided there is no other change in the other components of aggregate demand.

FIGURE 16.4 Changes in Net Exports and Aggregate Demand
In Panel (a), an increase in net exports shifts the aggregate demand curve to the right by an amount equal to the multiplier times the initial change in net exports. In Panel (b), an equal reduction in net exports shifts the aggregate demand curve to the left by the same amount.

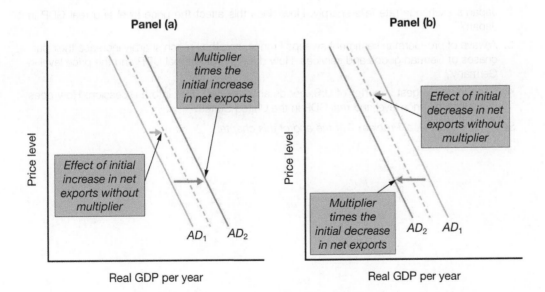

Changes in net exports that shift the aggregate demand curve can have a significant impact on the economy. The United States, for example, experienced a slowdown in the rate of growth in real

GDP in the second and third quarters of 1998—virtually all of this slowing was the result of a reduction in net exports caused by recessions that staggered economies throughout Asia. The Asian slide reduced incomes there and thus reduced Asian demand for U.S. goods and services. In the next section, we'll see another mechanism through which difficulties in other nations can cause changes in a nation's net exports and its level of real GDP in the short run.

Key Takeaways

- International trade allows the world's resources to be allocated on the basis of comparative advantage and thus allows the production of a larger quantity of goods and services than would be available without trade.
- Trade affects neither the economy's natural level of employment nor its real wage in the long run; those are determined by the demand for and the supply of labor.
- Growth in international trade has outpaced growth in world output over the past five decades.
- The chief determinants of net exports are domestic and foreign incomes, relative price levels, exchange rates, domestic and foreign trade policies, and preferences and technology.
- A change in the price level causes a change in net exports that moves the economy along its aggregate demand curve. This is the international trade effect. A change in net exports produced by one of the other determinants of net exports will shift the aggregate demand curve by an amount equal to the initial change in net exports times the multiplier.

Try It!

Draw graphs showing the aggregate demand and short-run aggregate supply curves in each of four countries: Mexico, Japan, Germany, and the United States. Assume that each country is initially in equilibrium with a real GDP of Y_1 and a price level of P_1. Now show how each of the following four events would affect aggregate demand, the price level, and real GDP in the country indicated.

1. The United States is the largest foreign purchaser of goods and services from Mexico. How does an economic expansion in the United States affect real GDP and the price level in Mexico?
2. Japan's exchange rate falls sharply. How does this affect the price level and real GDP in Japan?
3. A wave of pro-German sentiment sweeps France, and the French sharply increase their purchases of German goods and services. How does this affect real GDP and the price level in Germany?
4. Canada, the largest importer of U.S. goods and services, slips into a recession. How does this affect the price level and real GDP in the United States?

See related Numerical Problem 7 at the end of this chapter.

Case in Point: Canadian Net Exports Survive the Loonie's Rise

Source: Spiroview Inc/Shutterstock.com

Throughout 2003 and the first half of 2004, the Canadian dollar, nicknamed the loonie after the Canadian bird that is featured on its one-dollar coin, rose sharply in value against the U.S. dollar. Because the United States and Canada are major trading partners, the changing exchange rate suggested that, other things equal, Canadian exports to the United States would fall and imports rise. The resulting fall in net exports, other things equal, could slow the rate of growth in Canadian GDP.

Fortunately for Canada, "all other things" were not equal. In particular, strong income growth in the United States and China increased the demand for Canadian exports. In addition, the loonie's appreciation against other currencies was less dramatic, so Canadian exports remained competitive in those markets. While imports did increase as predicted, exports grew at an even faster rate, so net exports ended up increasing on the whole.

In sum, Canadian net exports grew, although not by as much as they would have had the loonie not appreciated. As Beata Caranci, an economist for Toronto Dominion Bank, put it, "We might have some bumpy months ahead but it definitely looks like the worst is over. While Canadian exports appear to have survived the loonie's run-up, their fortunes would be much brighter if the exchange rate were still at 65 cents."

See related Concept Problem 2 at the end of this chapter.

Source: Based on Steven Theobald, "Exports Surviving Loonie's Rise: Study," Toronto Star, July 13, 2004, p. D1.

Answers to Try It! Problems

1. Mexico's exports increase, shifting its aggregate demand curve to the right. Mexico's real GDP and price level rise, as shown in Panel (a).

2. Japan's net exports rise. This event shifts Japan's aggregate demand curve to the right, increasing its real GDP and price level, as shown in Panel (b).

3. Germany's net exports increase, shifting Germany's aggregate demand curve to the right, increasing its price level and real GDP, as shown in Panel (c).

4. U.S. exports fall, shifting the U.S. aggregate demand curve to the left, which will reduce the price level and real GDP, as shown in Panel (d).

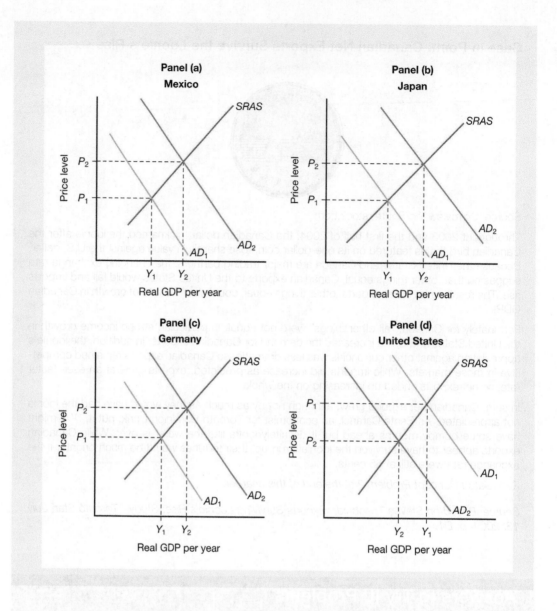

16.3 International Finance

Learning Objectives

1. Define a country's balance of payments, and explain what is included on the current and capital accounts.
2. Assuming that the market for a country's currency is in equilibrium, explain why the current account balance will always be the negative of the capital account balance.
3. Summarize the economic arguments used to counter public opposition to a current account deficit and a capital account surplus.

There is an important difference between trade that flows, say, from one city to another and trade that flows from one nation to another. Unless they share a common currency, as some of the nations of the European Union do, trade among nations requires that currencies be exchanged as well as goods and services. Suppose, for example, that buyers in Mexico purchase silk produced in China. The Mexican buyers will pay in Mexico's currency, the peso; the manufacturers of the silk must be paid in China's currency, the yuan. The flow of trade between Mexico and China, then, requires an exchange of pesos for yuan.

This section examines the relationship between spending that flows into a country and spending that flows out of it. These spending flows include not only spending for a nation's exports and imports, but also payments to owners of assets in other countries, international transfer payments, and purchases of foreign assets. The balance between spending flowing into a country and spending flowing out of it is called its **balance of payments**.

Keeping track of the balance of payments can sometimes be a real workout. We'll simplify our analysis in two ways:

- We'll ignore international *transfer payments*, which occur when an individual, firm, or government makes a gift to an individual, firm, or government in another country. Foreign aid is an example of an international transfer payment. International transfer payments play a relatively minor role in the international financial transactions of most countries; ignoring them won't affect our basic conclusions.

- We'll treat payments to foreign owners of factors of production used in a country as imports and payments received by owners of factors of production used in other countries as exports.

These two simplifications leave two reasons for demanding a country's currency. First, foreigners may want to purchase a country's goods and services (that is, its exports). Second, foreigners may want to purchase assets in the country—maybe stocks, bonds, or real estate. Of course, when an American goes to the foreign exchange market seeking, say, British pounds, that same American is supplying dollars to that market.

That accounts for the demand for dollars. But what about the supply—where does that come from? It comes from Americans, who take their dollars to the foreign exchange market in hopes of exchanging them for foreign currencies—say, British pounds—because they want to buy British goods, services, or assets.

In general, exchange rates are determined by the forces of demand and supply. Because exchange rates tend to adjust quickly, it's safe to assume, at any given moment, that the quantity of a currency demanded equals the quantity of the currency supplied. In other words, generally, the markets for most countries' currencies are in equilibrium.

Equilibrium in the market for a country's currency implies that the quantity of a particular country's currency demanded equals the quantity supplied:

EQUATION 16.2

$$\text{Quantity of Currency Demanded} = \text{Quantity of Currency Supplied}$$

As we mentioned above, the quantity of a currency *demanded* stems from export demand from the rest of the world (R.O.W.) and rest-of-world purchases of domestic assets. The quantity of a currency supplied stems from domestic demand for imports from the rest of the world and domestic purchases of rest-of-world assets. That lets us rewrite Equation 16.2 as:

EQUATION 16.3

$$\text{Exports} + \text{R.O.W. Purchases of Domestic Assets} =$$
$$\text{Imports} + \text{Domestic Purchases of R.O.W. Assets}$$

Unlike this young lady's checkbook, the balance of payments is *always* in balance—at least when the foreign exchange market is freely functioning.

Source: Nicoleta Ionescu/ Shutterstock.com

Accounting for International Payments

In this section, we'll build a set of accounts to track international payments. To do this, we'll use the equilibrium condition for foreign exchange markets given in Equation 16.3. With a bit of rearranging, we can rewrite that relationship as:

EQUATION 16.4

$$\text{Exports} - \text{Imports}$$
$$= -[(\text{R.O.W. Purchases of Domestic Assets}) - (\text{Domestic Purchases of R.O.W. Assets})]$$

Equation 16.4 represents an important relationship. The left side of the equation is net exports. It is the balance between spending flowing from foreign countries *into* a particular country for the purchase of its goods and services and spending flowing *out of* the country for the purchase of goods and services produced in other countries.

The **current account** is an accounting statement that includes all spending flows across a nation's border except those that represent purchases of assets. The **balance on current account** equals spending flowing into an economy from the rest of the world on current account less spending flowing from the nation to the rest of the world on current account. Given our two simplifying assumptions—that there are no international transfer payments and that we can treat rest-of-world purchases of domestic factor services as exports and domestic purchases of rest-of-world factor services as imports—the balance on current account equals net exports.

When the balance on current account is positive, spending flowing in for the purchase of goods and services exceeds spending that flows out, and the economy has a **current account surplus** (i.e., net exports are positive in our simplified analysis). When the balance on current account is negative, spending for goods and services that flows out of the country exceeds spending that flows in, and the economy has a **current account deficit** (i.e., net exports are negative in our simplified analysis).

current account

An accounting statement that includes all spending flows across a nation's border except those that represent purchases of assets.

balance on current account

Spending flowing into an economy from the rest of the world on current account less spending flowing from the nation to the rest of the world on current account.

current account surplus

Situation that occurs when spending flowing in for the purchase of goods and services exceeds spending that flows out.

current account deficit

Situation that occurs when spending for goods and services that flows out of the country exceeds spending that flows in.

Negative net exports? No worries—your current account deficit will be balanced against a capital account surplus!

Source: Andrii Yalanskyi/Shutterstock.com

A country's **capital account** reflects spending flows into and out of the country during a particular period for purchases of assets. The term in brackets on the right side of Equation 16.4 gives the balance between rest-of-world purchases of domestic assets and domestic purchases of rest-of-world assets; this balance is a country's **balance on capital account**. A positive balance on capital account is a **capital account surplus**. A capital account surplus means that buyers in the rest of the world are purchasing more of a country's assets than buyers in the domestic economy are spending on rest-of-world assets. A negative balance on capital account is a **capital account deficit**. It implies that buyers in the domestic economy are purchasing a greater volume of assets in other countries than buyers in other countries are spending on the domestic economy's assets. (Remember that the balance on capital account is the term *inside* the brackets on the right-hand side of Equation 16.4, and that there is a minus sign *outside* the parentheses.)

Equation 16.4 tells us that a country's balance on current account equals the negative of its balance on capital account.

EQUATION 16.5

$$\text{Current Account Balance} = -(\text{Capital Account Balance})$$

Let's see how that works. Suppose, for example, that buyers in the rest of the world are spending $100 billion per year acquiring assets in the United States, while U.S. buyers are spending $70 billion per year to acquire assets in the rest of the world. The United States, then, has a capital account surplus of $30 billion per year. Equation 16.5 tells us that the United States must have a current account deficit (net exports less than zero, or imports greater than exports) of $30 billion per year.

Alternatively, suppose buyers from the rest of the world acquire $25 billion in U.S. assets per year and that buyers in the United States buy $40 billion per year in assets in other countries. The economy has a capital account deficit of $15 billion (its capital account balance equals –$15 billion). Equation 16.5 tells us that the United States must have a current account surplus of $15 billion.

Assuming the market for a nation's currency is in equilibrium,

- A capital account surplus necessarily means a current account deficit. A capital account deficit necessarily means a current account surplus.

- Similarly, a current account surplus implies a capital account deficit; a current account deficit implies a capital account surplus.

Whenever the market for a country's currency is in equilibrium, and it virtually always is in the absence of exchange rate controls, Equation 16.5 is an identity—it must be true. Any surplus or deficit in the current account means the capital account has an offsetting deficit or surplus.

The accounting relationships underlying international finance hold as long as a country's currency market is in equilibrium. But what are the economic forces at work that cause these equalities to hold? Consider the global turmoil in 1997 and 1998, discussed in the chapter opener. Holders of foreign-denominated (especially Asian) assets, including currencies, were understandably concerned that the values of those assets might fall. To avoid a plunge in the values of their own holdings, many of them purchased U.S. assets. Those purchases of U.S. assets increased the U.S. surplus on capital account. To buy those assets, foreign purchasers had to purchase dollars: The demand for dollars increased.

At the same time, U.S. citizens became less willing to hold foreign (Asian, primarily) assets, and their preference for holding U.S. assets increased. As a result, United States citizens supplied fewer dollars to the foreign exchange market. The increased demand for dollars and the decreased supply of dollars sent the U.S. exchange rate higher, as shown in Panel (a) of Figure 16.5.

capital account

An accounting statement of spending flows into and out of the country during a particular period for purchases of assets.

balance on capital account

The balance between rest-of-world purchases of domestic assets and domestic purchases of rest-of-world assets.

capital account surplus

A positive balance on capital account.

capital account deficit

A negative balance on capital account.

Accountants may not be as interesting as economists, but they have their uses when it comes to international finance.

Source: alphaspirit.it/Shutterstock.com

FIGURE 16.5 A Change in the Exchange Rate Affected the U.S. Current and Capital Accounts in 1997 and 1998

Turmoil in currency markets all over the world in 1997 and 1998 increased the demand for dollars and decreased the supply of dollars in the foreign exchange market. That caused an increase in the U.S. exchange rate, as shown in Panel (a). Panel (b) shows actual values of the U.S. exchange rate during that period; Panel (c) shows U.S. balances on current and capital accounts. Notice that the balance on capital account generally rose while the balance on current account generally fell.

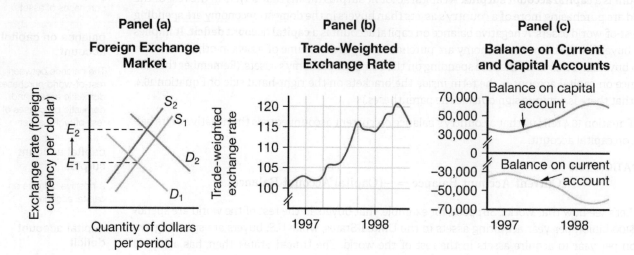

Panel (b) shows the actual movement of the U.S. exchange rate in 1997 and 1998. Notice the sharp increases in the exchange rate throughout most of the period. A higher exchange rate in the United States reduced U.S. exports and increased U.S. imports, which widened the current account deficit. Panel (c) shows the movement of the current and capital accounts in the United States in 1997 and 1998. Notice that as the capital account surplus increased, the current account deficit rose. A decrease in the exchange rate at the end of 1998 coincided with a movement of these balances in the opposite direction.

Deficits and Surpluses: Good or Bad?

For the past quarter century, the United States has had a current account deficit and a capital account surplus. Is this good or bad?

Viewed from the perspective of consumers, neither phenomenon seems to pose a problem. A current account deficit is likely to imply a trade deficit. That means more goods and services are flowing into the country than are flowing out. A capital account surplus means more spending is flowing into the country for the purchase of assets than is flowing out. It is hard to see the harm in any of that.

Public opinion, however, appears to regard a current account deficit and capital account surplus as highly undesirable, perhaps because people associate a trade deficit with a loss of jobs. But that is erroneous; employment in the long run is determined by forces that have nothing to do with a trade deficit. An increase in the trade deficit (that is, a reduction in net exports) reduces aggregate demand in the short run, but net exports are only one component of aggregate demand. Other factors—consumption, investment, and government purchases—affect aggregate demand as well. There is no reason a trade deficit should imply a loss of jobs.

What about foreign purchases of U.S. assets? One objection to such purchases is that if foreigners own U.S. assets, they will receive the income from those assets—spending will flow out of the country. But it is hard to see the harm in paying income to financial investors. When someone buys a bond issued by Microsoft, interest payments will flow from Microsoft to the bond holder. Does Microsoft view the purchase of its bond as a bad thing? Of course not! Despite the fact that Microsoft's payment of interest on the bond and the ultimate repayment of the face value of the bond will exceed what the company originally received from the bond purchaser, Microsoft is surely not unhappy with the arrangement. It expects to put that money to more productive use; that's the reason it issued the bond in the first place.

A second concern about foreign asset purchases is that the United States in some sense loses sovereignty when foreigners buy its assets. But why should this be a problem? Foreign-owned firms competing in U.S. markets are at the mercy of those markets, as are firms owned by U.S. nationals. Foreign owners of U.S. real estate have no special power. What about foreign buyers of bonds issued by the U.S. government? Foreigners owned about 33% of these bonds at the end of December 2020; they are thus the creditors for about one third of the national debt. But this position hardly puts them in control of the government of the United States. They hold an obligation of the U.S. government to pay them a certain amount of U.S. dollars on a certain date, nothing more. A foreign owner could sell his or her bonds, but more than $100 billion worth of these bonds are sold every day. The resale of U.S. bonds by a foreign owner will not likely have any significant effect on the U.S. government.

Some deficits can prove challenging . . . but a trade deficit isn't a bad thing at all.

Source: Hananeko_Studio/Shutterstock.com

In short, there is no economic justification for concern about having a current account deficit and a capital account surplus—nor would there be an economic reason to be concerned about the opposite state of affairs. The important feature of international trade is its potential to improve living standards for people. It is not a game in which current account balances are the scorecard.

Key Takeaways

- The balance of payments shows spending flowing into and out of a country.
- The current account is an accounting statement that includes all spending flows across a nation's border except those that represent purchases of assets. In our simplified analysis, the balance on current account equals net exports.
- A nation's balance on capital account equals rest-of-world purchases of its assets during a period less its purchases of rest-of-world assets.
- Provided that the market for a nation's currency is in equilibrium, the balance on current account equals the negative of the balance on capital account.
- There is no economic justification for viewing any particular current account balance as a good or bad thing.

Try It!

Compute the variables given in each of the following. Assume that the market for a nation's currency is in equilibrium and that the balance on current account equals net exports.

1. Suppose U.S. exports equal $300 billion, imports equal $400 billion, and rest-of-world purchases of U.S. assets equal $150 billion. What is the U.S. balance on current account? The balance on capital account? What is the value of U.S. purchases of rest-of-world assets?

2. Suppose Japanese exports equal ¥200 trillion (¥ is the symbol for the yen, Japan's currency), imports equal ¥120 trillion, and Japan's purchases of rest-of-world assets equal ¥90 trillion. What is the balance on Japan's current account? The balance on Japan's capital account? What is the value of rest-of-world purchases of Japan's assets?

3. Suppose Britain's purchases of rest-of-world assets equal £70 billion (£ is the symbol for the pound, Britain's currency), rest-of-world purchases of British assets equal £90 billion, and Britain's exports equal £40 billion. What is Britain's balance on capital account? Its balance on current account? Its total imports?

4. Suppose Mexico's purchases of rest-of-world assets equal $500 billion ($ is the symbol for the peso, Mexico's currency), rest-of-world purchases of Mexico's assets equal $700 billion,

and Mexico's imports equal $550 billion. What is Mexico's balance on capital account? Its balance on current account? Its total exports?

See related Numerical Problem 3 at the end of this chapter.

Case in Point: Alan Greenspan on the U.S. Current Account Deficit

Former Fed Chairperson Alan Greenspan always tells it like it is.

Source: Rob Crandall/Shutterstock.com

Large U.S. current account deficits have generated considerable alarm. But, is there cause for alarm? In a speech in December 2005, former Federal Reserve Chairman Alan Greenspan analyzed what he felt were the causes of the growing deficit and explained how the U.S. current account deficit may, under certain circumstances, decrease over time without a crisis.

"In November 2003, I noted that we saw little evidence of stress in funding the U.S. current account deficit even though the real exchange rate for the dollar, on net, had declined more than 10% since early 2002. . . . Two years later, little has changed except that our current account deficit has grown still larger. Most policy makers marvel at the seeming ease with which the United States continues to finance its current account deficit.

"Of course, deficits that cumulate to ever-increasing net external debt, with its attendant rise in servicing costs, cannot persist indefinitely. At some point, foreign investors will balk at a growing concentration of claims against U.S. residents . . . and will begin to alter their portfolios. . . . The rise of the U.S. current account deficit over the past decade appears to have coincided with a pronounced new phase of globalization that is characterized by a major acceleration in U.S. productivity growth and the decline in what economists call home bias. In brief, home bias is the parochial tendency of persons, though faced with comparable or superior foreign opportunities, to invest domestic savings in the home country. The decline in home bias is reflected in savers increasingly reaching across national borders to invest in foreign assets. The rise in U.S. productivity attracted much of those savings toward investments in the United States. . . .

"Accordingly, it is tempting to conclude that the U.S. current account deficit is essentially a byproduct of long-term secular forces, and thus is largely benign. After all, we do seem to have been able to finance our international current account deficit with relative ease in recent years.

"But does the apparent continued rise in the deficits of U.S. individual households and nonfinancial businesses themselves reflect growing economic strain? (We do not think so.) And does it matter how those deficits of individual economic entities are being financed? Specifically, does the recent growing proportion of these deficits being financed, net, by foreigners matter? . . .

"If the currently disturbing drift toward protectionism is contained and markets remain sufficiently flexible, changing terms of trade, interest rates, asset prices, and exchange rates will cause U.S. saving to rise, reducing the need for foreign finance, and reversing the trend of the past decade toward increasing reliance on it. If, however, the pernicious drift toward fiscal instability in the United States and elsewhere is not arrested and is compounded by a protectionist reversal of globalization, the adjustment process could be quite painful for the world economy."

See related Concept Problem 7 at the end of this chapter.

Source: Based on Alan Greenspan, "International Imbalances" (speech, Advancing Enterprise Conference, London, England, December 2, 2005), available at http://www.federalreserve.gov/ boarddocs/speeches/2005/200512022/default.htm.

Answers to Try It! Problems

1. All figures are in billions of U.S. dollars per period. The left-hand side of Equation 16.4 is the current account balance

   Exports − imports = \$300 − \$400 = −\$100

   The balance on capital account is

   −\$100 = −(capital account balance)

   Solving this equation for the capital account balance, we find that it is \$100. The term in parentheses on the right-hand side of Equation 16.4 is also the balance on capital account. We thus have

   \$100 = \$150 − U.S. purchases of rest-of-world assets

   Solving this for U.S. purchase of rest-of-world assets, we find they are \$50.

2. All figures are in trillions of yen per period. The left-hand side of Equation 16.4 is the current account balance

   Exports − imports = ¥200 − ¥120 = ¥80

   The balance on capital account is

   ¥80 = −(capital account balance)

   Solving this equation for the capital account balance, we find that it is −¥80. The term in parentheses on the right-hand side of Equation 16.4 is also the balance on capital account. We thus have

   −¥80 = rest-of-world purchases of Japan's assets − ¥90

   Solving this for the rest-of-world purchases of Japan's assets, we find they are ¥10.

3. All figures are in billions of pounds per period. The term in parentheses on the right-hand side of Equation 16.4 is the balance on capital account. We thus have

   £90 − £70 = £20

   The balance on current account is

   Current account balance = −(£20)

   The left-hand side of Equation 16.4 is also the current account balance

   £40 − imports = −£20

   Solving for imports, we find they are £60. Britain's balance on current account is −£20 billion, its balance on capital account is £20 billion, and its total imports equal £60 billion per period.

4. All figures are in billions of pesos per period. The term in parentheses on the right-hand side of Equation 16.4 is the balance on capital account. We thus have

   \$700 − \$500 = \$200

   The balance on current account is

   Current account balance = −(\$200)

   The left-hand side of Equation 16.4 is also the current account balance

   Exports − \$550 = −\$200

   Solving for exports, we find they are \$350.

16.4 Exchange Rate Systems

Learning Objectives

1. Define the various types of exchange rate systems.
2. Discuss some of the pros and cons of different exchange rate systems.

Exchange rates are determined by demand and supply. But governments can influence those exchange rates in various ways. The extent and nature of government involvement in currency markets define alternative systems of exchange rates. In this section we will examine some common systems and explore some of their macroeconomic implications.

There are three broad categories of exchange rate systems. In one system, exchange rates are set purely by private market forces with no government involvement. Values change constantly as the demand for and supply of currencies fluctuate. In another system, currency values are allowed to change, but governments participate in currency markets in an effort to influence those values. Finally, governments may seek to fix the values of their currencies, either through participation in the market or through regulatory policy.

Free-Floating Systems

free-floating exchange rate system

System in which governments and central banks do not participate in the market for foreign exchange.

In a **free-floating exchange rate system**, governments and central banks do not participate in the market for foreign exchange. The relationship between governments and central banks on the one hand, and currency markets on the other, is much the same as the typical relationship between these official institutions and stock markets. Governments may regulate stock markets to prevent fraud, but stock values themselves are left to float in the market. The U.S. government, for example, does not intervene in the stock market to influence stock prices.

The concept of a completely free-floating exchange rate system is a theoretical one. In practice, all governments or central banks intervene in currency markets in an effort to influence exchange rates. Some countries, such as the United States, intervene only to a small degree, so that the notion of a free-floating exchange rate system comes close to what actually exists in the United States.

Exchange rates are fully flexible in a free-floating system.

Source: fizkes/Shutterstock.com

A free-floating system has the advantage of being self-regulating. There is no need for government intervention if the exchange rate is left to the market. Market forces also restrain large swings in demand or supply. Suppose, for example, that a dramatic shift in world preferences led to a sharply increased demand for goods and services produced in Canada. This would increase the demand for Canadian dollars, raise Canada's exchange rate, and make Canadian goods and services more expensive for foreigners to buy. Some of the impact of the swing in foreign demand would thus be absorbed in a rising exchange rate. In effect, a free-floating exchange rate acts as a buffer to insulate an economy from the impact of international events.

The primary difficulty with free-floating exchange rates lies in their unpredictability. Contracts between buyers and sellers in different countries must not only reckon with possible changes in prices and other factors during the lives of those contracts, but also consider the possibility of exchange rate changes. An agreement by a U.S. distributor to purchase a certain quantity of Canadian lumber each year, for example, will be affected by the possibility that the exchange rate between the Canadian dollar and the U.S. dollar will change while the contract is in effect. Fluctuating exchange rates make international transactions riskier and thus increase the cost of doing business with other countries.

Managed Float Systems

Governments and central banks often intervene in foreign exchange markets to increase or decrease their exchange rates by buying or selling their own currencies. Exchange rates are still generally free to float, but governments try to influence their values. Government or central bank participation in a floating exchange rate system is called a **managed float**.

Countries that have a floating exchange rate system intervene from time to time in the currency market. Typically, the purpose of such intervention is to prevent sudden large swings in the value of a nation's currency. Such intervention is likely to have only a small impact, if any, on exchange rates. Roughly $1.5 trillion worth of currencies changes hands every day in the world market; it is difficult for any one agency—even an agency the size of the U.S. government or the Fed—to force significant changes in exchange rates.

Still, governments or central banks can sometimes influence their exchange rates. Suppose the price of a country's currency is rising very rapidly. The country's government or central bank might want to stave off further increases in order to prevent a major reduction in net exports. An announcement that a further increase in its exchange rate is unacceptable, followed by large sales of that country's currency by the central bank in order to bring its exchange rate down, can sometimes convince other participants in the currency market that the exchange rate will not rise further. That change in expectations could reduce demand for and increase supply of the currency, and hold the exchange rate down.

In a managed float, the government generally lets exchange rates go where they want . . . but sometimes gives them a little nudge.

Source: Four Oaks/Shutterstock.com

> **managed float**
> Government or central bank participation in a floating exchange rate system.

Fixed Exchange Rates

In a **fixed exchange rate system**, the exchange rate between two currencies is set by government policy. There are several mechanisms through which fixed exchange rates may be maintained. Whatever the system for maintaining these rates, however, all fixed exchange rate systems share some important features.

> **fixed exchange rate system**
> System in which the exchange rate between two currencies is set by government policy.

A Commodity Standard

In a **commodity standard system**, countries fix the value of their respective currencies relative to a certain commodity or group of commodities. With each currency's value fixed in terms of the commodity, currencies are fixed relative to one another.

For centuries, the values of many currencies were fixed relative to gold. Suppose, for example, that the price of gold were fixed at $20 per ounce in the United States. This would mean that the government of the United States was committed to exchanging 1 ounce of gold with anyone who handed over $20. (That was the case in the United States—and $20 was roughly the price—up to 1933.) Now suppose that the exchange rate between the British pound and gold was £5 per ounce of gold. With £5 and $20 both trading for 1 ounce of gold, £1 would exchange for $4. No one would pay more than $4 for £1, because $4 could always be exchanged for 1/5 ounce of gold, and that gold could be exchanged for £1. And no one would sell £1 for less than $4, because the owner of £1 could always exchange it for 1/5 ounce of gold, which could be exchanged for $4. In practice, actual currency val-

> **commodity standard system**
> System in which countries fix the value of their respective currencies relative to a certain commodity or group of commodities.

ues could vary slightly from the levels implied by their commodity values because of the costs involved in exchanging currencies for gold, but these variations are slight.

When each country fixes the price of gold in its home currency, the exchange rate ends up being fixed, too.

Source: kwarkot/Shutterstock.com

Under the gold standard, the quantity of money was regulated by the quantity of gold in a country. If, for example, the United States guaranteed to exchange dollars for gold at the rate of $20 per ounce, it could not issue more money than it could back up with the gold it owned.

The gold standard was a self-regulating system. Suppose that at the fixed exchange rate implied by the gold standard, the supply of a country's currency exceeded the demand. That would imply that spending flowing out of the country exceeded spending flowing in. As residents supplied their currency to make foreign purchases, foreigners acquiring that currency could redeem it for gold, since countries guaranteed to exchange gold for their currencies at a fixed rate. Gold would end up flowing out of a country running a deficit. Given an obligation to exchange the country's currency for gold, a reduction in a country's gold holdings would force it to reduce its money supply. That would reduce aggregate demand in the country, lowering income and the price level. But both of those events would increase net exports in the country, eliminating the deficit in the balance of payments. Balance would be achieved, but at the cost of a recession. A country with a surplus in its balance of payments would experience an inflow of gold. That would boost its money supply and increase aggregate demand. That, in turn, would generate higher prices and higher real GDP. Those events would reduce net exports and correct the surplus in the balance of payments, but again at the cost of changes in the domestic economy.

Because of this tendency for imbalances in a country's balance of payments to be corrected only through changes in the entire economy, nations began abandoning the gold standard in the 1930s. That was the period of the Great Depression, during which world trade virtually ground to a halt. World War II made the shipment of goods an extremely risky proposition, so trade remained minimal during the war. As the war was coming to an end, representatives of the United States and its allies met in 1944 at Bretton Woods, New Hampshire, to fashion a new mechanism through which international trade could be financed after the war. The system was to be one of fixed exchange rates, but with much less emphasis on gold as a backing for the system.

Fixed Exchange Rates Through Intervention

The Bretton Woods Agreement called for each currency's value to be fixed relative to other currencies. The mechanism for maintaining these rates, however, was to be intervention by governments and central banks in the currency market.

Again suppose that the exchange rate between the dollar and the British pound is fixed at $4 per £1. Suppose further that this rate is an equilibrium rate, as illustrated in Figure 16.6. As long as the fixed rate coincides with the equilibrium rate, the fixed exchange rate operates in the same fashion as a free-floating rate.

Now suppose that the British choose to purchase more U.S. goods and services. The supply of pounds increases, and the equilibrium exchange rate for the pound (in terms of dollars) falls to, say, $3. Under the terms of the Bretton Woods Agreement, Britain and the United States would be required to intervene in the market to bring the exchange rate back to the rate fixed in the agreement, $4. If the adjustment were to be made by the British central bank, the Bank of England, it would have to purchase pounds. It would do so by exchanging dollars it had previously acquired in other transactions for pounds. As it sold dollars, it would take in checks written in pounds. When a central bank sells an asset, the checks that come into the central bank reduce the money supply and bank reserves in that country. We saw in the chapter explaining the money supply, for example, that the sale of bonds by the Fed reduces the U.S. money supply. Similarly, the sale of dollars by the Bank of England would reduce the British money supply. In order to bring its exchange rate back to the agreed-to level, Britain would have to carry out a contractionary monetary policy.

FIGURE 16.6 Maintaining a Fixed Exchange Rate Through Intervention
Initially, the equilibrium price of the British pound equals $4, the fixed rate between the pound and the dollar. Now suppose an increased supply of British pounds lowers the equilibrium price of the pound to $3. The Bank of England could purchase pounds by selling dollars in order to shift the demand curve for pounds to D_2. Alternatively, the Fed could shift the demand curve to D_2 by buying pounds.

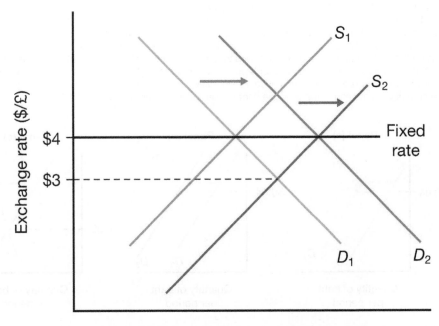

Quantity of British pounds per period

Alternatively, the Fed could intervene. It could purchase pounds, writing checks in dollars. But when a central bank purchases assets, it adds reserves to the system and increases the money supply. The United States would thus be forced to carry out an expansionary monetary policy.

Fixed exchange rate systems offer the advantage of predictable currency values—when they are working. But for fixed exchange rates to work, the countries participating in them must maintain domestic economic conditions that will keep equilibrium currency values close to the fixed rates. Sovereign nations must be willing to coordinate their monetary and fiscal policies. Achieving that kind of coordination among independent countries can be a difficult task.

When exchange rates are fixed but fiscal and monetary policies are not coordinated, equilibrium exchange rates can move away from their fixed levels. Once exchange rates start to diverge, the effort to force currencies up or down through market intervention can be extremely disruptive. And when countries suddenly decide to give that effort up, exchange rates can swing sharply in one direction or another. When that happens, the main virtue of fixed exchange rates, their predictability, is lost.

Thailand's experience with the baht illustrates the potential difficulty with attempts to maintain a fixed exchange rate. Thailand's central bank had held the exchange rate between the dollar and the baht steady, at a price for the baht of $0.04. Several factors, including weakness in the Japanese economy, reduced the demand for Thai exports and thus reduced the demand for the baht, as shown in Panel (a) of Figure 16.7. Thailand's central bank, committed to maintaining the price of the baht at $0.04, bought baht to increase the demand, as shown in Panel (b). Central banks buy their own currency using their reserves of foreign currencies. We have seen that when a central bank sells bonds, the money supply falls. When it sells foreign currency, the result is no different. Sales of foreign currency by Thailand's central bank in order to purchase the baht thus reduced Thailand's money supply and reduced the bank's holdings of foreign currencies. As currency traders began to suspect that the bank might give up its effort to hold the baht's value, they

In the Bretton Woods adjustable peg system, countries used monetary policy to peg the value of their currency to the U.S. dollar.

Source: David Pereiras/
Shutterstock.com

sold baht, shifting the supply curve to the right, as shown in Panel (c). That forced the central bank to buy even more baht—selling even more foreign currency—until it finally gave up the effort and allowed the baht to become a free-floating currency. By the end of 1997, the baht had lost nearly half its value relative to the dollar.

FIGURE 16.7 The Anatomy of a Currency Collapse

Weakness in the Japanese economy, among other factors, led to a reduced demand for the baht, as shown in Panel (a). That put downward pressure on the baht's value relative to other currencies. Committed to keeping the price of the baht at $0.04, Thailand's central bank bought baht to increase the demand, as shown in Panel (b). However, as holders of baht and other Thai assets began to fear that the central bank might give up its effort to prop up the baht, they sold baht, shifting the supply curve for baht to the right, as shown in Panel (c), which put even more downward pressure on the baht's price. Finally, in July of 1997, the central bank gave up its effort to prop up the currency. By the end of the year, the baht's dollar value had fallen to about $0.02.

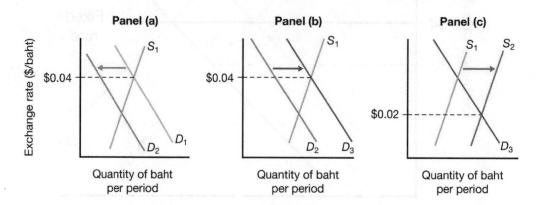

As we saw in the introduction to this chapter, the plunge in the baht was the first in a chain of currency crises that rocked the world in 1997 and 1998. International trade has the great virtue of increasing the availability of goods and services to the world's consumers. But financing trade—and the way nations handle that financing—can create difficulties.

The difficulty of maintaining fixed exchange rates, coupled with the loss of control over the money supply that maintaining a fixed exchange rate requires, ultimately brought about the demise of the Bretton Woods system. Japan and West Germany gave up the effort to maintain the fixed values of their currencies in the spring of 1971 and announced they were withdrawing from the Bretton Woods system. President Richard Nixon pulled the United States out of the system in August of that year, and the system collapsed. An attempt to revive fixed exchange rates in 1973 collapsed almost immediately, and the world has operated largely on a managed float ever since.

The fact that coordination of monetary and fiscal policies is difficult does not mean it is impossible. Eleven members of the European Union not only agreed to fix their exchange rates to one another, they agreed to adopt a common currency, the euro. The new currency was introduced in 1998 and became fully adopted in 1999. Since then, eight other nations have joined. The nations that adopted it agreed to strict limits on their fiscal policies. Each continues to have its own central bank, but these national central banks operate similarly to the regional banks of the Federal Reserve System in the United States. The new European Central Bank conducts monetary policy throughout the area. Details of this revolutionary venture and the extraordinary problems it has encountered in recent years are provided in "Case in Point: The Euro".

Key Takeaways

- In a free-floating exchange rate system, exchange rates are determined by demand and supply.

- In a managed-float system, exchange rates are determined by demand and supply, but governments intervene as buyers or sellers of currencies in an effort to influence exchange rates.

- In a fixed exchange rate system, exchange rates among currencies are not allowed to change. The gold standard and the Bretton Woods system are examples of fixed exchange rate systems.

Try It!

Suppose a nation's central bank is committed to holding the value of its currency, the mon, at $2 per mon. Suppose further that holders of the mon fear that its value is about to fall and begin selling mon to purchase U.S. dollars. What will happen in the market for mon? Explain your answer carefully, and illustrate it using a demand and supply graph for the market for mon. What action will the nation's central bank take? Use your graph to show the result of the central bank's action. Why might this action fuel concern among holders of the mon about its future prospects? What difficulties will this create for the nation's central bank?

See related Concept Problem 13 at the end of this chapter.

Case in Point: The Euro

Just like the fifty states all share the dollar, the nineteen member nations of the eurozone all share this colorful currency.

Source: D-VISIONS/Shutterstock.com

It was the most dramatic development in international finance since the collapse of the Bretton Woods system. A new currency, the euro, began trading among eleven European nations—Austria, Belgium, Finland, France, Germany, Ireland, Italy, Luxembourg, the Netherlands, Portugal, and Spain—in 1999. During a three-year transition, each nation continued to have its own currency, which traded at a fixed rate with the euro. Today, most of Europe now operates as the ultimate fixed exchange rate regime, a region with a single currency.

To participate in this radical experiment, the nations switching to the euro had to agree to give up considerable autonomy in monetary and fiscal policy. While each nation continues to have its own central bank, those central banks operate more like regional banks of the Federal Reserve System in the United States; they have no authority to conduct monetary policy. That authority is vested in a new central bank, the European Central Bank.

The participants also agreed in principle to strict limits on their fiscal policies. Their deficits could be no greater than 3% of nominal GDP, and their total national debt could not exceed 60% of nominal GDP.

The fact that many of the euro nations had disregarded these limits became a major problem for the new currency when the recession and financial crisis hit in 2008. The biggest "sinner" turned out to be Greece, but there were others, such as Italy, that also had not adhered to the agreement. The fiscal situation of other countries, such as Ireland, went sour as the recession and financial problems deepened. The countries that seemed most at risk of being unable to pay their sovereign (government) debts as they became due came to be known as the PIIGS—Portugal,

Ireland, Italy, Greece, and Spain—but there was a period in 2011 when even the interest rate on French bonds was abnormally high. The whole world seemed to be waiting throughout most of 2011 to see if the euro would hold together and, in particular, if Greece would default on its debt.

Finally, in early 2012, the situation seemed to calm down. The European Union nations (excluding the United Kingdom and the Czech Republic, which were not part of the eurozone) agreed to a new treaty that again requires fiscal discipline but this time has more enforcement associated with it. The European Union was setting up the European Stability Mechanism: a fund to help out with short-term liquidity problems that nations might encounter. Greece agreed to tough demands to reduce its deficit and then became eligible for a second EU bailout. It also managed to negotiate a debt-restricting deal with its private-sector lenders.

The euro has been a mixed blessing for eurozone countries trying to get through this difficult period. For example, guarantees that the Irish government made concerning bank deposits and debt have been better received, because Ireland is part of the euro system. On the other hand, if Ireland had a floating currency, the country could allow its value to fall during periods of recession, boosting net exports and aggregate demand. The euro exchange rate has probably benefited German exports, since a German currency would probably trade at a premium over the euro, but it has hurt exports from countries whose single-nation currencies would likely be weaker.

Also, even though there is a single currency, each country in the eurozone issues its own debt. The smaller market for each country's debt, each with different risk premiums, makes them less liquid, especially in difficult financial times. In contrast, the U.S. government is a single issuer of federal debt.

Even with general regulation of overall parameters, fiscal policy for the nineteen nations is largely a separate matter. Each has its own retirement and unemployment insurance programs, for example. In the United States, if one state is experiencing high unemployment, more federal unemployment insurance benefits will flow to that state. But if unemployment rises in Portugal, for example, its budget deficit will be negatively impacted, and Portugal will have to undertake additional austerity measures to stay within the EU-imposed deficit limit.

The fate of the euro remains uncertain. Even with the restructuring and bailouts, will Greece be able to meet its debt obligations? In early 2017 there were renewed worries that Greece could default on debt payments due in the summer, and the interest rate on Greek bonds again spiked. Is Grexit, Greek exit from the eurozone, on the horizon? If that happens, what changes for the euro might follow? For example, the value of the currency might appreciate if Greece and possibly other weaker economies in the eurozone left the arrangement. Or might the whole experiment collapse? Agreements to get through crises have tended to form at the eleventh hour, and this one may end in the same way, or maybe . . .

See related Concept Problem 12 at the end of this chapter.

Answer to Try It! Problem

The value of the mon is initially $2. Fear that the mon might fall will lead to an increase in its supply to S_2, putting downward pressure on the currency. To maintain the value of the mon at $2, the central bank will buy mon, thus shifting the demand curve to D_2. This policy, though, creates two difficulties. First, it requires that the bank sell other currencies, and a sale of any asset by a central bank is a contractionary monetary policy. Second, the sale depletes the bank's holdings of foreign currencies. If holders of the mon fear the central bank will give up its effort, then they might sell mon, shifting the supply curve farther to the right and forcing even more vigorous action by the central bank.

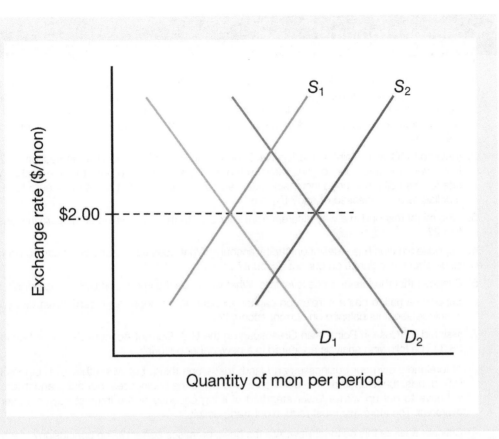

16.5 Review and Practice

Summary

In this chapter we examined the role of net exports in the economy. Export and import demand are influenced by many different factors, the most important being domestic and foreign income levels, changes in relative prices, the exchange rate, and preferences and technology. An increase in net exports shifts the aggregate demand curve to the right; a reduction shifts it to the left.

In the foreign exchange market, the equilibrium exchange rate is determined by the intersection of the demand and supply curves for a currency. Given the ease with which most currencies can be traded, we can assume this equilibrium is achieved, so that the quantity of a currency demanded equals the quantity supplied. An economy can experience current account surpluses or deficits. The balance on current account equals the negative of the balance on capital account. One reason for the current account deficit in the United States is the U.S. capital account surplus; the United States has attracted a great deal of foreign financial investment.

The chapter closed with an examination of floating and fixed exchange rate systems. Fixed exchange rate systems include commodity-based systems and fixed rates that are maintained through intervention. Exchange rate systems have moved from a gold standard, to a system of fixed rates with intervention, to a mixed set of arrangements of floating and fixed exchange rates.

Concept Problems

1. David Ricardo, a famous English economist of the nineteenth century, stressed that a nation has a comparative advantage in those products for which its efficiency relative to other nations is the highest. He argued in favor of specialization and trade based on comparative, not absolute, advantage. From a global perspective, what would be the "advantage" of such a system?

2. (Related to "Case in Point: Canadian Net Exports Survive the Loonie's Rise" in Section 28.2.) For several months prior to your vacation trip to Naples, Italy, you note that the exchange rate for the dollar has been increasing relative to the euro (that is, it takes more euro to buy a dollar). Are you pleased or sad? Explain.

3. Who might respond in a way different from your own to the falling value of the euro in Question 2?

4. Suppose a nation has a deficit on capital account. What does this mean? What can you conclude about its balance on current account?

5. Suppose that the foreign price level falls. What would be the impact on U.S. net exports?

6. Suppose a nation has a surplus on capital account. What does this mean? What can you conclude about its balance on current account?

7. (Related to "Case in Point: Alan Greenspan on the U.S. Current Account Deficit" in Section 28.3.) The following analysis appeared in a newspaper editorial:

   "If foreigners own our businesses and land, that's one thing, but when they own billions in U.S. bonds, that's another. We don't care who owns the businesses, but our grandchildren will have to put up with a lower standard of living because of the interest payments sent overseas. Therefore, we must reduce our trade deficit."

   Critically analyze this editorial view. Are the basic premises correct? The conclusion?

8. In the years prior to the abandonment of the gold standard, foreigners cashed in their dollars and the U.S. Treasury "lost gold" at unprecedented rates. Today, the dollar is no longer tied to gold and is free to float. What are the fundamental differences between a currency based on the gold standard and one that is allowed to float? What would the United States "lose" if foreigners decided to "cash in" their dollars today?

9. Can there be a deficit on current account and a deficit on capital account at the same time? Explain.

10. Suppose the people of a certain economy increase their spending on foreign-produced goods and services. What will be the effect on real GDP and the price level in the short run? In the long run?

11. Now suppose the people of a certain economy reduce their spending on foreign-produced goods and services. What will be the effect on real GDP and the price level in the short run? In the long run?

12. (Related to "Case in Point: The Euro" in Section 28.4.) Canada, Mexico, and the United States have a free trade zone. What would be some of the advantages of having a common currency as well? The disadvantages? Do you think it would be a good idea? Why or why not?

13. (Related to "Try It!" in Section 28.4.) Suppose that the government of Japan has fixed the exchange rate between its yen and the U.S. dollar at 100 yen/$. If the equilibrium exchange rate in a freely floating system were 120 yen/$, would the Japanese central bank accumulate or lose dollar reserves? Can this situation create the opportunity for a speculative attack against the yen?

Numerical Problems

1. For each of the following scenarios, determine whether the aggregate demand curve will shift. If so, in which direction will it shift and by how much?

a. A change in consumer preferences leads to an initial $25 billion decrease in net exports. The multiplier is 1.5.

b. A change in trade policies leads to an initial $25 billion increase in net exports. The multiplier is 1.

c. There is an increase in the domestic price level from 1 to 1.05, while the price level of the country's major trading partner does not change. The multiplier is 2.

d. Recession in a country's trading partner lowers exports by $20 billion. The multiplier is 2.

2. Fill in the missing items in the table below. All figures are in U.S. billions of dollars.

	U.S. Exports	U.S. Imports	Domestic Purchases of Foreign Assets	Rest-of-world Purchases of U.S. Assets
a.	100	100	400	
b.	100	200		200
c.	300		400	600
d.		800	800	1,100

3. (Related to "Try It!" in Section 28.3.) Suppose the market for a country's currency is in equilibrium and that its exports equal $700 billion, its purchases of rest-of-world assets equal $1,000 billion, and foreign purchases of its assets equal $1,200 billion. Assuming it has no international transfer payments and that output is measured as GDP:

a. What are the country's imports?

b. What is the country's balance on current account?

c. What is the country's balance on capital account?

4. Suppose that the market for a country's currency is in equilibrium and that its exports equal $400 billion, its imports equal $500 billion, and rest-of-world purchases of the country's assets equal $100 billion. Assuming it has no international transfer payments and that output is measured as GDP:

a. What is the country's balance on current account?

b. What is the country's balance on capital account?

c. What is the value of the country's purchases of rest-of-world assets?

5. The information below describes the trade-weighted exchange rate for the dollar (standardized at a value of 100) and net exports (in billions of dollars) for an eight-month period.

Month	Trade-weighted Exchange Rate	Net Exports
January	100.5	−9.8
February	99.9	−11.6
March	100.5	−13.5
April	100.3	−14.0
May	99.6	−15.6
June	100.9	−14.2
July	101.4	−14.9
August	101.8	−16.7

a. Plot the data on a graph.

b. Do the data support the expected relationship between the trade-weighted exchange rate and net exports? Explain.

6. The graph below shows the foreign exchange market between the United States and Japan before and after an increase in the demand for Japanese goods by U.S. consumers.

a. If the exchange rate was free-floating prior to the change in demand for Japanese goods, what was its likely value?

b. After the change in demand, the free-floating exchange rate would be how many yen per dollar?

c. If the Japanese central bank wanted to keep the exchange rate fixed at its initial value, how many dollars would it have to buy?

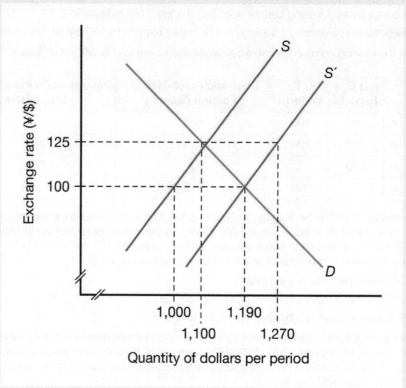

7. (Related to "Try It!" in Section 28.2.) Suppose Japan relaxes its restrictions on imports of foreign goods and services and begins importing more from the United States. Illustrate graphically how this will affect the U.S. exchange rate, price level, and level of real GDP in the short run and in the long run. How will it affect these same variables in Japan? (Assume both economies are initially operating at their potential levels of output.)

8. Suppose U.S. investors begin purchasing assets in Mexico. Illustrate graphically how this will affect the U.S. exchange rate, price level, and level of real GDP in the short run and in the long run. How will it affect these same variables in Mexico? (Assume both economies are initially operating at their potential levels of output.)

9. Suppose foreigners begin buying more assets in the United States. Illustrate graphically how this will affect the U.S. exchange rate, price level, and level of real GDP in the short run and in the long run. (Assume the economy is initially operating at its potential output.)

Endnotes

1. NAFTA was renegotiated under the Trump administration; the new agreement is called the U.S. – Mexico – Canada Agreement (USMCA).

2. Brexit was finalized December 31, 2020.

3. For an interesting history of this remarkable development, see Marc Levinson, *The Box: How the Shipping Container Made the World Smaller and the World Economy Bigger* (Princeton: Princeton University Press, 2006).

CHAPTER 17

A Brief History of Macroeconomic Thought and Policy

17.1 Start Up: Three Revolutions in Macroeconomic Thought

It is the 1930s. Many people have begun to wonder if the United States will ever escape the Great Depression's cruel grip. Forecasts that prosperity lies just around the corner take on a hollow ring.

The collapse seems to defy the logic of the dominant economic view—that economies should be able to reach full employment through a process of self-correction. The old ideas of macroeconomics just don't seem to work anymore; it's not clear what new ideas should replace them.

In Britain, Cambridge University economist John Maynard Keynes is struggling with ideas that he thinks will stand conventional wisdom on its head. He's confident that he has found the key not only to understanding the Great Depression, but also to correcting it: The careful use of government's powers to tax and spend can offset the animal spirits that create recessions.

Fast forward: It is the 1960s, and by now most economists believe that Keynes's ideas best explain the business cycle. The tools Keynes suggested are in widespread use by governments all over the world; fiscal policy management in the United States appears to have been a spectacular success. But at the University of Chicago, economist Milton Friedman is fighting a lonely battle against the economics of Keynes. He insists that fiscal policy cannot work, and that money, not fiscal policy, more powerfully influences aggregate demand. Paradoxically, Friedman then suggests that the central bank should *not* use monetary policy to guide the economy back to its potential output. Instead, the monetary authorities should adopt a policy of steady money growth, leaving the economy to adjust to long-run equilibrium on its own.

It is 1970. The economy has just taken a startling turn: Real GDP is falling, but inflation is rising. A young economist at Carnegie–Mellon University, Robert E. Lucas, Jr., finds this a paradox, one that he thinks cannot be explained by Keynes's theory. He begins work on a radically new approach to macroeconomic thought, one that will challenge Keynes's views head-on. Lucas suggests a world in which self-correction is swift, rational choices by individuals generally cancel the impact of fiscal and monetary policies, and stabilization efforts are likely to slow economic growth.

John Maynard Keynes, Milton Friedman, and Robert Lucas each helped to establish a major school of macroeconomic thought. Although their ideas clashed sharply, and although there remains considerable disagreement among economists about a variety of issues, a broad consensus among economists concerning macroeconomic policy seemed to emerge in the 1980s, 1990s, and early 2000s. That consensus, which took the better part of a century to reach, lasted only a few years, shattered by the Great Recession and the financial crisis of 2007–2008.

In this chapter we'll examine the macroeconomic developments of six decades: the 1930s, 1960s, 1970s, 1980s, 1990s, and 2000s. We'll use the aggregate demand–aggregate supply model to explain macroeconomic changes during these periods, and we'll see how the three major economic schools were affected by these events. We'll also see how these schools of thought affected macroeconomic policy. Finally, we'll see how the evolution of macroeconomic thought and policy influenced how economists designed policy prescriptions for dealing with the Great Recession of 2007, which at the time was the most severe downturn the country had seen since the Great Depression.

17.2 The Great Depression and Keynesian Economics

Learning Objectives

1. Explain the basic assumptions of the classical school of thought that dominated macroeconomic thinking before the Great Depression, and tell why the severity of the Depression struck a major blow to this view.
2. Compare Keynesian and classical macroeconomic thought, discussing the Keynesian explanation of prolonged recessionary and inflationary gaps as well as the Keynesian approach to correcting these problems.

The Great Depression exacted an enormous economic and human toll. Destitute pea-picker Florence Owens Thompson holds several of her children in this iconic photo, "Migrant Mother."

Source: Dorothea Lange, "Migrant Mother." Derived from the Farm Security Administration Collection, Library of Congress Prints and Photographs Division: https://www.loc.gov/pictures/item/2017762891/. Retouched and reproduced via Firebrace on Wikimedia: https://commons.wikimedia.org/wiki/File:Lange-MigrantMother02.jpg.

It's hard to imagine that anyone who lived during the Great Depression was not profoundly affected by it. From the beginning of the Depression in 1929 to the time the economy hit bottom in 1933, real GDP plunged nearly 30%. Real per capita disposable income sank nearly 40%. With more than 12 million people thrown out of work, the unemployment rate soared from 3% in 1929 to 25% in 1933. Some 85,000 businesses failed. Over 30% of the nation's banks failed, taking the life savings of hundreds of thousands of families with them. Hundreds of thousands of families lost their homes. By 1933, about half of all mortgages on all urban, owner-occupied houses were delinquent.[1]

This was not, of course, the first time the economy had slumped. But never had the U.S. economy fallen so far and for so long a period. Prior to the Great Depression, recessions lasted an average of less than two years. Recovery from the Great Depression lasted for more than a decade.[2] Figure 17.1 shows the course of real GDP compared to potential output during the Great Depression. The economy didn't approach potential output until 1941, when the pressures of world war forced sharp increases in aggregate demand.

FIGURE 17.1 The Depression and the Recessionary Gap
The red-shaded area shows real GDP from 1929 to 1942, the upper line shows potential output, and the orange-shaded area shows the difference between the two—the recessionary gap. The gap remained open for over ten years; ramping up production for WWII closed the gap by 1941.

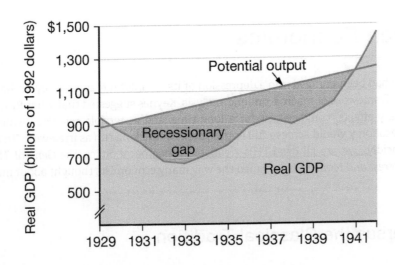

The Classical School and the Great Depression

The Great Depression came as a shock to what was then the conventional wisdom of economics. To see why, let's go back to the classical tradition of macroeconomics that dominated the economics profession when the Depression began.

Classical economics is the body of macroeconomic thought associated primarily with nineteenth-century British economist David Ricardo. His *Principles of Political Economy and Taxation*, published in 1817, established a tradition that dominated macroeconomic thought for over a century. Ricardo focused on the long run and on the forces that determine and produce growth in an economy's potential output. He emphasized the ability of flexible wages and prices to keep the economy at or near its natural level of employment.

According to the classical school, achieving what we now call the natural level of employment and potential output is not a problem; the economy can do that on its own. Classical economists recognized, however, that the process would take time: Ricardo admitted that there could be *temporary* periods in which employment would fall below the natural level. But his emphasis was on the long run, and in the long run (as you saw in our chapter on aggregate demand and aggregate supply) all would be set right by the smooth functioning of the price system.

classical economics

The body of macroeconomic thought, associated primarily with nineteenth-century British economist David Ricardo, that focused on the long run and on the forces that determine and produce growth in an economy's potential output.

Most famous for his theory of comparative advantage, David Ricardo had a profound influence on the behavior of the macroeconomy.

Source: Proesi via Stefan Bernd. "David Ricardo(1)." Via Wikimedia: https://commons.wikimedia.org/wiki/File:David_Ricardo(1).jpg.

Savvy investor, iconoclast, and brilliant economist: John Maynard Keynes revolutionized economic thought.

Source: International Monetary Fund. "John Maynard Keynes." Reproduced via Wikimedia: https:///commons.wikimedia.org/wiki/File:John_Maynard_Keynes.jpg.

Keynesian economics

The body of macroeconomic thought that asserts that changes in aggregate demand can create gaps between the actual and potential levels of output, and that such gaps can be prolonged. It stresses the use of fiscal and monetary policy to close such gaps.

Economists of the classical school saw the massive slump that occurred in much of the world in the late 1920s and early 1930s as a short-run aberration. The economy would right itself in the long run, returning to its potential output and to the natural level of employment.

Keynesian Economics

In Britain, which had been plunged into a depression of its own, John Maynard Keynes had begun to develop a new framework of macroeconomic analysis. Keynes suggested that what Ricardo considered "temporary effects" could persist for a long time, and at terrible cost. He dismissed the notion that the economy would achieve full employment in the long run as irrelevant: "In the long run," he wrote acidly, "we are all dead." His treatise on macroeconomics, *The General Theory of Employment, Interest and Money*, transformed the way many economists thought about macroeconomic problems.

Keynes versus the Classical Tradition

In a nutshell, we can say that Keynes's book shifted the thrust of macroeconomic thought from the concept of aggregate supply to the concept of aggregate demand. Ricardo's focus on the tendency of an economy to reach potential output inevitably stressed the supply side—an economy tends to operate at a level of output dictated by the position of the long-run aggregate supply curve. Keynes, in contrast, argued that what we now call recessionary or inflationary gaps could be created by shifts in aggregate demand. He argued that prices in the short run are quite sticky and suggested that this stickiness could block adjustments to full employment.

Keynes's work spawned a new school of macroeconomic thought, the Keynesian school. **Keynesian economics** asserts that changes in aggregate demand can create gaps between the actual and potential levels of output, and that such gaps can be prolonged. Keynesian economists stress the use of fiscal and monetary policy to close such gaps.

Keynesian Economics and the Great Depression

The experience of the Great Depression certainly seemed consistent with Keynes's argument. A reduction in aggregate demand took the economy from above its potential output to below its potential output, and, as we saw in Figure 17.1, the resulting recessionary gap lasted for more than a decade. Let's take a look at the perfect storm of events that pushed aggregate demand far to the left.

- The plunge in aggregate demand began with a collapse in investment. An investment boom during the 1920s had left firms with an expanded stock of capital. With the capital stock near its desired level, firms slowed investment spending. The stock market crash of 1929 was another blow: With business confidence shaken, real gross private domestic investment plunged nearly 80% between 1929 and 1932.

- Other factors contributed to the sharp reduction in aggregate demand. The stock market crash reduced the wealth of just a small fraction of the population (just 5% of Americans owned stock at that time), but it certainly reduced the consumption of the general population. The crash also shook consumer confidence, resulting in lower consumption spending.

- With consumption and incomes falling, governments at all levels found their tax revenues falling. They responded by raising tax rates in an effort to rebalance their budgets. The federal government, for example, doubled income tax rates in 1932, and total government tax revenues as a percentage of GDP shot up from 10.8% in 1929 to 16.6% in 1933. Higher tax rates, however, left consumers with less disposable income: Consumption and aggregate demand fell.

- The depression was global, with other countries suffering declining incomes that reduced foreign demand for U.S. goods and services. The United States responded to domestic producers' concerns by passing the Smoot–Hawley tariff, which raised the average tariff rate on imports to an astonishing 60%. As other countries retaliated, world trade collapsed: U.S. real exports fell 46% between 1929 and 1933.

- As if all this were not enough, the Federal Reserve's monetary policy during the early years of the recession was sharply contractionary. The money supply collapsed, and the Fed abdicated its responsibility to serve as a lender of last resort to the banking system. A wave of bank failures swept the country; households' life savings evaporated (reducing consumption) and vital credit flows to businesses were choked off (reducing investment).

Figure 17.2 shows the shift in aggregate demand between 1929, when the economy was operating just above its potential output, and 1933. The plunge in aggregate demand produced a recessionary gap. The *AD/AS* model tells us that a recessionary gap will eventually cause wages to fall: That happened, with nominal wages plunging roughly 20% between 1929 and 1933. That shifted the *SRAS* curve to the right, but that shift was swamped by the magnitude of the decrease in aggregate demand. Ultimately, the increase in *SRAS* simply wasn't large enough to bring the economy back to potential output.

FIGURE 17.2 Aggregate Demand and Short-Run Aggregate Supply: 1929–1933
Slumping aggregate demand brought the economy well below the full-employment level of output by 1933. The short-run aggregate supply curve increased as nominal wages fell. In this analysis, and in subsequent applications in this chapter of the model of aggregate demand and aggregate supply to macroeconomic events, we are ignoring shifts in the long-run aggregate supply curve in order to simplify the diagram.

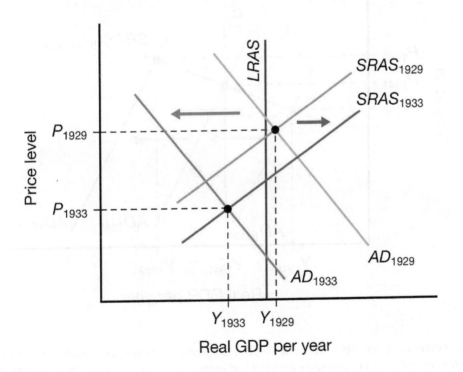

Not your ordinary bass boat: The money the U.S. government spent to build the Pacific Fleet from scratch dragged the economy out of the depression and into prosperity.

Source: Everett Collection/Shutterstock.com

To restore the economy to full employment, wages needed to decrease even more. Unfortunately, government policy stood in the way of that happening: President Franklin Roosevelt, thinking that falling wages and prices were in large part to blame for the Depression, implemented policies to block further reductions in wages and prices. That prevented any further self-correction. With recovery blocked from the supply side and no policy in place to boost aggregate demand, it's easy to see now why the economy remained in recession for so long.

Keynes, witnessing the American experience during the Great Depression, argued that expansionary fiscal policy represented the surest tool for bringing the economy back to full employment. Roosevelt's New Deal policies *did* seek to stimulate employment through a variety of federal programs. But, with state and local governments continuing to cut purchases and raise taxes, net government spending didn't change much at all, rising from $9.8 billion in 1920 to only $10.2 billion by 1933. World War II changed that, however: In 1941 government expenditures nearly doubled; by 1945 the government was spending more than $100 billion each year—a tenfold increase from 1933 levels.[3] As Figure 17.3 shows, expansionary fiscal policies forced by the war brought output back to potential by 1941, and by 1942 the economy had entered an inflationary gap.

FIGURE 17.3 World War II Ends the Great Depression
Increased U.S. government purchases, prompted by the beginning of World War II, ended the Great Depression. By 1942, increasing aggregate demand had pushed real GDP beyond potential output.

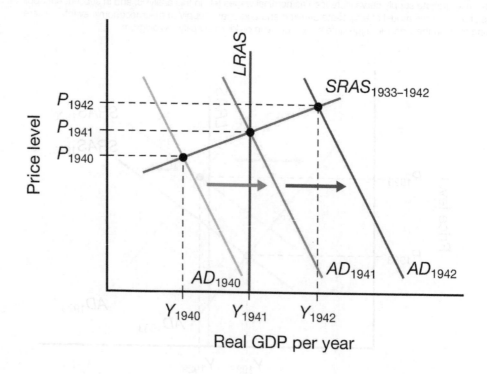

For Keynesian economists, the Great Depression provided impressive confirmation of Keynes's ideas. A sharp reduction in aggregate demand had gotten the trouble started. The recessionary gap created by the change in aggregate demand had persisted for more than a decade. And expansionary fiscal policy had put a swift end to the worst macroeconomic nightmare in U.S. history—even if that policy had been forced on the country by a war that would prove to be one of the worst episodes of world history.

Keynes's work prompted a slow reimagining of government's role in the economy, from passive acceptance to active management. That legacy has stood the test of time: Even today, governments around the world use the tools of monetary and fiscal policy to keep their economies operating as close as possible to potential.

Key Takeaways

- Classical economic thought stressed the ability of the economy to achieve what we now call its potential output in the long run. It thus stressed the forces that determine the position of the long-run aggregate supply curve as the ultimate determinants of income.
- Keynesian economics focuses on changes in aggregate demand and their ability to create recessionary or inflationary gaps. Keynesian economists argue that sticky prices and wages would make it difficult for the economy to adjust to its potential output.
- Because Keynesian economists believe that recessionary and inflationary gaps can persist for long periods, they urge the use of fiscal and monetary policy to shift the aggregate demand curve and to close these gaps.
- Aggregate demand fell sharply in the first four years of the Great Depression. As the recessionary gap widened, nominal wages began to fall, and the short-run aggregate supply curve began shifting to the right. These shifts, however, were not sufficient to close the recessionary gap. World War II forced the U.S. government to shift to a sharply expansionary fiscal policy, and the Depression ended.

Try It!

Imagine that it is 1933. President Franklin Roosevelt has just been inaugurated and has named you as his senior economic adviser. Devise a program to bring the economy back to its potential output. Using the model of aggregate demand and aggregate supply, demonstrate graphically how your proposal could work.

See related Concept Problem 11 at the end of this chapter.

Case in Point: Early Views on Stickiness

Philosopher, historian, economist: David Hume wrote about the ability of an increase in the quantity of money to boost short-run output.

Source: © Shutterstock, Inc.

Although David Ricardo's focus on the long run emerged as the dominant approach to macroeconomic thought, not all of his contemporaries agreed with his perspective. Many eighteenth- and nineteenth-century economists developed theoretical arguments suggesting that changes in aggregate demand could affect the real level of economic activity in the short run. Like the new Keynesians, they based their arguments on the concept of price stickiness.

Henry Thornton's 1802 book, *An Enquiry into the Nature and Effects of the Paper Credit of Great Britain*, argued that a reduction in the money supply could, because of wage stickiness, produce a short-run slump in output:

> *The tendency, however, of a very great and sudden reduction of the accustomed number of bank notes, is to create an unusual and temporary distress, and a fall of price arising from that distress. But a fall arising from temporary distress, will be attended probably with no correspondent fall in the rate of wages; for the fall of price, and the distress, will be understood to be temporary, and the rate of wages, we know, is not so variable as the price of goods. There is reason, therefore, to fear that the unnatural and extraordinary low price arising from the sort of distress of which we now speak, would occasion much discouragement of the fabrication of manufactures.[4]*

A half-century earlier, David Hume had noted that an increase in the quantity of money would boost output in the short run, again because of the stickiness of prices. In an essay titled "Of Money," published in 1752, Hume described the process through which an increased money supply could boost output:

> *At first, no alteration is perceived; by degrees the price rises, first of one commodity, then of another, till the whole at last reaches a just proportion with the new quantity of (money) which is in the kingdom. In my opinion, it is only in this interval or intermediate situation . . . that the encreasing quantity of gold and silver is favourable to industry.[5]*

Hume's argument implies sticky prices; some prices are slower to respond to the increase in the money supply than others.

Economists of the eighteenth and nineteenth centuries are generally lumped together as adherents to the classical school, but their views were anything but uniform. Many developed an analytical framework that was quite similar to the essential elements of new Keynesian economists today. Economist Thomas Humphrey, at the Federal Reserve Bank of Richmond, marvels at the insights shown by early economists: "Today economists and textbook writers perpetuate the myth by disseminating a caricature 'classical' macromodel in which money is always neutral. . . . On the contrary, except for Ricardo and one or two others, the classicals believed that money had powerful temporary real effects and perhaps some residual permanent effects as well. In the view of the classicals, nonneutrality typified the short run and neutrality at best held approximately in the long run only."

See related Concept Problem 12 at the end of this chapter.

Source: Based on Thomas M. Humphrey, "Nonneutrality of Money in Classical Monetary Thought," Federal Reserve Bank of Richmond Economic Review 77, no. 2 (March/April 1991): 3–15, and personal interview.

Answer to Try It! Problem

An expansionary fiscal or monetary policy, or a combination of the two, would shift aggregate demand to the right as shown in Panel (a), ideally returning the economy to potential output. One piece of evidence suggesting that fiscal policy would work is the swiftness with which the economy recovered from the Great Depression once World War II forced the government to carry out such a policy. An alternative approach would be to do nothing. Ultimately, that should force nominal wages down further, producing increases in short-run aggregate supply, as in Panel (b). We do not know if such an approach might have worked; federal policies enacted in 1933 prevented wages and prices from falling further than they already had.

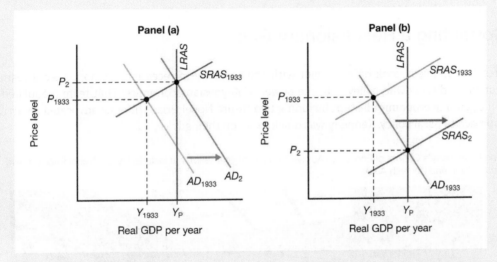

17.3 Keynesian Economics in the 1960s and 1970s

Learning Objectives

1. Summarize the economic climate in the 1960s and describe the monetary and fiscal policy responses to those economic challenges.
2. Describe the monetarist school of thought that emerged in the 1960s, and discuss how the experiences of the 1960s and 1970s seemed to be broadly consistent with it.
3. Describe the new classical school of thought that emerged in the 1970s, and discuss how the experiences of the 1970s seemed to be broadly consistent with it.
4. Summarize the lessons that economists learned from the economic experience of the 1970s.

The Great Depression and its policy response led to the widespread acceptance of Keynesian ideas among economists. Its acceptance as a basis for economic policy, however, was slower. Presidents Roosevelt, Truman, and Eisenhower all rejected the notion that fiscal policy could or should be used to manipulate real GDP, with Truman vetoing a 1948 Republican-sponsored tax cut aimed at stimulating the economy after World War II and Eisenhower resisting stimulative measures to deal with the recessions of 1953, 1957, and 1960. It was President John F. Kennedy who first used fiscal policy to steer the economy toward potential output. Kennedy's willingness to embrace Keynes's ideas changed the nation's approach to fiscal policy for the next two decades.

Expansionary Policy in the 1960s

The macroeconomic history of the 1960s can be divided into two distinct phases. The first showed the power of Keynesian policies to correct economic difficulties. The second showed the power of these same policies to create them.

Correcting a Recessionary Gap

President Kennedy took office in 1961 with the economy in recession. He appointed a team of economic advisers who believed in the power of Keynesian economics. That team (populated by some genuine economic all-stars, including two future Nobel Prize winners) advocated an activist approach to fiscal policy. Kennedy was quick to act on their advice.

John F. Kennedy's Council of Economic Advisers was an all-star team that included future Nobel Prize winners James Tobin and Kenneth Arrow.

Source: Abbie Rowe. White House Photographs."Meeting with the Council of Economic Advisers and their staff, 11:35AM." 1962 May 10. [Accession Number AR7225-A]. John F. Kennedy Presidential Library and Museum, Boston. Retrieved from: https://www.jfklibrary.org/asset-viewer/archives/JFKWHP/1962/Month 05/Day 10/JFKWHP-1962-05-10-C.

Expansionary policy to combat the recession dovetailed nicely with the administration's foreign-policy goals. Kennedy, arguing that the United States was falling behind the Soviet Union in military preparedness, won approval from Congress for sharp increases in defense spending in 1961. The Kennedy administration also pursued stimulative tax changes. Those changes reduced individual income taxes, bringing the top marginal rate down from 91% to 70%. Kennedy's tax plan also revised the corporate tax code: In addition to cutting the top corporate income tax rate, the plan allowed firms to accelerate depreciation expenses on new capital and extended an investment tax credit that allowed corporations to reduce their income taxes by 10% of their investment in any one year.

The combination of increased defense spending and tax measures to stimulate investment provided a quick boost to aggregate demand. That expansionary policy got support from the Fed, which shifted to an expansionary policy stance in 1961, ramping up the growth rate of the M1 and M2 money supplies.

As shown in Panel (a) of Figure 17.4, the expansionary fiscal and monetary policies of the early 1960s had pushed real GDP to its potential by 1963. But the concept of potential output had not been developed by 1963; Kennedy administration economists had defined full employment to be an unemployment rate of 4%. Given 1963's actual unemployment rate of 5.7%, the perception at the time was that the economy needed more stimulus.

FIGURE 17.4 The Two Faces of Expansionary Policy in the 1960s
Expansionary fiscal and monetary policy early in the 1960s closed a recessionary gap, as shown in Panel (a). Continued expansionary policy through the 1960s created an inflationary gap, as shown in Panel (b). Wages rose as part of the economy's attempt to self-correct, shifting the short-run aggregate supply curve to the left. But strong expansionary policy continued to shift aggregate demand to the right, and kept the economy locked into an inflationary gap.

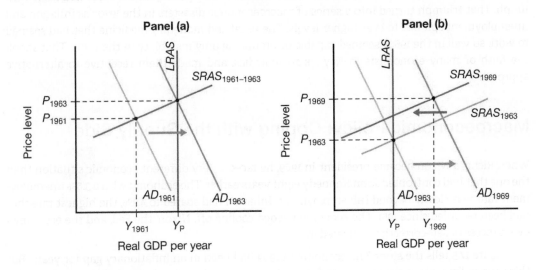

Expansionary Policy and an Inflationary Gap

Kennedy's tax plan was passed by Congress in 1964, just after the president had been assassinated. In retrospect, we may regard the tax cut as representing a kind of recognition lag—policymakers did not realize the economy had already reached what we now recognize was its potential output. Instead of closing a recessionary gap, the tax cut helped push the economy into an inflationary gap, as illustrated in Panel (b) of Figure 17.4.

The demand-side stimulus of the Vietnam War, coupled with high rates of money growth, pushed the U.S. economy into an inflationary gap.

Source: Chueasuwan Phunsawat/Shutterstock.com

The expansionary policies, however, did not stop with the tax cut. Continued increases in federal spending for the newly expanded war in Vietnam and for President Lyndon Johnson's agenda of domestic programs, together with continued high rates of money growth, sent the aggregate demand curve further to the right. While President Johnson's Council of Economic Advisers recommended contractionary policy as early as 1965, macroeconomic policy remained generally expansionary through 1969. Wage increases began shifting the short-run aggregate supply curve to the left, but expansionary policy continued to increase aggregate demand and kept the economy in an inflationary gap for the last six years of the 1960s.

Panel (b) of Figure 17.4 shows expansionary policies pushing the economy beyond its potential output after 1963.

The 1960s had demonstrated two important lessons about Keynesian macroeconomic policy. First, stimulative fiscal and monetary policy could be used to close a recessionary gap. Second, fiscal policies could have a long implementation lag. The tax cut recommended by President Kennedy's economic advisers in 1961 was not enacted until 1964—after the recessionary gap it was designed to fight had been closed. The tax increase recommended by President Johnson's economic advisers in 1965 was not passed until 1968—after the inflationary gap it was designed to close had widened.

Macroeconomic policy after 1963 pushed the economy into an inflationary gap. That push did produce rising employment and increases in real GDP. But the inflation that came with that economic expansion created real difficulties for the economy and for macroeconomic policy in the 1970s.

The 1970s: Troubles from the Supply Side

For many observers, the use of Keynesian fiscal and monetary policies in the 1960s had been a triumph. That triumph turned into a series of macroeconomic disasters in the 1970s as inflation and unemployment spiraled to ever-higher levels. The fiscal and monetary medicine that had seemed to work so well in the 1960s seemed capable of producing only instability in the 1970s. That shook the faith of many economists in Keynesian remedies, and made them receptive to alternative approaches.

Macroeconomic Policy: Coping with the Supply Side

When Richard Nixon became president in 1969, he faced a very different economic situation than the one that had confronted John Kennedy eight years earlier. The economy, with a 3.6% unemployment rate, was clearly beyond full employment. Inflation had soared to 4.3%, the highest rate that had been recorded since 1951. The economy needed cooling off. Nixon, the Fed, and the economy's own process of self-correction delivered it.

Figure 17.5 tells the story. The economy in 1969 had been in an inflationary gap for years. But this time, policymakers were no longer forcing increases in aggregate demand to keep it there. The adjustment in short-run aggregate supply brought the economy back to potential output.

What we can see now as a simple adjustment, however, seemed anything but simple in 1970. Economists didn't think in terms of shifts in short-run aggregate supply: Keynesian economics focused on shifts in aggregate *demand*, not supply.

For the Nixon administration, the slump in real GDP in 1970 as the economy self-corrected was perceived as a recession. But, as recessions go, it was an odd one. The price level had risen sharply. That was not, according to the Keynesian story, supposed to happen; there was simply no reason to expect the price level to soar when real GDP and employment were falling.

The administration dealt with the recession by shifting to an expansionary fiscal policy. That pushed the economy back into an inflationary gap by 1973. But 1974 brought another jolt: The Organization of Petroleum Exporting Countries (OPEC) tripled the price of oil. That supply shock shifted the short-run aggregate supply to the left, pushing the economy into recession and fueling another jump in the price level.

The second half of the decade was, in some respects, a repeat of the first. The Ford and Carter administrations, along with the Fed, pursued expansionary policies to stimulate the economy. Those efforts helped boost output, but they also pushed up prices. By the end of the decade, inflation was running at double-digit levels.

FIGURE 17.5 The Economy Closes an Inflationary Gap
The Nixon administration and the Fed joined to end the expansionary policies that had prevailed in the 1960s; aggregate demand did not rise in 1970, but the short-run aggregate supply curve shifted to the left as the economy responded to an inflationary gap.

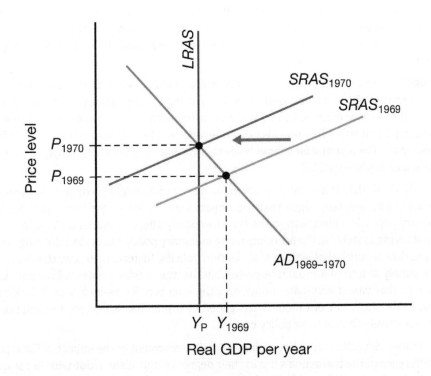

FIGURE 17.6 The Energy Supply Shocks of the 1970s
In 1973, oil prices rose five-fold, to $10 per barrel. By 1980, they'd quadrupled again to $40. Fighting cost-push inflation became job #1 for incoming Fed Chair Paul Volcker.

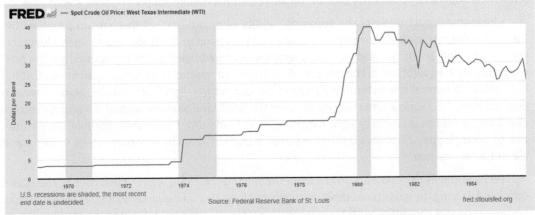

Source: Federal Reserve Bank of St. Louis, Spot Crude Oil Price: West Texas Intermediate (WTI) [WTISPLC], retrieved from FRED, Federal Reserve Bank of St. Louis; https://fred.stlouisfed.org/series/WTISPLC.

The 1970s presented a challenge not just to policymakers, but also to economists. Demand-focused Keynesian policy couldn't reconcile the sharp changes in real GDP and in the price level. Economists grappling to explain what was happening ultimately produced the model we've been using to explain the macroeconomy, a model with broad consensus. But before that consensus was reached, two additional pieces of the puzzle had to be fit into place. The first piece was the role of monetary policy; the second was role of aggregate supply in both the short run and the long run.

The Monetarist Challenge

The idea that changes in the money supply are the primary determinant of the nominal value of output is one of the oldest in economic thought, implied by David Hume and formalized in the equation of exchange. Classical economists, particularly interested in emphasizing the long run, were quick to point out that changes in the price level were ultimately linked to changes in the money supply.

At roughly the same time Keynesian economics was emerging as the dominant school of macroeconomic thought, some economists were exploring the importance of money in determining the level of economic activity. Led by Milton Friedman, these economists argued that because of crowding out, fiscal policy had no effect on the economy. Their "money rules" doctrine led to the name *monetarists*. The **monetarist school** holds that changes in the money supply are the primary cause of changes in nominal GDP.

You might think that, if money is so powerful, monetarists might favor activist monetary policy. But monetarists generally argue that the impact lags of monetary policy—the lags from the time monetary policy is undertaken to the time the policy affects nominal GDP—are so long and variable that trying to stabilize the economy using monetary policy can be destabilizing. As a result, most monetarists are critical of activist stabilization policies. Instead, they urge the Fed to increase the money supply at a fixed annual rate, preferably the rate at which potential output rises. With stable velocity, that would eliminate inflation in the long run. Recessionary or inflationary gaps could occur in the short run, but monetarists generally argue that self-correction will take care of them more effectively than activist policy can.

While monetarists differ from Keynesians in their assessment of the impact of fiscal policy, the primary difference in the two schools lies in their degree of optimism about whether stabilization policy can, in fact, be counted on to bring the economy back to its potential output. For monetarists, the complexity of economic life and the uncertain nature of lags mean that efforts to use monetary policy to stabilize the economy can be destabilizing. Monetarists argued that the difficulties encountered by policymakers as they tried to respond to the dramatic events of the 1970s demonstrated the superiority of a policy that simply increased the money supply at a slow, steady rate.

Monetarists could also cite the apparent validity of an adjustment mechanism proposed by Milton Friedman in 1968. As the economy continued to expand in the 1960s, and as unemployment continued to fall, Friedman asserted that unemployment had fallen below its natural rate, the rate consistent with equilibrium in the labor market. Friedman insisted the unemployment couldn't be held below its natural rate indefinitely. Instead, he said, with a tight labor market, workers would demand higher nominal wages that would cause the price level to shoot up and unemployment to rise. That, of course, is precisely what happened in 1970 and 1971. Friedman's notion of the natural rate of unemployment buttressed the monetarist argument that the economy moves to its potential output on its own.

Perhaps the most potent argument from the monetarist camp was the behavior of the economy itself. During the 1960s, monetarist and Keynesian economists alike could argue that economic performance was consistent with their respective views of the world. Keynesians could point to expansions in economic activity that they could ascribe to expansionary fiscal policy. Yet, economic activity *also* moved closely with changes in the money supply, just as monetarists predicted.

During the 1970s, however, it became difficult for Keynesians to argue that policies affecting aggregate demand were having the predicted impact on the economy. Changes in aggregate supply had repeatedly pushed the economy off a Keynesian course. But monetarists, once again, could point to a consistent relationship between changes in the money supply and changes in economic activity.

Figure 17.7 shows the movement of nominal GDP and M2 during the 1960s and 1970s. In the figure, annual percentage changes in M2 are plotted against subsequent percentage changes in

monetarist school

The body of macroeconomic thought that holds that changes in the money supply are the primary cause of changes in nominal GDP.

Milton Friedman highlighted the power of money and the importance of expectations.

Source: The Friedman Foundation for Educational Choice. "Portrait of Milton Friedman." Retrieved from: https://commons.wikimedia.org/wiki/File:Portrait_of_Milton_Friedman.jpg. Reproduced via Public Domain dedication: https://creativecommons.org/publicdomain/zero/1.0/deed.en.

nominal GDP.[6] There was, at least during these years, a strong relationship between changes in the quantity of money and changes in nominal GDP.

FIGURE 17.7 M2 and Nominal GDP, 1960–1980
The chart shows annual rates of change in M2 and in nominal GDP one year later. The two variables were strongly linked in the 1960s and 1970s: A change in money in one year was followed by a similar change in nominal GDP in the next year.

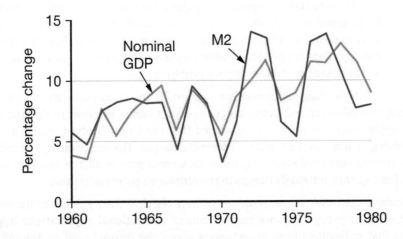

Monetarist doctrine emerged as a potent challenge to Keynesian economics in the 1970s largely because of the close correspondence between nominal GDP and the money supply. The next section examines another school of thought that came to prominence in the 1970s.

New Classical Economics: A Focus on Aggregate Supply

Much of the difficulty policymakers encountered during the 1970s resulted from shifts in aggregate supply. Keynesian economics (and, to a lesser degree, monetarism) had focused on aggregate demand. As it became clear that an analysis incorporating the supply side of the economy was an essential part of the macroeconomic puzzle, some economists turned to an entirely new way of looking at macroeconomic issues.

These economists started with what we identified at the beginning of this text as a distinguishing characteristic of economic thought: a focus on individuals and their decisions. Keynesian economics employed aggregate analysis and paid little attention to individual choices. Monetarist doctrine was based on the analysis of individuals' maximizing behavior with respect to money demand, but it didn't extend that analysis to the decisions that affect aggregate supply. The new approach, in contrast, explored individual choices across the entire spectrum of economic activity.

These economists rejected the entire framework of conventional macroeconomic analysis. In fact, they rejected the very term: For them, there *is* no macroeconomics, nor is there something called microeconomics! For them, there is *only* economics, the analysis of behavior based on individual maximization. In their eyes, analyzing inflation and unemployment becomes an application of basic economic theory rather than a separate body of thought. This approach to macroeconomic analysis, built on a foundation of individuals making maximizing choices, is called **new classical economics**.

> **new classical economics**
>
> The approach to macroeconomic analysis built from an analysis of individual maximizing choices and emphasizing wage and price flexibility.

New classical economists believe the macroeconomy is the product of individuals' maximizing behaviors.

Source: Elnur/Shutterstock.com

rational expectations hypothesis

Individuals form expectations about the future based on the information available to them, and they act on those expectations.

Rational Expectations: If anticipated, stabilization policy is like a sphere—pointless.

Source: valdis torms/Shutterstock.com

Like classical economic thought, new classical economics focuses on the determination of long-run aggregate supply and the economy's ability to reach this level of output quickly. But the similarity ends there. Classical economics emerged in large part before economists had developed sophisticated mathematical models of maximizing behavior. New classical economics puts high-level mathematics to work in adding up individual maximizers to arrive at aggregate results.

The new classical approach suggests that the economy will remain at or near its potential output, which implies that the changes we observe in economic activity result not from changes in aggregate demand but from changes in long-run aggregate supply. New classical economics suggests that economic *changes* don't necessarily imply economic *problems*.

New classical economists pointed to the supply-side shocks of the 1970s (both from changes in oil prices and from changes in expectations), as evidence that the emphasis on aggregate supply was on the mark. They argued that the large observed swings in real GDP reflected underlying changes in the economy's potential output. The recessionary and inflationary gaps that so perplexed policymakers during the 1970s weren't gaps at all, the new classical economists insisted. Instead, they reflected changes in the economy's potential output.

Two particularly controversial propositions of new classical theory relate to the impacts of monetary and of fiscal policy. Both are implications of the **rational expectations hypothesis**, which assumes that individuals form expectations about the future based on the information available to them, and that they act on those expectations.

The rational expectations hypothesis suggests that monetary policy, even though it will affect the aggregate demand curve, might have no effect on real GDP. This possibility, which was suggested by Robert Lucas, is illustrated in Figure 17.8. Suppose the economy is initially in equilibrium at point A in Panel (a), with real GDP equal to potential output, Y_P. Now suppose a reduction in the money supply causes aggregate demand to fall to AD_2. In our AD/AS model, the short-run equilibrium shifts to point B, with price level P_2 and real GDP Y_2. At point B there is a recessionary gap, but in the long run, the short-run aggregate supply curve shifts to $SRAS_2$, the price level falls to P_3, and the economy returns to equilibrium at its potential output at point C.

The new classical story, told in Panel (b), is quite different. Consumers and firms observe that the money supply has fallen and anticipate the eventual reduction in the price level to P_3. They adjust their expectations accordingly. Workers quickly agree to lower nominal wages, and the short-run aggregate supply curve shifts to $SRAS_2$. This occurs *at the same time as aggregate demand decreases*, which means that the economy moves straight down the $LRAS$ curve from point A to point C without the temporary departure (the costly recessionary gap) to Y_2.

In this new classical world, there is only one way for a change in the money supply to affect output, and that is for the change to take people by surprise. An unexpected change won't affect expectations, so the short-run aggregate supply curve wouldn't shift in the short run: In that case, events play out as in Panel (a). Monetary policy can affect output, but only if it takes people by surprise.

The new classical school offers an even stronger case against the operation of fiscal policy. It argues that fiscal policy does not shift the aggregate demand curve at all! Consider, for example, an expansionary fiscal policy. Such a policy involves an increase in government purchases or transfer payments or a cut in taxes. Any of these policies will increase the deficit or reduce the surplus. New classical economists argue that households, when they observe the government carrying out a policy that increases the debt, will anticipate that they, or their children, or their children's children, will end up paying more in taxes. According to new classical economists, these households will reduce their consumption as a result, socking away the money they would have spent on consumption goods to help cover the future increase in taxes. This means that any new government spending will be offset by decreases in consumption; any tax cut to consumers will simply be saved to cover future tax liabilities; neither will result in any stimulus.

FIGURE 17.8 Contractionary Monetary Policy: With and Without Rational Expectations

Panels (a) and (b) show an economy operating at potential output (point A); a contractionary monetary policy shifts aggregate demand to AD_2. Panel (a) shows the kind of response we have studied up to this point: Real GDP falls to Y_2 (point B) and the economy enters recession. The recessionary gap is closed in the long run by falling nominal wages that increase short-run aggregate supply; the new long-run equilibrium is at point C. Panel (b) shows the rational expectations argument. People anticipate the impact of the contractionary policy when it is undertaken, so that the short-run aggregate supply curve shifts to the right at the same time the aggregate demand curve shifts to the left. The result is a reduction in the price level but no change in real GDP. Equilibrium moves straight down the $LRAS$ curve from point A to point C.

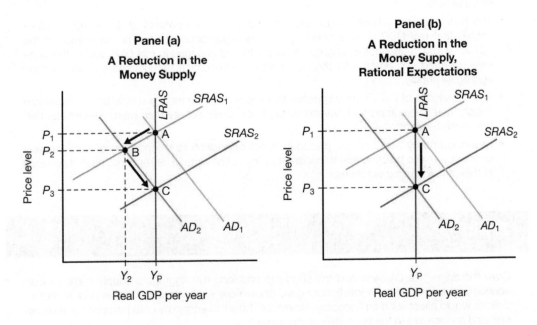

Lessons from the 1970s

The 1970s put Keynesian economics and its prescription for activist policies on the defensive. The period lent considerable support to the monetarist argument that changes in the money supply are the primary determinant of changes in the nominal level of GDP. A series of dramatic shifts in aggregate supply gave credence to the new classical emphasis on long-run aggregate supply as the primary determinant of real GDP.

For economists, the period offered some important lessons. These lessons, as we will see in the next section, forced a rethinking of some of the ideas that had dominated Keynesian thought. The experience of the 1970s suggested the following:

1. The short-run aggregate supply curve could not be viewed as something that provided a passive path over which aggregate demand could roam. The short-run aggregate supply curve could shift in ways that clearly affected real GDP, unemployment, and the price level.

2. Money mattered more than Keynesians had previously suspected. Keynes had expressed doubts about the effectiveness of monetary policy, particularly in the face of a recessionary gap. Work by monetarists suggested a close correspondence between changes in M2 and subsequent changes in nominal GDP, convincing many Keynesian economists that money was more important than they had thought.

3. Stabilization was a more difficult task than many economists had anticipated. Shifts in aggregate supply could frustrate the efforts of policymakers to achieve certain macroeconomic goals.

Key Takeaways

- Beginning in 1961, expansionary fiscal and monetary policies were used to close a recessionary gap; this was the first major U.S. application of Keynesian macroeconomic policy.
- The experience of the 1960s and 1970s appeared to be broadly consistent with the monetarist argument that changes in the money supply are the primary determinant of changes in nominal GDP.
- The new classical school's argument that the economy operates at its potential output implies that real GDP is determined by long-run aggregate supply. The experience of the 1970s, in which changes in aggregate supply forced changes in real GDP and in the price level, seemed consistent with the new classical economists' arguments that focused on aggregate supply.
- The experience of the 1970s suggested that changes in the money supply and in aggregate supply were more important determinants of economic activity than many Keynesians had previously thought.
- Keynesian policy activism was placed in direct opposition to the position of new classical economists, who believed that transparent policy actions would be rendered neutral because of their effects on expectations.

Try It!

Draw the aggregate demand and the short-run and long-run aggregate supply curves for an economy operating with an inflationary gap. Show how expansionary fiscal and/or monetary policies would affect such an economy. Now show how this economy could experience a recession and an increase in the price level at the same time.

See related Concept Problem 9 at the end of this chapter.

Case in Point: Tough Medicine Is Hard to Stomach: Macroeconomic Policy in the 1960s

Source: Palmer Kane LLC/Shutterstock.com

The Keynesian prescription for an inflationary gap seems simple enough. The federal government applies contractionary fiscal policy, or the Fed applies contractionary monetary policy, or both. But what seems simple in a graph can be maddeningly difficult in the real world. The medicine for an inflationary gap is tough, and it is tough to take.

In 1965, President Johnson's new chairman of the Council of Economic Advisers, Gardner Ackley, urged the president to adopt fiscal policies aimed at nudging the aggregate demand curve back to the left. The president reluctantly agreed and called in the chairman of the House Ways and Means Committee to see what he thought of the idea. Wilbur Mills flatly told Johnson that he wouldn't even hold hearings to consider a tax increase. For the time being, the tax boost was dead.

The Federal Reserve System did slow the rate of money growth in 1966, but fiscal policy remained sharply expansionary. Ackley continued to press his case, and in 1967 President Johnson proposed a temporary 10% increase in personal income taxes. Representative Mills now endorsed the measure, and the temporary tax increase went into effect the following year. The Fed, concerned that the tax hike would be *too* contractionary, countered the administration's contractionary fiscal policy with a policy of vigorous money growth in 1967 and 1968.

The late 1960s suggested a sobering reality about the new Keynesian orthodoxy: stimulating the economy was politically more palatable than contracting it. Expansionary policies like the Kennedy tax cuts were relatively quick to implement, which made closing recessionary gaps fairly straightforward. But even a mild and temporary tax increase like Johnson's faced fierce opposition and took years to put in place. That made inflationary gaps tough to close. As a result, the second half of the 1960s was marked by persistent efforts to boost aggregate demand, efforts that kept the economy in an inflationary gap. It was that inflationary gap which would usher in a series of supply-side troubles in the next decade.

See related Concept Problem 13 at the end of this chapter.

Answer to Try It! Problem

Even with an inflationary gap, it is possible to pursue expansionary fiscal and monetary policies, shifting the aggregate demand curve to the right, as shown. The inflationary gap will, however, produce an increase in nominal wages, reducing short-run aggregate supply over time. In the case shown here, real GDP rises at first, then falls back to potential output with the reduction in short-run aggregate supply.

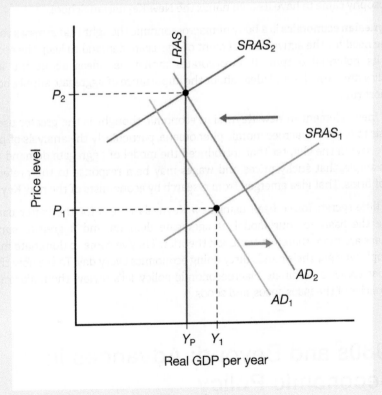

17.4 Macroeconomics for the Twenty-first Century

Learning Objectives

1. Discuss how the Fed incorporated a strong inflation constraint and lags into its policies from the 1980s onward.
2. Describe the fiscal policies that were undertaken from the 1980s onwards and their rationales.
3. Discuss the challenges that events from the 1980s onwards raised for the monetarist and new classical schools of thought.
4. Summarize the views and policy approaches of the new Keynesian school of economic thought.

Following the recession that ended in 1982, the United States enjoyed a long period of low inflation and economic growth that led many, economists included, to believe that the business cycle had been tamed. Those twenty-five years, often referred to as the Great Moderation, weren't recession-free, but the downturns were fairly mild and short-lived. There was a strong sense that evolving macroeconomic theories and policies, drawing on elements of Keynesian, monetarism, and new classical economics, had been responsible for this economic bliss. That synthesis of economic theory and philosophy came to have its own name: the New Keynesian School.

New Keynesian economics is a body of macroeconomic thought that stresses the stickiness of prices and the need for the active management of aggregate demand to keep the economy operating close to its potential output. It incorporates monetarist ideas about the importance of monetary policy and new classical ideas about the importance of aggregate supply, both in the long and in the short run.

Another "new" element in new Keynesian economic thought is the greater use of microeconomic analysis to explain macroeconomic phenomena, particularly the analysis of price and wage stickiness. We saw in the chapter that introduced the model of aggregate demand and aggregate supply, for example, that sticky prices and wages may be a response to the preferences of consumers and of firms. That idea emerged from research by economists of the new Keynesian school.

Here's a little secret: You've been using new Keynesian ideas for the better part of a semester—they are the basis for our model of aggregate demand and aggregate supply. But new Keynesian ideas are more than just textbook theories: They've come to dominate macroeconomic policy for people who get their hands dirty doing economics every day. To see how the new Keynesian school has come to dominate macroeconomic policy, let's review the major macroeconomic events and policies of the 1980s, 1990s, and 2000s.

new Keynesian economics

A body of macroeconomic thought that stresses the stickiness of prices and the need for the active management of aggregate demand to keep the economy operating close to its potential output. It incorporates monetarist ideas about the importance of monetary policy and new classical ideas about the importance of aggregate supply, both in the long run and in the short run.

The 1980s and Beyond: Advances in Macroeconomic Policy

The economic events of the 1970s and the challenges those events posed for policymakers provided the impetus for a rethinking of both policy objectives and the tools used to meet those objectives. By the late 1970s, macroeconomists had shown increasing interest in using monetary policy to deal with inflationary and recessionary gaps.

The Revolution in Monetary Policy

The monetary policy revolution of the last two decades began on July 25, 1979, when President Jimmy Carter appointed Paul Volcker to be chairman of the Fed's Board of Governors. Volcker, with President Carter's support, charted a new direction for the Fed. That new direction damaged Carter politically, but it ultimately produced dramatic gains for the economy.

Oil prices rose sharply in 1979 as war broke out between Iran and Iraq. On its own, such an increase would shift the short-run aggregate supply curve to the left, causing the price level to rise, real GDP to fall, and a recessionary gap to open. But expansionary fiscal and monetary policies pushed aggregate demand up at the same time. As a result, real GDP stayed at potential output, while the price level soared. CPI inflation rose 13.5%, the highest inflation rate recorded in the twentieth century. People came to expect high inflation and began incorporating those expectations into wage and contract negotiations.

New Fed Chairman Volcker made getting inflation under control job one. He charted a monetarist course of fixing the growth rate of the money supply to bring inflation down. After the high rates of money growth of the past, this new policy was sharply contractionary. With less money available in the money market, interest rates skyrocketed, sharply depressing investment and consumption and shifting the aggregate demand curve to the left. Continued oil price increases produced more leftward shifts in the short-run aggregate supply curve. The combined effects of decreasing aggregate demand and decreasing aggregate supply pushed the economy into recession by 1980, while inflation remained high. Figure 17.9 shows how the combined shifts in aggregate demand and short-run aggregate supply produced a reduction in real GDP and an increase in the price level.

FIGURE 17.9 The Fed's Fight Against Inflation
By 1979, expansionary fiscal and monetary policies had brought the economy to its potential output. Then war between Iran and Iraq caused oil prices to increase, shifting the short-run aggregate supply curve to the left. In the second half of 1979, the Fed launched an aggressive contractionary policy aimed at reducing inflation. The Fed's action shifted the aggregate demand curve to the left. The result in 1980 was a recession with continued inflation.

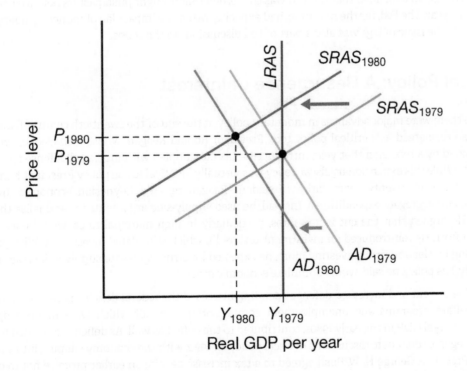

Volcker knew that until expectations could be re-anchored at a lower level, he would be unsuccessful at beating inflation. He stuck to his contractionary guns, and the inflation rate finally began to ratchet its way downward in 1981. But the recession worsened. Unemployment soared, shooting above 10% late in the year. It was, up to that point, the worst recession since the Great Depression. The inflation rate, though, fell sharply in 1982, and the Fed began to shift to a modestly expansionary policy in 1983. Inflation, however, had been licked, dropping to just 4.1% that year, the lowest since 1967.

In the 1980s, Fed Chair Paul Volcker made wringing inflation out of the economy his most urgent priority.

Source: Alvarezroure. "Portrait of Paul A. Volcker by Luis Alvarez Roure." Via Wikimedia: https:// commons.wikimedia.org/wiki/ File:Portrait_of_Paul_A._Volcker_ by_Luis_Alvarez_Roure.jpg. Reproduced via Creative Commons Attribution-ShareAlike 3.0 Unported (CC BY-SA 3.0) license: https://creativecommons. org/licenses/by-sa/3.0/deed.en.

The Fed's actions represented a sharp departure from those of the previous two decades. Faced with soaring unemployment, the Fed did not shift to an expansionary policy until inflation was well under control. Inflation continued to edge downward through most of the remaining years of the twentieth century and into the new century. The Fed has clearly shifted to a stabilization policy with a strong inflation constraint, shifting to expansionary policy when the economy has a recessionary gap, but only if it regards inflation as being under control.

In fact, inflation is now one of the Fed's official targets of policy. This concern about inflation was evident again when the U.S. economy began to weaken in 2008, and there was initially discussion among the members of the Federal Open Market Committee about whether or not easing would contribute to inflation. At that time, it looked like inflation was becoming a more serious problem, largely due to increases in oil and other commodity prices. Some members of the Fed, including then Chairman Ben Bernanke, argued that these price increases were likely to be temporary, and the Fed began using expansionary monetary policy early on. By late summer and early fall, inflationary pressures had subsided, and all the members of the FOMC were behind continued expansionary policy. Indeed, at that point, the Fed let it be known that it was willing to do anything in its power to fight the current recession.

The next major advance in monetary policy came in the 1990s, under then Federal Reserve Chairman Alan Greenspan. When Iraq's invasion of Kuwait in 1990 sent oil prices soaring, the Fed shifted to an expansionary policy as the economy slipped into a recession. By early 1994, real GDP was rising, but the economy remained in a recessionary gap. Nevertheless, the Fed announced on February 4, 1994, that it had shifted to a contractionary policy, selling bonds to boost interest rates and to reduce the money supply. While the economy had not reached its potential output, Chairman Greenspan explained that the Fed was concerned that it might push past its potential output within a year. The Fed, for the first time, had explicitly taken the impact lag of monetary policy into account. The issue of lags was also a part of Fed discussions in the 2000s.

Fiscal Policy: A Resurgence of Interest

While there were major advances in monetary policy at the end of the twentieth century, fiscal policy also reemerged as a critical policy tool. President Ronald Reagan, whose 1980 election victory was aided by a recession that year, introduced a tax cut coupled with increased defense spending in 1981. While this expansionary fiscal policy was virtually identical to the policy President Kennedy had introduced twenty years earlier, President Reagan rejected Keynesian economics (which focused on aggregate expenditures). Instead, he used supply-side arguments to rationalize the tax cuts. He argued that the cut in tax rates, particularly in high marginal rates, would encourage work effort. He reintroduced an investment tax credit, which stimulated investment. With people working harder and firms investing more, he expected long-run aggregate supply to increase more rapidly. His policy, he said, would stimulate economic growth.

The tax cut and increased defense spending increased the federal deficit. Increased spending for welfare programs and unemployment compensation, both of which were induced by the plunge in real GDP in the early 1980s, contributed to the deficit as well. As deficits continued to rise, they began to dominate discussions of fiscal policy. In 1990, with the economy slipping into a recession, President George H. W. Bush agreed to a tax increase despite an earlier promise not to do so. President Bill Clinton, whose 1992 election resulted largely from the recession of 1990–1991, introduced another tax increase in 1994, with the economy still in a recessionary gap. Both tax increases were designed to curb rising deficits.

At that time, deficits were a major concern for policymakers—so concerning that in the aftermath of the 1990 recession, a Democratic Congress rejected a Clinton stimulus package of increased government investment and tax cuts designed to stimulate private investment. The deficit acted like a straitjacket for fiscal policy. The Bush and Clinton tax increases, coupled with spending restraint and increased revenues from economic growth, brought an end to the deficit in 1998.

Initially, it was expected that the budget surplus would continue well into the new century. But that picture changed rapidly. President George W. Bush campaigned on a platform of large tax cuts, arguing that less government intervention in the economy would be good for long-term economic growth. Tax cuts in 2001 and 2003, coupled with large increases in government spending related to the Iraq War and a new Medicare drug benefit, pushed the government back into deficit . . . where it has been ever since.

Check, Please: When the government runs a deficit, it borrows what it needs. This clock, at One Bryant Park in New York City, keeps track of that borrowing. As of February 13, 2019, your future family is on the hook for over $400,000.

Source: rblfmr/Shutterstock.com

At the end of the second Bush administration, the economy began to weaken. An over-exuberant decade of investment in housing, fueled by new financial instruments, low interest rates, and a lot of real estate speculation, was starting to show cracks. (For more about this, see "Case in Point: Not-So-Great Financial Instruments Touch Off Great Recession".) With that weakness came a resurgence of interest in using discretionary increases in government spending. Three factors were paramount: (1) A set of temporary tax cuts had provided only a minor amount of stimulus to the economy; sizable portions of those tax cuts had been saved rather than spent; (2) expansionary monetary policy, while useful, had not seemed adequate—many of the new reserves created during the Fed's quantitative easing program were simply piled up in bank vaults rather than being used to extend credit; and (3) the recession threatening the global economy was larger than those in recent economic history.

The Rise of New Keynesian Economics

New Keynesian economics emerged in the twenty-first century as the dominant school of macroeconomic thought. There are two reasons why this happened. First, it successfully incorporated important monetarist and new classical ideas into Keynesian economics. Second, developments in the 1980s and 1990s shook economists' confidence in the ability of the monetarist or the new classical school alone to explain macroeconomic change.

Monetary Change and Monetarism

Look again at Figure 17.7. The close relationship between M2 and nominal GDP in the 1960s and 1970s helped win over many economists to the monetarist camp. Now look at Figure 17.10. It shows the same two variables, M2 and nominal GDP, from the 1980s through 2015. The tidy relationship between the two seems to have vanished. What happened?

The sudden change in the relationship between the money stock and nominal GDP has resulted partly from public policy. Deregulation of the banking industry in the early 1980s produced sharp changes in the ways individuals dealt with money, thus changing the relationship of money to economic activity. Banks have been freed to offer a wide range of financial alternatives to their customers. One of the most important developments has been the introduction of bond funds offered by banks. These funds allowed customers to earn the higher interest rates paid by long-term bonds while at the same time being able to transfer funds easily into checking accounts as needed. Balances in these bond funds are not counted as part of M2. As people shifted assets out of M2 accounts and into bond funds, velocity rose. That changed the once-close relationship between changes in the quantity of money and changes in nominal GDP.

FIGURE 17.10 M2 and Nominal GDP, 1980–2015

The close relationship between M2 and nominal GDP a year later that had prevailed in the 1960s and 1970s seemed to vanish from the 1980s onward.

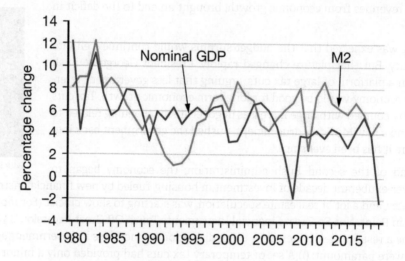

Source: Data from Federal Reserve System and Bureau of Economic Analysis, accessed through Federal Reserve Economic Data (FRED) at https://fred.stlouisfed.org/series/M2SL and https://fred.stlouisfed.org/series/GDP.

Many monetarists have argued that the experience of the 1980s, 1990s, and 2000s reinforces their view that the instability of velocity in the short run makes monetary policy an inappropriate tool for short-run stabilization. They continue to insist, however, that the velocity of M2 remains stable in the long run. But the velocity of M2 appears to have diverged in recent years from its long-run path. Although it may someday return to its long-run level, the stability of velocity remains very much in doubt. Because of this instability, in 2000, when the Fed was no longer required by law to report money target ranges, it discontinued the practice.

FIGURE 17.11 M2 Velocity, 1960–2020

M2 velocity was relatively stable from 1960 to 1990. Since 1990, velocity has made dramatic swings—first up, then down. The link between M2 and nominal GDP is no longer stable and predictable!

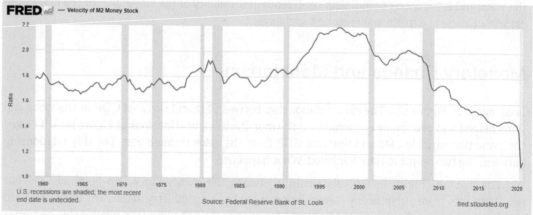

Source: Federal Reserve Bank of St. Louis, Velocity of M2 Money Stock [M2V], retrieved from FRED, Federal Reserve Bank of St. Louis; https://fred.stlouisfed.org/series/M2V.

The New Classical School and Responses to Policy

New classical economics suggests that people should have responded to the fiscal and monetary policies of the 1980s in predictable ways. They did not, and that has created new doubts among economists about the validity of the new classical argument.

The rational expectations hypothesis predicts that if a shift in monetary policy by the Fed is anticipated, it will have no effect on real GDP. The slowing in the rate of growth of the money supply over the period from 1979 to 1982 was surely well known. The Fed announced at the outset what it was going to do and then did it. It had the full support first of President Carter and then of President Reagan. But the policy plunged the economy into what was then its worst recession since the Great Depression. The experience hardly seemed consistent with new classical logic. New classical economists argued that people may have doubted the Fed would keep its word, but the episode still cast doubt on the rational expectations argument.

The public's response to the huge deficits of the Reagan era also seemed to belie new classical ideas. One new classical argument predicts that people will increase their savings rate in response to an increase in public-sector borrowing. The resultant reduction in consumption will cancel the impact of the increase in deficit-financed government expenditures. But the private savings rate in the United States, stable for years, began to *fall* during the 1980s, and continued falling, even through the high-deficit Iraq War years until the beginning of the Great Recession. New classical economists contend that standard measures of saving do not fully represent the actual savings rate, but the experience of the 1980s, 1990s, and 2000s did not seem to support the new classical argument.

The events of the 1980s and beyond do not suggest that either monetarist or new classical ideas should be abandoned, but those events certainly raised doubts about relying solely on these approaches. Similarly, doubts about Keynesian economics raised by the events of the 1970s led Keynesians to modify and strengthen their approach.

A Macroeconomic Consensus?

While there is less consensus on macroeconomic policy issues than on some other economic issues (particularly those in the microeconomic and international areas), surveys of economists generally show that the New Keynesian approach has emerged as the preferred approach to macroeconomic analysis. About 80% of economists agree that expansionary fiscal measures can deal with recessionary gaps, which suggests that most economists can be counted in the New Keynesian camp, as neither monetarist nor new classical analysis would support such measures.

Ironically, during the Great Moderation of the mid-1980s to early 2000s, about 70% of economists felt that discretionary fiscal policy should be avoided and that the business cycle should be managed by the Fed. A similar survey after the Great Recession, however, showed that many economists had become more sympathetic to using discretionary fiscal policy. Perhaps economists generally feel that monetary policy should do the heavy lifting during typical recessions but that both fiscal and monetary policy should be used during severe recessions.[7]

And those severe recessions have taught economists something. To combat the Great Recession, the government and the Fed coordinated to mount a recession-fighting program of unprecedented scale. (See our chapters on monetary and fiscal policy for more information on the nature of those programs.) That program of monetary and fiscal policy coordination was successful in staving off a complete meltdown in the financial system—a meltdown that would likely have created something much more depression-like.

That experience definitely affected economists' views concerning macroeconomic policy. According to a 2010 survey of economic policy given to members of the National Association for Business Economics (NABE), almost 60% were supportive of monetary policy at that time, which was strongly expansionary.[8] There was less agreement about fiscal policy: 22% characterized it as "about right," another third found it too restrictive, and about one third found it too stimulative. Nearly 75% of the economists surveyed ranked promotion of economic growth as more important than deficit reduction; roughly two thirds supported the extension of unemployment benefits; and 60% agreed that awarding states with federal assistance funds from the 2009 stimulus package was appropriate. Taken together, the new Keynesian approach still seems to reflect the dominant opinion.

That growing consensus served as a guide to policy during the coronavirus crisis in early 2020. Without delay, the Federal Reserve launched a massive bond-buying effort to pump reserves into the financial system; at the same time, the Treasury was implementing a set of fiscal measures—including tax rebates, stimulus checks, and extensions and supplements to unemployment insurance—that had been used before, but not in such a coordinated way and not on so large a scale. That coordinated effort, of course, did not prevent the COVID-19 recession, but it did spark a turnaround unprecedented in its speed and size. In short, the economic authorities have learned that stabilization policy is not an "either/or" proposition; nor is it the "nothing can solve this unless you surprise them" conclusion of the rational expectations camp. Instead, economists have come to realize that both monetary and fiscal policy have power; and that power can be highly effective even in *very* troubled times when the response is forceful and coordinated.

Pop! Goes the Econ: Keynes versus Hayek

This econ rap presents the economic philosophies of John Maynard Keynes and his greatest critic, Friedrich Hayek. Look for key points of the Keynesian school in Keynes's rap . . . and then try to decide which school of thought Hayek belongs to (if any!) and why. Be sure to watch through the credits—learning what these men thought about economics and economists is a great way to end a semester studying macroeconomics!

View in the online reader

Is the Great Moderation Over?

You have now lived through two major economic crises—arguably the two largest crises of the last eighty years. Between the Great Depression and the first of these crises, the United States (and much of the rest of the world—at least the developed world) experienced stable growth, occasionally interrupted by recession but rarely by full-fledged economic crisis.

The crises of 2007–2009 and the COVID-19 pandemic represent a departure from that stability. Is this pattern of huge economic busts likely to continue? Is it the new normal? Or were these crises extraordinary and unlikely events—like flipping twenty heads in a row—that just *happened* to occur in relatively back-to-back fashion?

Economist Todd Clark at the Federal Reserve Bank of Kansas City attempted to answer this question.[9] He first looked at three broad reasons for the stability of the U.S. economy during the twenty-five-year period that preceded the Great Recession: structural changes, improved monetary policy, and good luck. While there is disagreement in the literature as to the relative importance of each of these, Clark argues that there's no reason to assume that structural changes and better monetary policy will not continue to have moderating influences. For example, one positive structural change has been better inventory management, and Clark sees no reason why firms should become *less* able to manage inventories well in the future. Similarly, in the future, monetary authorities should be able to continue to make the better decisions that they made during the Great Moderation.

The element that can vary, of course, is luck. It's both unfortunate and rare that the price of oil skyrockets from $54 per barrel to $134 per barrel, as it did between January 2007 and June 2008. It's unfortunate and rare that a speculative asset bubble forms, then bursts, as housing prices did in the Great Recession. And it's an incredibly rare event when one person on the other side of the planet happens to get sick with a new virus—one with just the right characteristics to make managing it nearly impossible—that spread across the globe. Clark says, "Accordingly, once the crisis subsides and the period of very bad luck passes, macroeconomic volatility will likely decline. In the future, the permanence of structural change and improved monetary policy that occurred in years past should ensure that low volatility is the norm."[10]

Key Takeaways

- The actions of the Fed starting in late 1979 reflected a strong inflation constraint and a growing recognition of the impact lag for monetary policy.
- Reducing the deficit dominated much of fiscal policy discussion during the 1980s and 1990s.
- The events of the 1980s and early 1990s do not appear to have been consistent with the hypotheses of either the monetarist or new classical schools.
- New Keynesian economists have incorporated major elements of the ideas of the monetarist and new classical schools into their formulation of macroeconomic theory.

Try It!

Show the effect of an expansionary monetary policy on real GDP

1. according to new Keynesian economics.
2. according to the rational expectations hypothesis.

In both cases, consider both the short-run and the long-run effects.

See related Concept Problem 14 at the end of this chapter.

Case in Point: Steering on a Difficult Course

Source: © Shutterstock, Inc.

Imagine that you are driving a test car on a special course. You get to steer, accelerate, and brake, but you cannot be sure whether the car will respond to your commands within a few feet or within a few miles. The windshield and side windows are blackened, so you cannot see where you are going or even where you are. You can only see where you have been with the rear-view mirror. The course is designed so that you will face difficulties you have never experienced. Your job is to get through the course unscathed. Oh, and by the way, you have to observe the speed limit, but you do not know what it is. Have a nice trip.

Now imagine that the welfare of people all over the world will be affected by how well you drive the course. They are watching you. They are giving you a great deal of often-conflicting advice about what you should do. Thinking about the problems you would face driving such a car will give you some idea of the obstacle course fiscal and monetary authorities must negotiate. They cannot know where the economy is going or where it is—economic indicators such as GDP and the CPI only suggest where the economy has been. And the perils through which it must steer can be awesome indeed.

One policy response that most acknowledge as having been successful was how the Fed dealt with the financial crises in Southeast Asia and elsewhere that shook the world economy in 1997 and 1998. There were serious concerns at the time that economic difficulties around the world would bring the high-flying U.S. economy to its knees and worsen an already difficult economic situation in other countries. The Fed had to steer through the pitfalls that global economic crises threw in front of it.

In the fall of 1998, the Fed chose to accelerate to avoid a possible downturn. The Federal Open Market Committee (FOMC) engaged in expansionary monetary policy by lowering its target for the federal funds rate. Some critics argued at the time that the Fed's action was too weak to counter the impact of world economic crisis. Others, though, criticized the Fed for undertaking an expansionary policy when the U.S. economy seemed already to be in an inflationary gap.

In the summer of 1999, the Fed put on the brakes, shifting back to a slightly contractionary policy. It raised the target for the federal funds rate, first to 5.0% and then to 5.25%. These actions reflected concern about speeding when in an inflationary gap.

But was the economy speeding? Was it in an inflationary gap? Certainly, the U.S. unemployment rate of 4.2% in the fall of 1999 stood well below standard estimates of the natural rate of unemployment. There were few, if any, indications that inflation was a problem, but the Fed had to recognize that inflation might not appear for a very long time after the Fed had taken a particular course. This was also a time when the once-close relationship between money growth and nominal GDP seemed to be breaking down. The shifts in demand for money created unexplained and unexpected changes in velocity.

The outcome of the Fed's actions has been judged a success. While with 20/20 hindsight the Fed's decisions might seem obvious, in fact it was steering a car whose performance seemed less and less predictable over a course that was becoming more and more treacherous.

That brings us to the Great Recession—an episode in which the coordinated actions of the Fed and Treasury were used in unprecedented ways and on an unprecedented scale. The Fed responded with a "no holds barred" approach, moving aggressively to lower the federal funds rate target and engaging in a variety of other measures to improve liquidity to the banking system, to lower other interest rates by purchasing longer-term securities (such as ten-year treasuries and those of Fannie Mae and Freddie Mac), and, working with the Treasury Department, to provide loans related to consumer and business debt.

Fiscal authorities matched the Fed's efforts step for step. In addition to working with the Fed to bail out troubled financial institutions, the Obama administration passed a massive spending and tax relief package of more than $800 billion.[11] Janet Yellen, then president of the Federal Reserve Bank of San Francisco, commented, "The new enthusiasm for fiscal stimulus, and particularly government spending, represents a huge evolution in mainstream thinking."[12] A notable convert to using fiscal policy to deal with this recession was Harvard economist and former adviser to President Ronald Reagan, Martin Feldstein. His spending proposal encouraged increased military spending, and he stated, "While good tax policy can contribute to ending the recession, the heavy lifting will have to be done by increased government spending."

Of course, not all economists jumped onto the fiscal policy bandwagon. Many raised concerns so-called "shovel-ready" projects could really be implemented in time, whether government spending would crowd out private spending, whether monetary policy alone was providing enough stimulus, and whether the spending would flow efficiently to truly worthwhile projects. Those controversies persist. But the importance and usefulness of aggressive monetary and fiscal policy was, at least in this episode, not particularly in doubt. The policy response in the Great Recession has shaped the policy response to the coronavirus, and will continue to serve as a guide for crisis management decades into the future.

See related Concept Problem 15 at the end of this chapter.

Sources: Based on Ben S. Bernanke, "The Crisis and the Policy Response" (speech, London School of Economics, January 13, 2009); Louis Uchitelle, "Economists Warm to Government Spending but Debate Its Form," The New York Times, January 7, 2009, p. B1.

Answers to Try It! Problems

Panel (a) shows an expansionary monetary policy according to new Keynesian economics. Aggregate demand increases, with no immediate reduction in short-run aggregate supply. Real GDP rises to Y_2. In the long run, nominal wages rise, reducing short-run aggregate supply and returning real GDP to potential. Panel (b) shows what happens with rational expectations. When the Fed increases the money supply, people anticipate the rise in prices. Workers and firms agree to an increase in nominal wages, so that there is a reduction in short-run aggregate supply at the same time there is an increase in aggregate demand. The result is no change in real GDP; it remains at potential. There is, however, an increase in the price level.

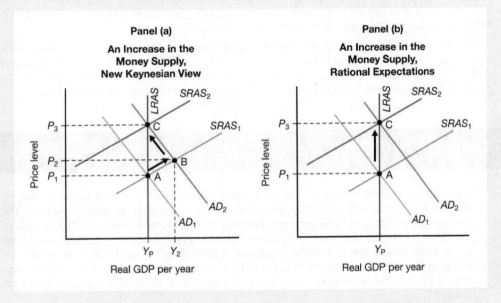

17.5 Review and Practice

Summary

We have surveyed the experience of the United States in light of the economic theories that prevailed or emerged during more than five decades. We have seen that events in the past century have had significant effects on the ways in which economists look at and interpret macroeconomic ideas.

Before the Great Depression, macroeconomic thought was dominated by the classical school. That body of theory stressed the economy's ability to reach full employment equilibrium on its own. The severity and duration of the Depression caused many economists to rethink their acceptance of natural equilibrating forces in the economy.

John Maynard Keynes issued the most telling challenge. He argued that wage rigidities and other factors could prevent the economy from closing a recessionary gap on its own. Further, he showed that expansionary fiscal and monetary policies could be used to increase aggregate demand and move the economy to its potential output. Although these ideas did not immediately affect U.S. policy, the increases in aggregate demand brought by the onset of World War II did bring the economy to full employment. Many economists became convinced of the validity of Keynes's analysis and his prescriptions for macroeconomic policy.

Keynesian economics dominated economic policy in the United States in the 1960s. Fiscal and monetary policies increased aggregate demand and produced what was then the longest expansion in U.S. history. But the economy pushed well beyond full employment in the latter part of the decade, and inflation increased. While Keynesians were dominant, monetarist economists argued that it was monetary policy that accounted for the expansion of the 1960s and that fiscal policy could not affect aggregate demand.

Efforts by the Nixon administration in 1969 and 1970 to cool the economy ran afoul of shifts in the short-run aggregate supply curve. The ensuing decade saw a series of shifts in aggregate supply that contributed to three more recessions by 1982. As economists studied these shifts, they developed further the basic notions we now express in the aggregate demand–aggregate supply model: that changes in aggregate demand and aggregate supply affect income and the price level; that changes in fiscal and monetary policy can affect aggregate demand; and that in the long run, the economy moves to its potential level of output.

The events of the 1980s and beyond raised serious challenges for the monetarist and new classical schools. New Keynesian economists formulated revisions in their theories, incorporating many of the ideas suggested by monetarist and new classical economists. The new, more powerful theory of macroeconomic events has won considerable support among economists today.

Concept Problems

1. Suppose you read the following: "For many years, the hands-off fiscal policies advocated by the classical economists held sway with American government. When times were hard, the prevailing response was to tough it out, awaiting the 'inevitable' turnaround. The lessons of the Great Depression and a booming wartime economy have since taught us, however, that government intervention is sometimes necessary and desirable—and that to an extent, we can take charge of our own economic lives." Evaluate this statement based upon the discussion in this chapter. How would you classify the speaker in terms of a school of economic thought?

2. In his 1982 *Economic Report of the President*, Ronald Reagan said, "We simply cannot blame crop failures and oil price increases for our basic inflation problem. The continuous, underlying cause was poor government policy."[13] What policies might he have been referring to?

3. Many journalists blamed economic policies of the Reagan administration for the extremely high levels of unemployment in 1982 and 1983. Given the record of the rest of the decade, do you agree that President Reagan's economic policies were a failure? Why or why not?

4. The day after the U.S. stock market crash of October 19, 1987, Federal Reserve Board Chairman Alan Greenspan issued the following statement: "The Federal Reserve, consistent with its responsibilities as the nation's central bank, affirmed today its readiness to serve as a source of liquidity to support the economic and financial system."[14] Evaluate why the Fed chairman might have been prompted to make such a statement.

5. Compare the rationale of the Reagan administration for the 1981 tax reductions with the rationale behind the Kennedy–Johnson tax cut of 1964, the Bush tax cut of 2001, and the Bush tax cut of 2003.

6. If the economy is operating below its potential output, what kind of gap exists? What kinds of fiscal or monetary policies might you use to close this gap? Can you think of any objection to the use of such policies?

7. If the economy is operating above its potential output, what kind of gap exists? What kinds of fiscal or monetary policies might you use to close this gap? Can you think of any objection to the use of such policies?

8. In *General Theory*, Keynes wrote of the importance of ideas. The world, he said, is ruled by little else. How important do you think his ideas have been for economic policy today?

9. (Related to "Try It!" in Section 29.3.) State whether each of the following events appears to be the result of a shift in short-run aggregate supply or aggregate demand, and state the direction of the shift involved.

   a. The price level rises sharply while real GDP falls.

   b. The price level and real GDP rise.

   c. The price level falls while real GDP rises.

   d. The price level and real GDP fall.

10. Explain whether each of the following events and policies will affect the aggregate demand curve or the short-run aggregate supply curve, and state what will happen to the price level and real GDP.

   a. Oil prices rise

   b. The Fed sells bonds

   c. Government purchases increase

   d. Federal taxes increase

   e. The government slashes transfer payment spending

   f. Oil prices fall

11. (Related to "Try It!" in Section 29.2.) Using the model of aggregate demand and aggregate supply, illustrate an economy with an inflationary gap. Show how a policy of nonintervention would ultimately close the gap. Show the alternative of closing the gap through stabilization policy.

12. (Related to "Case in Point: Early Views on Stickiness" in Section 29.2.) Using the model of aggregate demand and aggregate supply, illustrate an economy with an inflationary gap. Show how a policy of nonintervention would ultimately close the gap. Show the alternative of closing the gap through stabilization policy. What advantage does stabilization policy hold over nonintervention as a means to close the gap? Does price stickiness play a role in creating that advantage?

13. (Related to "Case in Point: Tough Medicine Is Hard to Stomach: Macroeconomic Policy in the 1960s" in Section 29.3.) Why might monetary policy be a more popular means to close an inflationary gap than fiscal policy? Refer to the general tools of each kind of policy in your answer.

14. (Related to "Try It!" in Section 29.4.) Explain why, if expectations are rational, both monetary and fiscal policy might be rendered powerless. Use an aggregate demand/aggregate supply graph to illustrate your answer.

15. (Related to "Case in Point: Steering on a Difficult Course" in Section 29.4.) Suppose the economy experiences an adverse supply shock that throws the economy into a recession. Using the *AD/AS* model, explain the importance of the government and the central bank agreeing on economic priorities and coordinating their fiscal and monetary policy responses.

Endnotes

1. David C. Wheelock, "The Federal Response to Home Mortgage Distress: Lessons from the Great Depression," *Federal Reserve Bank of St. Louis Review* 90, no. 3 (Part 1) (May/June 2008): 133–48.

2. Technically, the Great Depression only lasted from 1929 to 1933. But the recession was so deep that even during the recovery, the economy was in worse shape than it was at the peak of the Great and COVID-19 recessions. And in the midst of that recovery? Yes, you've got it: Another year-long recession in 1937–38.

3. For a discussion of fiscal policy during the Great Depression, see E. Cary Brown, "Fiscal Policy in the 'Thirties: A Reappraisal," *American Economic Review* 46, no. 5 (December 1956): 857–79.

4. Henry Thomas, *An Enquiry into the Nature and Effects of the Paper Credit of Great Britain* (Philadelphia: James Humphreys, 1802).

5. *The World's Classics XXXIII: The Works of David Hume: Essays: Moral, Political and Literary by David Hume* (London: Grant Richards, 1903).

6. Because changes in the money stock can take a while to influence economic activity, today's change in the money stock is graphed with *next year's* change in GDP.

7. Dan Fuller and Doris Geide-Stevenson, "Consensus among Economists — An Update," *Journal of Economic Education* 45:2 (2014): 131–146.

8. National Association for Business Economics, Economic Policy Surveys, March 2009 and August 2010, available at http://www.nabe.com.

9. Todd E. Clark, "Is the Great Moderation Over? An Empirical Analysis," *Federal Reserve Bank of Kansas City Economic Review* 94, no. 4 (Fourth Quarter 2009): 5–42.

10. Ibid., 27.

11. Not all troubled financial institutions were bailed out, however—most notable among them commercial bank Washington Mutual (see the associated Case in Point in our chapter on banking and the money supply) and investment bank Lehman Brothers.

12. Louis Uchitelle, "Economists Warm to Government Spending but Debate Its Form," *The New York Times*, January 7, 2009, p. B1.

13. Ronald Reagan, "Message to the Congress Transmitting the Annual Economic Report of the President" (speech, February 10, 1982). Retrieved from: https://www.reaganlibrary.gov/archives/speech/message-congress-transmitting-annual-economic-report-president.

14. Donald Bernhardt and Marshall Eckblad, Federal Reserve Bank of Chicago. "Stock Market Crash of 1987." Retrieved from: https://www.federalreservehistory.org/essays/stock-market-crash-of-1987.

CHAPTER 18
Inequality, Poverty, and Discrimination

18.1 Start Up: Occupy Wall Street; Change the World?

It all began in September 2011, when thousands of demonstrators unhappy with the nature of the U.S. economy—the distribution of income, Wall Street greed, bank bailouts, the winner-take-all nature of capitalism, and a variety of other issues—converged on Wall Street to make their voices heard. The protestors, many of whom were struggling in the wake of the Great Recession, commandeered a small park near the canyons of Wall Street, pitching tents where they'd live for the next few months while protesting by day. That long-term commitment to daily protest gave the movement its name: Occupy Wall Street.

During the Occupy movement, "We are the 99%" was a popular catchphrase protesting the increasing wealth of the top 1%.

Source: Rena Schild/Shutterstock.com

The Occupy movement soon became an international phenomenon. By mid-October, the *Economist* reported demonstrations in more than 900 cities and in more than 80 countries. The demonstrators were bound by a shared dissatisfaction, but the sources of that dissatisfaction varied. Pollster Douglas Schoen interviewed about 200 Occupy protesters early in the movement, and found that they were generally committed to a radical redistribution of income and sharp increases in government regulation of the economy, with 98% supporting civil disobedience to further their aims and 31% advocating violence if necessary. How was the rest of the country feeling about the protests? A Pew survey found Americans divided in their opinion, with nearly 40% in support and about 35% opposed.[1]

The Occupy movement eventually lost steam, but it clearly brought the issues examined in this chapter—poverty, discrimination, and the distribution of income—to the forefront of public attention. So attuned was America to the income distribution in the wake of the Great Recession and the Occupy protests that economist Thomas Piketty's *Capital in the Twenty-First Century*—a 700-page tome on the history and nature of economic inequality—spent weeks at the top of the 2014 New York Times bestseller list.[2]

Well, their intentions were good, but most readers likely abandoned Thomas Piketty's *Capital* by page 26.

Just as the Occupy movement was gaining traction, the poverty rate was hitting a decades-high rate of 15.1%. Over 46.2 million Americans were living below the $22,000 poverty line, the highest number ever recorded in the history of the United States. Decades after President Lyndon B. Johnson declared a "War on Poverty," the problem remained, despite trillions of dollars in federal antipoverty spending, including stepped-up federal aid to low-income people, an expanded health-care program for the poor, new housing subsidies, expanded federal aid to education, and job training programs.

Source: Ssilverartist/Shutterstock.com

This chapter explores both poverty and inequality. It also takes a closer look at discrimination, because the bottom end of the economic ladder is disproportionately occupied by racial minorities and women, and it's important to sort out the extent to which that stems from discrimination.

Questions of fairness often accompany discussions of income inequality, poverty, and discrimination. Answering them ultimately involves value judgments: They are normative questions, not positive ones, and they're questions this chapter can't answer for you. You must decide for yourself if a particular distribution of income is fair, or if society has made adequate progress toward reducing poverty or discrimination. The data and ideas about the origins of poverty, inequality, and discrimination that you'll find in this chapter may help inform those decisions.

18.2 Income Inequality

Learning Objectives

1. Explain how the Lorenz curve and the Gini coefficient provide information on a country's distribution of income.
2. Discuss and evaluate the factors that may explain changes in the distribution of income in the United States.

Income inequality in the United States has soared in the last half-century. According to the U.S. Census Bureau, between 1975 and 2019, real (inflation-adjusted) average household income rose 64%. But not everybody saw their real income increase by 64%: The top 5% of the population saw their real incomes increase an average of 128%, while the top 20% of the population almost doubled its real income with a 95% gain. Meanwhile, the bottom fifth of the population, poorer to start with, saw slower growth as well, with real income rising by only about 21%.[3]

The faster growth at the top end of the income distribution points toward increasing inequality over time. Let's take a look at various slices of the population and see exactly how unequal the income distribution is.

TABLE 18.1 The Distribution of Household Income, 2019
The bottom 20% of households had an average household income of $15,286, and took home 3.1% of the country's total income. The top 5% of households had average income of over $450,000 and took home 23% of the country's total income.

	Bottom 20%	Second 20%	Middle 20%	Fourth 20%	Top 20%	Top 5%
Limits	$0–$28,084	$28,085–$53,503	$58,504–$86,488	$86,489–$142,501	$142,502+	$270,002+
Average Income	$15,286	$40,652	$68,938	$111,112	$254,449	$451,122
Share of Total Income, 2019	3.1%	8.3%	14.1%	22.7%	51.9%	23.0%
Share of Total Income, 1967	4%	10.8%	17.3%	24.2%	43.6%	17.2%

Source: Data from Bureau of the Census Historical Income Tables H-1, H-2, and H-3.

Table 18.1 sorts the nation's households into five equal groups, each ranked by income. If your household income was $28,084 or less in 2019, you were in the bottom fifth of all earners. Among that group, the average income was $15,286. On the other hand, if your household income was more than $270,002, you were in the top 5% of all earners; you and your peer group had an average income of over $450,000.

Table 18.1 also shows the overall share of income earned by each of these groups of households. The poorest 20% of households lived on 3.1% of the nation's total income. Meanwhile, the top fifth of earning households snagged over half of the economic pie, and almost half of that slice (23% of total income) went to the top earning 5% of households. The U.S. income distribution is uneven, indeed. And it's getting more uneven over time: The last row of Table 18.1 shows the share of income flowing to each 20% of households a half-century ago. Those numbers reveal growing inequality: Each of the first four quintiles is receiving a smaller slice of the economic pie than they did in 1967. Only the top quintile (and its subgroup, the top 5%) is taking home a bigger share than before.

We're all born with equal rights, but we're not all created equal. Everyone has different abilities, aptitudes, social skills, connections, beauty, circumstances, and luck; all things that can create differences in income.

Source: Lightspring/Shutterstock.com

A Changing Distribution of Income

The changing income-share statistics in Table 18.1 show that the income distribution has become less equal over time. In this section, we'll see how to assess the degree of inequality with a single summary statistic, one that is often used to compare inequality across place and time. One quick reminder: We're focusing only on how the pie is divided, setting aside the important fact that the economic pie has been growing over time (for more on society's overall economic progress, see Chapter 9).

Measuring Inequality

The method we used to highlight the unequal distribution of income above—dividing households into ranked groups and then summarizing the income of each group—is commonplace. That data can be presented graphically using a **Lorenz curve**, a graph that shows cumulative shares of income received by individuals or groups.

To plot the curve, which is shown in blue in Figure 18.1:

- Begin with the lowest quintile (20%) of households. That group brings home 3.1% of total income, so plot a point at 3.1% (point A).

- The bottom 40% of all earners (the first two quintiles) collectively bring home 11.4% of total income (3.1% + 8.3%). That point is plotted as point B.

- The first 60% of all earners bring home 25.5% of all income (3.1% + 8.3% + 14.1%), point C.

- The first 80% of all earners bring home 48.2% of all income, point D.

- All five quintiles bring home 100% of all income, point E.

Figure 18.1 also shows two other curves. The orange curve is the line of perfect equality, where each quintile brings home exactly 20% of the country's total income: The bottom 20% of households would receive 20% of income; the bottom 40% would receive 40%, and so on. The more skewed a country's income distribution is, the smaller the share of income that will be received by each quintile, and the farther a country's Lorenz curve will be from the line of perfect equality.[4] The third curve in Figure 18.1 is the Lorenz curve for 1967, shown in grey. Because the 2019 curve is farther from the line of perfect equality than the 1967 curve, we know that income inequality is growing.

Lorenz curve

A curve that shows cumulative shares of income received by individuals or groups.

FIGURE 18.1 The Distribution of U.S. Income, 1967 and 2019
The distribution of income among households in the United States became more unequal from 1967 to 2019. The shares of income received by each of the first four quintiles fell, while the share received by the top 20% rose sharply. The Lorenz curve for 2019 was more bowed out than was the curve for 1967, indicating greater inequality.

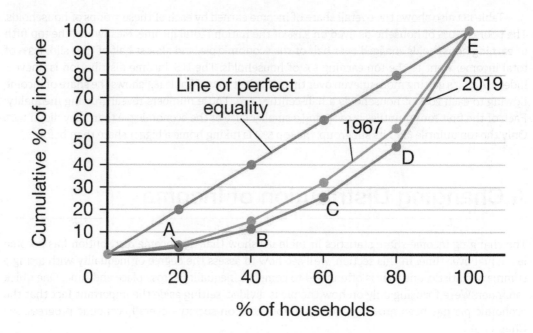

Source: Data from U.S. Census Bureau

Liberté, egalité, fraternité: In France, they're so proud of their freedom, unity, and low Gini coefficient that even the public toilets brag about it!

Source: Sergey_Bogomyako/Shutterstock.com

Gini coefficient

A measure of inequality expressed as the ratio of the area between the Lorenz curve and a 45° line and the total area under the 45° line.

The Lorenz curve is the basis for an often-used summary measure of income inequality. The **Gini coefficient** measures the size of the gap between the line of perfect equality and the Lorenz curve, as a percentage of the total area under the line of perfect equality. In Figure 18.1, it is the area between the orange and blue curves, divided by the total area under the orange curve.

Larger Gini coefficients indicate greater inequality. The more equal the income distribution, the closer the blue line will be to the orange, and the closer to zero the Gini coefficient will be. On the other hand, if there were perfect *inequality* (nobody gets any income at all except one person who gets everything), the gap between orange and blue would be the same size as the area under the line of perfect equality; the Gini coefficient would be 1. The Census Bureau reports that the Gini coefficient was 0.397 in 1967 and 0.484 in 2019—indicating growing income inequality.[5]

The U.S. Gini coefficient is not the highest in the world, but it's still high by world standards. Among developed countries, the U.S. Gini coefficient is similar to those in Hong Kong and Singapore, but much higher than the 0.25 in egalitarian Sweden, or Germany's 0.27. Developing countries sometimes have more inequality than the United States (South Africa's Gini is 0.625), but many have less (see Pakistan and Egypt, which have Gini indices in the neighborhood of 0.3).

Mobility and Income Distribution

The people who occupy a given income quintile change from year to year. Some families who are in the bottom quintile one year move up to higher quintiles in subsequent years; other families move down. Because people move up and down the distribution, we get a quite different picture of income change when we look at the incomes of a fixed set of persons over time rather than comparing average incomes for a particular quintile at a particular point in time, as was done in Figure 18.1.

Generally speaking, increasing inequality isn't that much of a problem as long as economic mobility—the ability to move up and down the income ladder—is high. Economists generally measure income mobility in two ways. First, they may look at *intergenerational mobility*—the ability of a child to escape his or her parents' circumstances—by looking for correlations between parents' and children's incomes. Second, they may follow particular individuals for a long stretch of time to see how those persons' incomes change, and then measure the probability of a person's jumping from one part of the income distribution to another.

In the most comprehensive study of income mobility to date, Harvard economists Raj Chetty and Nathaniel Hendren, along with Berkeley economists Patrick Kline and Emmanuel Saez and Nicholas Turner of the Department of the Treasury, examined more than 40 million tax records (with identifying information removed) of people born in the U.S. between 1971 and 1993. Contrary to public perception that mobility is declining, they found little change in recent decades. In 1971, a child born into the lowest-income quintile had an 8.4% chance of making it to the top quintile. By 1986, there was a 9% chance of making that same leap. Their conclusion—that income mobility had changed little over the past fifty years—confirmed several less-sophisticated studies that had reached the same conclusion.

Chetty's study also confirmed that economic mobility in the United States is lower than in many other developed countries.[6] And in a second study spun off from the original project, the authors determined that even economic mobility in the United States depends a lot on geography: A child born into the bottom quintile of the income distribution in San Jose has a 12.9% chance of reaching the top quintile; a similar child in Atlanta has only a 4.5% chance.

The authors pinpoint five factors that are correlated with economic mobility:

1. **Segregation by race or income.** The more segregated (by race or income) the city, the lower the associated economic mobility.

2. **Family structure.** A higher prevalence of single-parent households in a community is correlated with lower economic mobility.

3. **School quality.** Areas with higher test scores, lower dropout rates, and smaller class sizes had greater mobility.

4. **Social capital.** Greater religious and civic participation are positively correlated with economic mobility.

5. **Economic inequality.** Smaller income gaps among the middle class were associated with greater income mobility.

It is easy to understand why a widening income distribution is discouraging to those at the bottom of the income ladder. But the work of Chetty, Hendren, Kline, Saez, and Turner suggests that those who start at the bottom of the income ladder don't have to remain there. Their research also informs those who are interested in preserving or improving economic mobility about some potential policy targets.

Irrelevant inequality: If economic mobility is high, then everyone has a chance to claw their way to the top.

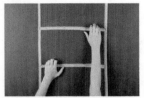

Source: stockfour/Shutterstock.com

Explaining Inequality

Everyone agrees that the distribution of income in the United States generally became more equal during the first two decades after World War II and that it has become more unequal since the mid-1960s. That has left many wondering why the distribution changed. Let's take a look at some of the explanations.

Family Structure

Clearly, an important source of rising inequality since the 1960s has been the sharp increase in the number of families headed by women. In 2019, the median income of families headed by married couples was twice that of families headed by women without a spouse.[7] Given that the proportion of families headed by women with no spouse present has nearly doubled since 1968, it's not surprising that inequality across households is increasing.

Globalization

globalization

The increasing integration of the world's economies.

A second fundamental change in the economy has been increasing **globalization**, the increasing integration of the world's economies. For many, globalization has been a wonderful thing: It's given U.S. producers access to larger markets, and it brings consumers greater variety at lower cost. Additionally, being forced to compete with foreign-produced goods has led domestic producers to improve the quality of their products.

For all of its virtues, globalization has not been kind to America's low-skilled workers. It turns out that the world is full of low-skilled workers capable of doing the same jobs as low-skilled American workers, often at a fraction of the cost. Ultimately, globalization (like everything else) has costs and benefits. It has created opportunities for people with special skills to expand who they sell to, but it has also closed doors and reduced wages for those who don't have special skills. On net, it's a possible culprit in the widening gap between rich and poor.

Technological, Education, and Managerial Change

A century ago, this man would have been in high demand. Today, not so much . . . what with tow trucks and all.

Source: semyon lorberg/Shutterstock.com

One hundred years ago, work was very different: It consisted of hard, physical labor that didn't require a lot of skill. As the century unfolded, a lot of that difficult, back-breaking work was automated, with humans replaced by capital. That has affected the demand for labor. Specifically, the demand for unskilled labor has decreased, while the demand for skilled labor has risen. The result of those changing demands has been an increase in the gap between the wages of skilled and unskilled workers; similar forces are producing a widening gap between college- and high-school-educated workers.

Technological change has also meant the integration of computers into virtually every aspect of production. That's made workers more productive, and it has increased the demand for workers with the knowledge to put new methods to work. That has increased the demand for workers with lots of human capital—education and training.

Along with new technologies that require greater technical expertise, firms are adopting new management styles that require stronger communication skills. The use of production teams, for example, shifts decision-making authority to small groups of assembly-line workers. That means those workers need more than the manual dexterity that was required of them in the past. They must write effectively, speak effectively, and interact effectively with other workers. Workers who cannot do so simply are not in demand to the degree they once were.

The result of those changing demands for labor—decreases in the demand for unskilled and under-educated workers, and increases in the demand for skilled and educated workers—is widening inequality. Wages are shrinking at the bottom end of the skills spectrum and rising near the top. Evidence of this is found in the college wage gap, which is near an all-time high: In 2020, a college graduate can expect to earn $1.80 for every dollar earned by someone with just a high-school diploma.

Increasingly, education is the key to a better material life. The 80% gap between the average annual incomes of high school graduates and those with a bachelor's degree has increased substantially over the last half century. In fact, it's risen a lot just in the past twenty years. Unfortunately, education is not an equal opportunity employer: A student from a family in the upper end of the income distribution is much more likely to get a college degree than is a student whose family is in the lower end of the income distribution.[8]

Pop! Goes the Econ: The Race Between Education and Technology

In this politically charged clip, the men of *South Park* are faring poorly in the race between education and technology. What is the trade-off between jobs for everyone and economic progress? Would you sacrifice your technology to help keep someone employed?

The inequality resulting from education and skill acquisition perpetuates itself in a second way, too. College graduates tend to marry other college graduates; high-school dropouts who marry tend to marry other high-school dropouts . . . and are also more likely to have children out of wedlock or never marry at all. The income distribution widens, and then gets wider still in the next generation; two-parent, wealthier households are often better able to provide opportunities for their children to build social and cultural capital (club sports, music lessons, even bedtime reading) that greatly increase the chances of educational success later in life.[9]

Tournament-Style Markets

Each year, tens of thousands of high-school students head off to college on sports scholarships. Of those players, only a tiny fraction will become professional athletes. For most, the years of sacrifice and the dream of going pro end when they receive their diplomas.

Economist Sherwin Rosen likens labor markets like this to tournaments: The people who enter them know they are likely to lose but are hoping to be lucky enough or skilled enough to win. Winning, of course, takes some luck. But odds are that the winner of a tournament creates success by having exactly the right blend of qualities in sufficient amounts. Of course, in today's digital economy, it's not just pro athletes who "win." It's actors and actresses looking for a starring role in Hollywood; it's singers hoping to win *The Voice*, and it's social influencers like Rosanna Pansino or Jeffree Star hoping to create internet empires out of lifestyle blogs. Many of those people are talented, but few are so complete and so super-talented that they have the mass appeal necessary to achieve stardom and the income that stardom produces.

The bigger the market, the bigger the rewards to stardom. Globalization, as mentioned before, means bigger markets. But so does technology. The technologically interconnected world gives the especially talented new ways to leverage their stardom. First, technology allows superstars to reach more people. Today, people in Outer Mongolia can watch Taylor Swift sing on their iPhones; twenty years ago, they wouldn't have known who the top American recording stars *were*. Second, technology has created new ways for superstars to earn income: Taylor Swift collects a tiny share of Google's ad revenue each time an Outer Mongolian plays one of her YouTube videos.

So, globalization has provided increased opportunities for higher-skilled labor, and growing technology has done the same. But both have produced outsized, exponential rewards for superstar talents. That's true for superstars like Taylor Swift and Steph Curry, but it's also true for corporate superstars: Since 1982, the pay of corporate chief executive officers (CEOs) has grown from forty times the typical worker's wages to over 280 times the typical worker's wages. CEOs of the top 500 companies made an average of $11.7 million in 2018.

"After a hard day of hunting, there's nothing better than kicking back in the yurt with a charcoal face mask and Spotify's T-Swifty channel."

Source: Stella sophie/ Shutterstock.com

Tax Policy

Did tax policy contribute to rising inequality over the past four decades? The tax changes most often cited in the fairness debate are the Reagan tax cuts introduced in 1981 and the Bush tax cuts introduced in 2001, 2002, and 2003.[10]

An analysis of the Bush tax cuts by the Tax Foundation combines the three Bush tax cuts and assumes they occurred in 2003. Table 18.2 gives the share of total income tax liability for each quintile before and after the Bush tax cuts. It also gives the share of the Bush tax cuts received by each quintile.

TABLE 18.2 Income Tax Liability Before and After the Bush Tax Cuts
The share of total tax relief received by the first four quintiles was modest, while those in the top quintile received more than two-thirds of the total benefits of the three tax cuts. However, the share of income taxes paid by each of the first four quintiles fell as a result of the tax cuts, while the share paid by the top quintile rose.

Quintile	Share of Income Tax Liability before Tax Cuts (%)	Share of Income Tax Liability after Tax Cuts (%)	Share of Total Tax Relief (%)
First quintile	0.5	0.3	1.2
Second quintile	2.3	1.9	4.2
Third quintile	5.9	5.2	9.4
Fourth quintile	12.6	11.6	17.5
Top quintile	78.7	81.0	67.7

Source: Based on data from William Ahern, "Comparing the Kennedy, Reagan, and Bush Tax Cuts," Tax Foundation Fiscal Facts, August 24, 2004.

Tax cuts under George W. Bush were widely criticized as being tilted unfairly toward the rich. And certainly, Table 18.2 shows that the share of total tax relief received by the first four quintiles was modest, while those in the top quintile garnered more than two-thirds of the total benefits of the three tax cuts. Looking at the second and third columns of the table, however, gives a different perspective. The share of income taxes paid by each of the first four quintiles fell as a result of the tax cuts, while the share paid by the top quintile rose. Further, we see that each of the first four quintiles paid a very small share of income taxes before and after the tax cuts, while those in the top quintile ended up shouldering more than 80% of the total income tax burden. We saw in Figure 18.1 that those in the top quintile received just over half of total income. After the Bush tax cuts, they paid 81% of income taxes. Others are quick to point out that those same tax cuts were accompanied by reductions in expenditures for some social service programs designed to help lower-income families. Still others point out that the tax cuts contributed to an increase in the federal deficit and, therefore, are likely to have distributional effects over many years and across several generations. Whether these changes increased or decreased fairness in society is ultimately a normative question.

Methodology

The method by which the Census Bureau computes income shares has been challenged by some observers. For example, quintiles of households do not contain the same number of people. Rea Hederman of the Heritage Foundation, a conservative think tank, notes that the top 20% of households contains about 25% of the population—making their size-adjusted incomes a bit smaller. Starting in 2006, the Census Bureau report began calculating a measure called "equivalence-adjusted income" to take into account family size. While the Gini coefficient for 2010 using this adjustment fell slightly from 0.469 to 0.457, the trend over time in the two Gini coefficients is similar. Two other flaws pointed out by Hederman are that taxes and benefits from noncash programs that help the poor are not included. While some Census studies attempt to take these into account and report lower inequality, other studies do not receive as much attention as the main Census annual report.[11]

Even studies that look at incomes over a decade may not capture lifetime income. For example, people in retirement may have a low income, but their consumption may be bolstered by drawing on their savings. Younger people may be borrowing to go to school, buy a house, or for other things. The annual income approach of the Census data does not capture this, and even the ten-year look in the mobility study mentioned above is too short a period. This suggests that more-precise measurements may provide more insight into explaining inequality.

Key Takeaways

- The distribution of income can be illustrated with a Lorenz curve. If all households had the same income, the Lorenz curve would be a 45° line. In general, the more equal the distribution of income, the closer the Lorenz curve will be to the 45° line. A more bowed out curve shows a less equal distribution. The Gini coefficient is another method for describing the distribution of income.
- The distribution of income has, according to the Census Bureau, become somewhat more unequal in the United States during the past forty years.
- The degree of mobility up and down the distribution of income appears to have declined in recent years.
- Among the factors explaining increased inequality have been changes in family structure and changes in the demand for labor that have rewarded those with college degrees and have penalized unskilled workers.
- Assessing the fairness of tax-policy changes is a normative issue that could include looking at how a new policy affects the share of taxes paid by different quintiles as well as its impact on other variables such as government deficits and social programs.

Try It!

The accompanying Lorenz curves show the distribution of income in a country before taxes and welfare benefits are taken into account (curve *A*) and after taxes and welfare benefits are taken into account (curve *B*). Do taxes and benefits serve to make the distribution of income in the country more equal or more unequal?

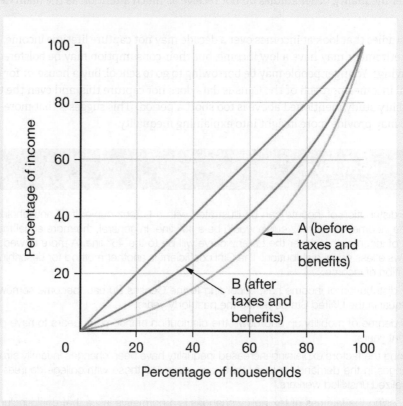

See related Numerical Problem 2 at the end of this chapter.

Case in Point: Attitudes and Inequality

"C'mon, man, this is America—now get ahold of those bootstraps and pull, pull, pull!"

Source: NILTON AKIRA IKUNO/Shutterstock.com

In a fascinating examination of attitudes in the United States and in continental Western Europe, economists Alberto Alesina of Harvard University and George-Marios Angeletos of the Massachusetts Institute of Technology suggest that attitudes about the nature of income earning can lead to quite different economic systems and outcomes concerning the distribution of income.

The economists cite survey evidence from the World Values Survey, which concludes that 71% of Americans, and only 40% of Europeans, agree with the proposition: *"The poor could become rich if they just tried hard enough."* Further, Americans are much more likely to attribute material success to hard work, while Europeans tend to attribute success to factors such as luck, connections, and even corruption. The result, according to Professors Alesina and Angeletos, is that Americans select a government that is smaller and engages in less redistributive activity than that selected by Europeans. Government in continental Western Europe is 50% larger than that in the United States, the tax system in Europe is much more progressive than that in the United States, regulation of labor and product markets is more extensive in Europe, and redistributive programs are more extensive in Europe than those in the United States. As a result, the income distribution in Europe is much more equal than in the United States.

People get what they expect. The economists derive two sets of equilibria. Equilibrium in a society in which people think incomes are a result of luck, connections, and corruption turns out to be precisely that. And, in a society in which people believe incomes are chiefly the result of effort and skill, they are. In the latter society, people work harder and invest more. In the United States, the average worker works 1,600 hours per year. In Europe, the average worker works 1,200 hours per year.

So, who is right—Americans with their "you get what you deserve" or Europeans with their "you get what luck, connections, and corruption bring you" attitude? The two economists show that people get, in effect, what they expect. European values and beliefs produce societies that are more egalitarian. American values and beliefs produce the American result: a society in which the distribution of income is more unequal, the government smaller, and redistribution relatively minor. Professors Alesina and Angeletos conclude that Europeans tend to underestimate the degree to which people can improve their material well-being through hard work, while Americans tend to overestimate that same phenomenon.

See related Concept Problem 10 at the end of this chapter.

Source: Based on Alberto Alesina and George-Marios Angeletos, "Fairness and Redistribution," American Economic Review 95:4 (September, 2005) 960–80.

Answer to Try It! Problem

The Lorenz curve showing the distribution of income after taxes and benefits are taken into account is less bowed out than the Lorenz curve showing the distribution of income before taxes and benefits are taken into account. Thus, income is more equally distributed after taking them into account.

18.3 The Economics of Poverty

Learning Objectives

1. Distinguish between relative and absolute measures of poverty and discuss the uses and merits of each.
2. Describe the demographics of poverty in the United States.
3. Describe the forms of welfare programs in the United States and the reform of welfare in the mid-1990s.
4. Discuss the factors that have been looked at to explain the persistence of poverty in the United States.

Poverty in the United States is something of a paradox. Per capita incomes in this country are among the highest on Earth; even the lowest-earning 5% of U.S. households make more than 60% of households in the rest of the world. Despite that apparent well-being, the United States has a greater percentage of its population below the official poverty line than do most other industrialized nations. How can a nation that is so rich have so many people who are poor?

There is no single answer to the question of why so many people are poor. A good place to begin our discussion is to see exactly how we *define* poverty.

Defining Poverty

Suppose you were asked to determine whether a particular family was poor or not poor. How would you do it? You might begin by listing the goods and services that would be needed to provide a minimum acceptable standard of living, and then figure out whether the family's income was large enough to purchase those items. If not, you might conclude that the family was poor. Alternatively, you might examine the family's income relative to the incomes of other families in the community or in the nation. If the family was on the low end of the income scale, you might classify it as poor.

absolute income test

Income test that sets a specific income level and defines a person as poor if his or her income falls below that level.

relative income test

Income test in which people whose incomes fall at the bottom of the income distribution are considered poor.

These two approaches represent two bases on which poverty is defined. The first is an **absolute income test**, which sets a specific income level and defines a person as poor if their income falls below that level. The second is a **relative income test**, in which people whose incomes fall at the bottom of the income distribution are considered poor. For example, we could rank households according to income as we did in the previous section on income inequality and define the lowest one-fifth of households as poor. By that definition, in 2019, any U.S. household with an annual income below $28,084 was below the poverty line.

> ## Pop! Goes the Econ: *Young Sheldon* and Rich v. Poor
>
> This clip from *Young Sheldon* compares and contrasts the ideas of absolute income and relative income. It runs counter to the way most economists have likely been trained, but in the real world, relative comparisons seem to matter a great deal.

poverty line

Amount of annual income below which the federal government defines a household as poor.

In contrast, to determine who is poor according to the absolute income test, we define a specific level of income, independent of how many households fall above or below it. The federal government defines a household as poor if the household's annual income falls below a dollar figure called the **poverty line**. In 2019, the poverty line for a family of four was an income of $25,750. Table 18.3 shows the poverty line for various family sizes.

TABLE 18.3 Weighted Average Poverty Thresholds in 2019, by Size of Family
This table contains the poverty threshold for various family sizes. Because the cost of living varies in different states, this national-level data is a weighted average of each state's calculated poverty line.

Number of People in Household	Poverty Line ($)
One	12,490
Two	16,910
Three	21,330
Four	25,750
Five	30,170
Six	34,590
Seven	39,010
Eight	43,430

Source: U.S. Department of Health and Human Services

The concept of an absolute poverty line grew out of a Department of Agriculture study in 1955 showing that families spent one-third of their incomes on food. With that one-third figure as a guide, the department then selected food plans that met the minimum daily nutritional requirements established by the federal government. The cost of the least expensive plan for each household size was multiplied by three to determine the poverty line for that size household. The government used this method to count the number of poor people from 1959 to 1969. After 1969, the poverty line was adjusted annually by the average percentage price change for all consumer goods, not just changes in the price of food.

There are some definite weaknesses to using this "food times three" method to define poverty. It makes no attempt to establish the income needed to provide other basic necessities, like shelter, clothing, and health care. In fact, it doesn't even attempt to establish what those necessities might be! Further, the day has long passed when the average household devoted one-third of its income to food purchases; today food purchases account for less than one-seventh of household income. Still, it's useful to have *some* threshold that is consistent from one year to the next so that progress in the fight against poverty can be measured; the "food times three" method provides a clear benchmark. In addition, the U.S. Census Bureau and the Bureau of Labor Statistics have begun working on more broad-based alternative measures of poverty. A new Supplemental Poverty Measure is based on expenses for food, clothing, shelter, and utilities; it adjusts for geographic differences; adds in various in-kind benefits such as school lunches, housing subsidies, and energy assistance; factors in tax credits; and then subtracts out taxes, work expenses, and out-of-pocket medical expenses. The Supplemental Poverty Rate tracks the official poverty rate fairly well, but generally shows that the official poverty rate understates the true poverty rate by about two percentage points.[12]

That **poverty rate** measures the percentage of the population that falls below the poverty line. Figure 18.2 shows the poverty rate from 1959 to 2019. In ordinary times, the poverty rate tends to hover in the 12%–13% range. But it rises during recessions, and tends to decline during long expansions.

poverty rate

The percentage of the population that falls below the poverty line.

FIGURE 18.2 The Poverty Rate in the United States, 1959–2019
These graphs show the number of people (in millions) living below the poverty line (top panel) and the percentage of people living below the poverty line (bottom panel) between 1959 and 2019. The poverty rate declined greatly throughout the 1960s, settling between 10% and 15%. The poverty rate tends to rise during recessions and fall during long expansions.

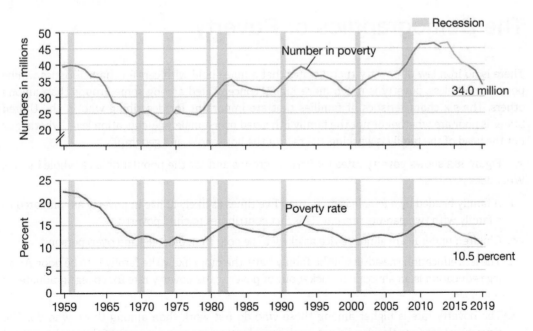

Source: Jessica Semega, Melissa Kollar, Emily A. Shrider, and John F. Creamer, "Income and Poverty in the United States: 2019," Figure 7. Report Number P60-270, September 15, 2020. U.S. Census Bureau. Retrieved from: https://www.census.gov/content/dam/Census/library/publications/2020/demo/p60-270.pdf.

School's Out: Poverty in the United States often looks a lot different than poverty elsewhere in the world. This young Indian boy works full time scrounging for recyclables in trash heaps.

Source: clicksabhi/Shutterstock.com

Despite its shortcomings, measuring poverty using an absolute measure allows for the possibility of progress in reducing it. Using a relative measure of poverty, however, does not: There will always be a lowest 1/5 or 1/10 (however you choose to define relative poverty) of the population. But relative measures do make an important point: Poverty is, in large part, a relative concept. In the United States, people defined as poor have much higher incomes than most of the world's people or even than average Americans did as recently as the early 1970s. By international and historical standards, the average poor person in the United States is rich! The material possessions of America's poor would be considered lavish in another time and in another place. For example, based on survey data from 2005 to 2009, 42% of *poor* households in the United States owned their own homes, nearly 75% owned a car, 64% had cable or satellite TV, and over 80% had air conditioning. Forty years ago, only 36% of the *entire* population in the United States had air conditioning. The average poor person in the United States has more living space than the average person—*rich or poor*—in London, Paris, Vienna, or Athens.[13]

But people judge their incomes relative to incomes of people around them, not relative to people everywhere on the planet or to people in years past. You may feel poor when you compare yourself to some of your classmates who may have fancier cars or better clothes. A family of four with an annual income of $18,000 living in Chicago surely doesn't feel rich, even though its income is many times higher than the average family income in Ethiopia. While the material possessions of poor Americans are vast by Ethiopian standards, they are low in comparison to how the average American lives. What we think of as poverty clearly depends more on what people around us are earning than on some absolute measure of income.

Both the absolute and relative income approaches are used in discussions of the poverty problem. When we speak of the number of poor people, we are typically using an absolute income test of poverty. When we speak of the problems of those at the bottom of the income distribution, we are speaking in terms of relative income. In the rest of this section, we focus on the absolute income test of poverty used in the United States.

The Demographics of Poverty

There is no iron law of poverty that dictates that a household with certain characteristics will be poor. Nonetheless, poverty is much more highly concentrated among some groups than among others. The six characteristics of families that are important for describing who in the United States is poor are whether or not the family is headed by a female, age, education level, whether or not the head of the family is working, the race of the household, and geography.

Figure 18.3 shows poverty rates for various groups and for the population as a whole in 2019. What does it tell us?

1. A family headed by a female is more than five times as likely to live in poverty as compared to a family with two parents present. This fact contributes to child poverty.

2. Children under 18 are almost twice as likely to be poor than older (65 and over) persons.

3. The less education the adults in the family have, the more likely the family is to be poor. A college education is an almost sure ticket out of poverty; the poverty rate for college graduates is under 4%.

4. The poverty rate is higher among those who do not work than among those who do. The poverty rate for people who did not work is twelve times the poverty rate of those who worked full time.

5. The poverty rate in cities is higher than that in suburbia.

6. The prevalence of poverty varies by race and ethnicity. The poverty rate for whites (non-Hispanic origin) was less than half that of Hispanics and blacks.

FIGURE 18.3 The Demographics of Poverty in the United States, 2019
Poverty rates in the United States vary significantly according to a variety of demographic factors. The lowest rates of poverty are found in married-couple families, those with college degrees, those working full time, those living in the suburbs, and those of Asian descent.

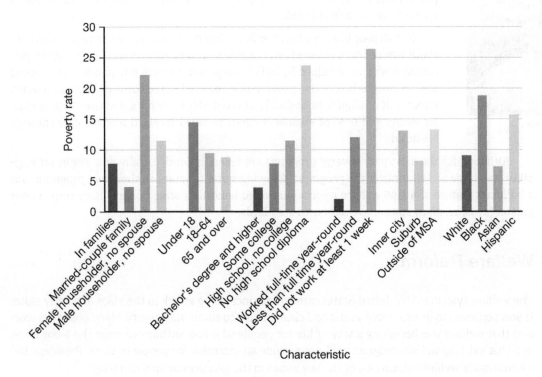

Source: Based on data from Jesssica Semega, Melissa Kollar, Emily A. Shrider, and John F. Creamer. "Income and Poverty in the United States: 2019." Report Number P60–270, September 15, 2020. U.S. Census Bureau. Retrieved from: https://www.census.gov/library/publications/2020/demo/p60-270.html.

We've just broken down poverty rates by single characteristics—race, education, etc. When those characteristics are combined, the poverty rate can soar. For example, the poverty rate for families with children that are headed by women who lack a high school education is higher than 50%.

Government Policy and Poverty

Consider a young single parent with three small children. The parent is unemployed and has no support from other relatives. For families like these, the government has created an array of **welfare programs** to help alleviate and ameliorate poverty.

The primary form of cash assistance is likely to come from a program called Temporary Assistance for Needy Families (TANF). This program began with the passage of the Personal Responsibility and Work Opportunity Reconciliation Act of 1996. It replaced Aid to Families with Dependent Children (AFDC). TANF is funded by the federal government but administered through the states. Eligibility is limited to two years of continuous payments and to five years in a person's lifetime, although 20% of a state's caseload may be exempted from this requirement.

In addition to this assistance, the family is likely to qualify for food assistance through the Supplemental Nutrition Assistance Program—commonly called SNAP benefits. Those benefits, loaded onto an easy-to-use EBT card, can be used to purchase qualified food items. Our representative fam-

welfare programs

The array of programs that government provides to alleviate poverty.

ily may also receive rent vouchers that can be used as payment for private housing, and the family may qualify for Medicaid, a program that pays for physician and hospital care as well as for prescription drugs.

Nobody's getting rich on welfare benefits, but it's sure nice to have a helping hand.

Source: bluedog studio/Shutterstock.com

A host of other programs provide help ranging from counseling in nutrition to job placement services. The parent may qualify for federal assistance in attending college. The children may participate in the Head Start program, a program of preschool education designed primarily for low-income children. If the poverty rate in the area is unusually high, local public schools the children attend may receive extra federal aid.

Not all people whose incomes fall below the poverty line received aid. In 2019, about 75% of those counted as poor received *some* form of aid. However, the percentages who were helped by individual programs were much lower. Only about 20% of people below the poverty line received some form of cash assistance. About half of eligible households received SNAP benefits, and over 70% of eligible adults and 90% of eligible children received received medical care through Medicaid.

Although for the most part poverty programs are federally funded, individual states set eligibility standards and administer the programs. Allowing states to establish their own programs was a hallmark feature of a 1996 welfare reform (discussed below). As state budgets have come under greater pressure, many states have tightened standards.

Welfare Reform

The welfare system in the United States came under increasing attack in the 1980s and early 1990s. It was perceived to be expensive, and it had clearly failed to eliminate poverty. Many observers worried that welfare was becoming a way of life for people who had withdrawn from the labor force, and that existing welfare programs did not provide an incentive for people to work. President Bill Clinton made welfare reform one of the key issues in the 1992 presidential campaign.

The Personal Responsibility and Work Opportunity Reconciliation Act of 1996 was designed to move people from welfare to work. It eliminated the entitlement aspect of welfare by defining a maximum period of eligibility. It gave states considerable scope in designing their own programs. In the first years following welfare reform, the number of people on welfare dropped by several million. Research on the impact of reform showed that caseloads declined and employment increased, with no net adverse effect on poverty or the well-being of children. This positive outcome seemed to be the combined result of larger-than-expected behavior response to the welfare reforms, a robust economy, and an expansion of the earned income tax credit.[14]

Advocates of welfare reform proclaimed victory, while critics pointed to the booming economy, the tight labor market, and the general increase in the number of jobs over the same period. The recession that began at the end of 2007 and the ensuing slow recovery in the unemployment rate provided a real-time test of the effects of the reform. Economists Marianne Bitler and Hilary Hoynes analyzed the impact of welfare reform during the Great Recession on nonelderly families with children. They found that participation in cash assistance programs seemed less responsive to the downturn but that participation in noncash safety net programs, particularly the food assistance program, had become more responsive. They did find some evidence that the increase in poverty or near-poverty status might have been greater than it would have been without the reform.[15]

Explaining the Persistence of Poverty

Just as the increase in income inequality begs for explanation, so does the question of why poverty seems so persistent. Shouldn't poverty have fallen in the long economic expansions during 1980s, 1990s, early 2000s, and 2010s?

It's clear that some of the same factors that have contributed to rising income inequality have also contributed to the persistence of poverty. One factor is an increase in the number of single-parent households over the past several decades: In 1960, 88% of children lived in a home with two parents; today, only about 68% do. Four out of five single-parent households are headed by a woman; those households are also statistically the most likely to be below the poverty line. A second factor contributing to persistent poverty is the growing wage gap between skilled and unskilled workers: Increases in trade and automation have made unskilled labor particularly vulnerable to poverty.

Tax and Transfer Policy

Tax policy changes, on the other hand, have reduced the extent of poverty. In addition to general reductions in tax rates, the Earned Income Tax Credit, which began in 1975 and which was expanded in the 1990s, provides people below a certain income level with a supplement for each dollar of income earned. This supplement, roughly 30 cents for every dollar earned, is received as a tax refund at the end of the year.

Taken together, though, transfer payment and tax programs in the United States are less effective in reducing poverty than are the programs of other developed countries. Figure 18.4 shows the share of households, after adjusting for size, with incomes below half the national median. The figure shows this share before (in blue) and after tax and transfer payment programs are considered (in red). The United States is fairly typical in terms of the number living in poverty before social programs are considered. However, it ranks last in terms of the number living in poverty even after the various forms of public assistance are considered.

FIGURE 18.4 Share of Individuals Living in Households with Income Below Half of Household-Size-Adjusted Median Income, Various Countries
List of major countries with the pre-tax and transfer and post-tax and transfer percentages shown on graph.

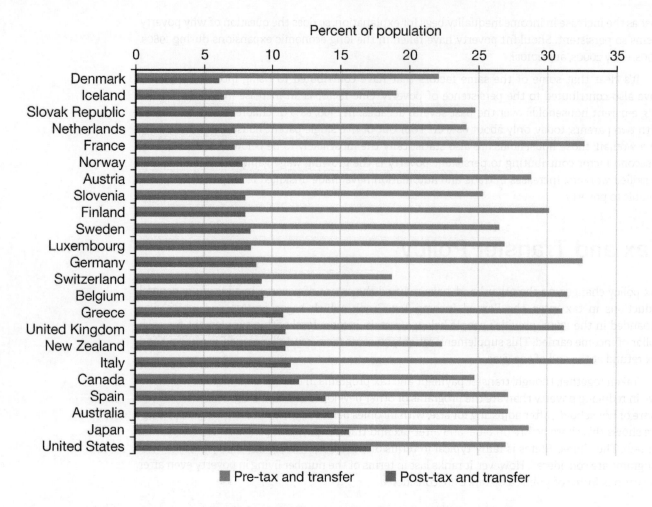

Source: Based on data from Economic Policy Institute. 2012. "Relative poverty rate in the United States and selected OECD countries, late 2000s" [chart] and "Extent to which taxes and transfer programs reduce the relative poverty rate, selected OECD countries, late 2000s." The State of Working America. Washington, D.C.: Economic Policy Institute. October 16, 2016. http://stateofworkingamerica.org/chart/swa-poverty-figure-7w-relative-poverty-rate/ and http://stateofworkingamerica.org/chart/swa-poverty-figure-7z-effect-taxes-transfer/.

Poverty and Work

Can poverty be reduced, not by social programs, but simply by providing more work opportunities to the poor? How does poverty relate to work? Look back at Figure 18.3. Many of the poor are children or adults over age 65 and some are already working full time. Taken together, these three groups represent more than half of those in poverty. Also included among the poor are people who are ill or disabled, people who do not work due to family or home reasons, and people who are in school. The Census Bureau found in 2010 that of the nation's 46.2 million poor people, nearly 3 million reported they were not working or worked only part of the year or part time because they could not find full-time work.[16] So, while more employment opportunities would partly alleviate poverty, reducing unemployment is clearly only part of the answer.

Key Takeaways

- Poverty may be defined according to a relative or an absolute definition.
- Official estimates of the number of people who are "poor" are typically based on an absolute definition of poverty, one that many view as inadequate and dated.
- Several demographic factors appear to be associated with poverty. Families headed by single women are three times as likely to be poor as are other families. Poverty is also associated with low levels of education and with minority status.
- There is a wide range of welfare programs; the majority of welfare spending is for noncash assistance. Those receiving this aid do not have it counted as income in the official calculations of poverty.
- Welfare reform has focused on requiring recipients to enter the labor force. Many poor people, however, are not candidates for the labor force.

Try It!

The Smiths, a family of four, have an income of $27,500 in 2019. Using the absolute income test approach and the data given in the chapter, determine if this family is poor. Then, use the relative income test to determine if this family is poor.

See related Numerical Problem 4 at the end of this chapter.

Case in Point: A Basic Solution to the Welfare-to-Work Problem

"Oh, *SNAP!* Worked too many hours, now they're cutting my food assistance."

Source: Pressmaster/Shutterstock.com

Most people agree that as a society, it's both smart and humane to provide the less fortunate with *some* sort of safety net. Government programs like the Children's Health Insurance Program (CHIP), the Supplemental Nutrition Assistance Program (SNAP), Medicaid, the Earned Income Tax Credit (EITC), and Temporary Assistance for Needy Families (TANF) all help make life just a bit easier for both lower-income parents and their children.

The assistance provided through those programs declines, however, as a participant's income increases. That process, called *means testing*, helps ensure that your hard-earned tax dollars aren't being used to support someone who is perfectly capable of supporting himself. In our politically polarized, market-based economy, it's highly unlikely that most people (or their elected representatives) would vote in favor of a welfare program without it being means tested.

Unfortunately, the very nature of means testing has an unintended consequence: It results in the poor facing extremely high marginal tax rates. That may seem silly, given the fact that the lowest income tax bracket is just 10%, and we're talking about the poor. But that 10% is just the *statutory* income tax rate. The real problem is the *implicit* taxes the poor pay as they work their way out of poverty.

Let's use an example to see why means testing creates high implicit taxes. Low-income worker Simon decides he wants to work an extra hour this week, and during that hour he earns $10. He'll have to pay $1 to the government to cover his income tax, and about $0.70 to cover his Social Security and Medicare taxes. Simon's statutory tax burden, then, is $1.70 on $10 of income, for an overall tax rate of 17%.

But Simon, with his low income, is also receiving some means-tested public assistance. Because he's earning just enough, the extra income Simon earns during that additional hour will cause his SNAP benefits to decline by $1. He'll also see his earned income tax credit decline by $0.50, and $1.50 of his health insurance exchange subsidy will disappear. None of those losses will show up on his pay stub, of course. But they *will* show up (or, more accurately, fail to show up) in his bank balance at the end of the month. Ultimately, Simon only finds himself $6.30 better off because of his decision to earn $10; his overall tax rate is not a modest 17%; it's an astonishingly high 47%.

Economist C. Eugene Steuerle has calculated the effective tax rate faced by the poor, a rate that includes both statutory income taxes and the implicit taxes caused by means testing. For a tax-payer with children earning around $20,000 per year, the effective marginal tax rate is almost 100%—much higher than even the 37% marginal rate paid by the richest of the rich.

Steuerle's numbers show that, because of means testing, an extra hour of work for a low-income individual can result in absolutely *zero* change in his bank balance. That may help explain why once someone enters poverty, they often remain there: *If working doesn't make you any wealth-ier, why do it?* Steuerle credits the implicit taxes of means-tested social programs with creating a long-term assistance dependence for about one-third of recipients.

If, as a society, we want to reduce poverty, a good starting point is to make it *easier* to return to work rather than harder. If the impediment is the high implicit taxes of means testing, then perhaps the solution is to *eliminate the means testing*. One way to do that would be to replace today's web of overlapping means-tested social programs with a simple cash payment sufficient to cover a bare minimum of necessities—say, $1,000 each month. Eliminating means testing, though, means that *everyone* would receive that benefit—from the poorest single mother to the richest dot-com billionaire.

In America, of course, we're used to the "you get what you work for" ethos. This kind of Universal Basic Income (UBI) program, proposed by presidential hopeful Andrew Yang in 2020 Democra-tic primaries, looks suspiciously like a handout: People get their check whether they work ninety hours a week or **gasp** not at all!

That's going to make such a program a very hard sell in Washington, D.C., where its most vocal opponents are certain to declare that UBI will encourage the poor to work less. But because the benefits of UBI are never phased out, the implicit taxes of means testing disappear. That means that the poor will get to take home just as much of their income as anyone else, an important step in encouraging them, paradoxically, to work not less, but more!

See related Concept Problem 6 at the end of this chapter.

Source: Based on C. Eugene Steuerle's report to the House of Representatives, "Labor Force Participation, Taxes, and the Nation's Social Welfare System," 2013.

Answer to Try It! Problem

According to the absolute income test, the Smiths are not poor because their income of $27,500 falls above the 2019 poverty threshold of $25,750. According to the relative income test, how-ever, they *are* poor, because their $27,500 income is below the upper limit of the lowest quintile, $28,084.

18.4 The Economics of Discrimination

Learning Objectives

1. Define discrimination, identify some sources of it, and illustrate Becker's model of discrimination using demand and supply in a hypothetical labor market.
2. Assess the effectiveness of government efforts to reduce discrimination in the United States.

Being a female head of household or being a member of a racial minority increases the likelihood of being at the low end of the income distribution and of being poor. In the real world, we know that, on average, women and members of racial minorities receive different wages from white male workers, even though they may have similar qualifications and backgrounds. They might be charged different prices or denied employment opportunities. This section examines the economic forces that create such discrimination, as well as the measures that can be used to address it.

Discrimination in the Marketplace: A Model

Discrimination occurs when people with similar economic characteristics experience different economic outcomes because of their race, sex, or other noneconomic characteristics. A black worker whose skills and experience are identical to those of a white worker but who receives a lower wage is a victim of discrimination. A woman denied a job opportunity solely on the basis of her gender is the victim of discrimination. To the extent that discrimination exists, a country will not be allocating resources efficiently; the economy will be operating inside its production possibilities curve.

discrimination

When people with similar economic characteristics experience different economic outcomes because of their race, sex, or other noneconomic characteristics.

Pop! Goes the Econ: What's in a Name?

Will your very name keep you from getting called back for a job? This clip from Freakonomics explores the "blackness" of names and its impact on success in the labor market.

Digital Downloads

Freakonomics_Can Your Name Hurt Your Job Opportunities Transcript.docx
https://catalog.flatworldknowledge.com/a/35275/
Freakonomics_Can_Your_Name_Hurt_Your_Job_Opportunities_Transcript-9f83.docx

Pioneering work on the economics of discrimination was done by Gary S. Becker, an economist at the University of Chicago, who won the Nobel Prize in economics in 1992. He suggested that discrimination occurs because of people's preferences or attitudes. If enough people have prejudices against certain racial groups, or against women, or against people with any particular characteristic, the market will respond to those preferences.

In Becker's model, discriminatory preferences drive a wedge between the outcomes experienced by different groups. Discriminatory preferences can make salespeople less willing to sell to one group than to another, or they may make consumers less willing to buy from the members of one group than from another, or make workers of one race or sex or ethnic group less willing to work with those of another race, sex, or ethnic group.

Let's explore Becker's model by examining labor-market discrimination against black workers. First, assume that no discriminatory preferences or attitudes exist. For simplicity, suppose that the supply curves of black and white workers are identical; they are shown as the single red curve in Figure 18.5. Let's also assume that all workers have identical marginal products; they are equally productive. In the absence of racial preferences, the demand for workers of both races would be D: Black and white workers would each receive a wage W per unit of labor, and a total of L black workers and L white workers would be employed.

FIGURE 18.5 Prejudice and Discrimination
If employers, customers, or employees have discriminatory preferences, and those preferences are widespread, then the marketplace will result in discrimination. Here, black workers receive a lower wage and fewer of them are employed than would be the case in the absence of discriminatory preferences.

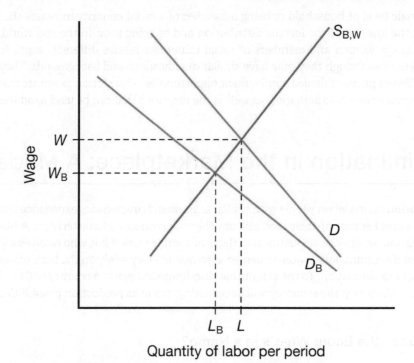

Now suppose that employers have discriminatory attitudes that cause them either to (1) assume that a black worker is less productive than an otherwise similar white worker, or (2) not care that black workers are equally productive, but instead indulge a taste for bigotry against blacks. Now employers have a lower demand, D_B, for black than for white workers. Employers pay black workers a lower wage, W_B, and employ fewer of them (L_B instead of L) than they would in the absence of discrimination.

Sources of Discrimination

As illustrated in Figure 18.5, racial prejudices on the part of employers produce discrimination against black workers, who receive lower wages and have fewer employment opportunities than white workers. But that isn't the only source of discrimination:

- One source of discriminatory prejudices is other workers. Suppose, for example, that white workers prefer not to work with black workers and require a wage premium for doing so. Such preferences would, in effect, raise the cost to the firm of hiring black workers. Firms would respond by demanding fewer of them, and wages for black workers would fall.

- Another source of discrimination against black workers could come from customers. If the buyers of a firm's product prefer not to deal with black employees, the firm might respond by demanding fewer of them. In effect, prejudice on the part of consumers would lower the revenue that firms can generate from the output of black workers.

Whether discriminatory preferences exist among employers, employees, or customers, the impact on the group discriminated against will be the same. Fewer members of that group will be employed, and their wages will be lower than the wages of other workers whose skills and experience are otherwise similar.

Competition may force a businessman with a taste for discrimination to put his money where his mouth is.

Source: Marcel Suliman/ Shutterstock.com

The impact on employers, however, might be different. If an employer is indulging his taste for bigotry, he might choose to hire less-productive white employees rather than more-productive black employees. The employer's profits will fall as a result, or those profits will be lower than his non-discriminating competitors' profits. The employer indulges his taste for bigotry, but at a cost. On the other hand, if an employer discriminates in hiring because his customers don't like being served by a black worker, then refusing to hire black workers might cause that employer's profits to rise relative to his non-discriminating competitors.

There's another type of discrimination an employer might engage in that isn't motivated by bigotry but by profitability. That type of discrimination, in which the characteristics of a group are ascribed to an individual, is called **statistical discrimination**. That definition is a little opaque; let's use an example to clarify. Suppose an employer is interviewing candidates for a job, and has narrowed the field to two—one woman and one man. The employer muses, "*Hmmmm . . . if I hire the woman, I'm probably looking at a paid maternity leave in the future, and she may leave her job to raise kids until they're in school. All the training I give her will be lost. But men—men don't bear children! I'd better go with the man.*"

statistical discrimination

Discrimination that results from assigning the characteristics of a group to all of the individuals in that group.

You may not like that reasoning (or the employer) for thinking that way, but it's true: Women bear children, not men; women generally have less job tenure and take more time-outs in their career arcs. The employer is properly assessing the characteristics of the group. However, the employer may be making an error in assigning those characteristics to the female applicant: Not only does she have no interest in having children, but she also is career-oriented pit bull who gets so energized by work that she'll put in hundred-hour weeks for years straight just to ensure a shot at a corner office.

Words You'll Never Hear in a Job Interview: "Hate kids. Can't stand 'em. You'll never have to worry about *me* taking maternity leave."

Source: Africa Studio/Shutterstock.com

You might be thinking that the employer's choice of the man will harm profits, forcing the employer to pay for the discrimination. In this case, that's true. But the employer is making a solid call, on average (at least where profits are concerned), which means that statistical discrimination generally pays off and makes firms more profitable rather than less. In other words, statistical discrimination is unlikely to disappear on its own.

We've used both race and sex in our examples of discrimination. But those aren't the only bases for discrimination. Other documented examples of discrimination include height discrimination, weight discrimination, beauty discrimination, and discrimination based on disability or sexual preference. Whenever discrimination occurs, it implies that employers, workers, or customers have, for one reason or another, discriminatory preferences. For the effects of such preferences to be felt in the marketplace, they must be widely shared.

Discrimination in the United States Today

Discrimination hasn't always been frowned upon by society. Nor has it always been illegal. Beginning in the 1950s, however, demands for social change brought action by the federal government. In 1954, the U.S. Supreme Court rendered its decision that so-called separate but equal schools for black and white children were inherently unequal, and the Court ordered that racially segregated schools be integrated. The Equal Pay Act of 1963 requires employers to pay the same wages to men and women who do substantially the same work. Federal legislation was passed in 1965 to ensure that minorities were not denied the right to vote.

Separate is not Equal.

Source: Everett Collection/Shutterstock.com

Congress passed the most important federal legislation against discrimination in 1964. The Civil Rights Act barred discrimination on the basis of race, sex, or ethnicity in pay, promotion, hiring, firing, and training. An Executive Order issued by President Lyndon Johnson in 1967 required federal contractors to implement *affirmative action* programs—training programs, outreach efforts, and other positive steps to ensure that members of minority groups and women are given equal opportunities in employment.[17] The practical effect of the order was to require that these employers increase the percentage of women and minorities in their work forces. Affirmative action programs for minorities followed at most colleges and universities.

What has been the outcome of these efforts to reduce discrimination? A starting point is to look at wage differences among different groups. Gaps in wages between males and females and between blacks and whites have fallen over time. In 1955, the wages of black men were about 60% of those of white men; in 2015, they were 74% of those of white men. For black men, the reduction in the wage gap occurred primarily between 1965 and 1973. In contrast, the gap between the wages of black women and white men closed more substantially, and progress in closing the gap continued after 1973, albeit at a slower rate. Specifically, the wages of black women were about 35% of those of white men in 1955, 58% in 1975, and 68% in 2019, a slightly lower fraction than a few years earlier. For white women, the pattern of gain is still different. The wages of white women were about 65% of those of white men in 1955 and fell to about 60% from the mid-1960s to the late 1970s. The wages of white females relative to white males have improved, however, over the last forty years. In 2019, white female wages were 80% of white male wages. While there has been improvement in wage gaps between black men, black women, and white women vis-à-vis white men, a substantial gap still remains. Figure 18.6 shows the wage differences for the period 1970–2015.

FIGURE 18.6 The Wage Gap

The exhibit shows the wages of white women, black women, and black men as a percentage of the wages of white men from 1970–2015. The graph shows the gap has closed considerably, but there remains a substantial gap between the wages of white men and those of other groups in the economy. Part of the difference is a result of discrimination.

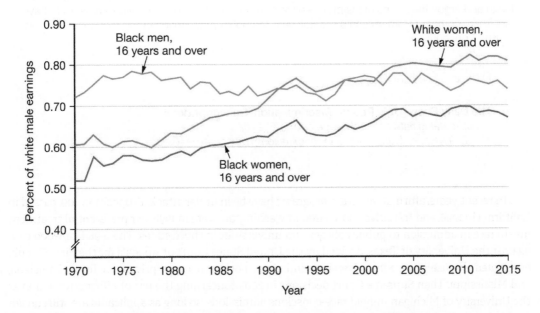

Source: Based on data from Current Population Survey, Table 37. Median weekly earnings of full-time wage and salary workers, by selected characteristics, Bureau of Labor Statistics, Available at http://www.bls.gov/cps/tables.htm.

One question that economists try to answer is the extent to which the gaps are due to discrimination and the extent to which they reflect other factors, such as differences in education, job experience, or choices that individuals in particular groups make about labor-force participation. Once these factors are accounted for, the amount of the remaining wage differential due to discrimination is less than the raw differentials presented in Figure 18.6 would seem to indicate.

There is evidence as well that the wage differential due to discrimination against women and blacks, as measured by empirical studies, has declined over time. For example, a number of studies have concluded that black men in the 1980s and 1990s experienced a 12% to 15% loss in earnings due to labor-market discrimination.[18] University of Chicago economist James Heckman denies that the entire 12% to 15% differential is due to racial discrimination, pointing to problems inherent in measuring and comparing human capital among individuals. Nevertheless, he reports that the earnings loss due to discrimination similarly measured would have been between 30% and 40% in 1940 and still over 20% in 1970.[19]

Can civil rights legislation take credit for the reductions in labor-market discrimination over time? To some extent, yes. A study by Heckman and John J. Donohue III, a law professor at Northwestern University, concluded that the landmark 1964 Civil Rights Act, as well as other civil rights activity leading up to the act, had the greatest positive impact on blacks in the South during the decade following its passage. Evidence of wage gains by black men in other regions of the country was, however, minimal. Most federal activity was directed toward the South, and the civil rights effort shattered an entire way of life that had subjugated black Americans and had separated them from mainstream life.[20]

Pop! Goes the Econ: Affirmative Action for the Ugly

In this clip from *The Daily Show*, economist Dan Hamermesh documents discrimination against unattractive people . . . and then recommends an interesting policy solution. Get together with a friend and argue the merits of his proposed reform over a refreshing drink; you'll be sure to have fun. Then, compare Hamermesh's solution with the policy prescription in this famous short story by Kurt Vonnegut.

Digital Downloads

The Daily Show_Ugly People Discrimination Transcript.docx
https://catalog.flatworldknowledge.com/a/35275/
The_Daily_Show_Ugly_People_Discrimination_Transcript-da40.docx

In recent years, affirmative action programs have been under attack. Proposition 209, passed in California in 1996, and Initiative 200, passed in Washington State in 1998, bar preferential treatment due to race in admission to public colleges and universities in those states. The 1996 Hopwood case against the University of Texas, decided by the United States Court of Appeals for the Fifth Circuit, eliminated the use of race in university admissions, both public and private, in Texas, Louisiana, and Mississippi. Then Supreme Court decisions in 2003 concerning the use of affirmative action at the University of Michigan upheld race-conscious admissions, so long as applicants are still considered individually and decisions are based on multiple criteria. A similar federal court ruling upheld Harvard's race-conscious admissions policy in 2019.

Controversial research by two former Ivy League university presidents, political scientist Derek Bok of Harvard University and economist William G. Bowen of Princeton University, concluded that affirmative action policies have created the backbone of the black middle class and taught white students the value of integration. The study focused on affirmative action at twenty-eight elite colleges and universities. It found that while blacks enter those institutions with lower test scores and grades than those of whites, receive lower grades, and graduate at a lower rate, after graduation blacks earn advanced degrees at rates identical to those of their former white classmates and are more active in civic affairs.[21]

While stricter enforcement of civil rights laws or new programs designed to reduce labor-market discrimination may serve to further improve earnings of groups that have been historically discriminated against, wage gaps between groups also reflect differences in choices and in "pre-market" conditions, such as family environment and early education. Some of these premarket conditions may themselves be the result of discrimination.

The narrowing in wage differentials may reflect the dynamics of the Becker model at work. As people's preferences change, or are forced to change due to competitive forces and changes in the legal environment, discrimination against various groups will decrease. However, it may be a long time before discrimination disappears from the labor market, not only due to remaining discriminatory preferences but also because the human capital and work characteristics that people bring to the labor market are decades in the making. While the election of Barack Obama as president of the United States in 2008 and the subsequent election of Kamala Harris as vice president in 2020 are important hallmarks of progress, events of the last few years indicate that the long and continued struggle against discrimination will continue for some time.

Key Takeaways

- Discrimination means that people of similar economic characteristics experience unequal economic outcomes as a result of noneconomic factors such as race or sex.
- Discrimination occurs in the marketplace only if employers, employees, or customers have discriminatory preferences and if such preferences are widely shared.
- Competitive markets will tend to reduce discrimination if enough individuals lack such prejudices and take advantage of discrimination practiced by others.
- Government intervention in the form of antidiscrimination laws may have reduced the degree of discrimination in the economy. There is considerable disagreement on this question, but wage gaps have declined over time in the United States.

Try It!

Use a production possibilities curve to illustrate the impact of discrimination on the production of goods and services in the economy. Label the horizontal axis as consumer goods per year. Label the vertical axis as capital goods per year. Label a point A that shows an illustrative bundle of the two which can be produced given the existence of discrimination. Label another point B that illustrates the gain to society from eliminating discrimination.

See related Concept Problem 14 at the end of this chapter.

Case in Point: Early Intervention Programs

Source: wee dezign/Shutterstock.com

Many authors have pointed out that differences in "pre-market" conditions may account for differences in market outcomes for people in different groups. One potential path to reducing poverty may lie in improving the educational opportunities available to minority and low-socioeconomic-status children. But when is the best time to intervene? Economist and Nobel Prize winner James Heckman argues that the key to improving student performance and adult economic outcomes is intervening *before* a child enters formal schooling.

Heckman notes that spending on children after they are already in school has little impact on their later success. Reducing class sizes, for example, doesn't appear to boost future college attendance or adult income. That may be because, by the age of eight, differences in learning abilities are essentially fixed. But early intervention to improve cognitive and non-cognitive abilities (including qualities such as perseverance, motivation, and self-restraint) has been shown to produce significant benefits. In an experiment begun several decades ago, four-year-old children from disadvantaged homes participated in pre-school programs designed to improve their chances for success in school. Evaluations of the program forty years later found a 15% to 17% wage gap between program participants and those from similar backgrounds who did not participate. Heckman argues that even earlier intervention among disadvantaged groups would be desirable—perhaps as early as six months of age.

Economists Rob Grunewald and Art Rolnick of the Federal Reserve Bank of Minneapolis have gone so far as to argue that because of the high returns to early childhood development programs (which they estimate at 12% per year), state and local governments would do more to promote economic development if they subsidized early childhood programs instead of offering subsidies to attract new businesses or build new sports stadiums. Turns out, throwing money at a problem really can work, as long as you throw it in the right direction!

See related Concept Problem 11 at the end of this chapter.

Sources: Based on James Heckman, "Catch 'em Young," The Wall Street Journal, January 10, 2006, p. A-14; Rob Grunewald and Art Rolnick, "Early Childhood Development on a Large Scale," Federal Reserve Bank of Minneapolis The Region, June 2005.

Answer to Try It! Problem

Discrimination leads to an inefficient allocation of resources and results in production levels that lie inside the production possibilities curve (*PPC*) (point A). If discrimination were eliminated, the economy could increase production to a point on the *PPC*, such as B.

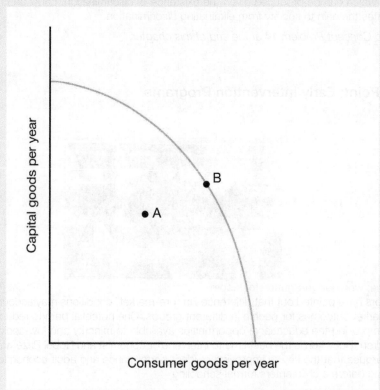

18.5 Review and Practice

Summary

In this chapter, we looked at three issues related to the question of fairness: income inequality, poverty, and discrimination.

The distribution of income in the United States has become more unequal in the last four decades. Among the factors contributing to increased inequality have been changes in family structure, technological change, and tax policy. While rising inequality can be a concern, there is a good deal of movement of families up and down the distribution of income.

Poverty can be measured using an absolute or a relative income standard. The official measure of poverty in the United States relies on an absolute standard. This measure tends to overstate the poverty rate because it does not count noncash welfare aid as income. The new supplemental poverty measures have begun to take these programs into account. Poverty is concentrated among female-headed households, minorities, people with relatively little education, and people who are not in the labor force. Children have a particularly high poverty rate.

Welfare reform in 1996 focused on moving people off welfare and into work. It limits the number of years that individuals can receive welfare payments and allows states to design the specific parameters of their own welfare programs. Following the reform, the number of people on welfare fell dramatically. The long-term impact on poverty is still under investigation.

Federal legislation bans discrimination. Affirmative action programs, though controversial, are designed to enhance opportunities for minorities and women. Wage gaps between women and white males and between blacks and white males have declined since the 1950s. For black males, however, most of the reduction occurred between 1965 and 1973. Much of the decrease in wage gaps is due to acquisition of human capital by women and blacks, but some of the decrease also reflects a reduction in discrimination.

Concept Problems

1. Explain how rising demand for college-educated workers and falling demand for high-school-educated workers contributes to increased inequality of the distribution of income.

2. Discuss the advantages and disadvantages of the following three alternatives for dealing with the rising inequality of wages.

   a. Increase the minimum wage each year so that wages for unskilled workers rise as fast as wages for skilled workers.

   b. Subsidize the wages of unskilled workers.

   c. Do nothing.

3. How would you define poverty? How would you determine whether a particular family is poor? Is the test you have proposed an absolute or a relative test?

4. Why does the failure to adjust the poverty line for regional differences in living costs lead to an understatement of poverty in some states and an overstatement of poverty in others?

5. The text argues that welfare recipients could achieve higher levels of satisfaction if they received cash rather than in-kind aid. Use the same argument to make a case that gifts given at Christmas should be in cash rather than specific items. Why do you suppose they usually are not?

6. (Related to "Case in Point: A Basic Solution to the Welfare-to-Work Problem" in Section 16.3.) Suppose a welfare program provides a basic grant of $10,000 per year to poor families but reduces the grant by $1 for every $1 of income earned. How would such a program affect a household's incentive to work? Accounting for income and payroll taxes, is it possi-

ble that the worker would end up poorer by working? What would that worker's effective tax rate be in that case?

7. Welfare reform calls for a two-year limit on welfare payments, after which recipients must go to work. Suppose a recipient with children declines work offers. Should aid be cut? What about the children?

8. How would you tackle the welfare problem? State the goals you would seek, and explain how the measures you propose would work to meet those goals.

9. Suppose a common but unfounded belief held that people with blue eyes were not as smart as people with brown eyes. What would we expect to happen to the relative wages of the two groups? Suppose you were an entrepreneur who knew that the common belief was wrong. What could you do to enhance your profits? Suppose other entrepreneurs acted in the same way. How would the wages of people with blue eyes be affected?

10. (Related to "Case in Point: Attitudes and Inequality" in Section 16.2.) This case argues that people in the United States attribute success to hard work and skill, while people in continental western Europe attribute success to connections, luck, and corruption. With what set of views do you agree? Explain.

11. Related to "Case in Point: Early Intervention Programs" in Section 16.4.) James Heckman advocates a program of early intervention targeted at low-income families. What are the advantages of such an approach? The disadvantages?

12. Give five reasons that the income distribution in the United States has become more unequal in the last several decades. Do you regard this as a problem for society? Why or why not?

13. Suppose that all welfare aid were converted to programs of cash assistance. Total spending on welfare would remain unchanged. How would this affect the poverty rate? Why?

14. (Related to "Try It!" in Section 16.4.) Make the argument that discrimination economically harms the discriminator, the one being discriminated against, and society as a whole. Explain your reasoning.

Numerical Problems

1. In the Republic of Atlantis, the shares of income received by each quintile are, in order: 10%, 15%, 20%, 25% and 30%.

   a. On a piece of graph paper, construct a Lorenz curve for Atlantis.

   b. Bonus: Approximate the Gini coefficient. (*Hint*: Count squares on your graph paper.)

2. (Related to "Try It!" in Section 16.2.) Here are income distribution data for three countries from the World Bank for 2015–2017. Here, we report only four data points rather than the five associated with each quintile. These data emphasize the distribution at the extremes of the distribution.

	Poorest 10%	Poorest 20%	Richest 20%	Richest 10%
Panama	1.1	3.4	54.2	37.7
Sweden	3.0	8.2	37.6	22.9
South Africa	0.9	2.4	68.2	50.5

   a. Plot the Lorenz curves for each in a single graph.

   b. Compare the degree of inequality for the three countries. (Do not forget to convert the data to cumulative shares; e.g., the lowest 80% of the population in Panama receives 45.8% of total income.)

   c. Compare your results to the Lorenz curve given in the text for the United States. Which country in your chart appears closest to the United States in terms of its income distribution?

3. Looking at Figure 18.5 suppose the wage that black workers are receiving in a discriminatory environment, W_B, is $25 per hour, while the wage that white workers receive, W, is $30 per

hour. Now suppose a regulation is imposed that requires that black workers be paid $30 per hour also.

   a. How does this affect the employment of black workers?

   b. How does this affect the wages of black workers?

   c. How does this affect their total income? Explain.

4. (Related to "Try It!" in Section 16.3.) Suppose the poverty line in the United States was set according to the test required in the European Union: a household is poor if its income is less than 60% of the median household income. Here are annual data for median household income in the United States for the period 2006–2019. The data also give the percentage of the households that fall below 60% of the median household income.

	Median Household Income in the U.S.	Percent of Households with Income below 60% of Median
2006	61,268	30.0
2007	62,090	30.9
2008	59,877	30.6
2009	59,458	30.7
2010	57,904	28.0
2011	57,021	28.1
2012	56,912	28.2
2013	58,904	31.5
2014	58,001	28.3
2015	60,987	31.5
2016	62,898	30.8
2017	64,007	31.1
2018	64,324	30.5
2019	68,703	30.3

Source: Data from U.S Census Bureau, Current Population Reports, P60-270; Income in 2019 CPI-U-RS adjusted dollars; column 3 estimated by authors using Table A-2.

   a. Plot the data on a graph.

   b. Is this a relative or an absolute definition of poverty?

   c. Why do you think the percent of households with incomes below 60% of the median fell from 2010 to 2012 and has risen since?

   d. Discuss the measurement issues involved in the data you have presented.

   e. Discuss the elements of the system of counting the incomes of low-income people in the United States and explain how it relates to your answer in (d).

5. Consider the following model of the labor market in the United States. Suppose that the labor market consists of two parts, a market for skilled workers and a market for unskilled workers, with different demand and supply curves for each as given below. The initial wage for skilled workers is $20 per hour; the initial wage for unskilled workers is $7 per hour.

   a. Draw the demand and supply curves for the two markets so that they intersect at the wages given above.

   b. How does increased demand for skilled workers and a reduced demand for unskilled workers affect the initial solution?

   c. How is the Lorenz curve for the United States economy affected by this development? Illustrate the old and the new Lorenz curves.

   d. Suppose there is an increase in immigration from Mexico. How will this affect the two markets for labor?

e. Suppose Professor Heckman's recommendation for early intervention for low-income children is followed and that it has the impact he predicts. How will this affect the two markets today? In twenty years? Illustrate and explain how the demand and/or supply curves in each market will be affected.

f. What would the impact of the change in (d) be on the Lorenz curve for the United States twenty years from now?

Endnotes

1. "Not Quite Together," *Economist*, October 22, 2011; Douglas Schoen, "Polling the Occupy Wall Street Crowd," *Wall Street Journal Online*, October 18, 2011; "Public Divided Over Occupy Wall Street Movement," Pew Charitable Trust Pew Research Center for the People & the Press, http://www.people-press.org/2011/10/24/public-divided-over-occupy-wall-street-movement/.

2. While *Capital* sold a lot of copies, few were actually read. See "The Summer's Most Unread Book Is..." *Wall Street Journal*, July 3, 2014, for an amusing yarn about how we know.

3. See Bureau of the Census table H-3.

4. If the distribution of income were completely unequal, with one household receiving all the income and the rest zero, then the Lorenz curve would be shaped like a backward L, with a horizontal line across the bottom of the graph at 0% income and a vertical line up the right-hand side.

5. See the Census Bureau's Historical Statistics on Income Table H-4.

6. See "Is the United States Still a Land of Opportunity? Recent Trends in Intergenerational Mobility," NBER Working Paper Series 19844, 2014, which finds little change in the ability of a person in any quintile to reach the top quintile over a relatively long time horizon. For an international comparison of income mobility, see Miles Corak's "Inequality from Generation to Generation: The United States in Comparison," in *The Economics of Inequality, Poverty, and Discrimination in the 21st Century*, 2012.

7. Median household income for married couples is $102,308, while median household income for single-female headed households is $48.098. See the Census Bureau's Historical Statistics on Income tables hinc04-7 and hinc04-10.

8. Economists Lawrence Katz and Claudia Goldin say that technology, rather than trade, is the primary driver of increasing inequality. Their landmark book, *The Race Between Education and Technology*, argues that the demand for skilled labor is outstripping the supply, driving up wages at the high end of the income distribution.

9. See David Autor and Melanie Wasserman, "Wayward Sons: The Emerging Gender Gap in Labor Markets and Education," at https://economics.mit.edu/files/8754

10. The Trump administration made a fairly major overhaul of the individual income tax in 2017. Those changes went into effect in 2018, but data are not yet out on the share of tax relief received by different groups.

11. Rea S. Hederman, Jr., "Census Report Adds New Twist to Income Inequality Data," Heritage Foundation, Policy Research and Analysis, No. 1592, August 29, 2007.

12. For more on the supplemental poverty measure, see https://www.census.gov/library/publications/2020/demo/p60-272.html

13. Robert Rector and Rachel Sheffield, "Understanding Poverty in the United States: Surprising Facts about America's Poor," Heritage Foundation, Policy Research & Analysis, No. 2607, September 13, 2011.

14. Marianne P. Bitler and Hilary W. Hoynes, "The State of the Social Safety Net in the Post-Welfare Reform Era," *Brookings Papers on Economic Activity* (Fall 2010): 71–127.

15. Marianne P. Bitler and Hilary W. Hoynes, "The State of the Social Safety Net in the Post-Welfare Reform Era," *Brookings Papers on Economic Activity* (Fall 2010): 71–127.

16. Current Population Survey, Annual Social and Economic Supplement 2010, Table POV24.

17. Affirmative action programs are required of government and of entities that are financially linked to the federal government. That said, many private firms have voluntarily adopted affirmative action programs of their own. See https://www.dol.gov/general/topic/hiring/affirmativeact for more on this subject.

18. William A. Darity and Patrick L. Mason, "Evidence on Discrimination in Employment," *Journal of Economic Perspectives* 12:2 (Spring 1998): 63–90.

19. James J. Heckman, "Detecting Discrimination," *Journal of Economic Perspectives* 12:2 (Spring 1998): 101–16.

20. John J. Donohue III and James Heckman, "Continuous Versus Episodic Change: The Impact of Civil Rights Policy on the Economic Status of Blacks," *Journal of Economic Literature* 29 (December 1991): 1603–43.

21. Derek Bok and William G. Bowen, *The Shape of the River: Long-Term Consequences of Considering Race in College and University Admissions* (Princeton, N.J.: Princeton University Press, 1998).

APPENDIX A
Graphs in Economics

If you've taken a quick peek through the pages of this book, you've probably noticed a lot of graphs. That's pretty standard—graphs are an important tool in almost any economics course because they are clear and unambiguous, which makes them an excellent way to present complicated ideas. A graph really is worth a thousand words! If you are already familiar with graphs, you'll likely have little difficulty seeing graphs' value and using them to answer economic questions. If you haven't used graphs before, or have not used them in some time, this appendix will help you feel comfortable with the graphs you'll encounter in this text.

A.1 Graphs in Economics

Learning Objectives

1. State how graphs show the relationship between two or more variables and explain how a graph demonstrates the nature of the relationship.
2. Define the slope of a curve.
3. Distinguish between a movement along a curve, a shift in a curve, and a rotation in a curve.

Much of the analysis in economics deals with relationships between variables. A variable is simply a quantity whose value can change. A **graph** is a pictorial representation of the relationship between two or more variables. The key to understanding graphs is knowing the rules that apply to their construction and interpretation. This section defines those rules and explains how to draw a graph.

Drawing a Graph

Let's use a hypothetical example to see how a graph is constructed from numerical data. Suppose a college campus has a ski club that organizes day-long bus trips to a ski area about 100 miles from the campus. The club leases the bus and charges $10 per passenger for a round trip to the ski area. In addition to the revenue the club collects from passengers, it also receives a grant of $200 from the school's student government for each day the bus trip is available; the club would receive $200 even if no passengers wanted to ride on a particular day.

Table A.1 shows the relationship between two variables: the number of students who ride the bus on a particular day and the revenue the club receives from a trip. In the table, each combination is assigned a letter (A, B, etc.); we'll use these letters when we transfer the information from the table to a graph.

A graph helps you see relationships between variables in a way that simply looking at numbers on a page cannot.

Source: Sergey Granev/
Shutterstock.com

graph

A pictorial representation of the relationship between two or more variables.

TABLE A.1 Ski Club Revenues
The ski club receives $10 from each passenger riding its bus for a trip to and from the ski area plus a payment of $200 from the student government for each day the bus is available for these trips. The club's revenues from any single day, then, are $200 plus $10 times the number of passengers. The table relates various combinations of the number of passengers and club revenues.

Combination	Number of Passengers	Club Revenue ($)
A	0	200
B	10	300
C	20	400
D	30	500
E	40	600

We can illustrate the relationship shown in Table A.1 with a graph. The procedure for depicting the relationship between variables graphically is illustrated in Figure A.1. Let's look at the steps involved.

FIGURE A.1 Plotting a Graph
Here we see how to show the information given in Table A.1 in a graph.

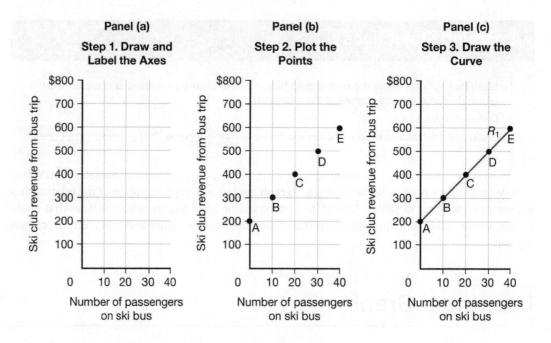

Step 1. Draw and Label the Axes

The two variables shown in the table are the number of passengers taking the bus on a particular day and the club's revenue from that trip. We begin our graph in Panel (a) of Figure A.1 by drawing two axes to form a right angle. Each axis will represent a variable. The axes should be carefully labeled to reflect what is being measured on each axis.

origin

The point at which the axes of a graph intersect.

When two variables are related, the *dependent variable* changes in response to changes in the *independent variable*. Here, the amount of revenue the club receives depends on the number of passengers, so revenue is the dependent variable and passengers are the independent variable. It's customary to place the independent variable (the number of passengers) on the horizontal axis, and the dependent variable (revenue) on the vertical axis.[1] The point at which the axes intersect is called the **origin** of the graph. Notice that in Figure A.1 the origin has a value of zero for each variable.

In drawing a graph showing numeric values, we also need to put numbers on the axes. For the axes in Panel (a), we have chosen numbers that correspond to the values in the table. The number of passengers ranges up to 40 for a trip; club revenues from a trip range from $200 (the payment the club receives from student government) to $600. We've extended the vertical axis just a bit further (to $800) to allow for some changes that we'll consider a bit later. The choice of the interval on each axis is mainly a matter of convenience in drawing and reading the graph; we've chosen intervals of 10 passengers on the horizontal axis and $100 on the vertical axis because they correspond to the intervals given in the table. Finally, we've drawn vertical lines from each of the values on the horizontal axis and horizontal lines from each of the values on the vertical axis. These lines, called *gridlines*, will help us in Step 2.

Step 2. Plot the Points

Each of the rows in Table A.1 gives a combination of the number of passengers on the bus and club revenue from a particular trip. We can plot these values in our graph.

Let's start with row A, where zero passengers ride the bus, but the club receives $200 of revenue from the student government. Read up from zero passengers on the horizontal axis, and over from $200 on the vertical axis; then plot point A at the intersection.

The second combination, B, tells us that if 10 passengers ride the bus, the club receives $300 in revenue from the trip—$100 from the $10-per-passenger charge plus the $200 from student government. Start at 10 passengers on the horizontal axis and follow the gridline up; then start at $300 on the vertical (revenue) axis and follow the gridline over. Plot point B where those gridlines intersect. Now, it's just a matter of repeating the same process to plot points C, D, and E. Check to be sure that you see that each point corresponds to the values of the two variables given in the corresponding row of the table.

We've already mentioned that points in a graph relate values of the variables on the two axes to each other. Sometimes it's convenient to read them in both directions. For example, you can read from passengers to revenue: If 30 passengers ride the bus, the club's revenue will be $500. but you can also read them the other direction, from revenue to passengers: Starting on the vertical axis and then reading to the horizontal, if the ski club needs to raise $500 in revenue, it needs to attract 30 passengers.

The graph in Panel (b) is called a scatter diagram, or scatter plot. A **scatter diagram** shows individual points relating values of the variable on one axis to values of the variable on the other.

scatter diagram

A graph that shows individual points relating values of the variable on one axis to values of the variable on the other.

Step 3. Draw the Curve

The final step is to draw the curve that shows the relationship between the number of passengers who ride the bus and the club's revenues from the trip. The term "curve" is used for any line in a graph that shows a relationship between two variables.

To draw the curve, simply connect the dots. In this case, the curve through points A through E is an upward-sloping straight line. Our curve, which we'll call R_1, shows club revenues. Notice that R_1 intersects the vertical axis at $200 (point A). The point at which a curve intersects an axis is called the **intercept** of the curve. We often refer to the vertical or horizontal intercept of a curve; such intercepts sometimes play a special role in describing economic relationships. The vertical intercept in this case shows the revenue the club would receive on a day it offered the trip and no one rode the bus.

intercept

The point at which a curve intersects an axis.

To check your understanding of these steps, try drawing a set of axes and gridlines on a sheet of paper and plotting curve R_1 for yourself. Then, for more practice, have a go at this section's [Unsupported Reference Type: appendix-note] problem.

The Slope of a Curve

Some curves are steep; others are pretty flat. The steepness or flatness of a curve is reflected in its *slope*. The slopes of curves tell an important story: They show *how much* your dependent variable will change if your independent variable changes. In this section, we'll see how to compute the slope of a curve.

> **slope**
>
> The ratio of the change in the value of the variable on the vertical axis to the change in the value of the variable on the horizontal axis measured between two points on the curve.

The **slope** of a curve equals the ratio of the change in the value of the variable on the vertical axis to the change in the value of the variable on the horizontal axis, measured between two points on the curve. You may have heard this described as "rise over run." In equation form, we can write the definition of the slope as

EQUATION A.1

$$\text{Slope} = \frac{\text{vertical change}}{\text{horizontal change}}$$

Equation A.1 is the first equation in this text. While economists don't use as many equations as graphs (at least at the principles-of-economics level), they do pop up from time to time. Many equations in economics begin in the form of Equation A.1, with the statement that one thing (in this case the slope) equals another (the vertical change divided by the horizontal change). In this example, the equation is written in words, though sometimes we use symbols instead. The basic idea though, is always the same: The term represented on the left side of the equals sign equals the term on the right side. In Equation A.1 there are three variables: the slope, the vertical change, and the horizontal change. If we know the values of two of the three, we can compute the third.

Let's do a sample calculation. First, let's choose two points—say, B and D—in the graph, and calculate the slope between them. Figure A.2 shows how this is done.

1. Compute the horizontal change. Point B corresponds to 10 passengers on the bus and point D corresponds to 30, so the change in the horizontal axis when we go from B to D is 20 passengers.

2. Compute the vertical change. Point B corresponds to club revenues of $300; point D corresponds to club revenues of $500. The change in the vertical axis equals $200.

3. Calculate the slope by dividing the vertical change by the horizontal change: $200/20 passengers, or $10/passenger.

We can compute the slope of R_1 between *any* two points on the curve. Consider, for example, points A and E. The vertical change between these points is $400 (we go from revenues of $200 at A to revenues of $600 at E). The horizontal change is 40 passengers (from zero passengers at A to 40 at E). The slope of R_1 between A and E is $400/(40 passengers) = $10/passenger—exactly the same as we got before! In fact, we'll get the same slope *regardless* of which pair of points on R_1 we choose, because R_1 is a straight line, which means that the slope never changes. When the curve showing the relationship between two variables has a constant slope, we say there is a **linear relationship** between the variables. A **linear curve** is a curve with constant slope.

> **linear relationship**
>
> Relationship that exists between two variables when the curve between them has a constant slope.

> **linear curve**
>
> A curve with constant slope.

> **positive relationship**
>
> Relationship that exists between two variables when both variables move in the same direction.

The slope of R_1 tells us how much revenues change (+$10) for each additional passenger the club carries. A curve whose slope is positive is upward sloping: As we travel up and to the right along R_1, both passengers and revenues increase. A **positive relationship** or *direct relationship* between two variables is one in which both variables move in the same direction. There is a positive relationship between club revenues and passengers on the bus. We'll look at a graph showing a negative relationship between two variables in the next section.

FIGURE A.2 Computing the Slope of a Curve

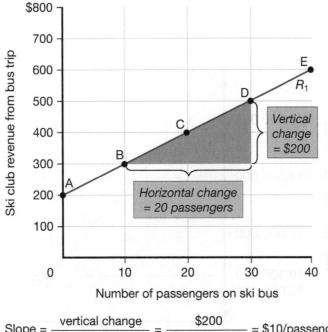

$$\text{Slope} = \frac{\text{vertical change}}{\text{horizontal change}} = \frac{\$200}{20 \text{ passengers}} = \$10/\text{passenger}$$

A Graph Showing a Negative Relationship

A **negative relationship** is one in which two variables move in opposite directions. A negative relationship is sometimes called an *inverse relationship*. The slope of a curve describing a negative relationship is always negative; a curve with a negative slope is always downward sloping.

As an example of a graph of a negative relationship, let's look at the impact the 1998–1999 NBA labor dispute had on the earnings of one player: Shaquille O'Neal. During the 1998–1999 season, O'Neal was the center for the Los Angeles Lakers.

O'Neal's salary with the Lakers in 1998–1999 would have been about $17,220,000 had the 82 scheduled games of the regular season been played. But the contract dispute between owners and players resulted in 32 games being canceled. Shaq's salary worked out to roughly $210,000 per game, so the labor dispute cost him well over $6 million. Presumably, he was able to eke out a living on his lower income, but the canceled games cost him a great deal.

The relationship between the number of games canceled and O'Neal's 1998–1999 basketball earnings is shown graphically in Figure A.3. Canceling games reduced his earnings, so the number of games canceled is the independent variable and goes on the horizontal axis. O'Neal's earnings are the dependent variable and go on the vertical axis. The graph assumes that his earnings would have been $17,220,000 had no games been canceled (point A, the vertical intercept). Assuming that his earnings fell by $210,000 per game canceled, the 32 canceled games reduced his earnings for the season to $10,500,000 (point B). We can draw a line between these two points to show the relationship between games canceled and O'Neal's 1998–1999 earnings from basketball. In this graph, we've inserted a break in the vertical axis near the origin. That allows us to expand the scale of the axis over the range from $10,000,000 to $18,000,000. Because there are no earnings values below $10,000,000, it also prevents a large blank space between the origin and where Shaq's income begins.

negative relationship

Relationship that exists between two variables when the variables move in opposite directions.

"If only we'd played the whole season, I would be shilling hamburgers for a cruise line."

Source: lev radin/Shutterstock. com

FIGURE A.3 Canceling Games and Reducing Shaquille O'Neal's Earnings
If no games had been canceled during the 1998–1999 basketball season, Shaquille O'Neal would have earned $17,220,000 (point A). Assuming that his salary for the season fell by $210,000 for each game canceled, the cancellation of 32 games during the dispute between NBA players and owners reduced O'Neal's earnings to $10,500,000 (point B).

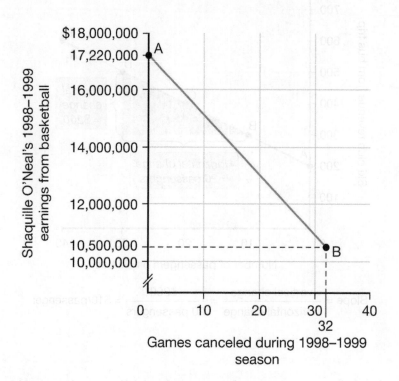

What is the slope of the curve in Figure A.3? We have data for two points, A and B. At A, O'Neal's basketball salary would have been $17,220,000. At B, it is $10,500,000. The vertical change between points A and B equals –$6,720,000. The change in the horizontal axis is from zero games canceled at A to 32 games canceled at B. The slope is thus

$$\text{Slope} = \frac{\text{vertical change}}{\text{horizontal change}} = \frac{-\$6,720,000}{32 \text{ games}} = -\$210,000/\text{game}$$

This time, the slope is negative, indicating the downward slope of Shaq's earnings curve. As we travel down and to the right along the curve, the number of games canceled rises and O'Neal's salary falls. The slope of O'Neal's salary curve is also constant, indicating a linear relationship between games canceled and his 1998–1999 basketball earnings. In this case, the slope tells us the rate at which O'Neal lost income as games were canceled; each game canceled cost Shaq another $210,000.

Shifting a Curve

When we draw a graph showing the relationship between two variables, we make an important assumption. We assume that all of the other variables that might affect the relationship between the variables in our graph are unchanged. When one of those other variables changes, the relationship changes, and the curve showing that relationship shifts.

Consider, for example, the ski club that sponsors bus trips to the ski area. The graph we drew in Figure A.1 shows the relationship between club revenues from a particular trip and the number of passengers on that trip, assuming that all other variables that might affect club revenues are unchanged.

Now, let's change one! Suppose the school's student government increases the payment it makes to the club to $400 for each day the trip is available (the payment was $200 when we drew the original graph). Panel (a) of Figure A.4 shows how the increase in the payment affects Table A.1; Panel (b) shows how the curve shifts. Each of the new observations in the table has been labeled with a prime: A′, B′, etc. The curve R_1 shifts upward by $200 as a result of the increased payment. A **shift in a curve** implies new values of one variable at each value of the other variable. The new curve is labeled R_2. With 10 passengers, for example, the club's revenue was $300 at point B on R_1. With the increased payment from the student government, its revenue with 10 passengers rises to $500 at point B′ on R_2.

shift in a curve

Change in the graph of a relationship between two variables that implies new values of one variable at each value of the other variable.

FIGURE A.4 Shifting a Curve: An Increase in Revenues

The table in Panel (a) shows the new level of revenues the ski club receives with varying numbers of passengers as a result of the increased payment from student government. The new curve is shown in dark purple in Panel (b). The old curve is shown in light purple.

Panel (a)

Combination	Number of Passengers	Club Revenue (with $400 Payment from Student Government)
A′	0	$400
B′	10	500
C′	20	600
D′	30	700
E′	40	800

Panel (b)

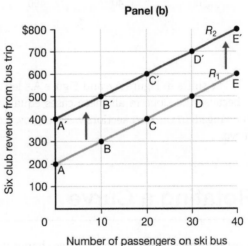

It's important to distinguish between shifts in curves and movements along curves. A **movement along a curve** is a change from one point on the curve to another. A movement along the curve is caused by a change in the independent variable. If, for example, the student government is paying the club $400 each day it makes the ski bus available and 20 passengers ride the bus, the club is operating at point C′ on R_2. If the number of passengers increases to 30, the club will be at point D′ on the curve. This is a movement along a curve; the curve itself does not shift.

What if, instead of increasing its payment, the student government *eliminates* its payments to the ski club? The club's only revenue from a trip now comes from its $10/passenger charge. We have again changed one of the variables that we were holding unchanged, so we get another shift in our revenue curve. The table in Panel (a) of Figure A.5 shows how the reduction in the student government's payment affects club revenues. The new values are shown as combinations A″ through E″ on the new curve, R_3, in Panel (b). Once again we have a shift in a curve, this time from R_1 to R_3.

movement along a curve

Change from one point on the curve to another that occurs when the dependent variable changes in response to a change in the independent variable.

FIGURE A.5 Shifting a Curve: A Reduction in Revenues
The table in Panel (a) shows the impact on ski club revenues of an elimination of support from the student government for ski bus trips. The club's only revenue now comes from the $10 it charges to each passenger. The new combinations are shown as A″ – E″. In Panel (b) we see that the original curve relating club revenue to the number of passengers has shifted down.

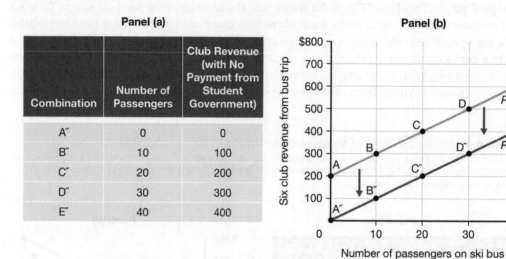

Panel (a)

Combination	Number of Passengers	Club Revenue (with No Payment from Student Government)
A″	0	0
B″	10	100
C″	20	200
D″	30	300
E″	40	400

The shifts in Figure A.4 and Figure A.5 left the slopes of the revenue curves unchanged. That is because the slope in all these cases equals the price per ticket, and the ticket price remains unchanged. In the next section, we'll see how a change in the ticket price affects the club's revenue curve.

Rotating a Curve

rotation of a curve

Change in a curve that occurs when its slope changes with one point on the curve fixed.

A **rotation of a curve** occurs when we change its slope, with one point on the curve fixed. Suppose, for example, the ski club changes the price of its bus rides to the ski area to $30 per trip, and the payment from the student government remains $200 for each day the trip is available. This means the club's revenues will remain $200 if it has no passengers on a particular trip. Revenue will, however, be different when the club has passengers. Because the slope of our revenue curve equals the price per ticket, the slope of the revenue curve changes.

Panel (a) of Figure A.6 shows what happens to the original revenue curve, R_1, when the price per ticket is raised. Point A does not change; the club's revenue with zero passengers is still $200. But with 10 passengers, the club's revenue would rise from $300 (point B on R_1) to $500 (point B′ on R_4). With 20 passengers, the club's revenue would equal $800 (point C′ on R_4).

The new revenue curve R_4 is steeper than the original curve. Panel (b) shows the computation of the slope of R_4 between points B′ and C′. As R_1 changes to R_4, the slope increases to $30 per passenger—the new price of a ticket. The greater the slope of a positively sloped curve, the steeper it will be.

We've now seen how to draw a graph of a curve, how to compute the curve's slope, and how to shift and rotate a curve. We've also examined both positive and negative linear relationships. In the next section, we'll look at curves that actually curve—what we call nonlinear relationships.

FIGURE A.6 Rotating a Curve
A curve is said to rotate when a single point remains fixed while other points on the curve move; a rotation always changes the slope of a curve. Here an increase in the price per passenger to $30 would rotate the revenue curve from R_1 to R_4 in Panel (a). The slope of R_4 is $30 per passenger.

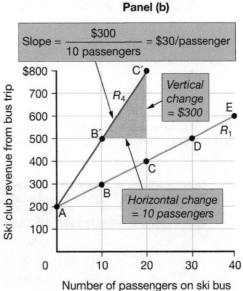

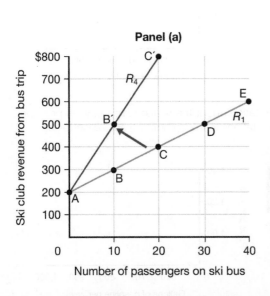

Panel (a)

Panel (b)

Key Takeaways

- A graph shows a relationship between two or more variables.
- An upward-sloping curve indicates a positive relationship between two variables. A downward-sloping curve shows a negative relationship between two variables.
- The slope of a curve is the ratio of the vertical change to the horizontal change between two points on the curve. A curve whose slope is constant indicates a linear relationship between two variables.
- A change from one point on a curve to another produces a movement along the curve. Movements along a curve are caused by changes in the independent variable.
- A shift in a curve implies new values of the dependent variable for each value of the independent variable. A rotation in a curve implies that one point remains fixed while the slope of the curve changes.

Try It!

The following table shows the relationship between the number of gallons of gasoline people in a community are willing and able to buy per week and the price per gallon. Plot these points in the grid provided and label each point with the letter associated with the combination. Notice that there are breaks in both the vertical and horizontal axes of the grid. Draw a line through the points you have plotted. Does your graph suggest a positive or a negative relationship? What is the slope between A and B? Between B and C? Between A and C? Is the relationship linear?

Combination	Price per Gallon ($)	Number of Gallons (per Week)
A	1.00	1,000
B	1.20	900
C	1.40	800

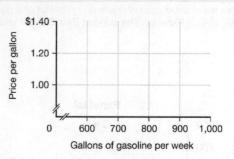

Now suppose you are given the following information about the relationship between price per gallon and the number of gallons per week gas stations in the community are willing to sell.

Combination	Price per Gallon ($)	Number of Gallons (per Week)
D	1.00	800
E	1.20	900
F	1.40	1,000

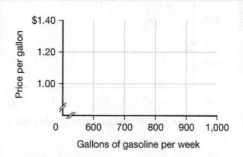

Plot these points in the grid provided and draw a curve through the points you have drawn. Does your graph suggest a positive or a negative relationship? What is the slope between D and E? Between E and F? Between D and F? Is this relationship linear?

Answer to Try It! Problem

The top panel in the figure below shows the graph of peoples' gasoline purchases. The curve's downward slope tells us there is a negative relationship between price and the quantity of gasoline people are willing and able to buy. This curve, by the way, is a demand curve (the next one is a supply curve). We will study demand and supply soon; you will be using these curves a great deal. The slope between A and B is −0.002.

$$(\text{slope} = \text{vertical change/horizontal change} = -0.20/100)$$

The bottom panel graphs the second set of data, indicating producers' willingness to sell gasoline. Economists call this a supply curve. Its upward slope tells us there is a positive relationship between price per gallon and the number of gallons per week gas stations are willing to sell. The slope between D and E is 0.002.

$$(\text{slope} = \text{vertical change/horizontal change} = 0.20/100)$$

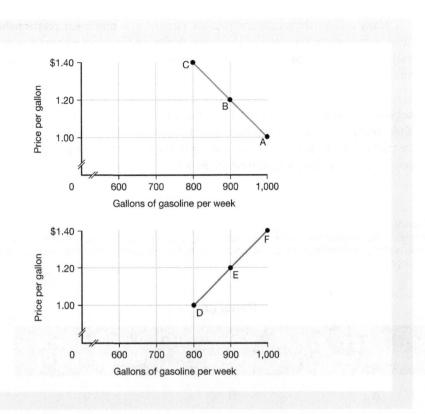

A.2 Nonlinear Relationships and Graphs without Numbers

Learning Objectives

1. Define nonlinear relationships and explain how they are illustrated with nonlinear curves.
2. Explain how to estimate the slope at any point on a nonlinear curve.
3. Explain how graphs without numbers can be used to understand the nature of relationships between two variables.

In this section we will extend our analysis of graphs in two ways. First, we will explore the nature of nonlinear relationships. Then, we'll have a look at graphs drawn without numbers.

Graphs of Nonlinear Relationships

In the previous section's graphs, increasing the independent variable by one unit always had the same effect on the dependent variable. When we added a passenger riding the ski bus, the ski club's revenues always rose by the $10 price of a ticket; when we canceled one more NBA game, Shaquille O'Neal's earnings always fell by $210,000. The slopes of the curves describing the relationships we have been discussing were constant; the relationships were linear.

Many relationships in economics are nonlinear. A **nonlinear relationship** between two variables is one where the slope of the curve depicting the relationship changes as the independent variable changes. A **nonlinear curve** is a curve whose slope changes as the value of one of the variables changes.

Here's an example: Felicia Alvarez owns a bakery, and she has recorded the relationship between her firm's daily output of bread and the number of bakers she employs. The relationship she's recorded is given in the table in Panel (a) of Figure A.7. The corresponding points are plotted in Panel (b). Clearly, we cannot draw a straight line through these points. Instead, we have to draw a nonlinear curve, like the one shown in Panel (c).

FIGURE A.7 A Nonlinear Curve

The table in Panel (a) shows the relationship between the number of bakers Felicia Alvarez employs per day and the number of loaves of bread produced per day. This information is plotted in Panel (b). This is a nonlinear relationship; the curve connecting these points in Panel (c), Loaves of bread produced, has a changing slope.

Panel (a)

Combination	Bakers per Day	Loaves of Bread Produced per Day
A	0	0
B	1	400
C	2	700
D	3	900
E	4	1,000
F	5	1,050
G	6	1,075

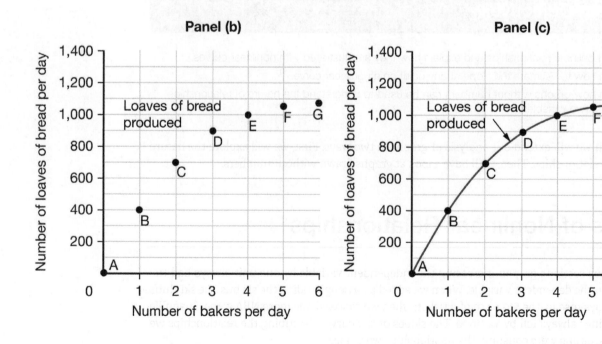

The curve for loaves of bread produced is always upward sloping, suggesting a positive relationship between the number of bakers and the output of bread. But the curve becomes flatter as we travel up and to the right along it; it describes a nonlinear relationship.

How can we estimate the slope of a nonlinear curve? After all, the slope of such a curve changes as we travel along it. We can deal with this problem in two ways. One is to consider two points on the curve and to compute the slope between those two points. Another is to compute the slope of the curve at a single point.

When we compute the slope of a curve between two points, we are really computing the slope of a straight line drawn between those two points. In Figure A.8, we have computed slopes between pairs of points A and B, C and D, and E and F on our curve for loaves of bread produced. These slopes equal 400 loaves/baker, 200 loaves/baker, and 50 loaves/baker, respectively. They are the slopes of the dashed-line segments shown. These dashed segments lie close to the curve, but they clearly are not on the curve. After all, the dashed segments are straight lines. Our curve relating the number of bakers to daily bread production is not a straight line; the relationship between the bakery's daily output of bread and the number of bakers is nonlinear.

FIGURE A.8 Estimating Slopes for a Nonlinear Curve
We can estimate the slope of a nonlinear curve between two points. Here, slopes are computed between points A and B, C and D, and E and F. When we compute the slope of a nonlinear curve between two points, we are computing the slope of a straight line that connects those points.

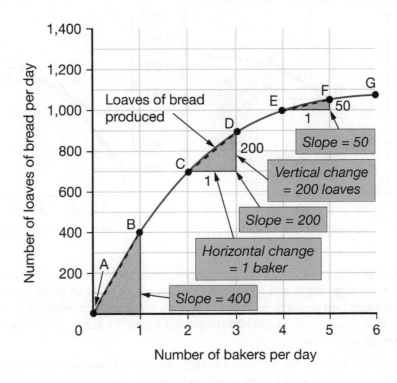

Every point on a nonlinear curve has a different slope. To get a precise measure of the slope of such a curve, we need to consider its slope at a single point. To do that, we draw a line tangent to the curve at that point. A **tangent line** is a straight line that touches, but does not intersect, a nonlinear curve at only one point. The slope of a tangent line equals the slope of the curve at the point at which the tangent line touches the curve.

tangent line

A straight line that touches, but does not intersect, a nonlinear curve at only one point.

Tangents: Useful in graphing; excruciating in lectures.

Source: ESB Professional/ Shutterstock.com

Consider point D in Panel (a) of Figure A.9. We have drawn a tangent line that just touches the curve showing bread production at this point. It passes through points labeled M and N (those points are not on the curve, but they're convenient points we've chosen to help us measure the slope of the tangent line). The vertical change between M and N is 300 loaves of bread; the horizontal change is two bakers. The slope of the tangent line, then, is 150 loaves of bread/baker (300 loaves/ 2 bakers). The slope of our bread production curve at point D equals the slope of the line tangent to the curve at this point. In Panel (b), we have sketched lines tangent to the curve for loaves of bread produced at points B, D, and F. Notice that these tangent lines get successively flatter, suggesting again that the slope of the curve is falling as we travel up and to the right along it.

FIGURE A.9 Tangent Lines and the Slopes of Nonlinear Curves

Because the slope of a nonlinear curve is different at every point on the curve, the precise way to compute slope is to draw a tangent line; the slope of the tangent line equals the slope of the curve at the point the tangent line touches the curve. In Panel (a), the slope of the tangent line is computed for us: It equals 150 loaves/baker. Generally, we will not have the information to compute slopes of tangent lines. We will use them as in Panel (b), to observe what happens to the slope of a nonlinear curve as we travel along it. In Panel (b), the slope falls (the tangent lines become flatter) as the number of bakers rises.

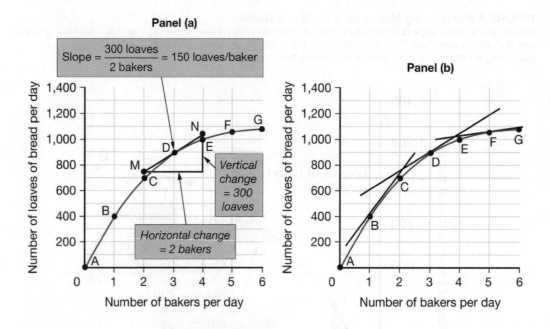

Notice that we don't have the information we need to compute the slopes of the tangent lines touching the curve at points B and F (but if you had a bigger sheet of graph paper with a lot of gridlines, you could get a decent estimate). That's ok, though: Often, we're more interested in using tangent lines qualitatively, to describe the general shape of a curve, rather than using them to generate precise measurements.

In our bread-baking case, the fact that the slope of the curve decreases (meaning the curve, while still positively sloped, gets flatter) as we increase the number of bakers suggests a phenomenon important in both microeconomic and macroeconomic analysis. As we add workers (in this case bakers), output (in this case loaves of bread) rises, but by smaller and smaller amounts. Another way to describe the relationship between the number of workers and the quantity of bread produced is to say that as the number of workers increases, output increases at a decreasing rate. In Panel (b) of Figure A.9 we express this idea with a graph, and we can gain this understanding by looking at the tangent lines, even though we do not have specific numbers. That's not unusual—much of our work with graphs will not require numbers at all.

Graphs Without Numbers

We know that a positive relationship between two variables can be illustrated with an upward-sloping curve in a graph, while a negative relationship can be illustrated with a downward-sloping curve. Some relationships are linear and some are nonlinear. We illustrate linear relationships using curves with constant slope, while nonlinear relationships are illustrated with curves with changing slope. Using these basic ideas, we can illustrate hypothesized relationships graphically, even in cases where we don't have numbers to work with.

Here's an example: Medical researchers hypothesize that eating more fruits and vegetables each day increases life expectancy. Let's show this idea graphically. Daily fruit and vegetable consumption (measured, say, in grams per day) is the independent variable; life expectancy (measured in years) is the dependent variable. Panel (a) of Figure A.10 illustrates the hypothesized positive relationship between the two variables. Notice the vertical intercept on the curve we have drawn; it implies that even people who eat no fruit or vegetables can expect to live at least a while!

Panel (b) illustrates another hypothesis we hear often: smoking cigarettes reduces life expectancy. Here the number of cigarettes smoked per day is the independent variable; life expectancy is the dependent variable. The hypothesis suggests a negative relationship, so we draw a downward-sloping curve.

Now consider a general form of the hypothesis suggested by the example of Felicia Alvarez's bakery: Adding more bakers means more output of bread, but the increases in output get successively smaller. As we saw in Figure A.7, this hypothesis suggests a positive, nonlinear relationship. Panel (c) illustrates this relationship with a positive, nonlinear curve that looks very much like the curve for bread production in Figure A.9.

Finally, consider a refined version of our smoking hypothesis. Suppose we assert that smoking cigarettes does reduce life expectancy, and that increasing the number of cigarettes smoked per day reduces life expectancy by larger and larger amounts. Panel (d) shows this case. Again, our life expectancy curve slopes downward. But now it suggests that life expectancy only falls a little bit when you smoke just a few cigarettes per day, but falls by more and more as the number of cigarettes smoked per day increases.

We have sketched lines tangent to the curve in Panel (d). The slopes of these tangent lines are negative, suggesting the negative relationship between smoking and life expectancy. They also get steeper as the number of cigarettes smoked per day rises. Whether a curve is linear or nonlinear, a steeper curve is one for which the absolute value of the slope rises as the value of the variable on the horizontal axis rises. When we speak of the absolute value of a negative number such as -4, we ignore the minus sign and simply say that the absolute value is 4. The absolute value of -8, for example, is greater than the absolute value of -4, and a curve with a slope of -8 is steeper than a curve whose slope is -4.

You've just acquired a solid understanding of graphs that show relationships between variables. In the next section, we'll look at graphs that show how one or more variables change over a period of time and graphs that show the values of one or more variables at a single point in time.

FIGURE A.10 Graphs Without Numbers

We often use graphs without numbers to suggest the nature of relationships between variables. The graphs in the four panels correspond to the relationships described in the text.

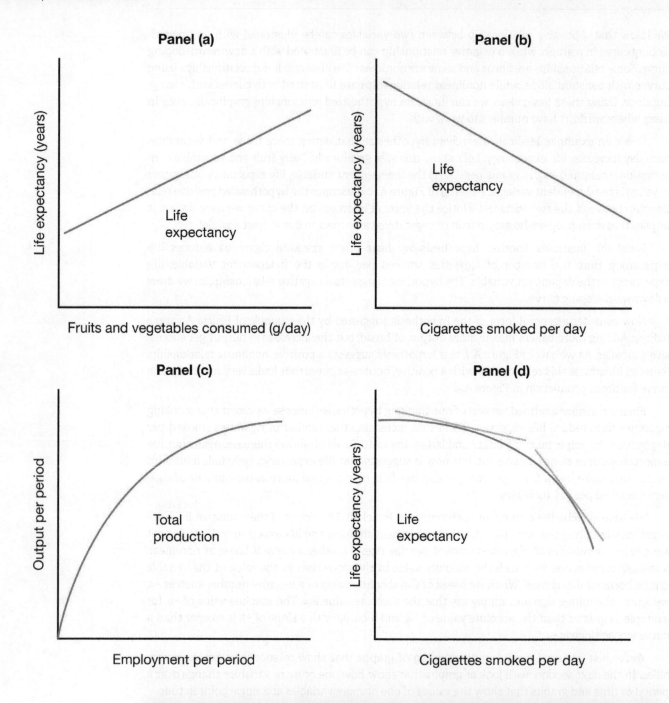

Key Takeaways

- The slope of a nonlinear curve changes as the value of one of the variables in the relationship shown by the curve changes.
- A nonlinear curve may show a positive or a negative relationship.

- The slope of a curve showing a nonlinear relationship can be estimated by computing the slope between two points on the curve. The slope at any point on such a curve equals the slope of a line drawn tangent to the curve at that point.

- We can illustrate hypotheses about the relationship between two variables graphically, even if we are not given numbers for the relationships. We need only draw and label the axes and then draw a curve consistent with the hypothesis.

Try It!

Consider the following curve drawn to show the relationship between two variables, A and B. Explain whether the relationship between the two variables is positive or negative, linear or nonlinear. Sketch two lines tangent to the curve at different points on the curve, and explain what is happening to the slope of the curve.

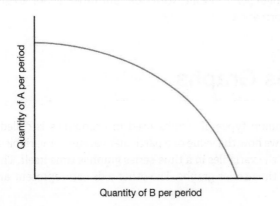

Answer to Try It! Problem

The relationship between variable A (shown on the vertical axis) and variable B (shown on the horizontal axis) is negative: As B increases, A gets smaller. In this case, the relationship is non-linear; the slope changes as you move along the curve. In this case, the slope becomes steeper as we move downward to the right along the curve, as shown by the two tangent lines that have been drawn. As the quantity of B increases, the quantity of A decreases, and it decreases at an increasing rate.

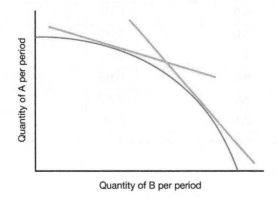

A.3 Using Graphs and Charts to Show Values of Variables

Learning Objective

1. Recognize and use time-series graphs, tables, pie charts, and bar charts to illustrate data and relationships among variables.

You often see pictures representing numerical information. These pictures may take the form of graphs that show how a particular variable has changed over time, or charts that show values of a set of variables at a single point in time. We'll close our introduction to graphs by looking at both ways of conveying information.

Time-Series Graphs

time-series graph

A graph that shows how the value of a particular variable or variables has changed over some period of time.

One of the most common types of graphs used in economics is called a time-series graph. A **time-series graph** shows how the value of a particular variable or variables has changed over some period of time. One of the variables in a time-series graph is time itself. Time is typically placed on the horizontal axis in time-series graphs. The other axis can represent any variable whose value changes over time.

Table A.2 shows annual values of the unemployment rate, a measure of the percentage of workers who are looking for and available for work but are not working, in the United States from 2005 to 2020. These values are plotted in Figure A.11. Notice that the vertical axis is scaled from 3% to 11%, instead of beginning with zero. Time-series graphs are often presented with the vertical axis scaled over a certain range. The result is the same as introducing a break in the vertical axis, as we did in Figure A.3.

TABLE A.2 Unemployment Rate, 2005–2020

Date	Unemployment Rate (%)	Date	Unemployment Rate (%)
2005	5.1	2013	7.4
2006	4.6	2014	6.2
2007	4.6	2015	5.3
2008	5.8	2016	4.9
2009	9.3	2017	4.3
2010	9.6	2018	3.9
2011	8.9	2019	3.7
2012	8.1	2020	8.1

Source: Bureau of Labor Statistics, accessed through Federal Reserve Economic Data (FRED) at https://fred.stlouisfed.org/series/UNRATE.

FIGURE A.11 A Time-Series Plot

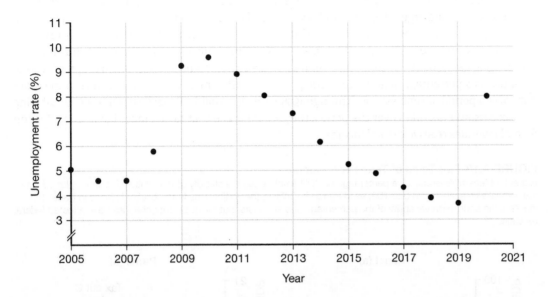

Often, individual values in a time-series graph are connected with a curve. That's done here in Figure A.12. The curve shows that the unemployment rate was rising between 2007 and 2009, falling from about 2010 through 2019, and then spiking sharply upward during the coronavirus crisis year, 2020.

FIGURE A.12 Time-Series Line Graph of Unemployment Rate

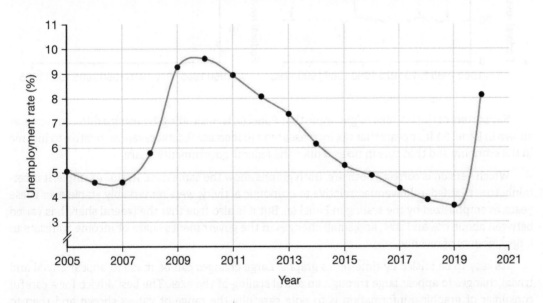

Source: Bureau of Labor Statistics, accessed through Federal Reserve Economic Data (FRED) at https://fred.stlouisfed.org/series/ UNRATE.

Scaling the Vertical Axis in Time-Series Graphs

The scaling of the vertical axis in time-series graphs can give very different views of economic data. We can make a variable appear to change a great deal, or almost not at all, depending on how we scale the axis. For that reason, it is important to note carefully how the vertical axis in a time-series graph is scaled.

Consider, for example, the issue of whether an increase or decrease in income tax rates has a significant effect on federal government revenues. Suppose a president proposes an increase in income tax rates and argues that this will boost federal revenues. Critics of the president's proposal might argue that changes in tax rates have little or no effect on federal revenues. Higher tax rates, they argue, would cause some people to scale back their income-earning efforts and thus produce only a small gain—or even a loss—in revenues. These critics might put together a graph of federal revenues as a percentage of gross domestic product (GDP), a measure of total income in the economy, over a period of time, say 1960 through 1995, similar to that in Panel (a) of Figure A.13. Labeling the tax cuts and tax hikes over the period, they would argue that tax changes have little effect on federal revenues relative to total income.

FIGURE A.13 Two Tales of Taxes and Income

A graph of federal revenues as a percentage of GDP emphasizes the stability of the relationship when plotted with the vertical axis scaled from 0 to 100, as in Panel (a). Scaling the vertical axis from 16% to 21%, as in Panel (b), stresses the short-term variability of the percentage and suggests that major tax rate changes have affected federal revenues.

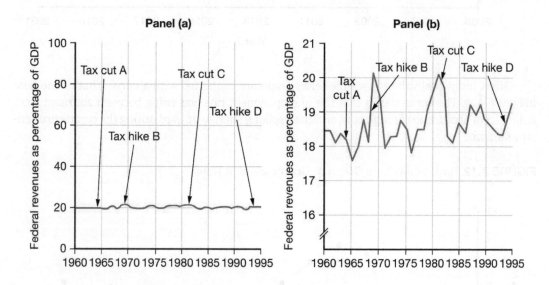

Supporters of the tax hike might argue that Panel (a) is misleading. By using a different scale, as shown in Panel (b), it appears that tax increases tend to increase federal revenues relative to income in the economy and that cuts in taxes reduce the federal government's share.

Which version is correct? Both are. Both graphs show the same data. In this example, it is certainly true that federal revenues, relative to economic activity, were remarkably stable over these years, as emphasized by the scaling in Panel (a). But it is also true that the federal share has varied between about 17% and 20%, and small changes in the government's share of income translate to large amounts of revenue.

It's easy to be misled by time-series graphs. Large changes can be made to appear trivial and trivial changes to appear large through an artful scaling of the axes. The best advice for a careful consumer of graphical information is to note carefully the range of values shown and then to decide whether the changes are really significant.

Sometimes it's not the size that matters, but the scale.

Source: Gunay Abbas/ Shutterstock.com

Testing Hypotheses with Time-Series Graphs

In 1936, economist John Maynard Keynes proposed a hypothesis about total spending for consumer goods in the economy. He theorized that consumer spending was positively related to the income households receive. One way to test such a hypothesis is to draw a time-series graph of both variables to see whether they do, in fact, tend to move together. Figure A.14 shows the values of consumption spending and disposable income, which is after-tax income received by households. Annual values of consumption and disposable income are plotted for the period 1980–2019. Notice that both variables have tended to move quite closely together. The close relationship between consumption and disposable income is consistent with Keynes's hypothesis that there is a positive relationship between the two variables.

FIGURE A.14 A Time-Series Graph of Disposable Income and Consumption
Plotted in a time-series graph, disposable income and consumption appear to move together. This is consistent with the hypothesis that the two are directly related.

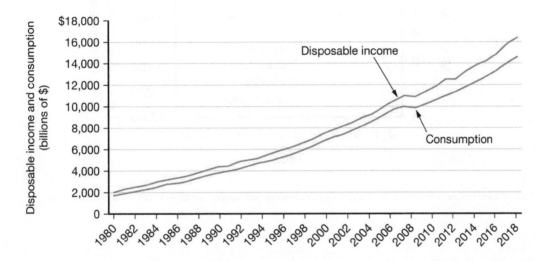

Source: Data from Bureau of Economic Analysis, accessed through Federal Reserve Economic Data (FRED) at https://fred.stlouisfed. org/series/DSPI and https://fred.stlouisfed.org/series/PCE.

The fact that two variables tend to move together in a time series does not by itself prove that there is a systematic relationship between the two. Figure A.15 shows a time-series graph of monthly values in 1987 of the Dow Jones Industrial Average, an index that reflects the movement of the prices of common stock. Notice the steep decline in the index beginning in October, not unlike the steep decline in October 2008.

It would be useful, and certainly profitable, to be able to predict such declines. Figure A.15 also shows the movement of monthly values of a "mystery variable," *X*, for the same period. The mystery variable and stock prices appear to move closely together. Was the plunge in the mystery variable in October responsible for the stock crash? Not likely, as the mystery value is the monthly average temperature in San Juan, Puerto Rico! Attributing the stock crash in 1987 to the weather in San Juan would be an example of the fallacy of false cause, which we discuss in the first chapter of this book.

Notice that Figure A.15 has two vertical axes. The left-hand axis shows values of temperature; the right-hand axis shows values for the Dow Jones Industrial Average. Two axes are used here because the two variables, San Juan temperature and the Dow Jones Industrial Average, are scaled in different units.

"Crazy hot out there. Market oughta be booming."

Source: Thaninee Chuensomchit/ Shutterstock.com

FIGURE A.15 Stock Prices and a Mystery Variable
The movement of the monthly average of the Dow Jones Industrial Average, a widely reported index of stock values, corresponded closely to changes in a mystery variable, X. Did the mystery variable contribute to the crash?

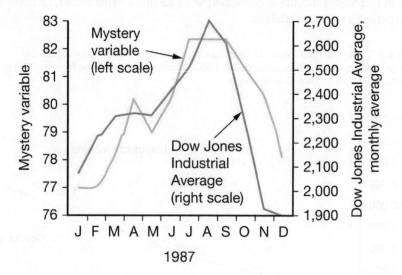

Source: Based on data from Dow Jones Industrial Averages historical data available at http://finance.yahoo.com/quote/^DJI/history?p=^DJI.

Descriptive Charts

We can use a table to show data. For example, each year the U.S. National Center for Education Statistics calculates the percentage of bachelor's degrees awarded in various fields. Table A.3 shows those percentages for 2018. In the groupings given, economics is included among the social sciences.

TABLE A.3 Bachelor's Degrees by Major, 2018

Field of Study	Percentage of Bachelor's Degrees (%)
Biological and Biomedical	6.0
Business	19.5
Communication, journalism, and related	4.7
Education	4.2
Engineering and engineering technologies	7.1
Health professions and related clinical sciences	12.4
Liberal arts and sciences, general studies, and humanities	2.2
Psychology	5.9
Social sciences and history	8.1
Visual and performing arts	4.5
Computer and information sciences	4.0
Parks, recreation, leisure, and fitness	2.7
Other	18.7

Source: Based on data from National Center for Education Statistics at https://nces.ed.gov/programs/digest/d20/tables/dt20_322.10.asp.

We can get a better sense of how those degree programs compare by showing the slice of the "degree pie" that each major claimed. In fact, one type of graph we can use to do that is called a pie chart. The data in the table above are graphed as shares of a complete "pie" in Figure A.16.

FIGURE A.16 Bachelor's Degrees Awarded by Major, 2018

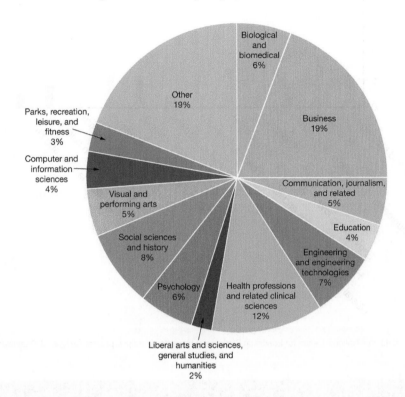

Source: Based on data from National Center for Education Statistics at https://nces.ed.gov/programs/digest/d20/tables/dt20_322.10. asp.

The same kind of information can be just as easily conveyed by using a column or bar chart. In our pie chart, the size of slices gave us a sense of which majors accounted for a large share of degrees and which did not; in a column chart, it's the height of the columns that relates that information.

FIGURE A.17 Bachelor's Degrees Awarded by Major, 2018
The graph here conveys the same information as the table and pie chart immediately above.

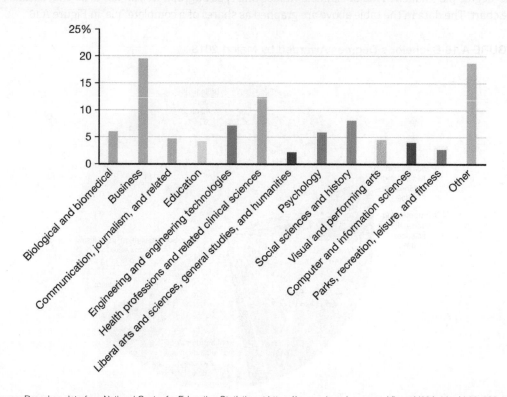

Source: Based on data from National Center for Education Statistics at https://nces.ed.gov/programs/digest/d20/tables/dt20_322.10.asp.

Key Takeaways

- A time-series graph shows changes in a variable over time; one axis is always measured in units of time.
- One use of time-series graphs is to plot the movement of two or more variables together to see if they tend to move together or not. The fact that two variables move together does not prove that changes in one of the variables cause changes in the other.
- Values of a variable may be illustrated using a table, a pie chart, or a bar chart.

Try It!

The table in Panel (a) shows a measure of the inflation rate, the percentage change in the average level of prices below.[2] Panels (b) and (c) provide blank grids. We have already labeled the axes on the grids in Panels (b) and (c). It is up to you to plot the data in Panel (a) on the grids in Panels (b) and (c). Connect the points you have marked in the grid using straight lines between the points. What relationship do you observe? Has the inflation rate generally increased or decreased? What can you say about the trend of inflation over the course of the 1990s? Do you tend to get a different "interpretation" depending on whether you use Panel (b) or Panel (c) to guide you?

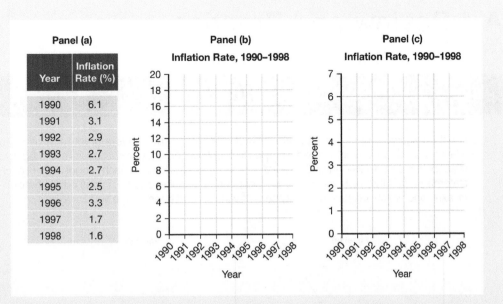

Answer to Try It! Problem

Here are the time-series graphs, Panels (b) and (c), for the information in Panel (a). The first thing you should notice is that both graphs show that the inflation rate generally declined throughout the 1990s (with the exception of 1996, when it increased). The generally downward direction of the curve suggests that the trend of inflation was downward. Notice that in this case we do not say negative, since in this instance it is not the slope of the line that matters. Rather, inflation itself is still positive (as indicated by the fact that all the points are above the origin) but is declining. Finally, comparing Panels (b) and (c) suggests that the general downward trend in the inflation rate is emphasized less in Panel (b) than in Panel (c). This impression would be emphasized even more if the numbers on the vertical axis were increased in Panel (b) from 20 to 100. Just as in Figure A.13, it is possible to make large changes appear trivial by simply changing the scaling of the axes.

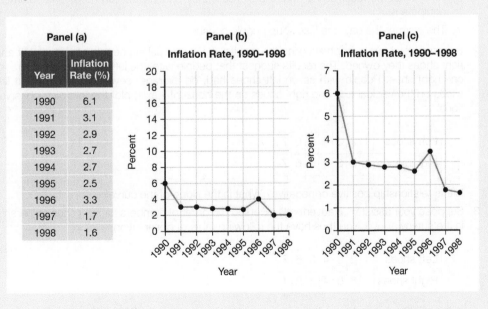

A.4 Review and Practice

Numerical Problems

1. Panel (a) shows a graph of a positive relationship; Panel (b) shows a graph of a negative relationship. Decide whether each proposition below demonstrates a positive or negative relationship, and decide which graph you would expect to illustrate each proposition. In each statement, identify which variable is the independent variable and thus goes on the horizontal axis, and which variable is the dependent variable and goes on the vertical axis.

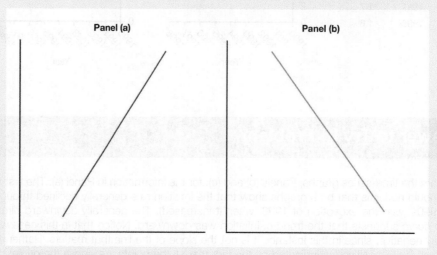

Panel (a)   **Panel (b)**

   a. An increase in national income in any one year increases the number of people killed in highway accidents.

   b. An increase in the poverty rate causes an increase in the crime rate.

   c. As the income received by households rises, they purchase fewer beans.

   d. As the income received by households rises, they spend more on home entertainment equipment.

   e. The warmer the day, the less soup people consume.

2. Suppose you have a graph showing the results of a survey asking people how many left and right shoes they owned. The results suggest that people with one left shoe had, on average, one right shoe. People with seven left shoes had, on average, seven right shoes. Put left shoes on the vertical axis and right shoes on the horizontal axis; plot the following observations:

Left shoes	1	2	3	4	5	6	7
Right shoes	1	2	3	4	5	6	7

Is this relationship positive or negative? What is the slope of the curve?

3. Suppose your assistant inadvertently reversed the order of numbers for right shoe ownership in the survey above. You thus have the following table of observations:

Left shoes	1	2	3	4	5	6	7
Right shoes	7	6	5	4	3	2	1

Is the relationship between these numbers positive or negative? What's implausible about that?

4. Suppose some of Ms. Alvarez's kitchen equipment breaks down. The following table gives the values of bread output that were shown in Figure A.7 It also gives the new levels of bread output that Ms. Alvarez's bakers produce following the breakdown. Plot the two curves. What has happened?

	A	B	C	D	E	F	G
Bakers/day	0	1	2	3	4	5	6
Loaves/day	0	400	700	900	1,000	1,050	1,075
Loaves/day after breakdown	0	380	670	860	950	990	1,005

5. Steven Magee has suggested that there is a relationship between the number of lawyers per capita in a country and the country's rate of economic growth. The relationship is described with the following Magee curve.

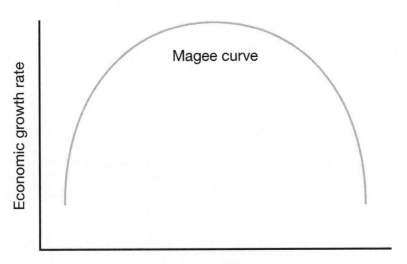

What do you think is the argument made by the curve? What kinds of countries do you think are on the upward-sloping region of the curve? Where would you guess the United States is? Japan? Does the Magee curve seem plausible to you?

6. Draw graphs showing the likely relationship between each of the following pairs of variables. In each case, put the first variable mentioned on the horizontal axis and the second on the vertical axis.

  a. The amount of time a student spends studying economics and the grade he or she receives in the course

  b. Per capita income and total expenditures on health care

  c. Alcohol consumption by teenagers and academic performance

  d. Household income and the likelihood of being the victim of a violent crime

Endnotes

1. In some cases, the variables in a graph cannot be considered independent or dependent. In those cases, the variables may be placed on either axis; we will encounter such a case in the chapter that introduces the production possibilities model. In other cases, economists simply ignore the rule; we will encounter that case in the chapter that introduces the model of demand and supply. The rule that the independent variable goes on the horizontal axis and the dependent variable goes on the vertical usually holds, but not always.

2. Bureau of Labor Statistics, All Urban Consumers CPI-U, 1982-84 = 100, Dec.-Dec. inflation rate.

APPENDIX B
The Solow Model of Economic Growth

B.1 Capital Accumulation and Economic Growth

Learning Objectives

1. Illustrate catching-up growth with the Solow growth model.
2. Use the Solow growth model to show how technological progress fuels cutting-edge growth.
3. List and explain three ingredients critical to fueling sustained economic growth.

In our chapter on economic growth, we looked at two drivers of economic growth—improvements in technology and increases in the size of the labor force. Those two drivers sent mixed messages about the typical person's standard of living...technology-driven growth improved the standard of living (or a reasonable proxy, the real wage), and labor-force-driven growth reduced it.

But for most of us, isn't improving the standard of living the entire point of economic growth? The evidence supports this, incidentally: real GDP per capita has trended steadily upward for the past 200 years, interrupted only by a few periods of recession. How can we explain that kind of persistent growth? One place to start is to release one of the factors of production that we held constant in our earlier analysis, and one that's changed a lot over the course of our country's history: capital. This appendix introduces a new model of economic growth that holds slow-growing labor constant, but allows capital to change. That model offers great insight into some major sources of economic growth.

Looking at growth through a different lens will offer us new perspectives on the nature of economic prosperity.

Source: Roman Zaiets/Shutterstock.com

Capital Isn't Constant! The Solow Growth Model

In our previous analysis of economic growth, we generally held capital constant and let labor vary. That makes sense—after all, the population *is* growing over time, and humans *are* productive. But the population grows pretty slowly, and pretty steadily. So what if we turned the tables by holding the population constant, but allowed the amount of capital to change?

This Thai stone carver knows that to get the job done right, you need the right tools.

Source: SasinTipchai/ Shutterstock.com

Those assumptions are the foundation of the Solow model of economic growth.[1] The Solow model, like the model in our growth chapter, begins with a production function, like the one shown as PFK_1 in Figure B.1. In this case, however, we hold the labor input constant and we let *capital* (denoted K) vary, which is why we've added a "K" to our production function, PFK_1. With labor constant, the more capital there is in the economy, the more capital is available to each worker and the more productive those workers will be. So, the production function slopes upward: With K_1 units of capital, output is Y_1; with K_2 units of capital, output increases to Y_2. Of course, having a lot of capital at their disposal makes workers more productive, but the most valuable units of capital are the first ones—both because workers are likely to acquire the most useful capital first, and because, with only limited capital, that capital is likely to see a lot of use. Additions to capital are likely to be less productive. For that reason, our production function displays diminishing returns; the slope flattens as we move to the right along PFK_1.

FIGURE B.1 A Production Function with a Capital Input

The production function PFK_1 shows the real output generated for various sizes of the capital stock. The production function shows a positive relationship between capital and output, but displays diminishing marginal returns to capital. The labor input is held constant.

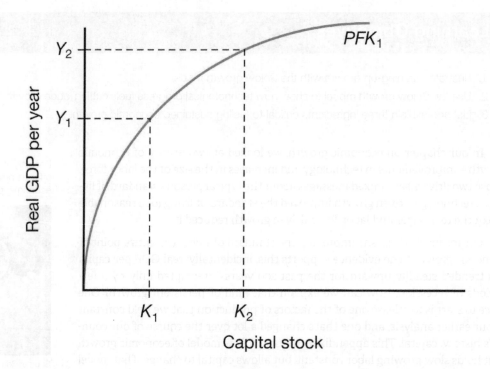

So our workers are now using their capital to produce goods and services. But what will happen to those goods and services? Some will undoubtedly be consumed by households—that's consumption spending, C. To keep things simple, let's assume there are no government purchases, so that once households' consumption desires have been met each year, any leftover production capacity is used to make investment goods, I. Those investment goods are new capital that can be added to the existing capital stock . . . *and used to produce more stuff next year!*

FIGURE B.2 Consumption and Investment in the Solow Growth Model
In the Solow growth model, output Y is divided between consumption (C) and investment (I). Investment is a constant fraction of output, s. Here, K_1 units of capital are used to produce Y_1 units of output, C_1 of which are consumed and I_1 of which are investment goods that will be added to next year's capital stock.

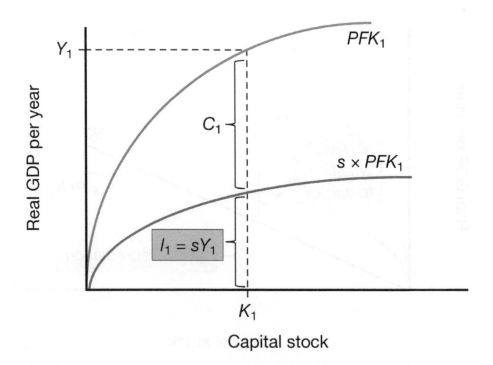

This division of output between consumption and investment goods is shown in Figure B.2, where the capital stock K_1 is combined with labor to produce Y_1 units of output. Some of that output will be consumed (C_1); the rest will be devoted to investment (I_1). The red curve in Figure B.2 (which we'll call the investment function) shows how much investment will take place for any level of the capital stock, K. If we assume that investment is a constant fraction s of the production function, PFK, then $I = s \times Y = s \times PFK$.[2]

The Solow model is notable for its appreciation of depreciation.

Source: demamiel62/Shutterstock.com

Any new investment this year will be added to the already-existing capital stock. That suggests that, in Figure B.2, next year's capital stock will be the existing capital stock (K_1) plus this year's investment (sY_1). One of the key insights of the Solow growth model, however, is that capital doesn't last forever: It wears out, or *depreciates*: Roads crumble, machines break, harbors silt up. So some of this year's newly produced investment goods won't be devoted to *increasing* the capital stock, but instead will simply *replace* capital that has worn out. Let's assume that some constant fraction of the capital stock, δ, wears out each year, so that each year's total depreciation, δK, will have to be fully replaced before the capital stock can actually grow. That's illustrated by the black line in Figure B.3, which shows the total amount of capital that will depreciate for every possible level of capital in the economy.

FIGURE B.3 Consumption and Net Investment
With capital stock K_1, Y_1 units of output are generated. C_1 units are consumed, the rest (below the red curve) is investment. Some of the investment goes to replace depreciated capital stock (δK_1); anything beyond that is added to next year's capital stock.

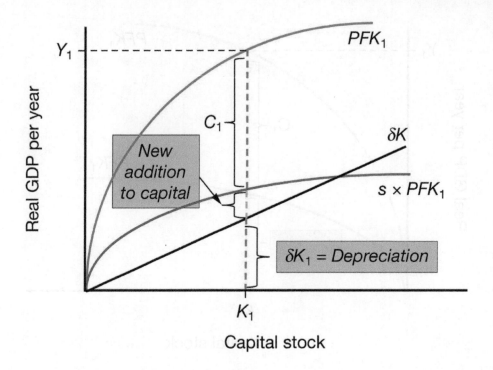

Let's use Figure B.3 to look at a specific example. Suppose K_1 units of capital are used to produce Y_1 units of output. That output is split between consumption (C_1, indicated by the green dashes) and investment (indicated by the blue and yellow dashes) below the investment function. Some of that investment spending will be used to replace depreciated capital (δK_1, indicated by blue dashes). Everything left over (the yellow dashes) constitutes new *net* investment that will be added to the capital stock to produce goods next year.

Capital Accumulation and Economic Growth

You've just seen the nuts and bolts of the Solow growth model. But you might be left wondering why it's called a "growth" model—after all, we haven't shown any growth yet! The right building blocks are in place, though. Let's start the clock and let time move forward to see our model economy grow.

In Figure B.3 we showed how new investment in an economy was divided between replacing capital that had worn out and generating new net capital that could be used to produce goods and services. Let's revisit a slightly cleaner version of that figure, starting in period 1, but letting time then move forward one click to see what unfolds.

The key to growth in the Solow model (and, frankly, most economies in the real world) is the accumulation of capital. As we just saw, an economy that starts with K_1 units of capital will devote some of its investment to replacing depreciated capital, but because overall investment is greater than the amount that wore out, there will some left over ($I_1 - \delta K_1$, indicated by yellow dashes at K_1) that will cause the capital stock to grow. In Figure B.4, we flip those yellow dashes on their side and lay them down on the horizontal axis. That tells us how big next year's capital stock K_2 will be: the amount we started with in year 1, plus the quantity of investment goods created, minus the capital goods that had to be replaced because of depreciation:

EQUATION B.1

$$K_2 = K_1 + I_1 - \delta K_1$$

FIGURE B.4 Capital Accumulation in the Solow Growth Model

In the Solow growth model, any investment beyond what was needed to replace depreciated capital is added to next year's capital stock. In period 1, with capital stock K_1, the yellow dashes show the net new addition to capital. Adding those yellow dashes to K_1 on the horizontal axis gives us next year's capital stock, K_2. With more capital available in the economy, output rises from Y_1 to Y_2.

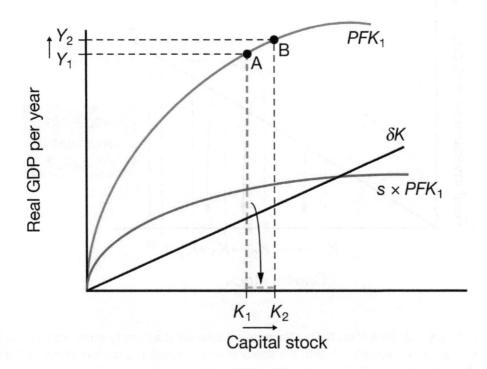

So, in year 2, the economy has more capital (K_2) than it did in year 1. With a bigger capital stock, the economy moves along the production function from A to B, and output rises from Y_1 to Y_2. That's economic growth! And because we assumed a fixed population, it's meaningful growth that raises output per capita and improves the standard of living—something that happens because each worker, armed with more capital, becomes more productive!

The Limits to Growth?

As long as the economy keeps adding capital, workers will come to the factory with more capital, productivity will rise, output will grow, and the standard of living will increase. Unfortunately, capital accumulation might not last forever. As the capital stock grows, more of it depreciates each year, and a greater amount of investment is required simply to replace the capital that wears out.

Let's zoom in on just the investment function and the depreciation line to see why this happens. Figure B.5 shows that in year 1, six yellow dashes worth of net investment goods are added to the capital stock to begin year 2 with. In year 2, only four green dashes of net capital are added; in year three, only three red dashes are added, and so on. Each year, the additions to capital get smaller and smaller, until finally no new capital is added at all: At K^{SS}, all investment goods produced are devoted to replacing worn out capital, with nothing left over to help the capital stock and the economy grow. That special place, where the investment function crosses the depreciation line, is called the **steady-state level of capital**.

steady-state level of capital

The level of the capital stock where all investment goods produced replace depreciated capital, with no net addition to the capital stock.

FIGURE B.5 Approaching the Steady State

As the capital stock grows, a greater proportion of the year's investment is devoted to replacing depreciated capital goods, and a smaller proportion is left to build the capital stock. In the steady state, net new investment decreases to zero and the capital stock stops growing; all investment simply replaces depreciated capital.

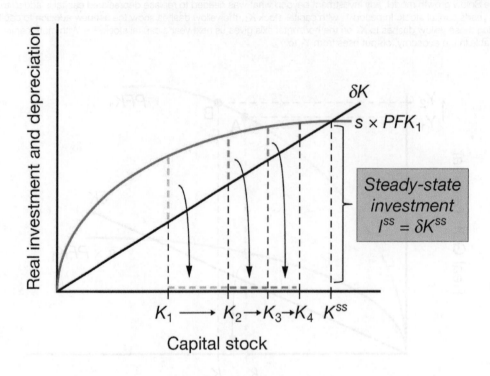

Steady State: Go ahead—add all the tea you want. You'll never have more to drink than can fit in that cup.

Source: Watchara Samsuvan/Shutterstock.com

The steady-state level of capital is a long-run equilibrium: If a country starts with less capital than K^{SS}, capital will accumulate until the steady state is reached. If a country starts with *more* than the steady-state level of capital, then more capital depreciates each year than is being replaced, and the capital stock shrinks to its steady-state level. (*Verify this for yourself—to the right of K^{SS}, the black depreciation line is above the red investment function, so more capital wears out than is replaced.*)

If capital converges to a long-run level, then so does everything that springs from capital. The economy's output, as shown in Figure B.6, converges to Y^{SS}. That steady-state output is divided between steady-state consumption (C^{SS}), shown in green dashes, and steady-state investment, I^{SS}, shown in black dashes.

The fact that output and consumption converge to a steady state has subtle, but important implications. The first is that, holding all else constant, as a country's capital accumulates, its economic growth typically slows (*thanks, diminishing returns*), and when it reaches the steady state, it grinds to a halt completely. In other words, there are potentially limits to growth!

The second major implication of the Solow growth model is that as long as all economies have access to the same production technology and devote the same fraction of their output to investment, those economies will eventually reach the same steady-state levels of capital, output, and consumption. In other words, countries will eventually converge to the same standard of living![3]

FIGURE B.6 Steady-State Output, Consumption, and Investment
The economy's capital stock converges to its steady-state level, K^{SS}. With that capital stock, steady-state output is Y^{SS}, steady-state investment is I^{SS}, and steady-state consumption is C^{SS}.

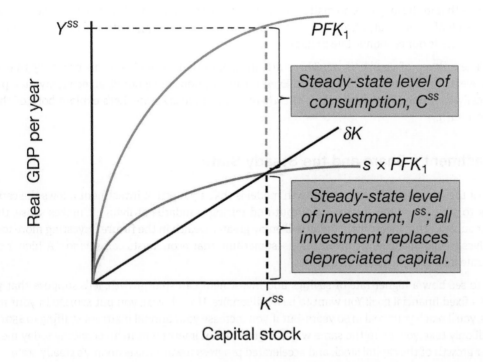

Not all countries, of course, are in the same stage of development. Some, like the United States, have a lot of capital already—the typical American worker has access to about $360,000 worth of capital. Others have less: Workers in India only have access to about $50,000 of capital, on average. Those differing stages of development matter a great deal for the pace of economic growth, and they do so for two reasons. First, capital will likely accumulate more rapidly in India than in the United States. Second, because of diminishing returns, the Solow model predicts rapid growth in India's output as capital accumulates in big doses, and slower growth in the United States, where capital is accumulating more slowly and diminishing returns have set in.

The fact that economies with lots of capital that are nearing the steady state will grow slowly, while economies farther away from the steady state will grow quickly means that the less-developed economies will close the gap between poor and rich fairly rapidly. For that reason, economists call growth driven by capital accumulation *catching-up growth*.

This young Bangladeshi woman is breaking bricks into gravel for road construction. If she is able to save up for a power tool, her output (and her wages) can increase dramatically.

Growth Unlimited? Prescriptions for Continued Progress

The discussion in the previous section makes it seem like our economic outcomes are predetermined—that in the long run, no matter where we are on the planet, we'll all reach the same steady-state levels of capital, output, and consumption, and that eventually growth will grind to a halt. But is that true? Is our economic fate sealed?

The answer, of course, is no. There are, in fact, options available to an economy that can improve its steady-state level of output. Even if those options are ignored, an economy may, paradoxically, *continue to grow even if it's already reached its steady state*! Let's explore both of those ideas in turn.

Investment's Share and the Steady State

One of the key ideas of the Solow growth model is that a pattern of investment allows the capital stock to grow over time, increasing output and raising standards of living. It makes sense, then, that countries that invest more today will enjoy greater wealth in the future. Investing more today involves foregoing current consumption—something that economists call *saving*.[4] A higher savings rate means more investment.

To see how a higher rate of savings and investment can spur growth, let's suppose that you have a fixed financial goal: You want to be a millionaire. If, each year, you put $20,000 in your mattress, you'll reach your goal in 50 years. But if you increase your annual mattress-stuffing to $50,000, it will only take you 20! In the same way, a higher rate of investment in an economy today means faster growth of the capital stock and accelerated progress toward the economy's steady state.

That accelerated progress means greater growth for economies that are not yet at their steady state. But there's a big added bonus to a higher savings rate: By ramping up your annual mattress-stuffing from $20,000 to $50,000, it becomes possible to achieve even greater economic success. In 40 years, a $50,000 saver can have $2 million in his mattress, an amount that lies beyond reach (and ordinary life expectancy) for a $20,000 saver.

In the same way, a country that saves/invests a higher fraction of its output can achieve a higher steady-state level of output than a country that doesn't devote much of its output to investment. It's also possible for a country to do a hard reset on its steady state by implementing policies that encourage greater saving. To see why, consider Figure B.7. Suppose the economy is in its steady state at point A, with a capital stock of K^{SS}_1 and output Y^{SS}_1. If that economy increases its savings rate from s_1 to s_2, the investment function will shift upward. Immediately, capital will start accumulating … and bringing economic growth with it! The new steady state is found at B, with a bigger capital stock K^{SS}_2 and higher steady-state output Y^{SS}_2. Most important, the standard of living gradually increases: Steady-state consumption, indicated by the length of the green dashes, is larger at B than at A.[5]

FIGURE B.7 Savings and the Steady State
By increasing the share of output devoted to investment goods (the savings rate), an economy can achieve a higher steady-state level of capital and a higher steady-state level of output. Initially, the economy has savings rate s_1 and is in the steady state at point A, with capital stock K^{SS}_1 and output Y^{SS}_1. Increasing the share of output devoted to investment to s_2 shifts the investment function upward, pushing the economy to a new steady state at point B, with capital stock K^{SS}_2 and output Y^{SS}_2. Consumption (measured by the green dashes at each level of capital) increases.

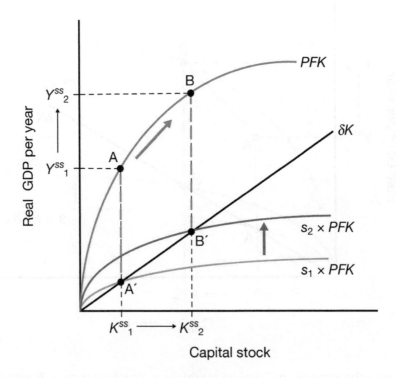

This means that mature economies nearing their steady states don't have to simply accept low growth as a fact of life: It's possible for those economies to kick-start a spurt of growth by consuming less and saving more. Policies that encourage more saving, such as tax-deductible savings plans to fund retirement, can give an economy a boost. That long-run boost, unfortunately, comes at the expense of current consumption: While the economy is still at K^{SS}_1, greater saving means less consumption and a temporarily lower standard of living.

Technology and the Steady State

Increasing the savings rate is one way to spur capital accumulation and nudge an economy to a higher steady-state level of output. But there's a second way for an economy that has reached its steady state to spur growth, and it's the way most mature, developed economies have sustained growth over time: figuring out ways to squeeze more output from the same inputs, what economists call *improvements in technology*. The effects of an improvement in technology are shown in Figure B.8.

FIGURE B.8 Technology and Growth

The economy is initially in the steady state at A and A'. An improvement in technology shifts the production function upward from PFK_1 to PFK_2. With a constant saving and investment rate, s, the shift in the production function causes the investment function to shift upward. The economy moves to a new steady state at B and B', with a higher capital stock (K^{SS}_2), higher output (Y^{SS}_2), and higher consumption (indicated by the green dashes).

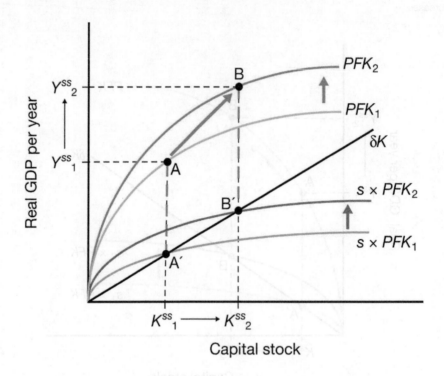

Let's suppose the economy in Figure B.8 is initially at its steady state at A, with steady-state capital stock K^{SS}_1 (point A'), steady-state output Y^{SS}_1, and steady-state consumption indicated by the green dashes.

The improvement in technology shifts the production upward from PFK_1 to PFK_2, *which immediately increases income even with no change in the capital stock!* But the capital stock *does* start to change: The shift in the production function drags the investment function along with it, shifting upward from $s \times PFK_1$ to $s \times PFK_2$. That means more investment today—more than enough to replace the depreciated capital at K^{SS}_1. With net investment now positive, capital begins to accumulate, eventually pushing the economy to a new steady state at points B and B'. In its new steady state, the economy not only has a higher capital stock, K^{SS}_2, but it also uses that capital more productively, jumping from PFK_1 to PFK_2. The result is an increase in steady-state output to Y^{SS}_2, and an increase in steady-state consumption (indicated by the green dashes at point B).[6]

That's a lot of technical detail, but the lessons, we hope, are clear:

- Even when an economy has reached its steady state, improvements in technology can immediately increase output and the standard of living.

- Improvements in technology will touch off a sustained spurt of capital accumulation.

- Improvements in technology will result in increased steady-state levels of capital and steady-state output that can continue to increase the standard of living.

This is good news for the developed world, which has already accumulated large quantities of capital and is likely nearing the steady state. Residents of developed countries don't have to stand by and accept eventual stagnation: Their standard of living will likely continue to increase as long as technological progress continues. That kind of growth, which comes not by throwing more power at a problem, but instead by having new ideas, is often called *cutting-edge growth*.

It's often easier to solve a problem by throwing more power at it rather than thinking of a better way to attack it. But sooner or later, economies run out of brute-force power; that's exactly what happens in the steady state. At that point, the easy growth disappears, and the only option available to solve the growth problem is to work smarter (figuring out how to squeeze more lemonade from the same number of lemons) rather than harder (trying to grow lemon trees in Norway).

The lessons the Solow model teaches are clear: Economic growth has two major sources—catching-up growth comes through capital accumulation; cutting-edge growth stems from technological improvements. Let's summarize some of the Solow model's key insights:

You can't escape the steady state by working harder . . . but you can leave it behind if you work smarter!

Source: sun ok/Shutterstock.com

1. Without improvements in technology, an economy with a fixed savings/investment rate will grow because of capital accumulation, and will eventually converge to the same capital stock, output, and standard of living as similar countries that began with larger capital stocks.

2. Because of diminishing returns, countries with small capital stocks enjoy potentially faster growth than similar countries beginning with large capital stocks (*catching-up growth*).

3. Economies can accelerate their growth by increasing the share of output devoted to investment (*the savings rate*). Additional saving boosts catching-up growth.

4. Countries with higher savings rates will enjoy higher steady-state levels of capital, output, and (likely) consumption.

5. Even when an economy has reached its steady state, improvements in technology can immediately increase the standard of living, and can sustain long-run economic growth for as long as advances continue (*cutting-edge growth*).

Key Takeaways

- A primary engine for economic growth has been the accumulation of capital. Capital makes workers more productive, increasing output and the standard of living.

- Countries with small capital stocks tend to grow rapidly as capital accumulates. Countries with large capital stocks grow more slowly, because capital doesn't accumulate as quickly, and because of diminishing marginal returns to additional capital.

- When a country reaches the steady state, growth of the capital stock, output, and consumption stop. Countries that have not reached the steady state will tend to catch up with those more-developed countries.

- Countries in the steady state can fuel additional growth by increasing their savings/investment rate.

- Once the steady state is reached, technological progress can continue to be an engine for growth.

Khan Academy Link

Economic growth and investment

B.2 Review and Practice

Summary

The Solow growth model illustrates the importance of capital in creating economic growth. The more a country saves (refrains from consuming), the greater the country's investment and the larger next year's capital stock will be. The economic growth created through the accumulation of capital is called catching-up growth.

Eventually, however, new investment will be completely devoted to replacing capital that depreciates or wears out, and capital accumulation will cease. That long-run outcome is called the steady state.

Countries can shift to new steady states by changing their savings rates or by improving their production technology. The growth that stems from technological improvements is called cutting-edge growth.

Concept Problems

1. Suppose the people in a certain economy decide to stop saving and instead use all their income for consumption. They do nothing to add to their stock of human or physical capital. Discuss the prospects for growth of such an economy.

2. Singapore has a savings rate that is roughly three times greater than that of the United States. Its greater savings rate has been one reason why the Singapore economy has grown faster than the U.S. economy. Suppose that if the United States increased its savings rate to, say, twice the Singapore level, U.S. growth would surpass the Singapore rate. Would that be a good idea?

3. Suppose an increase in air pollution causes capital to wear out more rapidly, doubling the rate of depreciation. How would this affect economic growth?

4. Suppose technology stops changing. Explain the impact on economic growth. Draw on the *AD/AS* model or the Solow model in your explanation.

5. "Given the rate at which scientists are making new discoveries, we will soon reach the point that no further discoveries can be made. Economic growth will come to a stop." Using the Solow growth model, discuss the validity of this statement.

6. Suppose that for some country it was found that its economic growth was based almost entirely on increases in quantities of factors of production. Why might such growth be difficult to sustain? Which model of growth will you use to frame your results?

Numerical Problems

1. Robinson Crusoe is the sole inhabitant of a tropical island. His production function is $Y = 10\sqrt{K}$. He currently has 16 units of capital, and each year, 10% of his capital depreciates. He devotes 10% of his output to investment and consumes the rest.

   a. How much is Robinson producing?

   b. How much is Robinson consuming?

   c. How much is Robinson investing in new capital?

   d. How much capital is depreciating?

2. In Numerical Problem 1 above, how much capital will Robinson begin next year with? What will happen to Robinson's

a. production

b. consumption

c. investment

d. standard of living

3. Robinson Crusoe is the sole inhabitant of an island. His production function is as follows: $Y = 10\sqrt{K}$. He devotes 10% of his output to investment and consumes the rest. Each year, 10% of his capital depreciates.

   a. Equate investment and depreciation to find the steady-state level of capital.

   b. Find steady-state levels of output, consumption, and depreciation.

   c. Suppose a technological improvement changes Robinson's production function to $Y = 11\sqrt{K}$. Find the new steady-state levels of capital, output, and consumption. Has the tech improvement increased Robinson's standard of living?

4. *YOLO!* After emerging from a deadly pandemic, consumers celebrate by reducing their saving and spending more on all the things they'd been missing: travel, dining out, clubbing, and lavish holiday parties. Use the Solow growth model to discuss the immediate and long-term implications of this change in behavior on the capital stock, output, and consumption. (Hint: Assume the economy is initially at its steady state. Then, shift the saving/investment function.)

Endnotes

1. The Solow (pronounced like Han Solo) model was developed by Nobel Prize winner Robert Solow. His more mathematically complex version of the model presented here incorporates population growth. You'll likely see that more-complete model when you take an intermediate-level course in macroeconomic theory.

2. Assuming that investment is a constant fraction of income is equivalent to saying that households save a constant fraction of their income. In a world with no government spending or taxes, (Y − C) represents households' aggregate saving: Each month you receive income, and what you don't consume ends up getting saved in your checking account (or in a slit in your mattress). Financial markets channel that saving to firms that want to build factories and buy equipment, so aggregate saving ends up equaling aggregate investment. You'll see how this happens in our chapter on financial markets.

3. In the model presented here, output depends on both capital and labor, and we've held the economy's labor at a fixed size. Of course, in the real world, the size of the labor force matters to the level of steady-state output. Solow's original model accounted for this by putting everything in per-worker terms: output per worker, capital per worker, investment per worker, consumption per worker. You'll likely deal with that added complexity in a second course in macroeconomics. The model here assumes all countries have the same labor available because it makes the math simpler and still yields the same basic takeaways.

4. Technically, saving (S) is the amount households earn less the amount they consume, or $S = Y − C$. Because income in our simple world is divided between consumption and investment, $Y = C + I$. That means that $S = (C + I) − C$, or $S = I$. In other words, the more households save, the greater the economy's overall investment. Our chapter on financial markets makes it clear how this happens.

5. You can measure the distance between the production and investment functions to see that consumption increases from 4.5 green dashes to 6 green dashes. Technically, there's a single steady-state level of capital that makes consumption as large as it can possibly be. That steady state is called the *golden rule steady state* and you'll likely learn how to find it in a second course in macroeconomics.

6. Increases in capital and output don't necessarily imply increases in consumption. As a hypothetical, consider an economy that invests 100% of its output. In the steady state, that economy will have the highest possible capital stock and therefore the highest level of sustainable output, but all of its output will be devoted to replacing depreciated capital, and its consumers will get nothing. Better for an economy like that to save less and have a lower capital stock: With less depreciated capital to replace each year, there might be something left for consumers to enjoy! The saving rate that maximizes consumption (and there is only one in this model!) is called the *golden rule level of saving*.

Extensions of the Aggregate Expenditures Model

In this appendix, we'll extend the aggregate expenditures model in two ways. First, instead of using graphs, we'll express the model in algebraic form and show how to solve it for the equilibrium level of real GDP. The advantage of using general algebraic expressions in place of the specific numbers that we used in the chapter is that we can then use the results to solve for any specific value that may pertain to a given economy. Second, we'll show how the aggregate expenditures model can be used to analyze the impact of fiscal policy measures—changes in government expenditures and in taxes—on the economy.

C.1 Extensions of the Aggregate Expenditures Model

In our chapter on aggregate expenditures, we represented the economy graphically, using a few specific equations as we went. But any time we draw a graph, it's possible to represent that graph with a more general algebraic expression. Our purpose in this section is to take the components of aggregate expenditure (consumption, investment, government spending, and net exports) and translate each into a mathematical form that we can then use to solve for equilibrium output. Taking that extra care in specifying our model will let us predict with greater precision the effects on output of changes in the economy.

Let's dive right in to our model-building exercise with a look at consumption:

EQUATION C.1

$$C = C_a + bY_d$$

As in our specific example in the chapter, Equation C.1 represents the consumption function. Total consumption has an autonomous component (C_a); it describes consumption that would take place even if there were no income (people might, for example, draw down their savings to buy food). It also includes an induced component (bY_d), where b is the marginal propensity to consume (MPC), and Y_d is disposable income. The induced component captures the idea that as our disposable income increases, we tend to consume more. In the example in the chapter, C_a was $300 billion and the MPC, or b, was 0.8.

Equation C.2 shows that total taxes, T, include an autonomous component T_a (for example, property taxes, licenses, fees, and any other taxes that do not vary with the level of income) and an induced component that is a fraction of real GDP, Y. That fraction is the tax rate, t.

EQUATION C.2

$$T = T_a + tY$$

Disposable personal income is just the difference between real GDP and total taxes, as shown in Equation C.3:

EQUATION C.3

$$Y_d = Y - T$$

In this model, planned investment (I_p) is assumed to be autonomous—it doesn't depend on income, interest rates, or any other factor. In Equation C.4 we denote autonomous investment as I_a.

EQUATION C.4

$$I_p = I_a$$

We'll also assume that government expenditures are autonomous—set by Congress rather than being determined by other factors in the economy. That's shown in Equation C.5, where government expenditures (G) are set autonomously (G_a).

EQUATION C.5

$$G = G_a$$

Net exports (X_n) are also autonomous, and do not depend on income, exchange rates, or other factors in the model. Those autonomous net exports are denoted by X_{n_a} in Equation C.6.

EQUATION C.6

$$X_n = X_{n_a}$$

Let's use the equations that describe each of the components of aggregate expenditure to solve for the equilibrium level of real GDP. Equilibrium in the aggregate expenditures model is found where aggregate expenditures equal real GDP, or:

EQUATION C.7

$$Y = AE$$

where aggregate expenditures (AE) are the sum of spending for consumption, planned investment, government purchases, and net exports. We can replace the right-hand side of Equation C.7 with those terms to get:

EQUATION C.8

$$Y = C + I_p + G + X_n$$

But we can make even more substitutions to ensure we account for the behavior of each component of aggregate expenditure. Consumption is described in Equation C.1, investment in Equation C.4, government spending in Equation C.5, and net exports in Equation C.6. Replacing the right-hand-side terms in Equation C.8 with those expressions, we have:

EQUATION C.9

$$Y = C_a + bY_d + I_a + G_a + X_{n_a}$$

Everything in Equation C.9 is autonomous except for Y and Y_d—we don't know those yet. That, unfortunately, leaves us with one equation containing two unknowns; we can only solve that equation if we can express one in terms of the other. That's easy to do by combining Equation C.3 and Equation C.2:

$$Y_d = Y - (T_a + tY)$$

which can be simplified further by distributing the negative sign and removing the parentheses:

EQUATION C.10

$$Y_d = Y - T_a - tY$$

Let's group all of the Y terms on the right together and factor:

EQUATION C.11

$$Y_d = (1 - t)Y - T_a$$

If we substitute the expression on the right for Y_d in Equation C.9, we'll get rid of the Y_d term and be left with a single equation in a single unknown, Y.

$$Y = C_a + b[(1 - t)Y - T_a] + I_a + G_a + X_{n_a}$$

Now just expand some terms:

EQUATION C.12

$$Y = C_a - bT_a + b(1 - t)Y + I_a + G_a + X_{n_a}$$

The first two terms ($C_a - bT_a$) show that overall consumption depends positively on autonomous consumption, but negatively on the level of autonomous taxes. For example, suppose T_a is $10 billion. To pay those taxes, households have to reduce consumption. If households' marginal propensity to consume is 0.8, then consumption will be $8 billion less than it would have been in the absence of autonomous taxes.

Equation C.12 contains a lot of autonomous terms that, because they are autonomous, won't change with other changes in the model. Let's group them all together in brackets, and then simplify our equation by representing the collection of autonomous terms with one letter, $\overline{A}$

$$y = [C_a - bT_a + I_a + G_a + X_{n_a}] + b(1 - t)Y$$

Letting $\overline{A}$ stand for the autonomous terms in brackets, we can simplify:

EQUATION C.13

$$Y = \overline{A} + b(1 - t)Y$$

The coefficient of real GDP (Y) on the right-hand side of Equation C.13, $b(1 - t)$, is the fraction of an additional dollar of real GDP that will be spent for consumption. It is the slope of the aggregate expenditures function in this model of the economy. The aggregate expenditures function for the simplified economy that we presented in the chapter had a slope that was simply the marginal propensity to consume, b. What's the difference here? This model incorporates taxes, which most definitely affect the willingness of consumers to spend. In this more realistic model, the marginal propensity to consume measures how much consumers will spend out of each additional dollar of *after-tax* income. That flattens the aggregate expenditure function; the slope decreases by a factor of (1 - t).

Now, we're ready to solve Equation C.13 for Y. To do that, first gather all of the Y terms on the left-hand side:

$$Y - b(1 - t)Y = \overline{A}$$

Then, factor out Y:

$$Y[1 - b(1 - t)] = \overline{A}$$

And finally, divide both sides by the term in brackets to isolate Y:

EQUATION C.14

$$Y = \frac{1}{1 - b(1 - t)} \overline{A}$$

In Equation C.14, $1/[1 - b(1 - t)]$ is the multiplier. Equilibrium real GDP is achieved at a level of income equal to the multiplier times the amount of autonomous spending. Notice that because the slope of the aggregate expenditures function is less than it would be in an economy without induced taxes, the value of the multiplier is also less, all other things the same. In this representation of the economy, the value of the multiplier depends on the marginal propensity to consume and on the tax rate. The higher the tax rate, the lower the multiplier; the lower the tax rate, the higher the multiplier.

For example, suppose the marginal propensity to consume is 0.8. If the tax rate were 0, then the multiplier would be 5. If the tax rate were 0.25, then the multiplier would be 2.5.

C.2 The Aggregate Expenditures Model and Fiscal Policy

Let's use the aggregate expenditures model to explain the impact of fiscal policy on aggregate demand. We already looked at various types of policy options in our chapter on fiscal policy. Including taxes and building our model with equations will let us look at those policy options in more detail.[1]

Changes in Government Purchases

All other things unchanged, a change in government purchases shifts the aggregate expenditures curve by an amount equal to the change in government purchases. A $200 billion increase in government purchases, for example, shifts the aggregate expenditures curve vertically upward by $200 billion. A $75 billion decrease in government purchases shifts the aggregate expenditures curve vertically downward by that amount.

Panel (a) of Figure C.1 shows an economy that is initially in equilibrium at an income of $7,000 billion (where AE_1 crosses the 45-degree line). Suppose that the slope of the aggregate expenditures function, $b(1 - t)$, is 0.6, so that the multiplier is 2.5. An increase of $200 billion in government purchases shifts the aggregate expenditures curve vertically upward by that amount to AE_2. In the aggregate expenditures model, real GDP increases by an amount equal to the multiplier times the change in autonomous aggregate expenditures. Real GDP in that model thus rises by 2.5 × $200 billion, or $500 billion. The economy ends up with real GDP of $7,500 billion.

One of the shortcomings of the aggregate expenditures model is that it assumes that prices are sticky or inflexible. In the real world, however, strong increases in aggregate demand often cause the price level to increase. So, to get a more complete picture of what happens as a result of the fiscal stimulus, we switch to the model of aggregate demand and aggregate supply, as shown in the right-hand panel.

In the model shown in Panel (b), the initial price level is P_1, and the initial equilibrium real GDP is $7,000 billion. The aggregate expenditures model assumes that prices are frozen at P_1, so the $200 billion increase in government purchases increases the total quantity of goods and services demanded at that price level by $500 billion. That's represented by a $500 billion rightward shift of the aggregate demand curve. But, if we relax the assumption of sticky prices, that additional demand will put upward pressure on prices, so part of the impact of the increase in aggregate demand will result in higher output, but some will be absorbed by higher prices. In our *AD/ AS* model, we end up at price level P_2, and at an equilibrium real GDP of $7,300, rather than the $7,500 predicted by the sticky-price *AE* model.

A reduction in government purchases would have the opposite effect. All other things unchanged, aggregate expenditures would shift downward by an amount equal to the reduction in aggregate purchases. In the model of aggregate demand and aggregate supply, the aggregate demand curve would shift to the left by an amount equal to the initial change in autonomous aggregate expenditures times the multiplier. Real GDP and the price level would fall, and fall by less than we'd see if the price level stayed constant.

FIGURE C.1 An Increase in Government Purchases
The economy shown here is initially in equilibrium at a real GDP of $7,000 billion and a price level of P_1. In Panel (a), an increase of $200 billion in the level of government purchases shifts the aggregate expenditures curve upward by that amount to AE_2, increasing the equilibrium level of income in the aggregate expenditures model by $500 billion, to $7,500 billion. In Panel (b), the aggregate demand curve shifts to the right by $500 billion to AD_2. The equilibrium level of real GDP rises to $7,300 billion, while the price level rises to P_2.

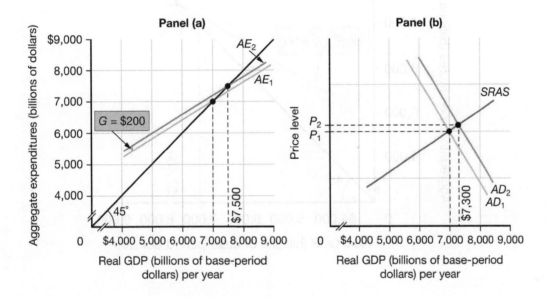

In the remainder of this appendix, we will focus on the shift in the aggregate expenditures curve. To determine what happens to equilibrium real GDP and the price level, we must look at the intersection of the new aggregate demand curve and the short-run aggregate supply curve, as we did in Panel (b) of Figure C.1.

Change in Autonomous Taxes

A change in autonomous taxes shifts aggregate expenditures in the opposite direction of a change in government purchases. If the autonomous taxes go up, for example, aggregate expenditures go down by a *fraction* of the change. Because the initial change in consumption is less than the change in taxes (because it is multiplied by the *MPC*, which is less than 1), the shift caused by a change in taxes is smaller than the shift caused by an equivalent change in government purchases.

Let's consider a cut in autonomous taxes of $200 billion, as shown in Figure C.2. If the marginal propensity to consume is 0.8, then the aggregate expenditures curve AE_1 will shift vertically upward by $160 billion (0.8 × $200 billion) to AE_2. (As we saw earlier, a $200 billion increase in government purchases shifted the aggregate expenditures curve up by the full $200 billion—so just as we claimed above, a $200 billion tax cut has a smaller effect than a $200 billion increase in government expenditures.)

What's the overall impact of the tax cut? Assuming a multiplier of 2.5, the $200 billion decrease in autonomous taxes causes equilibrium real GDP in the aggregate expenditures model to rise from

Elon Musk may be able to avoid income taxes, but nobody escapes the autonomous tax.

Source: Nick_Raille_07/ Shutterstock.com

$7,000 billion to $7,400 billion, a $400 billion increase. This is, as mentioned above, less than the $500 billion change that would be caused by a $200 billion increase in government purchases.

FIGURE C.2 A Decrease in Autonomous Taxes

A decrease of $200 billion in autonomous taxes shifts the aggregate expenditures curve upward by the marginal propensity to consume of 0.8 times the changes in autonomous taxes of $200 billion, or $160 billion, to AE_2. The equilibrium level of income in the aggregate expenditures model increases by $400 billion to $7,400 billion.

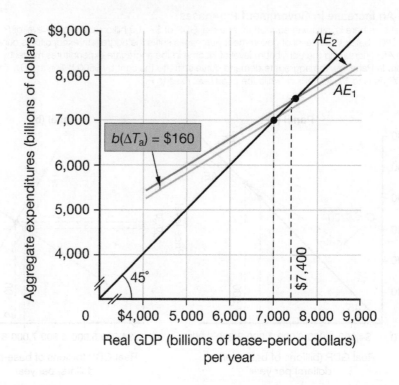

An increase in autonomous taxes works just the same way, but in the opposite direction. An increase, for example, of $75 billion would shift the aggregate expenditures curve downward by $60 billion (= 0.8 × $75 billion) and cause the equilibrium level of real GDP to decrease by $150 billion (= 2.5 × $60 billion).

Changes in Income Tax Rates

One way government can stimulate or slow the economy is by changing autonomous taxes, which you'll remember don't depend on peoples' current income. They're a lot like a fixed cost: The amount of taxes you owe this year will have to be paid whether you earn like Jeff Bezos or like your local trench-digger. But there's another way the government can manipulate your tax bill: It can change the tax *rate* applicable to your income, so that every dollar you earn will increase your overall tax bill; every day you take off will reduce it.

When government purchases or autonomous taxes change, the aggregate expenditures curve shifts up or down; the new aggregate expenditures curve has the same slope as the old curve, and the multiplier is the same after the change as it was before. But when income tax rates change, the *slope* of the aggregate expenditures curve changes, and the multiplier itself changes with it.

We saw in the first section of this appendix that when taxes are related to income, the multiplier, $1/[1 - b(1 - t)]$, depends on both the marginal propensity to consume (b) and the tax rate (t). An increase in income tax rates will reduce the multiplier and make the aggregate expenditures curve flatter. Reducing the income tax rate makes the multiplier larger and the aggregate expenditures curve steeper.

Let's see how this works. Suppose that our economy has an initial income tax rate of 25% (0.25), and an initial real GDP of $7,000 billion. To simplify, we will assume there are no autonomous taxes (that is, $T_a = 0$). So $T = tY$, and disposable personal income Y_d is 75% of real GDP:

$$T = 0.25Y$$

$$Y_d = Y - T = 0.75Y$$

Suppose the marginal propensity to consume is 0.8. Then a $1 change in real GDP produces an increase in disposable personal income of $0.75, and that in turn produces an increase in consumption of $0.60 (= $1 × 0.75 × 0.8). If the other components of aggregate expenditures are autonomous, then the multiplier is:

$$\frac{1}{1 - .8(1 - .25)} = \frac{1}{1 - 0.6} = 2.5$$

The impact of a tax rate change is illustrated in Figure C.3. It shows the original aggregate expenditures curve AE_1 intersecting the 45-degree line at the income of $7,000 billion. The curve has a slope of 0.6. Now suppose that the tax rate is increased to 0.375. The higher tax rate will rotate this curve downward, making it flatter. The slope of the new aggregate expenditures curve AE_2 will be 0.5 (= 1 − 0.8[1 − 0.375]). The value of the multiplier thus falls from 2.5 to 2 (= 1 / [1 − 0.5]).

FIGURE C.3 The Impact of an Increase in Income Tax Rates
An increase in the income tax rate rotates the aggregate expenditures curve downward by an amount equal to the initial change in consumption at the original equilibrium value of real GDP found in the aggregate expenditures model, $7,000 billion in this case, assuming no other change in aggregate expenditures. It reduces the slope of the aggregate expenditures curve and thus reduces the multiplier. Here, an increase in the income tax rate from 0.25 to 0.375 reduces the slope from 0.6 to 0.5; it thus reduces the multiplier from 2.5 to 2. The higher tax reduces consumption by $700 billion and reduces equilibrium real GDP in the aggregate expenditures model by $1,400 billion.

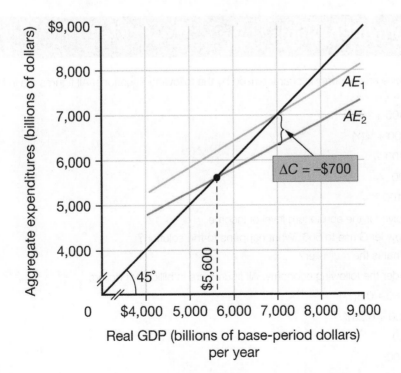

At the original level of income, $7,000 billion, tax collection equaled $1,750 billion (again, for this example, we assume T_a = 0, so T = 0.25 × $7,000). At the new tax rate and original level of income, tax collection would be $2,625 billion (0.375 × $7,000 billion). That means that disposable personal income at a real GDP of $7,000 billion declines by $875 billion, and with a marginal propensity to consume of 0.8, consumption drops by $700 billion (= 0.8 × $875 billion). So, at the original income level of $7,000, the vertical distance between AE_1 and AE_2 is $700 billion.

Before the tax rate increase, an additional $1 of real GDP induced $0.60 in additional consumption. At the new tax rate, an additional $1 of real GDP creates $0.625 in disposable personal income ($1 in income minus $0.375 in taxes), and additional consumption of only $0.50 (= [$1 × (0.8 × 0.625)]). The new aggregate expenditures curve, AE_2 in Figure C.3, shows the end result of the tax rate change in the aggregate expenditures model. As the aggregate expenditures curve flattens, the equilibrium level of real GDP falls to $5,600 billion from its original $7,000 billion. The $1,400 billion reduction in equilibrium real GDP in the aggregate expenditures model is equal to the $700 billion initial reduction in consumption at the original equilibrium level of real GDP times the new multiplier of 2.[2]

In the model of aggregate demand and aggregate supply, a tax rate increase will shift the aggregate demand curve to the left by an amount equal to the initial change in aggregate expenditures induced by the tax rate boost times the *new* value of the multiplier. Similarly, a reduction in the income tax rate rotates the aggregate expenditures curve upward by an amount equal to the initial increase in consumption (at the original equilibrium level of real GDP found in the aggregate expenditures model) created by the lower tax rate. It also increases the value of the multiplier. Aggregate demand shifts to the right by an amount equal to the initial change in aggregate expenditures times the new multiplier.

C.3 Review and Practice

Numerical Problems

1. Suppose an economy is characterized by the following equations. All figures are in billions of dollars.

   $C = 400 + ⅔(Y_d)$

   $T = 300 + ¼(Y)$

   $G = 400$

   $I = 200$

   $X_n = 100$

   a. Solve for the equilibrium level of income.
   b. Now let G rise to 500. What happens to the solution?
   c. What is the multiplier?

2. Consider the following economy. All figures are in billions of dollars.

   $C = 180 + 0.8(Y_d)$

   $T = 100 + 0.25Y$

   $I = 300$

   $G = 400$

   $X_n = 200$

   a. Solve for the equilibrium level of real GDP.

   b. Now suppose investment falls to $200 billion. What happens to the equilibrium real GDP?

   c. What is the multiplier?

3. Consider the following economy:

   $C = 400 + \frac{2}{3}(Y_d)$

   $T = 300$

   $I = 200$

   $G = 400$

   $X_n = 100$

   a. Solve for the equilibrium level of real GDP.

   b. Suppose government increases spending by $100, and pays for the additional spending with an accompanying $100 tax increase. Solve for the equilibrium level of real GDP after these changes.

   c. Does income grow with the new policies? By how much? Relate the change, if any, to the multiplier.

4. Suppose an economy has a consumption function $C = \$100 + \frac{2}{3} Y_d$. Autonomous taxes, T_a, equal 0, the income tax rate is 10%, and $Y_d = 0.9Y$. Government purchases, investment, and net exports each equal $100. Solve the following problems.

   a. Draw the aggregate expenditures curve, and find the equilibrium income for this economy in the aggregate expenditures model.

   b. Now suppose the tax rate rises to 25%, so $Y_d = 0.75Y$. Assume that government purchases, investments, and net exports are not affected by the change. Show the new aggregate expenditures curve and the new level of income in the aggregate expenditures model. Relate your answer to the multiplier effect of the tax change.

   c. Compare your result in the aggregate expenditures model to what the *AD/AS* model would show.

5. Suppose a program of federally funded public-works spending was introduced that was tied to the unemployment rate. Suppose the program was structured so that public-works spending would be $200 billion per year if the economy had an unemployment rate of 5% at the beginning of the fiscal year. Public-works spending would be increased by $20 billion for each percentage point by which the unemployment rate exceeded 5%. It would be reduced by $20 billion for every percentage point by which unemployment fell below 5%. If the unemployment rate were 8%, for example, public-works spending would be $260 billion. How would this program affect the slope of the aggregate expenditures curve?

Endnotes

1. The possibility of crowding out was discussed in the fiscal policy chapter and will not be repeated here. To incorporate that possibility, we'd need to have investment depend on the level of interest rates, which in turn would need to depend on the level of government borrowing. That's a much more complex model—more than we're ready to tackle here!

2. If you relax the sticky price assumption and carry this result through to the *AD/AS* model, the aggregate demand curve will shift to the left by $1,400 billion.

Index